April 20–21, 2017
Cambridge, MA, USA

I0036676

**Association for
Computing Machinery**

Advancing Computing as a Science & Profession

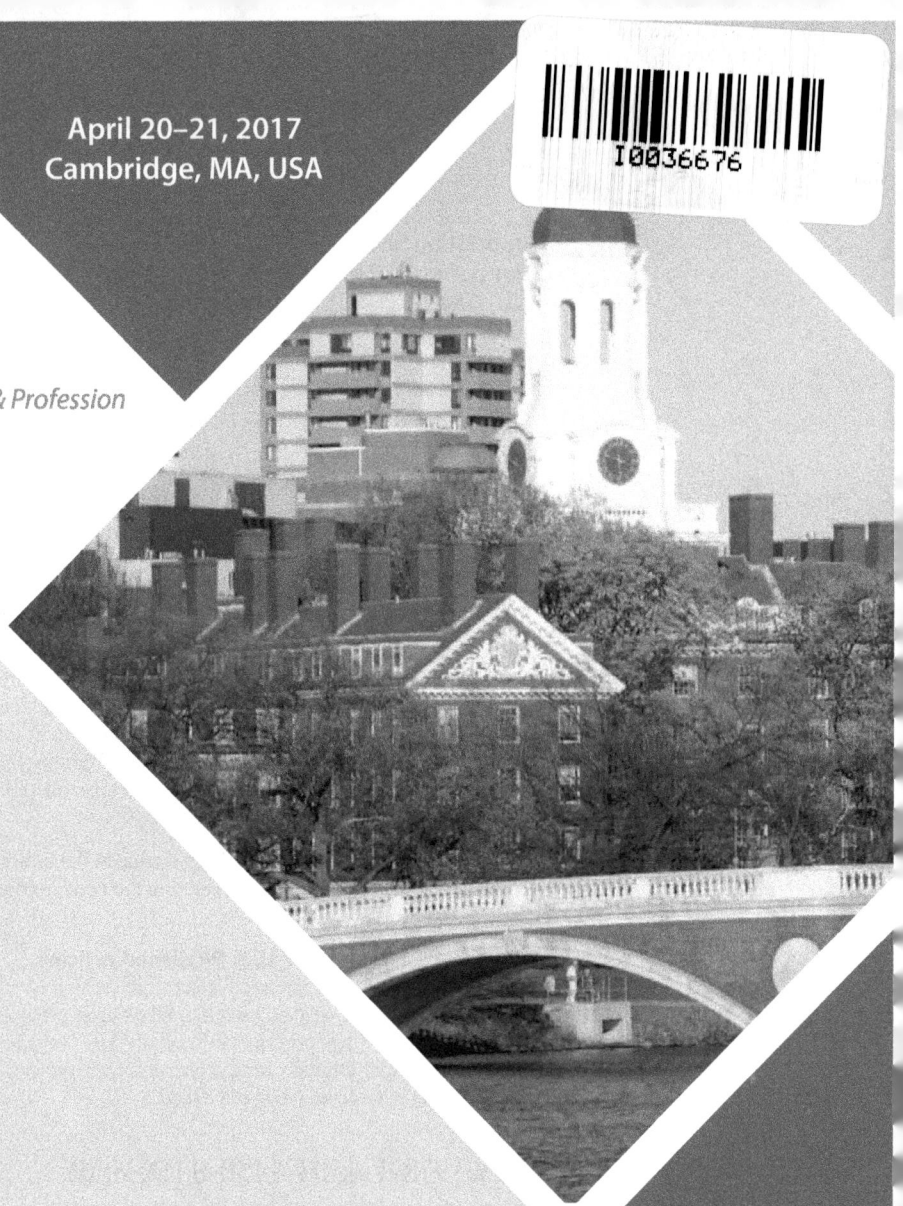

L@S'17

Proceedings of the Fourth (2017) ACM Conference on
Learning @ Scale

Sponsored by:
ACM

Supported by:
Oracle Academy, Google, and edX

**Association for
Computing Machinery**

Advancing Computing as a Science & Profession

The Association for Computing Machinery
2 Penn Plaza, Suite 701
New York, New York 10121-0701

ISBN: 978-1-4503-4450-0 (Digital)

ISBN: 978-1-4503-5472-1 (Print)

Additional copies may be ordered prepaid from:

ACM Order Department
PO Box 30777
New York, NY 10087-0777, USA

Phone: 1-800-342-6626 (USA and Canada)
+1-212-626-0500 (Global)
Fax: +1-212-944-1318
E-mail: acmhelp@acm.org
Hours of Operation: 8:30 am – 4:30 pm ET

Printed in the USA

Learning at Scale 2017 Preface

It is our great pleasure to present the Proceedings of the Fourth Annual ACM Conference on Learning at Scale, L@S 2017, held on April 20-21 at the Massachusetts Institute of Technology, Cambridge, MA, USA.

Learning at Scale investigates large-scale, technology-mediated learning environments. The conference was created by the Association for Computing Machinery (ACM), inspired by the emergence of Massive Open Online Courses (MOOCs) and the accompanying shift in thinking about education. While the conference was originally inspired by the emergence of MOOCs, large-scale technology mediated learning environments are very diverse and the conference series is a venue for discussion of the highest quality research on how learning and teaching can be transformed by that diversity of environments. Intelligent tutoring systems, open learning courseware, learning games, citizen science communities, collaborative programming communities, community tutorial systems, and the countless informal communities of learners are all examples of learning at scale. These systems either depend upon large numbers of learners, or they are enriched through use of data generated by the previous use of many learners. They share a common purpose–to increase human potential--and a common infrastructure of data and computation to enable learning at scale.

Investigations of learning at scale naturally bring together two different research communities. Learning scientists are drawn to these innovative environments to study established and emerging forms of knowledge production, transfer, modeling, and co-creation. Computer scientists are drawn to the field as powerful site for the development and application of advanced computational techniques. At its very best, the Learning at Scale community supports the interdisciplinary investigation of these important sites of learning and human development.

The goal of the Learning at Scale community is the understanding and enhancement of human learning. In emerging education technology genres, researchers often use a variety of proxy measures for learning, including measures of participation, persistence, completion, satisfaction, and activity. In the early stages of investigating a technological genre, it is entirely appropriate to begin lines of research by investigating these proxy outcomes. As lines of research mature, however, it is important for the community of researchers to hold each other to increasingly high standards and expectations for directly investigating thoughtfully constructed measures of learning. In the early days of research on MOOCs, many researchers documented correlations between measures of activity (videos watched, forums posted, clicks) and outcome proxies including participation, persistence, and completion. As learning at scale research matures, studies that document these kinds of correlations should give way to studies of student learning that produce evidence of instructional techniques, technological infrastructures, learning habits, and experimental interventions that improve learning. As a community, we believe that that the very best of our early papers define a foundation to build upon but are not an established standard to which to aspire.

The call for papers attracted submissions from all over the world, covering a broad range of topics from the theoretical to the pragmatic. We received submissions on a variety of topics including: novel assessments of learning, drawing on computational techniques for automated, peer, or human-assisted assessment; new methods for validating inferences about human learning from established measures, assessments, or proxies; experimental interventions in large-scale learning environments that show evidence of improved learning outcomes; domain independent interventions inspired by social psychology, behavioral economics, and related fields with the potential to benefit learners in diverse fields and disciplines; domain specific interventions inspired by discipline-based educational research that have the potential to advance teaching and learning of specific ideas, misconceptions, and theories within a field; tools or techniques for personalization and adaptation, based on log data, user modeling, or choice; usability studies and effectiveness studies of design elements for students or instructors; tools and pedagogy to promote community, support learning, or increase retention in at-scale environments; new tools and techniques for learning at scale; best practices in the archiving and reuse of learner data in safe, ethical ways; innovations in platforms for supporting learning at scale; and tools and techniques for managing privacy of learning data. In all topics, we encourage the use of best practices in open science, including pre-planning and pre-registration as well as a particular focus on contexts and populations that have been historically not well served.

The overall submission numbers were greater than those of previous years. All papers were reviewed according to stringent criteria. Full Papers were reviewed by at least three program committee members, Work-In-Progress Papers and Demonstration Descriptions by two. Final decisions for acceptance of Full Papers were made by the program committee as a whole, often after extensive discussion of the merits of the paper. Whereas Full Papers present work that is innovative and mature, WiPs and Demos offer a forum for the newest and emerging work at earlier stages, offering pointers to future directions. As may be clear from the following analytics, the conference is highly selective in the work it accepts.

	Full Papers	Work in Process & Demos
Submitted	105	79
Accepted	14	35
Accepted as Posters	17	
Acceptance Rate	13%	44%

Learning at Scale 2017 was truly a community effort. We thank the authors for their creativity and rigor. We are grateful to the program committee and all the reviewers for their thoughtful and constructive evaluation of the submitted papers, and their careful shepherding. We thank the steering committee and ACM for their guidance and support. Finally, the conference received invaluable sponsorship from Oracle Academy at the gold level, from Google at the Silver level, and from edX, at the bronze level.

We trust that the conference will be a forum for interesting exchanges among researchers and practitioners from institutions around the world. While the proceedings may not capture the live excitement, they present a permanent record. May they be a valuable resource for many researchers interested in Learning at Scale in the years to come!

Justin Reich
L@S2017 Program Co-chair
MIT, USA

Candace Thille
L@S2017 Program Co-chair
Stanford University, USA

Claudia Urrea
L@S2017 Conference Chair
MIT, USA

Table of Contents

Session: Keynote Address
Session Chair: Claudia Urrea *(Massachusetts Institute of Technology)*

Session: Engineering Learning Environments
Session Chair: Mary Ellen Wiltrout *(Massachusetts Institute of Technology)*

Session: Learn to Code
Session Chair: Susan Singer *(Rollins University)*

Session: Predicting and Explaining Learning
Session Chair: Nia Dowell *(University of Memphis)*

Session: Feedback for Improving Learning
Session Chair: Amy Ogan *(Carnegie Mellon University)*

Works in Progress

Learning@Scale 2017 Organization

General Chair: Claudia Urrea *(Massachusetts Institute of Technology, USA)*

Program Chair: Justin Reich *(Massachusetts Institute of Technology, USA)*
Candace Thille *(Stanford University, USA)*

Steering Committee Chair: Gregor Kiczales *(University of British Columbia, Canada)*

Steering Committee: Vincent Alevan *(Carnegie Mellon University, USA)*
Ryan Baker *(University of Pennsylvania, USA)*
Armando Fox *(University of California at Berkeley, USA)*
Marti Hearst *(University of California at Berkeley, USA)*
Judy Kay *(University of Sydney, Australia)*
Scott Klemmer *(University of California at San Diego (USA)*
Ken Koedinger *(Carnegie Mellon University, USA)*
John Mitchell *(Stanford University, USA)*
Carolyn Penstein Rosé *(Carnegie Mellon University, USA)*
Ido Roll *(University of British Columbia, Canada)*
Jeremy Roschelle *(SRI International, USA)*
Daniel Russell *(Google, USA)*
Mehran Sahami *(Stanford/ex officio ACM Ed Board, USA)*
Karen Swan *(Univ of Illinois, Springfield, USA)*
Yan Timanovsky *(ACM Staff Liaison, USA)*
Beverly P. Woolf *(University of Massachusetts Amherst, USA)*

Program Committee: Vincent Alevan *(Carnegie Mellon University, USA)*
Andrew Bernat *(Computing Research Association, USA)*
Marie Bienkowski *(SRI International, USA)*
Gautam Biswas *(Vanderbilt University, USA)*
Christopher Brooks *(University of Michigan, USA)*
Eric Bruillard *(ENS Cachan, France)*
Emma Brunskill *(Carnegie Mellon University, USA)*
Bodong Chen *(University of Minnesota, USA)*
Chris Dede *(Harvard University, USA)*
Pierre Dillenbourg *(École Polytechnique Fédérale de Lausanne, Switzerland)*
Matthew Easterday *(Northwestern University, USA)*
Kobi Gal *(Ben Gurion University, Israel)*
Dragan Gasevic *(University of Edinburgh, UK)*
Lee Giles *(Pennsylvania State University, USA)*
Irene Grief *(International Business Machines, USA)*
Marti Hearst *(University of California at Berkeley, USA)*
Neil Heffernan *(Worcester Polytechnic Institute, USA)*
Iris Howley *(Stanford University, USA)*
Geert-Jan Houben *(TU Delft, Netherlands)*
Judy Kay *(University of Sydney, Australia)*
Juho Kim *(KAIST, Korea)*
Rene Kizilcec *(Stanford University, USA)*

Learning@Scale 2017 Organization

General Chair: Claudia Urrea *(Massachusetts Institute of Technology, USA)*

Program Chair: Justin Reich *(Massachusetts Institute of Technology, USA)*
Candace Thille *(Stanford University, USA)*

Steering Committee Chair: Gregor Kiczales *(University of British Columbia, Canada)*

Steering Committee: Vincent Alevan *(Carnegie Mellon University, USA)*
Ryan Baker *(University of Pennsylvania, USA)*
Armando Fox *(University of California at Berkeley, USA)*
Marti Hearst *(University of California at Berkeley, USA)*
Judy Kay *(University of Sydney, Australia)*
Scott Klemmer *(University of California at San Diego (USA)*
Ken Koedinger *(Carnegie Mellon University, USA)*
John Mitchell *(Stanford University, USA)*
Carolyn Penstein Rosé *(Carnegie Mellon University, USA)*
Ido Roll *(University of British Columbia, Canada)*
Jeremy Roschelle *(SRI International, USA)*
Daniel Russell *(Google, USA)*
Mehran Sahami *(Stanford/ex officio ACM Ed Board, USA)*
Karen Swan *(Univ of Illinois, Springfield, USA)*
Yan Timanovsky *(ACM Staff Liaison, USA)*
Beverly P. Woolf *(University of Massachusetts Amherst, USA)*

Program Committee: Vincent Alevan *(Carnegie Mellon University, USA)*
Andrew Bernat *(Computing Research Association, USA)*
Marie Bienkowski *(SRI International, USA)*
Gautam Biswas *(Vanderbilt University, USA)*
Christopher Brooks *(University of Michigan, USA)*
Eric Bruillard *(ENS Cachan, France)*
Emma Brunskill *(Carnegie Mellon University, USA)*
Bodong Chen *(University of Minnesota, USA)*
Chris Dede *(Harvard University, USA)*
Pierre Dillenbourg *(École Polytechnique Fédérale de Lausanne, Switzerland)*
Matthew Easterday *(Northwestern University, USA)*
Kobi Gal *(Ben Gurion University, Israel)*
Dragan Gasevic *(University of Edinburgh, UK)*
Lee Giles *(Pennsylvania State University, USA)*
Irene Grief *(International Business Machines, USA)*
Marti Hearst *(University of California at Berkeley, USA)*
Neil Heffernan *(Worcester Polytechnic Institute, USA)*
Iris Howley *(Stanford University, USA)*
Geert-Jan Houben *(TU Delft, Netherlands)*
Judy Kay *(University of Sydney, Australia)*
Juho Kim *(KAIST, Korea)*
Rene Kizilcec *(Stanford University, USA)*

Program Committee (continued): Scott Klemmer *(University of California, Berkeley, USA)*
Kenneth Koedinger *(Carnegie Mellon University, USA)*
Chinmay Kulkarni *(Carnegie Mellon University, USA)*
Colleen Lewis *(Harvey Mudd College, USA)*
Rose Luckin *(The London Knowledge Lab, UK)*
Taylor Martin *(O'Reilly Media, USA)*
Manolis Mavrikis *(The London Knowledge Lab, UK)*
Christoper Meniel *(Hasso Plattner Institute, Germany)*
Robert Miller *(Massachusetts Institute of Technology, USA)*
John Mitchell *(Stanford University, USA)*
Zachary Pardos *(University of California at Berkeley, USA)*
Beverly Park Woolf *(University of Massachusetts, USA)*
Chris Piech *(Stanford University, USA)*
Ido Roll *(University of British Columbia, Canada)*
Yigal Rosen *(Harvard University, USA)*
Daniel Russell *(Google, USA)*
Mehran Sahami *(Stanford University, USA)*
Eileen Scanlon *(Open University, UK)*
Emily Schneider *(Stanford University, USA)*
Daniel Seaton *(Massachusetts Institute of Technology, USA)*
Susan Singer *(Rollins University, USA)*
George Velesianos *(Royal Roads University, Canada)*
Jacob Whitehill *(Worcester Polytechnic University, USA)*
Astrid Wichmann *(Ruhr-University Bochum, Germany)*
Joseph Jay Williams *(Harvard University, USA)*
Alyssa Wise *(New York University, USA)*

Additional reviewers:

Seth Adjei
Anthony F. Botelho
Benedict Du Boulay
Amanda Carr
Heeryung Choi
Yi Cui
Ben Domingue
Yi Dong
Carrie Demmans Epp
Josh Gardner
John Hansen
Wayne Holmes
Petr Johanes
Yoon Jeon Kim
Yasmine Kotturi
Vitomir Kovanovic
David Lang

Chen Liang
Phoebe Liang
Alexander Ororbia
Korinn Ostrow
Thanaporn Patikorn
Mar Pérez-Sanagustín
Kaska Porayska-Pomsta
Kristin Stephens-Martinez
Steven Tang
Meredith Thompson
Josh Underwood
Shuting Wang
Xiaolu Xiong
Biao Yin
Liang Zhang
Ningyu Zhang
Siyuan Zhao

Learning@Scale 2017 Sponsor & Supporters

Sponsor: **Association for Computing Machinery**

Gold Supporter: **ORACLE ACADEMY**

Silver Supporter: **Google**

Bronze Supporter: **edX**

Learning Engineering: The Art of Applying Learning Science at Scale

Bror Saxberg
Chief Learning Officer, Kaplan, Inc.
Fort Lauderdale, FL
Bror.Saxberg@Kaplan.com

ABSTRACT

There's a lot of excitement about how technology can transform education, and how the data created by all this technology can create a new era of amazingly motivating personalized instruction. However, the history of technology in education suggests we need to be skeptical: radio in the 1930's, film in the 1950's, on and on through the decades. – all promised much, but never reached traction. What makes this time different?

A key difference, if we choose to put it to work, is the availability of good, evidence-based principles about how learning seems to work, derived in many laboratories using randomized controlled trials over many years.

Unfortunately, as with any set of deeply researched ideas, the narrowly specific conditions of most research studies don't answer the question, "How do I build a better math/composition/history course" in any direct way. What we need is an engineering approach – a way to take evidence-based principles and ideas, and apply them at scale to solve (with plenty of uncertainties and iterative tweaking) real-world situations – "learning engineering."

Doing this in an organization that is itself at scale is non-trivial: you may have hundreds of people who should alter their thinking and practice around learning, making this a major change project on top of the series of new engineering challenges that evidence-based work creates.

One approach involves taking a series of steps within the organization over time:

- Exposure
- Education
- Effort
- Evaluation

By drawing from the evidence that exists already, showing examples within the organization of how these principles make a difference, training developers to use the principles for design and managers to use a version of the principles to evaluate resource priorities, and building continuous evaluation into the whole operation, we can move down the path to becoming a "learning engineering" organization.

Author Keywords

Learning engineering, applied cognitive science, education technology, evidence-based instructional design, e-learning

BIOGRAPHY

Bror Saxberg is the Chief Learning Officer for Kaplan, Inc., a leading global provider of educational services. Saxberg is responsible for the support of innovative, evidence-based learning strategies, technologies and products across Kaplan's full range of educational services offerings. He is the co-author of **Breakthrough Leadership in the Digital Age: Rebooting Schooling Using Learning Science** with Frederick M. Hess, and has published a number of articles related to "learning engineering."

He helped found and acted as Chief Learning Officer at K12, Inc., a virtual education company. Before this, he was a Vice President at Knowledge Universe, and a General Manager for DK Multimedia US. He began working at McKinsey & Company, Inc.

Saxberg holds a B.A. in Mathematics and B.S. in Electrical Engineering from the University of Washington, an M.A. in Mathematics from Oxford University, a Ph.D. in Electrical Engineering and Computer Science from MIT, and an M.D. from Harvard Medical School.

L@S 2017, April 20–21, 2017, Cambridge, MA, USA.
ACM ISBN 978-1-4503-4450-0/17/04.
http://dx.doi.org/10.1145/3051457.3054019

Robust Evaluation Matrix
Towards a More Principled Offline Exploration of Instructional Policies

Shayan Doroudi
Computer Science Department
Carnegie Mellon University
shayand@cs.cmu.edu

Vincent Aleven
Human-Computer Interaction
Institute
Carnegie Mellon University
aleven@cs.cmu.edu

Emma Brunskill
Computer Science Department
Carnegie Mellon University
ebrun@cs.cmu.edu

ABSTRACT
The gold standard for identifying more effective pedagogical approaches is to perform an experiment. Unfortunately, frequently a hypothesized alternate way of teaching does not yield an improved effect. Given the expense and logistics of each experiment, and the enormous space of potential ways to improve teaching, it would be highly preferable if it were possible to estimate in advance of running a study whether an alternative teaching strategy would improve learning. This is true even in learning at scale situations, since even if it is logistically easier to recruit a large number of subjects, it remains a high stakes environment because the experiment is impacting many real students. For certain classes of alternate teaching approaches, such as new ways to sequence existing material, it is possible to build student models that can be used as simulators to estimate the performance of learners under new proposed teaching methods. However, existing methods for doing so can overestimate the performance of new teaching methods. We instead propose the Robust Evaluation Matrix (REM) method which explicitly considers model mismatch between the student model used to derive the teaching strategy and that used as a simulator to evaluate the teaching strategy effectiveness. We then present two case studies from a fractions intelligent tutoring system and from a concept learning task from prior work that show how REM could be used both to detect when a new instructional policy may not be effective on actual students and to detect when it may be effective in improving student learning.

Author Keywords
instructional policies; reinforcement learning; off-policy; policy estimation; policy selection

L@S 2017, April 20 - 21, 2017, Cambridge, MA, USA

© 2017 Copyright held by the owner/author(s). Publication rights licensed to ACM.
ISBN 978-1-4503-4450-0/17/04. . . $15.00

DOI: http://dx.doi.org/10.1145/3051457.3051463

INTRODUCTION
The gold standard for identifying more effective pedagogical approaches is to perform an experiment. Unfortunately, frequently a hypothesized alternate way of teaching does not yield an improved effect. Given the expense and logistics of each experiment, and the enormous space of potential ways to improve teaching, it would be highly preferable if it were possible to estimate in advance of running a study whether an alternative teaching strategy would improve learning. This is true even in learning at scale situations, since even if it is logistically easier to recruit a large number of subjects, it remains a high stakes environment because the experiment is impacting real students, and likely many more than in standard classroom environments.

It is possible to build student models that can be used as simulators to estimate the performance of learners under a variety of proposed teaching methods. In particular, one important open question in education is whether and how the sequencing of a given set of course activities impacts student learning. There are an enormous possible set of ways to sequence material, including the use of adaptive policies (like cognitive mastery learning [5] or reinforcement learning based policies [1, 3, 21, 24, 17, 15] which map representation of the current student state to a next pedagogical activity). Indeed prior work has suggested that the pedagogical activity to provide in terms of maximizing learning gains may depend on the student state [12], and offer significant benefits over randomly or suboptimally selecting such activities [5, 3, 15, 21]. To help estimate the potential performance of new sequencing approaches, we can build a student model, and use it as a simulator to approximate what the student learning outcomes might be when taught using the new sequencing policy. In particular, a common approach is to estimate the efficacy of a policy a priori by simulating its performance using a student model that is identical to the one used to compute the policy itself[1] [3, 17, 25]. Unfortunately, such an approach can overestimate the performance of the policy [16, 15], and relies on students

---

[1]Note that this simulation process can in fact be done in multiple ways, and often the process used to compute the policy given a student model may itself directly also yield an estimate of the performance (the student learning outcomes) of the policy assuming the student model it uses is in fact how students learn in the real world. (For example, in reinforcement learning, value iteration or policy iteration would yield such an estimate.)

really learning in the same way as the student model assumes. While we hope that we have good models of student learning, student modeling is an active area of research, and different models of student learning with similar predictive accuracies can yield very different policies or outcomes for students [23, 13, 28].

In contrast, in this paper, we present the robust evaluation matrix (REM) method for estimating the potential impact of a new way of teaching (focusing on sequencing strategies) in advance of an experiment. REM seeks to make our predictions more robust to model mismatch, the situation where the student model used to derive a policy is not the same as the true model that underlies student learning where the policy will be deployed. We present two case studies to show how REM can be used in practice. In the first, we demonstrate that our method can help correctly predict when a new policy would not be effective in improving student learning while standard model-based evaluation predicts otherwise. In the second, we show that REM could be used to detect policies that will do better than baselines in a concept learning domain when deployed on actual students, and again can detect cases where policies are likely to be ineffective in the real world.

We believe REM could be used to more cautiously estimate the potential impact of new strategies, and thereby has the potential to help guide and potentially reduce the number of experiments needed to find promising new teaching methods.

OFF-POLICY POLICY ESTIMATION AND SELECTION
We are interested in the related problems of off-policy policy estimation and off-policy policy selection: the setting where we have access to prior data collected using some policy, and we want to use that data to make inferences about one or more *other* (instructional) policies. Off-policy policy estimation can be used to estimate the performance of a new instructional policy without (or in advance of) running an experiment. Such counterfactual reasoning is important not just in education, but in a wide swath of other areas including economics, healthcare, and consumer modeling [27, 29]. Off-policy policy estimation is often a critical part of off-policy policy selection: determining which policy from among a set of candidate policies would have the highest expected performance if deployed in the future. We are primarily interested in the problem of off-policy policy selection, as it can have practical implications with respect to what we do in practice. We consider the problem of off-policy policy estimation in so far as it helps us achieve the former. As we will show, while the two have been tightly coupled in the literature, we present a method that does not necessarily give us reliable estimates of the performance of instructional policies but could still be used to compare instructional policies.

An important class of instructional policies that we focus on in this paper are policies that determine what problem/activity to present to a student at any given time based on features of a student's state (e.g., the student's performance on past problems, how long the student has spent on the system, the student's level of prior knowledge etc.). The performance of an instructional policy might be how much it improves student learning, which is often assessed in educational experiments

by how well students do on a posttest given after instruction, or how much faster it helps students learn a fixed amount of material, which is often what is optimized in mastery learning contexts. We now discuss approaches to doing off-policy policy estimation and selection, including how this problem has been tackled in education settings as well as in some of the broader reinforcement learning literature.

Model-Based Evaluation
To leverage the data collected from another policy, a common approach to doing off-policy policy estimation is to first use that data to fit the parameters of a statistical (student) model [3, 17, 21]. Given such a model, we can then use that model as a simulator to evaluate the performance of any compatible alternate (instructional) policy. Compatibility here involves two aspects. The first is that the student simulator model must be a generative model capable of simulating any observations required by the instructional policy. For example, for the following instructional policy,

---
if *student took* > 100 *seconds to complete previous problem*
  then
  | give multiplication problem
else
  | give division problem

---

the student simulator model must be capable of generating the amount of time a simulated student takes to do each problem. Second, the alternate policy can only select an activity given a student state which the model is capable of simulating an outcome for. Implicitly, this means that the data used to train the model parameters must have included making a similar decision for another student in that state, and observing some outcome. This indicates that the collected data supports the alternate policy. More intuitively, consider collecting data from an instructional policy (call it policy 0) that randomly either gives a student a worked example or a short video whenever the student first logs into the educational software. Now consider a new instructional policy (call it policy A) that provides a student with a quiz when he first logs into the educational software. The old policy never provided students with a quiz upon logging in to the system, and so a model of student learning and the impact of activities on the student's learning state will not include any estimate of what it would be like if the student were to get a quiz in this situation. In this situation, the alternate policy cannot be simulated. In contrast, consider another new instructional policy (policy B) that always provides students with a worked example when they first log in to the tutoring software. In this case, we can simulate the potential performance of policy B, because the statistical student model of learning that was estimated from policy 0 includes an estimate of potential outcomes that could occur in this setting. Throughout the rest of this paper, we will focus our attention on considering instructional policies that are compatible with the previously collected data– that is, policies whose outcomes could be simulated by a generative student learning model estimated from the collected data.

In model-based off-policy estimation, two immediate questions arise: (1) given a particular (student) model class and a dataset, how do we estimate the performance of a policy, and (2) how do we select which model class to choose? Here, model class refers to the type of statistical model used to represent student learning. There are many models of student learning considered in the literature, including Bayesian Knowledge Tracing [6], logistic regression models like performance factors analysis [18], Markov decision processes (MDPs) [3, 25], partially observable MDPs (POMDPs) [21], and Deep Knowledge Tracing [19].

Given a model class and a dataset, the typical approach is to use machine learning to fit the parameters that best model the available data (such as finding the maximum likelihood model, or a model that minimizes a desired loss function). Using the resulting fit model parameters, we can then simulate how a student might learn under a desired compatible policy. To assess how good a policy is, we also need a way to evaluate the student learning outcomes generated under a specific policy. In reinforcement learning this is typically known as the reward model, which could, for example, provide a positive reward when a student gets a test question correct. Together the student learning model and reward model can be used to both simulate a student's learning under a compatible policy, and evaluate the quality of the resulting simulated outcomes. If the student learning model plus the reward model constitute a Markov decision process, there exist well known algorithms (such as value iteration or policy iteration) for computing an instructional policy that achieves the maximal expected policy performance under that student learning model and reward function. This approach has been leveraged in multiple educational data mining research projects and reinforcement learning settings [3, 17, 25].

There are at least two issues that arise with this approach. First, given finite data, the estimated model parameter values will be approximate, and these parameter uncertainties can result in error in the resulting estimated performance of a policy, especially when that policy is designed to maximize performance for that model [16]. There do exist multiple techniques to quantify the amount of error in the resulting estimated policy performance due to parameter uncertainty, some of which have been previously considered in the educational technology literature [16, 3]. In addition, large scale datasets like those collected when learning at scale reduce parameter uncertainty, as in general the more data we have the more precise our parameter estimates will be.

The other, larger issue, is that the chosen model class may be a poor approximation of how students learn, and may yield misleading estimates of the performance of a proposed policy. This relates to the second critical issue: how do we select which model class to choose?

Indeed, there is a vast amount of research on student modeling, and a common way to evaluate and compare potential student model classes is by their predictive accuracy, such as using cross validation root mean squared error on an input dataset. One natural idea then is to select the model class with the smallest predictive error, and then compute an instructional

policy with the highest predicted performance for the given model class as fit to the available data. Unfortunately, even if two different student model classes have similar predictive accuracy when fit to a particular dataset, they may have very different implications for what instructional policy will be most effective [23, 13, 28]. Moreover, prior work has shown that just selecting the student model with the highest accuracy on an input dataset may not be the model whose best associated policy has the highest performance for real student learning [15]. Other work has shown the limitations of considering model accuracy and how it does not capture the information most meaningful for decision making [2, 9]. All of this suggests that model accuracy alone is not sufficient for deciding which model class to select.

A second approach is to select the student model and instructional policy that under that student model is expected to have the best performance (e.g. best student learning outcomes). This requires deriving a policy for each model under consideration (often the optimal policy or an approximation of the optimal policy for that model) and evaluating that policy by simulating it on the model used to derive it. We call this **direct model-based evaluation**. This approach has been used to compare and select among different student learning models and their optimal policies. Chi et al. used this approach to select an instructional policy, by comparing different student learning models represented as Markov decision processes with different student features and the resulting instructional policy that yielded the best expected performance for a given model [3]. Similarly, Rowe et al. estimated the predicted performance of instructional policies that were designed to maximize performance under particular student models and compared them to some hand designed baseline policies and a random policy by evaluating these policies under the same student models. Unsurprisingly, the policy that was computed to have the best predicted performance for a given student model was also estimated to to out-perform the baseline policies under that same model [25].

This approach is quite appealing, as it is more directly getting at what we often care about: estimating the performance of policies in order to select a policy with the best expected performance. Unfortunately, since any student model will not generally capture the way that real students learn (even given infinite amounts of data used to estimate the model parameters), evaluating a policy assuming the model it was derived under is correct will generally not provide an accurate estimate of the value of a policy if it were to be used with real students. Comparing the estimated performance of policies when each policy is evaluated using a different simulated student model can therefore yield misleading conclusions. Indeed Mandel et al. have shown that *even if* the real world can be accurately modeled as a complex Markov decision process, it is possible that the optimal policy for an alternate statistical model that is incorrect might have a higher estimated performance than the optimal policy of the true MDP, even with an infinite amount of data[2] [15]. Therefore, this is not a problem that learning at scale alone can solve.

---

[2]This is because the alternate statistical model may not satisfy the Markov property.

Indeed, the limitations of evaluating the performance of a policy with the student model used to derive the policy has been observed previously. In simulation, Rowe et al. estimated a new instructional policy would have a performance of 25.4 in contrast to a random policy that was estimated to have a performance of 3.6, where performance was measured as a function of students' normalized learning gains[3] beyond the median student and the performance of both policies was simulated with the student model used to derive the new instructional policy[25]. In contrast, in an experiment with real students, there was no significant difference between the performance of students taught by the two policies [24]. While there are many factors in any experiment with real students, estimating performance using the assumed student model may particularly lead to overly optimistic estimates of the resulting performance. In this paper, we will present other situations where doing so incorrectly predicts a difference in performance between policies that is not found in an actual experiment, but where our alternate procedure (to be described shortly) would have correctly anticipated no significant difference in performance among the policies.

Importance Sampling

Using prior data to obtain an estimator of an instructional policy's performance in advance of deploying the new policy that is not biased by assuming particular statistical student model could seem rather difficult. However, there does exist an elegant solution: importance sampling, an approach that does not require building a student model, but rather re-weighs past data to compute an estimate of the performance of a new policy [20]. Importance sampling is statistically consistent and unbiased. In prior work, Mandel et al. used importance sampling to find an instructional policy in an educational game that significantly outperformed a random policy and even an expert-designed instructional policy [15]. Unfortunately, importance sampling tends to yield highly variable estimates of a new policy's performance when evaluating instructional policies that are used for many sequential decisions, such as students interacting with a tutoring system across many activities. Intuitively this issue arises when a new policy is quite different from a previous policy, and so the old data consists of quite different student trajectories (sequences of pedagogical activities given and student responses) than what would be expected to be observed under a new policy. Mathematically, this is because importance sampling yields unbiased but high variance estimates, unlike direct-model based evaluation which can yield very biased estimates (due to choosing an inaccurate model class) with potentially low variance (when we have enough data).

It is true that with more data, the variance of the importance sampling estimator will decrease, so one may assume this should be the method of choice for learning at scale, but this is not the case when one has to make a large number of sequential decisions. For example, consider some educational software that presents 20 activities to students and only needs to choose between one of two options at any given time (for example,

[3]The normalized learning gain for a student is the difference between the posttest score and pretest score of the student divided by the maximum possible difference.

whether to give the student a worked example or a problem-solving exercise). Suppose we have collected existing data from a policy that randomly chose each option for each of the 20 decisions and want to use this for off-policy policy estimation. If we want to evaluate a deterministic instructional policy (i.e., a policy with no randomness), then only one out of every 2^{20} (over one million) students would encounter a trajectory that matches the policy of interest, which means we need millions of students to get a decent estimate of the policy. If the software were to make 50 decisions, then we would need over 10^{15} students!

Finding a statistical estimator that offers the best of both approaches (model-based evaluation and importance sampling estimators) is an active area of research in the reinforcement learning community [8, 11, 26] but remains a challenge whenever the (instructional) policies may be used to make a large number of decisions, as highlighted above.

ROBUST EVALUATION MATRIX (REM)

Ideally we want a method for off-policy policy estimation that combines the statistical efficiency of (student) model based estimators with the agnosticism of importance sampling techniques which allows them to be robust to the choice of student model used to derive a particular policy. As we previously argued, this is important even given an enormous amount of data. One potential avenue is to focus on designing better student models, a key effort in the educational data mining and artificial intelligence in education communities. However, since these model classes will still likely be approximate models of student learning, we propose an alternative approach that may not enable us to achieve accurate estimates, but can still help inform comparisons among different policies: using many models we expect to be wrong, rather than using one model we hope to be right.

Our robust evaluation matrix (REM) is a tool for more conservatively evaluating the potential performance of a new policy in relation to other policies during off-policy policy selection. As shown in Algorithm 1, the simple idea is to estimate the performance of different instructional policies by simulating them using multiple plausible student models whose model parameters were fit using previously collected data. The rows of the matrix are different student models and the columns of the matrix are the various policies one wants to estimate the performance of. An entry in the matrix represents the expected performance of a particular instructional policy when simulated under a particular student model. As the student model simulators have parameters that are fit based on the previously collected data, they will often represent reasonable possible ways of modeling the dynamics of student learning. If we restrict our comparison to models with similar predictive accuracy (e.g., as evaluated using cross validation or a test set constructed from the available data), it is unclear which model is better, but the REM method can be used to assess trends in performance across policies that are consistent across multiple possible ways that students may learn in the real environment (e.g., Bayesian Knolwedge Tracing, Performance Factors Analysis, Deep Knowledge Tracing etc.).

Simulating the potential performance of instructional policies under multiple student models to inform off-policy policy selection has been previously underexplored. There has been some prior work that analyzes the interaction of student models and instructional policies (that may have been derived with a particular student model) [21, 13, 23, 9, 4], but such work has often been done to understand the general differences between policies run on various models, rather than as a tool to inform whether a new policy may offer benefits over previous ones before conducting experiments or embedding a policy in a tutoring system. One exception is work by Clement et al., where they investigate the case where the knowledge graphs (i.e., prerequisite relations between knowledge components) used to learn models used to compute policies are not the same as the ones underlying student learning [4]. The authors found that a particular model that does not have parameters fine-tuned to the knowledge graph performs best when there is a mismatch in the policy's representation of knowledge graph and true knowledge graphs of students. Their work differs from our current paper in that the authors only consider robustness of policy's of varying complexity in light of the knowledge graph changing but do not consider student models that differ more wildly and the authors do not present a general method for off-policy policy estimation or selection. Moreover, they only presented results from simulations with hand-crafted parameters rather than models and policies fit to real data. Nonetheless, we can consider this work as an example of REM being used in the past to inform policy selection. The most closely related work is by Rafferty et al.[21], which analyzed the potential performance of various instructional policies derived from different models of student concept learning under various student concept learning models that were fit from a previously collected dataset. However, unlike our current paper, they presented this idea primarily to understand the interaction between the policies and the models of student learning (e.g. could a policy assuming a very simple model of student learning still do well if the real student exhibits much more complicated student learning), rather than as a generic tool for off-policy policy estimation and selection. In the next section, we reinterpret their results as a positive use case of REM. Moreover, while Rafferty et al. consider simulating policies only on models of student learning that were used to derive some of the policies, REM could simulate policies on other models of student learning, even if one does not derive any policies from those student models. We present one example of this in the next section.

REM can be used in several ways. If one or more student models in the matrix suggest that a new policy is no better or even worse than other (baseline) policies, then it would suggest a new policy may not yield a significant improvement in learning outcomes. On the other hand, if the student models agree that one policy appears to be better than others (and these student models are indeed quite different from each other[4]), then it should increase our confidence that the policy will actually out-perform the other policies. Recall that we are

---

Input: Set of models $m = 1\ldots M$ and policies $p = 1\ldots P$
REM ← $m \times p$ matrix
for *model* $m = 1\ldots M$ **do**
    for *policy* $p = 1\ldots P$ **do**
        if *model m compatible with policy p* **then**
            mean, stddev ← Estimate performance of policy p on model m // For example by simulating many times
            REM[m][p] ← mean, stddev

return *REM*

Algorithm 1: Pseudocode for algorithm to fill in robust evaluation matrix.

interested in the joint problems of off-policy policy estimation and off-policy policy selection. We propose that REM can help with addressing the second problem, even though it does not necessarily help us with the first. That is, if we find a policy that robustly does better than another policy according to various student models, then we may decide to choose to implement that policy in practice; however, if different student models have very different predictions as to how well the new policy will perform, then we may not have a good estimate of its performance a priori. But having an estimate of a policy we are confident will do well a priori may not be necessary if we are planning on testing it on actual students anyways. This makes REM differ from off-policy policy selection techniques in the existing literature, which aim to use imperfect methods of policy estimation as a way to do policy selection. Rather, REM aims to help the researcher make decisions about what policy to select without directly trying to get a good estimate of a policy's performance.

CASE STUDIES

We now present two case studies to ground the discussion and illustrate how REM can inform what instructional policies may yield improved performance, given prior data. The first is an experimental study we ran in which we used old data to derive a new policy we estimated to be better than a standard baseline, but which yielded equivalent performance in a subsequent student study. Our post hoc analysis suggests we could have predicted this result by using a REM analysis. In the second case study, we will look at the results of a paper by Rafferty et al. where they perform an analogue of REM to better understand how various instructional policies might perform under different student models [21]. Although their paper did not suggest using such a method for off-policy policy selection, we show two examples of how it could have been used both to predict that several policies were likely to do well when tested on real students and to predict that another policy may perform poorly (a result that would not have been predicted if a policy's performance was only estimated assuming that the student model used to derive the policy was in fact how students truly learn).

---

[4]The difference in student models could be based difference in theory, for example a Bayesian Knowledge Tracing model and a Deep Knowledge Tracing model make rather different assumptions about

student learning—or based on empirically observing that simulating the same instructional policy on two different models results in reasonably different trajectories quantified in some way.

Case Study 1: Fractions Tutor Experiment

We ran an experiment to test five instructional policies in an intelligent tutoring system (ITS) designed to teach fractions to elementary school students [22, 7].

There were two main goals to the experiment: (1) to test whether adaptive problem selection based on an individual student's knowledge state makes a difference (in terms of improving student learning), and (2) to test whether supporting a variety of activity types in an ITS leads to more robust learning. Additionally, we were interested in testing whether we could improve upon the traditional form of adaptive instruction used in ITSs: cognitive mastery learning using Bayesian Knowledge Tracing (BKT). Namely, we were interested in testing whether reasoning about (prerequisite) relationships between skills when deciding what problem to give a student to solve improves student learning beyond simply giving problems until a student masters each skill independently. We therefore developed a new student model that treats the correctness on the last two steps of each skill as the state of a student's knowledge of that skill, and then predicts the student's next state of a skill based on the student's knowledge of that skill as well as prerequisite skills. Prerequisite skills were identified using the G-SCOPE algorithm [10]. Our models used a skill model that was inferred using the weighted Chinese restaurant process technique developed by Lindsey et al. [14], which was seeded with a hand-crafted skill model. Model parameters were fit given access to data that was previously collected using a semi-random instructional policy to teach over 1,000 students, who used the tutor for four to six days, with most students completing between 20 and 100 problems out of a potential set of 156 problems. Student learning was assessed using identical pretests and posttests composed of 16 questions.

We iterated over multiple potential adaptive instructional policies, seeking to identify a policy that we estimated would yield improved performance over both strong baseline non-adaptive policies, and equal or better performance to a state-of-the-art policy based on mastery teaching. Since each student completed many problems using the tutor, typically more than 20, importance sampling techniques for estimating the student learning outcomes under an alternate instructional policy (that adaptively sequenced activities in a different way) were infeasible (see example above). Instead, we relied on simulating a policy's performance based on a student learning model. We choose adaptive policies that we estimated would yield a significant improvement over the non-adaptive baselines. This lead us to choose the following adaptive policies for use in a future experiment, policies that we believed had a good chance of yielding a significant improvement,

- Adaptive Policy 1 (**AP-1**): greedily maximize the number of skills that students learn with each problem assuming the fit G-SCOPE model.

- Adaptive Policy 2 (**AP-2**): Selects problems to myopically maximize the student's posttest score under a fit G-SCOPE student model.

These were to compared to the following baselines

- Baseline 1: Instructional policy that selects standard (induction and refinement) problems, in a reasonable non-adaptive order, based on spiralling through the curriculum.

- Baseline 2: Instructional policy that selects among a diverse set of problem types, in a reasonable non-adaptive order, based on spiralling through the curriculum.

- BKT Mastery Policy (**BKT-MP**): This is a state-of-the-art cognitive mastery learning policy used with a Bayesian Knowledge Tracing model which has been previously shown to yield substantial improvements in student learning [6].

Row 1 of Table 1 shows the estimated performance of the above policies, where each adaptive policy was simulated using the student model used to derive the policy. Since the first two policies are non-adaptive, they were not derived using a student model. We used the G-SCOPE student model to simulate the performance of these baseline non-adaptive policies. All evaluations assumed each (simulated) student completed 40 problems, and we repeated this process with 1,000 simulated students.

Using these off-policy policy performance estimates, the predicted Cohen's d effect size of AP-2 vs. Baseline 2 is 3.66 and the predicted effect size of AP-2 vs. Baseline 1 is 4.14, indicating that the new adaptive policies may yield a large improvement in robust student learning.

However, in our subsequent experiments there was no significant difference in the performance of students taught in the different policies as shown in Row 2 of Table 1.

We now consider the insight we could have obtained by using REM. We apply REM to our policies by evaluating them on three models: (1) the G-SCOPE model (which was used to derive AP-1 and AP-2), (2) the BKT student model (which was used to derive BKT-MP), and (3) a Deep Knowledge Tracing (DKT) model [19]. The results are shown in Table 2.

Using the BKT student model, we see that all the policies appear to have much more similar expected performance than when using the G-SCOPE student model, though the new adaptive policies are still expected to be as good or better than the state-of-the-art BKT mastery policy in either situation, and an improvement over the non-adaptive policies. Therefore, were we only to simulate policies under the models used to derive the policies, we might still expect that the new adaptive policies would yield improved performance.

The key distinction comes up when we also simulate under another plausible student model, which was not used to derive a particular student policy. In contrast to the other student models, simulating using a Deep Knoweldge Tracing student model actually predicts that Baseline 1 will yield the highest expected student learning performance, and be substantially higher than the predicted performance of the adaptive instructional policies.[5] Since three student models (BKT, G-SCOPE

---

[5]This Deep Knowledge Tracing model was introduced by Piech et al. [19] after these experiments were conducted, so interestingly, we could not have done this analysis prior to running our experiment.

	Instructional Policies				
	Baseline 1	Baseline 2	BKT-MP	AP-1	AP-2
Direct Model-Based Evaluation Results	5.87 ± 0.90	6.10 ± 0.97	7.03 ± 1.00	7.85 ± 0.98	9.10 ± 0.80
Actual Experimental Results	5.52 ± 2.61	5.14 ± 3.22	5.46 ± 3.0	5.57 ± 3.27	4.93 ± 1.8

Table 1. The first row shows the estimated expected performance of a student when taught under each policy, assuming either the student model used to derive the policy, or, in the case of the non-adaptive policies, using the estimated G-SCOPE student model. The second row shows the results of our actual experiment. Note that the posttest was out of sixteen points.

		Instructional Policies				
		Baseline 1	Baseline 2	BKT-MP	AP-1	AP-2
Student Models	New Student Model	5.87 ± 0.90	6.10 ± 0.97	N/A	7.85 ± 0.98	9.10 ± 0.80
	BKT Student Model	6.46 ± 0.78	6.65 ± 0.95	7.03 ± 1.00	6.82 ± 0.94	7.04 ± 0.96
	DKT Student Model	9.89 ± 1.45	8.69 ± 1.82	8.55 ± 2.08	8.31 ± 2.22	8.58 ± 2.13

Table 2. Robust evaluation matrix showing predictions of the five policies in our experiment according to the new student model as well as the BKT student model and a DKT student model. Notice that BKT-MP was not simulated on the new student model since they were not exactly compatible due to a nuance in the way they represent steps.

and DKT) are all seemingly reasonable choices of student models with similar predictive accuracies (RMSE between 0.41 and 0.44), our robust evaluation matrix suggests that we should not have been confident that new adaptive policies would yield a large effect size improvement over non-adaptive baselines or even necessarily be better than the non-adaptive policies (thus consistent with the lack of difference in the true experimental results).

Therefore, in this case REM could have served as a diagnostic tool to identify that our new proposed adaptive policies might not yield the significant improvement we hoped for, by explicitly considering whether this improvement is robust across many plausible student models.

Case Study 2: Concept Learning

In Rafferty et al. [21], the authors consider three instructional policies for concept learning. The models are derived under three different partially observable Markov decision process (POMDP) student learning models of varying complexity inspired from the cognitive science literature: a memoryless model in which a learner maintains a single potential concept until evidence contradicts the correctness of this concept, a discrete model with memory which augments the memoryless model to prevent the learner from forgetting prior negative evidence about the potential concepts, and a continuous model which assigns probabilities to different potential concepts [21]. The model parameters were fit with data the authors collected from students given a random policy. The performance of a policy is measured in how long (time in seconds) it takes for students to learn a series of rules or a concept.

Like REM, the authors first simulate each policy on each of the three student models, but unlike REM, the authors only consider models that are used to derive some instructional policy (and no other student learning models). This is because the authors are interested in the interaction of student models with policies derived from student models and what that says about human learning, rather than using this simulation as an off-policy policy selection tool to help decide which instructional policies may offer a benefit over existing benchmarks.

Indeed, Rafferty et al. test all policies with real students. We reinterpret their results in terms of insights REM would have offered about the relative expected performance among the policies.

In the first experiment, the authors find that in simulation, all three student models agree that the three policies induced by the POMDPs would enable student to learn the rules faster than a random policy (i.e., the memoryless, discrete with memory, and continuous policies do better than the random policy *in all three rows* of the robust evaluation matrix). We propose this should lead a practitioner to believe that these three policies will likely do better than a random policy when presented to actual students (if the student models are believed to be decent). Indeed, in their experiments, the authors found that all three POMDP policies induced a smaller average time to mastering the rules than the policy which selects activities randomly, two of which were statistically significantly faster.

In this situation REM consistently estimated that the adaptive policies would have higher performance than the random activity selection policies, under 3 different student models, and this result was confirmed experimentally. This shows a situation where REM consistently identified a predicted improvement, under a variety of student models.

We now consider another example from this work where REM could have helped predict that a policy would likely not work well in practice, but evaluating policies only under the models used to derive that policy would fail to identify this issue.

In their Experiment 3, Rafferty et al. compare various policies on three concept learning tasks both in simulation (under all three student models) and in an actual experiment. The following result is of most interest to us: when using the continuous POMDP model to simulate student learning, they find that a heuristic greedy policy derived from this model—the maximum information gain policy—does significantly better than both the random-action-selection policy and the two POMDP polices derived from other POMDP models. This was estimated to hold in all three concept learning tasks. However, in the actual experiment with students, the maximum information gain policy yields lower student performance than the random action selection policy and all the POMDP policies for all three concept learning tasks. This result could have been detected using REM, as both the memoryless model and the discrete model with memory estimated that the performance of the maximum information gain policy would be lower than the estimated performance of the random-action-selection instructional policy in at least one concept learning task. In this situation REM would have restricted the confidence with which one could expect the new policy to yield a big improvement in performance.

DISCUSSION

In some cases, REM might result in one being overly-conservative by not deploying an instructional policy that is actually worthwhile, but at the end of the day, it is up to each researcher to decide if they want to try a policy they think might result in improved student learning, even if they do not have strong evidence that it will, or if they would rather find a policy they are confident would result in an improvement. One can attain such confidence (although not in any statistically precise sense) if one finds a policy that does very well under various student models as we saw an example of in Case Study 2. However, as we have emphasized several times, this confidence depends on being convinced that our choice of student models to use in the matrix was good. As we mentioned, we do not expect any of these student models to be correct, so what does it mean for a model to be "good"? A necessary condition is that such a model should be able to differentiate between different policies. For example, a model that predicts students are always in the same state (perhaps determined by their prior knowledge or pretest scores) and never learn would not be a good model to use in REM, because it would predict all instructional policies result in equal student outcomes. One way to avoid such "bad" models is to avoid models with bad predictive accuracy; even if high predictive accuracy is not a good indicator of a model's ability to suggest good instructional policies, an especially low predictive accuracy should be a red flag.

So far we have been discussing how REM can help address the problem of wrong classes of student models. But notice that REM can also help address two other related issues that may arise in educational contexts and certainly did arise in Case Study 1. First, recall that in the fractions tutor case study, the off-policy estimation was based on assuming students would do 40 problems each (i.e., we simulated trajectories of 40 problems). In reality, trajectories will be of varying length due to a number of factors: some students work faster than others, some students spend less time working or may be absent on certain days of our experiment, etc. However, even if we consider the variance in trajectory lengths that existed in our past data, the evaluation results would be similar. But one thing we did not consider is that the distribution of trajectory lengths varies for different instructional policies. For example, students who had the Baseline 1 policy, did around 48 problems on average, whereas for all the other policies, the average was 28 problems or less. This is, at least in part, because Baseline 1 only gives problems of a particular activity type (induction

and refinement), which tended to be the activity type that took the least amount of time on average. This could explain why Baseline 1 did as well as the other policies in our experiment; these students simply had more problems, which could make up for the lack of diversity or adaptivity of problems. To tackle this problem, we can consider different generative models of how many problems students will do given a particular instructional policy (for example by taking into account how long problems took students in our past data); we can then use these various models as different student models (i.e., different rows in our matrix) and see if any policies robustly do well with respect to these differences.

The second issue is that the classrooms that we ran this experiment in were very different from the classrooms we had collected data from previously to fit the models (and hence policies) used in this experiment. This mismatch in student population could mean that our student models learned from students of one population may not generalize to other student populations. For example, students in low-performing schools may have lower learning rates than students in high-performing schools, even if the model class could accurately model student learning. To our knowledge, this is an issue that is not well studied or solved in the education literature. To tackle the problem of mismatched student populations, we can fit our various student models to different subsets of our data corresponding to different student populations (assuming we have data from multiple student sub-populations), and then have these different models (of the same model class) form new rows in our matrix. Interestingly, Clement et al. cast their work as training models on different student populations (characterized by student's with certain knowledge graphs) and seeing how that generalizes to other populations of students (with different knowledge graphs) [4]; their work would be an instance of using REM to explore robustness of policies to different student populations in simulation. Table 3 shows a hypothetical matrix depicting how REM could potentially be used to tackle the various issues of general student model mismatch, varying trajectory lengths, and generalization of student population in tandem.

We wish to highlight that the case studies we have examined were retrospective. We hope that future studies will explore REM's use in a prospective manner, and how it might be leveraged to inform instructional design decisions for later use.

At this point we do not make any universal recommendations for how to use the robust matrix method to determine which instructional policy to use in the future. It is possible that one policy does not consistently do better than all other policies for every row of the matrix, but that it tends to do better, or that on average it does better. In this case, should we be confident in that policy? The answer must be determined on a case-by-case basis. The matrix might help reveal trends that can help the researcher determine whether a policy should be deployed or not. It is not an algorithm that will tell the researcher what to do; it is a heuristic that can help inform the researcher to make better decisions.

	Policy 1	Policy 2	Policy 3	Policy 4

Student Model 1 with Time Model 1 fit to data from Low Performing Students
Student Model 2 with Time Model 1 fit to data from Low Performing Students
Student Model 1 with Time Model 1 fit to data from **High Performing Students**
...

Table 3. Hypothetical robust evaluation matrix that incorporates both various student model classes, different generative time models of how many problems students will do in a fixed time, and models that are fit to different demographics.

CONCLUSION

We have introduced the robust evaluation matrix, a method to support off-policy policy selection. Interestingly, even though REM cannot enable the user to accurately assess the impact of a policy, it can help a researcher determine when a policy should or should not be deployed. We have shown how REM could have been used before running our own experiment to test new adaptive policies to reduce our confidence that any of the policies we were testing would do better than any other, and perhaps dissuade us from running the experiment until we found a better policy. We additionally showed how prior work [21] has indirectly provided evidence that REM could potentially be used to help gain confidence that a policy will actually improve student performance (beyond baseline policies). This could have implications to the learning at scale community as personalization is one of the most important fronts for learning at scale researchers, and as we have seen, current techniques in policy estimation and policy selection are not sufficient, even at scale. Moreover, this new method could prove promising to the reinforcement learning community, beyond its impact in the domain of education. For ourselves, we have helped turn hindsight into foresight; we hope this foresight will guide future researchers towards more rapidly discovering effective adaptive instructional policies.

ACKNOWLEDGMENTS

The research reported here was supported, in whole or in part, by the Institute of Education Sciences, U.S. Department of Education, through Grants R305A130215 and R305B150008 to Carnegie Mellon University. The opinions expressed are those of the authors and do not represent views of the Institute or the U.S. Dept. of Education.

REFERENCES
1. Joseph Beck, Beverly Park Woolf, and Carole R Beal. 2000. ADVISOR: A machine learning architecture for intelligent tutor construction. *AAAI/IAAI* 2000 (2000), 552–557.

2. Joseph Beck and Xiaolu Xiong. 2013. Limits to accuracy: how well can we do at student modeling?. In *Educational Data Mining 2013*.

3. Min Chi, Kurt VanLehn, Diane Litman, and Pamela Jordan. 2011. Empirically evaluating the application of reinforcement learning to the induction of effective and adaptive pedagogical strategies. *User Modeling and User-Adapted Interaction* 21, 1-2 (2011), 137–180.

4. Benjamin Clement, Pierre-Yves Oudeyer, and Manuel Lopes. 2016. A Comparison of Automatic Teaching Strategies for Heterogeneous Student Populations. *International Educational Data Mining Society* (2016).

5. Albert Corbett. 2000. *Cognitive mastery learning in the ACT programming tutor*. Technical Report. AAAI Technical report, SS-00-01.

6. Albert T Corbett and John R Anderson. 1994. Knowledge tracing: Modeling the acquisition of procedural knowledge. *User modeling and user-adapted interaction* 4, 4 (1994), 253–278.

7. Shayan Doroudi, Kenneth Holstein, Vincent Aleven, and Emma Brunskill. 2015. Towards Understanding How to Leverage Sense-Making, Induction and Refinement, and Fluency to Improve Robust Learning. *International Educational Data Mining Society* (2015).

8. Miroslav Dudík, John Langford, and Lihong Li. 2011. Doubly robust policy evaluation and learning. *arXiv preprint arXiv:1103.4601* (2011).

9. José P González-Brenes and Yun Huang. 2015. " Your Model Is Predictive–but Is It Useful?" Theoretical and Empirical Considerations of a New Paradigm for Adaptive Tutoring Evaluation. *International Educational Data Mining Society* (2015).

10. Assaf Hallak, COM François Schnitzler, Timothy Mann, and Shie Mannor. 2015. Off-policy Model-based Learning under Unknown Factored Dynamics. In *Proceedings of the 32nd International Conference on Machine Learning (ICML-15)*. 711–719.

11. Nan Jiang and Lihong Li. 2015. Doubly Robust Off-policy Evaluation for Reinforcement Learning. *arXiv preprint arXiv:1511.03722* (2015).

12. Slava Kalyuga, Paul Ayres, Paul Chandler, and John Sweller. 2003. The expertise reversal effect. *Educational psychologist* 38, 1 (2003), 23–31.

13. Jung In Lee and Emma Brunskill. 2012. The Impact on Individualizing Student Models on Necessary Practice Opportunities. *International Educational Data Mining Society* (2012).

14. Robert V Lindsey, Mohammad Khajah, and Michael C Mozer. 2014. Automatic discovery of cognitive skills to improve the prediction of student learning. In *Advances in neural information processing systems*. 1386–1394.

15. Travis Mandel, Yun-En Liu, Sergey Levine, Emma Brunskill, and Zoran Popovic. 2014. Offline policy evaluation across representations with applications to educational games. In *Proceedings of the 2014*

international conference on Autonomous agents and multi-agent systems. International Foundation for Autonomous Agents and Multiagent Systems, 1077–1084.

16. Shie Mannor, Duncan Simester, Peng Sun, and John N Tsitsiklis. 2007. Bias and variance approximation in value function estimates. *Management Science* 53, 2 (2007), 308–322.

17. Christopher M Mitchell, Kristy Elizabeth Boyer, and James C Lester. Evaluating State Representations for Reinforcement Learning of Turn-Taking Policies in Tutorial Dialogue. In *Proceedings of the Fourteenth Annual SIGDIAL Meeting on Discourse and Dialogue (SIGDIAL-2013)*. 339–343.

18. Philip I Pavlik Jr, Hao Cen, and Kenneth R Koedinger. 2009. Performance Factors Analysis–A New Alternative to Knowledge Tracing. *Online Submission* (2009).

19. Chris Piech, Jonathan Bassen, Jonathan Huang, Surya Ganguli, Mehran Sahami, Leonidas J Guibas, and Jascha Sohl-Dickstein. 2015. Deep knowledge tracing. In *Advances in Neural Information Processing Systems*. 505–513.

20. Doina Precup. 2000. Eligibility traces for off-policy policy evaluation. *Computer Science Department Faculty Publication Series* (2000), 80.

21. Anna N Rafferty, Emma Brunskill, Thomas L Griffiths, and Patrick Shafto. 2015. Faster Teaching via POMDP Planning. *Cognitive Science* (2015).

22. Martina A Rau, Vincent Aleven, and Nikol Rummel. 2013. Complementary effects of sense-making and fluency-building support for connection making: A

matter of sequence?. In *International Conference on Artificial Intelligence in Education*. Springer, 329–338.

23. Joseph Rollinson and Emma Brunskill. 2015. From Predictive Models to Instructional Policies. *International Educational Data Mining Society* (2015).

24. Jonathan P Rowe and James C Lester. 2015. Improving student problem solving in narrative-centered learning environments: A modular reinforcement learning framework. In *International Conference on Artificial Intelligence in Education*. Springer, 419–428.

25. Jonathan P Rowe, Bradford W Mott, and James C Lester. 2014. Optimizing Player Experience in Interactive Narrative Planning: A Modular Reinforcement Learning Approach.. In *AIIDE*.

26. Philip S Thomas and Emma Brunskill. 2016. Data-Efficient Off-Policy Policy Evaluation for Reinforcement Learning. *arXiv preprint arXiv:1604.00923* (2016).

27. Philip S Thomas, Georgios Theocharous, and Mohammad Ghavamzadeh. 2015. High-Confidence Off-Policy Evaluation.. In *AAAI*. 3000–3006.

28. Michael Yudelson and Steve Ritter. 2015. Small Improvements for the Model Accuracy — Big Improvements for the Student. In *International Conference on Artificial Intelligence in Education*. Springer, 903–905.

29. Li Zhou and Emma Brunskill. 2016. Latent Contextual Bandits and their Application to Personalized Recommendations for New Users. *arXiv preprint arXiv:1604.06743* (2016).

A Visual Approach towards Knowledge Engineering and Understanding How Students Learn in Complex Environments

Lauren Fratamico
University of British Columbia
Vancouver, Canada
fratamic@cs.ubc.ca

Sarah Perez
University of British Columbia
Vancouver, Canada
sarah.perez@ubc.ca

Ido Roll
University of British Columbia
Vancouver, Canada
ido.roll@ubc.ca

ABSTRACT

Exploratory learning environments, such as virtual labs, support divergent learning pathways. However, due to their complexity, building computational models of learning is challenging as it is difficult to identify features that (i) are informative with respect to common learning strategies, (ii) abstract similar actions beyond surface differences, and (iii) differentiate groups of learners. In this paper, we present a visualization tool that addresses these challenges by facilitating a novel analytic approach to aid in the knowledge engineering process, focusing on five main capabilities: data-driven hypotheses raising, visualizing behavior over time, easily grouping related actions, contrasting learners' behaviors on these actions, and comparing the behaviors of groups of learners. We apply this analytic approach to better understand how students work with a popular interactive physics virtual lab. By splitting learners by learning gains, we found that productive learners performed more active testing and adapted more quickly to the task at hand by focusing on more relevant testing instruments. Implications for online virtual labs and a broader class of complex learning environments are discussed throughout.

ACM Classification Keywords

H.5.3. Information Interfaces and Presentation (e.g. HCI): Group and Organization Interfaces; K.3.1. Computers and Education: Computer Uses in Education

Author Keywords

Visual analytics; Exploratory data analysis; Interactive virtual labs; Exploratory learning environments; Learning strategies; Temporal data; Educational data mining; Learning analytics

INTRODUCTION

Online learning environments are increasingly complex. One aspect of this complexity is the diversity of instructional activities and their affordances. In addition, many environments move away from prescribed linear trajectories to support (and

L@S 2017, April 20-21, 2017, Cambridge, MA, USA
© 2017 ACM. ISBN 978-1-4503-4450-0/17/04...$15.00
DOI: http://dx.doi.org/10.1145/3051457.3051468

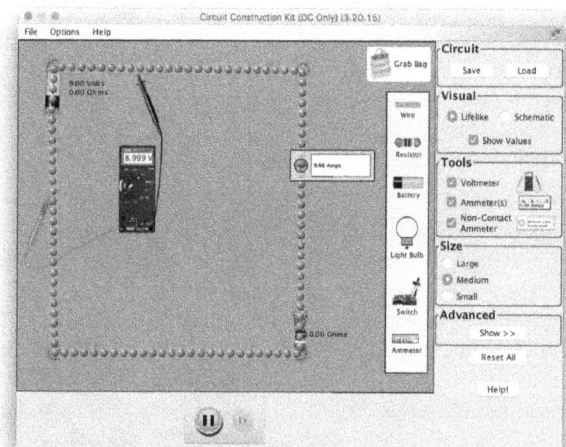

Figure 1. The PhET CCK interface, an unstructured learning environment. A complete circuit has been built in the workspace with a battery, resistor, and some wires. Also seen are two of the testing instruments: voltmeter (measuring voltage) and ammeter (measuring current).

encourage) user-driven exploration. Another aspect is the variety of learners, their goals, and engagement patterns. Overall, this complexity and diversity add a significant challenge to the interpretation of log data from learning trajectories. In short, how can we interpret learners' interactions in online learning environments? More specifically, how can we identify strategies, infer intentions, assess learning, or evaluate quality of engagement? For example, Figure 1 shows a virtual lab in which learners construct and test electric circuits with the goal of learning about DC circuits. This virtual lab has 124 different actions available to learners, and is part of a family of virtual labs that are used over 50 million times a year [1]. How can one use log data to evaluate student's attitudes and knowledge when the design space is unlimited and the solution space is underdefined? Furthermore, how can this be applicable to learners with diverse backgrounds and goals?

To interpret learner behaviors, researchers create models of learning in the environment. Common approaches for knowledge engineering rely on expert analysis and learning theories. However, all too often, this process is not well-informed by empirical data. Machine learning approaches, on the other hand, make extensive use of empirical data, yet often ignore expert knowledge and learning theories. In this paper we seek to combine the benefits of theory-driven (top down) knowledge engineering and data-driven (bottom up) knowledge discovery to make sense of data from complex systems. We propose a workflow, supported by a system, which allows researchers to hypothesize patterns based on data and quickly test these hypotheses. By doing so, we infuse the knowledge discovery process with insights based on available data.

A main goal for this work is to strengthen the bridge between data sciences, learning sciences, and instructional design. The tool, Tempr, helps its users raise hypotheses about what actions are related and how. It then allows them to quickly test their hypotheses by visualizing the relationship between engagement behaviors and other student-level factors (such as knowledge level). Tempr facilitates an analytic process that is based on the following approaches: iterative hypothesis raising and testing regarding grouping of related actions, informed by data; temporal analysis of log data; and visual comparisons between groups of learners.

We begin by describing the challenge of knowledge engineering in complex environments. We then review related literature from the education and visualization communities. We highlight key capabilities of Tempr that address many of the identified challenges, and demonstrate its utility by presenting the results of using Tempr to analyze authentic data from the virtual lab shown in Figure 1. Last, we describe how Tempr could assist with knowledge engineering in other complex learning environments, such as Massive Open Online Courses (MOOCs).

BACKGROUND

A first step towards modeling learning in new environments is to better understand it. That is, researchers should be able to label patterns in the data and assign meaning to sequences of actions. Overall, there are two common methodologies for contextualizing our understanding of what learning looks like in a target environment. While these typically apply to model the domain knowledge, they can also be applied to modeling the learning process [19]. Knowledge engineering refers to a theory-driven top-down process, often based on expert analysis [2]. For example, in a problem solving environment, fast repeat failed attempts can be labeled as guessing. This label is based on our understanding of how students learn, not on empirical data. Similarly, knowledge engineering can be used successfully to interpret other aspects of the learning process, such as help seeking [2, 18]. However, knowledge engineering becomes harder as the design space in the environment grows. For example, in a virtual lab such as the one shown in Figure 1, it is nearly impossible to define what actions constitute different testing strategies, given the multitude of testing actions. Similarly, in a MOOC setting, interpreting navigation events is challenging given their diversity. A common alternative to knowledge engineering is knowledge discovery, in which machine learning and statistical approaches are used to extract patterns from the data. For example, a knowledge-discovery approach to identify guessing in a problem-solving environ-

ment revealed two different types of guessing [4]. Knowledge discovery has been found to be very successful in certain domains [10], including in complex environments [3, 8]. However, while knowledge discovery can often be applied to predict overall learning from an environment, it has several major shortcoming. First, it is often hard to interpret the detected trends, and thus, while accurate, does not inform theory [2, 19]. Second, it is effective for skills that are easy to label, but less for divergent strategies [3, 21]. Last, the detected models may be overly specific to context and populations [8].

Several existing visualization systems address similar challenges to the ones identified above. A few systems support temporal analysis of log data and visual comparisons between groups [12, 14, 16, 24]. A number of these systems allow for iterative hypothesis raising and testing regarding grouping of related actions. One such system is CoCo [14], which allows users to test their hypotheses about which events, or sequences of events, describe different clusters of learners. However, CoCo's design works best when investigating log data with a small number of possible events. Thus, applying the tool to data from environments with a large variety of actions is challenging. Similarly, MatrixWave [24] allows for the comparison of log events between two groups. Specifically, it allows for the exploration of how one webpage is navigated in two different conditions. This allows researchers to form hypotheses regarding the differences between the two conditions. However, again, this tool works best when researchers have a small set of events to study, it does not allow the researcher to combine multiple events together to explore how different types of events relate to each other.

Other visualization systems have made an attempt at explicitly highlighting informative features from the data. For example, INFUSE [11] visualizes the result of feature selection, showing the user the most predictive features. While this is an important step, the system does not support the next steps, in which analysis is preformed on grouped events. FeatureInsights [6] helps users to engineer features from their text data, highlighting the features that distinguish two groups. However, this system also does not allow users to group multiple features. Others allow for detection and automated grouping of similar features [9, 23], an approach more similar to knowledge discovery. Yet, we advocate for a process in which the researcher can form their own groups of features as is desired in feature engineering. Other researchers attempted to group log event features for their visualization of clickstream data in semantic ways, including tf-idf and LDA, but resorted to relying on experts to perform the grouping manually, as none of the automated groupings produced acceptable results [13]. Thus, while addressing the challenge of making meaning of complex data is shared in many existing environments, it seems that these often lack the ability for the user to group different types of actions, evaluate that grouping over time, and analyze how the newly-formed groups are used by different clusters of learners. Tempr and the analytic workflow that it facilitates address that need.

VISUALIZATION TOOL

We have developed Tempr, a visual analytic approach, to assist with knowledge engineering. The main goal of this tool is to inform the top-down knowledge engineering process with patterns that emerge bottom up. Tempr does so iteratively: researchers investigate different types of behaviors and use the tool to identify patterns in the data and informative groupings of actions. Assigning meaning to these patterns can facilitate additional hypothesis testing and grouping in Tempr. The outputs of this exploratory process are intended to inform additional analysis, likely more statistical in nature.

Capabilities

The tool is built to support five main capabilities, presented below.

Surfacing big picture patterns

It is important to give researchers an overview of the data upfront, so that they may better discover and interpret emerging patterns. A global view of the data allows researchers to assess the scope and scale of the data [22], in terms of, for example, the number of available actions in a virtual lab or other learning environment. Acknowledging the size and scale of a dataset will help put discovered patterns in perspective. Finally, an overview of the data allows researchers to prioritize the aspects or features of the data they wish to explore.

Visualizing learning over time

While researchers often look at data by learner, too often data across entire sessions (or even entire courses) are combined, ignoring trends over time. However, learning in complex environments has a temporal nature [7]. For example, while an early pause in a student's actions may be a sign of planning, a later pause is more likely a sign of reflection. Analyzing a student's overall pausing behavior ignores possible strategic use of pauses over time. Thus, Tempr visualizes how learning unfolds over the duration of the activity.

Supporting exploratory grouping of related actions

One of the main challenges in exploratory environments, as described above, is the large diversity of actions. These could be merged into fewer types of actions, skills, or strategies. However, identifying which actions should be merged together in order to abstract learner behaviors is not a trivial task. As an example, in the case of a MOOC, correct problem-solving attempts may show similar trends to incorrect ones, and may be grouped to create an "attempt" category. However, perhaps these actions are qualitatively different, as they hint at different knowledge levels and entail different subsequent actions. Thus, quick evaluation of grouping of actions is of interest. Similarly, in an interactive virtual lab such as the one shown in Figure 1, grouping and then visualizing all "building" types of actions may be more meaningful than individually visualizing actions that are associated with building a circuit, such as adding a wire, connecting a light bulb, or connecting a resistor. Tempr supports quick evaluation of potential grouping of actions to facilitate the evaluation of learning strategies.

Contrasting of actions

While some actions need to be grouped, other types of actions need to be contrasted. For example, in a MOOC context,

```
==========================================
user.wire.addedComponent
user.battery.addedComponent
user.resistor.addedComponent
user.junction.movedJunction
user.battery.movedComponent
...
user.redProbe.drag
user.redProbe.endDrag
user.blackProbe.startDrag
model.voltmeterBlackLeadModel.connectionFormed
user.blackProbe.drag
user.blackProbe.endDrag
model.voltmeterModel.measuredVoltageChanged
==========================================
user.wire.addedComponent
user.wire.addedComponent
model.junction.junctionFormed
user.junction.movedJunction
user.resistor.addedComponent
model.junction.junctionFormed
...
```

Figure 2. Input to Tempr. All users for each group are placed in one ".txt" file. Each action they took while working with the environment is listed one after the other, with users separated by "======".

one may wish to compare how learners engage differently with graded versus ungraded problems, quizzes in different course modules, lecture videos in different course modules, etc. In a virtual lab, one may wish to understand what the relationship is between building circuits and testing them. The tool supports visual contrasts by simultaneously displaying the distribution of relevant actions over time, and, in so doing, enables researchers to evaluate these actions as part of effective or ineffective learning strategies.

Comparing groups of learners

In many exploratory environments there is no one correct way to engage with the course. For example, how should learners make use of self-tests in MOOCs? How should they use testing instruments in a virtual lab? Tempr has a built-in ability to show how different groups of learners interact with the environment differently. This could be used to compare learners with different outcome attributes (such as comparing successful learners to less successful ones), or incoming attributes (such as comparing the behavior of learners with different prior knowledge, attitudes, or backgrounds).

Tempr's architecture

The main Tempr interface can be seen in Figure 4. It was built using JavaScript[17], and, specifically, D3.js [5] for the graphs. Tempr is available for download on Github under the GNU license: https://github.com/fratamico/Tempr---A-visual-knowledge-engineering-tool.

Data Input

Tempr was designed with flexibility and generality in mind. The requirements in terms of data input reflect this design by enabling the use of log data from diverse sources with varying analysis goals. Tempr takes input in the form of two

".txt" files, one for each group of learners. Each file is comprised of the sequence of log events for each user in that group. An example of the input is shown in Figure 2. In terms of format, users' action sequences are separated by equals signs and each line is a logged event for that user. The researcher can choose which and how many arguments within a logged event they want to include, and should separate the selected arguments with a period. For example, in the virtual lab shown above, we chose to include the following information in the event: actor (user or model), component (the component being operated on), and action (the action that was done). For MOOCs, this data can include module ID, component type, component ID, and event type, for example: Week1.video.Introduction_Video.PlayVideo. There are no requirements of event names. However, the terms in each line of the logged events can later be used for filtering and should include all meaningful contextual information available in the logged event. Notably, the input data files contain sequences of events and do not include duration information. While this compromises the ability to analyze actions by duration, it makes data entry to Tempr more straightforward and permissible to log data without time stamps.

As mentioned above, Tempr takes two files, one for each group of learners. Learners can be grouped in different ways. In the example below we split learners into two groups based on learning gains from an activity in a virtual lab. However, learners could be divided in other ways too, for example, based on incoming attributes (knowledge, attitudes) or whether they completed the MOOC or not. Any qualitative or quantitative factor can be used to split students into groups and these groups need not be of the same size.

An overview of Tempr

Tempr has three main panels:

1. The Heatmap Panel. This panel supports hypothesis raising. It provides an overview of all actions in the tool over time and helps to identify which actions show similar patterns and could be further investigated.

2. The Merging Panel. This panel supports exploration of different groupings of actions. This is key for knowledge engineering, as it helps to see what combined actions may highlight the differences in how groups of students learn.

3. The Visualization Panel. This panel enables the comparison of an action or merged sets of actions by groups of students over time.

The next sections present the utility of these panels by demonstrating how users can quickly raise hypotheses, identify and design the comparisons they wish to make, discover differences in learning behaviors of student groups, and test their hypotheses.

Heatmap Panel

The heatmap panel offers users the big picture of their data. It visualizes differences in the frequency of action use at certain time intervals. This helps users raise hypotheses about learning in their environment. For example, users may be curious about

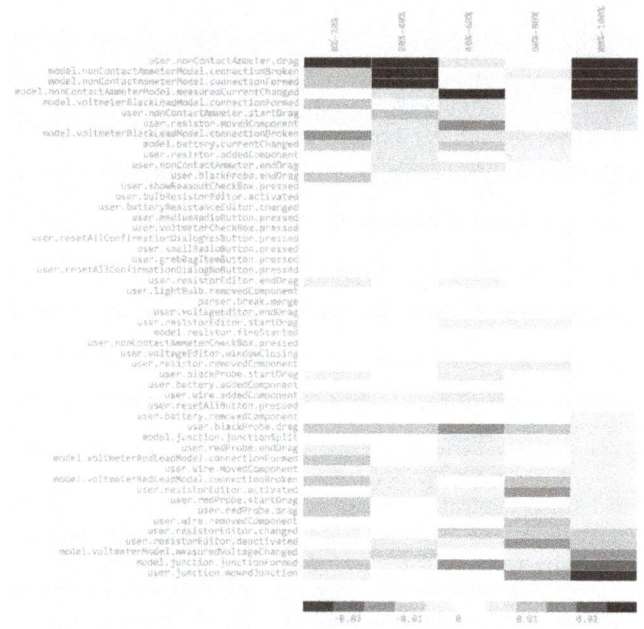

Figure 3. The heatmap panel of the Tempr interface. Blue hues indicate that high learners (HL) performed the action more, and brown hues indicate that low learners (LL) performed the action more. The darkness of the color indicates how much more that group performed the action.

which events are similar between different groups of learners. Similarly, the heatmap allows the comparisons of actions based on the use of the action by student groups. Finally, potential groupings of actions can be determined by identifying actions sharing similar use patterns over time.

The heatmap panel can be seen in Figure 3. Along the left are the raw log events. Raw log events are simply each event that is available in the logs of raw student action data. For virtual lab log data, one of these such events could be the action of manipulating a testing instrument. For MOOC data, this could be a play of video 1 in lesson 1. Across the top shows the percent of actions completed, normalized for each student. For example, the left column, labeled "0%-20%", summarizes the first 20% of actions that students took. The colors indicate which group of students performed the action more, and the darkness of the color indicates the how much more of it they performed.

This panel gives an overview of how groups of learners were performing over the course of interaction. We can quickly ignore the events where the heatmap shows white cells, as these are times when that event was used with a similar frequency by the two groups of learners. This allows users to focus on the more divergent events and form hypothesis about which actions should be combined to distinguish groups of learners while also developing potentially informative features.

Merging Panel

The merging panel allows users to group actions that they hypothesize are related. As mentioned in the introduction, in order to find patterns in data, a researcher may have to try looking at the data in a variety of different ways. To determine

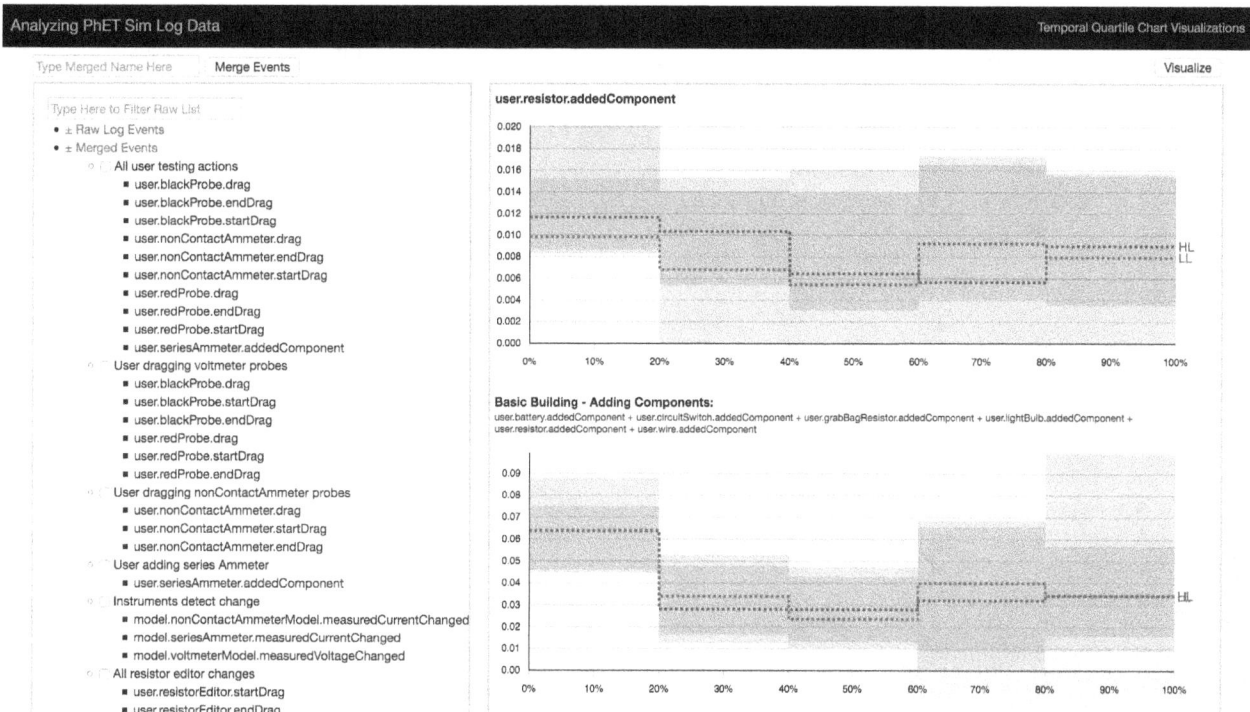

Figure 4. Tempr interface. The merging panel is on the left, and the visualization panel is on the right. The top graph shows the use of one action over time, specifically the use of the action "user.resistor.addComponent". The bottom graph shows the use of a group of merged actions over time, specifically the use of all actions that result in a circuit component being added, such as a light bulb, resistor, battery, wire, etc.

the best features to engineer, one may first want to abstract to a bigger picture (combining many raw log events), then dive in and explore different pieces that make up the bigger picture, then abstract out to a different bigger picture, etc. This iterative process is at the core of the Tempr workflow.

There are two portions of the merging panel which can both be seen on the left side of Figure 4: the raw log events portion and the merged events portion. There could be hundreds of different types of raw log events, as is often common in exploratory learning environments. This drives the need to combine raw events to understand how sets of actions are applied by different groups of learners throughout the interaction. Merged events are comprised of multiple raw log events. To merge raw log events together with Tempr, a researcher can first select the raw log events in the top of the left panel by checking the box next to them, then merge them by clicking on the "Merge Events" button above. Subsequently, the merged action will appear under the "Merged Events" list and all the raw log events that comprise it will be listed below it. This feature allows for an iterative procedure for hypothesis testing. Users can quickly group actions to test hypotheses about what impacts different groups of combined raw log actions will have on learner behavior, and revise accordingly, combining bottom-up and top-down analytic processes: expert knowledge guides the data mining, by choosing which combinations to test; patterns in the data then guide the expert knowledge, by revealing which show consistent and coherent terms.

Visualization Panel

The visualization supports comparing different groups of learners on different sets of actions over time. Both merged events and raw log events (top graph, right side) can be plotted, as shown in the right hand side of Figure 4. The bolded title gives the name of what is graphed, and the subtitle below, if any, tells what raw events were combined to make up the graph. The bottom graph in Figure 4 is the visualization of the "Basic Building - Adding Components" set. To comprise this feature, 6 raw log events, all related to adding components to the learning environment, were merged. In this way, Tempr allows a researcher to gain a visual understanding of how different combinations of raw events reveal learning patterns for different groups of students.

Each chart is an overlay of two plots, corresponding to the two groups of learners. The y-axis is frequency of that action, that is, the percent of this action out of all actions per student during that time slice, averaged across students. For example, if a student performed 20 actions while interacting with the environment, and 2 of them were testing actions, then the frequency for that student would be 0.1. The presented value is the average frequency across students in that group. The x-axis across the bottom shows percent of actions completed, normalized for each student. In this way, with Tempr, users can compare student performance over the learning process and see how student groups perform differently over the course of interacting with the learning environment. The visualization over task progression is an essential piece as it helps us understand how learning unfolds over time. Furthermore, differences in frequency of actions taken can often be washed out if only looking over the overall interaction patterns over the entire activity. Visualizing task progression allows users to see things such as changes in frequency for each student group over time, differences between the two groups of learners, and frequency of sets of actions in specific time slices relative to frequency of other actions. For example, in Figure 4, we can see from the bottom graph that adding components to a circuit in the PhET virtual lab is done more frequently at the beginning of interaction than it is at any other point throughout interaction.

The graph itself shows distribution within groups. The dashed lines are the median frequency of that action for users in each group, and the shaded regions shade the region between the 25th and 75th percentile for each group (one may think about it as box-and-whisker plots for each group at each time slot, without the whiskers). This representation shows both central tendency and distribution, and is less sensitive to outliers. The two groups can be quickly identified based on the colors. In this way, users can quickly compare the frequency with which most users in each group are performing each action. There is also a green area in the middle where the two groups of learners are overlapping. This is common, and it can be common for the green area to be large; for the most part, but depending how students were grouped, many students act fairly similarly throughout interacting with the environment. That's one of the challenges in finding the right features that differentiate between groups of learners. However, with Tempr, since the medians are also graphed and since the area between the quartiles can extend past each other (eg, the 75th percentile for one group may be higher than it is for the other group, as it is in the first 20% of interaction in the top graph in Figure 4), we can still easily understand these subtle differences in how the groups of students are learning. It is important to emphasize that data sets with large and statistically significant effect sizes still have much overlap in their distributions. Overall, the visualization panel of Tempr allows for easy comparison for how different groups of students are performing.

RESULTS

In this section we discuss the application of Tempr to facilitate analysis on students working through the PhET CCK learning environment. We first describe the PhET CCK and its dataset. We then demonstrate how Tempr is able to abstract and evaluate learner strategies from user log data.

CCK Simulation

PhET is a family of over a hundred interactive virtual labs in STEM topics, used by students at the kindergarten through university level [1]. It is the most popular family of virtual labs, having over 50 million runs a year. These virtual labs offer learners opportunities to engage in authentic inquiry, and teachers create a variety of activities around these. These are often shared in the teaching community.

The PhET Circuit Construction Kit (CCK) is the most commonly used virtual lab in the PhET family. Students in CCK construct and test DC electric circuits by using a variety of components that include batteries, wires, light bulbs, resistors, and measurement instruments such as ammeters and voltmeters. Overall, there are 124 different types of actions that students can perform at each moment. These actions include adding, moving, joining, splitting, and removing components, as well as changing the attributes of components (such as resistance). Additional actions relate to the interface (such as changing views or zooming in and out), or the virtual lab itself (such as pausing or resetting the virtual lab). The outcomes of these actions depend on the state of the virtual lab. These outcomes manifest themselves in the logs in the form of model actions. For example, the user action of changing the resistance of a component will, if that component is connected to a live circuit, trigger a model action of changing the current of the circuit. A second model action in this scenario may be a change to the ammeter reading, if one is connected to the circuit.

User Study

One hundred students from first-year physics courses at the University of British Columbia volunteered for a study which took place outside their normal classroom hours [20]. The study included an activity on the topic of DC circuits, which took 30 minutes. The activity asked students to explain the effect of connecting multiple resistors on the voltage and current of a circuit. Students received this general learning goal and a general recommendation to explore several resistors within the same circuit loop, on different circuit loops, and a combination of the two. Pre- and post- tests were given to each student so that we could measure learning gains across the activity.

Processing the Log Data

To prepare the data, we extracted the sequential list of actions logged as each student interacted with the virtual lab. As mentioned above, this was a combination of student-originated actions and the resulting model actions. Classifying learners to two groups was done by calculating their learning gains [15]. We then applied a tertiary split, comparing the high learning gain group (HL) to the students with low learning gains (LL), ignoring the middle third.

CCK Simulation Analysis with Tempr

Overall, our analysis was driven by the following question: How do students learn by testing? Without Tempr, one may settle for merging all testing events, looking for testing more vs. less frequently during the entire activity. However, as shown in Figure 5, this does not reveal interesting results: HL test slightly more than LL at the beginning and end of interaction, but during the rest of interaction, it appears they test fairly similarly. Instead, we want to better understand how testing instruments are used by learners of both groups with the goal of identifying effective and ineffective testing strategies. Specifically, we looked to better understand: (i) How do learners use different testing instruments? For example, are they all treated equally, or do different groups gravitate to different instruments? (ii) How do learners use the instruments? Do they leave them connected to passively test other changes in the circuit, or do they test actively by moving them around? Do we observe the same patterns for measuring voltage and measuring current? Answering these questions can

All Testing Events:
model.nonContactAmmeterModel.connectionBroken + model.nonContactAmmeterModel.connectionFormed +
model.nonContactAmmeterModel.measuredCurrentChanged + model.seriesAmmeter.measuredCurrentChanged + model.voltmeterBlackLeadModel.connectionBroken +
model.voltmeterBlackLeadModel.connectionFormed + model.voltmeterRedLeadModel.measuredVoltageChanged + model.voltmeterRedLeadModel.connectionBroken +
model.voltmeterRedLeadModel.connectionFormed + user.blackProbe.endDrag + user.blackProbe.startDrag + user.nonContactAmmeter.drag +
user.nonContactAmmeter.endDrag + user.nonContactAmmeter.startDrag + user.redProbe.endDrag + user.redProbe.startDrag +
user.seriesAmmeter.addedComponent + user.seriesAmmeter.movedComponent + user.seriesAmmeter.removedComponent

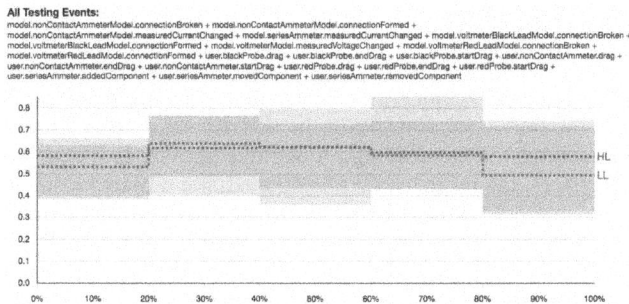

Figure 5. Merging all testing results does not reveal interesting results. It appears as though HL and LL test similarly for the majority of interaction.

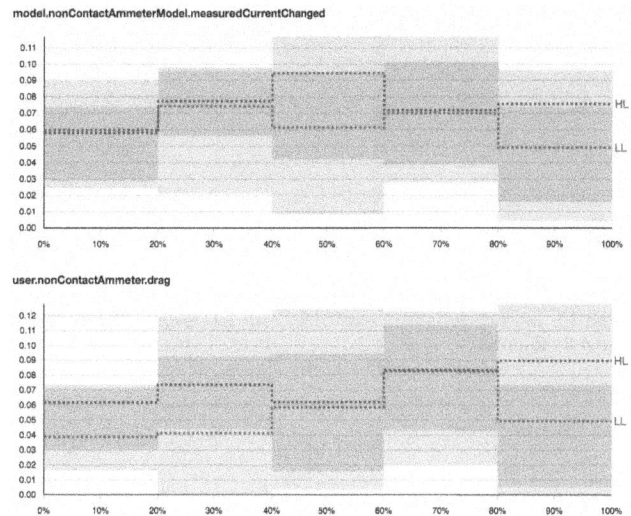

Figure 6. Measuring current change with an ammeter vs actively using the ammeter. Low Learners drag the ammeter less frequently than they observe current changes, likely engaging in less explicit testing compared with High Learners.

reveal what critical testing events look like. In other words, what testing events correspond with productive learning, and how are they performed?

The heatmap visualization provides an overview of the differences between the two learner groups. Figure 3 shows the heatmap sorted by the last column, to emphasize differences between common actions of HL vs. LL during the last 20% of the interaction.

In regards to the types of testing, since the heatmap is sorted, we see that the top seven events are ones that HL perform more frequently than LL. 5 of those 7 relate to testing with the ammeter. Conversely, 7 of the 16 events that LL perform more frequently relate to voltmeter testing. Already, we see that there might be a difference in which testing instruments each group of students prefers.

In regards to the way testing was done, HL are both performing a larger amount of moving the ammeter device and measuring current changes with it. LL are the opposite: performing a larger amount of moving the voltmeter device and measuring voltage changes with it. Thus, the heatmap reveals different preferences with regard to the instrument, but not for the manner in which it is used. Next we examine these two questions in detail using the main Visualization and Merging panels, starting with the open question about the manner in which students test.

How does productive testing look like?
A first step in trying to understand what testing events are important would be to assess whether active moving of the testing device is similar to observing a change in reading of the testing device while connected.

Here we describe testing with the ammeter as an example to answer this question. We can visualize this with Tempr without needing to do any merging as moving the testing device (user.nonContactAmmeter.drag) and the resulting change in reading of the testing device (model.nonContactAmmeterModel.measuredCurrentChanged) were logged actions in the CCK Simulation. It is important to note that drag events that end in connections being formed or broken lead to a change in reading. Thus, the two events are related. Figure 6 shows these two actions with Tempr. The lower graph, describing dragging, shows that HL tend to be

dragging the ammeter more than LL. This is highly visible as the blue HL shading (representing the 75th percentile) extends above the LL brown shading. On closer inspection, we also see that the medians differ for dragging the testing instrument. For example, in the first 20% of interaction, both HL and LL measured current change for about 6% of the actions that took place (top chart). Additionally, HL also dragged the ammeter for 6% of the actions, while LL dragged the ammeter for only 4% of actions in that time period. This is a lower number than the number of actions that they observed current change, meaning that they observed more current changes than they actually moved the testing instrument. This is an indication of passive testing. It's likely that they left the testing instrument on the circuit as they were modifying the circuit, hence obtaining current changes without moving the device. One problem with this kind testing is that LL were not necessarily actually observing the changes in the testing device.

With Tempr, we were able to visually explore these two initially seemingly equivalent manifestations of testing and understand that, in fact, they are not the same. It also gave deeper insight into how the two groups test, allowing us to see that HL are engaging in more explicit testing while LL are partaking in more passive testing.

What testing instruments do different groups use?
Based on the heatmap shown above, one can conjecture that HL students use the ammeter more than the voltmeter, while LL do the opposite. However, this conjecture is based on data from the last 20% of the interaction, across all testing events. Here we would like to evaluate this, focusing on the more significant active testing events. Our initial hypothesis was that HL test more than LL. To evaluate this, we merge all active movement of the three types of testing devices and plot this combination. Because we previously saw that moving the testing device is more important than detecting the measure-

All user testing actions:
user.blackProbe.drag + user.blackProbe.endDrag + user.blackProbe.startDrag + user.nonContactAmmeter.drag + user.nonContactAmmeter.endDrag + user.nonContactAmmeter.startDrag + user.redProbe.drag + user.redProbe.endDrag + user.redProbe.startDrag + user.seriesAmmeter.addedComponent

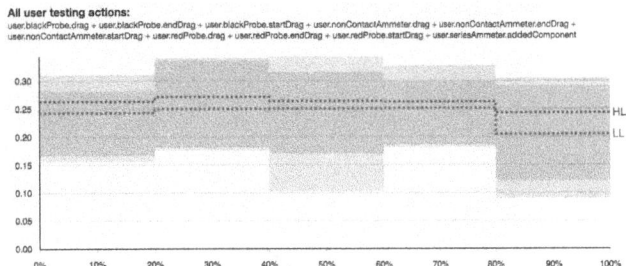

Figure 7. Merging all testing device manipulation events. Note that HL and LL are nearly indistinguishable, with LL testing slightly less frequently than HL.

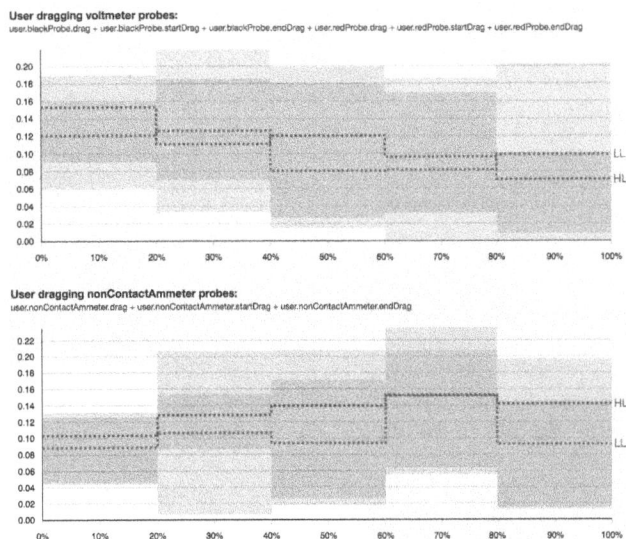

User dragging voltmeter probes:
user.blackProbe.drag + user.blackProbe.startDrag + user.blackProbe.endDrag + user.redProbe.drag + user.redProbe.startDrag + user.redProbe.endDrag

User dragging nonContactAmmeter probes:
user.nonContactAmmeter.drag + user.nonContactAmmeter.startDrag + user.nonContactAmmeter.endDrag

Figure 8. The result of decomposing the different types of testing. Interesting to note that HL decrease their use of voltmeter (top graph) and increase their use of ammeter (bottom graph) over the course of the interaction, showing their ability to adapt to a new environment better than LL.

ment change, we'll focus on these moving the testing device actions.

The result of this is shown in Figure 7. As can be seen, HL and LL are nearly indistinguishable. LL testing drops off at the end of interaction, but during the rest, the median lines are roughly equivalent. Both have quartiles that are roughly equivalent, with LL behaving less consistently in the middle of the interaction.

Since we did not find much difference in the previously explored level of abstraction, we can dive into each of the raw log events that comprise that merged event. Tempr allows us to easily try other combinations of features, such as manipulating the different types of testing events in the PhET CCK virtual lab: voltmeter and ammeter. If we visualize each of these with Tempr, the result is the graphs in Figure 8.

It is interesting to compare the difference in use of the ammeter and the voltmeter as it does appear that there are differences in how HL and LL are testing their circuits over time. We see

is that the HL students increase the use of the ammeter over the course of interaction (see bottom graph in Figure 8).

The intent of Tempr is to reveal patterns that can be explained and understood. Revisiting the activity suggests a clear explanation for this finding. Since this activity is focused on resistors, the more useful testing instrument to use would be the ammeter. This is because changes to the resistor's resistance change the current but not the voltage. Additionally, we see that the HL use of the voltmeter actually decreased over the course of interaction (see top graph in Figure 8). That is, HL began using both instruments, and then favored the ammeter over the voltmeter. We can compare this to the LL whose use of the voltmeter only decreases very slightly from beginning to end of interaction. From this, it appears that HL are adapting to their environment. As mentioned, the students completed another activity before the one we are using the data from. This earlier activity was on understanding light bulbs, and the more fit testing instrument to use in that activity would have been the voltmeter. It makes sense that learners would start with using the voltmeter, since that was beneficial to their understanding in the first activity, but then that only the productive students would come to realize while interacting with the learning environment that the voltmeter would not be as useful here and that the ammeter was the better tool. LL instead continue to use the voltmeter, and appear to have not adapted as well to this activity.

DISCUSSION AND CONCLUSION

We introduced a visualization tool that facilitates a novel exploratory analytic approach. It allows for the combination of bottom-up and top-down processes when engineering features to highlight differences in how different groups of students learn over time. We demonstrated, through a case study with the PhET CCK learning environment, how the tool help us (i) hypothesize what actions correspond with productive engagement, (ii) evaluate different sets of actions, (iii) compare groups of learners on these sets, and (iv) do so in the context of a temporal analysis.

With the aid of Tempr, we were able to use the heatmap to raise hypotheses and pinpoint the questions we wanted to answer regarding the instruments that students used (ammeter vs voltmeter) and the way in which testing was done (actively moving the device vs passively leaving the testing device connected). After investigation of these two with Tempr, we found that HL perform more active testing compared to LL. By visualizing use over time we also found that HL adapt more successfully to characteristics of the activity. This was found using Temper's ability to visualize combinations of raw events at different levels of abstraction - finding minimal differences in how students test when all testing events were merged, but discovering richer differences once we reduced to the different types of testing events.

We are currently using Tempr to analyze data from other complex environments such as MOOCs. While technically data from a variety of environments can be entered into Tempr, its utility across types of learning environments needs to be evaluated. For example, what is the dependency of Tempr on granularity of data? We hypothesize that Tempr is beneficial especially with data with high resolution, as a main advantage of the tool is its ability to identify and group sets of actions. However, this hypothesis is yet to be tested. It is also of interest to evaluate Tempr with hierarchical data. While using search terms in the merging panel can support the grouping of hierarchical data, presently Tempr lacks a structural support for levels in data. Tempr also focuses solely on ordinal information and lacks timing data. This choice was made to simplify its data structure, as Tempr takes simple lists of events. However, this compromises the ability to analyze by duration of events. This is relevant especially when data includes events of widely varying duration, such as video watching (often minutes) and problem attempts (often seconds) in MOOCs.

We are currently working to extend Tempr's capabilities to further support researchers in their ability to use data to understand more about how groups of learners are learning. Specifically, Tempr will soon support identifying and evaluating sequences of actions. For example, rather than merely merging actions (action *A or* action *B*), it may be of interest to sequence actions (action *A followed by* action *B*). This will allow researchers to use grammatical structures and reveal more complex patterns.

Overall, Tempr is not intended to replace the expert. Instead, it is a powerful tool to be used by experts who seek to obtain a more detailed understanding of learning trajectories in the target environment.

ACKNOWLEDGMENTS

We would like to thank Kathy Perkins and the rest of the PhET team for their invaluable collaboration and feedback.

REFERENCES

1. 2016. PhET Interactive Virtual Labs for Science and Math. (2016). `https://phet.colorado.edu/`

2. Vincent Aleven, Ido Roll, Bruce M McLaren, and Kenneth R Koedinger. 2016. Help helps, but only so much: research on help seeking with intelligent tutoring systems. *International Journal of Artificial Intelligence in Education* 26, 1 (2016), 205–223.

3. Ryan S.J.d. Baker and Jody Clarke-Midura. 2013. Predicting successful inquiry learning in a virtual performance assessment for science. In *International Conference on User Modeling, Adaptation, and Personalization*. Springer, 203–214.

4. Ryan S.J.d. Baker, Albert T Corbett, Ido Roll, and Kenneth R Koedinger. 2008. Developing a generalizable detector of when students game the system. *User Modeling and User-Adapted Interaction* 18, 3 (2008), 287–314.

5. Michael Bostock. 2015. Visualizations with D3. (2015).

6. Michael Brooks, Saleema Amershi, Bongshin Lee, Steven M Drucker, Ashish Kapoor, and Patrice Simard. 2015. FeatureInsight: Visual support for error-driven feature ideation in text classification. In *Visual Analytics Science and Technology (VAST), 2015 IEEE Conference on*. IEEE, 105–112.

7. Bodong Chen, Alyssa F. Wise, Simon Knight, and Britte Haugan Cheng. 2016. Putting Temporal Analytics into Practice: The 5th International Workshop on Temporality in Learning Data. In *Proceedings of the Sixth International Conference on Learning Analytics & Knowledge (LAK '16)*. ACM, New York, NY, USA, 488–489.

8. Cristina Conati, Lauren Fratamico, Samad Kardan, and Ido Roll. 2015. Comparing representations for learner models in interactive simulations. In *International Conference on Artificial Intelligence in Education*. Springer, 74–83.

9. Diansheng Guo. 2003. Coordinating computational and visual approaches for interactive feature selection and multivariate clustering. *Information Visualization* 2, 4 (2003), 232–246.

10. Hogyeong Jeong, Amit Gupta, Rod Roscoe, John Wagster, Gautam Biswas, and Daniel Schwartz. 2008. Using hidden Markov models to characterize student behaviors in learning-by-teaching environments. In *International Conference on Intelligent Tutoring Systems*. Springer, 614–625.

11. Josua Krause, Adam Perer, and Enrico Bertini. 2014. INFUSE: interactive feature selection for predictive modeling of high dimensional data. *IEEE transactions on visualization and computer graphics* 20, 12 (2014), 1614–1623.

12. Heidi Lam, Daniel Russell, Diane Tang, and Tamara Munzner. 2007. Session viewer: Visual exploratory analysis of web session logs. In *Visual Analytics Science and Technology, 2007. VAST 2007. IEEE Symposium on*. IEEE, 147–154.

13. Zhicheng Liu, Yang Wang, Mira Dontcheva, Matthew Hoffman, Seth Walker, and Alan Wilson. 2017. Patterns and sequences: Interactive exploration of clickstreams to understand common visitor paths. *IEEE Transactions on Visualization and Computer Graphics* 23, 1 (2017), 321–330.

14. Sana Malik, Ben Shneiderman, Fan Du, Catherine Plaisant, and Margret Bjarnadottir. 2016. High-Volume Hypothesis Testing: Systematic Exploration of Event Sequence Comparisons. *ACM Transactions on Interactive Intelligent Systems (TiiS)* 6, 1 (2016), 9.

15. Jeffrey D Marx and Karen Cummings. 2007. Normalized change. *American Journal of Physics* 75, 1 (2007), 87–91.

16. Megan Monroe, Rongjian Lan, Hanseung Lee, Catherine Plaisant, and Ben Shneiderman. 2013. Temporal event sequence simplification. *IEEE transactions on visualization and computer graphics* 19, 12 (2013), 2227–2236.

17. T. Powell. 2004. *JavaScript: The Complete Reference* (2 ed.). McGraw-Hill, New York, NY, USA.

18. Ido Roll, Ryan S.J.d. Baker, Vincent Aleven, and Kenneth R Koedinger. 2014. On the benefits of seeking (and avoiding) help in online problem-solving environments. *Journal of the Learning Sciences* 23, 4 (2014), 537–560.

19. Ido Roll, Ryan S.J.d. Baker, Vincent Aleven, Bruce M McLaren, and Kenneth R Koedinger. 2005. Modeling students' metacognitive errors in two intelligent tutoring systems. In *International Conference on User Modeling*. Springer, 367–376.

20. Ido Roll, N Yee, and A Cervantes. 2014. Not a magic bullet: the effect of scaffolding on knowledge and attitudes in online simulations. In *International Conference of the Learning Sciences*.

21. Michael A Sao Pedro, Ryan S.J.d. Baker, Janice D Gobert, Orlando Montalvo, and Adam Nakama. 2013. Leveraging machine-learned detectors of systematic inquiry behavior to estimate and predict transfer of inquiry skill. *User Modeling and User-Adapted Interaction* 23, 1 (2013), 1–39.

22. Ben Shneiderman. 1996. The Eyes Have It: A Task by Data Type Taxonomy for Information Visualizations *(VL '96)*. IEEE Computer Society, 336–.

23. Jing Yang, Wei Peng, Matthew O Ward, and Elke A Rundensteiner. 2003. Interactive hierarchical dimension ordering, spacing and filtering for exploration of high dimensional datasets. In *Information Visualization, 2003. INFOVIS 2003. IEEE Symposium on*. IEEE, 105–112.

24. Jian Zhao, Zhicheng Liu, Mira Dontcheva, Aaron Hertzmann, and Alan Wilson. 2015. MatrixWave: Visual comparison of event sequence data. In *Proceedings of the 33rd Annual ACM Conference on Human Factors in Computing Systems*. ACM, 259–268.

Enabling Real-Time Adaptivity in MOOCs with a Personalized Next-Step Recommendation Framework

Zachary A. Pardos
UC Berkeley
Berkeley, CA
zp@berkeley.edu

Steven Tang
UC Berkeley
Berkeley, CA
steventang@berkeley.edu

Daniel Davis
TU Delft
Delft, Netherlands
d.j.davisattudelft.nl

Christopher Vu Le
UC Berkeley
Berkeley, CA
chrisvle@berkeley.edu

ABSTRACT

In this paper, we demonstrate a first-of-its-kind adaptive intervention in a MOOC utilizing real-time clickstream data and a novel machine learned model of behavior. We detail how we augmented the edX platform with the capabilities necessary to support this type of intervention which required both tracking learners' behaviors in real-time and dynamically adapting content based on each learner's individual clickstream history. Our chosen pilot intervention was in the category of adaptive pathways and courseware and took the form of a navigational suggestion appearing at the bottom of every non-forum content page in the course. We designed our pilot intervention to help students more efficiently navigate their way through a MOOC by predicting the next page they were likely to spend significant time on and allowing them to jump directly to that page. While interventions which attempt to optimize for learner achievement are candidates for this adaptive framework, behavior prediction has the benefit of not requiring causal assumptions to be made in its suggestions. We present a novel extension of a behavioral model that takes into account students' time spent on pages and forecasts the same. Several approaches to representing time using Recurrent Neural Networks are evaluated and compared to baselines without time, including a basic n-gram model. Finally, we discuss design considerations and handling of edge cases for real-time deployment, including considerations for training a machine learned model on a previous offering of a course for use in a subsequent offering where courseware may have changed. This work opens the door to broad experimentation with adaptivity and serves as a first example of delivering a data-driven personalized learning experience in a MOOC.

Author Keywords

Adaptivity; Personalization; Real-time intervention; MOOC; RNN; Behavioral modeling; Navigational efficiency; edX

INTRODUCTION

The path towards a more democratized learner success model for MOOCs has been hampered by a lack of capabilities to provide a personalized experienced to the varied demographics MOOCs aim to serve. Primary obstacles to this end have been insufficient support of real-time learner data across platforms and a lack of maturity of recommendation models that accommodate the learning context and breadth and complexity of subject matter material in MOOCs. In this paper we address both shortfalls with a framework for augmenting a MOOC platform with real-time logging and dynamic content presentation capabilities as well as a novel course-general recommendation model geared towards increasing learner navigational efficiency. We piloted this intervention in a portion of a live course as a proof-of-concept of the framework. The necessary augmentation of platform functionality was all made without changes to the open-edX codebase, our target platform, and instead only requires access to modify course content via an instructor role account.

The organization of the paper begins with related work, followed by technical details on augmentation of the platform's functionality, a description of the recommendation model and its back-tested prediction results, and finally an articulation of the design decisions that went into deploying the recommendation framework in a live course.

RELATED WORK

In searching for answers to the problem of dismal completion rates in MOOCs, previous research has shown that MOOC learners often feel lost or isolated in their learning experience [9]. So far, the attempts to address this problem have largely come in the form of self-regulated learning (SRL) support interventions. For example, [10] tested the effectiveness of recommending self-regulating learning strategies to MOOC learners in the pre-course survey, but did not observe any significant changes in behavior as a result. As an example of a MOOC experiment integrated in the course content, [5] ran experiments in two MOOCs evaluating the effectiveness of providing learners with retrieval cues (to facilitate the active retrieval of information from memory) and study planning support (planning and reflecting on one's learning activities each week)—both foundational techniques in self-regulation. However, in both studies the authors report null results, with no evidence that providing this support to learners was beneficial. Another approach to instructional interventions in MOOCs is found in [17] where the authors manipulated the course discussion forum. In one condition, the course instructor was active in the discussion forum and provided support to the learners in answering their questions; in the other, the instructor was absent and the learners were on their own to discuss amongst themselves. Just as in the previous two studies, this yielded no significant change in behavior between the conditions.

To address the challenge of implementing a real-time, adaptive intervention in a MOOC, we act on the need to find a way to effectively support learners in improving their navigational efficiency with the course materials. We here present a new form of support for MOOC learners in our next step recommendation system, as prior work has shown a strong relationship between the success of a MOOC learner (measured by course completion) and the characteristics of their learning path through the course [4, 6, 18]. While novel to the MOOC context specifically, such

L@S 2017, April 20-21, 2017, Cambridge, MA, USA
© 2017 ACM. ISBN 978-1-4503-4450-0/17/04…$15.00
DOI: http://dx.doi.org/10.1145/3051457.3051471

recommender systems have been applied to educational settings in the past, namely in intelligent tutoring systems (ITS). Both [1] and [101] provide an overview of the various approaches used to recommend and adapt course content and resources to learners in the context of ITS.

To highlight some example use cases of learning path adaptivity in prior research, we begin with an early example of real-time "task-loop adaptivity" (defined in [1] as the guiding of learners from task to task) offered in [2]. The authors here present a tutoring system which models a student's learning path in terms of correct and incorrect actions, and would adaptively intervene to guide students back to the correct path of action with immediate feedback.

The authors in [13, 12] provide real-time adaptive hints to coding assignments in the context of computer programming MOOCs. Both approaches are "step-loop" [1] in that they provide adaptive hints regarding the learners' problem solving process. However, they take different approaches in doing so; [13] models the ideal process of solving the problem in a "Problem Solving Policy," as defined by an expert, and guides learners towards this behavior. [12], on the other hand, leverages the scale of MOOCs and proposes algorithms which use the surrounding context of a code snippet to identify the problem and recommend a solution to the learner. The authors in [8] present a personalized navigation support system in the context of a JavaScript programming course. By monitoring the learner's performance on previous problems, the system presented learners with a next-step suggestion to try problems of the appropriate, or "optimal," difficulty level. By addressing the issue of learners navigating themselves to tasks that are too easy or too difficult, this system increased learner achievement and engagement.

[15], [3], and [16] describe the design and deployment of an adaptive hint generator in an ITS on the topic of logic. This system uses past learner activity data as input for a Markov decision process which, when prompted by the learner requesting a hint, provides personalized support based on the current progress through the problem. This step-loop adaptivity was empirically tested in [16] where, compared to a tutor system without adaptive hints, learners receiving the adaptive hint system earned higher grades, tried more problems, and persisted deeper into the course. While the next-step recommender system we present here does not provide hints about how to solve a given quiz or assessment problem, the suggestions we provide can be thought of as hints on how to most efficiently navigate the course.

The next-step recommendation system proposed here is course content-general and concerned solely with modeling learner behavior from the navigational patterns of peers from previous offerings of the course. This is in contrast to studies described above which are based on modeling a learner's mastery of the course topic/domain or helping them through a given task. It also differs in that the system does not acknowledge any "correct" or "incorrect" learning path as described in [2]. The system could be trained to bias towards the behaviors of certificate earners but this would miss out on serving those who do not intend to complete but nevertheless wish to make use of portions of the courseware. While the objective of the recommender is not explicitly focused on improving cognitive aspects, as was attempted to be modelled in [8], it will facilitate this in so far as past behavior has been a means to these ends, for example by recommending resources for review before a quiz. These considerations are key when it comes to the eventual evaluation of recommendation quality. A review of the work in the area of recommender systems suggests that every

context in which a system operates has its own special aspects against which both the system and its success metrics must be evaluated [7] Although outside of the scope of this paper, future evaluation of this intervention might include: increasing navigational efficiency (clicks per performance), affective experience (feeling supported), as well as common outcomes such as grade and completion rate.

Thinking back to the challenge of addressing MOOC learners feeling lost in the course, we propose next-step recommendations as a service that could reach learners most in need of engagement. Pointing to recent findings from HCI research, [14] found that people are stimulated and respond positively to recommendations when they are bored. The potentially-overwhelming selection of possible next steps in a MOOC compounded with the complexity of course content can, understandably, leave a learner frustrated. A friendly next-step recommendation can be the support they need to move forward and persist.

PLATFORM AUGMENTATION

Several technical hurdles had to be overcome in order to add base functionality that would enable at-scale deployment of a real-time recommendation system within the edX platform. All solutions can be achieved without modification to open-edx and only require standard instructional design team / instructor access to edit course material.

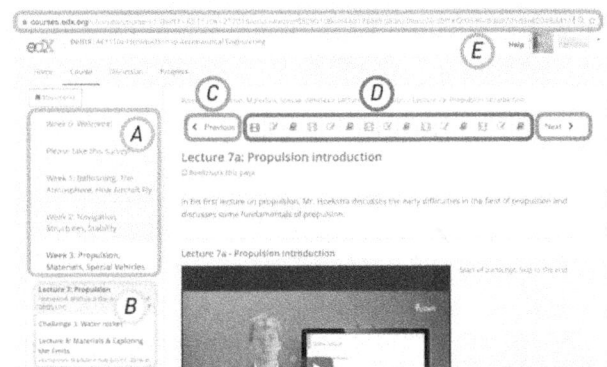

Figure 1. Annotated breakdown of edX interface components. Label (A) shows what is henceforth referred to as "Chapters," (B) refers to "Sequentials," (C) refers to navigation/goto buttons, (D) refers to "Verticals," and (E) is the page URL.

Enabling real-time logging

Our real-time recommendation requires knowledge of the student's most recent navigational events, some of which may have occurred only seconds earlier. The edX platform provides a daily event log delivery to its X consortium members but does not have a real-time data API. In order to enable access to real-time learner event logs, we set up a JavaScript logger within the xml of every page in the course which communicated to the recommendation server which events to store in the logging database. This process is illustrated in Figure 2.

The client side logging, which we describe as the sensor code, was written in JavaScript. The sensor code was responsible for gathering four items of information from the client at every page: (1) the learner's userID (2) the page's chapter (3) the page's sequential (4) the page's vertical.

The learner's anonymous ID can be queried simply enough from Segment's analytics library used by edX:

```
userid = analytics.user().anonymousId();
```

The anonymosId call has the shortcoming that it will change if the user switches devices or browsers. A non-anonymized userID call is also available, which will remain stationary throughout.

Next is the retrieval of chapter and sequential ID, both of which can be parsed from the browser URL:

```
var url = window.location.href;
var split = url.split("/");
chap = split[6];
seq = split[7];
```

The vertical ID, also known as the position ID within a sequential, is non-trivial to retrieve. While verticals can be accessed by adding the vertical number to the sequential URL, this is rarely how verticals are accessed in the course. They are most commonly accessed via the "next" and "previous" arrow buttons which are graphical navigational elements on either side of the sequential accordion view. When these "seq" events are triggered, the desired page's content dynamically replaces the current page. This dynamic loading keeps the browser URL the same (cf Figure 1) which means that the vertical position must be queried from a different source. We find this vertical position information in the edX document object model (DOM[1]).

```
var block = $('#sequence-list .nav-item.active').data('id');
vert = block.split("@").pop();
```

Arbitrarily clicking on a vertical in the accordion triggers a "seq_goto" event which is much the same as the next and previous events in how they load the page.

With all of these elements now stored, the full description of the page a learner is on can be described:

```
origin = chap+"/"+seq+"/"+vert;
```

The userID and origin are sent to a local server for logging via a cross domain aJax POST method.

Row ID	Anon Stu. ID	Origin	Rec	Followed	Previous ID	Timestamp	Time Category
100	C103	5	6	0	99	1477142712	2
101	C103	35	45	1	100	1477142732	1
102	C548	89	101	0	82	1477142736	2

Table 1. Example of entries in local mongo database

Table 1 shows the columns stored in the logging database and a few example entries. At the time of the event, only the following columns are populated: row id (transaction id), stu_id, origin, timestamp, and previous ID (the previous transaction id of the user). The remainder of the columns are populated on the subsequent event. Full client side javascript can be found here[2].

---

[1] All DOM related function calls used in this work are undocumented by edX and subject to change. After conducting this pilot study of the framework, we contacted edX in regards to the supportability of our approach, including providing persistent anon IDs. This support is currently under review.

[2] https://github.com/CAHLR/adaptive_mooc_LAS/

Enabling real-time recommendation

An html <div> container is inserted at the bottom of every page which contains a template of the recommendation text. The container is marked as hidden using "display: none" until a recommendation is received successfully, upon which time the template is populated with the actual page being recommended and its title. By hiding the template until a recommendation is received, we are able to fail gracefully and shield learners from any error that may occur along the recommendation pipeline; in the case of an unsuccessful recommendation request, the page would appear to the user the same way as it would as if no intervention was added.

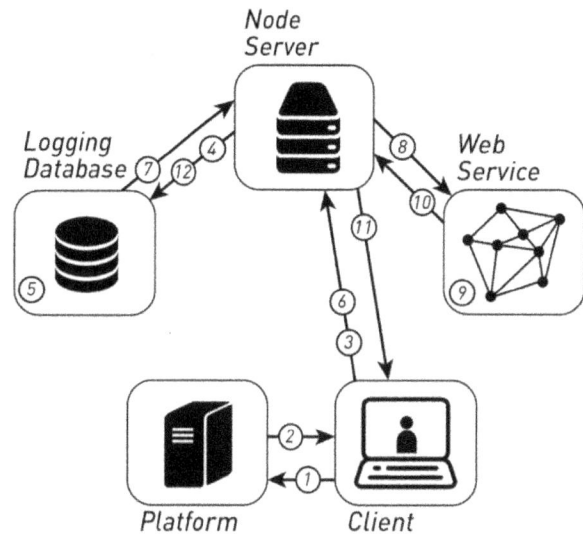

Figure 2. Diagram visualizing the entire process of delivering a recommendation to the learner. The circled numbers correspond to the numbered steps below.

The recommendation URL and title is populated by (i) sending an aJax POST to the recommendation server, which in turn (ii) looks up the learner's event history from the logging server and then (iii) passes that information to a web service which interfaces with the machine learned model. The model returns a recommendation which is passed back through to the web service. This is then sent to the recommendation server and then to the requesting client. At this point, the "Rec" column of Table 1 is filled in representing the internal index of the recommended URL, and "Followed" is set to 0. If the learner clicks on the recommended URL, a request is sent to the recommendation server, the "Followed" is set to 1, and the learner is redirected to the recommended URL. Upon loading a subsequent page, either by following the recommendation or clicking on a different navigational component, the sensor code will look up the previous event of the learner and update the time category of the past event. This is necessary since it is unknown how long the learner will spend on the page when it is first logged.

1. The learner requests a page in the course
2. The platform sends the page to the client. In the case of a "seq" event, the page is loaded in dynamically.
3. Client sensor code sends a logging event to the server
4. The server writes the event to a Mongo database
5. If a previous event exists for this student, the time category of that event is calculated and updated.
6. Client sends a request to the server for recommendation

7. The database is queried for all of the learner's past events and respective time categories.

8. The server relays this information to a Flask web service that parses the information and passes it along to the machine learned model written in python.

9. The machine learned model predicts forward until it finds a page that the user is predicted to spend more than 10 seconds on.

10. The recommended page is returned to the server.

11. The server sends this page to the client which parses a valid "200" response into a proper hyperlink and populates the <div> to display the recommendation.

12. The server will update the logging database for this learner with the recommendation simultaneously

13. If user clicks on the recommendation, the server is contacted and the database is updated to indicate that user followed the recommendation.

The term "learner" is used when an event is triggered due to a deliberate action on the part of a human, such as clicking on a link. The term "client" is used when actions are initiated, invisible to the learner (e.g. sending a logging request), by code processed by their web browser.

Choice of Technology

In order to create this live intervention, we used a range of different technologies. NodeJS and Express were used to create the server API; Python Flask served as a light-weight web service; Python Keras was used to create the machine learned model; and Mongo was used for persistent database storage.

Server - NodeJS with Express

We decided to create our server using Node primarily because it is fast and performs well under stress. It handles operations asynchronously and facilitates a large number of simultaneous connections very well. It integrates nicely with MongoDB and can easily create routes with the Express framework.

Our API has several local lookup tables including a mapping of url to index (used for the machine learned model), index to url, url to edX path, and edX path to display name.

When the server receives a post request from the client it creates a new event with a unique user_id, origin, and timestamp. It will then check if the student has had a previous entry. If yes, the server will update the previous the timeSeq column of the previous entry and update the Recents database with this current entry. If no previous entry exists, it will skip the update in the Events database and go straight to updating the Recents database for this student. It will create an entry in the Recents database if this is the student's very first event.

After successful logging and updating, the client will ask for a recommendation for this particular student. The server will then take the student's unique user_id and query the Events database for the sequence of events and timeSeqs connected with this student. The output will then be sent to the Python web service for a recommendation.

When the web service responds, the response is checked. A lookup is then done to go from index to url as well as Edx path to name and then sent back to the client. The final JSON response will have the url, Sequential display name, and Vertical display name of the recommendation.

Web Service - Python & Flask

We decided to create web service using Python and Flask because our machine learning model was written using Python. It made it easiest to get the input into the correct format and parse the output into a simple response. Flask also allowed us to create multiple processes for parallelizability.

The web service is called after the server requests for a recommendation for a particular student. It takes in a list of the student's events and associated time categories, and then queries the machine learned model. It will receive either a -1 or an index from the machine learned model. If the response is a -1, then there is no valid recommendation (i.e., no recommendations meet the minimum time anticipated for the learner to spend on the page).

Machine Learned Model - Python Keras

Keras is a neural network machine learning framework providing functions for fast model prototyping. It has the option of utilizing Theano or tensorflow for the backend computations, both of which can utilize GPUs for accelerated training.

Database - MongoDB

We decided to use Mongo as our database of persistent storage because it is scalable and quickly handles simultaneous queries. It also has fast in-place updates and has documents stored in JSON, which makes it efficient to work with our client and server code.

Choice of Course

This framework is generally applicable to different backend recommendation algorithms with different objectives. For our purposes of navigational behavior recommendation, there were several criteria that we anticipated as important in selecting a reasonable pilot course.

Given our objective of increasing the navigational efficacy of learners, courses with more numerous pages to navigate are better candidates for demonstrating the utility of navigational recommendation. In order to learn non-trivial navigational patterns from past course events, we also wanted a course with a high amount of variation in navigational pathways exhibited by its learners. To measure this variation, we chose to treat student paths through a particular course as a Markov chain and then computed the entropy of the transition probability matrix for each course [26]. There were 13 courses evaluated offered by our deployment University partner, DelftX. Table 2 shows the entropy calculated for a variety of courses where entropy was 20 or greater. A higher amount of entropy indicates larger amounts of non-linear navigation. Since the Intro to Aeronautical Engineering course had both a high entropy and candidate assets to recommend, we selected that course for deployment.

Course	Entropy	Assets	Normalized Entropy+Assets
Intro to Aeronautical Engineering (2014)	343	1175	1.782
Intro to Water & Climate (2013)	149	1503	1.434
Intro to Drinking Water treatment (2015)	86	745	0.806
Economics of Cybersecurity (2015)	78	323	0.746

Table 2. Course suitability evaluation based on navigational entropy and asset quantity

MODELING

Modeling Navigation Behavior

The literature on cognition and learning has several theories for describing how knowledge acquisition develops over time. Far fewer theories exist for behavior, however, as it is an amalgam of many cognitive and affective factors. As such, the lack of existing theory to adequately predict navigational behavior to a high degree of accuracy means that there is also a lack of knowledge of which manually engineered features may capture student behavior. As such, we use a model that makes no assumption about behavior and instead learns these features from the raw time series data itself.

To model student navigation behavior, we chose to use the Recurrent Neural Network (RNN) architecture. RNNs are able to model time sensitive dependencies between events in arbitrarily long sequences without the need for manual feature engineering.

To provide an example, an RNN can be given a sequence of URLs a learner has already visited. The RNN maintains a hidden, continuous state that represents the past behavior exhibited by the learner. The RNN model can then output a probability distribution over the next URL the student is likely to visit. Thus, we can then take the output of the RNN as a potential recommendation to serve to the learner. The output can be augmented to also be able to predict the amount of time that a learner will spend on the resource. With this augmentation, we can then choose to only provide recommendations where there is expected to be a significant amount of time spent on the URL. This helps expedite the learner's navigation through the course by skipping less useful content.

To use an RNN model, the logs of student actions must be parsed so that each student can be represented by a single list which contains each unique course URL the student has visited. Additionally, the timestamp associated with each course URL visit is also tracked. These timestamps are used to create a proxy for the amount of time spent on a resource. We investigate whether adding time spent as an input to the RNN model improves its predictive accuracy, and investigate two model modifications to incorporate time spent as an input.

Understanding edX logging of navigational events

Parsing a data log of student actions is not trivial. In this work, the ultimate goal of parsing through the data log is to obtain the sequence of course URLs that each student has visited, as well as the timestamp associated with each visit. The data log contains other student events, such as pausing videos and answering quiz questions. For this work, such rows were dropped. Thus, only navigation events were kept, where navigation is defined as visiting a specific course URL. These navigation events were then parsed to resolve to a specific course URL. Each URL contains a chapter hash, a sequential hash (which refers to sections within a chapter), and a vertical hash (which refers to a specific course page within a section). For example, a URL represented by 'abc123/zzz444/2' would have a chapter hash of 'abc123', a sequential hash of 'zzz444', and a vertical value of '2'. Thus, each navigation event in the edX data log can be resolved to a specific URL. However, each event in the raw log unfortunately does not directly map to a URL without an extra step of processing. Navigation events can be found in rows where either:

1. The row is a **seq event**. Seq events include *seq_next*, *seq_prev*, or *seq_goto*. Next and prev refer to moving directly forward or backwards one vertical. Goto is a jump to any vertical within a single sequential.

OR

2. The row contains a direct course page URL. In the URL, the vertical may be given directly, or the vertical may be missing.

Both types of navigation events mentioned above have data processing quirks. *Seq_next* and *seq_prev* events contain the sequential hash and the vertical that is navigated to. Using the sequential hash, the chapter hash can be inferred, since there is only one sequential hash per section in the course, and each section only belongs to one chapter. The vertical displayed by the row, however, may need to be additionally processed when *seq_prev* is invoked on the first vertical in a section or *seq_next* is invoked on the last vertical in a section. For example, the row in the data log may contain a *seq_next* to vertical 7 in a particular section. However, that section might only contain 6 verticals. This event should actually point to vertical 1 of the next section. Thus, the processing code must be able to handle when navigating to the previous and next sections when the current vertical is at the beginning or the end of the section. Once the corresponding sequential, chapter, and vertical hashes are resolved, a URL can be constructed to represent the URL that the student is now at in this row.

For the second type of navigation event, where the row contains a direct course URL, when the vertical is included in the row, the URL can be directly taken from the row itself. When the vertical is not included in the row, which means that the row contains a chapter hash and a sequential hash, but no vertical value, then the vertical must be inferred from the student's past actions. The server stores the most recent vertical a student was at for each section in the course. Thus, the processing code must keep track of the most recent vertical accessed for each section in the course, and when a row contains a direct course URL without a vertical, the vertical must be inferred from the previously stored most recent vertical for that section.

One other important note is that the rows of the original data file may not actually be sorted, ascending order by time. In our processing, we found that while some rows seemed to be in ascending order, some rows were actually sorted in descending order.

Thus, each student is associated with a list of URLs they visited, processed from the original data log. There are a fixed number of possible course page URLs, which can be represented by the possible combinations of chapter, sequential, and vertical hashes. If there are 200 unique URLs in a course, then the indices from 1 to 200 can each correspond to one of the URLs. Once this mapping between index and URL is established, each student's set of actions can be represented as a list of indices.

Recommendation model design

This sub-section provides context to how the RNN and LSTM architectures function. RNNs maintain an ongoing latent hidden state that persists between each input to the model. This latent state can provide a representation of what has already been seen in the input sequence. Long Short-Term Memory (LSTM) is a modification of the RNN architecture, where the hidden latent state is replaced with a more powerful memory component. We chose to use LSTMs due to their stronger performance in modeling longer range dependencies [19, 20].

RNNs maintain a latent, continuous state, represented by h_t in the equations below. This latent state persists in the model between inputs, such that the prediction at x_{t+1} is influenced by the latent state h_t. The RNN model is parameterized by the input weight matrix W_x, recurrent weight matrix W_h, initial state h_0, and output matrix W_y. b_h and b_y are biases for the latent and output units.

$$h_t = tanh(W_x x_t + W_h h_{t-1} + b_h)$$

$$y_t = \sigma(W_y h_t + b_y)$$

LSTMs, a popular variant of the RNN, augment the latent, continuous state with additional gating logic that helps the model learn longer range dependencies. The gating logic learns when to retain and when to forget information in the latent state. Each hidden state h_t is instead replaced by an LSTM cell unit with the additional gating parameters. The update equations for an LSTM are:

$$f_t = \sigma(Wf_x x_t + W_{fh} h_{t-1} + b_f)$$

$$i_t = \sigma(W_{ix} x_t + W_{ih} h_{t-1} + b_i)$$

$$C'_t = tanh(W_{Cx} x_t + W_{Ch} h_{t-1} + b_C)$$

$$C_t = f_t \times C_{t-1} + i_t \times C'_t$$

$$o_t = \sigma(W_{ox} x_t + W_{oh} h_{t-1} + b_o)$$

$$h_t = o_t \times tanh(C_t)$$

f_t, i_t, and o_t represent the gating mechanisms used by the LSTM to determine when to forget, input, and output data from the cell state, C_t. C'_t represents an intermediary candidate cell state that is gated to update the next cell state.

LSTM Model Description and Training

LSTM models have several hyperparameters, which refer to values that affect how the model performs on a given set of data. Evaluating which hyperparameters work best for a given model and dataset can be done in one of several ways, and is usually resolved with some empirical experimentation. For this analysis, we varied the following hyperparameters: number of LSTM layers and number of hidden nodes per LSTM layer. Each model was trained using either 1, 2, or 3 LSTM layers, as well as 64, 128, and 256 nodes per LSTM layer. Thus, each LSTM model is trained with 9 different hyperparameter sets.

To create a behavior prediction LSTM model, the model needs to be trained to predict the next URL given a prior sequence of URLs visited. This is our baseline LSTM model, where the inputs and outputs are simply indices corresponding to unique URL accesses. The model is trained in batches of 64 student sequences at a time using back propagation through time [21]. Categorical cross entropy is used to calculate loss and RMSprop is used as the optimizer. Drop out layers were added between LSTM layers as a method to curb overfitting [22]. An embedding layer with 160 dimensions is added to convert input indices to a continuous multi dimensional space, a technique commonly used in language modeling [23]. LSTM models were created using Keras [24], a Python library built on top of Theano [25].

Figure 3 details an example pipeline where the first two timesteps of a student sequence of URL accesses is shown. The two URLs in the student's sequence are converted to an index representation of that URL, which is then fed to the LSTM model. The index is implicitly converted to a one-hot vector representation by the embedding layer used by the Keras LSTM model. The output of the model uses the softmax function to normalize the outputs to sum to 1, so that the values within the output vector could be thought of as probabilities of that index being the predicted next URL. If there are 300 unique course URLs, for example, then the output vector would be of length 300, where each value of the vector corresponds to the probability that the next URL in the sequence will be that index value. Thus, to find the most likely next URL, one needs to find the index of the vector that has the

maximum probability, and then consult the one to one mapping between indices and URLs to find which URL that index corresponds to. Note that in the example figure, index 32 of the softmax output in timestep 1 has the highest probability. Thus, according to the model, the most likely next URL would be the URL corresponding to index 32. In the example, this prediction turns out to be correct, as it is shown that the actual input in the next timestep is associated with that URL.

Incorporating time into the model

The previous subsection described a baseline LSTM model, where only the sequence of URL visits was modeled. We hypothesize that prediction accuracy of the next URL can go up if the model were to incorporate the amount of time spent on each resource. Unfortunately, there is no way to know exactly how much time the student is truly paying attention to a particular URL. We can approximate time spent, however, by calculating the time difference between each URL visit. Thus, we approximate the time spent on a URL by taking the time difference before accessing the next URL.

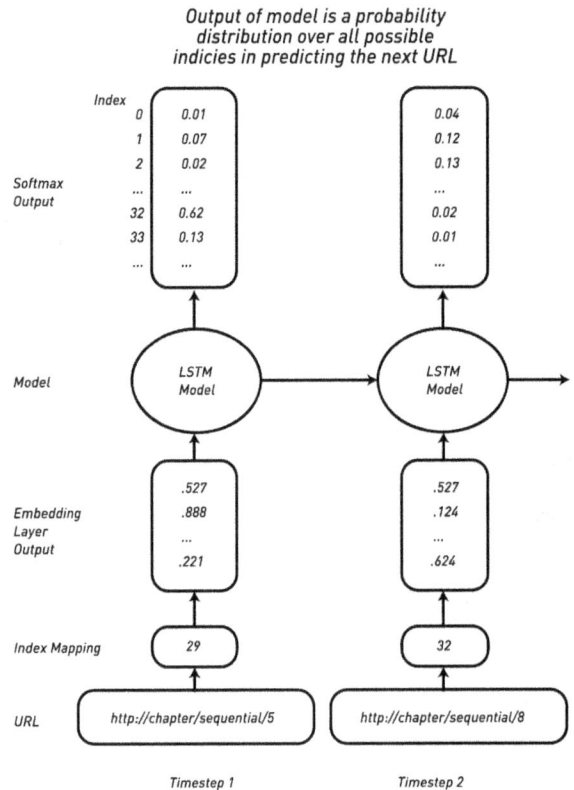

Figure 3. Depiction of baseline LSTM architecture

The baseline LSTM model [20] can be augmented to be able to incorporate time spent in addition to the standard input and output of the current and next URL index.

We propose two methods for incorporating time spent into the input of the model. These two methods are referred to as bucketed-time-input and normalized-time-input. These two methods of input are explained next.

Bucketed-time-input refers to an augmented input, where an additional one-hot vector is concatenated with the original baseline input. Figure 4 depicts this additional time input processing step in a graphical format. This additional one-hot vector indicates the amount of time spent on the resource relative to four pre-determined buckets: between 0-10 seconds, 11-60 seconds, 61-1799 seconds, and finally 1800 and beyond seconds. These buckets were chosen qualitatively, rather than with a data driven approach, to be able to prescribe real world interpretation to the time buckets.

Normalized-time-input refers to an augmented input where an additional two-dimensional vector is concatenated with the original baseline input. Figure 4 depicts how the normalized-time-input is incorporated into the architecture. The first dimension of this vector takes a value between 0 and 1, which is calculated by dividing the time spent on the resource by 1800, or if the time spent is greater than 1800, then the value is taken to simply be 1. Thus, a time spent of 900 seconds would be converted to 0.5. This is considered normalizing the time by 1800 seconds. The second dimension of the vector is simply 1 if the time spent is over 1800 seconds, and 0 otherwise.

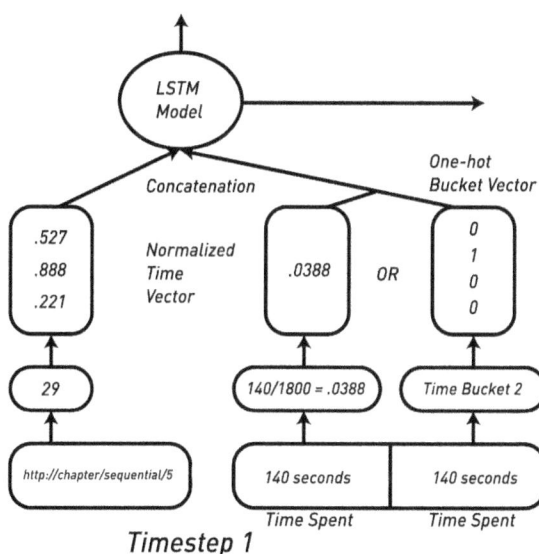

Figure 4. Depiction of two methods of adding dwell time to the model; Normalized continuous (0-1) and time bucketed (1-4)

It is also possible to incorporate time into the output of the model. The non-time version is referred to as non-concatenated-output, while the time incorporated version is referred to as concatenated-output.

Non-concatenated-output refers to the standard output, where the object of prediction is simply an index, where each index has a one-to-one mapping with a course URL. Concatenated-output refers to an output space where the number of indices possible is multiplied by four, so that one could think of a time bucket being concatenated with each index. Each possible course URL now has four associated indices with it, where each index represents a course URL and the amount of time spent on that URL, where time spent is bucketed in the same fashion as the bucketed-time-input. We can compute the overall likelihood for a particular URL by adding the probabilities among all four indices associated with a particular URL. Since each output is also associated with a time, one can look at only indices associated with a particular time bucket. Thus, the output can now be queried to find the most likely URL to visit among each possible time category.

With these methods of input and output defined, we propose the following models:

Attributes:

(a) Input time treated as continuous
(b) Input time treated as categorical
(c) Input time concatenation with vertical after embedding
(d) Time category concatenated with vertical in the output

1. Baseline LSTM model: Inputs and outputs are indices, where each index has a one to one mapping to a unique course URL.

2. Bucketed-time-input, nond-concatenated-output (b,c)

3. Bucketed-time-input, concatenated-output (b,c,d)

4. Normalized-time-input, non-concatenated-output (a,c)

5. Normalized-time-input, concatenated-output (a,c,d)

Deployment Course Dataset and Prediction Results
The pilot course, DelftX Intro to Aeronautical Engineering 2015, contained log data from 27024 unique learner ids. However, for the purposes of behavior recommendation, we chose to filter the data to only include learners who attempted at least one problem check, resulting in data logs from 9,172 learners. From the data logs, we again filter the data to only include data regarding course page navigations, thus excluding events related to lecture video pausing, problem viewing, and so on. We chose to also filter out contiguous repeats of URL accesses. This means that if there are multiple visits to the same URL in a row, we removed duplicates such that there only remained one access to that URL for a student sequence representation. For the time spent associated with sole URL used in place of the duplicate contiguous URLs, we took the maximum time spent among the duplicated URL accesses. Time spent is calculated, in general, by taking the timestamp of a URL access and calculating the future difference to the timestamp of the next URL access in the sequence. There were 336127 navigation events in the 0-10 second bucket, 248918 in the 11-60 second bucket, 338144 events in the 61-1799 bucket, and 123287 events in the 1800 seconds and beyond bucket.

There was a total of 286 possible course URLs, which means there were 286 possible unique verticals to model, spread over 38 sequentials. The median number of verticals in a sequential was 6, with a maximum of 19. The course was self-paced, which means that assignment due dates were not fixed, and all of the course content was released at the beginning of the course. Log data was filtered to only include data from roughly the time period that the course officially ran, from May 31, 2015 to June 3, 2016.

Hill-climbing Validation Early Stopping
The 5 LSTM models described in the previous section were each trained under the 9 different hyperparameter settings described in section 3.1.4. The data was split into two sets, a training set and a held-out test set. The training set comprised sequences from a randomly selected 70% of the users, while the test set contained the remaining 30%. Within the training set, 10% of the sequences were held out as a hill-climbing validation set. During training of a particular model, if the loss calculated on the hill-climbing set did not obtain a best result for 3 consecutive epochs, then training was halted for that model and the best result was recorded. This was our early stopping criterion.

Baselines
An n-gram model is included as another sequential model for comparison. N-gram models capture the structure of sequences through the statistics of *n*-sized sub-sequences. The model predicts each sequence state x_i using the estimated conditional probability that x_i follows the previous *n-1* states in the training set. We trained n-grams with values of n between 2 and 10, while

also instituting a "back-off" policy when there are too few subsequences. For each n-gram, we instituted back-off policies of between 0 and 10 occurrences, so that a particular sub-sequence of size n must occur at least the number of times as the back-off policy, or else that sub-sequence is not used. The back-off policy prevents the n-gram model from using very sparse data, requiring a minimum number of occurrences for that sub-sequence to be used. If there are too few occurrences of a particular n-sized sub-sequence, the model "backs off" and uses the values for the (n-1)-gram model, and so on. The best performing n-gram model on the validation set had an n-value of 7 and a back-off value of 8. A 2-gram model is also included, representing a model predicting the most common URL following a particular URL. We call this model the "Next most common" model. The last baseline is dubbed the "Next syllabus URL" model, which predicts the next URL in the course structure; this is equivalent to the page learners are taken to when they click on the "Next" button in the native edX interface.

Back-tested Prediction Results
Validation accuracy and test set accuracy is shown in Table 2. For each model, the hyperparameter set that reached the highest validation accuracy was used. Thus, for each LSTM model listed in the table, only the highest achieving hyperparameter set results are shown, where training stopped according to the early stopping rules described previously. Accuracy refers to average accuracy per student sequence; thus a next URL prediction accuracy is established per student sequence, and then the averages from all students are averaged together. For baseline outputs, the models produce an index which has a one to one mapping with a URL. Thus, if the most likely index produced by the model matches the actual next URL in the sequence, that is counted as a correct prediction within a student sequence. For concatenated outputs, the models produce an index which has a four to one mapping with a URL, meaning there are four possible indices that all correspond to the same URL, just with a different time spent predicted. For the purpose of accuracy, as long as the URL mapping of the index is correct, then the prediction is counted as correct. Thus, accuracy for concatenated outputs drops the time component from the output in calculating correctness.

Model Input / Output	Validation Acc.	Test Set Acc.
Bucket /Non-Concat.	63.5	64.0
Norm / Concat.	62.6	63.5
Bucket / Concat.	63.0	63.3
Norm / Non-Concat.	62.9	63.3
Baseline LSTM	62.0	62.5
Best *n*-gram (7)	61.6	61.7
Next most common	55.1	55.6
Next syllabus URL	51.5	52.0

Table 2. Prediction accuracy results

REAL-TIME DEPLOYMENT

Recommendation Interface
This section describes our rationale for how to best integrate the recommendations the learner's course experience. We primarily consider two key aspects of the interface: (i) the visual appearance of the recommendations and (ii) the linguistic framing of the accompanying text.

Visual Appearance
As the interface is housed within the edX platform and course materials, it is important that the appearance of the recommendations is seamless. This ensures both a sense of trust from the user---in that it looks like it's a natural part of the edX course---and assuages the risk that the recommendations act as distractions to the learners. Given the simplicity of the edX user interface design, this was not hard to achieve. And to make following the recommendations more intuitive, we also add a "Go" button that learners can use as an alternative to clicking on the plain text link. These appear at the bottom of every page in the course---made directly available to the learner at all times.

Linguistic Framing
Just as we did not want the visual appearance of the recommendation to be too overwhelming in the existing course interface, we likewise aimed to present the accompanying text in a way that clearly communicates the benefit of this resource while not sounding overly authoritative. While definitely an avenue for future experimentation (what is the most effective way to frame such recommendation text to learners?), we eventually decided on "Suggestion for you… Consider visiting: [Recommended next-step]." This text accomplishes the task of communicating to the learner that this recommendation is indeed personalized and unique to him or her (without explaining how) and also making it clear that following this recommendation is optional. Figure 5 shows the final design of the recommendation interface.

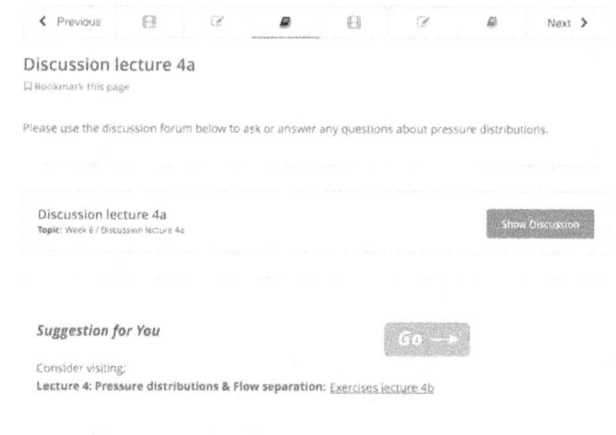

Figure 5. Final design of the recommendation interface

We are able to show the text of sequential and vertical being suggested through a lookup table we created from the course xml.

Model Usage Considerations

Training a model based on a previous offering of the course
Since the navigation behavior model proposed in this paper is behavior and data driven, a requirement to deploy such a model in a live course is that behavior from the course must already exist. To perform our live case study, we selected a MOOC that had multiple offerings over time so that we could use behavior from a completed iteration of the course to train our behavior models. Since the model is trained on a specific structure of course URLs, the current iteration of the course should not deviate too much, preferably at all, from the iteration that the model was trained on.

To deploy our behavior model in the 2016 offering of the Aeronautics Engineering course, we trained on the behavior data from the 2015 offering of the course.

Taking into Account Changes in The Courseware

In our case study, the majority of the course structure was held exactly the same. However, the first chapter to the course was re-ordered. Our behavior model implicitly incorporates the ordering of the course in its predictions, so that any re-ordering of course content would adversely affect its prediction. Therefore, we chose to drop all events related to the first chapter of the course from both the training and the live recommendation data sets. This was deemed acceptable since the first chapter for this course was an introduction to the course staff and logistics.

Additionally, one unique URL was added to the current version of the course. Thus, the trained model has no knowledge or ability to recommend that URL. However, the actual recommendation code can be altered so that when it is detected that a student is near the new URL, the recommendation code can choose to temporarily suspend usage of the behavior model and either suggest going to the new URL directly or simply not suggesting a URL temporarily.

Any deviation in course structure from the training environment needs consideration in handling. Special recommendation logic must be put in place when the live version of the course differs in ways that the original model cannot account for.

Description of the Recommendation Engine

The machine learned model is the contact point between the underlying LSTM behavioral model and the code that serves a clickable link on the learner's browser. The LSTM model has been trained to produce an output that contains a probability distribution over all possible course pages. Our time-concatenated output LSTM models additionally contain time information in each of the output indices. With this time-concatenated probability distribution, it is reasonable to simply take the most likely page and serve that as the model's recommendation. With the time-augmented output, however, the recommendation engine can instead be configured to recommend a URL that the learner is likely to spend a significant amount of time on, for example between 10 seconds and 30 minutes. The hypothesis behind this logic is that if the model only expects the learner to spend fewer than 10 seconds on a resource, then it may be the case that the learner is trying to skip over it on her way to the eventual resource of interest. The recommender gives the learner the skip directly to that eventual resource of interest. It could be reasonable to recommend pages where the learner is expected to spend more than 30 minutes on; However, we chose not to include these as part of our recommendation engine configuration, since it could be possible that such a lengthy time spent on a page could really be indicative of a time-out event, where the learner has actually just left the page, potentially after consulting an ineffective page.

Another method for producing a recommendation could instead be to repeatedly query the behavioral model until the most likely page corresponds to a desirable time bucket, where each repeated query has a "hypothetical action" appended as the most recent event. For example, if a student is currently at a quiz page (Figure 6), then the behavioral model would be queried using that student's past behavior as well as the current quiz page. The time spent on the current quiz page is not known yet since the learner has not navigated away from that page at the time of the query. Thus, time spent on the current page must be approximated in some way; we use the modal time bucket as a place holder (11-60 seconds) and the real time spent is filled in after the next navigation event. The model then produces a probability distribution over time-concatenated indices, as usual. If the most probable page is in a desirable time bucket range, then the engine

recommends that URL. However, if the most probable page is not in a desirable time bucket range, then instead of recommending this page, the engine temporarily appends it to the student's "hypothetical" path until a desirable time bucket recommendation is reached. Thus, through repeated querying of the model, eventually a page in the desirable time bucket range would be reached, and the engine would use this as the recommendation. The reasoning behind such a model would be, for example, to skip through many URL accesses that are under ten seconds (undesirably short time spent) and instead recommend a URL that the student would likely have eventually dwelled on. We refer to this as a forward-stepping process, where we create hypothetical forward steps to the model. The page used in the case shown in Figure 6 is *Video 1*, a recommendation which is inserted into the page after the query completes and which the student followed in this example. After the learner in the example visits *Video 1*, she is suggested to return to the quiz but instead navigates to *Text 3*.

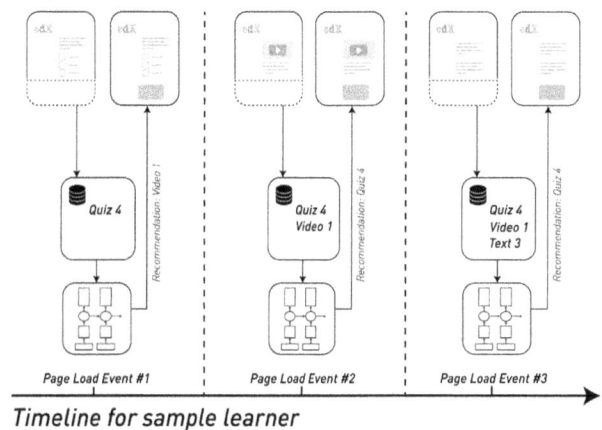

Timeline for sample learner

Figure 6. An example of the framework delivering three recommendations at three consecutive page visits for a learner

We chose to use the time-bucketed-input with time-concatenated output model discussed previously. For the live recommendation pilot, we chose to retrain the LSTM model on the entire set of the previous course offering's data, as opposed to the original training only using 70% of the data. We only used the validation set's best hyperparameters.

Our next step recommendation can be seen as predicting what page a learner wants or will eventually want, and directly linking them to that page in advance. When to consider if what learners want is different from what they need to achieve their goals or the goals of the course is a matter for consideration by future work as well as the appropriate role of a platform, courseware, and personalization in facilitating these goals.

CONTRIBUTIONS

In this paper, we made three contributions to adaptive personalization in a MOOC. The first was to solve the issue of real-time learner event logging required for data-driven intervention with a client side JavaScript solution that records learner navigational events. The second was to introduce a novel behavioral model which predicted the next page a learner was likely to spend significant time on which outperformed existing prediction baselines. Lastly, we combined the first two contributions to provide the first proof-of-concept realization of a real-time data-driven recommendation framework in a live MOOC along with the edge cases and design considerations that needed to be handled in order to deploy.

ACKNOLWEDGEMENTS
We would like to acknowledge our use of the edX partner's Research Data Exchange (RDX) program and the support contributed by the edX data team. We also acknowledge the support from TU Delft's Office of Online Learning, its director, and the DelftX Aeronautics Engineering course team for their cooperation.

REFERENCES

1. Aleven, V., McLaughlin, E., Glenn, R. A., and Koedinger, K. (2016) Instruction based on adaptive learning technologies. *Handbook of research on learning and instruction*. Routledge.

2. Anderson, J. R., Corbett, A. T., Koedinger, K. R., and Pelletier, R. Cognitive tutors: Lessons learned. *The Journal of the Learning Sciences* 4, 2 (1995), 167–207.

3. Barnes, T., and Stamper, J. Toward automatic hint generation for logic proof tutoring using historical student data. In *International Conference on Intelligent Tutoring Systems*, Springer (2008), 373–382.

4. Davis, D., Chen, G., Hauff, C., and Houben, G.-J. Gauging mooc learners adherence to the designed learning path (2016) In *Proceedings of the 9th International Conference on Educational Data Mining (EDM)*. 54–61.

5. Davis, D., Chen, G., van der Zee, T., Hauff, C., and Houben, G. J. (2016) Retrieval practice and study planning in moocs: Exploring classroom-based self-regulated learning strategies at scale. In *European Conference on Technology Enhanced Learning, Springer*. 57–71.

6. Guo, P. J., & Reinecke, K. (2014). Demographic differences in how students navigate through MOOCs. In *Proceedings of the first ACM conference on Learning@ scale conference* (pp. 21-30). ACM.

7. Herlocker, J. L., Konstan, J. A., Terveen, L. G., & Riedl, J. T. (2004). Evaluating collaborative filtering recommender systems. *ACM Transactions on Information Systems (TOIS)*, 22(1), 5-53.

8. Hsiao, I.-H., Sosnovsky, S., and Brusilovsky, P. (2010) Guiding students to the right questions: adaptive navigation support in an e-learning system for java programming. *Journal of Computer Assisted Learning* 26, 4, 270–283.

9. Khalil, H., and Ebner, M. (2014) Moocs completion rates and possible methods to improve retention-a literature review. In *World Conference on Educational Multimedia, Hypermedia and Telecommunications*, no. 1, 1305–1313.

10. Kizilcec, R. F., Pérez-Sanagustin, M., & Maldonado, J. J. (2016). Recommending self-regulated learning strategies does not improve performance in a MOOC. In *Proceedings of the Third ACM Conference on Learning@ Scale* (pp. 101-104). ACM.

11. Kopeinik, S., Kowald, D., and Lex, E. (2016) Which algorithms suit which learning environments? A comparative study of recommender systems in tel. *In European Conference on Technology Enhanced Learning*, Springer, 124–138.

12. Nguyen, A., Piech, C., Huang, J., and Guibas, L. (2014) Codewebs: scalable homework search for massive open online programming courses. In *Proceedings of the 23rd international conference on World wide web, ACM*. 491–502.

13. Piech, C., Sahami, M., Huang, J., & Guibas, L. (2015). Autonomously generating hints by inferring problem solving policies. In *Proceedings of the Second ACM Conference on Learning@ Scale* (pp. 195-204). ACM.

14. Pielot, M., Dingler, T., Pedro, J. S., and Oliver, N. When attention is not scarce-detecting boredom from mobile phone usage. In *Proceedings of the 2015 ACM International Joint Conference on Pervasive and Ubiquitous Computing*, ACM (2015), 825–836.

15. Stamper, J., Barnes, T., Lehmann, L., and Croy, M. The hint factory: Automatic generation of contextualized help for existing computer aided instruction. In *Proceedings of the 9th International Conference on Intelligent Tutoring Systems Young Researchers Track* (2008), 71–78.

16. Stamper, J., Eagle, M., Barnes, T., and Croy, M. Experimental evaluation of automatic hint generation for a logic tutor. *International Journal of Artificial Intelligence in Education* 22, 1-2 (2013), 3–17.

17. Tomkin, J. H., & Charlevoix, D. (2014). Do professors matter?: Using an a/b test to evaluate the impact of instructor involvement on MOOC student outcomes. In *Proceedings of the first ACM conference on Learning@ scale conference* (pp. 71-78). ACM.

18. Wen, M., and Rosé, C. P. Identifying latent study habits by mining learner behavior patterns in massive open online courses. In *CIKM '14* (2014), 1983–1986.

19. Bengio, Y., Simard, P., and Frasconi, P. Learning long-term dependencies with gradient descent is difficult. *Neural Networks, IEEE Transactions on*, 5(2):157-166, 1994.

20. Gers, F. A., Schmidhuber, J., and Cummins, F. Learning to forget: Continual prediction with lstm. *Neural computation*, 12(10):2451-2471, 200.

21. Werbos, P. J. Generalization of backpropagation with application to a recurrent gas market model. *Neural Networks*, 1(4):339-356, 1988.

22. Pham, V., Bluche, T., Kermorvant, C., and Louradour, J. Dropout improves recurrent neural networks for handwriting recognition. In *Frontiers in Handwriting Recognition (ICFHR), 2014 14th International Conference on*, pages 285-290. IEEE, 2014.

23. Mikolov, T., Karafiat, M., Burget, L., Cernocky, J., and Khudanpur. Recurrent neural network based language model. In *INTERSPEECH*, volume 2, page 3, 2010.

24. Chollet, F. Keras. https://github.com/fchollet/keras, 2015.

25. Bergstra, J., Breuleux, O., Bastien, F., Lamblin, P., Pascanu, R., Desjardins, G., Turian, J., Warde-Farley, D., and Bengio, Y. Theano: a CPU and GPU math expression compiler. In *Proceedings of the Python for Scientific Computing Conference (SciPy)*, June 2010. Oral Presentation.

26. Reddy, S., Labutov, I., and Joachims, T. Latent skill embedding for personalized lesson sequence recommendation. *CoRR*, abs/1602.07029, 2016.

27. Tang, S., Peterson, J. C., & Pardos, Z. A. (2016). Modeling Student Behavior using Granular Large Scale Action Data from a MOOC. *arXiv preprint arXiv:1608.04789*.

28. Pardos, Z.A., Bergner, Y., Seaton, D., Pritchard, D.E. (2013) Adapting Bayesian Knowledge Tracing to a Massive Open Online College Course in edX. D'Mello, S. K., Calvo, R. A., and Olney, A. (eds.) *Proceedings of the 6th International Conference on Educational Data Mining* (EDM). Memphis, TN. Pages 137--144.

Learning to Code in Localized Programming Languages

Sayamindu Dasgupta[*†]
*MIT Media Lab
Cambridge, MA 02142
sayamindu@media.mit.edu

Benjamin Mako Hill[†]
†University of Washington
Seattle, WA, 98195
{sdg1, makohill}@uw.edu

ABSTRACT

Education research suggests that learning in one's local language can have a positive impact on learning outcomes. We offer a quantitative test of the association between local language use and the rate at which youth learn to program. Using longitudinal data drawn from five countries and over 15,000 users of Scratch, a large informal learning community, we find that novice users who code with their programming language keywords and environment localized into their home countries' primary language demonstrate new programming concepts at a faster rate than users from the same countries whose interface is in English. We conclude with a discussion of the implications of our findings for designers of online learning systems.

ACM Classification Keywords

H.5.2 Information Interfaces and Presentation (e.g. HCI): User Interfaces; K.3.2 Computer and Information Science Education: Computer Science Education

Author Keywords

learning; programming language education; localization; learning in local languages; linguistic accessibility; Scratch

INTRODUCTION

A large body of education research and theory suggests that learning in one's local language at the primary and secondary levels supports positive learning outcomes [20, 4, 13]. As early as 1953, UNESCO's publication on "the use of vernacular languages in education" [20] argued for instruction in students' mother tongues both as early, and as late, as possible:

> On educational grounds, we recommend that the use of the mother tongue be extended to as late a stage in education as possible. In particular, pupils should begin their schooling through the medium of the mother tongue because they understand it best [...]

A 2008 study that covered 26 countries and 153 linguistic groups found that attendance in educational institutions was positively related with the availability of mother-tongue instruction [18]. Another study in Guatemala showed that

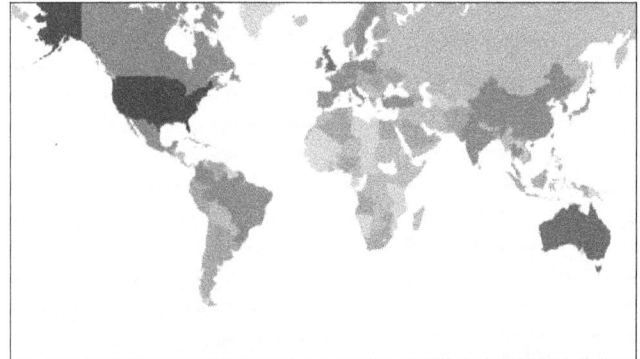

Figure 1: Choropleth map showing the distribution of Scratch users worldwide as indicated by self-reported country information. Countries are shaded from lightest to darkest in terms of the number of Scratch users in the country along a log-linear scale [10].

schools that offered bilingual education in students' mother tongues have higher attendance and promotion rates and lower repetition and dropout rates [12].

As the audiences for large-scale digital learning tools and environments become more global, the potential benefit of supporting local languages in these systems has grown. Despite prior work in HCI highlighting the need for localized[1] user interfaces [15, 9], localization can be complex and expensive [7]. As a result, many online learning systems are offered only in English. When interfaces are localized, it is often only into a small number of languages spoken by large populations. For speakers of other languages, especially for those belonging to small or marginalized linguistic groups, the only option is to use English.

The use of English is particularly pronounced in programming education. In nearly every widely used programming language, the names of symbols and keywords (e.g., for, while, if, else) are borrowed from English. In this paper, we examine the relationship between the rate at which young people learn to code and their use of localized programming languages and user interfaces. Using longitudinal data on the learning trajectories of 15,015 users of the Scratch online community from five countries, we find that, controlling for differing

L@S 2017, April 20-21, 2017, Cambridge, MA, USA
ACM 978-1-4503-4450-0/17/04.
http://dx.doi.org/10.1145/3051457.3051464

---

[1]In this paper we use the term "localization" to mean translated user interfaces. However, localization often consists of more than translation—for example, customized UI icons, customized representations of numbers, locale appropriate units, support for local calendars, and so on.

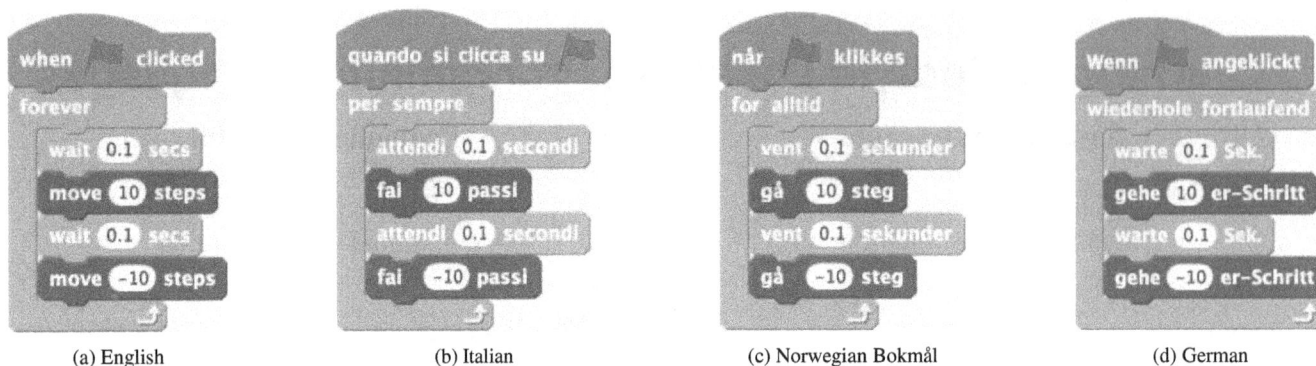

| (a) English | (b) Italian | (c) Norwegian Bokmål | (d) German |

Figure 2: Functionally identical Scratch code represented in four different languages.

levels of activity and socialization, learners who code with localized programming language keywords and environments demonstrate new programming concepts at a faster rate relative to users from the same countries who use otherwise identical interfaces in English. We conclude with a discussion of our findings, the relatively small size of our estimated effect, and implications of our study for designers of online learning systems.

Our empirical setting is Scratch [14], a programming language and online community designed for children aged 8-16. In Scratch, programs are constructed by dragging and dropping visual blocks to define the behavior of on-screen graphical objects called sprites (Figure 2). The Scratch language is supported by a large online community launched in 2007 [11], where creators can share their projects, comment on each others' work, and remix projects created by their peers. Although participation in Scratch is generally open-ended and self-directed, Scratch is used in formal educational settings as well [2].

When Scratch users register they are asked to list their home country. Scratch's 16 million users come from all over the world (Figure 1). The Scratch programming editor, website, and programming blocks are translated into a number of languages by volunteer translators through a web-based translation portal. When a user visits the Scratch website, the interface language is automatically selected based on the user's browser configuration. In previous studies, this mechanism has been used to identify English as a Second Language (ESL) users in MOOCS [19]. Scratch users can also select their language manually from a menu in the website or code-editor interface. The language choice persists across browser sessions through a HTTP cookie-based mechanism. In exploratory analysis, we found that a majority of the users (approx. 88%) use a single language throughout their interactions with the site.

In Scratch, a single piece of code can be represented in different languages depending on the language selected by the user. Figure 2 shows the same Scratch code, from the same project, represented in four different languages. For example, when a user of the localized Japanese interface creates a project and shares it, they do so entirely in Japanese. If a user of the Italian

localized interface were to view or edit the Japanese user's project, the code would appear in Italian.

Scratch reflects a unique source of observational data to answer questions about the effect of localization on learning for several reasons: it is among the largest websites where young people learn to program, it is used by large numbers of users around the world, and it has been localized into dozens of languages by a large team of volunteer translators. Given education research that suggests that local language use will lead to better learning outcomes, our hypothesis is that *Scratch users will learn programming concepts more rapidly when their programming language keywords and environments are localized into their own languages.*

DATA AND MEASURES

Blocks in Scratch are the equivalent of tokens in text-based programming languages and can be used to make a character on the screen (sprite) move, to change a variable, to repeat a set of instructions, and so on. For example, in Figure 2, blocks for making a sprite move back and forth are enclosed in an outer "forever" loop block that is connected to an event-handler block ("when green flag clicked"). In previous research on Scratch and other block-based programming languages such as App Inventor, learning has been modeled as growth in the cumulative repertoire of blocks, similar to a measure of demonstrated vocabulary, which may grow more or less quickly over time [22, 5, 21]. We follow a similar approach and construct a longitudinal measure that represents a cumulative block repertoire over time for each user in our dataset. The cumulative block repertoire is updated for every *de novo* (i.e., non-remix) project shared and incremented by the number of types of blocks in each project that the user had never used previously. For example, if a given project uses two instances of the `if` block, and if the user has not used the `if` block before in previous projects, we increase the cumulative block repertoire by one. We use this measure (*Cumulative Block Repertoire$_{up}$*) as our measure of learning and as the dependent variable in our analysis. The subscript "*up*" reflects the fact that the variable is at the level of the project, clustered within user.

A central independent variable in our analysis is a measure of whether users are interacting with Scratch using a localized interface. To construct this variable, we seek to exploit varia-

Country	Language	% average translation	# users	% users w/ local language	# projects
Portugal	Portuguese	98.9	2,630	90.2	13,178
Italy	Italian	98.5	3,820	87.3	19,875
Brazil	Brazilian Portuguese	96.5	4,353	88.0	26,170
Germany	German	95.8	2,666	75.2	14,339
Norway	Norwegian Bokmål	95.5	1,546	84.6	6,372

Table 1: Countries included in the dataset used in this paper, along with the corresponding primary language, average translation level, number of users, proportion of users who use Scratch in the local language, and total number of projects (with usable language data) per country.

tion in the agreement between users' local language and their interface language. For example, we seek to compare Italian-speaking youths using Italian interfaces to Italian-speaking youths using non-localized English interfaces. Constructing this variable using observation data means we must separately infer each user's primary language and interface language.

There are several reasons why a user might use an interface in a language other than their primary language. One set of reasons is related to the fact that the Scratch website attempts to infer users' language preference on their first visit using metadata sent by the users' web browser. If a user's computer is not configured to send language preference data when a user first visits Scratch, or if any number of technical issues prevent this from happening correctly, users will end up using Scratch in English. When this happens, users may not change the language because they are not aware of the existence of the menu for switching their interface language manually. In another scenario, a learner who has a working knowledge of English may choose to use the system in English because of external factors (e.g., the instructional material being followed may be in English).

Identifying a users' interface language in Scratch is relatively straightforward. When a Scratch user creates a project, the language choice of the user at that moment is recorded. We use this information to determine each user's interface language. Because a large majority of users (88%) never change their language, we set each user's language to what they have used for more than 50% of their published *de novo* projects.

A Scratch user's primary language, independent of their interface, is not possible to observe directly. As a proxy, we first identify the countries that users' self-report as their home at the time that they create their accounts. We then associate languages with countries using *Ethnologue: Languages of the World* [8] to identify the most widely-spoken languages in each country. We treat these national languages as users' primary language. At this point, we excluded all users from countries where English is the mostly widely spoken language as well as users from countries without a single language spoken by a majority of the population.

Since translation in Scratch is volunteer driven, there are only a few languages into which the Scratch website, the Scratch code editor, and the Scratch programming blocks are fully translated. Additionally, the Scratch website and the editor are being continuously developed and updated with bug fixes

and new features. Frequently, these updates cause translations to become out of date, which causes coverage to vary over time. Because we are interested in the effect of translated interfaces, we attempt to identify a set of languages into which the Scratch interface (website, code-editor, and programming blocks) was fully translated. Toward this end, we calculate the translation coverage in all languages twice, at the beginning of our data-collection period and at the end. Although no languages were 100% translated at both points, five languages had at least 95% average translation coverage: Portuguese, Italian, Brazilian Portuguese, German and Norwegian Bokmål. As a result, we restrict our analysis to users who reported their home countries as Portugal, Italy, Brazil, Germany, and Norway, respectively.

Using these measures of users' inferred interface and primary language, we construct a dummy variable (*Localized?$_u$* with a subscript u because it does not vary across users) set to 1 if a user's inferred interface language matches their home country's most widely used language (i.e., Portuguese, Italian, Brazilian Portuguese, German, and Norwegian Bokmål, respectively). Table 1 shows the number of users from each country in the resulting dataset who use Scratch in their local language. As an additional robustness check of our study, we did a similar analysis with languages above the 90% translation level threshold with two additional countries (France and Slovenia). The overall results remained similar in magnitude and sign. Next, we construct a continuous variable that represents the cumulative number of *de novo* projects shared by the user prior to the observation (*De Novo Projects$_{up}$*). The interaction between these two variables constitutes our key question predictor.

We also construct a series of controls used by Dasgupta *et al.* [5]. We construct a control for the cumulative number of blocks used in users' *de novo* projects (*Total Blocks$_{up}$*). To control for social activity, we construct a control for the number of comments that projects' creators have left on Scratch at the time that they shared the project (*Comments$_{up}$*). To capture the effect of remixing, we construct a control for users' numbers of remixes (*Remixed Projects$_{up}$*). Dasgupta *et al.*, whose dataset was drawn from an earlier version of Scratch, used a count of downloads as a measure of users' exposure to other users' source code. In the newer version of Scratch used in our analysis, downloading has been replaced with 'See Inside" functionality that allows users to view source code directly on the website. Hence, we add a control for the number of times users have seen inside another user's projects (*See Insides$_{up}$*). Finally, we construct controls for users' tenures on the site in days (*Experience$_{up}$*) and self-reported age measured in years (*User Age$_{up}$*).

For our analysis, we constructed a dataset that contains all projects shared by users from the five focal countries who signed up between May 15, 2015 and May 15, 2016. We chose May 15, 2015 as the data collection start date as the Scratch software started to log language information just prior to that date. As we rely on longitudinal measures for our study, we consider only those users who have shared more than one *de novo* project during our period of analysis. Out of a total of 15,339 users from this period who shared more than one *de novo* project, we discard 324 who were found to have used Scratch in a language that is neither the local language of that country nor English. Our final dataset includes a total of 90,859 projects shared between May 15, 2015 to July 8, 2016 by the remaining 15,015 users.

Variable	Range	μ	M	σ
Cumulative Block Repertoire	[0, 139]	27	25	18
De Novo Projects	[1, 744]	6	3	12
Remixed Projects	[0, 570]	1	0	7
Comments	[0, 2771]	4	0	41
Total Blocks	[0, 72461]	487	138	1909
Experience	[0, 415]	62	39	71
User Age	[4, 89]	19	15	12

Table 2: Summary statistics for users in our dataset at the point of the final project included in the dataset. Columns report variables' range, mean (μ), median (M), and standard deviation (σ).

Among these projects, 10,768 are missing language information. Another 157 projects are missing all data in the Scratch database. Examination of randomly chosen projects where language information is missing suggests that these were projects uploaded from the standalone Scratch offline client, which though localized, does not include language information with project uploads. For the 157 projects without any data at all, it is hard to pinpoint a reason that data is missing. One possibility is that the Scratch website's project upload or auto-save mechanism failed for these projects. As an additional data cleanup measure, we mark 2,389 projects as having missing age information, where the user age was found to be self-reported as less than 4 years, or more than 90 years of age. As with any online-activity dataset all our variables of interest are highly skewed, and we provide summary statistics for each user in our dataset (post cleanup) in Table 2 at the point when users shared their final projects.

ANALYTIC PLAN
Our analytic plan closely follows the approach used by Dasgupta *et al*. Our dataset is structured so that our unit of analysis is the *de novo* Scratch project. Of course, measures of cumulative block repertoire within a particular user are not independent of each other, and this introduces an important threat

of serial correlation of standard errors. The most common technique for addressing this threat is the use of multi-level models [17]. Dasgupta *et al*. [5] addressed this with user-level fixed effects, which control for all observed and unobserved qualities that have a consistent effect across projects shared by a user. This strategy is not possible in this study because a key question predictor (*Localized?$_u$*) does not vary across users' projects. Instead, we include a random intercept term. Since our dependent variable is a count, we model growth in block repertoire using mixed-effects Poisson regression models using the lme4 package in R [1]. As we are concerned about over-dispersion in the dependent variable, we fit a negative binomial regression model as well, and the results are similar. Since the distributions of the continuous independent variables are skewed, we log-transform all of them except for *User Age$_{up}$*.

In our first model (M1), we consider only three variables. First, we include our dummy variable, which indicates whether the user in question is creating projects with a localized interface (*Localized?$_u$*). Second, we include our continuous variable that represents the cumulative number of shared *de novo* projects (*De Novo Projects$_{up}$*). Finally, because our hypothesis is that the growth of repertoires for users using localized interfaces will be faster, we include an interaction term between *Localized?$_u$* and *De Novo Projects$_{up}$*, which allows us to estimate the difference in slope associated with a localized interface. The formal version of M1 is presented below:

$$\text{Cumulative Block Repertoire}_{up} = \beta_0 +$$
$$\beta_1 \ln \text{Localized?}_u + \beta_2 \ln \text{De Novo Projects}_{up} +$$
$$\beta_3 \text{Localized?}_u \times \ln \text{De Novo Projects}_{up} + [u_{0i} + \varepsilon_{up}]$$

In our second model (M2), we add the series of controls described above. Formally, M2 can be represented as:

$$\text{Cumulative Block Repertoire}_{up} = \beta_0 +$$
$$\beta_1 \text{Localized?}_u + \beta_2 \ln \text{De Novo Projects}_{up} +$$
$$\beta_3 \text{Localized?}_u \times \ln \text{De Novo Projects}_{up}$$
$$+ \beta_4 \ln \text{Remixed Projects}_{up} + \beta_5 \ln \text{See Insides}_{up} +$$
$$\beta_6 \ln \text{Comments}_{up} + \beta_7 \ln \text{Total Blocks}_{up} +$$
$$\beta_8 \ln \text{Experience}_{up} + \beta_9 \text{User Age}_{up} + [u_{0i} + \varepsilon_{up}]$$

RESULTS
Shown in Table 3, the results of parameter estimates for both models suggest a positive effect of localization on the rate at which block repertoire increases. Because the addition of controls in M2 does not alter our results substantively, we discuss only the results from M2 below. The main effect of *Localized?* is negative ($\beta = -0.056$, $SE = 0.015$, $p < 0.01$). This suggests that, everything else equal, the first projects by users of the localized interface have a lower diversity of blocks. Given that a user's cumulative repertoire cannot decrease, it is unsurprising that we estimate that the main effect of *De Novo Projects* is positive ($\beta = 0.012$, $SE = 0.005$, $p < 0.001$).

	Cumulative Block Repertoire	
	M1	M2
Localized?$_u$	−0.109*	−0.056*
	(0.020)	(0.015)
ln De Novo Projects$_{up}$	0.517*	0.012*
	(0.003)	(0.005)
Localized?$_u$ × ln De Novo Projects$_{up}$	0.091*	0.027*
	(0.004)	(0.004)
ln Remixed Projects$_{up}$		−0.033*
		(0.002)
ln See Insides$_{up}$		0.020*
		(0.002)
ln Comments$_{up}$		−0.048*
		(0.002)
ln Total Blocks$_{up}$		0.371*
		(0.002)
ln Experience$_{up}$		0.052*
		(0.001)
User Age$_{up}$		−0.001*
		(0.0004)
Constant	2.119*	1.045*
	(0.019)	(0.016)
Observations	79,934	77,545
Log Likelihood	-284,220.000	-246,430.700

Note: *p<0.01

Table 3: Results of fitting mixed-effects Poisson regression models M1 and M2.

Our key question predictor is the interaction term between *De Novo Projects* and *Localized?*, which captures the difference in the rate of repertoire growth between users of localized and English interfaces. Our estimates are small but positive ($\beta = 0.027$, $SE = 0.004$, $p < 0.001$). Although we estimate that users of non-localized interfaces begin with higher repertoires, our model predicts that users who have shared 2 log units more projects will have the same repertoire as otherwise identical users of non-localized interfaces and that this gap will widen as users share more.

Because our model is a non-linear model, because most of our our independent variables are log-transformed, and because our key predictor is an interaction, interpreting the coefficients in our model directly can be challenging. We find it useful to interpret the results by describing model-predicted values for "prototypical" users. For example, M2 predicts that a user who has shared 16 projects (95th percentile in our dataset) with median values for all of our control variables would have a repertoire that would be 37.1 if they had used English but 37.9 if they had used a localized interface instead. Though the difference of less than 1 block is small, the negative main effect of *Localized?*$_u$ masks some of the differences in the rate of change.

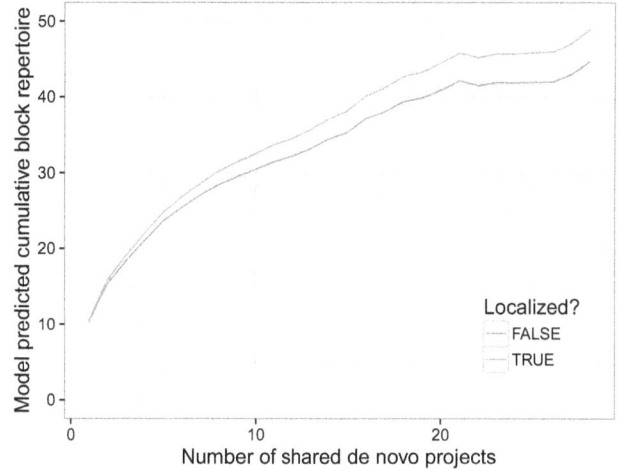

Figure 3: Model-derived predicted values (from model M2) for *Cumulative Block Repertoire* for two prototypical users across a range of values of *de novo* projects. The main effect of localized language use is set to zero. All other predictor variables are set to median values for the corresponding value of *de novo* project share count.

To further aid in interpretation, we visualize a range of these model-predicted values drawn from M2 in Figure 3 for two such prototypical users: one who uses a localized interface and the other who does not. The x-axis represents the number of *de novo* projects shared (up to the 98th percentile in our dataset), and the y-axis represents the users' model-predicted cumulative block repertoire. Since all other predictor variables tend to increase over time, we set each of of our controls to the median value across all projects with the same value of *De Novo Projects* (e.g., the median for users' 1st, 2nd, 3rd, ... etc. projects). To make it easier to interpret the effect of the interaction, we also set the main effect of *Localized?* to 0 so that both prototypical users start with identical repertoires. A user who has shared 16 projects (95th percentile in our dataset) with median values for all of our control variables would have a repertoire that would be 37.1 if they had used English but 40.1 if they had used a localized interface instead.

All of the parameter estimates for our controls are well estimated. Drawn from a very different version of Scratch and from a non-US sample, several of our estimates for our controls are different in sign from those found in the earlier study by Dasgupta *et al.* [5]. Most important for the previous work, Dasgupta *et al.* found a positive relationship between remixing activity and learning, and we estimate a negative association. Although this might be explained by revisions to Scratch that changed the way that code is shared and reused, our model points to an important area for further study. In terms of our papers' findings, the addition of the controls in M2 attenuate the size of our effect but does not alter the sign or substantive takeaway.

LIMITATIONS

Of course, the validity of our findings and results could be affected by a number of potential threats to validity. First, cumulative block repertoire can increase at a faster rate for reasons unrelated to, but correlated with, users' use of a localized interface. In other words, although our results can be understood as evidence in support of the hypothesis that local language use can cause users to learn about new programming blocks more quickly, our results describe correlation, not causation. We have attempted to address this threat by including a number of variables in our model as controls for productivity, social activity, and age, but there may be other important variables that we have omitted. For example, wealthier individuals are often more likely to be more fluent with English [6]. If relatively wealthier users within a country are more likely to use a non-localized interface, they might also learn faster or slower than their less wealthy peers for reasons other than the language of the Scratch interface.

Second, it is unclear what effect the English-dominated nature of the Scratch online community has on learning. In our analysis, we choose languages where translation coverage is very high, meaning that the website is localized almost completely. However, the content on the Scratch website includes prompts within projects, comments, and project descriptions. Based on our unscientific observations, most of this material—with the exception of language specific forums—is in English. If social learning within Scratch is supported by English fluency, we might expect English users to be at a relative advantage compared to users relying on localization. Ultimately, however, the implication of this is unknown.

Third, our analysis relies on a series of assumptions that we know are not always true. Central to our construction of our variable *Localized?* is the assumption that everyone in each country in our dataset speaks the same language (e.g., that in Germany, everyone speaks German). This is clearly not always true. In future work, it may be possible to use language-detection algorithms [16] to infer users' primary languages from their submitted content (e.g., project titles, comments, variable names in projects). However, the presence of English-speaking users in our dataset using the non-localized interfaces seems most likely to lead to under-estimates of the effect of localization on learning because these English-speaking users in non-English-speaking countries would be using their preferred language and would not be at a relative disadvantage.

Finally, our measure of block repertoire cannot detect whether a block is used correctly or if a user actually understands the function of the block. This is a challenge with quantitative measures of learning in general, and it has been shown through qualitative work [3] that there are scenarios where a learner uses a given Scratch block by trial and error without necessarily understanding how it works. We present our work in the hope that future research will critique and build upon our approach and measures.

DISCUSSION

This paper's contribution is support for the theory that novice learners have better learning outcomes when learning in their own language. We present models that estimate a positive association between the growth rate of users' repertoires of programming blocks and the translation of their programming language and interface into their local languages. We do not know if these results are generalizable beyond the users and countries in our dataset. We believe that our work points to the possible benefits of supporting localization for designers of educational programming languages and environments.

Our estimated effect size is small and reflects a difference of only several blocks over the full trajectory of some of Scratch's most active users. However, we remain optimistic about these results for two reasons. First, a single block reflects a very large proportion of most users' repertoires. Second, there are several plausible scenarios, discussed above, that might lead to an underestimation of our effect. Of course, as we explain in our limitations, establishing a causal effect remains a goal for future work.

Perhaps more important is the effect that localization has on the degree to which engagement and learning is possible in the first place. After all, Scratch is almost unique among programming languages in that it provides a completely localized interface, including a translated version of the programming language itself. Although we have presented evidence in support of the claim that young programmers learn more quickly using localized interfaces, the most important effect of localization, not captured by our analysis, may be that being able to engage in ones' primary language supports users who would otherwise not learn to code at all.

ACKNOWLEDGMENTS

We are grateful to the Lifelong Kindergarten group at the MIT Media Lab for creating Scratch and for continuing to support the growth of the community and the technical platform. We would also like to acknowledge Mitchel Resnick, Natalie Rusk, Nathan TeBlunthuis, and our anonymous reviewers for their support and thoughtful feedback on this paper. Financial support for this work came from the National Science Foundation (grants DRL-1417663 and DRL-1417952).

REFERENCES

1. Douglas Bates, Martin Mächler, Ben Bolker, and Steve Walker. 2015. Fitting Linear Mixed-Effects Models Using lme4. *Journal of Statistical Software* 67, 1 (2015), 1–48. DOI:http://dx.doi.org/10.18637/jss.v067.i01

2. Karen Brennan. 2012. ScratchEd: Developing support for educators as designers. *Designing with teachers: Participatory approaches to professional development in education* (2012), 67–77.

3. Karen Brennan and Mitchel Resnick. 2012. New frameworks for studying and assessing the development of computational thinking. In *Proceedings of the 2012 annual meeting of the American Educational Research Association*. AERA, Vancouver, Canada. http://scratched.gse.harvard.edu/ct/files/AERA2012.pdf

4. Dörthe Bühmann and Barbara Trudell. 2008. *Mother tongue matters: Local language as a key to effective learning*. Technical Report. United Nations Educational, Scientific and Cultural Organization (UNESCO), Paris, France. http://unesdoc.unesco.org/images/0016/001611/161121e.pdf

5. Sayamindu Dasgupta, William Hale, Andrés Monroy-Hernández, and Benjamin Mako Hill. 2016. Remixing As a Pathway to Computational Thinking. In *Proceedings of the 19th ACM Conference on Computer-Supported Cooperative Work & Social Computing (CSCW '16)*. ACM, New York, NY, USA, 1438–1449. DOI:
http://dx.doi.org/10.1145/2818048.2819984

6. Janina Kahn-Horwitz, Joseph Shimron, and Richard L. Sparks. 2006. Weak and strong novice readers of english as a foreign language: Effects of first language and socioeconomic status. *Annals of Dyslexia* 56, 1 (2006), 161–185. DOI:
http://dx.doi.org/10.1007/s11881-006-0007-1

7. Luis A. Leiva and Vicent Alabau. 2015. Automatic Internationalization for Just In Time Localization of Web-Based User Interfaces. *ACM Trans. Comput.-Hum. Interact.* 22, 3 (May 2015), 13:1–13:32. DOI:
http://dx.doi.org/10.1145/2701422

8. M Paul Lewis, Gary F Simons, and Charles D Fennig (Eds.). 2016. *Ethnologue: Languages of the world (online edition)*. Vol. 19. SIL International, Dallas, TX.
http://www.ethnologue.com/

9. Aaron Marcus, Nuray Aykin, Apala Lahiri Chavan, Donald L. Day, Emilie West Gould, Pia Honold, and Masaaki Kurosu. 2000. Cross-cultural User-interface Design: What? So What? Now What?. In *CHI '00 Extended Abstracts on Human Factors in Computing Systems (CHI EA '00)*. ACM, New York, NY, USA, 299–299. DOI:http://dx.doi.org/10.1145/633292.633468

10. MIT Scratch Team. 2013. Scratch Statistics. (2013).
https://scratch.mit.edu/statistics/ Accessed: 2016-10-03.

11. Andrés Monroy Hernández. 2007. ScratchR: sharing user-generated programmable media. In *Proceedings of the 6th international conference on Interaction design and children (IDC '07)*. ACM, New York, NY, USA, 167–168. DOI:
http://dx.doi.org/10.1145/1297277.1297315

12. Harry Anthony Patrinos and Eduardo Velez. 2009. Costs and benefits of bilingual education in Guatemala: A partial analysis. *International Journal of Educational Development* 29, 6 (2009), 594 – 598. DOI:
http://dx.doi.org/10.1016/j.ijedudev.2009.02.001

13. Helen Pinnock and Gowri Vijayakumar. 2009. *Language and Education: The Missing Link: How the Language Used in Schools Threatens the Achievement of Education for All*. CfBT Education Trust, Reading; London.
http://www.unesco.org/education/EFAWG2009/LanguageEducation.pdf

14. Mitchel Resnick, John Maloney, Andrés Monroy-Hernández, Natalie Rusk, Evelyn Eastmond, Karen Brennan, Amon Millner, Eric Rosenbaum, Jay Silver, Brian Silverman, and Yasmin Kafai. 2009. Scratch: Programming for All. *Commun. ACM* 52, 11 (Nov. 2009), 60–67. DOI:http://dx.doi.org/10.1145/1592761.1592779

15. Patricia Russo and Stephen Boor. 1993. How Fluent is Your Interface?: Designing for International Users. In *Proceedings of the INTERACT '93 and CHI '93 Conference on Human Factors in Computing Systems (CHI '93)*. ACM, New York, NY, USA, 342–347. DOI:
http://dx.doi.org/10.1145/169059.169274

16. Nakatani Shuyo. 2010. Language detection library for Java. (2010).
http://code.google.com/p/language-detection

17. Judith D. Singer and John B. Willett. 2003. *Applied Longitudinal Data Analysis: Modeling Change and Event Occurrence*. Oxford University Press, USA.

18. Jeroen Smits, Janine Huisman, and Karine Kruijff. 2008. Home language and education in the developing world. *Paper commissioned for the EFA Global Monitoring Report 2009, Overcoming Inequality: why governance matters* (2008). http://unesdoc.unesco.org/images/0017/001787/178702e.pdf

19. Judith Uchidiuno, Amy Ogan, Kenneth R. Koedinger, Evelyn Yarzebinski, and Jessica Hammer. 2016. Browser Language Preferences As a Metric for Identifying ESL Speakers in MOOCs. In *Proceedings of the Third (2016) ACM Conference on Learning @ Scale (L@S '16)*. ACM, New York, NY, USA, 277–280. DOI:
http://dx.doi.org/10.1145/2876034.2893433

20. UNESCO. 1953. *The Use of Vernacular Languages in Education*. Technical Report 8. United Nations Educational, Scientific and Cultural Organization (UNESCO), Paris, France. http://unesdoc.unesco.org/images/0000/000028/002897eb.pdf

21. Benjamin Xie and Hal Abelson. 2016. Skill Progression in MIT App Inventor. In *2016 IEEE Symposium on Visual Languages and Human-Centric Computing (VL/HCC)*. IEEE, Cambridge, UK. DOI:
http://dx.doi.org/10.1109/VLHCC.2016.7739687

22. Seungwon Yang, Carlotta Domeniconi, Matt Revelle, Mack Sweeney, Ben U. Gelman, Chris Beckley, and Aditya Johri. 2015. Uncovering Trajectories of Informal Learning in Large Online Communities of Creators. In *Proceedings of the Second (2015) ACM Conference on Learning @ Scale (L@S '15)*. ACM, New York, NY, USA, 131–140. DOI:
http://dx.doi.org/10.1145/2724660.2724674

Teaching Students to Recognize and Implement Good Coding Style

Eliane S. Wiese,
Michael Yen,
Antares Chen
UC Berkeley
Berkeley, USA
{eliane.wiese, mayen,
antaresc} @berkeley.edu

Lucas A. Santos
Federal University of São
Carlos
São Carlos, SP, Brazil
lukeaugusto@berkeley.edu

Armando Fox
UC Berkeley
Berkeley, USA
fox@cs.berkeley.edu

ABSTRACT

Teaching students to write code with good style is important but difficult: in-depth feedback currently requires a human. AutoStyle, a style tutor that scales, offers adaptive, real-time holistic style feedback and hints as students improve their code. An in-situ study with 103 undergraduate students in a CS class compared AutoStyle to a control tutor which only offered ABC score. While students improved the style of their code in both cases, students working with AutoStyle were more likely to use an appropriate language idiom and to improve their recognition of good style. However, students struggled to implement style improvements, even when hints recommended specific functions.

Author Keywords

Computer science education; programming style tutor; in-situ experiments

INTRODUCTION: ENCOURAGING BEAUTIFUL CODE

It's hard to teach programmers to write beautiful code, but it's vitally important. We use the term *beautiful code* to mean code that is elegant, efficient, idiomatic, and revealing of design intent [5, 2].

Beautiful code is crucial in professional settings. As Knuth put it in 1984, "Instead of imagining that our main task is to instruct a *computer* what to do, let us concentrate rather on explaining to *human beings* what we want a computer to do" (emphasis in the original) [12]. The importance of human-readable code has been borne out quantitatively. Robert Martin, a thought leader in software engineering, recounts replaying a keystroke log of one of his own programming sessions in his book *Clean Code* [17]. He discovers that when he creates new code, he spends only 10% of his time typing it out. 90% of his time is spent reading existing code that the new code would interact with. Since the vast majority of his time is

L@S 2017, April 20–21, 2017, Cambridge, MA, USA

© 2017 Copyright held by the owner/author(s). Publication rights licensed to ACM.
ISBN 123-4567-24-567/08/06...$15.00

DOI: http://dx.doi.org/10.475/123_4

spent reading existing code, he concludes that it is imperative for programmers to write beautiful code that is easy to read. Indeed, the dominant cost incurred during the lifecycle of a successful (long-lived) software system is not bug fixing, but rather maintenance and enhancement of legacy code [8]. Code that is functional but stylistically poor incurs high maintenance costs because it is difficult and time-consuming for a new programmer to understand and modify poor-quality code written by someone else.

Measuring the Beauty of Code

Beautiful code goes beyond simply adhering to syntactic coding standards such as indentation, use of whitespace, and the placement of delimiters (e.g., braces). Ward Cunningham is quoted in [17] as stating that beautiful code "makes it look like the language was made for the problem." The Related Work section reviews both quantitative and qualitative methods used by professional programmers to assess the beauty of their code, but these do not eliminate an expert programmer's subjective judgment, including the ability to recognize where improvements in beauty are possible. For novice programmers, therefore, we start at the level of individual methods (functions) and ask: What makes a short function (5–15 lines) beautiful, and can we teach students to recognize and improve code beauty at this level?

Cunningham's goal focuses on matching the problem to the facilities and abstractions available in the language and its core libraries. For example, while both JavaScript and Ruby have some features associated with functional languages, the use of collection idioms (e.g., `map`) is far more prevalent in Ruby, whereas the use of higher-order functions is much more frequent in JavaScript. As another example, both Python and Ruby include basic control flow constructs such as `if...then`, but Ruby also includes `unless`, and allows reversing the clauses in a conditional. As these examples illustrate, stylistic usages depend on the language. Therefore, language-independent guidelines are insufficient.

While Fowler and Beck have stated [7] that "no set of [code] metrics rivals informed human intuition" for improving code quality, Mäntylä et al. [15] found empirically that for the simple "code smells" at the method level, there was high inter-rater agreement between humans and source code metrics on what refactoring would be appropriate. Informal experimentation by teaching assistants in our intermediate programming courses has shown that the Assignment–Branch–Conditional (ABC) score [6], which measures a weighted sum of three basic types of statements within a function, is a good proxy for idiomatic code at the method level. ABC score rewards conciseness, and code with the best ABC score generally combines an efficient approach and appropriate language idioms. Consequently, ABC score is one of the metrics computed by virtually all tools that compute code metrics, including online services such as CodeBeat.com and CodeClimate.com. While we use ABC score to operationalize good style at the level of individual methods, we note that it does not capture all important style features (e.g., the usefulness of variable names and comments). As idiomatic code is important and often unsupported in introductory CS courses, it is our focus here.

Prior Work: The AutoStyle Tutor

Computing the ABC score does not tell students how to improve it. Providing holistic suggestions for improving style currently requires an instructor to hand-inspect code, a solution that is asynchronous and does not scale to large courses.

AutoStyle [4] is a research system that provides automated, adaptive style hints. The hints suggest syntax shortcuts and offer better approaches to solving the problem. Hints may also include code skeletons, in which the control flow is given but the student must fill in missing lines. AutoStyle's hints are intended to help the student improve their code's ABC score. A prior, randomized, controlled study of AutoStyle with 80 paid participants (students in an introductory computer science class) showed that AutoStyle helped students improve their code [4]. Students were given the standard "style manual" created for the course and were asked to write code that solved a programming problem and achieved a target ABC score. All students were allowed unlimited attempts, and received their ABC score after each one. The intervention group additionally received hints from the AutoStyle tutor [4]. In that study, 70% of the AutoStyle condition reached the style threshold, compared to 13% of the control group.

While this initial evaluation is promising, it examines performance, not learning - it does not demonstrate that students can apply new knowledge or practices outside of the tutor. A follow-up study [3] found that students could learn a coding idiom from AutoStyle and correctly apply while working independently, but it did not compare AutoStyle to a control condition. Finally, while both experiments measured how well students could write beautiful code, they did not examine how well students could *recognize* beautiful code. Recognizing beautiful code is important when deciding between different code implementations, and when identifying areas of one's own code for improvement.

Research Questions

We address our research questions by comparing AutoStyle to a control condition in which students see their ABC score but do not receive hints. Our research questions and brief summary of our results are as follows:

1. **RQ1.** Does working with a style tutor help students write beautiful code? *Yes, like [4], and students use more appropriate idioms with AutoStyle.*

2. **RQ2.** Does working with a style tutor help students write beautiful code independently? *No, unlike [3].*

3. **RQ3.** Does working with a style tutor improve students' ability to recognize beautiful code? *Yes, and students improve more with AutoStyle.*

To investigate these questions we conducted an *in situ* experiment during the summer offering of an introductory programming course. The experiment consisted of three parts: code improvement, multiple choice questions, and coding from scratch. After completing two coding assignments for the course, students were asked to improve the style of their code to meet an ABC score threshold. All students received their ABC score on each attempt, with some students assigned to receive additional hints from AutoStyle. Before and after the code improvement task, multiple-choice questions measured recognition of beautiful code by asking students to select the example with the best style. Finally, students did a code-from-scratch challenge without any feedback.

RELATED WORK

The existing literature on teaching coding style is sparse, both in terms of practical suggestions for teaching and theory for guiding future designs and experiments. This is in contrast to the literature and systems for teaching code correctness, which includes identification of student errors and synthesis of feedback that might help the student transform a defective program into a correct one. Real-time adaptive feedback is a hallmark of these systems, whether given by peer evaluation [13] or automated tools [10].

While automated, real-time feedback is an obvious instructional strategy for coding style, it has not been feasible to provide. Ideally, such feedback would offer personalized, holistic suggestions for improving style. However, currently there are few techniques and tools designed to offer any help on coding style at all.

Current style checkers similar to `lint` [11, 14] can provide style feedback, but only for relatively low-level stylistic problems such as redundant use of Boolean expressions (e.g. shortening `if (b!=false)` to `if (b)`) [1]. Another tool, Ugly-Code [18] can illustrate the importance of good style. Ugly-Code starts with good code and allows the student or teacher to apply transformations to obfuscate variable names, mess up indentation/line breaks, add useless comments, etc., to teach good style by uglifying a good piece of code rather than improving a bad one. Foobaz helps students choose useful variable names [9].

However, writing beautiful code goes beyond the low-level transformations addressed by these tools. Grady Booch, a pioneer in object-oriented design, writes: "Clean code is simple and direct. Clean code reads like well-written prose. Clean code never obscures the designers' intent but rather is full of crisp abstractions and straightforward lines of control" [2]. Adhering to low-level code formatting guidelines is insufficient to produce code with these properties.

Refactoring, in which the structure of code is improved without changing its behavior, is closely tied to good code style. However, most scientific work on analyzing refactoring has focused on identifying refactoring opportunities, either by using formal methods and tools or (more widespread) identifying *code smells*, which are (anti-)patterns in source code that increase the cost of maintaining and enhancing it by creating unnecessary complexity [19]. In contrast, the role of humans as decision makers in refactoring has been largely neglected in the professional software engineering literature [16].

OVERVIEW OF THE STYLE TUTOR
Pedagogical Framework
Coding with good style is a metacognitive task: it involves not just producing code, but assessing, planning, and evaluating changes. Closely related to practicing good coding style is *refactoring* - improving the structure of a piece of code without changing its functionality. While refactoring typically occurs across methods or classes, the techniques used can also be applied to individual methods. Our three-step process for improving style draws on a six-step process for refactoring: (1) recognize that a piece of code needs refactoring, (2) determine which refactoring techniques to apply, (3) ensure the refactoring preserves correct behavior, (4) apply the refactoring, (5) assess the effect on quality (i.e. whether further refactoring is needed), (6) modify related artifacts such as technical documentation to reflect the changes [19].

Our three steps for improving coding style are intended to guide assessment and instruction:

i **Assessment.** Identify areas for style improvement. A novice may have no basis for doing this step. This step is similar to step 1 for refactoring.

ii **Information Retrieval.** Efficiently search for a better idiom or strategy. This step is similar to step 2 for refactoring. While experienced programmers don't memorize every language idiom, they do know how to look for them. Novices may not know how to conduct such a search or how to recognize what information is likely to be helpful. Further, even when a novice is familiar with a useful language idiom, they may not realize that it is applicable to their current problem.

iii **Implementation.** Correctly apply the new idiom or strategy to the particular coding task. This step is similar to step 4 for refactoring. This step may be particularly difficult for a novice, as incorporating unfamiliar language idioms may introduce bugs.

This three-step procedure should be repeated as necessary (similar to step 5 for refactoring). This pedagogical framework was developed after AutoStyle was implemented. Consequently, AutoStyle performs step 1 (assessment), supports students in doing step 2 (information retrieval), and does not support step 3 (implementation). AutoStyle detects which aspect of the code should be improved and suggests a function

or an approach. When offering syntax hints, the tutor provides the name of a function and directs students to online documentation for more details. This is intended to give the students practice using documentation. AutoStyle does not offer hints on code that is not functionally correct.

Implementation
We briefly review the description of the style tutor; for further details see [4]. In order for AutoStyle to automatically generate hints, a corpus of several hundred previously collected submissions is needed to capture the style variations in students' submissions. Each submission's style is measured with the scalar quantity of Assignment–Branch–Condition (ABC) complexity, also known as ABC score.

Whereas [4] calculates the ABC score as the weighted L2 norm of the ABC vector, we used the equivalently weighted L1 norm, which allowed us to calculate ABC score gains and compare the progression of students' improvements. We preferred the linear properties of the L1 norm since code complexity should scale linearly with the number of operations. The original inventor of the ABC metric, who used the L2 norm, has stated that using a different vector norm may be preferable [6].

The corpus of submissions is clustered using density-based clustering, which is superior to K-means in that outliers far away from a cluster centroid are not "forced" into a cluster; this allows the instructor to identify students who may require more general guidance on problem strategy as opposed to hints for fine-tuning a sound strategy. Normalized tree edit distance is used as a distance metric. Previous studies have shown that clustering ASTs using this distance metric often captures groups of code with similar high-level design [4]. Through the instructor interface, an instructor can provide hints tailored to a specific cluster. In our implementation, AutoStyle provides instructor-written (A) *approach* hints that include links to resources such as language documentation, and (B) *skeletons* created by redacting a similar-but-correct submission from the corpus. Scale is effectively handled as instructor-created hints are proportional to the number of clusters, not the number of submissions, and in general the number of clusters and the number of submissions do not correlate [4].

Upon receiving a submission from a student, AutoStyle grades the submission for correctness by running a suite of test cases. If the code is functionally correct, its abstract syntax tree (AST) is extracted and compared to all other submissions to determine which cluster it would best fit into. Submissions mapping to "weak" clusters (poor ABC scores) are shown approach hints, skeletons, or both.

Submissions mapping to "strong" clusters are shown one or more automatically generated syntax hints. Syntax hints are generated by identifying another submission that has a similar structure but a better ABC score. Features that are present (or absent) from the superior submission are extracted and displayed to students as features they may want to add (or remove) from their submission. Hints can be provided until the student reaches the best ABC score in the corpus. Noted software engineer Michael Feathers says of clean code that "There is nothing obvious that you can do to make it better" [5].

43

His definition is operationalized by our approach, in which students improve their code style until reaching an optimal threshold determined by examining a corpus of submissions assumed to contain at least one "ideal" exemplar. AutoStyle supports students in improving their code incrementally, by pointing them to idioms and approaches that make their code slightly better. Students are not immediately pointed to the best style solution, since the differences between a poor solution and and the best one may be hard to understand in one jump. Figure 1 shows hints provided to an AutoStyle student.

EXPERIMENT

This study examined the effect of AutoStyle in the context of a large introductory CS course. On two selected homework problems, after writing a functional solution, students could work on improving their code's style for extra credit. Students who wanted the extra credit were invited to participate in the study (unpaid). Only study participants were given AutoStyle. Students did untutored problems as assessments.

Class Context and Materials

330 students were enrolled in the summer offering of the on-campus introductory CS course. This course, geared toward rising sophomores, is intended to be students' first CS class and is required for the major. Style is a component of this course, and students' large programming projects are hand-graded for style. Of the style features that determined students' style grades in the course, some overlap with measures that ABC captures (e.g., avoiding unnecessary function calls and variable assignments, avoiding code that is never called) while others are distinct (e.g., meaningful variable names, clear and useful comments). ABC was not used directly to determine style grades in the course.

In study sessions 1 and 2, students revised a completed homework problem to improve its style (`AddUp` and `Permute`). Instructors did not grade those problems for style. We selected these two problems because past students' answers had a wide range of style quality, suggesting both that students may benefit from style support and AutoStyle could construct chains to provide it automatically. For `AddUp` and `Permute`, we used approximately 500 historical submissions to set up the clustering and hints in the AutoStyle tutor. For sessions 1 and 2, students worked with a tutor to improve their style on their homework problems, and then independently did experimenter-created tasks that drew on key idioms and concepts targeted in the homework (`Letters` and `CountAnagrams`). For study session 3, students only did an untutored, experimenter-created coding task, which drew on functions from students' most recent homework. All of the problems in the study can be solved in 4-10 lines of Python. The tutored homework problems and independent coding challenges were:

(1) Session 1 - with tutoring. `AddUp`: Given an integer `n` and a list of integers `lst`, return true if there exists two unique elements in `lst` that add up to `n`.

(2) Session 1 - independent. `Letters`: Given a list of words `lst`, return a Python set of letters that are common amongst all words in `lst`.

(3) Session 2 - with tutoring. `Permute`: Given a list of unique integers `lst`, implement a Python generator that returns all possible permutations of `lst`.

(4) Session 2 - independent. `CountAnagrams`: Given a word `word` as well as a list of valid words `word_list`, return the number of anagrams for `word` that are also in `word_list`.

(5) Session 3 - assessment. `MaxDepth`: Write a function that takes a deep list, and determines its maximum depth. You may use any built-in python functions.

We chose these problems to examine AutoStyle in a natural setting with normal coursework. While we designed the tasks to be suitable for students' prior knowledge, the course had not taught students to use the target functions to minimize ABC score in their code. In these problems and throughout the course, instructors asked students to write their own logic rather than using built-in functions. While this gives students practice coding, it does not mimic professional practices.

The multiple-choice questions presented a programming problem and 6 or 7 solutions. Part one of each question asked students to select the correct solution with the best style (Figure 2). To see if students were overlooking good solutions because they mistakenly thought they were not functional, part two asked students to select all functionally correct solutions. To avoid ordering effects, the answer order was randomized at pre-test and post-test for each student.

Participants

200 students participated in at least one study activity. The analysis below only includes the 103 students who participated in study activities for sessions 1 and 2. 99 of those students also participated in session 3. Students were randomly assigned to three groups: (1) get AutoStyle for the first assignment only, (2) for both assignments, or (3) for none of the assignments. Students' random assignment into study conditions did not affect the instruction they received in class. Each study session was limited to a two-hour block (see Method), and students did not receive class instruction during the study sessions. Therefore, it is unlikely that any differences between conditions across the study, and especially within a single study session, were caused by the course instruction.

Method

For sessions 1 and 2, students began by writing a working solution to their homework problem and submitting it to the course auto-grader. This solution had to pass a set of instructor-written test cases. If the solution was correct, the student could open the extra-credit interface from the auto-grader and work on improving the code's style. At this point, students were invited to participate in the study.

Consenting students did a pretest of two-part multiple-choice questions (two questions in session 1 and and one in session 2). Then students worked with their assigned style tutor (AutoStyle or ABC score only) until they reached a target ABC score (9 or below; lower scores are better), or until 45 minutes elapsed. We used 9 as the score threshold after examining prior submissions. Those submissions showed acceptable

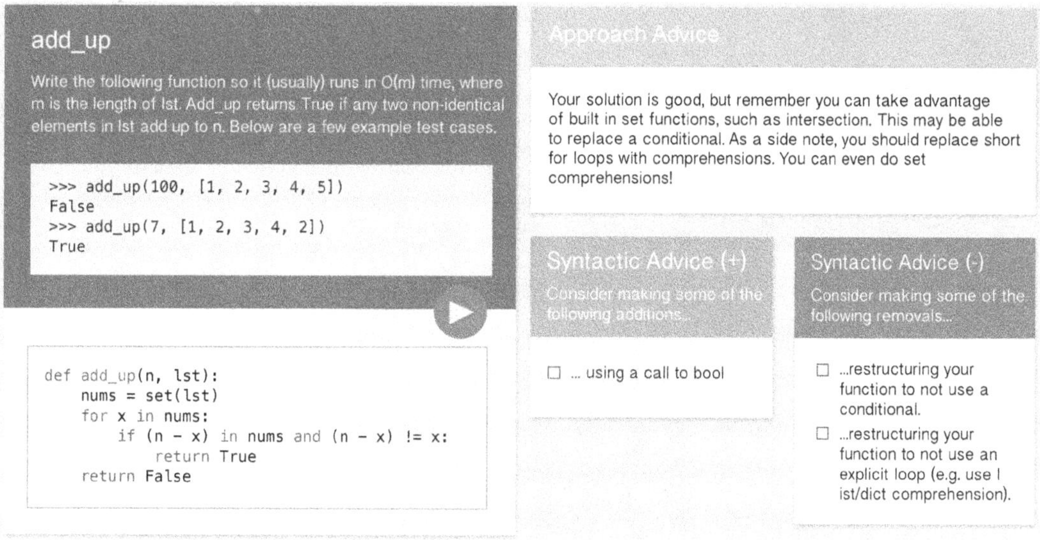

```
add_up

Write the following function so it (usually) runs in O(m) time, where
m is the length of lst. Add_up returns True if any two non-identical
elements in lst add up to n. Below are a few example test cases.

>>> add_up(100, [1, 2, 3, 4, 5])
False
>>> add_up(7, [1, 2, 3, 4, 2])
True
```

```
def add_up(n, lst):
    nums = set(lst)
    for x in nums:
        if (n - x) in nums and (n - x) != x:
            return True
    return False
```

Approach Advice

Your solution is good, but remember you can take advantage of built in set functions, such as intersection. This may be able to replace a conditional. As a side note, you should replace short for loops with comprehensions. You can even do set comprehensions!

Syntactic Advice (+)
Consider making some of the following additions...

☐ ... using a call to bool

Syntactic Advice (-)
Consider making some of the following removals...

☐ ...restructuring your function to not use a conditional.

☐ ...restructuring your function to not use an explicit loop (e.g. use l ist/dict comprehension).

Figure 1. A student's submission and AutoStyle hints. Students in both conditions are also shown their ABC score (not pictured here).

style, with the best ones scoring around 2. Students had unlimited submissions. After each functionally correct submission, students were shown their ABC score. If a submission was not functionally correct, students were shown the expected and received results of experimenter-written test cases.

After working with the style tutor, students did a post-test (with the same multiple-choice questions as the pre-test). Finally, students were given a coding challenge, where they were asked to solve a new programming problem, from scratch, without hints or ABC score feedback. Students had an unlimited submissions, and worked until their program passed all experimenter-written test cases, or until 2 hours had elapsed for the whole experiment session. The third study assignment was a cumulative assessment with multiple-choice questions (one each from the previous assignments and one novel) and an independent coding challenge.

RESULTS
103 students participated in sessions 1 and 2 (respectively, 72 AutoStyle and 31 Control, and 49 AutoStyle and 54 Control). One AutoStyle student and three Control students each from session 1 and 2 did not do session 3.

Coding Style Improved
On each problem, a few students (≤ 6) did not submit any functional solutions. Only students who submitted at least one functional solution are included in the analyses of coding style. Students improved their style when they worked with either tutor (AutoStyle or ABC score only), but did not improve their style on the untutored coding challenges. Most students submitted at least two unique, functional solutions for the tutored problems, indicating that the feedback prompted revisions. By their last submissions, most students surpassed the ABC threshold for the tutored problems (AddUp: Control - 71%, AutoStyle - 74%; Permute: Control - 75%, AutoStyle - 78%). Means for ABC scores improved from first to last attempts for the tutored problems (from 11.7 to 8.5 for AddUp

and from 11.3 to 8.7 for Permute). For the untutored problems Letters and CountAnagrams, few students submitted more than one functional solution, and scores did not improve on those problems. For the untutored problem MaxDepth, 7 AutoStyle students and one control student improved their code through revision, resulting in a slight improvement in scores for the AutoStyle condition but not the control. Table 1 shows how many students in each condition completed each problem and revised their work, along with initial and final style scores.

Although students' style scores do not satisfy the Shapiro-Wilk test for normality, we proceeded with ANOVAs and t-tests under the assumptions of the Central Limit Theorem since there were more than 30 students in each condition. Within-condition paired t-tests indicate significant differences in initial and final style scores on the tutored problems for both conditions, indicating that both tutors helped students improve through revision. The only untutored problem that showed a significant difference in initial and final style score was MaxDepth, and only for the AutoStyle condition, indicating that AutoStyle students improved their score through revision while working independently. However, while the result is statistically significant, the improvement was small (see table 1 for means, p-values, and t-values). To compare improvement on tutored vs. untutored problems, we ran separate repeated measures ANOVAs for ABC scores in study sessions 1 and 2. These ANOVAs followed the pattern suggested by the means: students in both conditions improved on the tutored problems but not the untutored ones, and there were no differences in improvement by condition. The repeated measures ANOVAs were run on students' ABC scores by submission time (first/last), if the problem was tutored (true/false), and by assigned condition (AutoStyle/Control). These analyses were done with the 101 students who submitted functionally correct code for both AddUp and Letters, and with the 97 students who submitted functionally correct code for both Permutation and CountAnagrams. Submission time

```
Supplementary Question                              ⓘ

Given two sets set1 and set2, how would you find their common
element

Choose all functionally correct answers.

                                              ▶
```

```
☐   def common(set1,set2):
        for elem in set1:
            if elem not in set2:
                set1.discard(elem)
        return set1
```

```
☐   def common(set1,set2):
        members = set()
        for elem1 in set1:
            for elem2 in set2:
                if elem1 == elem2:
                    members.add(elem1)
        return members
```

```
☐   def common(set1,set2):
        return set1 & set2
```

```
☐   def common(set1,set2):
        return set.intersection(set1,set2)
```

```
☐   def common(set1,set2):
        return set.union(set1,set2)
```

```
☐   def common(set1,set2):
        return set1 == set2
```

Figure 2. Answer options for a multiple choice question: Given two sets, set1 and set2, how would you find their common element? Students were asked to select the best style solution and then identify all functionally correct solutions. The middle two choices are the best stylistically, and the last two are not functionally correct.

($F(1) = 67.99; 41.9$), tutoring ($F(1) = 18.3; 209$), and their interaction ($F(1) = 69.1; 40.9$) were significant in both analyses (Pillai's Trace: $p < .001$ for all), while condition was not significant as a main effect ($F(1) = 1.1; .22, p = .3; .6$) or in interactions with submission time ($F(1) = .39; .31, p = .5; .5$; values are given for session 1 and 2, respectively). To compare condition differences in improvement on the untutored problem MaxDepth, we ran an ANOVA on data from the 98 students who completed the problem. We ran the ANOVA on final ABC score for MaxDepth, with initial ABC score as a covariate. Condition was not significant ($F(1) = 3.65, p = .059$). The t-test for the 70 students who had used AutoStyle was driven by 10 students who made two attempts on MaxDepth instead of one. Seven of those students improved their score, and three maintained their score. Of the 28 control students, five made more than one attempt. One student improved their score, one maintained it, and three worsened their score (note, students did not get ABC score as feedback on the coding challenges).

Students were allowed unlimited code submissions. Submissions that were not functionally correct were not given an ABC score. Further, some students submitted the same exact code several times in a row. Therefore, in examining students' attempts to improve their code, we consider an attempt to be a functional solution that is not a duplicate of the immediately-preceding submission. Across conditions, students averaged about 4 attempts when they worked with a style tutor (4.7 and 4.1 for AddUp and Permutation, respectively). 90% of AutoStyle students and 87% of control students made two or more attempts on AddUp. 67% of AutoStyle students and 64% of control students made two or more attempts on Permute (see table 1 for raw numbers). Most of the remaining students met the style threshold on their first attempts. Only one student in each condition (for AddUp) and one control student (for Permute) made only one attempt without meeting the style threshold. Repeating the ANOVAs above without students who met the style threshold on their first attempt does not change the significance levels of the results. Students averaged 1 attempt on the coding challenge, when they did not receive any feedback or have a style threshold (1.1, 1,1, and 1.2 for Letters, CountAnagrams, and MaxDepth). Fewer than 20% of students made multiple attempts on these problems.

Identification of Good Style Improved
Students improved in their identification of the best style solution from a given set. Multiple choice questions on each assignment were given before and after the tutored coding problem. These questions presented a coding problem and sample solutions, and asked which solution exhibited the best style. Answers were scored 1 if correct and 0 if incorrect or blank. Session 1 included two of these questions and session 2 had one. On AddUp question 2 and on the question for Permute, AutoStyle students improved more than the control, with no significant difference in improvement on AddUp question 1 (see table 2 for mean scores). Three separate logistic regressions on the post-test scores, with tutoring condition and corresponding pre-test score as factors, indicate significant effects for pre-test score (all $p < .015$), with significant effects for condition on question 2 for AddUp ($p = .04$) and on the question for Permute ($p = .03$), in favor of AutoStyle. Nagelkerke's pseudo R^2 for the three regressions are .15, .38 and .16, respectively. These analyses were done on all 103 students who participated in the study. Additional logistic regressions were run on scores from session 3, with corresponding pre-test scores from session 1 or 2 and exposure to AutoStyle as factors. Condition was not significant in any of those analyses, suggesting that AutoStyle outperformed the control on immediate learning but not longer term retention.

While students improved on their identification of the best coding style, they did not improve on their identification of which code blocks were functionally correct. After asking which solution exhibited the best style, a follow-up question asked which ones correctly solved the problem. For each of the 6 code samples, students got 1 point if they correctly identified it as functional or not. Students' improvement on these items were not significant from pre- to post-test or significantly different by condition, as indicated by a repeated measures ANOVA on the three questions (AddUp 1 and 2, and Permute)

Task	AutoStyle N	Mean Attempts	Initial style	Final style	Paired t-test	Control N	Mean Attempts	Initial style	Final style	Paired t-test
AddUp (tutored)	71 (64)	3.6 (2.4)	11.9 (6.4)	8.5 (5.7)	$p < .001$	31 (27)	7.2 (5.9)	11.4 (4.3)	8.4 (4.1)	$p < .001$
Letters (no tutor)	70 (2)	1.0 (0.17)	15.4 (9.2)	15.4 (9.2)	same mean	31 (6)	1.3 (0.63)	13.5 (4.5)	13.6 (4.4)	$p = .432$
Permute (tutored)	49 (33)	5.0 (6.07)	11.1 (4.6)	8.6 (2.70)	$p < .001$	53 (34)	3.4 (4.26)	11.5 (4.7)	8.7 (3.1)	$p < .001$
CountAnagrams (no tutor)	48 (2)	1.0 (0.20)	22.5 (7.4)	22.5 (7.4)	$p = .159$	49 (4)	1.1 (0.27)	21.4 (7.4)	21.4 (7.5)	$p = .322$
MaxDepth (no tutor)	70 (10)	1.1 (0.35)	18.3 (5.34)	18.1 (5.31)	$p = .017$	28 (5)	1.3 (0.59)	17.9 (4.7)	18.0 (4.8)	$p = .395$

Table 1. For each task, the number of students who submitted a functional solution (and who submitted at least two attempts). Means (and standard deviations) for number of attempts, and for initial and final ABC scores. Students are divided by condition. Paired t-tests compare the first and last ABC scores of each problem, by condition, to determine if the improvement is significant. t-values for each test are (left to right): 7.9, 4.7, NA, -.80, 4.4, 4.9, -1.4, 1.0, 2.4, -.86. In session 3 (MaxDepth, untutored), students who had used AutoStyle previously improved their score with revision.

Multiple Choice	Group	Pre-test	Post-test	Session 3	Condition (pre-post)
AddUp Q1	AS	.86	.92	NA	$p = .7$
	Control	.71	.90		
AddUp Q2	AS	.28	.46	.44	$p = .04$
	Control	.26	.26	.36	
Permute	AS	.18	.31	.31	$p = .03$
	Control	.17	.13	.24	

Table 2. Multiple-choice questions at pre- and post-test asked students which code example was stylistically best (two questions for session 1, one for session 2). Two of these questions were repeated at session 3. Percent correct for each condition shows more improvement for AutoStyle. Logistic regressions on post-test scores with pre-test as a covariate show that the greater improvement in the AutoStyle condition for AddUp Q2 and for Permute are significant. This table includes all participants.

by test time (pre or post), with condition as a fixed factor ($p > .05$ for test time, test time * question, condition, and condition * test time; n = 103).

STUDENTS' INTERACTIONS WITH THE TUTORS
AutoStyle is intended to help students by pointing them to new style idioms and approaches, which the student ideally implements. Case studies illustrate how students actually interacted with AutoStyle and the control tutor. Our case studies come from three categories: AutoStyle students who improved their code and met the style threshold on their last attempt; AutoStyle students who did not meet the style threshold despite multiple attempts; and Control students who improved their code and met the style threshold on their last attempt. We selected one student from each group, choosing cases where we felt most confident interpreting students' intentions and where students' actions highlighted shortcomings of AutoStyle. These case studies are from AddUp (session 1).

Implementation Is Hard. Case Study: Diligent Student
The Diligent Student begins with an acceptable solution: using a for-loop over all elements in lst, which yields an ABC score of 11.6 (slightly higher than the goal, 9). AutoStyle suggests using the Python built-in function list. This change would make the code better incrementally, but would not immediately lead to the best solution. The student tries to implement the suggestion, but makes a very simple typo. The student has a

variable 1st, and calls 1st instead of list. This introduces a bug, and the code does not compile. It takes the student six submissions to fix this bug (see figure 3). From the code alone, it is not clear if the student misunderstood the hint, or if the student made a typo and struggled to identify it. While no students in the control condition made this exact error, 5 other students in the AutoStyle condition did (8.5% of the AutoStyle condition).

In many ways, this student exemplifies the ideal user of the system. After 45 minutes of working with the tutor, students could still get extra credit even if their code did not meet the threshold. Diligent Student continues to struggle with implementing some hints, working beyond the required 45 minutes. Ultimately, Diligent Student implements hints designed for strong clusters, and achieves an ABC score of 5.4, one of the top style solutions for the homework assignment. This case study illustrates that students cannot just write correct code and then move on to improving its style - even diligent students may regress to non-functional code in the process. For less-diligent students, the bugs they introduce may become insurmountable obstacles.

This student was not the only one who struggled to implement hints. On average, after an AutoStyle student receives a hint, it takes four tries for the student to implement the change in a functionally correct manner. The lack of hints for non-functional code is a weakness of AutoStyle.

Large Changes Are Hard. Case Study: Confused Student
AutoStyle requires students to start with working code. However, all working code is not equal. Confused Student started with a ABC score of 55.6, a big difference from Diligent Student's 11.6. Confused Student solved the homework problem by breaking the problem down into many (and sometimes redundant) edge cases instead of crafting one holistic solution. AutoStyle does not provide hints that are specific to that starting point, so Confused Student got the same hints as Diligent Student. Confused Student did not successfully implement any of AutoStyle's hints. Many attempts resulted in non-functional code, and the few submissions that were functionally correct actually made the ABC score worse.

```
def add_up(-, ---):
    - = list(set(---))
    for - in ---[::(- -)]:
        if (- - -) in ---[:(len(---) - -)]):
            return ----
    return -----
```
`typo occured`

[Approach] Make sure you take advantage of python's set operations. Python set documentation contains a lot of useful description for checking set membership. Try looking through it and finding something useful.

[Syntactic] Try using a call to bool, try restructuring your function to not use a conditional try restructuring your function to not use an explicit loop (e.g. use list/set comprehension)

```
def add_up(n, lst):                              1
    lst = list(set(lst))
    for i in lst:
        if (n - i) in lst[1:]:
            return True
    return
```

```
def add_up(n, lst):                              2
    l = set(lst)
    for i in l:
        if (n - i) in lst and (n - i) != i:
            return True
    return False
```

```
def add_up(n, lst):                              3
    new_set = {n-x for x in lst if x != n - x}
    return bool(new_set.intersection(set(lst)))
```

Figure 3. Diligent student gets a skeleton hint suggesting `list` (top left) and makes a typo in trying to implement it (top right). After correcting the typo, the student gets a hint to use `set`, which is implemented correctly (middle row). The student gets further hints throughout the session (bottom left) ending with a stylistically good solution (bottom right).

AutoStyle leads students down an incremental path of code improvement: suggestions point students to solutions that are a little bit better. The assumption underlying this approach is that students will not be able to implement drastic changes in one revision. Confused Student's interaction support this notion. In total, 13 students started AddUp with ABC scores above 20. Eight students exhausted the required 45 minutes and still had a score above 20 at the end. Two students ended between 20 and 9, and only one met the target threshold. Two students had ABC scores above 20 for the majority of their session, but achieved the best ABC score on their last submission (likely gaming the system).

The general lack of improvement for students who started with very poor code suggests that AutoStyle's current hints may only be advantageous for students who demonstrate a complete understanding of the preexisting assignment. Students may struggle when AutoStyle asks them to take a perspective that is radically different from the student's current understanding. Since starting with working code can inhibit large-scale changes [3], some students may benefit from approach hints before they start coding.

Self Assessment Is Hard. Case Study: Myopic Student

Myopic Student is a control student, and only received ABC score as feedback. Myopic Student did improve their code style, but demonstrated difficulty in assessing where and how to do so. The student's first submission is good: it solves the assignment using a for-loop and a call to Python's set operations, with an ABC score of 9.84. Myopic Student's initial submission has an identical control flow to Diligent Student's submission code block 2 in Figure 3. While Diligent Student has AutoStyle's suggestions to follow, Myopic Student demonstrates a lack of direction in attempts to improve coding style. The student makes a series of simple transformations by removing whitespace and adding redundant test cases in the for-loop body, which only serves to vary the student's ABC score between 9.84 and 10.92. At some points it seems like this student is just testing out what will make the ABC score go up or down. Shorter code is often more concise and our style metric rewarded students for using fewer lines. However, this measure is vulnerable to gaming, and several students "improved" their style by cramming the whole solution into one line. This brevity reward will not be used in future work. Myopic Student finds that shorter submissions (e.g., without blank lines) result in better ABC score, and then tries to shorten the code further re-ordering the control flow. However, Myopic Student never attempts to implement an operation that wasn't contained in the original submission. Myopic Student's submissions illustrate the difficulty in assessing what improvements can be made (step 1 in our pedagogical framework).

```
def add_up(n, lst):
    for num in lst:
        if ((n - num) in lst and (n - num) != num):
            return True
    return False
```

Figure 4. Myopic Student's final submission. The Python built-in function `list` does not yield the best style solution.

Although this student started with AutoStyle's suggested function, `set`, this student replaces it with a call to `list`. A solution using `list` allows the student to achieve an ABC score better than the threshold, but does not achieve the best solution (see figure 4). As students in the introductory programming course are taught how to use `list` before `set`, the student seems to fall back on previous knowledge instead of discovering new information on how to use `set` to achieve a more stylistic solution. This illustrates a student attempting to do step 2 (Information Retrieval) from prior knowledge, without the foresight of how the change will affect the code's style.

DISCUSSION

AutoStyle helped students write and recognize beautiful code. Students in both conditions improved their style while working with a tutor. However, overall, students' submissions on the coding challenges did not demonstrate that AutoStyle promoted better independent work. While students may not have learned enough from the tutor to make those revisions, another explanation is that students were not well-motivated to improve their style. Students received extra credit for writing any functional solution to the coding challenge, and there was no target ABC score.

Although AutoStyle and the ABC-only tutor produced similar style improvements, students' paths through the two tutors were different. Considering only the students who met the style threshold for AddUp, AutoStyle students were much more likely to use the target function set (11/22 with the control, 42/51 with AutoStyle). However, it was not the case that students were unfamiliar with set before working with AutoStyle. Almost all students used set in their independent coding challenge (where its relevance was more apparent), and students correctly identified functional solutions with set in the multiple-choice questions. Rather, it seems that without AutoStyle, proportionally more students did not recognize that set would be a good style choice for the AddUp problem. This underscores why the Information Retrieval step in our pedagogical framework applies to a student's prior knowledge as well as to new information.

Further, ABC score alone was not as helpful in teaching students to recognize good style. While students appeared to be at ceiling for the best-style multiple-choice question AddUp 1, the majority of students were not correct on AddUp 2 or Permute, even at post-test. Identifying good style is not trivial for novice students, likely because their conceptions of good style do not match those of experts. Students in the control condition, like Myopic Student, may have improved their ABC score through guess-and-check without uncovering the meaningful features that affect style. The easiest feature to uncover is superficial: shorter is usually better. Since AutoStyle provided text hints, students did not need to guess at which features mattered for style. This may explain why AutoStyle students improved more than the control on two of the three multiple-choice questions that asked students to select the best style solution. Recognizing good style was not cited as a goal of the original AutoStyle work [4, 3], illustrating how our pedagogical framework can improve the design of style assessments. Overall, students did not improve on their recognition of which options were functional, indicating that improvement on selecting the best style was driven by students' new ideas about style, not correctness.

Our data suggests that each step in our framework is indeed distinct. Many novices cannot easily identify good style on multiple-choice questions, or retrieve the information necessary to improve their style, even when that information resides in their own prior knowledge (e.g., Myopic Student). Finally, even when students know which function to use, implementation is not trivial (e.g., Diligent Student). These findings show initial validity for our framework, and suggest that style tutors should support all three steps.

Recommendations for CS Educators

If nothing else, show the student their style score while they're coding and provide a target score based on a reference solution. The quantitative results showed that students improved their code with ABC score alone. This suggests that simply making students aware that style can be measured, and telling them when there is room for improvement, seems to drive them to improve it. However, students are unlikely to learn what good style is with ABC feedback alone. Showing students example code of similar lengths and explaining why one has better style may dissuade students from simply thinking that shorter is better.

Future Work: Improving AutoStyle

Process measure and case studies illustrate where AutoStyle could provide more supportive feedback. First, students need style support even when their code is not functional. There is no clear distinction between getting code to work and improving the code's style. For the Diligent Student, the Confused Student, and many others, attempts to improve style introduced bugs. These bugs also show the difficulty of Implementation (step 3 in our pedagogical framework). Telling students what function to use is not always enough. In large-enrollment courses, students may make the exact same mistake when trying to implement a change (e.g., 8.5% of the AutoStyle condition tried to call a function with the typo lst instead of the name list). AutoStyle could provide specific feedback for common mistakes.

Second, when students start off with working but stylistically horrible code (like Confused Student), AutoStyle may be more effective if it tells the student to start from the beginning. Including one instructor-written approach hint for these cases may help students who otherwise wouldn't be able to start down the style-improvement path.

Third, while AutoStyle points students to documentation, it does not help them interpret the documentation. AutoStyle may be more effective if it scaffolds students in how to use online resources - this may also reduce the instance and severity of implementation errors. AutoStyle could also become more adaptive: if the student receives a hint but seems unable to successfully apply it to their own code upon resubmission, the student may need tutoring in interpreting the language documentation or in modifying an example in the documentation to apply it to their own code.

Future Work: Targeted Assessments

This study did not replicate the striking results from [4], where 70% of AutoStyle students vs. 13% of the control reached the best style solution. However, our non-replication was not because AutoStyle students did poorly, but rather because the control students did well. One explanation may be the differences between the particular problems and style thresholds in the two studies. In [4], students needed to use the AutoStyle-recommended syntax to get under the style threshold. In AddUp, students could reach the style threshold without using the syntax that AutoStyle recommended (though it was necessary for the best possible solution). Selecting a lower threshold may have resulted in stronger relative benefits for AutoStyle in our study. For Permute, the main style recommendations related to approach and control flow, not syntax. This made it more difficult to automatically detect the effect of AutoStyle in students' code. Additionally, AutoStyle's current approach hints may not be as effective as the syntax hints.

Likewise, we did not replicate the results from [3], where students demonstrated style improvements independently. The independent problems in [3] required the same syntax, used in the same way, as the corresponding tutored AutoStyle problem. This tight connection between the tutored problem and the independent problem was not present in the current study. Future work will develop a range of assessments that allow students to demonstrate both near and far transfer.

CONCLUSIONS

On course homework assignments, both AutoStyle and ABC feedback helped students improve their style. AutoStyle additionally helped students recognize code with good style. This *in situ* study shows AutoStyle's effectiveness in a large-enrollment course. Results from the style-recognition questions and from logged student interactions provide initial validation for our 3-step pedagogical framework by showing that the three steps are distinct, and students need support in each. Although AutoStyle was not designed to promote recognition of good style, students did improve on this measure, a key component of Assessment (step 1 in our framework). While an important aspect of AutoStyle is that it directs students to code documentation and online resources, this study showed the importance of helping students incorporate their own prior knowledge (part of Information Retrieval, step 2). Finally, case studies and log data show that students still struggle with Implementation (step 3) even when step 2 is complete.

Acknowledgements

This work was supported by an IBM Faculty Award, a gift from Google Inc, and the National Science Foundation (Grant No. DRL-1418423 and INT-1451604). Opinions, findings, conclusions, or recommendations expressed here are those of the authors and do not necessarily reflect the views of the NSF.

REFERENCES

1. Hannah Blau and J. Eliot B. Moss. 2015. FrenchPress Gives Students Automated Feedback on Java Program Flaws. In *Proceedings of the 2015 ACM Conference on Innovation and Technology in Computer Science Education (ITiCSE '15)*. ACM, New York, NY, USA, 15–20. DOI:http://dx.doi.org/10.1145/2729094.2742622

2. Grady Booch, Robert A. Maksimchuk, Michael W. Engle, Bobbi J. Young, Jim Conallen, and Kelli A. Houston. 2007. *Object-Oriented Analysis and Design with Applications (3rd Edition)*. Addison-Wesley Professional.

3. Antares Chen, Eliane Wiese, HeZheng Yin, Rohan Choudhury, and Armando Fox. 2016. Preliminary evidence for learning good coding style with AutoStyle. In *Third Symposium on Learning With MOOCs (LWMOOC III)*. Philadelphia, PA.

4. Rohan Roy Choudhury, HeZheng Yin, and Armando Fox. 2016. Scale-Driven Automatic Hint Generation for Coding Style. In *13th International Conference on Intelligent Tutoring Systems (ITS 2016)*. Zagreb, Croatia.

5. Michael Feathers. 2004. *Working Effectively with Legacy Code*. Prentice Hall.

6. J. Fitzpatrick. 2000. Applying the ABC Metric to C, C++, and Java. In *More C++ Gems*. Cambridge University Press, New York, NY, 245–264.

7. Martin Fowler, Kent Beck, John Brant, William Opdyke, and Don Roberts. 1999. *Refactoring: Improving the Design of Existing Code*. Addison-Wesley Professional.

8. Robert L. Glass. 2002. *Facts and Fallacies of Software Engineering*. Addison-Wesley Professional.

9. Elena L. Glassman, Lyla Fischer, Jeremey Scott, and Robert C. Miller. 2015. Foobaz: Variable Name Feedback for Student Code at Scale. In *Proceedings of the 28th Annual ACM Symposium on User Interface Software I& Technology*. ACM, Charlotte, NC, 609–617.

10. Petri Ihantola, Tuukka Ahoniemi, Ville Karavirta, and Otto Seppälä. 2010. Review of Recent Systems for Automatic Assessment of Programming Assignments. In *Proceedings of the 10th Koli Calling International Conference on Computing Education Research (Koli Calling '10)*. ACM, New York, NY, USA, 86–93. DOI:http://dx.doi.org/10.1145/1930464.1930480

11. S. Johnson. 1977. *Lint, a C program checker*. Technical Report 65. Bell Labs.

12. D. E. Knuth. 1984. Literate Programming. *Comput. J.* 27, 2 (1984), 97–111.

13. C. E. Kulkarni, M. S. Bernstein, and S. R. Klemmer. 2015. PeerStudio: Rapid Peer Feedback Emphasizes Revision and Improves Performance. In *Proceedings of the 2nd ACM Conference on Learning@Scale*. ACM, New York, NY, 75–84.

14. Jin-Su Lim, Jeong-Hoon Ji, Yun-Jung Lee, and Gyun Woo. 2011. Style Avatar: A Visualization System for Teaching C Coding Style. In *Proceedings of the 2011 ACM Symposium on Applied Computing (SAC '11)*. ACM, New York, NY, USA, 1210–1211. DOI:http://dx.doi.org/10.1145/1982185.1982451

15. M Mäntylä. 2005. An experiment on subjective evolvability evaluation of object-oriented software: explaining factors and interrater agreement.. In *ISESE*. 134–138. http://lib.tkk.fi/Diss/2009/isbn9789512298570/article3.pdf

16. M Mäntylä and Casper Lassenius. 2006. Drivers for software refactoring decisions. *Proceedings of the 2006 ACM/IEEE International Symposium on Empirical Software Engineering (ISESE)* (2006), 297–306. http://dl.acm.org/citation.cfm?id=1159778

17. Robert C. Martin. 2008. *Clean Code: A Handbook of Agile Software Craftsmanship*. Prentice Hall.

18. K McMaster, S Sambasivam, and Stuart Wolthuis. 2013. Teaching Programming Style with Ugly Code. In *Information Systems Educators Conference*. San Antonio, TX. http://citeseerx.ist.psu.edu/viewdoc/download?doi=10.1.1.400.9411&rep=rep1&type=pdf

19. Tom Mens and Tom Tourwé. 2004. A survey of software refactoring. *IEEE Transactions on Software Engineering* 30, 2 (2004), 126–139. DOI:http://dx.doi.org/10.1109/TSE.2004.1265817

Detecting Diligence with Online Behaviors on Intelligent Tutoring Systems

Steven Dang
HCI Institute
Carnegie Mellon University
Pittsburgh, PA, USA
stevenda@cs.cmu.edu

Michael Yudelson
HCI Institute
Carnegie Mellon University
Pittsburgh, PA, USA
yudelson@cs.cmu.edu

Kenneth R. Koedinger
HCI Institute
Carnegie Mellon University
Pittsburgh, PA, USA
koedinger@cmu.edu

ABSTRACT

The current study introduces a model for measuring student diligence using online behaviors during intelligent tutoring system use. This model is validated using a full academic year dataset to test its predictive validity against long-term academic outcomes including end-of-year grades and total work completed by the end of the year. The model is additionally validated for robustness to time-sample length as well as data sampling frequency. While the model is shown to be predictive and robust to time-sample length, the results are inconclusive for robustness in data sampling frequency. Implications for research on interventions, and understanding the influence of self-control, motivation, metacognition, and cognition are discussed.

Author Keywords

Self-Control; Self-Regulated Learning; Intelligent Tutoring Systems; Measurement; Noncognitive factors; Learning Analytics; Diligence; Motivation; Online Behaviors

INTRODUCTION

The oft-cited 10,000 hour rule, popularized by Malcolm Gladwell as the amount of time required to build expertise, does not completely describe an amateur's pathway to mastery [23]. Not just any practice will lead to expertise; practice that is at the edge of students' abilities will be most effective at improving abilities. This type of practice is typically referred to as "deliberate practice" [14], and because it demands the student to perform at the limits of his or her existing abilities, such practice can tax the student's mental and physical resources. Thus deliberate practice requires students to constantly regulate their learning and exercise self-control to remain focused. As learning shifts increasingly towards digital environments, students will be tempted by more distractions and it is

L@S 2017, April 20-21, 2017, Cambridge, MA, USA
© 2017 ACM. ISBN 978-1-4503-4450-0/17/04...$15.00
DOI: http://dx.doi.org/10.1145/3051457.3051470

important that they resist and remain diligent while learning.

In the past decade, there has been mounting evidence that self-control influences long-term academic outcomes[29]. In 2013, the US Department of Education released a report summarizing the evidence supporting the role of self-control and similar non-cognitive factors in academic performance. This new area of interest has led educators to push for interventions that promote greater self-control during learning. As these interventions proliferate, so does research to better understand their efficacy and interactions with other factors including motivation, metacognition, and cognition. Research in this field relies on survey-based measures of self-control [29]. Furthermore, with the push to include assessment as part of state standards, there is a need for a more robust measure [10]. This has created a demand for a validated behavioral measure to complement existing measures.

Digital courses present an opportunity to explore whether behavioral measures of self-control can be computed from the fine-grained, high-volume data generated by student actions in more interactive courses. If so, there is a great potential benefit relative to survey or specially-constructed behavioral assessments. Such a model could unobtrusively detect student levels of self-control as a natural consequence of course interaction. Key questions for such an exploration are what models can effectively convert raw interaction data into self-control measures and at what scale must data be collected, particularly in terms of the observations per student, for such measures to be reliable and have predictive validity.

In this study, we operationalize student diligence, a facet of self-control, and introduce a model for measuring student diligence using behaviors logged while learning with an intelligent tutoring system. We validate this measure using a year-long large-scale dataset (2.5 million observations) that has a modest scale in terms of students (108), but a large scale in terms of observations per student (about 15,000). The long time frame facilitates analysis of the measure's robustness variance in the time-sample length and volume of per student data. We also assess the convergent and divergent validity of the diligence measure with other self-regulated learning and self-control constructs assessed through associated surveys.

BACKGROUND

What is Diligence

Diligence has been defined as working assiduously on academic tasks which are beneficial in the long-run but tedious in the moment, especially in comparison to more enjoyable, less effortful diversions[16]. Thus, diligence is the domain-specific ability to maintain a high degree of focus on a given task within that domain. This highlights two important relations to the higher-level construct of self-control, domain-specificity and trait-like stability. Self-control is generally considered trait-like and is the broader ability of an individual to regulate emotions, behaviors, and thoughts especially under the temptation of desirable alternatives [30]. This trait-like quality is driven by the control facet of the "Big Five" personality trait, conscientiousness [22]. Therefore diligence should be stable across contexts in aggregate. However, while self-control should be relatively stable aggregated across contexts and domains, like many traits, it can have relatively low correlations between domains(r=.20-.30) [31]. Thus math diligence may vary greatly from athletic diligence, and it is important to measure the domain-specific self-control displayed to accurately capture its influence. This definition of diligence follows directly from the social and developmental psychology literatures which also use the terms willpower [24] and ego-resiliency [17] to refer to self-control. Alternatively, the cognitive and educational psychology communities have similar constructs that have been enumerated specifically for learning contexts. We describe some of these constructs next. We do so both because they give a sense of the rich landscape of related (hypothesized) psychological constructs and because the data we analyze includes survey measures corresponding not only to diligence but also to these other constructs.

Relation to Executive Function

Executive function is a cognitive function heavily implicated in self-control [5]. Similar to personality measures such as conscientiousness, executive function is a relatively constant cognitive resource that consists of three components: inhibitory control, working memory, and set shifting. All of these components are recruited collectively in diligent behaviors. However, associations between low-level executive function measures and self-control in real-world tasks are small [9].

Relations to Self-Regulated Learning

Self-regulated learning (SRL) is a framework from the education community that subsumes and integrates a wide range of beliefs, skills, and strategies that impact learning and originate from the self [33]. This framework views self-regulation as a set of motivational, metacognitive, and behavioral constructs that drive a plan-act-reflect cycle. Each construct has its own specific moderating relationship with self-control and diligence.

Self-Efficacy

Self-efficacy is defined as the belief in one's ability to perform at a given level on a range of tasks [4]. Self-Efficacy moderates self-control and thus ratings of self-efficacy should be correlated to measures of diligence.

Achievement Goals

Achievement goals are a cognitive knowledge construct defined by a 2x2 matrix where one axis is Performance versus Mastery and the other is Approach versus Avoidance [27]. Performance goals are those that define accomplishment relative to peer-derived standards while mastery goals are ones that are defined relative to personal standards and prior ability and knowledge. Approach orientation implies an individual is seeking attainment of those goals while avoidance orientation describes individuals more concerned with avoiding failure rather than goal attainment. Thus mastery approach describes individuals who work towards attaining greater knowledge or ability and performance avoidance describes individuals who work to avoid having lower grades than their peers [13]. As a cognitive knowledge construct, these are activated by the task context to moderate self-control. While mastery orientation should tend to focus executive function on task specific information, performance goals will have more variable influences on self-control depending on the dynamics of performance and the resulting behaviors and strategies employed [2].

Theory of Intelligence

Theory of Intelligence describes a mindset related to the nature of human intelligence [12]. Fixed mindset describes an individual's belief that intelligence and thus academic accomplishment is a fixed and predetermined trait (i.e. some people are smart others are not). Growth mindset describes the belief that intelligence can be developed. While it appears that mindsets should have an influence on self-control through ego-depletion [18], it turns out that mindsets are uncorrelated with conscientiousness [8] and thus are likely uncorrelated with diligence.

Effort Regulation

Effort Regulation is one scale from the MSLQ Self-regulated learning inventory [26]. It is defined as a students' ability to control their effort and attention in the presence of distractors. This construct is analogous to diligence as defined, and thus should be highly correlated.

Existing Measures

Each executive function has an associated behavioral task that has been validated such as the star-counting task measuring working memory. However, the predictive validity of such measures is low due to the weak association between these low level cognitive measures and more complex real-world tasks involving self-control [25].

SRL researchers have made a number of notable strides towards online measurements instruments. [32] created a note-taking, collaborative study-aid tool. This system found student judgments of their learning process to not reliably match assessments of online behaviors, thus raising questions of measured construct validity. [1] was able to identify help-seeking strategies as informed by SRL theories using log data collected from an intelligent tutoring system. [15] found conditional but no direct links in looking for online measures of achievement goals based on online hint-seeking and glossary-use behaviors.

For self-control measures, there are currently no online behavioral measures, but [16] introduce a math based behavioral task that served as inspiration for our investigation. In [16], the authors introduce the Academic Diligence Task (ADT), a math-based task that is targeted for high-school aged students and older. The ADT attempts to measure diligence by monitoring how long students engage in a tedious but beneficial math task versus a more immediately rewarding alternative, playing video games and watching videos. They are told "try to solve as many problems as quickly and accurately as you can" and "you are doing this activity because it can make you smarter" to create the expectation that they should do the math task and that it is good for them. More specifically, students are asked to solve single-digit subtraction problems for 4 five-minute windows. The computer interface is split between a math problem interface and video-watching/game-playing interface. During this task, the total time spent solving math problems as opposed to watching videos or playing games is logged. Also the total number of problems solved is logged. These two measures were correlated with self-control and conscientiousness, but not with other big five personality traits. They were also predictive of long-term outcomes including end-of-year grade, graduation, and 4-year college admission.

Adapting the Diligence Model for a Cognitive Tutor
The ADT utilized a low skill task in order to tax the mental facilities associated with self-control such that more diligent students would tend to stay on task more often, while less diligent students would tend to stray from the task. Thus more time on task and more problems solved translated to greater diligence.

The model proposed by the ADT would be as follows in (1):

$$Y_{dil} = \beta_0 X_{tot} + \beta_1 X_{prod} + \varepsilon \qquad (1)$$

Where Y_{dil} is the measured diligence. X_{tot} is the total time on task. X_{prod} is the total number of correct problems completed. ε is a Gaussian random error term.

By design, this task is able to differentiate the diligence of students who are very fluent in simple arithmetic, however, it is less likely to be able to differentiate students in the 1st grade who are only just learning how to subtract single digit numbers. Thus a more general model of student diligence would be valuable to assess a wider range of students.

Students are increasingly using highly interactive online course materials, such as intelligent tutoring systems, and logged student interactions with these systems are a rich source of student behavior during learning. The availability of such data provides an opportunity to explore whether these observations of naturalistic student learning behaviors can be utilized for the assessment of diligence. There are several challenges to using a cognitive tutor as a diligence assessment in place of the ADT. The first challenge is that cognitive tutors are designed to be adaptive to student's knowledge, moving on to the new material upon reaching mastery [28]. Thus students solving the same number of problems may actually have learned different amounts. Similarly, errors during learning will adjust the knowledge model and lead towards increased practice on a given problem type. Thus the raw number of problems completed, as proposed by the ADT, is not as directly comparable across students.

In contrast to the ADT, another challenge with using intelligent tutoring systems is that students are solving problems using a variety of learning processes including deliberate sense-making, inductive learning, and fluency-building cognitive processes [20]. In the ADT, the simple nature of the problem reduced the cognitive load to a fluency-building task, where time per problem solved should be nearly constant throughout the task. While working on cognitive tutors, students may pause for productive reasons such as reflection or sense-making [1], as well as for unproductive reasons such as socializing [3]. Thus interpreting time-on-task is trickier than it is in the ADT.

As with any cognitive task, greater prior-knowledge is going to enable superior task performance. Thus, this is also likely a factor that will have to be taken into account. Students with greater math ability will tend to solve more problems in the same amount of time as their peers with less ability.

Taking these factors into account, the following model is proposed as shown in (2).

$$Y_{dil} = \beta_0 X_{tot} + \beta_1 X_{work} + \beta_2 X_{prior} + \varepsilon \qquad (2)$$

Where Y_{dil} is the measured diligence. X_{tot} is the total time in the system as a sum of the duration of all steps in the sampled time period. X_{prod} is the total number of correct steps completed in the sampled time. X_{work} is the average work rate as computed by X_{prod} / X_{tot}. X_{prior} is the prior knowledge of the student, which in this work is equivalent to the grade from the previous year's math course. ε is a Gaussian random error term.

Fitting the model
For each model (1) and (2), diligence is assumed to be some linear combination of the measured behaviors from the intelligent tutoring system. In order to learn the context specific coefficients of these parameters, the normalized number of curriculum units mastered at the end of the year

by each student is used in place of Y_{dil}. Thus equations (3) and (4) are utilized to learn the values of β_0, β_1, and β_2 for (1) and (2) respectively. This defines the model as the components of the online behaviors along the student learning latent subspace.

$$Y_{out} = \beta_0 X_{tot} + \beta_1 X_{prod} + \varepsilon \qquad (3)$$

$$Y_{out} = \beta_0 X_{tot} + \beta_1 X_{work} + \beta_2 X_{prior} + \varepsilon \qquad (4)$$

Where Y_{out} is the number of curriculum units completed by the student.

The justification for this model is best understood with a few examples.

Varying Time-on-task
Comparing two students with the similar prior knowledge and who have been solving problems equally fast, the student who spends more time solving problems instead of quitting the application early, delaying getting started at the beginning of class, or taking more bathroom breaks, is the more diligent student.

Varying Work-Rate
Comparing two students with the similar prior knowledge and who have been solving problems for the same amount of time, the student who is solving more problems is likely doing so because they are focusing more and learning more per problem as a result. This makes the faster working student more diligent due to their increased exercising of self-control to focus on the task at hand.

Varying Prior-Knowledge
Comparing one student with less prior knowledge to one with more prior knowledge, the social pressure of the class context may encourage students to reach certain milestones. Students with more knowledge may feel less pressure to work as quickly, but when they are working just as fast and just as long as less knowledgeable students, they are demonstrating greater diligence.

THIS STUDY
In this study, we look to validate the proposed model as having superior model fit over the ADT for data from adaptive learning environments. We then characterize the predictive validity of the model for end-of-year grade and amount of material completed by the end of the year. We characterize the robustness of the model to data sampling from varying time-grain sizes. We look at convergent and discriminant validity with other motivation and metacognition constructs collected through surveys. Finally we finish with an analysis looking at the predictive validity of varying time-grains with sparser samples to characterize a lower bound on data required to support this model.

DATASET
This dataset [6] includes over 2.5M transactions from 108 students middle school students in pre-algebra class using a Carnegie Learning's Cognitive Tutor on a regular basis (two class-periods/week for the entire year). The data was collected as part of a different study [7], but we have

utilized here because it includes a long time-window as well as motivational and metacognitive survey measures. The students are all from a single middle class suburban school in a mid-Atlantic state. The dataset includes 87 seventh graders and 21 eighth graders. There are equal numbers of male and female students, and the population is predominantly Caucasian, with 104 Caucasian and 4 non-Caucasian students.

Carnegie Learning's Cognitive Tutor
While the model introduced is designed for more general online behavioral assessment, this study leverages Carnegie Learning's Cognitive Tutor (CT) dataset for the aforementioned reasons. The CT utilized in this dataset is an Intelligent Tutoring System for Pre-Algebra that is deployed across thousands of middle schools across the United States. The CT leverages computational cognitive models to provide adaptive problem selection and hint support and correctness feedback to the students. Problems are broken down into a multi-step process, which allows the system to identify independent skills and trace skill improvement over a fine-grained skill model of the domain. The system logs all interactions with the system including problem attempts, hint requests, response accuracy, and problem step time. In this study, transactions for all students over the course of an entire academic year are utilized.

Collected Metadata Measures
In addition to online behavior logs from the CT, each student's course grades for the previous year, each academic quarter, and the end-of-year course grade are reported alongside several surveys of motivation and metacognition completed at the beginning of the academic year before any course content was completed.

Self Efficacy
Self-efficacy was measured using a 5-question scale with a 5-point Likert rating assessing student's self-efficacy with respect to their performance in the math class.

Achievement Goal Orientation
Achievement goals for Mastery Approach, Performance Approach, and Performance Avoidance were assessed using the corresponding 9 questions from the AGQ-R 12-question scale [13] with a 5-point Likert rating.

Theory of Intelligence
Theory of Intelligence was assessed using a 6-question scale from [12] reported using a 5-point Likert rating.

Effort Regulation
Effort Regulation is measured using the 4-question scale from the MSLQ [26] using a 5-point Likert rating.

RESULTS

Comparing Model Fit
The proposed model was compared to the ADT model in order to determine which model had better fit to the data in the intelligent tutoring context. Linear fixed effect models

Model	AIC	BIC
(1) ADT Model	300.00	308.03
(2) Proposed Model	298.13	306.15

Table 1. Model fit for data from full academic year.

were constructed according to equations *(1)* and *(2)* with each proposed variable as fixed effects, intercepts were removed as insignificant extrapolations of the data, and number of units completed over the entire year was set as the dependent variable.

Both the Akaike Information Criterion (AIC) and the Bayesian Information Criterion (BIC) were calculated for each model. The AIC and BIC values for each model are shown in Table 1. In both cases, the proposed model is found to have better fit to the data, and thus all analysis moving forward was conducted using the proposed model.

Predictive Validity
We then tested the predictive validity of our diligence measure for both curriculum units completed in a year and end-of-year course grade using ordinary least-squares regression. In both models, gender, ethnicity, free or reduced lunch, interest in math, and previous math achievement are controlled for. All variables are normalized in order to facilitate interpretation of coefficients.

The results of the regressions are shown in Table 2. The diligence measure was predictive of both Final Grade ($R^2=0.53$) and Units Completed ($R^2=0.62$).

In order to gain insight into the nature of the models' predictions, the actual outcome measures and estimated outcome measures were divided into quintiles and the type and size of errors made by the model were analyzed. Tables 3 and 4 show the accuracy and error rate of the model for End-of-year Grade and Units Completed respectively. As expected given the models' R^2 values, there is a strong diagonal to both matrices implying both high accuracy and small magnitude errors at each level. One notable feature is that the models more accurately predict the correct class at the bottom and top quintiles(66% on average) as opposed to the middle three quintiles (35% on average).

Parameter	Final Grade β(p-value)	Units Completed β(p-value)
Gender	0.06(.58)	0.06(.55)
F&R Lunch	-0.17(.25)	-0.03(.80)
Ethnicity	0.28(.41)	0.26(.40)
Math Interest	0.12(.073)	0.15(.017)*
Prior Grade	0.20(<0.01)**	0.07(.217)
Diligence	1.89(<0.001)***	1.64(<0.001)***

Table 2. Regression model using full academic year data.

End-of-Year Grade	1st 20%	2nd 40%	3rd 60%	4th 80%	5th 100%
Correct Pos.	55%	24%	38%	33%	68%
Type I	12%	17%	14%	19%	8%
Type II	45%	76%	62%	67%	77%
Correct Neg.	88%	83%	86%	81%	80%

Table 3. Model Prediction Accuracy of End-of-Year Grade.

Units Completed	1st 20%	2nd 40%	3rd 60%	4th 80%	5th 100%
Correct Pos.	80%	45%	38%	33%	59%
Type I	7%	14%	14%	16%	18%
Type II	20%	55%	63%	67%	41%
Correct Neg.	93%	86%	86%	84%	82%

Table 4. Model Prediction Accuracy of Units Completed by Quintile.

However, a model that utilizes student work metrics across an entire year to predict end of the year grades is not as useful for informing interventions. Therefore, we repeated the analysis with models that only utilized a fraction of the data from the school year to determine their predictive validity of each of these models for end-of-year grade and units completed.

The full year of data was divided into academic quarters and then into sets of decreasing number of continuous quarters (1 through 4). Thus there are two 3-quarter subsets, Q1Q2Q3 and Q2Q3Q4, three 2-quarter subsets, Q1Q2, Q2Q3, and Q3Q4, and four 1-quarter subsets, Q1, Q2, Q3, and Q4. The model definition had to be adjusted accordingly to use more local measures of prior knowledge and work completion. Work completion was simply set to the total number of units completed during the sampled time. Prior knowledge was set to the grade earned in the quarter prior to the first quarter in the sample, or the grade from the prior year if the sample includes Q1.

The results of each regression are shown in Table 5. The diligence measure is significantly predictive of both end-of-

	End-of-Year Grade		Units Completed	
Samples	β (p-value)	R^2	β (p-value)	R^2
Q1	1.85(<.001)***	0.40	2.23(<.001) ***	0.43
Q2	1.69(<.001)***	0.45	1.72(<.001) ***	0.41
Q3	1.08(<.001) ***	0.45	1.16(<.001) ***	0.44
Q4	2.52(<.001) ***	0.51	2.09(<.001) ***	0.39
Q1Q2	1.93(<.001) ***	0.50	2.17(<.001) ***	0.52
Q2Q3	1.95(<.001)***	0.56	2.09(<.001) ***	0.56
Q3Q4	1.11(<.001) ***	0.56	1.18(<.001) ***	0.55
Q1Q2Q3	2.11(<.001) ***	0.59	2.36(<.001) ***	0.63
Q2Q3Q4	2.04(<.001) ***	0.62	2.16(<.001)***	0.62

Table 5. Predictive validity over varying sample time windows.

Samples	1st 20%	2nd 40%	3rd 60%	4th 80%	5th 100%
Q1	59%	30%	10%	22%	41%
Q2	59%	35%	25%	17%	55%
Q3	55%	25%	25%	26%	59%
Q4	79%	48%	32%	39%	50%
Q1Q2	64%	30%	30%	22%	55%
Q2Q3	55%	20%	30%	26%	64%
Q3Q4	59%	10%	40%	35%	68%
Q1Q2Q3	64%	25%	25%	22%	64%
Q2Q3Q4	59%	30%	10%	22%	41%

Table 6. Model Positive Classification Accuracy of End-of-Year Grade.

Samples	1st 20%	2nd 40%	3rd 60%	4th 80%	5th 100%
Q1	65%	45%	29%	19%	27%
Q2	55%	35%	46%	19%	59%
Q3	70%	30%	42%	29%	55%
Q4	58%	40%	42%	38%	50%
Q1Q2	65%	45%	38%	19%	45%
Q2Q3	65%	45%	46%	14%	59%
Q3Q4	75%	40%	42%	38%	82%
Q1Q2Q3	75%	55%	42%	29%	59%
Q2Q3Q4	70%	40%	42%	29%	73%

Table 7. Positive Classification Accuracy of Units Completed

year grade and total curriculum units completed in a year across all time subsets.

The quintile analysis was repeated for each of the time subsets. The percent of correct positive labels was calculated for each dataset and averaged across all the datasets. The top and bottom quintiles of the End-of-year Grade regression models had a mean accuracy of 63.8% with mean standard deviation of 8.6%. The middle three quintiles of the End-of-year Grade regression models had a mean accuracy of 27.0% with a mean standard deviation of 8.7%. The top and bottom quintiles of the Units Completed regression models had a mean accuracy of 61.5% with a mean standard deviation of 11.3%. The middle three quintiles of the End-of-year Grade regression models had a mean accuracy of 36.1% with a mean standard deviation of 6.9%. Thus even without a full year of data, the model retains its prediction accuracy at all quintiles, though as can be seen in Tables 6 & 7, the model estimates begin to have larger errors as data size decreases.

Understanding the Diligence Measure

We followed this analysis with a partial correlation analysis to validate the relationship between our diligence measure and other SRL constructs. The partial correlation analysis included gender, ethnicity, and free and reduced lunch in

Survey Measure	Correlation (p-value)
Math Interest	0.25(.01) **
Theory of Intelligence	0.05(.596)
Self-Efficacy	.258(.007) **
Mastery Approach	.284(.003) ***
Performance Approach	0.189(.051)
Performance Avoidance	.06(.52)
Effort Regulation	0.337(<.001) ***

Table 8. Partial Correlation with Diligence.

the models. The predicted diligence measure using the full year of data is compared with the survey measures and the results are shown in Table 8.

The diligence measure is significantly correlated with its analogous SRL construct, effort regulation, highlighting the predominant effect size of self-control on average during the usage of the tutor. There are also strong correlations with mastery goal orientation and self-efficacy ratings again supporting the hypothesis that these constructs moderate self-control. Likewise, both performance achievement goals were uncorrelated with diligence as anticipated. Furthermore, domain-interest is significant as expected because this is a domain-specific measure of self-control. Thus the agreement between the partial correlation analysis and theory bolsters the construct validity of this model.

Robustness to Data Sparsity

The robustness of the model to sparser data was tested through an initial analysis of a second data set from a set of 96 Geometry students from the same school and the same academic school year. The students in the geometry classes had about 5,000 transactions over the entire year, and thus had about 1/3 the data on average over any time-window compared to the Pre-Algebra dataset.

Samples	End-of-Year Grade	
	β (p-value)	R^2
Q1	.345(.17)	0.621
Q2	0.303(.43)	0.612
Q3	0.450(.31)	0.615
Q4	0.283(.18)	0.612
Q1Q2	0.259(.16)	0.618
Q2Q3	-0.618(.54)	0.612
Q3Q4	0.206(.46)	0.616
Q1Q2Q3	0.200(.26)	0.615
Q2Q3Q4	-0.391(.55)	0.612
Q1Q2Q3Q4	0.177(.30)	0.619

Table 9. Predictive validity over varying sample time windows using sparse samples.

The same ordinary least-squares regression was performed where the models included gender, ethnicity, free or reduced lunch, interest in math, and previous math achievement. All variables were normalized in order to facilitate interpretation of coefficients. The results of the regressions are shown in the Table 9. In this case the model shows that the smaller dataset was not significantly predictive of end-of-year grade at any time-window length.

DISCUSSION

In this paper, we introduced a model for measuring student diligence using online behavioral traces of an intelligent tutoring system. This method expands on an existing model by leveraging the characteristics of the intelligent tutoring system context to be able to draw inferences on quantity and quality of student effort. The result is a measure of diligent practice that has strong predictive ability on long-term academic outcomes even when only utilizing a relatively short time-sample. There is some initial evidence that the system needs a reasonably large sample of student activity in order to make more accurate predictions of long-term outcomes based on diligence measures. It remains uncertain based on the initial analysis conducted, whether this inaccuracy is because the data collected is sampled too infrequently to build an accurate picture of student diligence or because the student's measured diligence isn't reflective of an aggregation of all learning activities completed by the student.

The study found supporting evidence of how motivation and metacognitive measures such as achievement goals and self-efficacy influence diligence longitudinally. Interestingly, the higher predictive strength of this diligence measure at the extremes in contrast to the reduced predictive power at intermediate values is a result that is worth further investigation. Do intermediate diligence students have more varied academic exertion across academic activities? Are students in this range only measured as less diligent in the system, while they may tend to work more or less diligently on written homework or while studying for exams? Conversely, are extremely non-diligent and extremely diligent students more likely to apply constant effort and focus across all activities in the class? Is the varied diligence associated with academically relevant offline behaviors such as peer tutoring or frequently asking the teacher for help?

In this study, report card grades were utilized as prior knowledge measures, and therefore limited the extent to which smaller time-windows could be utilized to assess diligence. This leaves several open questions for future investigation. Many online courses do not span longer than a few months, and thus a diligence measure designed to identify potential low performers that requires 9 weeks of data is likely too slow to provide intervention support. Thus this model needs to be validated using alternative knowledge and progress measures that can be sampled more frequently. Knowledge tracing algorithms provide a much more fine grained picture of both prior knowledge and student learning, though they no longer capture learning gains from offline activities and thus may challenge the model accuracy. This is a promising avenue for future investigations into the robustness of the model to time-window length.

With an online behavioral measurement in hand, several new avenues of research can be opened. Especially in environments such as MOOCs where student motivation is a known problem [18], the proposed diligence instrument can be used to identify categories of low motivation and diligence students for more targeted study. Furthermore, interactions between diligence, self-regulated learning, and cognition can easily be explored through existing behavior-mining methods [19]. This instrument also creates opportunities to experiment at scale with a range of self-control interventions such as suggesting behavioral changes that alter the typical study context or scheduling [11], or encouraging more challenging learning activities [21].

CONCLUSION

This paper introduces a model that can measure student diligence unobtrusively through data generated when students interact with course materials. Furthermore, it can support more sophisticated research into the impact of various interventions on student diligence. Ultimately, the model can support the identification of patterns of diligent behaviors that lead to long-term academic success, uncovering a range of effective non-cognitive interventions and also elucidating the relationship between self-control based constructs, motivational states, and how micro-behaviors aggregate to produce specific long-term outcomes.

ACKNOWLEDGMENTS

The research reported here was supported in part by the Institute of Education Sciences, U.S. Department of Education through Grant #R305B150008 to Carnegie Mellon University. We would like to thank Carnegie Learning, Inc., for providing the Cognitive Tutor data supporting this analysis. The opinions expressed are those of the authors and do not represent the views of the Institute of the U.S. Department of Education.

REFERENCES

1. Vincent Aleven, Ido Roll, Bruce M McLaren, and Kenneth R Koedinger. 2010. Automated, Unobtrusive, Action-by-Action Assessment of Self-Regulation During Learning With an Intelligent Tutoring System. *Educational Psychologist* 45, 4: 224–233. http://doi.org/10.1080/00461520.2010.517740

2. Carole Ames and Jennifer Archer. 1988. Achievement goals in the classroom: Students' learning strategies and motivation processes. *Journal of Educational Psychology* 80, 3: 260–267. http://doi.org/10.1037/0022-0663.80.3.260

3. Ryan Shaun Baker, Albert T Corbett, and Kenneth R Koedinger. 2004. Detecting Student Misuse of Intelligent Tutoring Systems. In *Intelligent Tutoring Systems*. Springer Berlin Heidelberg, Berlin, Heidelberg, 531–540. http://doi.org/10.1007/978-3-540-30139-4_50

4. Albert Bandura. 1994. Self-efficacy In VS Ramachaudran (Ed.) Encyclopedia of Human Behavior, 4, 71-81.

5. Roy F Baumeister, Brandon Schmeichel, and Kathleen Vohs. 2003. Self-regulation and the executive function of the self. In *Social Psychology Handbook of basic Principles* (2nd ed.). New York, 197–217.

6. Matthew L Bernacki and Steven Ritter. 2013. Hopewell 2011-2012. Dataset 613 in DataShop. Retrieved from https://pslcdatashop.web.cmu.edu/DatasetInfo?datasetId=613.

7. Matthew L Bernacki, Timothy J Nokes-Malach, and Vincent Aleven. 2013. Fine-Grained Assessment of Motivation over Long Periods of Learning with an Intelligent Tutoring System: Methodology, Advantages, and Preliminary Results. In *International Handbook of Metacognition and Learning Technologies*. Springer New York, New York, NY, 629–644. http://doi.org/10.1007/978-1-4419-5546-3_41

8. Jeni L Burnette, Ernest H O'Boyle, Eric M VanEpps, Jeffrey M Pollack, and Eli J Finkel. 2013. Mind-sets matter: A meta-analytic review of implicit theories and self-regulation. *Psychological Bulletin* 139, 3: 655–701. http://doi.org/10.1037/a0029531

9. Angela L Duckworth and Laurence Steinberg. 2015. Unpacking Self-Control. *Child Development Perspectives* 9, 1: 32–37.

10. Angela L Duckworth and David Scott Yeager. 2015. Measurement matters assessing personal qualities other than cognitive ability for educational purposes. *Educational Researcher* 44, 4: 237–251.

11. Angela L Duckworth, Tamar Szabó Gendler, and James J Gross. 2016. Situational Strategies for Self-Control. *Perspectives on Psychological Science* 11, 1: 35–55. http://doi.org/10.1177/1745691615623247

12. Carol Dweck. 2000. *Self-theories: Their role in motivation, personality, and development. Psychology Press.*

13. Andrew J Elliot and Kou Murayama. 2008. On the measurement of achievement goals: Critique, illustration, and application. *Journal of Educational Psychology* 100, 3: 613–628. http://doi.org/10.1037/0022-0663.100.3.613

14. K Anders Ericsson, Ralf T Krampe, and Clemens Tesch-Römer. 1993. The role of deliberate practice in the acquisition of expert performance. *Psychological Review* 100, 3: 363–406. http://doi.org/10.1037/0033-295X.100.3.363

15. Stephen Fancsali, Matthew L Bernacki, Timothy J Nokes-Malach, Michael Yudelson, and Steven Ritter. 2014. Goal Orientation, Self-Efficacy, and" Online Measures" in Intelligent Tutoring Systems. *CogSci*.

16. Brian M Galla, Benjamin D Plummer, Rachel E White, David Meketon, Sidney K D'Mello, and Angela L Duckworth. 2014. The Academic Diligence Task (ADT): assessing individual differences in effort on tedious but important schoolwork. 39, 4: 314–325. http://doi.org/10.1016/j.cedpsych.2014.08.001

17. Veronika Job, Carol S Dweck, and Gregory M Walton. 2010. Ego Depletion—Is It All in Your Head? *Psychological Science* 21, 11: 1686–1693. http://doi.org/10.1177/0956797610384745

18. Hanan Khalil and Martin Ebner. 2014. MOOCs completion rates and possible methods to improve retention-a literature review. *World Conference on Educational Multimedia*.

19. John S Kinnebrew, Kirk M Loretz, and Gautam Biswas. 2013. A Contextualized, Differential Sequence Mining Method to Derive Students' Learning Behavior Patterns. *JEDM - Journal of Educational Data Mining* 5, 1: 190–219.

20. Kenneth R Koedinger, Albert T Corbett, and Charles Perfetti. 2012. The Knowledge-Learning-Instruction Framework: Bridging the Science-Practice Chasm to Enhance Robust Student Learning. *Cognitive Science* 36, 5: 757–798. http://doi.org/10.1111/j.1551-6709.2012.01245.x

21. Kenneth R Koedinger, Jihee Kim, Julianna Zhuxin Jia, Elizabeth A McLaughlin, and Norman L Bier. 2015. *Learning is Not a Spectator Sport: Doing is Better than Watching for Learning from a MOOC.* ACM, New York, New York, USA. http://doi.org/10.1145/2724660.2724681

22. Carolyn MacCann, Angela Lee Duckworth, and Richard D Roberts. 2009. Empirical identification of the major facets of Conscientiousness. *Learning and Individual Differences* 19, 4: 451–458. http://doi.org/10.1016/j.lindif.2009.03.007

23. Gladwell Malcolm. 2008. *Outliers: The story of success.* New York: Little.

24. Walter Mischel, Yuichi Shoda, and Monica L. Rodriguez. 1989. Delay of gratification in children. *Science* 244, 4907: 933–938. http://doi.org/10.1126/science.2658056

25. National Research Council. 2011. *Assessing 21st Century Skills*. National Academies Press, Washington, D.C. http://doi.org/10.17226/13215

26. Paul R Pintrich. 1991. A Manual for the Use of the Motivated Strategies for Learning Questionnaire (MSLQ).

27. Paul R Pintrich. 2000. An Achievement Goal Theory Perspective on Issues in Motivation Terminology, Theory, and Research. 25, 1: 92–104. http://doi.org/10.1006/ceps.1999.1017

28. Steven Ritter, John R Anderson, Kenneth R Koedinger, and Albert Corbett. 2007. Cognitive Tutor: Applied research in mathematics education. *Psychonomic Bulletin & Review* 14, 2: 249–255. http://doi.org/10.3758/BF03194060

29. Nicole Shechtman, Angela H DeBarger, Carolyn Dornsife, and Soren Rosier. 2013. *Promoting grit, tenacity, and perseverance: Critical factors for success in the 21st century*. Washington.

30. June P Tangney, Roy F Baumeister, and Angie Luzio Boone. 2004. High Self-Control Predicts Good Adjustment, Less Pathology, Better Grades, and Interpersonal Success. *Journal of personality* 72, 2: 271–324. http://doi.org/10.1111/j.0022-3506.2004.00263.x

31. Eli Tsukayama, Angela Lee Duckworth, and Betty Kim. 2013. Domain-specific impulsivity in school-age children. *Developmental Science* 16, 6: 879–893. http://doi.org/10.1111/desc.12067

32. Phillip H Winne, John C Nesbit, Vive Kumar, et al. 2006. Supporting self-regulated learning with gStudy software: The Learning Kit Project. *Technology* ....

33. Barry J Zimmerman. 2008. Investigating Self-Regulation and Motivation: Historical Background, Methodological Developments, and Future Prospects. *American Educational Research Journal* 45, 1: 166–183. http://doi.org/10.3102/0002831207312909

Epistemic Cognition: A Promising and Necessary Construct for Enriching Large-scale Online Learning Analysis

Petr Johanes
Stanford University
Stanford, CA, USA
pjohanes@stanford.edu

ABSTRACT

Epistemic cognition refers to the process of thinking about one's forms of knowledge and ways of knowing. Epistemic cognition becomes especially critical when learners need to, assess the validity, certainty, reliability, source, and limits of their knowledge, as when working through ill-structured problems or evaluating contradictory knowledge claims. This psychological construct is relevant to Massively Open Online Courses (MOOCs), for instance, in that researchers are modeling learner behavior and performance (i.e., how learners handle knowledge) based on inferred learner knowledge states. In this synthesis paper, I provide a brief account of epistemic cognition research, summarize the field's key findings and theories, and outline the affordances that epistemic cognition offers to online learning researchers. I also show that, without knowing it, online learning researchers have already engaged with epistemic cognition concepts and provide recommendations for future, more theoretically and practically enriching work.

Author Keywords

Online Learning; Epistemic Cognition; MOOC; Epistemology; Knowledge Modeling

INTRODUCTION

The rapid rise of Massively Open Online Courses (MOOCs) since 2012 has demonstrated the potential to bring together computer scientists, data scientists, learning scientists, and psychologists in a collaborative and coordinated manner. One of the main draws for these communities has been the promise of large, diverse, and continuous/periodic data sets that can provide the kind of sampling scale and variety to test hypotheses, run interventions, and inform theories more robustly [37]. This draw remains as attractive as ever thanks to researchers already demonstrating how the diversity and scale of these data sets can contribute to empirical as well as theoretical work.

One example is video learning, where MOOCs have produced large and varied data sets for investigating learner behavior generally [19], predicting dropout rates specifically [21], and examining interface navigation [33]. While researchers have had

L@S 2017, April 20 - 21, 2017, Cambridge, MA, USA
Copyright is held by the owner/author(s). Publication rights licensed to ACM.
ACM 978-1-4503-4450-0/17/04...$15.00
DOI: http://dx.doi.org/10.1145/3051457.3051462

to create proxies for various measures, namely engagement [19], the ubiquity of video in online learning makes it an attractive research site for testing and expanding on learning theories about video learning [29]. Another example is social psychology, where MOOCs have provided a platform for studying learners from different socioeconomic [11], geographic [4,20], and political backgrounds [56] while investigating motivation [40], growth mindset [52], and sense of social belonging [38], among other psychological constructs. Starting out as replications of previous investigations and interventions in a new context, this area of MOOC research is now starting to craft new variations and kinds of interventions to contribute to the offline-based social psychology intervention literature. Yet another example is in the area of adaptive and personalized learning, as online education platforms have produced data sets of sufficient scale and complexity to enable the use of machine learning and other methods to investigate human learning problems like never before [65]. A particularly exciting line of research is the creation of new models for predicting learner behavior [9,55] and for recommending how a student moves through the many possible learning assessments [55] as well as course materials [63]. Overall, then, large-scale and diverse data sets from online education platforms have successfully shown the potential to bring together previously isolated communities of researchers, opened up new sites/media for previously offline-only research, and provided new inputs for previously unfeasible data science research.

Searching for learning-relevant psychological constructs that could enrich current and future large-scale data science methods, one can find multiple promising candidates. One of these is the construct of epistemic cognition. In this synthesis paper, I briefly introduce the history, findings, and models of epistemic cognition research and then outline some affordances of epistemic cognition for researchers using data sets originating from large-scale, online learning environments for computer science, data science, and learning science purposes. Toward the end, I also recommend possible steps for increasing fruitful collaboration among epistemic cognition, data analytics, and online learning researchers. The motivation for writing this paper is to expose online learning researchers to epistemic cognition as a promising – and in some cases even necessary – construct for enhancing their future as well as already ongoing investigations.

THE STATE OF EPISTEMIC COGNITION RESEARCH

Epistemic cognition has coalesced into an umbrella term for an increasing amount of research activity investigating human intellectual development and beliefs about knowledge, among other objects of inquiry [26]. The "cognition" part of the construct refers to people's mental processes (or, thinking) and the "epistemic" part refers to people's views and frameworks regarding knowledge and knowing. Epistemic cognition research, then, is the study of people's thinking about knowledge and knowing, especially critical when learners need to assess the validity, certainty, reliability, source, and limits of their knowledge. As such, the research draws heavily for inspiration from both epistemological philosophy and educational psychology, a collaboration several researchers are calling for the two fields to strengthen [5,18,62]. Epistemic cognition manifests in a variety of tangible ways in people's everyday, academic, and professional lives. Are some kinds of knowledge more valuable than others for the knowledge production goals of a particular field? For instance, many professional mathematicians consider proofs (a deductive form of knowledge) to be the gold standard in advancing their field, but that does not mean that they completely discount large-sample, computational evidence (an empirical form of knowledge) for every conjecture [66]. Presented with contradictory knowledge claims from different sources, how does a student work with and evaluate those claims? For instance, as participants in one study [15], if a student read a claim about vitamin D in a biology textbook and another claim about vitamin D in a health magazine, does the student discount one over the other because of where the student found it (the source of knowledge)? Or does the student maybe delve deeper and discount one over the other because of the research methodology used in the studies that support those claims (the process of knowledge production)? Or maybe the student does not discount at all and believes them to be equally valid! As perhaps right now: When encountering new knowledge, how does one think about integrating it with one's prior knowledge?

The point is that these are not high-minded and abstract concerns, but cognitive acts we engage in daily, informing how we operate both as individuals consuming knowledge and as collective participants contributing knowledge. These seemingly small cognitive acts can lead to a pattern of preferential behavior for handling similar situations in the future, which can, in turn, lead to establishing a stable attitude toward certain forms of knowledge and ways of knowing. This could be all the more important in online environments, where the learner is largely reliant upon the learner's own self-regulation to engage in, monitor, execute, and interpret the epistemological implications of those cognitive acts.

While philosophical investigations of epistemology stretch back to antiquity, educational psychology investigations stretch back only a few decades. In that time, much work has been done, stemming originally from Perry's qualitative study of the intellectual development of Harvard undergraduates [54]. Hofer presents the development of the epistemic cognition field as occurring in three waves that produced three models: a developmental model (primarily qualitative study of stable, synchronous epistemological beliefs) [1,34,35,43,54]; a dimensional model (primarily quantitative study of independent, asynchronous dimensions of an epistemological belief profile) [27,49,58,59]; and a situated model (primarily qualitative study of the activation and use of standalone epistemological resources) [12,13,22,46]. Each wave re-cast epistemic cognition in a new theoretical model and with a different set of methodologies. Responding to the overt focus on an individual's epistemic cognition in these three models, Kelly recently proposed a fourth, sociocultural, model [30]. Here, the focus is on qualitatively studying epistemic practices, behaviors regarding knowledge one acquires through interaction within and across different groups (each of which has its own unique take on what knowledge counts and looks like) [30]. **Table 1** summarizes these models' main characteristics. Many researchers, including Hofer, believe that the field is on the cusp of a fourth wave of research that will be marked most probably by a conceptual clarification of the epistemic cognition construct, greater collaboration with other research communities, and new and creative ways of measuring epistemic cognition [26].

The reason that researchers remain excited about epistemic cognition is because of the findings of small-scale studies related to learning, education, and psychology. From these small-scale studies, two or three particular findings stand out in relation to online learning. First, Muis and Duffy showed that student epistemological belief profiles are malleable and change over time when they are in a classroom environment that has instruction based on a sophisticated epistemology [50]. A sophisticated epistemology in this context espouses more constructivist conceptions of learning in that knowledge is tentative and complexly structured (rather than a simple structure of isolated facts) and that meaning must be actively constructed by the learners (rather than passively absorbed from authority). Student belief profiles shift in the direction of the sophisticated epistemology in their environment (their epistemic climate), though it may take 6-8 weeks [50]. Second, difference (or direct misalignment) between the epistemology of a science text and that of a student can lead to students remembering less from the text

Attribute	Developmental Model	Dimensional Model	Situated Model	Sociocultural Model
Model Visualization				
Construct Definition	Stable, synchronous, naturally-occurring, and linearly-evolving beliefs	Independent, asynchronous dimensions of beliefs	Distinct, deployable, and context-sensitive mental resources/representations	Interactional, socialized, and group-based practices/habits
Measurement Methods	• Interviews • Discourse analysis • Longitudinal observation	• Likert-scale self-reports • Surveys • Activity performance	• Think-aloud protocols • Semi-structured interviews • Cognitive interviews	• Video analysis • Discourse analysis • Semi-structured interviews

Table 1. Shows a simple visualization, construct definition, and popular measurement methods for each of the four models currently dominating the epistemic cognition research literature.

and being less likely to change any prior misconceptions than under conditions of epistemic alignment [16]. Third, different sets of epistemological beliefs seem to influence student text comprehension [57] and multiple text comprehension [14,15].

While multiple quantitative and self-report measurement instruments exist for these experiments [28,60,61], the instruments' validity and reliability has been called into question in a systematic and robust manner [2,25] along methodological and measurement issues that researchers have identified over the last couple of decades [26,30,48,62]. The four dimensions [25,48] these quantitative studies tend to track now are: certainty of knowledge (ranging from knowledge being certain to knowledge being tentative); simplicity of knowledge (ranging from the structure of knowledge being simple to the structure of knowledge being complex); source of knowing (ranging from passive acquisition through authority to active construction by oneself); and justification for knowing (ranging from relying on authoritative sources to use of objective criteria for justification). It can happen that different instruments can produce opposite interaction effects between an epistemic belief measure and a learning outcome [31]. This, in turn, calls into question how coarse- or fine-grained the constructs researchers trying to measure are and if bipolar Likert-scales (from strongly disagree to strongly agree) that imply a desirable (read sophisticated) and an undesirable (read naïve) direction are the best measurement tools [3,48]. Especially in intervention research, lack of cultural diversity, lack of process data, lack of scale, and lack of instruction/environment control remain barriers for truly robust findings and analyses [3]. These problems would most probably not have arisen had the field not taken the quantitative turn from its qualitative roots, and researchers from both methodologies are now looking to re-explore and address them [18,30,48].

To that end, epistemic cognition researchers have proposed a variety of ways to move forward in terms of methodology and measurement. Multiple researchers suggest measuring epistemic cognition in a fine-grained and context-sensitive manner [3,5,48,62]. After all, the way a learner approaches quantum mechanics might be epistemologically different from how a learner approaches classical mechanics. Others suggest to focus on inferring epistemic cognition from action rather than from self-report [22,62]. The reasoning here is simple: what a learner believes might not be how a learner behaves…or at least not all of the time. This leads to another suggestion, which is to better contextualize epistemic cognition by also monitoring learner epistemic aims (i.e., one's goals for acquiring and producing knowledge) along with other psychological systems and processes (e.g., motivation, emotion) [3,59]. A learner might believe that engaging in mathematical proof is a way to arrive at the kind of understanding the learner genuinely wants, but the learner's emotional state might become a barrier to that exercise. Finally, there is a call for epistemic cognition research to focus on more culturally diverse populations and process-oriented data [3,5].

To sum up, a theoretical, empirical, and intuitive basis exists for further epistemic cognition research. As a concept, it appears to have promising explanatory and predictive potential in the context of learning processes. The field is now looking for new methods for collecting and analyzing data (that are more behavioral, process-oriented, finer-grained, and context-sensitive), new media in which to intervene (that are more scalable, editable, and replicable), and new populations which to investigate (that are larger, periodic/replenishable, and culturally diverse).

EPISTEMIC COGNITION AFFORDANCES TO LARGE-SCALE, ONLINE LEARNING RESEARCH

Building on this prior work in the field of epistemic cognition and at least two independent calls for a computer-based research agenda for epistemic cognition [17,41], I now want to make the case for two qualities of epistemic cognition that are well-matched specifically with online learning research priorities. I call these well-matched qualities affordances. For each affordance, I introduce a key concern within the online research literature, ground the concern with a specific example from prior work, re-cast the example via a narrative with an epistemological lens, and then describe possible ways to enhance the online learning research with the theoretical models from epistemic cognition. Using this structure, I hope to show both the value of the present investigative approach and the value added by an epistemologically-conscious approach.

Affordance #1 – Additional Explanatory Power for Learner States and Learning Tasks

The first affordance relates to algorithm design and data analysis methods. Online environments can offer the possibility of adapting what content and assessments a learner encounters. A key concern, then, is predicting (1) what each learner does know and does not know, (2) how each learner knows what that learner knows (this is non-trivial: one could know something, for instance, with a logic different from the instructor's and problematic for learning upcoming content), and also (3) what to present the learner with so that the learner moves from one state of knowledge to another. All three of these predictions are epistemic in nature, and yet online learning researchers have not brought philosophical or psychological epistemology to bear on them.

These predictions fall into the realm of knowledge modeling and knowledge tracing, and we can look to explanation generation, evaluation, and adoption as a prime use case. AXIS (the Adaptive eXplanation Improvement System) asks learners in MOOCs to generate explanations for statistics and mathematics problems they just finished solving that are then shown to and rated by other learners as they encounter difficulties with those problems [67]. As large-scale numbers of learners generate, assess the quality of, and refine explanations (through a process called learnersourcing [32]), the AXIS system continuously makes choices as to which explanations to show to which student based on ratings of explanations, subjective judgments regarding ability to solve future problems, and objective measures of accuracy when solving those problems [67]. This system and others like it, help externalize learner cognition and create a history of that cognition via the online interface. They also fundamentally deal with producing, communicating, and evaluating knowledge claims, thereby representing fertile ground for weaving in measures relevant to epistemic cognition to enhance the systems' pedagogical and research potential further.

Consider a learner who differentiates between formal reasoning (characterized by mathematical equations and algebraic formulae) and everyday reasoning (characterized by naturally-occurring phenomena and observations from one's direct experience). More importantly, the learner discounts in the context of learning statistics everyday reasoning as not useful and also not 'statistics-y' enough. Note that these learner qualities are actually based on those of a real-life college physics student that Lising and Elby observed during a qualitative case study [45]. Showing this learner the best possible explanation based on counting beans in a jar and predicting the color of a bean picked from said jar most likely does not represent the path of least resistance for a knowledge state transition. For instance, it could be that the top-ranked explanation genuinely works if its epistemology matches that of the learner (the dimensional beliefs model) or if it is activating the right set of epistemological resources for each learner (the situated resources model). Otherwise, we could be forcing explanations that further deepen and enforce epistemic misalignment without being aware of it and without providing appropriate supports for addressing the misalignment once it arises. From this perspective, learnersourced explanations work for facilitating knowledge state transition only insofar as those explanations are matched with learner-matched epistemologies.

Here is how online researchers could weave epistemic cognition into designing adaptive systems for predicting and facilitating knowledge state transitions to gain a more comprehensive view of the transition process. Using the dimensional beliefs model, researchers could deploy one of the existing questionnaires or survey instruments (e.g., Epistemological Beliefs Questionnaire, EQ [60]; Epistemic Beliefs Inventory, EBI [61]; Discipline-Focused Epistemological Beliefs Questionnaire, DFEBQ [25]) in their experiments and/or environments for pre- and post-testing. Researchers could then look for demonstrated effects (e.g., epistemically-mismatched explanations facilitating slower misconception correction in learning Newton's laws [16]) and new effects (e.g., alternating between epistemically-matched and mismatched explanations facilitates faster misconception correction in statistics than only presenting epistemically-matched explanations). The measurement instruments are scalable and modifiable, enabling researchers to investigate beliefs about the knowledge in a particular chapter, course, or discipline as well as across chapters, courses, or disciplines. Researchers could also likely use learners' rankings of (equally valid) explanations as a proxy for preference toward certain epistemologies and not others.

Using the situated resources model, researchers could also classify the epistemological resources and other constructs each assessment and explanation requires learners to activate in order to extract the intended learning outcome. Particularly easy early targets for this endeavor might be learning tasks that require the activation of constructs such as epistemic doubt in evaluation of explanations (or, knowledge claims) or epistemic value in revising explanations (or, knowledge claims). Especially by collecting learners' writing about evaluating and revising the explanations, researchers could employ qualitative analysis to identify an appropriate coding scheme with which to then train a classification algorithm. Researchers could even structure short writing prompts to specifically elicit these specific epistemic constructs. Learners' revisions to their own explanations in light of the explanations they have encountered since crafting their own can also act as a proxy for what kinds of epistemological resources which explanations activate if done in a controlled enough manner.

The purpose of the examples above is to show an illustrative (rather than an exhaustive) set of ways in which epistemic cognition can enhance the investigations already underway and systems already under construction by online learning researchers. The fact of the matter is that predicting learner knowledge states is fundamentally grounded in epistemology. Therefore, epistemic cognition necessarily has a worthwhile contribution to make to the knowledge modeling foundation.

Affordance #2 – Additional Insight into for Learner and Environment Development

The second affordance relates to the design of online pedagogy and online learning environments. MOOCs have a well-documented track record of attracting large numbers of learners who are predominantly not from Western, Educated, Industrialized, Rich, and Democratic (WEIRD) countries [24]. MOOCs also have a well-documented high dropout rate or, put another way, a learner persistence problem [21,40]. Understanding these trends and constructing online learning environments that are effectively inclusive (i.e., they work) and consciously inclusive (i.e., they work by design) is a prime concern for the online research community.

This is evidenced by the plethora of research into both the kinds of learners that MOOCs attract and those learners' various behaviors and qualities: demographic and geographic differences in course navigation [20], learner persistence and achievement [10,38,40], and socioeconomic differences in course completion of learners in the US [23], to name a few. One attempt at inclusiveness online can be the deployment of value and belonging affirmations to help close achievement gaps among various nationalities by reducing the social psychological barriers that members of these groups might feel in these environments (e.g., seeing themselves as less capable and, therefore, questioning their belonging to an online learning community centered around a Western elite institution) [8,37]. The intention here is to have learners write for a few minutes about something they genuinely value in their lives (e.g., family, sports, religion) as a way to buttress their self-worth before engaging in these potentially socially threatening environments [8]. Using these affirmations or their variations, an online environment can help psychologically support learners in the learning process from the start.

Consider now a learner who enters a physics online learning environment. From the welcome video to the opinions voiced in the discussion forums to the solutions for assessment items, everything points to the norm that mathematical proof is how physicists arrive at their understanding of physics knowledge. No one appears to have a problem with this. Except, it seems, for this one learner, who has always used computational methods to understand and verify the knowledge from physics teachers and textbooks. Maybe this is how the learner's high school physics teachers propounded how physicists learn and make sense of physics knowledge. When immersed in this online learning environment that seems to not value and also even not acknowledge the learner's way of knowing physics, the learner might feel genuinely confused and isolated. At the same time, unless the teaching team and the learning community are aware that this could be happening, then the course does not adapt to provide systematic supports for being more epistemologically inclusive.

There are various ways that epistemic cognition research can be strategic in creating and studying inclusiveness in online learning environments. Using the developmental stages model, online learning researchers can analyze discussion forum and chat exchanges for the ways that learners handle disagreements and reflect upon those disagreements. How dogmatic or inflexible learners might be about holding onto a singular way to evidence a knowledge claim, for instance, can be indicative of earlier stages of epistemological development [34,35,54]. On the other hand, claiming all knowledge claims to be of equal value, while certainly more open-minded, is also not the end-point of most developmental models because such an epistemological stance does not distinguish between knowledge produced by different means. Maggioni, VanSledright, and Alexander comprehensively review the four popular developmental models and map across the models' separate stages for easier theoretical navigation [47]. Analyzing (and in the future maybe even structuring) early forum conversations to understand where learners are in their epistemological development can inform both instruction preparation and test performance analysis.

Using the sociocultural practices model, online learning researchers can analyze the epistemic moves that the teaching team promotes and that learners adopt by coming into contact with the community. Through videos, discussions, and assessments, the instructional team is promoting a specific set of behaviors related to handling knowledge and knowledge claims both for the wider professional community of the field, but also for the tight learning community of the MOOC. Here, researchers can analyze the epistemic content especially of assessment items on homework assignments and on quizzes and examinations and look for replication of that epistemic content by learners. For instance, imagine that, in teaching physics online, an instructional team structures assignments such that the first move is to compute a numerical value, the second move is to verify that value with another computational example, and the third move is to create a generalized formula. The team further reinforces this three-step approach in online videos, solution sheets, and discussion forums (e.g., by asking learners to run through this process when addressing confusions). This could be considered an instantiation of an epistemic practice that learners can observe and partake in via interaction with the learning community and the wider epistemic climate. Online learning researchers can then investigate rates of adoption and accuracy of replication of this practice and of other practices. Based on prior work on MOOC sub-populations of interest, researchers could also segment these results by, for instance, gender [38], nationality [37], and academic background [6]. An added benefit of this approach to online learning researchers and instructors can of course be that they collectively gain a clearer and more comprehensive view of the epistemic practices within the environments that they are studying.

As with the first affordance, the examples above are meant to be illustrative, not exhaustive. Especially because large-scale online learning environments such as MOOCs attract diverse populations of learners with the aim of onboarding these learners into new knowledge and new knowledge-handling practices, neglecting the epistemic aspect of the enterprise can have unintended consequences. In the same way that the logo of an elite higher education institution could induce identity threat in someone who is might be from a low socioeconomic and non-American cultural background, course and instructional designers might be sending epistemic cues that contribute to early dropout rates (or, conversely, lack of high certification rates), a key problem in MOOC research [9,21]. Epistemic cognition can bring a new dimension to data already being collected (especially from instructional materials and discussion exchanges) and reveal new patterns in including or isolating certain learner sub-populations (based on learner development and community practices).

FUTURE WORK RECOMMENDATIONS

The most productive way to fully realize these two (and myriad other) affordances of epistemic cognition is for epistemic cognition researchers and online learning researchers to acknowledge each other's prior work and to collaborate with each

other on future work. In this section, I point out additional areas of latent intersection between the two research fields and then describe possible research directions based on successes originating from serious investigation of epistemic cognition in a field such as history education.

As I have already noted, online learning researchers are investigating aspects of epistemic cognition without necessarily realizing it. Research on confusion in discussion forums [69] and on online learner sentiment/affect in general [7,39] could be recast as research into epistemic affect/emotion [53] as long as the emotions are epistemic in nature (i.e., related to thinking about knowledge and knowing). Research incorporating reflection activities in online environments [51] – again, as long as epistemic in nature – could be recast as research into epistemic resources and epistemic practices (especially if in a public venue) [30]. The knowledge tracing models in general and ones that deal with classifying, labeling, and/or predicting higher-order cognitive and learning skills/behaviors are probably in epistemic cognition territory simply because higher-order skills tend to be synonymous with or requisite of epistemic cognition [3,36]. Finally, at least one study already used student opinion on the course's epistemology as a feature in trying to understand the environment itself [64], a framework that epistemic cognition researchers can help expand upon with the concept of epistemic climate. Reframed with this lens, online research has forayed into epistemic cognition territory already, but has done so without the theoretical and practical benefits of the epistemic cognition research community's efforts.

When history educators and history education researchers seriously delved into epistemology and epistemic cognition, the result was a brand-new instructional curriculum, learning materials, and pedagogy style today called Reading Like a Historian [70]. Stemming from Wineburg's work that identified in professional historians an epistemological inclination to view historical texts as human constructions that need to be interrogated [68], the curriculum centers around work with primary sources. The curriculum encourages specific epistemic practices (or, in the language of history education, heuristics): sourcing (considering the document's source and purpose), contextualizing (placing the document in the when and where of its existence), and corroborating (comparing and evaluating accounts of multiple sources) [68]. Students are, thus, onboarded into thinking historically.

Given that multiple online learning environments can cover similar disciplines and that a single online learning environment can attract a learner population from diverse backgrounds (disciplines, cultures, and so on), could we through epistemological analysis arrive at similar innovative curricula? For instance, although physics, chemistry, mechanical engineering, and materials science might all teach thermodynamics, the way these disciplines enculture their participants into specific epistemic practices could show up in the learning process and learning performance during a well-crafted, thermodynamics-related online learning environment. These differences in disciplinary epistemological enculturation might also show up in the paths that learners take both through the course itself and through the corresponding knowledge states. We could then scale that analysis to other MOOCs in order to 'MOOC-source' a discipline's epistemology (e.g., from video transcripts, assessment items, discussion forums) and notice variations across MOOCs (across individual MOOCs and/or across MOOCs grouped by institution type or continent, for instance). By combining the disciplinary variety and content overlap of MOOCs with the disciplinary and curricular prior work in epistemic cognition, we can entertain investigations into clarifying epistemic practices within different online learning cultures and streamlining future curriculum construction.

Of course, the online learning research community does not entirely have to follow the history education field's trajectory in leveraging epistemic cognition research. Many online learning environments possess capabilities that predispose them to certain kinds of future work. First, many online learning environments empower instructors and/or researchers to assign learners to groups according to certain criteria at scale for work [42] and for discussion [44]. How does epistemological diversity influence group work online? Some of the observational/qualitative studies of STEM students at work indicate that group dialogue can efficiently reveal epistemologies [13,30,45], but there does not seem to be in the literature of a serious learning-oriented observation of multiple teams constructed with epistemological diversity in mind. Given the learner population diversity and scale as well as the ease of assignment into groups, investigations of some kind of group work might be more beneficial to do online. Second, certain online learning environments (especially MOOCs) are beginning to employ advanced machine learning techniques such as recurrent neural networks that can help cluster learners and predict learning trajectories more efficiently than previous models [55]. These algorithms simply do not make sense in pen-and-paper or small-data settings. A few intriguing possibilities present themselves with these data analysis techniques: clustering learner trajectories by learner epistemologies; investigating whether or not certain sequences of knowledge state transitions also facilitate epistemological beliefs transitions; and collecting data around tacit (rather than only overt and/or self-reported) epistemic behaviors. All of these investigations have the potential to lend existing models greater explanatory power for clarifying how learners navigate the learning process. This is especially important for online learning research because it could add a new dimension through which to understand the online learners and because it could add a new variable with which to structure and predict mastery training. The overall point is that the online learning research community can as much translate methods from others' success as try investigative methods that only this community can uniquely attempt.

CONCLUSION

To advance their investigations, epistemic cognition researchers are calling for data sets, learning environments, and intervention possibilities that share the qualities that diverse, large-scale online learning environments offer. In turn, epistemic cognition affords online learning data and online learning researchers a fresh conceptual frame for understanding and describing online environments and a new variable for analyzing and predicting online behaviors. Various online learning researchers and data scientists either have already encountered or are about to encounter epistemic cognition in their research without realizing it and therefore not leveraging the literature of that field for its significant theoretical and practical value. Evidence of that value has been demonstrated in history education, where seriously investigating epistemic cognition produced a new and expanding pedagogy that teaches history while also giving students practice with thinking like a historian. Furthermore, it is clear especially from the discussion of the affordances of epistemic cognition to online learning research that we can use a wealth of existing data to conduct some of the investigations mentioned here. At the same

time, we also need to design activities and environments that render epistemic cognition readily observable and craft assessments that render epistemic cognition absolutely necessary. The research reviewed in this paper paints a picture of a significant overlap (present and future) between epistemic cognition research and online learning research, rendering the collaboration between the two fields seem not only unavoidable, but also indispensable.

ACKNOWLEDGMENTS
I would like to thank the Stanford Lytics Lab and the Stanford Office of the Vice Provost for Teaching and Learning for research support and mentorship.

REFERENCES

1. Marcia B. Baxter Magolda. 2004. Evolution of a Constructivist Conceptualization of Epistemological Reflection. *Educational Psychologist* 39, 1: 31–42. https://doi.org/10.1207/s15326985ep3901_4

2. Lisa D. Bendixen and Deanna C. Rule. 2004. An Integrative Approach to Personal Epistemology: A Guiding Model. *Educational Psychologist* 39, 1: 69–80. https://doi.org/10.1207/s15326985ep3901_7

3. Ivar Bråten. 2016. Epistemic cognition interventions. In *Handbook of epistemic cognition*, Jeffrey A Greene, William A Sandoval and Ivar Bråten (eds.). Routledge, New York, 360–371.

4. Christopher Brooks, Craig Thompson, and Stephanie Teasley. 2015. Who You Are or What You Do: Comparing the Predictive Power of Demographics vs. Activity Patterns in Massive Open Online Courses (MOOCs). 245–248. https://doi.org/10.1145/2724660.2728668

5. Clark A. Chinn, Luke A. Buckland, and Ala Samarapungavan. 2011. Expanding the Dimensions of Epistemic Cognition: Arguments From Philosophy and Psychology. *Educational Psychologist* 46, 3: 141–167. https://doi.org/10.1080/00461520.2011.587722

6. Gayle Christensen, Andrew Steinmetz, Brandon Alcorn, Amy Bennett, Deirdre Woods, and Ezekiel J. Emanuel. 2013. The MOOC phenomenon: who takes massive open online courses and why? *Available at SSRN 2350964*. Retrieved October 24, 2016 from http://papers.ssrn.com/sol3/papers.cfm?abstract_id=2350964

7. Jaye Clarkes-Nias, Juliet Mutahi, Andrew Kinai, Oliver Bent, Komminist Weldemariam, and Saurabh Srivastava. 2015. Towards Capturing Learners Sentiment and Context. 217–222. https://doi.org/10.1145/2724660.2728662

8. Geoffrey L. Cohen, Julio Garcia, Nancy Apfel, and Allison Master. 2006. Reducing the Racial Achievement Gap: A Social-Psychological Intervention. *Science* 313, 5791: 1307–1310. https://doi.org/10.1126/science.1128317

9. Cody A. Coleman, Daniel T. Seaton, and Isaac Chuang. 2015. Probabilistic Use Cases: Discovering Behavioral Patterns for Predicting Certification. 141–148. https://doi.org/10.1145/2724660.2724662

10. Jennifer DeBoer, Glenda S. Stump, Daniel Seaton, and Lori Breslow. 2013. Diversity in MOOC students' backgrounds and behaviors in relationship to performance in 6.002 x. In *Proceedings of the Sixth Learning International Networks*

Consortium Conference. Retrieved October 24, 2016 from http://tll.mit.edu/sites/default/files/library/LINC%20%2713.pdf

11. Tawanna R Dillahunt, Sandy Ng, Michelle Fiesta, and Zengguang Wang. 2016. Do Massive Open Online Course Platforms Support Employability? 232–243. https://doi.org/10.1145/2818048.2819924

12. Andrew Elby. 2001. Helping physics students learn how to learn. *American Journal of Physics* 69, S1: S54–S64. https://doi.org/10.1119/1.1377283

13. Andrew Elby and David Hammer. 2001. On the substance of a sophisticated epistemology. *Science Education* 85, 5: 554–567.

14. Leila E. Ferguson, Ivar Bråten, and Helge I. Strømsø. 2012. Epistemic cognition when students read multiple documents containing conflicting scientific evidence: A think-aloud study. *Learning and Instruction* 22, 2: 103–120. https://doi.org/10.1016/j.learninstruc.2011.08.002

15. Leila E. Ferguson, Ivar Bråten, Helge I. Strømsø, and Øistein Anmarkrud. 2013. Epistemic beliefs and comprehension in the context of reading multiple documents: Examining the role of conflict. *International Journal of Educational Research* 62: 100–114. https://doi.org/10.1016/j.ijer.2013.07.001

16. Gina M. Franco, Krista R. Muis, Panayiota Kendeou, John Ranellucci, Lavanya Sampasivam, and Xihui Wang. 2012. Examining the influences of epistemic beliefs and knowledge representations on cognitive processing and conceptual change when learning physics. *Learning and Instruction* 22, 1: 62–77. https://doi.org/10.1016/j.learninstruc.2011.06.003

17. Jeffrey A. Greene, Krista R. Muis, and Stephanie Pieschl. 2010. The Role of Epistemic Beliefs in Students' Self-Regulated Learning With Computer-Based Learning Environments: Conceptual and Methodological Issues. *Educational Psychologist* 45, 4: 245–257. https://doi.org/10.1080/00461520.2010.515932

18. Jeffrey A. Greene and Seung B. Yu. 2014. Modeling and measuring epistemic cognition: A qualitative re-investigation. *Contemporary Educational Psychology* 39, 1: 12–28. https://doi.org/10.1016/j.cedpsych.2013.10.002

19. Philip J. Guo, Juho Kim, and Rob Rubin. 2014. How video production affects student engagement: an empirical study of MOOC videos. 41–50. https://doi.org/10.1145/2556325.2566239

20. Philip J. Guo and Katharina Reinecke. 2014. Demographic differences in how students navigate through MOOCs. 21–30. https://doi.org/10.1145/2556325.2566247

21. Sherif Halawa, Daniel Greene, and John Mitchell. 2014. Dropout prediction in MOOCs using learner activity features. *Experiences and best practices in and around MOOCs* 7.

22. David Hammer and Andrew Elby. 2002. On the form of a personal epistemology. In *Personal epistemology: The psychology of beliefs about knowledge and knowing*, Barbara K Hofer (ed.). Erlbaum, Mahwah, NJ, 169–190.

23. John D Hansen and Justin Reich. 2015. Democratizing education? Examining access and usage patterns in massive open online courses. *Science* 350, 6265: 1245–1248.

24. Joseph Henrich, Steven J. Heine, and Ara Norenzayan. 2010. The weirdest people in the world? *Behavioral and Brain Sciences* 33, 2-3: 61–83. https://doi.org/10.1017/S0140525X0999152X

25. Barbara K. Hofer. 2000. Dimensionality and Disciplinary Differences in Personal Epistemology. *Contemporary Educational Psychology* 25, 4: 378–405. https://doi.org/10.1006/ceps.1999.1026

26. Barbara K Hofer. 2016. Epistemic cognition as a psychological construct: Advancements and challenges. In *Handbook of epistemic cognition*. Routledge, New York, 19–39.

27. Barbara K. Hofer and Paul R. Pintrich. 1997. The development of epistemological theories: Beliefs about knowledge and knowing and their relation to learning. *Review of educational research* 67, 1: 88–140.

28. Jihn-Chang J Jehng, Scott D Johnson, and Richard C Anderson. 1993. Schooling and students' epistemological beliefs about learning. *Contemporary educational psychology* 18, 1: 23–25.

29. Petr Johanes and Larry Randles Lagerstrom. 2016. Online Videos: What Every Instructor Should Know.

30. Gregory J Kelly. 2016. Methodological considerations for the study of epistemic cognition in practice. In *Handbook of epistemic cognition*, Jeffrey A Greene, William A Sandoval and Ivar Bråten (eds.). Routledge, New York, 393–408.

31. Dorothe Kienhues, Rainer Bromme, and Elmar Stahl. 2008. Changing epistemological beliefs: The unexpected impact of a short-term intervention. *British Journal of Educational Psychology* 78, 4: 545–565. https://doi.org/10.1348/000709907X268589

32. Juho Kim. 2015. Learnersourcing: improving learning with collective learner activity. Massachusetts Institute of Technology. Retrieved October 24, 2016 from http://dspace.mit.edu/handle/1721.1/101464

33. Juho Kim, Philip J. Guo, Carrie J. Cai, Shang-Wen (Daniel) Li, Krzysztof Z. Gajos, and Robert C. Miller. 2014. Data-driven interaction techniques for improving navigation of educational videos. 563–572. https://doi.org/10.1145/2642918.2647389

34. Patricia M King and Karen Strohm Kitchener. 1994. *Developing Reflective Judgment: Understanding and Promoting Intellectual Growth and Critical Thinking in Adolescents and Adults. Jossey-Bass Higher and Adult Education Series and Jossey-Bass Social and Behavioral Science Series*. Jossey-Bass, San Francisco.

35. Patricia M. King and Karen Strohm Kitchener. 2004. Reflective Judgment: Theory and Research on the Development of Epistemic Assumptions Through Adulthood. *Educational Psychologist* 39, 1: 5–18. https://doi.org/10.1207/s15326985ep3901_2

36. Karen S Kitchener. 1983. Cognition, metacognition, and epistemic cognition. *Human Development* 26, 4: 222–232.

37. René F. Kizilcec and Christopher Brooks. to appear. Diverse Big Data and Randomized Field Experiments in Massive Open Online Courses: Opportunities for Advancing Learning Research. In *Handbook on Learning Analytics & Educational Data Mining*, George Siemens and Charles Lang (eds.).

38. René F. Kizilcec and Sherif Halawa. 2015. Attrition and Achievement Gaps in Online Learning. 57–66. https://doi.org/10.1145/2724660.2724680

39. René F. Kizilcec, Kathryn Papadopoulos, and Lalida Sritanyaratana. 2014. Showing face in video instruction: effects on information retention, visual attention, and affect. 2095–2102. https://doi.org/10.1145/2556288.2557207

40. René F. Kizilcec, Chris Piech, and Emily Schneider. 2013. Deconstructing disengagement: analyzing learner subpopulations in massive open online courses. In *Proceedings of the third international conference on learning analytics and knowledge*, 170–179. Retrieved February 1, 2016 from http://dl.acm.org/citation.cfm?id=2460330

41. Simon Knight, Simon Buckingham Shum, and Karen Littleton. 2014. Epistemology, assessment, pedagogy: where learning meets analytics in the middle space. *Journal of Learning Analytics* 1, 2: 23–47.

42. Yasmine Kotturi, Chinmay E. Kulkarni, Michael S. Bernstein, and Scott Klemmer. 2015. Structure and messaging techniques for online peer learning systems that increase stickiness. 31–38. https://doi.org/10.1145/2724660.2724676

43. Deanna Kuhn, Richard Cheney, and Michael Weinstock. 2000. The development of epistemological understanding. *Cognitive development* 15, 3: 309–328.

44. Chinmay Kulkarni, Julia Cambre, Yasmine Kotturi, Michael S. Bernstein, and Scott R. Klemmer. 2015. Talkabout: Making Distance Matter with Small Groups in Massive Classes. 1116–1128. https://doi.org/10.1145/2675133.2675166

45. Laura Lising and Andrew Elby. 2005. The impact of epistemology on learning: A case study from introductory physics. *American Journal of Physics* 73, 4: 372. https://doi.org/10.1119/1.1848115

46. Loucas Louca, Andrew Elby, David Hammer, and Trisha Kagey. 2004. Epistemological Resources: Applying a New Epistemological Framework to Science Instruction. *Educational Psychologist* 39, 1: 57–68. https://doi.org/10.1207/s15326985ep3901_6

47. Liliana Maggioni, Bruce VanSledright, and Patricia A. Alexander. 2009. Walking on the Borders: A Measure of Epistemic Cognition in History. *The Journal of Experimental Education* 77, 3: 187–214. https://doi.org/10.3200/JEXE.77.3.187-214

48. Lucia Mason. 2016. Psychological perspectives on measuring epistemic cognition. In *Handbook of epistemic cognition*, Jeffrey A Greene, William A Sandoval and Ivar Bråten (eds.). Routledge, New York, 375–392.

49. Krista R. Muis, Lisa D. Bendixen, and Florian C. Haerle. 2006. Domain-Generality and Domain-Specificity in Personal Epistemology Research: Philosophical and Empirical Reflections in the Development of a Theoretical Framework. *Educational Psychology Review* 18, 1: 3–54. https://doi.org/10.1007/s10648-006-9003-6

50. Krista R. Muis and Melissa C. Duffy. 2013. Epistemic climate and epistemic change: Instruction designed to change students' beliefs and learning strategies and improve achievement. *Journal of Educational Psychology* 105, 1: 213–225. https://doi.org/10.1037/a0029690

51. Denise Nacu, Caitlin K. Martin, Michael Schutzenhofer, and Nicole Pinkard. 2016. Beyond Traditional Metrics: Using Automated Log Coding to Understand 21st Century Learning Online. 197–200. https://doi.org/10.1145/2876034.2893413

52. Eleanor O'Rourke, Erin Peach, Carol S. Dweck, and Zoran Popovic. 2016. Brain Points: A Deeper Look at a Growth Mindset Incentive Structure for an Educational Game. 41–50. https://doi.org/10.1145/2876034.2876040

53. Reinhard Pekrun. 2011. Emotions as Drivers of Learning and Cognitive Development. In *New Perspectives on Affect and Learning Technologies*, Rafael A. Calvo and Sidney K. D'Mello (eds.). Springer New York, New York, NY, 23–39. Retrieved October 24, 2016 from http://link.springer.com/10.1007/978-1-4419-9625-1_3

54. William G. Perry Jr. 1968. Patterns of Development in Thought and Values of Students in a Liberal Arts College: A Validation of a Scheme. Final Report. Retrieved October 24, 2016 from http://eric.ed.gov/?id=ED024315

55. Chris Piech, Jonathan Bassen, Jonathan Huang, Surya Ganguli, Mehran Sahami, Leonidas J. Guibas, and Jascha Sohl-Dickstein. 2015. Deep knowledge tracing. In *Advances in Neural Information Processing Systems*, 505–513. Retrieved October 24, 2016 from http://papers.nips.cc/paper/5654-deep-knowledge-tracing

56. Justin Reich, Brandon Stewart, Kimia Mavon, and Dustin Tingley. 2016. The Civic Mission of MOOCs: Measuring Engagement across Political Differences in Forums. 1–10. https://doi.org/10.1145/2876034.2876045

57. Michael P Ryan. 1984. Monitoring text comprehension: Individual differences in epistemological standards. *Journal of Educational Psychology* 76, 2: 248–258.

58. Marlene Schommer-Aikins. 2002. An evolving theoretical framework for an epistemological belief system. In *Personal epistemology: The psychology of beliefs about knowledge and knowing*, Barbara K Hofer and Paul R Pintrich (eds.). Lawrence Erlbaum Associates, In., Mahwah, NJ, 103–118.

59. Marlene Schommer-Aikins. 2004. Explaining the Epistemological Belief System: Introducing the Embedded Systemic Model and Coordinated Research Approach. *Educational Psychologist* 39, 1: 19–29. https://doi.org/10.1207/s15326985ep3901_3

60. Marlene Schommer. 1990. Effects of beliefs about the nature of knowledge on comprehension. *Journal of educational psychology* 82, 3: 498.

61. Gregory Schraw, Lisa D Bendixen, and Michael E Dunkle. 2002. Development and validation of the Epistemic Belief Inventory (EBI). In *Personal epistemology: The psychology of beliefs about knowledge and knowing*, Barbara K Hofer

and Paul R Pintrich (eds.). Jossey-Bass, Mahwah, NJ, 261–275.

62. Gale Sinatra. 2016. Thoughts on knowledge about thinking about knowledge. In *Handbook of epistemic cognition*, Jeffrey A Greene, William A Sandoval and Ivar Bråten (eds.). Routledge, New York, 479–491.

63. Tanmay Sinha and Justine Cassell. 2015. Connecting the Dots: Predicting Student Grade Sequences from Bursty MOOC Interactions over Time. 249–252. https://doi.org/10.1145/2724660.2728669

64. Karen Swan, Scott Day, and Leonard Bogle. 2016. Metaphors for Learning and MOOC Pedagogies. 125–128. https://doi.org/10.1145/2876034.2893385

65. Candace Thille, Emily Schneider, René F. Kizilcec, Christopher Piech, Sherif A. Halawa, and Daniel K. Greene. 2014. The future of data-enriched assessment. *Research & Practice in Assessment* 9. Retrieved October 24, 2016 from http://search.proquest.com/openview/9602ae685ff647d18a64a517a78ef5a2/1?pq-origsite=gscholar

66. Keith Weber, Matthew Inglis, and Juan Pablo Mejia-Ramos. 2014. How Mathematicians Obtain Conviction: Implications for Mathematics Instruction and Research on Epistemic Cognition. *Educational Psychologist* 49, 1: 36–58. https://doi.org/10.1080/00461520.2013.865527

67. Joseph Jay Williams, Juho Kim, Anna Rafferty, Samuel Maldonado, Krzysztof Z. Gajos, Walter S. Lasecki, and Neil Heffernan. 2016. AXIS: Generating Explanations at Scale with Learnersourcing and Machine Learning. 379–388. https://doi.org/10.1145/2876034.2876042

68. Samuel S. Wineburg. 1991. Historical problem solving: A study of the cognitive processes used in the evaluation of documentary and pictorial evidence. *Journal of educational Psychology* 83, 1: 73.

69. Diyi Yang, Miaomiao Wen, Iris Howley, Robert Kraut, and Carolyn Rose. 2015. Exploring the Effect of Confusion in Discussion Forums of Massive Open Online Courses. 121–130. https://doi.org/10.1145/2724660.2724677

70. Reading Like a Historian. *Stanford History Education Group*. Retrieved January 10, 2017 from https://sheg.stanford.edu/rlh

Scaling Expert Feedback: Two Case Studies

David A. Joyner
Georgia Institute of Technology
Atlanta, Georgia
david.joyner@gatech.edu

ABSTRACT

Traditionally, education relies on a linear relationship between enrollment and staff; rising enrollment dictates increases to staff with some expertise (such as teaching assistants, TAs) for evaluation. This relationship is expensive, so learning at scale has largely deemphasized expert evaluation and feedback. Two organizations, though, have used different models to scale up class size online while retaining this expert evaluation and feedback. In this paper, we analyze the methods these two organizations have used to increase enrollment while preserving scalability and feedback. We observe an academic program has scaled feedback with traditional TAs by relying on unique characteristics of its student body, while a commercial program has done so with a novel, network-based model. These successes show the potential of learning from experts at scale.

Author Keywords

Expert feedback; online higher education; microcredentials.

ACM Classification Keywords

Social and professional topics~Computer science education

INTRODUCTION

The rise of online education has been a boon for learning at scale, especially in higher education, due to the online environment's ability to resolve classical threats to scalable education, such as classroom size, geographic mobility, and synchronous scheduling. However, online delivery still may incur significant monetary costs to students because the most expensive piece of higher education is also one of its most pedagogically important: the presence of dedicated, expert-level feedback, such as that provided by by graduate teaching assistants (TAs) in many programs. Research shows students perceive these TAs as less authoritative than professors, but also as more engaging and interactive [14].

In online programs, this threat to scale has been handled in two main ways. One, many programs deliver traditional

curricula online for the same cost as residential programs. The similar cost lets classical models of grading by instructors and TAs persist. These costs, however, dampen the programs' scalability due to the massive and unevenly distributed barrier to entry presented by high tuition.

So, many efforts in learning at scale emphasize *removing* individual expert-level feedback, as seen in most MOOCs. While few people would argue this is a better learning experience, some argue the trade-off in affordability justifies the shift in approach to feedback.

Recently, efforts to reintroduce expert-level feedback into affordable programs have begun. MOOC host Coursera has begun leveraging volunteer mentors to provide expertise in forum interactions [26]. While paid graduate TAs do not possess the expertise of professors, their feedback sustains existing graduate programs; scaling it could preserve expert feedback while increasing accessibility and enrollment.

This paper provides case studies on two ongoing efforts to use scalable expert-level feedback in affordable online programs. One effort is in a major university's all-online Master's degree, which enrolls over 4,000 students in its online Master's program, while keeping the *total* cost of the degree around $7,000 [4]. Importantly, the program is identically accredited as the residential program, creating demand for the same feedback and endorsement residential students receive. The university has scaled by preserving the traditional model for expert feedback, but adapting it to rely on the unique motivations of online students.

The second effort is a company providing online programs in emerging fields like machine learning, enrolling over 10,000 students, while maintaining a lower (~$200/month) program cost than accredited institutions, boot camps, or certification programs. While the company does not have accreditation requirements, it has a similar pressure to provide expert-level feedback and endorsement due to a guarantee of employment for graduates. The company has scaled using a dramatically different model for expert evaluation than traditional higher education, leveraging a distributed network of freelance professionals.

These organizations are very different. The university is a century-old accredited academic and research institution; the company is a young Silicon Valley startup. However, they experience similar pressures to provide expert-level feedback and a reliable endorsement of the skills of their graduates. So, both have developed ways to scale their programs while preserving student ↔ expert interaction.

This paper first outlines reasons that methods for scaling used by other programs are insufficient given these pressures. It then gives case studies on two organizations: for each, it covers the setup for scaling feedback, and for the university, it examines the motivations of those experts. It concludes that scaling expert feedback while preserving affordability is possible.

MODELS FOR SCALABLE FEEDBACK

In examining the landscape around MOOCs, there are three common mechanisms for scaling feedback without additional hiring: automated, peer, and implicit feedback. These three require no additional investment of time from the teaching team as enrollment rises. All three also present valuable learning opportunities; there are challenges, however, in using them alone in programs with significant pressure for expert-level feedback and endorsement.

Automated Feedback

One approach to scalable feedback is automatic evaluation. Traditionally, this calls to mind negative connotations surrounding multiple-choice tests, but automated evaluation can evaluate complex problems and provide individualized feedback. Grading by simulation is one example, that has been used in fields like cyber-physical systems [11] and electrical engineering [25]. Similar initiatives, called virtual labs in the sciences, even predate MOOCs, e.g. [33]. The prevalence of online computer science education has led to initiatives for automatic code evaluation, e.g. [6, 27], although some initiatives predate online education [10].

Aside from scalability, automated feedback presents pedagogical advantages. It facilitates immediate feedback, allowing students to engage the valuable rapid revision cycles [3]. The entire field of intelligent tutoring systems [22] is built on immediate, individualized, automatic feedback [28], and research has found it can be nearly as effective as human tutoring [29], while presenting significant advantages in availability and integration.

However, automated evaluation presents three major challenges. First, construction of automated evaluators is typically expensive, a problem so apparent that dedicated efforts are underway to reduce production costs [1, 21]. Even when automated assessors can be built, equipping them with deep, expert-level feedback is an additional challenge. Second, they largely address closed answer spaces; the space may be large, but they struggle with entirely open-ended, student-driven, project-based learning, which is desirable and presents a demand for feedback [15]. Third, deserved or not, overreliance on automated evaluation may challenge the perception of the endorsement's authenticity and integrity. While automated evaluation has an important role, it cannot presently be solely responsible for feedback and endorsement.

Peer Feedback

Likely the most common approach taken to scaling evaluation online is peer feedback. Peer feedback entails having students evaluate classmates' work, then deriving a grade from those evaluations. Like automated evaluation, it is perfectly scalable: adding students also adds reviewers. Solutions for peer review are more easily constructed and domain-general, helping resolve the cost of construction.

Peer feedback has great pedagogical value. Research shows its positive effect on learning [2, 18, 31] due to the implicit feedback and learning-by-teaching paradigm; that the act of *giving* feedback itself has a positive effect on learning [20]; and that it can be valid under specific circumstances [5]. Efforts exist to improve its validity through machine learning [e.g. 17, 23] or expert meta-reviewing [e.g. 12].

Peer review is valuable; however, for supporting accredited or guaranteed programs, it presents challenges. First, as noted, it is valid only in specific circumstances, and research shows peer graders are often unreliable [32] and unmotivated [19]. Second, it also introduces perception issues: the notion that a student may graduate without any expert evaluation is problematic. While these two issues are likely resolvable with evidence of validity, a third challenge is more problematic: individual expert-level feedback provides expertise and targeted insights that peer review does not always capture. Experts' knowledge of the material translates to better feedback than peers alone. Thus, while it is pedagogically valuable to include peer review, it likely cannot solely support such high-stakes programs.

Implicit Feedback

Implicit feedback is providing resources from which learners can self-evaluate [9]. A common type of implicit feedback is supplying learners with exemplary assignments: by comparing their own work to the best work in the class, they can derive feedback on their performance. Worked examples are similar in formal domains [24, 30]. Peer review facilitates implicit feedback, too: it provides learners an opportunity to compare their work against other approaches, developing their understanding of its strengths and weaknesses.

Like peer and automated feedback, implicit feedback is perfectly scalable. It additionally may provide a richer set of feedback than the more closed set provided by automated evaluation by giving well-equipped students the data to generate detailed personal feedback. However, it presents drawbacks: it does not generate endorsement, it necessitates preexisting metacognitive skills, and it may raise more questions than it answers in the mind of the student.

Expert Feedback

These three feedback approaches – automated, peer, and implicit – are valuable pedagogical activities, but even combined, they struggle to provide expert-level formative assessment and reliable endorsement. The questions surrounding scaling expert feedback have never been about its value, but rather its practicality. Individual expert assessment is expensive. Some efforts have focused on scaling expert-level feedback by combining it with peer review [12] or seeding peer review to infer peer grader validity [17], but these still struggle with the fundamental benefit of expert feedback: that experts have greater domain knowledge, experience, and ability to provide individual feedback. For programs that must maintain accreditation (like this university) or a guarantee (like this company), scaling expert-level review remains highly desirable.

STUDY 1: A UNIVERSITY MASTER'S PROGRAM

The first case study here presents an online Master's program at a major university. The program is scalable, affordable, entirely online, and fully accredited. Its attempts to provide feedback at scale run into the challenges above: classes involve work that is too open-ended for automated grading alone, but too complex and high-stakes to rely on peer evaluations for grades and formative assessment. Expert-level feedback is needed, but how does it scale?

Methodology

The study began by synthesizing participant observation of the program and interviews with the program's instructors, administrators, and TAs. First, the participant observation consisted of retrospective analysis of three years of email exchanges on the challenges to scale and their solutions. This analysis traced a narrative from an initial emphasis on automated and peer grading to the ultimate redesign of the process of recruiting and hiring TAs at scale.

Second, interviews were conducted with the head TAs (13 individuals), and some professors (six individuals) via teleconference about the administration of each class and its reliance on TAs. Most of the head TAs were on-campus PhD students; thus, the level of expertise of the interview subjects was considerably higher than that of in-progress Master's students.

These interviews pointed to a need for continued involvement from traditional TAs. At the time of these interviews, online TAs had been hired, but sparingly. Based on the results of these interviews, we delivered a survey of the students applying to give feedback in the program, touching on their demographics, motivations, and experiences teaching in the program. This study covers the results of these interviews and surveys.

Program Background

The university's online Master's program launched in January 2014 with around 350 students, and has since grown to over 4,000 students. Three classes have graduated the program, and the average student should complete the program in three years. It is the largest such program in the United States, and has been projected to increase the annual output of Master's degrees in Computer Science by 8% [7].

Distinguishing Factors of the Online Program
While online Master's programs, and distance learning programs more generally, have been around for many years, this university's program differentiates itself in at least five significant ways [13]:

- Affordability. The entire degree costs around $7,000 [4], compared to $45,000 for out-of-state students in the residential program. Other online programs have tuitions comparable to residential tuition, e.g. Stanford's program costs approximately $63,000.

- Accessibility. Online programs naturally resolve issues of geographic accessibility, but this online program further resolves temporal accessibility by requiring no fully synchronous activities.

- Inclusivity. By removing the barriers of physical classrooms, the program can let in a greater percentage of applicants, providing opportunities to diverse groups of students who would not likely be selected with tighter space constraints.

- Custom-Built. Many programs use technology to copy processes used in person (like broadcasting live lectures), but this program constructed its courses from scratch to take advantage of the online medium.

- Accreditation. While the above factors apply to any MOOC, the key factor differentiating this online program its accreditation not only as a full Master's degree, but also as an identical degree to the residential program. There is no 'online' qualifier; the degree is the same as the one awarded on campus. This is bolstered by analysis showing that online students match or exceed residential students' performance on identical assignments [8].

These features create a unique pressure on this program: the low tuition creates a scarcity of resources with which to hire experts, but the accreditation demands a similar education and endorsement of graduates as the residential program.

Student Demographics: Anticipated Challenges to Scale
Traditionally, residential programs leverage TAs hired from the student body to support grading and feedback. To recreate the education and endorsement of residential graduates, using this same mechanism for expert feedback presents potential. Thus, to understand the challenges to scale, the demographics of the online students compared to the residential students are important. To evaluate this, some instructors begin their semesters with demographic surveys of their online and residential students.

Unsurprisingly, these surveys show dramatic differences between online and residential students. Online students are significantly older, with a median age of 38, compared to 23 among residential students. 29% of online students had previously obtained a Master's and 8% had previously obtained doctoral degrees, compared to 6% and 0%, respectively, among the residential students. Most notably, online students are far more likely to be employed: 90% reported full-time employment, compared to 5% for residential students. Finally, anecdotally, online students are far more likely to mention having children at home.

Based on these demographics and the listed tuition information, the strong hypothesis was that the online program could not scale by relying on online students the same way residential programs relied on residential students. First, the monetary incentive for online students to work as TAs is dramatically lower because residential students receive a full tuition waiver on top of their stipend. Second, the relative monetary incentive for online students is lower given their greater rate of full-time employment and existing career success. Third, the greater rate of employment and the observation that online students are more likely to support families raise the number of competing obligations; whereas residential TAs typically only balance taking classes with working as TAs, online students would also balance their family and work lives.

	Online Summer '15	On-Campus Fall '14
Median age	38	23
% previously obtaining a Master's degree	29%	6%
% previously obtaining a Doctoral degree	8%	0%
% working full-time	90%	5%
Estimated tuition per class	$510	$3,450
Estimated tuition per semester	$510	$13,800

Table 1. Demographic and tuition differences between online students in the Summer 2015 class and on-campus students in the Fall 2014 class. Online students take an average of one class per semester.

Given these observations, the assumption was that online students could not be relied upon to supply the necessary expert-level feedback; they have too many competing obligations and the financial incentive is too small. An alternative would be to hire residential students as TAs for online classes. However, it would take the entire tuitions of almost 40 online students to pay for the salary and tuition waiver of a single residential TA, and the residential program alone nearly exhausts the available TAs.

Realities of Scaling
This online program relied on residential students for TAs through the first year of the program, when it grew to around 2,000 students. This presented scaling challenges which threatened to escalate entering the summer of 2015 when most residential students leave for internships, leaving an even smaller body from which to draw.

Resolving Anticipated Challenges to Scale
Entering the summer 2015 semester, one class for the first time actively solicited teaching assistants from the online student body (two online teaching assistants had been hired for spring 2015 after they themselves expressed interest). The hypothesis remained that online students would not

work as TAs, but the hope was that even a couple additional applicants would help alleviate the load.

Instead, 57 online students applied to work as teaching assistants for the class, enough to potentially support 3,000 student enrollments in that class alone. 14% of all online students that had completed the class applied. 400 students enrolled, and 10 of the 57 teaching assistants were hired; not only were there sufficiently many applicants to scale the program, but that first semester of soliciting applicants from the online students, 80% were turned away because there were not enough positions. In the year since that experimental semester, hiring for this online program has shifted almost exclusively to online students, allowing the program to continue growing by 500 students per semester.

Pedagogical Benefits of Online Teaching Assistants
The presence of the actual numbers necessary to scale the program while maintaining expert feedback is only one part of the picture. Anecdotally, nearly every professor in the program has commented on the superior performance of online teaching assistants relative to residential ones. Through conversations around these students, this trend is likely attributed to two factors. First, as online students themselves, online teaching assistants are better positioned to understand the needs of their classmates.

Second and more remarkably, many of the online teaching assistants not only have significant professional experience, but specifically have experience in the classes they are assisting. A point has been raised that graduate teaching assistants are not "experts", but the prevalence of true experts among this body of teaching assistants is notable. The teaching assistants for the program's Educational Technology class, for example, have included an executive at a textbook publisher, two data analysts from EdTech companies, two college instructors at other schools, and a high school AP Computer Science teacher. A newly launched Human-Computer Interaction class was initially staffed by professional user experience designers and researchers from within the student body.

The expertise of these TAs far exceeds that of traditional teaching assistants. Even among more traditional former students, the number of applicants also allows professors to specifically choose the most highly-qualified former students to work as TAs in future offerings. In this way, scaling expert feedback has taken on two forms: maintaining the amount of expert feedback while increasing the size of the program, and increasing the expertise of the expert feedback through the scale and audience of the program.

Motivations of Online Teaching Assistants
The initial hypothesis was that online students would not work as teaching assistants due to low financial incentive and the more significant number of competing obligations. The justification of this hypothesis was true, but the conclusion was false; online students have applied to work

as teaching assistants in droves. There are three possible explanations for this: either (a) the online applicants are coming from the subset of students most similar to residential students, and the program size is sufficient for there to be many of them; (b) we were wrong about what motivates teaching assistants in general; or (c) online teaching assistants are motivated by different factors than residential teaching assistants.

Study Methodology

To investigate this, we performed a study of the applicants and teaching assistants who either applied to work or worked within the online program in 2016. A survey was administered asking a set of questions of all applicants, with a follow-up section asking questions specifically of those that were hired. Students were solicited to participate through the list of original applications to work in the program and the list of students that were ultimately hired. The survey was sent out twice: immediately following the combined application period for Summer and Fall 2016, and immediately following the application period for Spring 2017.

	Online Applicants	Residential Applicants
Age		
<25 years old	11%	65%
25 – 34 years old	48%	35%
35+ years old	40%	0%
First Language		
English	81%	49%
Other	19%	51%
Employment Status		
Employed full-time	86%	8%
Employed part-time	7%	13%
Not otherwise employed	7%	79%
Employment Area		
Tech Sector	78%	14%
Non-Tech Sector	14%	7%
Not Employed	7%	79%
# of Children at Home		
0	63%	96%
1-2	30%	2%
3+	7%	2%
Highest Prior Education		
Bachelor's	80%	91%
Master's	14%	9%
Doctoral	6%	0%
Prior Experience		
>5 Years Programming Experience	72%	59%
>2 Years Teaching Experience	46%	22%

Table 2. Demographic of applicants to work as teaching assistants in the online program. Employment status excludes employment as a teaching assistant.

234 applicants completed the survey: 136 during the first distribution, 97 during the second. 161 online students and

72 residential students completed the survey. Among these, 13 of the 72 residential students who replied were hired, while 54 of the 161 online students who replied were hired.

The survey was broken into three parts: a demographic and background survey, a motivations survey, and an experience survey. All students completed the first two portions; only those that were hired completed the third.

Demographic Comparison

To begin with, the survey evaluated the demographics the applicants for teaching assistant positions to check if the observed demographics of the online program carried over into the demographics of the applicants for teaching assistant positions more specifically. The full results of this survey are shown in Table 2.

The results of the demographic portion of the survey confirm that the general trends observed in the online body of students carry over to the applicants for teaching assistant positions. Both the raw values and the comparisons to the residential applicants mirror the comparisons between the general student bodies. This confirms that it is *not* the case that the online applicants are the subset of online students that is similar to the residential applicants.

Motivation Comparison

In the second section of the survey, applicants were asked to select their single primary motivation and multiple secondary motivations. 12 options were offered, as well as a free-response box. The 12 options were inspired by the literature on learner motivation in online courses [16], and were further developed through a pilot survey asking for purely open-ended responses. These responses were summarized and coded into the 12 provided to students. Options were displayed in random order. Table 3 reports the results of these questions; the first column 'Pri.' within each group is the percent of students within that group selecting that motivation as their single primary motivation, while the italicized second column 'Sec.' within each group is the percent of students within that group selecting that motivation as their primary or one of their secondary motivations. The motivations are grouped into three general categories: Extrinsic, Intrinsic, and Altruistic.

As noted, a free-response "other" option was also supplied. No responses to this box for primary motivations fell outside the 12 response categories provided; for secondary motivations, the free response replies that fell outside the 12 provided categories were: exploring academia (3 responses), exploring new challenges (1 response), exploring a teaching career (1 response), and general curiosity about the program's inner workings (1 response).Given the lesser financial incentive available to online teaching assistants, the shift in motivations is not surprising: with a lesser financial incentive, one would expect fewer applicants to be primarily motivated by the financial incentive.

	Online Applicants		Residential Applicants	
	Pri.	Sec.	Pri.	Sec.
To obtain a tuition waiver	0%	4%	53%	90%
To obtain the salary or stipend	9%	34%	1%	49%
Any Extrinsic	**9%**	**36%**	**54%**	**96%**
To improve my resume	8%	47%	3%	49%
To improve my teaching ability	11%	59%	4%	53%
To network with faculty	11%	53%	11%	49%
To network with classmates	4%	37%	1%	22%
To learn the material	19%	64%	10%	56%
Any Intrinsic	**53%**	**93%**	**29%**	**97%**
To help my classmates	8%	50%	11%	46%
To help the instructors	4%	39%	1%	32%
To improve the class	6%	46%	1%	38%
To use my professional experience	4%	38%	1%	38%
To help the online program	16%	70%	1%	17%
Any Altruistic	**38%**	**90%**	**17%**	**76%**

Table 3. Motivations of applicants to work as teaching assistants in the online program. The 'Pri.' column designates applicants' primary motivations, and the 'Sec.' column designates applicants' secondary motivations.

What *is* remarkable is that the number of applications from this body so dramatically increased *despite* the lacking financial incentive, and these data provides an explanation of why. Online teaching assistants were far more likely than residential teaching assistants to be primarily motivated intrinsically (53% to 29%) or altruistically (38% to 17%). While both groups shared near-universal rates of some intrinsic motivators, online teaching assistants were far less likely to possess an extrinsic motivator (36% to 96%) and notably more likely to possess an altruistic motivator (90% to 76%).

More specifically, these data also demonstrate the personal ownership these online students feel over the program, given the high incidence of applicants specifying 'To help the online program' as their primary (16%) or secondary (70%) motivation. These data also suggest online applicants use working as teaching assistants to break some of the isolation experience by online students, as indicated by the relatively high percentage noting 'To network with classmates' as a secondary motivation (37%) compared to residential applicants (22%).

Given these observations, we conclude that it is the case that online students retain different motivations for applying to work as teaching assistants than residential students. This finding on its own is unsurprising; however, when taken in combination with the significant number of applicants received from this audience, it provides guidance for ways to recruit and incentivize online students to help programs with high demands for expert feedback and endorsement.

Experience Comparison

As noted previously, 13 of the 72 residential respondents and 54 of the 161 online respondents to the survive were then hired to work as teaching assistants in the program. The final portion of the survey focused on their experience as teaching assistants. In this phase of the survey, there was relatively little difference between online and residential teaching assistants in terms of workload and responsibilities. Both primarily focused on manually grading assignments, projects, and exams, echoing the premise of this paper that the primary effect of this initiative is scaling expert feedback. Interestingly, residential teaching assistants reported a median workload per week of 12 hours, while online teaching assistants reported a median workload of 10 hours; this is notable because online teaching assistants are paid hourly, while residential teaching assistants are salaried with an assumption of 20 hours per week. If this ratio generalizes, this would cut the cost per teaching assistant even further.

As noted, anecdotally, most professors have noted superior engagement, ownership, and performance from online teaching assistants, although there are many exceptions. Generally, differing responsibilities make formal, direct comparisons difficult. However, one comparison corroborates these anecdotes. One class employed an all-residential teaching team one semester, and an all-online teaching team the next; the two teaching teams graded the same assignments, a set of six 1000-word essays. The all-online team gave an average of 130 words of feedback per assignment, while the residential team gave an average of 22 words per assignment. The least prolific online teaching assistant gave an average of twice as much feedback as the most prolific residential teaching assistant.

Conclusions of Study 1

This university's new online Master's program has, at a minimum, preserved the quantity of expert feedback while scaling an online Master's program to 4,000 students. Strong arguments can be made as well that the program has increased the volume and quality of that feedback in addition to merely preserving it with the growing program.

This growth has been made possible by an unanticipated audience of online students interested in giving back to the program as teaching assistants. The fact that these students are largely intrinsically or altruistically motivated is not on its own overly remarkable; many MOOC programs, such as Coursera's mentor program [26], have similarly noted similar student bodies. What makes this development in this online program notable is that this audience can actually support a fully accredited, rigorous, prestigious program with high standards for success. The program has relied on this audience to create a groundbreaking program [4] that preserves learning outcomes [8] and the student experience [13] while dramatically increasing size, affordability, and accessibility.

It is worth noting, as this is a case study, that there are questions as to the generalizability of these observations. As noted by the survey results, the vast majority of online applicants apply in part to help the program; this echoes a sense of ownership over the program. We hypothesize this comes from (a) the desire to participate with a revolutionary program [4], and, (b) a sense of gratitude toward an opportunity most students would not have otherwise had [13]. These motivations may not generalize in the same way to non-accredited programs, nor are they guaranteed to persist as programs like these become more common. Interestingly, however, this may also suggest that the accreditation and prestige of the program both dictates and resolves the need for increased expert-level feedback, as participating in that prestige may be part of students' motivations to help the program.

STUDY 2: AN INDUSTRY MICROCREDENTIAL
The second case study focuses on a for-profit online education provider that supplies project-based microcredential programs in fields like machine learning, virtual reality, and web development. Its programs generally offer students the opportunity to go at their own pace, paying a monthly subscription cost if they remain in the program. Most notably, the microcredential programs are entirely project-based, and typically feature open-ended, partially student-defined projects.

Unlike the university, the company's microcredential programs do not have the pressures of accreditation demanding the presence of expert-level feedback and endorsement. However, a similar pressure arises in a different form: the company offers a job guarantee for graduates from their programs in machine learning, web development, data analysis, and mobile development. With the promise that any learner completing the program would receive a job or their money would be refunded, the pressure to possess both authentic, project-based assessments and reliable endorsements of learner ability rose considerably. However, assessing and teaching through authentic, open-ended projects necessitated expert feedback.

Methodology
This case study emphasizes the mechanisms that give rise to this system of feedback and the results of the system in action. As such, the primary sources of information for this case study are the design documents of the system architecture and the data automatically generated during its regular use. In addition to evaluation of the design documents, three interviews were conducted via teleconference (notes taken by hand by the interviewer) with individuals involved in the system in some capacity: an engineer working on the system, a content developer creating content for the system, and a reviewer evaluating work through the system. These interviews focused on the goals of the system in achieving rapid, scalable, high-quality feedback. Although these interviews provided

valuable backdrop, the major takeaways below are the design of the system and the measurable results achieved.

Project Reviewer Infrastructure
Rather than rely on the traditional model of hiring on-staff teaching assistants to evaluate and give feedback on projects, the company instead developed a network model for providing expert reviews. This system leverages a distributed network of freelance project reviewers paid per project that they evaluated.

Training Project Reviewers
Project reviewers were drawn from three audiences: professionals working in the field, exemplary microcredential graduates, and course developers and managers that helped produce the programs in the first place. Once identified, new reviewers go through a training process. They participate in a general course on reviewing and giving feedback on projects, followed by some additional material specific to the field in which they will be reviewing, highlighting the type of feedback to give and the misconceptions to anticipate.

After the training course, prospective project reviewers are provided multiple sample projects to evaluate, and their evaluations are provided to a set of super-reviewers. These super-reviewers, themselves experienced project reviewers, give the prospective reviewers feedback on the degree to which the evaluation matched the evaluations expected (in both result and feedback), as well as what the strengths and weaknesses were of the feedback provided.

In this way, prospective project reviewers effectively participate as students in the review system, where their "projects" are reviews of others' projects. This plays two roles: not only does it provide the prospective reviewers with feedback to help ensure they align, both in quality and in conclusion, with the other reviewers, but it also allows them to experience the system from the student perspective.

Project Reviewing in Action
When a student in a microcredential program submits a project, the project becomes available on the dashboards for any reviewers approved to review that project. This process is instantaneous, a notable contrast to the traditional deadline- and batch-based grading methods used by many areas of higher education. This is afforded by the microcredential programs' self-paced nature.

Once a project appears on the dashboard to be reviewed, any certified reviewer can claim it. After claiming the project for review, the reviewer is supplied with the project itself (typically some source code with a written report or documentation), notes from the student, and a history of the project submission. In this way, reviewers can look at the historical submissions the student has made to evaluate the new submission in context. Reviewers were observed using this to comment on student progress specifically in the context of the progress that was already observed.

Projects are evaluated on a pass/fail basis across multiple criteria. For a project to pass, it must pass each individual criterion; if it does not, the reviewer provides feedback on what revisions will be necessary to meet the project's expectations.

Project Review Results

Four metrics are available for evaluating the success of this novel project review process: scale, turnaround time, learner satisfaction, and reviewer earnings.

Evaluation of the Project Reviewer System

First, the primary motivation of this system is to scale up the number of projects that can be evaluated. At time of writing, the project reviewer system described here is processing approximately 650 projects per day. Thus, in terms of scale, this system appears successful, reviewing an average of a project every two minutes.

Second, research shows that the speed at which feedback is received is a significant determinate of learning outcomes [3, 18]. This has presented a challenge for traditional deadline-based models of education because evaluation tends to wait until the deadline has passed, regardless of how far in advance of the deadline an individual submits their assignment. After a deadline has passed, it would typically take at least a day for the batch of feedback to be processed, if not far higher. Given that this project reviewer infrastructure is always-available and the microcredential programs themselves lack deadlines, these constraints are absent. Thus, a second metric for evaluating the system's effectiveness turns up similarly positive results: the median turnaround time for a project review is 92 minutes. Under this mechanism, a student could conceivably complete multiple iterations of a project in a single day, complete with expert feedback. Further research will evaluate the prevalence of this rapid revision.

Third, although student satisfaction does not guarantee positive learning outcomes, it nonetheless provides a glimpse into the learners' impressions of the system. Learners within this system are asked to meta-review each review they receive out of 5 points. The average rating assigned to reviews that are received is 4.9. This infrastructure also allows auditing of project reviewers if multiple subpar reviews are received.

Thus, this project review system generates many reviews rapidly that satisfy learners. The university covered in the first case study found similar results, but without a heavy financial incentive. Although no survey has yet been performed on the project reviewers within this company's system, we hypothesize the motivations in this case *are* extrinsic. First, the intrinsic or altruistic incentives present in the university's program do not appear to generalize here: there are no professors with whom to network, the project reviewers do not heavily collaborate with one another, and we do not see the same signs of a sense of ownership over the program among the company's project reviewers as we see in the university's teaching assistants. Second, the financial incentive in this company's project reviewer system is very significant; the top-paid project reviewer currently earns over $4,500 per week. This heavy earning potential creates a strong incentive to maintain high quality, given the threat of competition.

Pedagogical Benefits

It is worth noting that the metrics described above do not directly capture the learners' learning processes. That learners are satisfied with their reviews does not guarantee positive learning outcomes, and nor does rapid feedback guarantee quality feedback. The metrics demonstrate successful accomplishment of scale, but these metrics do not directly capture learning outcomes. For this, we analyzed more theoretically the pedagogy that results from this review system. Follow-up analyses will examine the prevalence of revision and the workflows involved therein.

In practice, several pedagogical benefits were observed emerging out of this system. First, research has shown that the speed with which feedback is received has a strong connection to learning; rapid feedback leads to better, more rapid learning [3, 18]. This project reviewing framework facilitates rapid feedback, as demonstrated by the 90-minute median turnaround time between submission and receipt of evaluation. That rapid feedback cycle is further enhanced by the second pedagogical benefit, the opportunity for revision. Rather than receiving a grade and moving on as is common in many learning environments, learners participating with this project review system can iterate on and improve their solutions. The strength of the rapid feedback cycle becomes even more pertinent because the feedback is directly applied to a revision of the same work.

These pedagogical benefits also enhance the positive effect seen from other elements of the programs' structures. For example, the self-paced nature of these programs removes the high-stakes grades, allowing learners the opportunity to iterate more naturally without the heavy extrinsic pressure of grades and deadlines. Additionally, and especially pertinent for the fields these programs address, the notion of iterating over a project is authentic to the domain. Learners thus learn the metacognitive knowledge involved in evaluation and revision that is similarly part of the domain skillset they are developing.

Conclusions of Study 2

Where the university described in the first study scaled up its enrollment while preserving the involvement of experts by relying on a shift in motivations to maintain a traditional system, the company here in the second study instead opts for a radically different system. Rather than traditional teaching teams under the direction of a single faculty member, this company uses a distributed network of on-demand project reviewers. This system has proved successful in dramatically increasing the number of projects evaluated daily, while introducing additional pedagogical benefits as well.

As with the first study, however, there are questions as to the generalizability of this second study. First, part of the flexibility to design a system like this comes from the company's non-academic nature; it is not governed by details of FERPA and other regulations, allowing more freedom to select its evaluators. Secondly, this type of system does rely on the presence of an existing body of experts capable of evaluating projects. Moreover, it relies on the ability to provide a sufficient financial incentive to such a body to have them contribute to reviewing projects. These challenges may threaten the ability of a system like the one described here to generalize to academic environments or other content domains.

CONCLUSION

These case studies do not aim to argue that expert feedback is "better" than the scalable feedback mechanisms used in other online programs, like automated feedback, peer feedback, and implicit feedback. Indeed, the academic program reviewed in this paper leverages all four types of feedback in its offering, and removing any one of these four would have detrimental effects. It is also worth noting that the importance of expert-level feedback is derived from the demands of public perception and documented weaknesses in alternative feedback methods; however, this analysis does not attempt to present evidence of superior learning gains from expert-level feedback compared to other methods. If it is the case that other feedback methods may present the same learning gains, then expert-level feedback may itself be unnecessary.

If expert-level feedback has value, however, there are three primary takeaways from these case studies. First, whether in accredited academic programs or in vocational industry programs, there remain pressures to supply expert-level feedback and reliable endorsement of graduates' abilities. Solely relying on automated, peer, or implicit feedback presents challenges to the pedagogy and perception of these programs. Even setting aside most common criticisms of these methods, these methods all struggle with providing expert-level, targeted, individualized feedback on open-ended projects at scale. This struggle presents a problem for programs that experience significant pressure to retain open-ended, authentic projects, expert-level feedback, and reliable endorsement.

To facilitate scale, many programs have dropped expert-level feedback altogether, and there exists a strong argument that the additional accessibility and affordability justify that loss. However, this paper shows two similar methods that have been successful at increasing scale while retaining expert-level feedback. The second takeaway of these case studies, then, is that it is possible – at least for now – to rely on the documented unique motivations of online students in these innovative programs to maintain or increase the amount of expert-level feedback while retaining a traditional structure, even as the financial incentives become several times less lucrative. The third

takeaway is that it is also possible to develop an entirely alternative model, based not around traditional teaching assistants but rather around a distributed network of reviewers, that radically increases the rate of feedback while preserving the ability to offer authentic projects in a highly affordable program. Both these methods are worth exploring in other domains and programs.

Taken all together, this analysis argues that there remains a need to have expert evaluation in high-stakes (accredited or otherwise guaranteed) programs. We have documented two options for this: One, maintaining the traditional model dictates that the financial incentives for traditional teaching assistants will be lower, but the shifting motivations of online students are sufficient to provide a strong pool of experts nonetheless. Two, throwing out the traditional model, it is possible to leverage a more agile distributed workforce to provide rapid expert feedback on open-ended projects while preserving affordability. These two methods cover some of the space surrounding scaling expert feedback; other methods that may be explored include relying strictly on a volunteer model (such as Coursera's mentorship program [26]). Given the role of altruistic and implicit motivations in scaling expert feedback, scale through a purely volunteer model may be possible if the necessary accountability can be duplicated while preserving these motivations.

REFERENCES

1. Aleven, V., Mclaren, B. M., Sewall, J., & Koedinger, K. R. (2009). A new paradigm for intelligent tutoring systems: Example-tracing tutors. *International Journal of Artificial Intelligence in Education, 19*(2), 105-154.

2. Boud, D., Cohen, R., & Sampson, J. (2001). *Peer Learning in Higher Education: Learning from & with Each Other*. Psychology Press.

3. Butler, D. L., & Winne, P. H. (1995). Feedback and self-regulated learning: A theoretical synthesis. *Review of educational research, 65*(3), 245-281.

4. Carey, K. (2016, October 5). Georgia Tech's $7,000 Online Master's Degree Could Start a Revolution. *New York Times*, pp. A15.

5. Falchikov, N., & Goldfinch, J. (2000). Student peer assessment in higher education: A meta-analysis comparing peer and teacher marks. *Review of Educational Research, 70*(3), 287-322.

6. Geigle, C., Zhai, C., & Ferguson, D. C. (2016, April). An Exploration of Automated Grading of Complex Assignments. In *Proceedings of the Third (2016) ACM Conference on Learning @ Scale* (pp. 351-360). ACM.

7. Goodman, J., Melkers, J., & Pallais, A. (2016). Can Online Delivery Increase Access to Education? HKS Faculty Research Working Paper Series RWP16-035.

8. Goel, A. & Joyner, D. A. (2016a). An Experiment in Teaching Cognitive Systems Online. In Haynes, D.

(Ed.) *International Journal for Scholarship of Technology-Enhanced Learning 1*(1).

9. Goel, A. & Joyner, D. (2016b). *Formative Assessment and Implicit Feedback in Online Learning.* Presentation, Learning with MOOCs III.

10. Hext, J. B., & Winings, J. W. (1969). An automatic grading scheme for simple programming exercises. *Communications of the ACM, 12*(5), 272-275.

11. Jensen, J. C., Lee, E. A., & Seshia, S. A. (2013, April). Virtualizing cyber-physical systems: Bringing CPS to online education. In *Proc. First Workshop on CPS Education (CPS-Ed).*

12. Joyner, D. A., Ashby, W., Irish, L., Lam, Y., Langston, J., Lupiani, I., ... & Bruckman, A. (2016, April). Graders as Meta-Reviewers: Simultaneously Scaling and Improving Expert Evaluation for Large Online Classrooms. In *Proceedings of the Third (2016) ACM Conference on Learning @ Scale* (pp. 399-408). ACM.

13. Joyner, D. A., Goel, A., & Isbell, C. (2016). The Unexpected Pedagogical Benefits of Making Higher Education Accessible. In *Proceedings of the Third (2016) ACM Conference on Learning @ Scale.* ACM.

14. Kendall, K., & Schussler, E. (2012). Does instructor type matter? Undergraduate student perception of graduate teaching assistants and professors. *CBE-Life Sciences Education, 11*(2), 187-199.

15. Kirschner, P., Sweller, J., & Clark, R. (2006). Why minimal guidance during instruction does not work: An analysis of the failure of constructivist, discovery, problem-based, experiential, and inquiry-based teaching. *Educational Psychologist, 41*(2), 75-86.

16. Kizilcec, R. F., & Schneider, E. (2015). Motivation as a lens to understand online learners: Toward data-driven design with the OLEI scale. *ACM Transactions on Computer-Human Interaction (TOCHI), 22*(2), 6.

17. Kolhe, P., Littman, M. L., & Isbell, C. L. (2016, April). Peer Reviewing Short Answers using Comparative Judgement. In *Proceedings of the Third (2016) ACM Conference on Learning @ Scale* (pp. 241-244). ACM.

18. Kulkarni, C., Bernstein, M. S., & Klemmer, S. (2015). PeerStudio: Rapid Peer Feedback Emphasizes Revision and Improves Performance. In *Proceedings from The Second ACM Conference on Learning @ Scale.* ACM.

19. Lu, Y., Warren, J., Jermaine, C., Chaudhuri, S., & Rixner, S. (2015, May). Grading the Graders: Motivating Peer Graders in a MOOC. In *Proceedings of the 24th International Conference on World Wide Web* (pp. 680-690). ACM.

20. Lundstrom, K., & Baker, W. (2009). To give is better than to receive: The benefits of peer review to the reviewer's own writing. *Journal of Second Language Writing, 18*(1), 30-43.

21. Murray, T., Blessing, S., & Ainsworth, S. (2003). Authoring tools for advanced technology learning environments: Toward cost-effective adaptive, interactive and intelligent educational software. Springer Science & Business Media.

22. Polson, M. C., & Richardson, J. J. (2013). *Foundations of intelligent tutoring systems.* Psychology Press.

23. Raman, K., & Joachims, T. (2015). Bayesian Ordinal Peer Grading. In *Proceedings from The Second ACM Conference on Learning @ Scale.* ACM. 149-156.

24. Renkl, A. (2002). Worked-out examples: Instructional explanations support learning by self-explanations. *Learning and Instruction, 12*(5), 529-556.

25. Salzmann, C., Gillet, D., & Piguet, Y. (2016, February). MOOLs for MOOCs: A first edX scalable implementation. In *2016 13th International Conference on Remote Engineering and Virtual Instrumentation (REV)* (pp. 246-251). IEEE.

26. Saraf, K. & Smith, C. (2016, October 5). "Coursera's superheroes: Meet the Mentor team." *Coursera Blog.* Retrieved from coursera.tumblr.com/post/151389966612/

27. Srikant, S., & Aggarwal, V. (2014, August). A system to grade computer programming skills using machine learning. In *Proceedings of the 20th ACM International Conference on Knowledge Discovery and Data Mining* (pp. 1887-1896). ACM.

28. VanLehn, K. (2006). The behavior of tutoring systems. *International Journal of Artificial Intelligence in Education, 16*(3), 227-265.

29. VanLehn, K. (2011). The relative effectiveness of human tutoring, intelligent tutoring systems, and other tutoring systems. *Educational Psychologist, 46*(4), 197-221.

30. Van Gog, T., & Rummel, N. (2010). Example-based learning: Integrating cognitive and social-cognitive research perspectives. *Educational Psychology Review, 22*(2), 155-174.

31. Van Zundert, M., Sluijsmans, D., & Van Merriënboer, J. (2010). Effective peer assessment processes: Research findings and future directions. *Learning and Instruction, 20*(4), 270-279.

32. Vogelsang, T., & Ruppertz, L. (2015, March). On the validity of peer grading and a cloud teaching assistant system. In *Proceedings of the Fifth International Conference on Learning Analytics and Knowledge* (pp. 41-50). ACM.

33. Yaron, D., Karabinos, M., Lange, D., Greeno, J. G., & Leinhardt, G. (2010). The ChemCollective—virtual labs for introductory chemistry courses. *Science, 328*(5978), 584-585.

Gradescope: a Fast, Flexible, and Fair System for Scalable Assessment of Handwritten Work

Arjun Singh
Gradescope, Inc.
Berkeley, CA
arjun@gradescope.com

Sergey Karayev
Gradescope, Inc.
Berkeley, CA
sergey@gradescope.com

Kevin Gutowski
Gradescope, Inc.
Berkeley, CA
kevin@gradescope.com

Pieter Abbeel
UC Berkeley
Berkeley, CA
pabbeel@cs.berkeley.edu

ABSTRACT

We present a system for online assessment of handwritten homework assignments and exams. First, either instructors or students scan and upload handwritten work. Instructors then grade the work and distribute the results using a web-based platform. Our system optimizes for three key dimensions: speed, consistency, and flexibility. The primary innovation enabling improvements in all three dimensions is a dynamically evolving rubric for each question on an assessment. We also describe how the system minimizes the overhead incurred in the digitization process. Our system has been in use for four years, with instructors at 200 institutions having graded over 10 million pages of student work. We present results as user-reported data and feedback regarding time saved grading, enjoyment, and student experience. Two-thirds of responders report saving 30% or more time relative to their traditional workflow. We also find that the time spent grading an individual response to a question rapidly decays with the number of responses to that question that the grader has already graded.

Author Keywords

education; learning assessment; rubric-based grading; computer-assisted instruction; scaling large courses

INTRODUCTION

Over the past few years, course sizes have gone up significantly at many higher education institutions. Although there have been many recent innovations in teaching that aim to help scale up courses (e.g. MOOCs), there are two primary components involved in teaching that are difficult to scale.

The first is personal interaction with instructors and tutors. The second is fair, informative assessment of student work without compromising on question quality. This is our focus.

Assessing student work is one of the most tedious and time consuming aspects of teaching. It is also one of the most important, being a primary feedback mechanism for students. One solution to scaling course sizes is to simply give assessments that can be graded automatically, such as multiple choice exams. Although these assessments can be valuable, there are many concepts that are better assessed by free response questions than multiple choice questions. Our system allows instructors to use exactly the same questions in a 1000 student course that they would in a 25 student course, and grade them quickly and consistently.

The primary benefits of our system are:

1. **Speed:** most users report that their grading is sped up by a third, versus paper-based grading.

2. **Consistency:** most users report they are able to grade more fairly while helping students learn from mistakes and providing transparency in grading.

3. **Flexibility:** users can modify rubrics as they encounter new mistakes, or revise earlier evaluations.

Our system is publicly available[1] and has been used in over two thousand higher-ed courses.

In this paper, we first give an overview of related work in Section 2. We then describe the system in detail in Section 3, and provide results for how the system performs in Section 4. Lastly, we discuss future work and share concluding thoughts in Section 5 and Section 6.

RELATED WORK

Grading assignments has always been a major pain point and bottleneck of instruction, especially in large courses and in distance education. The challenges of scaling grading are two-fold. The more students there are, the more graders are needed

---

[1] https://gradescope.com

Current Submission   Rubric

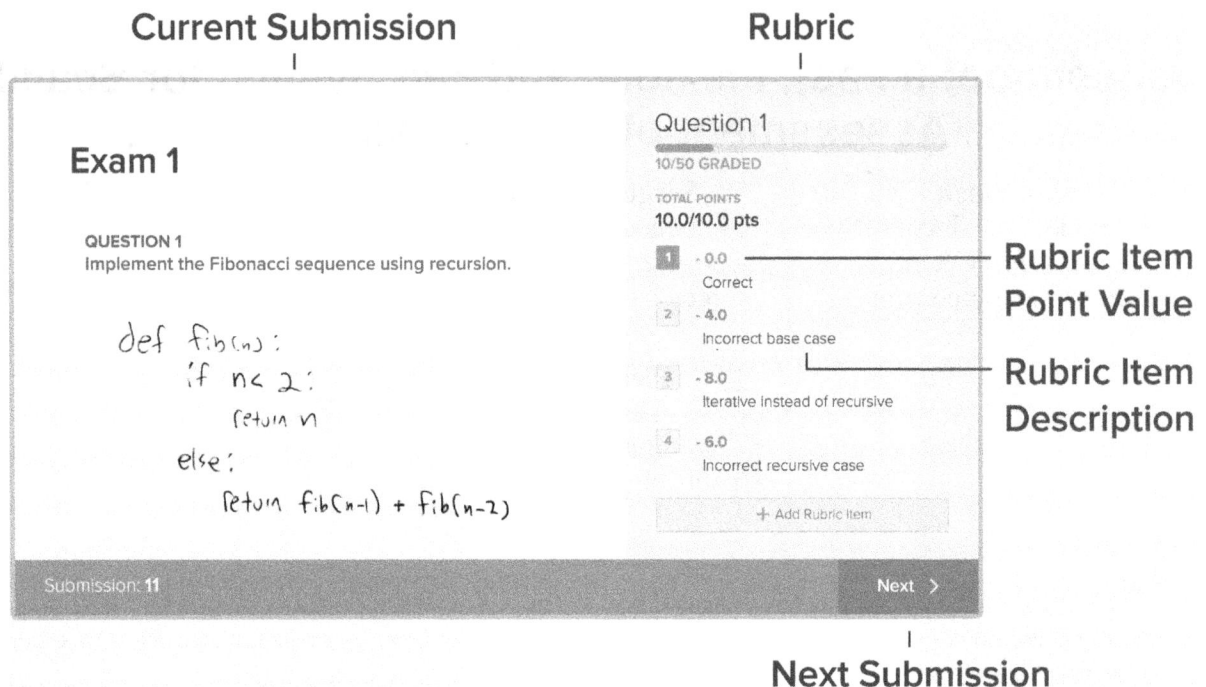

Figure 1: Our system's grading interface, simplified slightly and annotated for publication. On the left, the grader sees a single student's submission to the question they're grading. On the right, they see the rubric, composed of multiple rubric items that each have point values and descriptions. When finished grading, graders navigate to the next submission for the same question.

to deliver feedback in a timely manner. But the more graders are involved, the less consistent grading tends to become.

Automating assessment is one answer to the problem. There is a body of work aiming to automate more parts of computer science, engineering, and writing assessment. For computer science courses, focus has been on autograding of programming projects [11, 8, 3] and automated plagiarism detection [14]. For general engineering courses, notable new efforts include automatic grading of engineering drawings [10]. For grading essays and other student writing, software such as Canvas Speedgrader exists for entirely manual scoring, and both research and commercial systems for autograding have existed for over a decade [18, 4].

However, there are only a few systems focused on grading paper-based work. The one most similar to our system is a tablet-based paper exam grading (T-Pegs) system described by Bloomfield and Groves in 2008 [2]. Bloomfield described improvements to this system in 2010 [1]. In the original system, graders simply assigned a point value to each page in the scan. In the followup, the system was extended to allow graders to give a point value for each question, along with some textual feedback.

Park and Hagen [12] describe a fax-based system for managing large quantities of work being graded by hand on paper in a distance education setting. Schneider [15] describes a system for grading handwritten homework, in which students upload scans of their work to be graded. Instructors of a large business course also report their initial experiments with online marking of scanned assesments [5].

Our system has much in common with these: student work is scanned in and then digitally assessed, and graders can be in any physical location, and can grade in parallel. However, we have several key differentiators from work listed above:

1. We allow a much richer form of feedback due to the rubric. Rather than giving a single score with a bit of text as feedback, students are graded on a rubric, enabling transparency and consistency. Rubric-based grading, including sharing of the rubric with students, has been shown to both increase inter-grader reliability and improve student educational outcomes [17, 16, 13, 9].

2. We do not require the exams to be preprocessed in any way. An instructor can grade exams with our system without modifying their existing exams. Systems described in [1, 5] require exams to have special frontmatter sections in order to match scans with students.

3. We support both exams and homework in a single system.

4. We allow students to securely view their work online, potentially as soon as grading is completed. Prompt delivery of informative feedback on the student's work has been shown to increase learning in students [7].

5. Instructors can choose to allow students to submit regrade requests directly to their graders, to cut down on time spent during office hours on such requests.

6. We automatically expose detailed statistics to instructors, including which mistakes were made most frequently on every question on an assessment.

SYSTEM DETAILS

In this section, we describe our system in detail. First, we explain how to set up an assessment for grading. Next, we discuss how we minimize the overhead associated with scanning and digitizing students' paper assignments. We then describe the grading process, including the dynamic rubrics. We explain how students can view their graded work and request clarifications. Lastly, we describe how the system enables instructors to analyze their students' performance.

Setup

Assignments are generally one of two types: (1) worksheet-style, fixed-length assignments in which every student writes on a template and submits the same number of pages, and (2) variable-length assignments, in which students might be asked to answer questions out of a textbook and use an arbitrary number of pages.

Our system supports both types of assignments effectively. However, for clarity of explanation, we will assume that the instructor has a fixed-length assignment. We will describe the process for an exam (as opposed to a homework assignment), such that it is the instructors responsibility to digitize the students' work.

In order to optimize the workflow for a worksheet-style exam, the instructor first uploads a *template* of their exam, and then sets up the *assignment outline*. The template is simply a blank PDF of the exam. The assignment outline consists of the list of questions on the assignment, their point values, and the region on the template that corresponds to each question. They select the regions by drawing boxes on the exam, as shown in Figure 2. They also draw a box around the region where students write their name on the exam, which allows the instructor to quickly label each exam with a student, as described in Section 3.2.2.

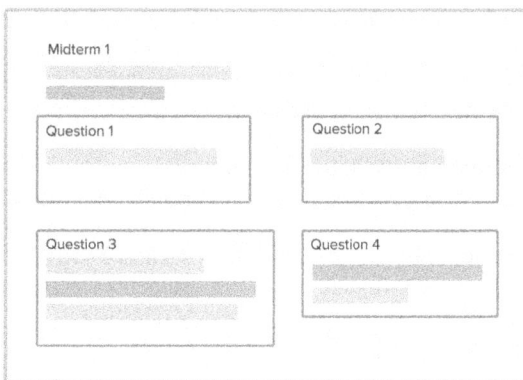

Figure 2: When creating the assignment outline, the user draws boxes corresponding to where on the page the student writes their responses to each question.

Scanning

One important constraint that we built into our system is that exams did not need to be altered in order to be graded online. Other systems, such as described in [1], require the exams to be preprocessed with bubble sections, QR codes, or other markers. For our system, the pre-exam workflow is exactly identical to grading on paper.

After the students write their answers on the exam template and return their work to the instructor, the exams have to be scanned and associated with the students. This is the largest upfront cost of our system. We reduce the time spent in this step of digitizing the exams in two ways.

Scanning in Batches

First, we allow instructors to scan the exams in batches. This can dramatically reduce the amount of time a scanner is sitting idle, waiting to be fed with the next exam. The system then automatically suggests how to split the batch into individual exams, as shown in Figure 3. The user is able to confirm that the split is correct, or merge, rearrange, or reorder pages.

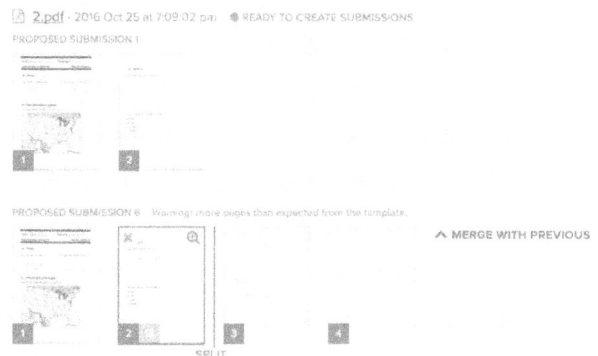

Figure 3: Screenshot of the scan splitting interface. The user is able to confirm that the split is correct, or alter the proposed split.

Assigning Names

We make the name assignment step fast, without automating it. This leads to a far lower error rate in name assignment than that shown by some of the automated systems [1]. In order to minimize time spent on this step, we show only the part of the page with the student's name on it, and autocomplete based on the roster, as shown in Figure 4.

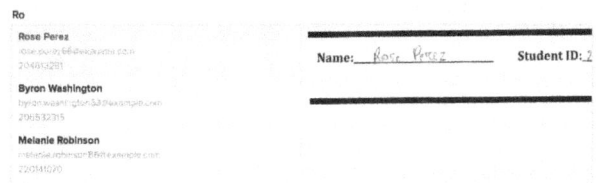

Figure 4: Screenshot of the submission naming interface. We show the area of the scan where the students write their names, and then autocomplete what the user has typed against the course roster.

Grading With a Rubric

Once the exam is set up and the scans are uploaded and split into submissions, users can start grading. Naming submissions is not required prior to grading. Graders can grade different responses to the same question (the system ensures that graders do not evaluate the same student) – or they can grade different questions altogether. They are able to grade in parallel, and they do not need to be in the same physical location.

The grading interface is shown in Figure 1. It consists of a single student's answer to a single question, as well as a *rubric* that is built up as the instructor grades.

The rubric is composed of one or more *rubric items*. Each rubric item has a point value and a description associated with it, as illustrated in Figure 5. The rubric can be subtractive (rubric items correspond to point deductions, or mistakes), or additive (rubric items correspond to point additions), and it can have a point value floor and ceiling. For clarity, we assume that the rubric is subtractive in this paper.

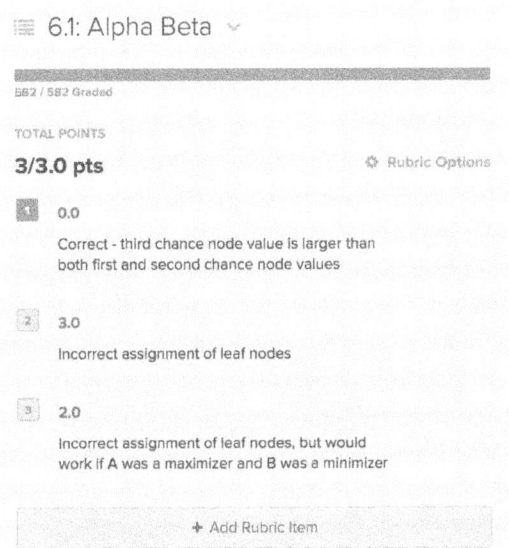

Figure 5: Screenshot of a rubric. The first item in the rubric is applied to this particular student, and the student received full credit.

One of the most common grading workflows is detailed below:

1. Look at the student answer and find any mistakes made.

2. If there are new types of mistakes that aren't yet in the rubric, create rubric items for each new type of mistake.

3. Apply each rubric item corresponding to each mistake made by the student.

4. Go to the next ungraded student answer *for the same question*.

5. Repeat steps 1-4 until this question is graded, and then move to the next question.

One important attribute of the system is that the rubric is *dynamic*. As graders find new types of mistakes, they can add new rubric items to the rubric. Furthermore, if a grader realizes that the point value associated with a rubric item should be changed, they can do so, and our system will retroactively update the grades given to all previous students for that question according to the updated rubric. This process is illustrated in Figure 6.

Although graders can build rubrics and grade work in any order, the above workflow has a few key benefits. First, it allows graders to focus on a single question at a time. Rather than needing to understand the rubric for all questions on the exam, they only need to worry about the question they are grading. Second, it helps enforce consistency: if all new mistakes are added to the rubric as they are seen, then graders can be confident that each instance of a mistake had the correct number of points deducted.

Additional grading features
Although the bulk of grading actions on our platform occur via the rubric, there are two more ways to provide feedback to students while grading: comments and free-form annotation of the scan. The grader is always able to leave a comment on a student submission that is only visible to that student. This feature is useful when, for example, an answer is wrong in a singular way that does not merit inclusion in the rubric. Alongside the comment, the grader can adjust the total score however they would like. Additionally, the grader can annotate the scan area with a free-form pen tool, which is especially useful when grading on a touch-screen or tablet device.

Analysis of Student Performance
In addition to simply saving a significant amount of time, digital grading enables analysis of student performance that is quite tedious with traditional paper-based grading. We can track per-assignment and per-question statistics, as the Bloomfield system also does [1]. In addition to this basic level of analysis, we additionally enable rubric-level statistics.

Because grading is done using a rubric in our system, instructors are able to see exactly *which* mistakes were made most often by students in our rubric-level statistics view (see Figure 7). This kind of analysis is nearly impossible with traditional paper-based grading, and it can give valuable insight into specific misconceptions that students developed.

Distribution of Work to Students
Once satisfied with how the exam is graded, the instructor can securely return the work to the students with a single click. In accordance with privacy regulations such as FERPA, students only have access to their own work. Students can see the scan of their exam and their score on every question.

By default, students can see which entries in the rubric applied to their answer, as well as the rest of the rubric. This allows them to understand all of the ways students could earn or lose points on the question. Although this is the default, the instructor can choose to limit student visibility of the rubric to either nothing or only applied items. Furthermore, the instructor is able to see whether each graded submission has been reviewed by the student.

Handling Regrade Requests
Often, students will have questions or feel that mistakes have been made in grading their work. With paper-based grading,

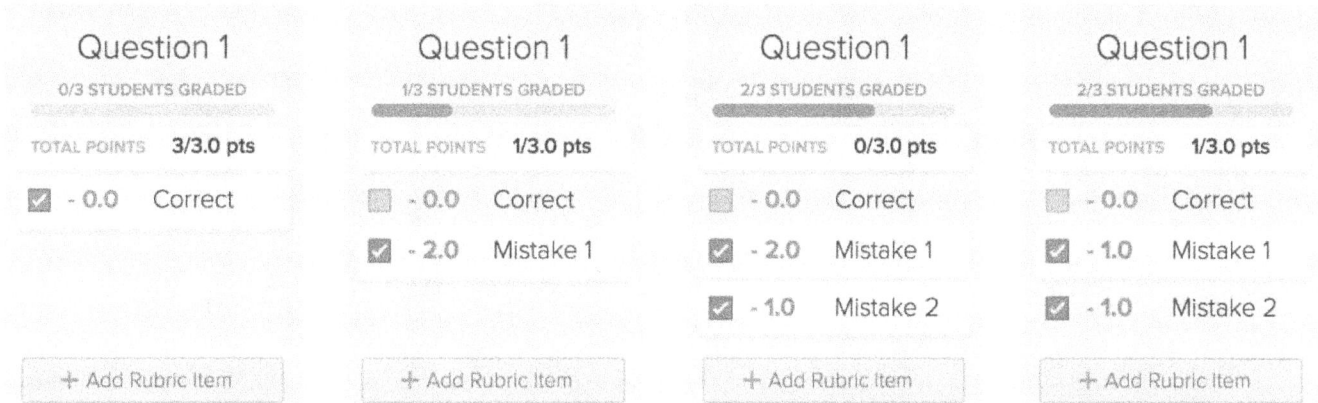

Figure 6: Illustration of the dynamic rubric. At first, the rubric contains only a single item. When a grader finds a new mistake, they add an item to the rubric. More than one rubric item may be applied to the same student's answer. The point value of any rubric item can be adjusted at any time, and the system will retroactively update the score assigned to any previously graded answers.

Figure 7: Screenshot of rubric statistics. Each rubric item is shown, along with its point value and the percentage of student answers it was applied to.

this typically leads to an unwieldy process, in which a student will email a request to their instructor and/or show up at their office hours. In large classes, the instructor they interact with is often not the person who graded that student's response. Getting the request into the hands of the correct grader often takes several days, leading to a long turnaround time for the student.

Our system tracks which grader graded each student's answer, and will notify the grader when a student requests a regrade. The status of each request is centrally tracked, so the instructor can confirm whether all outstanding requests have been handled. The student is also notified when a request is handled.

RESULTS
We analyze our system in two ways: a user survey, and statistics about usage.

Survey Results
We asked a series of questions to our instructor user base in 2014, consisting of faculty and teaching assistants. We report the detailed survey results in Tables 1 through 7. The majority of users agree or strongly agree that the system helps them grade more fairly, faster, and more enjoyably. Additionally, the majority of users agree or strongly agree that the system

simplified the regrade request process and helped students learn from the feedback.

To quantify the time savings of our system, we asked "How much time do you save grading with our system versus grading on paper?" As reported in Table 7, 67% of the users said that they cut down grading time by at least 30%.

Strongly Agree	**32 (46.4%)**
Agree	23 (33.3%)
Neutral	12 (17.4%)
Disagree	2 (2.9%)
Strongly Disagree	0 (0%)

Table 1: Does the system help you grade more fairly?

Strongly Agree	**42 (60.9%)**
Agree	18 (26.1%)
Neutral	4 (5.8%)
Disagree	4 (5.8%)
Strongly Disagree	1 (1.4%)

Table 2: Does the system save you time in grading?

Strongly Agree	18 (26.9%)
Agree	**22 (32.8%)**
Neutral	20 (29.9%)
Disagree	4 (6%)
Strongly Disagree	3 (4.5%)

Table 3: Does the system make grading more enjoyable?

Data Analysis
Our system has been used at over 200 different schools to grade over 10 million pages of student work. As shown in Figure 8, course sizes on our platform range from typical K-12 sizes of 20-30 students per course to over 1700 students in our largest course.

Strongly Agree	28 (41.2%)
Agree	22 (32.4%)
Neutral	8 (11.8%)
Disagree	9 (13.2%)
Strongly Disagree	1 (1.5%)

Table 4: Does the system simplify regrade requests?

Strongly Agree	12 (17.6%)
Agree	31 (45.6%)
Neutral	19 (27.9%)
Disagree	5 (7.4%)
Strongly Disagree	1 (1.5%)

Table 5: Does the displayed rubric help your students learn more from their mistakes?

Strongly Agree	26 (38.2%)
Agree	30 (44.1%)
Neutral	10 (14.7%)
Disagree	2 (2.9%)
Strongly Disagree	0 (0%)

Table 6: Does the system offer transparency to my students about the grading scheme?

Time saved vs. traditional grading	% of users
> 10%	91%
> 20%	88%
> 30%	67%
> 40%	49%
> 50%	40%
> 60%	19%
> 70%	12%
> 80%	7%
> 90%	3%

Table 7: How much time do you save grading with the system?

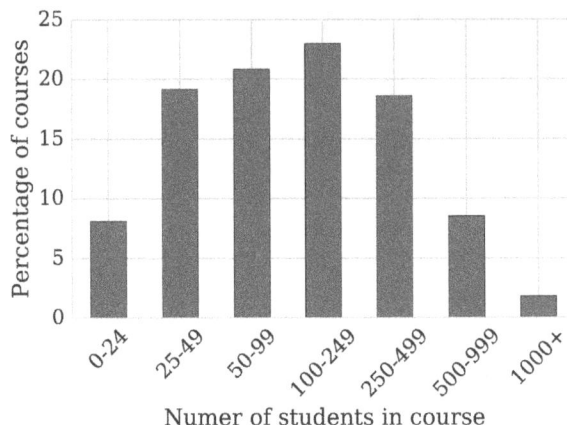

Figure 8: Percentage of courses in our system by number of students in the course.

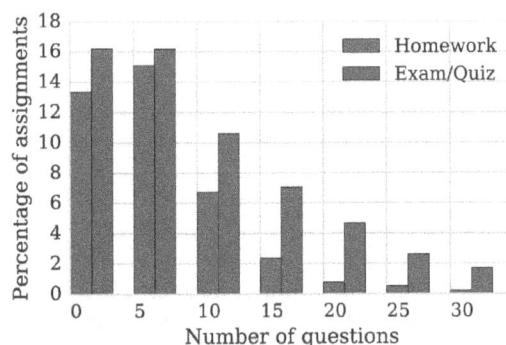

Figure 9: Histogram of the number of questions per assignment.

Assignments on our platform range from just a question or two to over 30 questions, as shown in Figure 9. Exams and quizzes (instructor-scanned assignments) tend to have more questions than homework (student-scanned assignments). Very few questions on our platform have been of the multi-page essay type.

Rubric usage statistics
For this analysis, we look at questions with at least 40 graded submissions.

First, we examine how instructors set up question rubrics: do they use the rubric to mark different types of mistakes, thereby providing feedback, or do they essentially ignore this feature of our system, and simply mark "correct/incorrect"?

Figure 10 shows that most questions average 5.6 rubric items, with standard deviation of 3.9. The median number of rubric items is 5. There are no meaningful differences in these statistics between subtractive and additive rubrics. More questions have 8 or more rubric items than have 2 or less. This shows

that instructors choose to give more detailed feedback than simply marking correct or incorrect, and that they do this for both additive and subtractive rubrics.

Grading time per submission
Second, we examine the relationship between time spent grading the average student answer and the number of student answers already graded. If the dynamic rubric works as described, then time per answer should go down with more and more answers graded.

For this plot, we look at a random set of 100 courses in Computer Science subjects in which our system was used for at least 2 assignments, each with at least 50 students. There are 596 assignments composed of 7,710 questions assessed in these courses. The vast majority of the questions (6,258) were graded by one person – but some questions were graded by many people (as many as 17 for one question).

Figure 11 shows that time spent per student answer rapidly decays with number of answers graded. Some details for this plot are in order. "Grading time" is measured as the interval between successive grading actions, per grader per question. Intervals of more than ten minutes are filtered out, as they

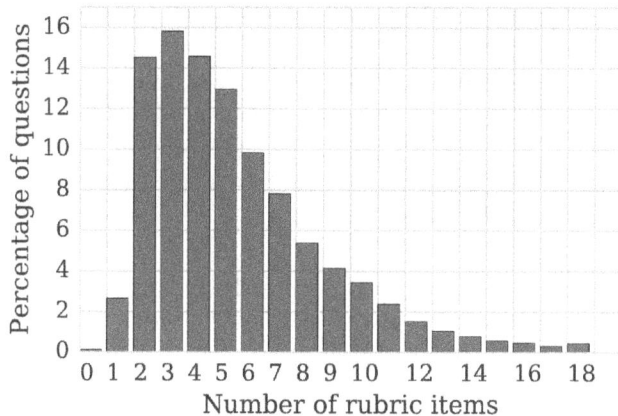

Figure 10: Histogram of the number of rubric items per question.

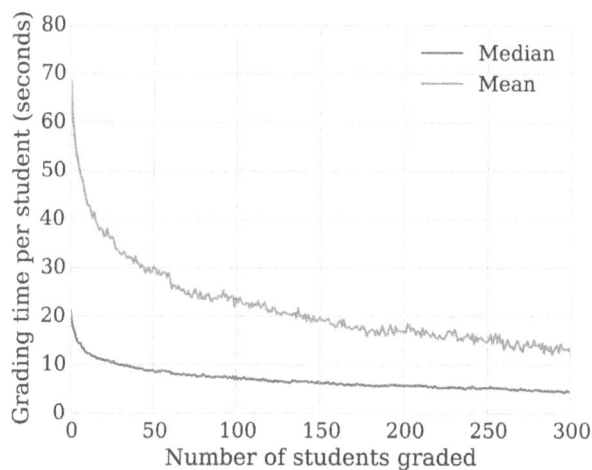

Figure 11: Time spent grading each submission vs number of graded submissions.

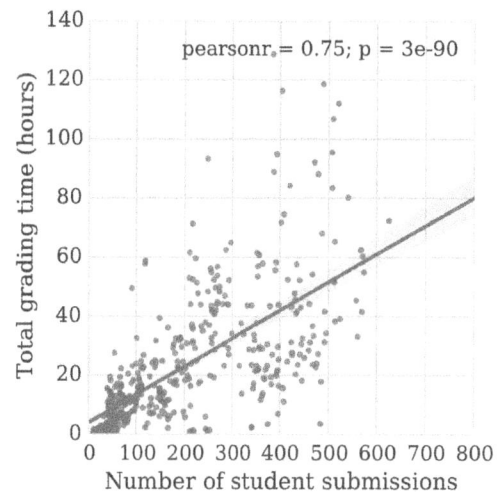

Figure 12: Total time spent grading the assignment in person-hours vs number of student submissions.

correspond to boundaries between distinct grading "sessions." Arranging the grading times in order of their execution, we compute the mean and median across all graders and questions.

Total grading time
Total grading time per assignment is a useful metric that is easy to obtain with our system. We plot it relative to the number of student submissions in Figure 12. The median assignment in our sample dataset has 14 questions, 141 student submissions, and took 14.6 person-hours to grade.

FUTURE WORK
Perhaps the most interesting consequence of grading digitally is that all of the grading data is also digitized, in a form that enables easy analysis. We plan to build tools that enable both students and instructors to benefit from this data.

First, we can allow users to tag questions with concepts. If all questions on the homework assignments and exams in a course are tagged with concepts, we can provide a dashboard illustrating how every student in a course is performing on each concept. In addition to the instructor, who will be able to adjust their teaching accordingly, students could benefit from seeing similar data about their performance. Roughly speaking, there are two ways for a student to receive an 80% on an assignment: get 80% partial credit on all questions, or to entirely miss one question out of five. If the missed question corresponds to one particular concept, the study plan for the next assignment should be very clear.

We also aim to point out to instructors which of their questions might be misleading. For this, some extensions of item response theory [6] are necessary for our rubric-based data.

Many of the student users of our system are enrolled in several courses using the system. This allows us to longitudinally track student performance throughout their academic careers, and yield insights into curricular development.

Lastly, we would like to support open-response assessment in online courses. In a brief pilot that allowed online students in UC Berkeley's CS188x edX offering to submit the same open-response, paper-based final as in-class students, we learned that MOOC students welcomed the opportunity to be tested more rigoruously than their usual automatic assessment allowed. We look forward to integrating with more MOOCs.

CONCLUSION
We described an online system for fast, fair, and flexible grading of handwritten assignments. In four years of usage, over 10 million pages of student work have been graded, corresponding to over 100 thousand questions. In survey, instructors report that our system enables them to provide higher quality feedback in less time than with traditional paper-based grading. With no additional effort, instructors also get detailed, actionable statistics on assignment, question, and rubric levels.

REFERENCES

1. Aaron Bloomfield. 2010. Evolution of a digital paper exam grading system. In *Frontiers in Education Conference (FIE)*. IEEE.

2. Aaron Bloomfield and James F Groves. 2008. A tablet-based paper exam grading system. In *ACM SIGCSE Bulletin*, Vol. 40. ACM, 83–87.

3. Brenda Cheang, Andy Kurnia, Andrew Lim, and Wee-Chong Oon. 2003. On automated grading of programming assignments in an academic institution. *Computers & Education* 41, 2 (2003), 121–131.

4. Ronan Cummins, Meng Zhang, and Ted Briscoe. 2016. Constrained Multi-Task Learning for Automated Essay Scoring. Association for Computational Linguistics.

5. Andrew Eberhard and Donald Sheridan. 2015. The Transition to Online Marking in Large Classes. In *EdMedia: World Conference on Educational Media and Technology*, Vol. 2015. 371–376.

6. Susan E Embretson and Steven P Reise. 2013. *Item response theory*. Psychology Press.

7. John Hattie. 2008. *Visible Learning: A Synthesis of Over 800 Meta-Analyses Relating to Achievement*. Taylor & Francis. `https://books.google.com/books?id=c2GbhdNoQX8C`

8. Michael T Helmick. 2007. Interface-based programming assignments and automatic grading of java programs. In *ACM SIGCSE Bulletin*, Vol. 39. ACM, 63–67.

9. Anders Jonsson and Gunilla Svingby. 2007. The use of scoring rubrics: Reliability, validity and educational consequences. *Educational research review* 2, 2 (2007), 130–144.

10. Youngwook Paul Kwon and Sara McMains. 2015. An Automated Grading/Feedback System for 3-View Engineering Drawings using RANSAC. In *Proceedings of the Second (2015) ACM Conference on Learning@ Scale*. ACM, 157–166.

11. David J Malan. 2013. CS50 sandbox: secure execution of untrusted code. In *Proceeding of the 44th ACM technical symposium on Computer science education*. ACM, 141–146.

12. James Park and John Hagen Jr. 2005. Managing Large Volumes of Assignments. *EDUCAUSE Quarterly* (2005).

13. Y Malini Reddy and Heidi Andrade. 2010. A review of rubric use in higher education. *Assessment & Evaluation in Higher Education* 35, 4 (2010), 435–448.

14. Saul Schleimer, Daniel S Wilkerson, and Alex Aiken. 2003. Winnowing: local algorithms for document fingerprinting. In *Proceedings of the 2003 ACM SIGMOD international conference on Management of data*. ACM, 76–85.

15. Susan C Schneider. 2014. "Paperless Grading" of Handwritten Homework: Electronic Process and Assessment. In *ASEE North Midwest Section Conference*.

16. Donald Sheridan and Lesley Gardner. 2012. From Cellulose to Software: The Evolution of a Marking System. In *World Conference on Educational Multimedia, Hypermedia and Telecommunications*, Vol. 2012. 454–461.

17. D.D. Stevens and A. Levi. 2005. *Introduction to Rubrics: An Assessment Tool to Save Grading Time, Convey Effective Feedback, and Promote Student Learning*. Stylus Pub. `https://books.google.com/books?id=LIxWgDn8_N0C`

18. Salvatore Valenti, Francesca Neri, and Alessandro Cucchiarelli. 2003. An overview of current research on automated essay grading. *Journal of Information Technology Education* 2 (2003), 319–330.

Writing Reusable Code Feedback at Scale with Mixed-Initiative Program Synthesis

Andrew Head[†*], Elena Glassman[†*], Gustavo Soares[†‡*],
Ryo Suzuki[§], Lucas Figueredo[‡], Loris D'Antoni[||], Björn Hartmann[†]

[†]UC Berkeley, [‡]UFCG, [§]CU Boulder, [||]UW-Madison

{andrewhead,eglassman,bjoern}@berkeley.edu, {gsoares@dsc,lucas.figueredo@ccc}.ufcg.edu.br,
ryo.suzuki@colorado.edu, loris@cs.wisc.edu

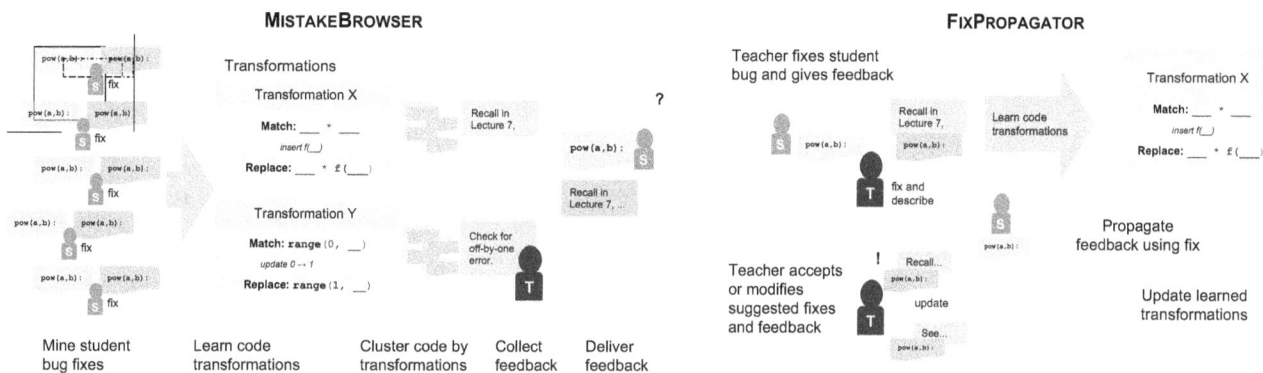

Figure 1. We contribute two interfaces that help teachers give feedback on incorrect student submissions using program synthesis. MISTAKEBROWSER learns code transformations from examples of students fixing bugs in their own code. Using these transformations, MISTAKEBROWSER clusters and fixes current and future incorrect submissions. The teacher adds feedback, one cluster at a time. FIXPROPAGATOR learns code transformations from examples of teachers fixing bugs in incorrect student submissions. The teacher annotates each fix with feedback. Using these annotated transformations, FIXPROPAGATOR propagates fixes and feedback to current and future incorrect submissions.

ABSTRACT

In large introductory programming classes, teacher feedback on individual incorrect student submissions is often infeasible. Program synthesis techniques are capable of fixing student bugs and generating hints automatically, but they lack the deep domain knowledge of a teacher and can generate functionally correct but stylistically poor fixes. We introduce a mixed-initiative approach which combines teacher expertise with data-driven program synthesis techniques.

We demonstrate our novel approach in two systems that use different interaction mechanisms. Our systems use program synthesis to learn bug-fixing code transformations and then cluster incorrect submissions by the transformations that correct them. The MISTAKEBROWSER system learns transformations from examples of students fixing bugs in their own submissions. The FIXPROPAGATOR system learns transformations from teachers fixing bugs in incorrect student submissions. Teachers can write feedback about a single submission

or a cluster of submissions and propagate the feedback to all other submissions that can be fixed by the same transformation. Two studies suggest this approach helps teachers better understand student bugs and write reusable feedback that scales to a massive introductory programming classroom.

Author Keywords
programming education; program synthesis

INTRODUCTION

One of the most common forms of instantaneous debugging assistance in Computer Science (CS) classes is the autograder. Typical autograders display the results of running a teacher-written test suite on student *submissions*, or solution attempts to programming exercises. However, feedback in the form of test results leaves students with a large gulf of evaluation [16] between the failed tests and bugs in their own submissions.

Recently developed techniques address this gulf by automatically generating or learning *bug fixes*, or code edits, for a submission such that a modified submission passes all tests [11, 19, 22, 20, 13]. From each fix, a personalized hint can be generated. The hints range from vague pointers, e.g., identifying the faulty line, to specific instructions about what new expression should replace the faulty one. Most of these approaches use program synthesis [7] to generate the fixes and hints.

*. These three authors contributed equally to the work.

```
1 1    def accumulate(combiner, base, n, term):
 2 +        if n==0:
 3 +            return base
2 4        if n==0:
3 5            return term(1)
4 6        else:
5 7            return accumulate(combiner,
                    combiner(base, term(n)), n-1, term)
```

Figure 2. A functionally correct but stylistically poor bug fix generated by program synthesis.

These automated techniques suffer from two key flaws. First, the hints lack the deep domain knowledge of a teacher. They do not address the underlying misconceptions of students or point to relevant principles or course materials. Second, the fixes can be functionally correct but stylistically poor and therefore potentially misleading when used as the basis of a hint. For example, Fig. 2 shows a bug fix synthesized with Refazer [20]. The fix inserts a nearly identical correct base case immediately before the incorrect base case. This is poor coding practice, and hints generated from this fix may be misleading. Specifically, hinting at this fix by its location, such as *Add code before line 2*, would be misleading because the bug is in the return statement on line 3. This is not a one-time occurrence: in our study, teachers rejected, on average, 19% ($\sigma = 18\%$) of the fixes synthesized by Refazer.

We introduce a mixed-initiative approach which allows teachers to combine their deep domain knowledge with the results of data-driven program synthesis techniques. The teacher and program synthesis back-end take turns applying their relative strengths in pursuit of the common goal of providing reusable, teacher-written feedback at scale. We demonstrate and evaluate this approach in two novel systems, MISTAKEBROWSER and FIXPROPAGATOR, which illustrate two different interaction mechanisms.

MISTAKEBROWSER and FIXPROPAGATOR both rely on Refazer, a data-driven program synthesis technique that learns *code transformations* from examples of bug fixes. Transformations are sequences of rewrite rules applied to the abstract syntax tree (AST) of a program. In our systems, we use transformations to: (1) cluster incorrect submissions, so cluster members may share a common bug or misconception; (2) generate bug fixes for each incorrect submission; (3) propagate teacher-written feedback to all incorrect submissions that are fixed by the same transformation. These learned code transformations can be reused to apply feedback to students through autograders or apply rubric items to exam submissions in current and future semesters.

In the MISTAKEBROWSER system, code transformations are learned from examples of student-written bug fixes. The history of student attempts is already available today in many autograding systems. In the MISTAKEBROWSER workflow, shown on the left in Figure 1, the teacher reviews the incorrect student submissions that were clustered offline by the code transformations that corrected them. Each submission is shown as a diff between its incorrect and corrected form. Even if some synthesized bug fixes are stylistically poor, the incorrect submissions in any one cluster may all share a misconception because the same code transformation corrected all of them. When reviewing the cluster, the teacher can infer the shared misconception and write feedback for the whole cluster that includes explanations, hints, or references to relevant course materials.

When submission histories are not available, FIXPROPAGATOR can learn code transformations from teachers fixing bugs in incorrect student submissions. As shown on the right in Figure 1, the process is cyclic and iterative. First, the teacher demonstrates a stylistically good fix that corrects a single incorrect submission. Then they annotate the fix with feedback. For each bug fix and annotation the teacher enters, a synthesis back-end learns and propagates these fixes and feedback to more incorrect submissions in the dataset. The teacher reviews these propagated fixes and feedback as pending suggestions and accepts them or modifies them as necessary. Modifications kick off another round of synthesis to learn and propagate the updated fix and feedback to more incorrect submissions.

Since MISTAKEBROWSER requires prior student data and the FIXPROPAGATOR workflow does not, the FIXPROPAGATOR system is most suitable for newly introduced homework or exam programming problems. While it is not currently standard practice for teachers to explicitly fix bugs in incorrect submissions, doing so with FIXPROPAGATOR allows teachers to scale their ability to provide manually written feedback — and grades — by propagating already authored feedback to current and future incorrect submissions.

We ran two user studies, one for each system. Seventeen current and former teachers from the staff of a massive introductory programming class participated. In both studies, the teachers were using MISTAKEBROWSER or FIXPROPAGATOR to interact with incorrect student submissions collected from previous semesters of the same class. The study of MISTAKEBROWSER suggests that the system helps teachers understand what mistakes and algorithms are common in student submissions. Teachers appreciated the generated fixes, but confirmed that a human in the loop is needed to review and annotate them with conceptual or high-level feedback. In the study of FIXPROPAGATOR, teachers wrote fixes and feedback for dozens of incorrect submissions, which the system propagated to hundreds of other submissions. Teachers generally accepted propagated fixes and feedback, although some feedback needed to be rewritten to generalize to additional submissions. Together, the studies suggest that our approach helps teachers better understand student bugs and provide scalable and reusable feedback.

This paper makes the following contributions:

- A technique for clustering incorrect submissions by the code transformations that correct them.

- A mixed-initiative approach in which teachers combine domain knowledge with the results of data-driven program synthesis.

- Two systems that demonstrate this approach with different interaction mechanisms.

- Two studies that suggest this approach helps teachers better understand student bugs and write reusable feedback that scales to a massive introductory programming classroom.

RELATED WORK

Feedback is critical to the learning experience [1], and teachers can be excellent sources of personalized, timely feedback [12]. As the class size grows, personal attention becomes infeasible; however, students in larger groups may share common errors and misconceptions [5]. Relevant prior work falls into two general categories: systems that rely on instructors to generate feedback, but provide better tools to do so; and systems that compute and display feedback automatically.

Tools that Support Instructor Feedback at Scale. Several user interfaces and systems empower teachers to manage large numbers of programming students. CodeOpticon [8] enables instructors to monitor many students simultaneously and provide situated help on code-in-progress. OverCode [6] and Foobaz [4] normalize and cluster correct student submissions so teachers do not need to read thousands of submissions to identify common and uncommon student choices about syntax and style. AutoStyle [14] clusters correct submissions using a metric of code complexity so that teachers can write hints how the code in a cluster can be written more simply. Singh et al. [21] define a problem-independent grammar of features; a supervised learning algorithm trained on teacher-graded examples can map new student code submissions to grades. However, these systems cannot give a teacher a high-level overview of the different, common misconceptions and bugs their own students have, like MISTAKEBROWSER can.

Clustering Student Submissions and Bugs. Identifying and clustering semantically similar student code submissions in a robust, general way is a challenge. Nguyen et al. [15] define probabilistic semantic equivalence to cluster functionally equivalent but syntactically distinct code phrases within submissions. Piech et al. [17] use neural networks to learn program embeddings and cluster submissions. Kaleeswaran et al. [11] cluster dynamic programming (DP) submissions by 'solution strategy,' using static analysis to detect how students manipulate arrays that store the results of subproblems in a DP solution. Earlier work relies on clustering student submissions using various distance metrics, like AST tree edit distance [10]. Instead of clustering code, Glassman et al.'s "learnersourcing" workflow [5] and HelpMeOut [9] cluster bug fixes by failed test cases, compiler errors, or runtime exceptions. Rather than clustering based on behaviorial or syntactic similiarity, our approach is to cluster incorrect submissions based on the transformation that corrects them.

Algorithmically Generating Debugging Feedback. Intelligent Tutoring Systems (ITS) seek to emulate one-on-one tutoring and provide personalized feedback by using rule-based or constraint-based methods [23]. However, traditional rule-based feedback requires much time and expert knowledge to construct [19]; it does not scale well for programming exercises, which have large and complex solution spaces.

Data-driven methods have recently been introduced to augment existing techniques. Rivers et al. [19] use student data to incrementally improve ITS feedback for Python assignments. Codewebs [15] and Codex [3] use machine learning to analyze large volumes of code, extract patterns, flag anomalies as possible errors, and, if deployed in an educational context, could

deliver feedback. These techniques can leverage the statistical properties of large numbers of student submissions, but they suffer from the cold-start problem. FIXPROPAGATOR enables teachers to provide examples to bootstrap hint generation.

Program Synthesis for Feedback Generation. Recent advances in program synthesis can help programming teachers and students in verifiably correct ways that statistical or rule-based techniques cannot. AutomataTutor [2] uses program synthesis to generate conceptual hints in the domain of automata constructions. Synthesized bug fixes have also been used to generate personalized hints for introductory-level programming assignments [11, 22]. AutoGrader [22] can find a minimal sequence of "repairs" that transforms a student's incorrect solution into a correct one; however, it requires that the teacher manually write down an error model of possible local modifications ahead of time. Instead of requiring a hard-coded error model, Lazar et al. [13] mine textual line edits from student interactions with a Prolog tutor, and synthesize code fixes by combining these edits. Rolim et al. [20] take an example-based approach to learn code fixes as abstract syntax tree transformations from pairs of incorrect and correct student submissions. We build on this technique in this paper.

WRITING REUSABLE CODE FEEDBACK WITH MIXED-INITIATIVE INTERFACES

We established the following design goals based on our literature review and our understanding of current pain points in large programming courses: **(1)** Help teachers better understand the distribution of common student bugs in introductory programming assignments. **(2)** Help teachers understand the nature of those bugs and ways to fix them. **(3)** Help teachers scale teacher-authored feedback to large numbers of students in a way that is reusable across semesters. We first briefly review how program synthesis enables MISTAKEBROWSER and FIXPROPAGATOR, then describe both systems.

Using Program Synthesis To Cluster Submissions

To reduce teacher burden, our systems automatically find groups of student submissions that exhibit the same underlying problem. We extract code transformations from pairs of incorrect and correct student submissions. We then check if a transformation can be successfully applied to other incorrect student submissions. Success is defined relative to an assignment's test suite: a transformation is successful if applying the transformation makes the corrected solution pass all tests.

In MISTAKEBROWSER, the pairs of incorrect and correct code come from histories of student submissions to an autograder that culminate in a correct submission. In FIXPROPAGATOR, the pairs of incorrect and correct code come from the small subset of incorrect student submissions that teachers choose to manually correct (see Figure 1).

Naïve extraction of code transformations through simple text differencing or abstract syntax tree differencing does not work well. Consider the two incorrect submissions in Figure 3, center column: while they are conceptually similar, and indeed exhibit the same underlying problem, they differ both in variable names and in code structure — one uses a loop with an index variable, and the other uses list iteration. Thus, it is important

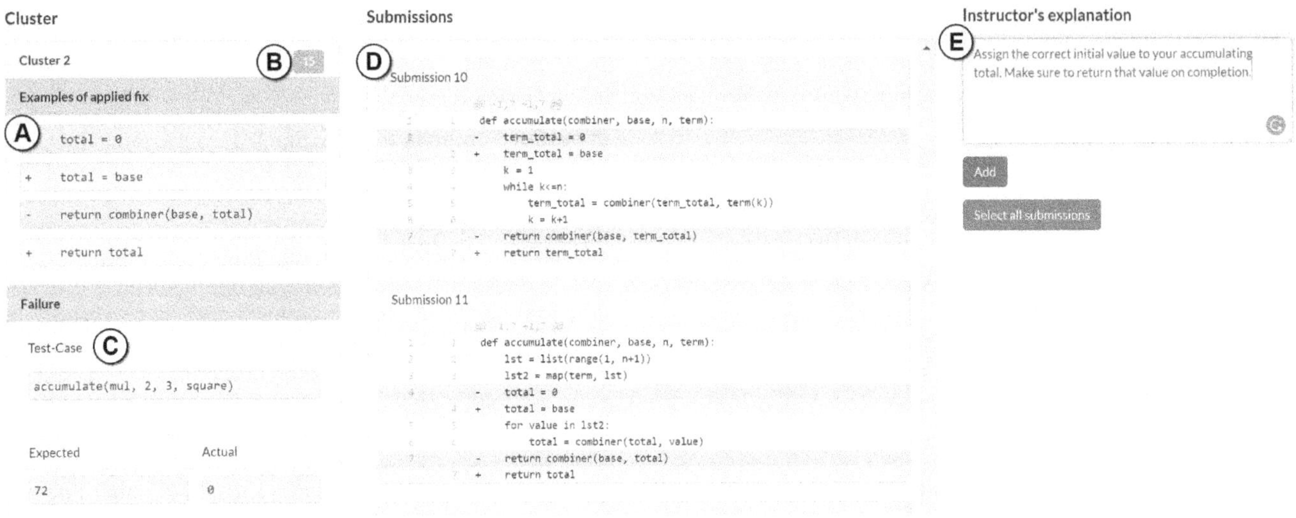

Figure 3. MISTAKEBROWSER interface: On the left panel, teachers can find information about the current cluster, such as an example of the synthesized fix (A); the total number of submissions in the cluster (B); the failing test case input, the expected output, and the actual output produced by the incorrect submissions (C). The center column shows the incorrect submissions before and after the synthesized fix (D). Finally, on the right panel, instructors can add explanations about student mistakes (E).

to find *abstract* transformations that capture edits at a level that can be reused across different students. In our example, the abstract transformation expresses that a student replaced the 0 on the right-hand-side of an assignment with function parameter `base`; and the function call inside the `return` statement should be replaced with the second argument inside that call (e.g., replace `return combiner(base, total)` to `total`).

We generate abstract code transformations using Refazer [20], which in turn builds on the PROSE synthesis framework [18]. Refazer uses a Domain-Specific Language (DSL) to specify transformations, and synthesizes transformations as programs in that DSL that map from incorrect to correct submissions. The language allows abstracting nodes in the Abstract Syntax Tree (AST) of a submission using a tree pattern matching language. It then offers common tree edit operations to modify nodes in the AST, such as *Insert*, *Delete*, *Update*, and *Move*. Returning to our example, the transformation synthesized by Refazer to fix submissions 10 and 11 in Figure 3 has 3 AST operations: (i) *Update* a constant value to `base`; (ii) *Delete* a function call with two name arguments located in a return statement and (iii) *Move* the second argument of this call to the beginning of the return statement.

Browsing Student Bugs

Consider the teaching staff of a massive introductory programming class, CS1, that have been using the same programming assignments for weekly 'finger exercises' every semester for years. These exercises are intended to reinforce new concepts introduced in class each week. Since teaching staff are not present when students attempt these exercises, they do not know what bugs and misconceptions are most common in student code, except through student forum posts.

Before the semester starts, Jamie, the lead teaching assistant (TA), loads student code snapshots from the prior semester from the class autograder into MISTAKEBROWSER, shown

in Figure 3. The back-end learns reusable abstract transformations from the bug fixes made by students in previous semesters. The MISTAKEBROWSER interface displays, one at a time, clusters of incorrect submissions that are corrected by the same transformation, along with their synthesized fixes. The center pane lists all incorrect submissions in that cluster, showing incorrect code fragments in red, and fixes in green in a common code difference view (Figure 3D). Jamie reviews each cluster and writes down conceptual feedback for each cluster. To explain the cluster's contents, the interface shows a compact representation of the fix for the cluster (Figure 3A), how many incorrect submissions comprise the cluster (Figure 3B), and the return value or exception of a representative submission for the first test case it fails to pass (Figure 3C). There are two clustering variants we consider in the user study that follows. Figure 3 shows the CLUSTERBYFIXANDTEST-CASE variant, in which incorrect submissions are clustered both by the transformation that fix them and by the return value of the first failed test case. In the CLUSTERBYFIX variant, incorrect submissions are clustered only by transformation.

After reviewing a cluster, Jamie composes high-level feedback in free-form text that applies to all submissions in the cluster (Figure 3E). For the cluster shown in Figure 3, she might write the hint, *Assign the correct initial value to your accumulating total, and make sure you return that value on completion.* When Jamie is satisfied that the most common and interesting clusters have been annotated with explanations, hints, or references to relevant course materials, MISTAKEBROWSER can be left running as part of the course autograder's back-end, where it can deliver the TAs' feedback to students during current and future semesters, along with the test case successes and failures, whenever an incorrect submission falls into an annotated cluster in MISTAKEBROWSER.

MISTAKEBROWSER clusters are based on program transformations synthesized by Refazer. For each homework assignment, the back-end keeps a list of Refazer transformations and the

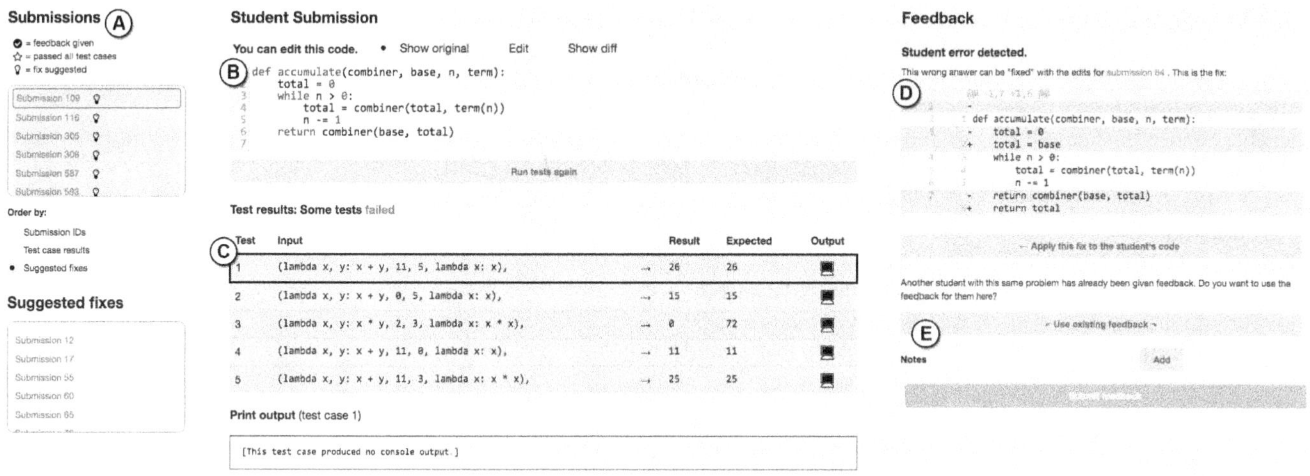

Figure 4. FIXPROPAGATOR interface: The left panel shows all of the incorrect submissions (A). When the teacher selects one, the submission is loaded into the Python code editor in the center of the interface (B). Then the teacher can edit the code, re-run tests, and inspect results. The bottom of the center panel shows the list of tests and console output (C). Once the teacher has fixed the submission, they add some hint that will be shown to current and future students fixed by the same transformation. The bottom of the left panel shows submissions for which the system is suggesting a fix. When the teacher selects a suggested fix, it is shown as a diff in the right panel (D). The teacher can reuse the previously written hint or create a new one (E).

assignment's test suite. Given an incorrect submission, the system iterates over the list of transformations, and for each transformation, tries to apply it and checks whether the code is fixed according to the test suite. As soon as the system finds a transformation that fixes the submission, it adds the submission to the cluster associated with this transformation. In the CLUSTERBYFIXANDTESTCASE, the system uses additional information provided by the tests related to the actual and expected outputs to create clusters.

Propagating a Teacher's Bug Fixes
Sam, the lead TA of a massive introductory programming class at another school, wants to deploy the same kind of high-level feedback on incorrect submissions that MISTAKEBROWSER enables. However, their course infrastructure only saves the most recent submission from each student, so there is no history of student bug fixes from which MISTAKEBROWSER could learn transformations. Instead, Sam uploads the incorrect submissions he has to FIXPROPAGATOR. Figure 4 shows the FIXPROPAGATOR user interface.

In the FIXPROPAGATOR interface, Sam looks at incorrect submissions by selecting them (Figure 4A), iteratively edits and executes the submission in an interactive code editor (Figure 4B) against the teacher's test suite (Figure 4C), and adds some high-level feedback for the student, such as explanations, hints, or pointers to relevant course materials. Ideally, this feedback should be worded so that future students in need of a similar fix would also find it beneficial (Figure 4E).

When Sam submits feedback, the system uploads the original incorrect submission, fixed submission, and high-level feedback to a synthesis back-end to learn generalized transformations from Sam's correction. FIXPROPAGATOR applies each transformation to the incorrect submissions that do not yet have feedback. Transformations that fix incorrect submissions turn into suggested fixes–along with the corresponding feedback–in the FIXPROPAGATOR interface (bottom of Figure 4A) that can be accepted with a single click (Figure 4D).

If accepted, the tests are run automatically and Sam sees that, indeed, this fix is just what the student needs to correct their submission. Sam clicks on a button to reuse the feedback from the submission that generated the fix (Figure 4E). If Sam judges the fix or the feedback as not appropriate, it can be modified in place. Changes to synthesized fixes become new bug fix examples that spur the generation of new transformations in the back-end. Sam alternates between reviewing suggestions and manually correcting more incorrect submissions. After a while, most submissions have suggestions.

Given the high cost of debugging student code, a teacher should be able to fix few incorrect submissions and see feedback propagate to many other students. We modified Refazer to synthesize generalizable fixes from just one fix. To improve generalization, Refazer produces multiple transformations of varying generality for each submitted fix. All generated rules are applied to all submissions that have not yet been fixed.

Furthermore, FIXPROPAGATOR needs to support online fix generation at interactive speeds. However, effectively searching a space of code transformations can be time-consuming; with the current synthesis back-end, it can take minutes to synthesize and apply fixes to other submissions. The user interface was decoupled from Refazer so that teachers can continue to fix and test code, produce feedback, and move on to other submissions while the back-end discovers fixes. All communication with the synthesis back-end aside from initialization is asynchronous: fixes are uploaded to and retrieved from Refazer using background threads.

Our implementation anticipates future modifications to support collaborative production of fixes and feedback. Communications with Refazer are moderated as "sessions" sharing a common set of submissions and synthesized transformations. We have made the code for both the web server and front end available under an open source license[1].

---

1. https://github.com/ace-lab/refazer4CSteachers

93

USER STUDIES

We ran two in-lab user studies with the teaching staff of a massive programming class, with one study per system. The studies evaluate how effective the interfaces are at helping teachers understand common bugs and write feedback to help students overcome them.

Participants

We recruited 17 teachers from the pool of current and former CS61a teaching staff members. CS61a is a massive introductory programming class at UC Berkeley with as many as 1,500 students enrolled per semester. All the teachers in our study are over 18 years old (average: 19.76 years old, σ =1.39). 16 of the 17 teachers are currently serving on the class teaching staff, and the remaining participant was previously a class teaching assistant for many semesters.

We split the pool of teachers into two groups of size 9 and 8. The first group (SS1-9) tested MISTAKEBROWSER, while the second group (ST1-8) tested FIXPROPAGATOR. The identifiers SS and ST reference the fact that bug fixes in MISTAKEBROWSER and FIXPROPAGATOR are student and teacher-generated, respectively. All teachers were qualified to try both tools, but we limited each teacher to one system due to the length of time required to thoroughly evaluate a system.

Dataset

Whenever a CS61a student submits code to be tested by the course autograder against the teacher-written test suite, the system logs the code, student ID, and test results. From one homework assigned in Spring 2015, we selected the three programming exercises below.

Product (data from 549 students): takes as parameters a positive integer n and a unary function *term*, and returns the product of the first n terms in a sequence: $term(1) * term(2) * ... * term(n)$.

Accumulate (668 students): takes as parameters the same n and *term* as Product as well as a binary function *combiner* for accumulating terms, and an initial value *base*. For example, $accumulate(add, 11, 3, square)$ returns $11 + square(1) + square(2) + square(3)$.

Repeated (720 students): takes as parameters a unary function f and a number n, and returns the nth application of f. For example, $repeated(square, 2)(5)$ returns $square(square(5))$, which evaluates to 625.

For each exercise, the interfaces were populated with incorrect submissions using a two-step process. First, we extracted each student's final correct solution and preceding incorrect submission. Using these submission pairs as examples, we trained Refazer to synthesize code transformations to fix common bugs. Second, for each student, we identified the earliest incorrect submission that the transformations could fix. These early, fixed submissions were shown to teachers in clusters of fixed submissions in MISTAKEBROWSER, or as incorrect submissions in FIXPROPAGATOR.

When pre-populating MISTAKEBROWSER, Refazer generated mostly small synthesized fixes for the dataset: on average, the tree edit distance between the abstract syntax trees of incorrect and fixed submissions was 4.9 ($\sigma = 5.1$).

Shared Protocol: Setup and Training

Teachers were invited to an on-campus lab for one hour and offered 20 US dollars in exchange for their time and expertise. The experimenter walked the teacher through the features of the interface they would see, demonstrating actions on one of the incorrect submissions that the teacher would be working on. This walk-through included a few minutes of explanation about the synthesis back-end. We chose to give this brief explanation because, during pilot studies, teachers who did not receive an explanation were distracted from the task by their own curiosity and theories about the back-end's inner workings. The tutorial took no more than five minutes. Finally, the experimenter walked the teacher through a brief description of the first programming exercise for which the teacher will see incorrect submissions: the purpose of the programming exercise, the test cases used to check the correctness of submissions, and the expected test case return values.

STUDY 1: MISTAKEBROWSER

The purpose of this user study was to evaluate the MISTAKEBROWSER system. We asked the following research questions: **(1)** How do teachers perceive the quality of synthesized fixes? **(2)** Do synthesis-based clusters help teachers write feedback? **(3)** How reusable is the cluster-based feedback?

Study Protocol

Teachers had 40 minutes to review clusters of incorrect submissions and write feedback for each cluster. They viewed two clustering interface variants, CLUSTERBYFIX and CLUSTERBYFIXANDTESTCASE, for 20 minutes each. The order of interface variants and choice of programming exercise from the three exercises were counterbalanced across teachers. Teachers were assigned an interface variant, problem, and cluster to start with. For each cluster, they marked all of the poor synthesized fixes to student submissions. They then answered a few questions about the semantic coherence of the cluster, e.g., "Do these incorrect submissions share the same misconception?" They were asked to "write the most precise short description [they] can of the fix [they] would suggest," which need not match the synthesized fix. The teacher also answered Likert scale questions about their confidence in their descriptions and the depth of domain knowledge they added in the process. As soon as they finished these tasks for a cluster, they could advance to the next of the largest three clusters in their assigned programming exercise and interface. After the second 20-minute period, teachers reflected on their experiences in a final survey.

Results

Refazer, our synthesis back-end, generated fixes for 87% of the students in our dataset, resulting in an average of 549 fixes across all three problems. On average, these fixes were grouped into 134 clusters in the CLUSTERBYFIX condition and 198 clusters in the CLUSTERBYFIXANDTESTCASE condition. Within the top three clusters for all programming exercises, the largest cluster contained, on average, 109 submissions and the smallest cluster contained 32 submissions.

Teachers saw an average of 3 ($\sigma = 1.4$) clusters containing 145 ($\sigma = 80.9$) incorrect submissions per hour-long session, where they spent 20 min in each clustering condition. They saw, on average, 72.9 ($\sigma = 53.4$) incorrect submissions in the CLUSTERBYFIX condition and 78.7 ($\sigma = 43.9$) incorrect submissions in the CLUSTERBYFIXANDTESTCASE condition.

Perceived quality of synthesized fixes. On average, 19% ($\sigma = 18$) of the synthesized fixes were considered poor by the teachers, and all teachers reported at least one poor fix. This corroborates our initial intuition that synthesis alone is not enough to generate high-quality hints.

For instance, SS2 and SS7 noticed a synthesized fix that did not match the approach teachers explicitly taught for coding recursive solutions. SS2 called the suggested fix "dangerous." SS2 also called some fixes "hot fixes" because, after application, the student submission returned the expected values but still had logical failures. In one example, the system suggested a fix that compensated for, rather than corrected, an incorrect variable initialization. Some fixes were not full fixes, even though the fixed code passed all the teacher-written test cases. For example, some incorrect submissions computed the product of $term(i)$ for $i = 1..n - 1$, instead of $1..n$. A synthesized "hot fix" changed the range of the loop to $i = 2..n$. However, this incorrect logic was not caught by the teacher's test suite: $term(1)$ returned 1 for all $term$ functions in the test cases, so it was impossible to detect if the student failed to call $term$ when $i = 1$. This result revealed limitations in the teacher-written test suite. SS8 noticed this and marked the entire cluster of fixes as poor.

The value of clustering by code transformation. While not all synthesized fixes were appropriate for students, teachers did appreciate seeing them. When completing free response questions about what they liked in the interfaces, two-thirds of teachers (six of nine) specifically named clustering by transformation as a feature they appreciated and two-thirds named the synthesized fixes directly. All nine teachers named at least one of those two features as what they appreciated most.

Teachers described how the synthesized fixes, shown as highlighted diffs, helped during their task: "highlight[ing] the part of the code that was incorrect ... made it much easier to quickly learn what was wrong with the code and how to fix it" (SS7). These diffs were "fast and easy to review" and "familiar" (SS3).

Subject SS1 wrote, "I thought it was interesting how grouping student answers by their common mistakes actually revealed something about the misconceptions they shared!" The utility of this clustering was apparent to SS3: "Seeing all of the similar instances of the same (or nearly the same) misconception was very useful, because it suggested ways to address common issues shared by many students." They agreed with the statement "These interfaces gave me insight into student mistakes and misconceptions" at the level of 6.2 ($\sigma = 0.44$) on a scale from 1 (strongly disagree) to 7 (strongly agree); no teacher rated their agreement as lower than a 6.

Several teachers' responses support the hypothesis that MISTAKEBROWSER gives a high-level view of the misconceptions

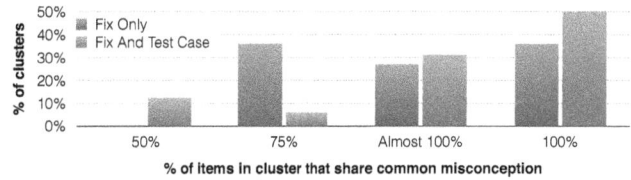

Figure 5. Distribution of clusters with respect to % of solutions that shared common misconceptions.

and bugs students labor under while solving the problem, like an OverCode [6] for incorrect submissions. SS9 liked that "it had a wide variety of student responses to the same problem." SS1 wrote, "I felt that being able to compare many different solutions (i.e. iterative, recursive, tail-recursive) was insightful as to how the students approached the problem."

Reusability of the feedback. To evaluate the reusability of feedback assigned to synthesis-based clusters, we asked teachers to report how many submissions in each cluster actually shared the same misconception. Figure 5 shows teachers' answers for the two cluster conditions, CLUSTERBYFIX and CLUSTERBYFIXANDTESTCASE. In both conditions, they reported that most submissions share the same misconceptions. However, they reported a greater proportion of CLUSTERBYFIXANDTESTCASE clusters as "100%" or "100% with a few exceptions" compared to CLUSTERBYFIX clusters. Seven out of nine teachers also mentioned in the final survey they preferred CLUSTERBYFIXANDTESTCASE cluster because the combination of fixes and test cases made it easier to check if the incorrect submissions share the same misconception.

One of the clusters for the CLUSTERBYFIXANDTESTCASE condition was reported to be less internally consistent than the others, with only "50%" of submissions sharing a common misconception. As we learned from teachers in the study, the provided test cases failed to reveal a bug that caused a subset of submissions to behave differently than the other submissions. Submissions with this bug required a different fix.

STUDY 2: FIXPROPAGATOR

The purpose of this user study was to evaluate FIXPROPAGATOR. Specifically, we had the following research questions:
(1) Can FIXPROPAGATOR propagate a small number of teacher-written fixes and feedback to many incorrect submissions?
(2) Can FIXPROPAGATOR's back-end perform fast enough to support real-time interaction?
(3) Do teachers accept propagated fixes and hints?

Study protocol

Each teacher was assigned to review student submissions for one of the three programming exercises. After a five-minute tutorial with the FIXPROPAGATOR interface, they were given thirty minutes to interact with the system to teach the system to fix and provide feedback on student code. This thirty-minute period was broken up into alternating five-minute tasks. In the first five-minute task, the teacher was asked to fix as many bugs as possible, to maximize the number of generated fixes. The experimenter told the teacher that simpler bug fixes may yield more suggested fixes. During the second five-minutes task, the

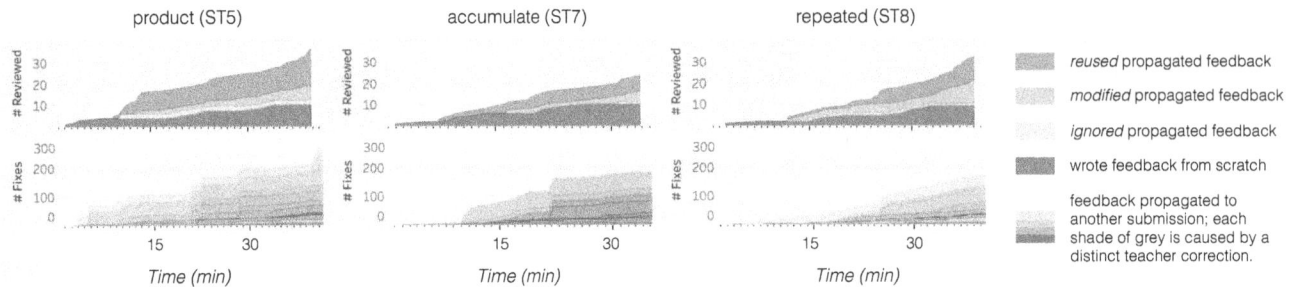

Figure 6. Top row: The number of incorrect submissions fo
The number of incorrect submissions that received propag

teacher reviewed pending fixes and then accepted
them, so that they could check whether the system
acceptable transformations for fixing incorrect s
they had not yet seen. After the thirty-minute peri
were asked to fill out a post-study reflection surve
Likert-scale and free response questions about their
with FIXPROPAGATOR.

Results
During this study, due to unforeseen circumstanc
thesis back-end was disabled for part of two teache
(ST1, ST4). Data described here was collected for
ing six teachers.

Bug fix propagation. Teachers provided examp
fixes in two ways: fixing incorrect submissions fr
and editing suggested fixes. They fixed a median
2.7) submissions from scratch and fixed 3 ($\sigma =$
after editing suggested fixes. During the time o
session and up to 40 minutes after the study, our syn
end was able to fix a median of 201 submissions
Figure 6 shows the propagation of fixes over tir
end of the study, a large portion of the submissions (average =
34.7%, $\sigma = 10.19\%$) had either been corrected by the teacher
or fixed by a synthesized transformation.

Performance. It took a median of 2 minutes and 20 seconds ($\sigma = 7m34s$) to successfully propagate a fix to another
submission after a teacher corrected an incorrect submission.
Although the current system does not immediately show teachers suggestions based on their corrections, teachers were able
to work on other submissions while waiting for synthesized
fixes. Figure 7 shows the interaction of one of the teachers
with FIXPROPAGATOR. Teachers alternated between fixing
and reviewing, but the effort invested in manual fixes allowed
them to accept a large number of auto-propagated fixes.

The value of synthesized fixes. Transformations learned
from teachers' manual corrections fixed new incorrect submissions in unexpected ways. They helped teachers better
understand the space of bug fixes and approaches to implementing the solution. For example, ST3 came across an incorrect submission which was very close to being correct. She
did not see the simple fix and instead wrote an elaborate fix
that was fundamentally different from the student's approach.
Later, a simpler synthesized fix to a similar incorrect submission was suggested, and she realized the submissions were

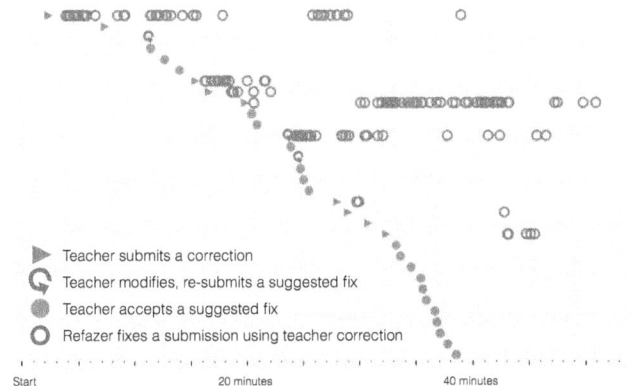

Figure 7. Timeline of the corrections a teacher (ST8) made to incorrect
submissions, and the subsequent synthesized fixes that were generated
from each correction.

using a different but valid approach to solving the problem.
After accepting the suggested fix, she reported she had learned
something about the space of solutions for the exercise.

Reusability. After contributing fixes and feedback for incorrect student submissions, teachers generally accepted the fixes
and feedback propagated to other submissions. Teachers were
more likely to reuse propagated fixes to the code verbatim
(median = 17 times, $\sigma = 8.9$) than to reuse feedback verbatim
(median = 11, $\sigma = 6.3$). Fixes were likely propagated correctly more often than feedback, as fixes were only propagated
if they allowed a submission to pass test cases that it failed
before. However, teachers' feedback did not always generalize to new submissions. Some feedback referred to arbitrary
implementation choices not present in other submissions. For
example, one teacher referenced a specific variable name when
writing, "Your starting value of z should be a function, not
an int." When proposed fixes and feedback were not enough,
teachers made modifications after applying suggested fixes
(median = 3, $\sigma = 2.9$), and modified the feedback (median =
6, $\sigma = 2.7$).

Survey responses confirmed our observations about the ac-
ceptability of fixes and feedback. Most teachers reported that
pending fixes were acceptable "100% of the time, with a few
exceptions." The proportion of acceptable feedback was one
category worse: teachers rated the suggested feedback as accurate "75%" of the time.

DISCUSSION

Our first design goal is to help teachers better understand the distribution of common student bugs in introductory programming exercises. MISTAKEBROWSER achieved this goal by clustering incorrect submissions by the transformation that corrects them. Given that the teachers in our studies had no comparable view of incorrect submissions, this added significant value. FIXPROPAGATOR achieved this goal indirectly, by helping teachers discover how many different incorrect submissions could be fixed with the same transformation.

Our second design goal is to help teachers understand the nature of student bugs and ways to fix them. Both MISTAKE-BROWSER and FIXPROPAGATOR achieve this goal by visualizing the synthesized fix as a diff for every incorrect submission in each cluster. By seeing the variety of submissions fixed by a common transformation, teachers begin to understand the essence of the underlying misconception, as well as the variety of submissions it can appear in.

Our third design goal is to give teachers a tool for composing high-level feedback and hints that scale to large numbers of students and can be reused in future semesters. Teachers can achieve this goal with either system, depending on the availability and quality of archives of student debugging activity. As seen in the first study, the existence of poor synthesized fixes within a cluster does not prevent teachers from composing high-level feedback that can be propagated to current and future incorrect submissions in that cluster. Clustering by transformation and test cases reduced cluster size but increased cluster purity, as in, there was more likely to be a single bug shared across all incorrect submissions in the cluster. Despite the smaller size of clusters in the CLUSTERBYFIXANDTEST-CASE variant of MISTAKEBROWSER, teachers still reviewed as many or more incorrect submissions. In the FIXPROPAGA-TOR system, after only a few minutes of manually fixing and providing feedback on a few incorrect submissions, teachers received bug fix and feedback suggestions for tens or hundreds of additional incorrect submissions. Even if only a large minority of students receive high-level feedback in which teachers can remind the student of relevant principles and course content, it is still a major advance over the status quo of feedback for students in massive programming classes.

One participant (SS3) mentioned that they used to hand-grade homework submissions, giving feedback as well as grades, until their class became too large. Now they only evaluate student homework based on a proxy for student effort, test cases passed, and spot-checks for composition. He thought that MISTAKEBROWSER could help the staff grade their massive class the same way they used to grade homework when the class was smaller. The FIXPROPAGATOR system can also be used for grading-through-debugging. Debugging a student exam submission is not a trivial activity, but FIXPROPAGA-TOR can potentially learn reusable transformations from every successful correction, simplifying adjustments to the grading rubric and point deductions during the grading process. If the exam problem is reused, the problem-specific rubric and point deduction for that problem can be reused and added to during

future exam grading sessions, bringing the staff closer to fully automatic submission grading.

Limitations. Our studies do not evaluate the impact of these systems on student learning outcomes. The study results show that teachers had some confidence that the transformations and feedback were appropriate for unseen current and future incorrect submissions in the cluster. However, we have not shown whether students find the feedback relevant to them or whether it improves their learning outcomes. There may be a trade-off between the generality and the relevance of the feedback teachers provide. Future studies can shed light onto how propagated feedback impacts student learning and inform how the systems could best help teachers to write feedback that is both general and pedagogically useful.

So far, our systems have only been shown to propagate feedback for small fixes. For MISTAKEBROWSER, this is due to the constraints of the training data: to build the training examples, we used a correct solution paired with the last incorrect submission from each student. It may be possible to synthesize larger fixes by learning transformations from correct solutions paired with incorrect submissions selected from earlier attempts in a student's submission history. While larger fixes may allow teachers to give feedback on more problems, there is an inherent tradeoff: larger fixes may be harder for teachers to understand and provide feedback for.

Our datasets have thus far only focused on fixing short functions typical of early exercises in an introductory programming class. The student solutions usually consist of just one main function, sometimes including a few helper functions. We have not tested how the systems' real-time performance will scale with more complex programs. Intuitively, the time to synthesize a fix for a given incorrect submission will depend on transformation size, the size of the incorrect submission, and the runtime of the test cases. The synthesis back-end is capable of learning and applying transformations for complex code bases (150K-1500K lines of code) [20], but tuning may be necessary to synthesize fixes for complex programs.

CONCLUSIONS AND FUTURE WORK

We presented two mixed-initiative systems for providing reusable feedback at scale with program synthesis. MIS-TAKEBROWSER learns transformations to fix incorrect submissions from examples of student-written bug fixes. MIS-TAKEBROWSER uses these transformations to cluster incorrect student submissions. Teachers can then review these clusters and write reusable feedback for current and future incorrect submissions. When examples of student fixes are not available, FIXPROPAGATOR allows teachers to write example bug fixes themselves. The system then learns from such fixes in real-time. We conducted two user studies with teaching assistants to evaluate our systems. Our results suggest that synthesized fixes, either from teachers' examples or previous students' bug fixes, can be useful for providing reusable feedback at scale.

As future work, we plan to deploy these systems in a massive programming course and evaluate the effectiveness of the generated feedback on helping students during programming assignments. To increase flexibility, we plan to combine workflows of FixPropagator and MistakeBrowser, allowing teachers to edit transformations learned from students' fixes by providing additional examples. To improve the interpretability of learned transformations, we plan to explore alternate visual and natural language interfaces to help teachers understand and modify synthesized code transformations. Finally, we have not yet investigated how to effectively combine both teacher-authored feedback and automatically synthesized hints in a student-facing interface. In future work, we plan to explore this design space of hybrid hints.

ACKNOWLEDGMENTS

We would like to thank the CS61a teaching staff for their time and perspective. This research was supported by the NSF Expeditions in Computing award CCF 1138996, NSF CAREER award IIS 1149799, CAPES 8114/15-3, an NDSEG fellowship, and a Google CS Capacity Award.

REFERENCES

1. Susan A. Ambrose, Michael W. Bridges, Michele DiPietro, Marsha C. Lovett, and Marie K. Norman. 2010. *How learning works: Seven research-based principles for smart teaching*. John Wiley & Sons.

2. Loris D'Antoni, Dileep Kini, Rajeev Alur, Sumit Gulwani, Mahesh Viswanathan, and Björn Hartmann. 2015. How can automatic feedback help students construct automata? *ACM-TOCHI* 22, 2 (2015), 1–24.

3. Ethan Fast, Daniel Steffee, Lucy Wang, Joel R. Brandt, and Michael S. Bernstein. 2014. Emergent, crowd-scale programming practice in the IDE. In *Proceedings of CHI*. ACM, 2491–2500.

4. Elena L. Glassman, Lyla Fischer, Jeremy Scott, and Robert C. Miller. 2015. Foobaz: Variable Name Feedback for Student Code at Scale. In *Proceedings of UIST*. ACM, 609–617.

5. Elena L. Glassman, Aaron Lin, Carrie J. Cai, and Robert C. Miller. 2016. Learnersourcing Personalized Hints. In *Proceedings of CSCW*. ACM, 1626–1636.

6. Elena L. Glassman, Jeremy Scott, Rishabh Singh, Philip J. Guo, and Robert C. Miller. 2015. OverCode: Visualizing variation in student solutions to programming problems at scale. *ACM-TOCHI* 22, 2 (2015), 1–35.

7. Sumit Gulwani. 2010. Dimensions in program synthesis. In *Proceedings of the Symposium on Principles and Practice of Declarative Programming*. ACM, 13–24.

8. Philip J. Guo. 2015. Codeopticon: Real-Time, One-To-Many Human Tutoring for Computer Programming. In *Proceedings of UIST*. ACM, 599–608.

9. Björn Hartmann, Daniel MacDougall, Joel Brandt, and Scott R. Klemmer. 2010. What would other programmers do: suggesting solutions to error messages. In *Proceedings of the CHI*. ACM, 1019–1028.

10. Jonathan Huang, Chris Piech, Andy Nguyen, and Leonidas Guibas. 2013. Syntactic and functional variability of a million code submissions in a machine learning MOOC. In *Proceedings of the First Annual Workshop on Massive Open Online Courses*. 25–32.

11. Shalini Kaleeswaran, Anirudh Santhiar, Aditya Kanade, and Sumit Gulwani. 2016. Semi-Supervised Verified Feedback Generation. In *Proceedings of FSE*. ACM, 739–750.

12. Chinmay E Kulkarni, Michael S Bernstein, and Scott R Klemmer. 2015. PeerStudio: rapid peer feedback emphasizes revision and improves performance. In *Proceedings of L@S*. ACM, 75–84.

13. Timotej Lazar and Ivan Bratko. 2014. Data-driven program synthesis for hint generation in programming tutors. In *International Conference on Intelligent Tutoring Systems*. Springer, 306–311.

14. Joseph Bahman Moghadam, Rohan Roy Choudhury, HeZheng Yin, and Armando Fox. 2015. AutoStyle: Toward Coding Style Feedback at Scale. In *Proceedings of L@S*. ACM, 261–266.

15. Andy Nguyen, Christopher Piech, Jonathan Huang, and Leonidas Guibas. 2014. Codewebs: scalable homework search for massive open online programming courses. In *Proceedings of WWW*. ACM, 491–502.

16. Donald A. Norman and Stephen W. Draper. 1986. *User Centered System Design; New Perspectives on Human-Computer Interaction*. L. Erlbaum Associates, Inc.

17. Chris Piech, Jonathan Huang, Andy Nguyen, Mike Phulsuksombati, Mehran Sahami, and Leonidas J. Guibas. 2015. Learning Program Embeddings to Propagate Feedback on Student Code. In *Proceedings of ICML*. IMLS, 1093–1102.

18. Oleksandr Polozov and Sumit Gulwani. 2015. FlashMeta: A Framework for Inductive Program Synthesis. In *Proceedings of OOPSLA*. ACM, 107–126.

19. Kelly Rivers and Kenneth R. Koedinger. 2015. Data-driven hint generation in vast solution spaces: a self-improving Python programming tutor. *IJAIED* (2015), 1–28.

20. Reudismam Rolim, Gustavo Soares, Loris D'Antoni, Oleksandr Polozov, Sumit Gulwani, Rohit Gheyi, Ryo Suzuki, and Björn Hartmann. 2017. Learning Syntactic Program Transformations from Examples. In *Proceedings of ICSE*. IEEE, in press.

21. Gursimran Singh, Shashank Srikant, and Varun Aggarwal. 2016. Question Independent Grading Using Machine Learning: The Case of Computer Program Grading. In *Proceedings of KDD*. ACM, 263–272.

22. Rishabh Singh, Sumit Gulwani, and Armando Solar-Lezama. 2013. Automated feedback generation for introductory programming assignments. *ACM SIGPLAN Notices* 48, 6 (2013), 15–26.

23. Kurt Vanlehn. 2006. The behavior of tutoring systems. *IJAIED* 16, 3 (2006), 227–265.

Creative Learning @ Scale

Mitchel Resnick
MIT Media Lab
Cambridge, USA
mres@media.mit.edu

Karen Brennan
Harvard Graduate School of
Education
Cambridge, USA
karen_brennan@gse.harvard.edu

Cristóbal Cobo
Center for Research – Ceibal
Foundation
Montevideo, Uruguay
ccobo@fundacionceibal.edu.uy

Philipp Schmidt
MIT Media Lab
Cambridge, USA
ps1@media.mit.edu

ABSTRACT

In today's fast-changing world, the ability to think and act creatively is more important than ever before. This panel will discuss tools, activities, and strategies for helping people develop as creative thinkers — and how to scale those efforts to engage learners around the world. The panel will draw on examples involving learners of many different ages, in many different places, both in school and out.

Keywords

Creative thinking; Scratch

BIOS

Mitchel Resnick, LEGO Papert Professor of Learning Research at the MIT Media Lab, develops new technologies and activities to engage people (particularly children) in creative learning experiences.

His Lifelong Kindergarten research group develops the Scratch programming software and online community (scratch.mit.edu), used by millions of young people around the world. The group also collaborates with the LEGO Company on the development of new educational ideas and products, including LEGO Mindstorms and WeDo robotics kits. Resnick co-founded the Computer Clubhouse project, an international network of 100 after-school learning centers where youth from low-income communities learn to express themselves creatively with new technologies.

Resnick earned a BA in physics at Princeton University (1978) and MS and PhD degrees in computer science at MIT (1988, 1992). He worked as a science-technology journalist from 1978 to 1983. He is author of Turtles, Termites, and Traffic Jams (1994), co-editor of Constructionism in Practice (1996), as well as co-author of Adventures in Modeling(2001) and The Official ScratchJr Book (2015). He was awarded the McGraw Prize in Education in 2011 and the AACE EdMedia Pioneer Award in 2013.

Karen Brennan is an Associate Professor at the Harvard Graduate School of Education. Her research is primarily concerned with the ways in which learning environments–in and out of school, online and face-to-face–can be designed to support young people's development as computational creators.

Many of Brennan's research and teaching activities focus on constructionist approaches to designing learning environments–encouraging learning through designing, personalizing, connecting, and reflecting, and fostering learner agency. Before joining HGSE, Brennan completed her PhD in Media Arts and Sciences at the MIT Media Lab.

Cristóbal Cobo (PhD) is Director of the Center for Research – Ceibal Foundation in Uruguay, and also an associate researcher at the Oxford Internet Institute, University of Oxford.

Cristobal has been distinguished by the British Council of Economic and Social Research (ESRC) and associate research fellow at the Centre on Skills, Knowledge and Organizational Performance, University of Oxford. He was Professor and director of Communication and New Technologies at the Latin American Faculty of Social Sciences, Mexico. He has served as external Evaluator for the Inter-American Development Bank; the National

Science Foundation and MIT Press (US), International Labor Organization (UN), and the International Development Research Centre (Canada). He has PhD "cum laudem" Communication Sciences at Universitat Autònoma de Barcelona. Co-author of the book Invisible Learning, his most recent books is "Innovación Pendiente" (Penguin Random House, 2016). He has been speaker in more than 30 countries (+ 4 TEDx).

Currently he collaborates with the Digitally Connected Network (a collaborative initiative between UNICEF and the Berkman Klein Center).

J. Philipp Schmidt is Director of Learning Innovation at the MIT Media Lab, where he leads the ML Learning initiative, teaches courses, and conducts research on learning communities. He is also a cofounder and board member of Peer 2 Peer University (P2PU), a non-profit organization that provides access to online higher education through public libraries. Philipp served on the founding board of the OpenCourseWare Consortium, co-authored the Cape Town Open Education Declaration, and is an advisor to a number of non-profit and for-profit education projects. He has received and Ashoka fellowships, and came to MIT as a Media Lab Director's fellow.

Preventing Keystroke Based Identification in Open Data Sets

Juho Leinonen
University of Helsinki
Department of Computer
Science
Helsinki, Finland
juho.leinonen@helsinki.fi

Petri Ihantola
Tampere University of
Technology
Department of Pervasive
Computing
Tampere, Finland
petri.ihantola@tut.fi

Arto Hellas
University of Helsinki
Department of Computer
Science
Helsinki, Finland
arto.hellas@cs.helsinki.fi

ABSTRACT

Large-scale courses such as Massive Online Open Courses (MOOCs) can be a great data source for researchers. Ideally, the data gathered on such courses should be openly available to all researchers. Studies could be easily replicated and novel studies on existing data could be conducted. However, very fine-grained data such as source code snapshots can contain hidden identifiers. For example, distinct typing patterns that identify individuals can be extracted from such data. Hence, simply removing explicit identifiers such as names and student numbers is not sufficient to protect the privacy of the users who have supplied the data. At the same time, removing all keystroke information would decrease the value of the shared data significantly.

In this work, we study how keystroke data from a programming context could be modified to prevent keystroke latency based identification whilst still retaining information that can be used to e.g. infer programming experience. We investigate the degree of anonymization required to render identification of students based on their typing patterns unreliable. Then, we study whether the modified keystroke data can still be used to infer the programming experience of the students as a case study of whether the anonymized typing patterns have retained at least some informative value.

We show that it is possible to modify data so that keystroke latency based identification is no longer accurate, but the programming experience of the students can still be inferred, i.e. the data still has value to researchers. In a broader context, our results indicate that information and anonymity are not necessarily mutually exclusive.

CCS Concepts

•**Security and privacy** → **Pseudonymity, anonymity and untraceability; Data anonymization and sanitization; Privacy protections;** •**Information systems** → *Data mining;* •**Social and professional topics** → Computing education;

Author Keywords

data privacy; data anonymization; keystroke dynamics; programming experience inference; source code snapshots

INTRODUCTION

Nowadays, a lot of data is shared openly for replication studies and novel analysis on existing data [3, 6, 18]. Still, privacy issues often prevent companies, governments, and (educational) institutions from sharing the data that they have collected [10]. Sharing non-anonymized data that could be used to identify individuals would violate the privacy of the users or parties from which the data has been collected. Anonymizing data by simply removing parts of the data – attributes – may not be sufficient as latent factors that can be used to identify individuals may exist.

Attributes that are not identifiers by themselves, but can be used for identification together with other attributes are called quasi-identifiers [10]. For example, Daries et al. [5] studied anonymization of MOOC data from a social science perspective, and defined the country, gender, age and level of education of a participant as quasi-identifiers. Similarly, keystroke timings found in programming snapshots are quasi-identifiers: a single keystroke timing does not reveal the identity of the typist, but together the timings can be used to construct a typing profile that can be used for identification [7, 11, 15, 21, 24]. Longi et al. [21] have showed that individual programmers can be identified from source code snapshots based on the times that the programmers take to move from one key to another, i.e. the typing pattern.

From a computer science education viewpoint, having fine-grained keystroke data provides a detailed picture of the students' learning process [30]. Research carried by Vihavainen et al. [31] found that keystroke level data can be used to conduct studies that are not possible with more coarse-grained data. Such data can also be used for inferring the programming experience of students [20].

L@S 2017, April 20 - 21, 2017, Cambridge, MA, USA

© 2017 Copyright held by the owner/author(s). Publication rights licensed to ACM.
ISBN 978-1-4503-4450-0/17/04. . . $15.00

DOI: http://dx.doi.org/10.1145/3051457.3051458

However, it is rare to include keystroke data in open data sets. While source code snapshot data is publicly available by, for example, the Blackbox-project [3], the data does not include keystroke level data. Thus, keystroke timing based studies (e.g. [2, 7, 20, 29]) are presently hard to replicate because such data is rarely collected and available. This has been acknowledged as a problem and there seems to be pressure (and a trend) for publishing more fine-grained learning data than what is available today [14]. Al-Zubidy et al. note that replication studies are essential for theory building and are therefore concerned about the lack of replication studies in the computer science education field [1].

Daries et al. [5] showed that in a social science context, the value of data can degrade significantly in the anonymization process – results on anonymized data differ from results on non-anonymized data. In this work, we study whether there is a similar effect in anonymizing source code snapshot data. More specifically, we investigate whether keystroke timing data in source code snapshots can be modified in a way that prevents typing pattern based identification, whilst other valuable information can still be inferred from the anonymized keystroke timing data. While identification could also be possible from other identifiers found in keystroke data such as text content (variable names, class names, etc.), we focus on preventing identification based on keystroke timings. Being able to modify keystroke timings so that they cannot be used for identification would remove a quasi-identifier from the data, which would maintain the possibility that anonymized keystroke timings could be included in open data sets and used for research.

It has been previously shown that programming experience can be inferred from keystroke timings to a degree [20]. Thus, we conduct a case study where programming experience is the valuable information we wish to be able to infer from anonymized keystroke timing data. Inferring programming experience from keystroke timings can be useful on data sets that do not include programming background information or with students who have not answered a background survey [20]. We conduct experiments using two anonymization procedures and compare identification accuracies with different degrees of anonymization. Furthermore, we seek to find a balance where programmers could not be identified based on keystroke timings but programming experience could still be inferred. Being able to infer programming experience but not the individuals would suggest that there is value for researchers in the data, while the privacy of the individuals would be preserved. This is a step towards releasing fine-grained source code snapshot data openly to others.

This article is organized as follows. First, we provide a summary of previous work related to identification using keystroke dynamics, inferring valuable information from keystroke timings, and data anonymization. Next, we outline our research methodology and data. Then, our experiments and their results are presented. Finally, a discussion of the results and conclusions are presented.

RELATED WORK

Here, we visit three streams of related work. First, we discuss articles where keystroke data has been used to infer the identity of a user, then we discuss articles related to inferring other information in addition to identity from keystroke timings, and finally, we visit data anonymization from a data sharing perspective.

Keystrokes and identity

Information recorded from typing, such as the duration of keystrokes, pressure of keystrokes, and keystroke latencies, has been used for identification purposes [7, 11, 15, 21, 22, 24]. From these especially the keystroke latencies between pairs of keys – digraphs – have been used extensively [7, 11, 21, 24]. For example, a study by Longi et al. [21] shows that the identity of programmers can be detected from keystroke data recorded during programming sessions. Using data from two separate courses, they observed that linking the students from one course to another – when using full course data from both courses – could be done with 98.6% accuracy. They note that keystroke identification is an especially convenient way of authentication in Massive Online Open Courses (MOOCs) as it is irrespective of location and thus perfect for distance learning. The MOOC platform Coursera is already using keystroke identification as they collect typing samples from students seeking to acquire a verified certificate for completing a course [4].

Identification results often vary significantly based on the data used. For example, in a study by Monrose and Rubin with 46 participants, the identification accuracy decreased significantly from 79% with transcribed text to 21% with free text [24]. It was suggested that this could be explained by the writer having to think about what they were going to write instead of just writing whatever was given to them. However, Killourhy and Maxion found no significant difference in classification results when using transcribed or free text [17].

Keystroke analysis has been applied successfully for identifying students in online exams [19, 22, 27]. Using data from 30 students taking examinations in a business school, Monaco et al. were able to correctly identify all the students [22]. Likewise, Leinonen et al. [19] were able to identify a large portion of the students in programming exams where students code on a computer. They showed that students can be identified quite reliably in both controlled and uncontrolled exam environments. In the controlled exam, the students were in a computer lab at the university and in the uncontrolled exam they could be in whatever setting they found most comfortable, e.g. at home.

Inferring information based on keystroke timing

In addition to identification and authentication, keystroke timings can be used for inferring other information. Thomas et al. have studied the relationship between keystroke latencies and programming performance [29]. They categorized digraphs, i.e. character pairs, into seven categories based on their type and calculated the mean latency by category. They found statistically significant correlations between the mean latencies of some categories and exam results. An explanation they provide is that skilled programmers type some digraphs faster than novice programmers.

More recently, Leinonen et al. [20] partially replicated the study by Thomas et al. [29] by analyzing the relationship between digraph latencies and programming performance. Furthermore, they described an experiment where they sought to identify students' past programming experience from keystroke latencies. Leinonen et al. note that inferring programming experience from keystroke latency data can be more reliable than a background questionnaire as some students may choose not to answer such questionnaires. After performing feature selection on digraph latencies and experimenting with a set of classifiers, they observed up to 77% classification accuracy and a Matthew's Correlation Coefficient of 0.54 in predicting whether a student had programmed previously or not. As an example, they showed that on average, experienced programmers move faster from the key i to the key +, i.e. experienced programmers type the digraph $i+$, faster than novice programmers and thus at least partially confirmed the suggestion by Thomas et al. Intuitively, this makes sense as the digraph $i+$ is something programmers type often when incrementing an index variable, while it rarely occurs in regular text.

Additionally, keystroke analysis has been used to detect boredom and engagement [2], stress [33], and emotional states [9].

Data anonymization
Anonymity in data is often achieved by removing attributes from the data [10, 25, 28], reducing the accuracy of the data, e.g. by grouping and smoothing [13, 16] and by adding noise or fake information [8, 16]. Sun and Upadhyaya have developed a rule-based data sanitization method to remove sensitive information such as social security numbers from keystroke data [28].

Fung et al. outline four different types of attributes in data which reserve privacy: explicit identifiers, quasi-identifiers, sensitive attributes, and non-sensitive attributes [10]. Quasi-identifiers are attributes that are not identifiers by themselves, but can be used for identification together with other quasi-identifiers. As an example of anonymizing data by removing explicit identifiers and quasi-identifiers, network measurement data could be anonymized by removing attributes such as packet payloads and ip-addresses [25]. Daries et al. [5] analyzed the anonymization of data collected on MOOCs. They found two explicit identifiers – username and ip-address – and six quasi-identifiers – country, age, gender, and level of education of a participant as well as course id and the amount of forum posts – in their data and removed them. Similarly, explicit identifiers such as student numbers and quasi-identifiers such as keystroke timestamp information could be removed from source code snapshot data. However, removing quasi-identifiers also reduces the value of the data as information that is possibly relevant for research can be lost in the process as Daries et al. noticed [5]. Thus, modifying such data in a way that preserves privacy but yields possibility for research would be optimal.

In addition to removing attributes, other approaches for preserving anonymity have been suggested. For example, He et al. [13] suggested anonymization of set-valued data by distributing the data into buckets. Their work was motivated by the fact that the previously suggested approaches work well only if a subject is associated with a single sensitive value at a time, which does not suit set-valued data well. Similarly, Samarati et al. suggested replacing values in the data by semantically consistent less precise alternatives [26], i.e. generalization or rounding. A challenge here is to find an optimal degree of anonymization where data is minimally distorted while identification of subjects is still made improbable.

Recently, Monaco and Tappert developed two obfuscation strategies in the context of a third party continuously recording keystroke data [23]. They were able to decrease identification accuracy on average by 20% by adding a 25 ms random delay to the keystroke events and found that a delay of 500 ms was needed to reduce identification accuracy by half. In the context of a constant flow of keystrokes, there is a constraint that the anonymization should not affect the user experience, e.g. an added delay can not be noticeably long. However, in our context of open data sets there is no such constraint, which allows calculating optimal degrees of anonymization post hoc.

METHODOLOGY
In this section, we outline our research questions, the context of the data we use, and our research methodology.

Research questions
In this work, we seek to determine how different degrees of anonymization of programming course data affects attributes that can be inferred from typing profiles. Our research questions are:

RQ 1. How does anonymization by rounding keystroke average latencies affect identification accuracy?

RQ 2. How does anonymization by bucketing affect identification accuracy?

RQ 3. How does anonymization affect inferring programming experience from typing profiles?

With the first research question, we seek to determine how rounding average latencies can be used to anonymize keystroke data. With the second research question, we explore whether splitting the data into even-sized buckets works for anonymization. Finally, with the third research question, we examine the extent of anonymization one can perform whilst still retaining information about programming experience. We are interested in finding an optimal amount of anonymization where identification is no longer practical, but programming experience can still be inferred.

Context
The data used in the experiments come from two similar introductory Java programming courses held in the autumns of 2014 and 2015 at University of Helsinki. One of the authors of this work was responsible for organizing the courses. Both courses lasted for 7 weeks. The courses taught the students

programming basics such as variables, loops, input, and output. Both data sets were used in the identification experiments, but only the autumn 2014 course had information available on students' programming background, and therefore was the only one included in the programming experience experiments. 41.2% of the students had at least some programming experience and 58.8% had none.

The students used an integrated development environment (IDE) for working on the course assignments. The IDE used the Test My Code -plugin [32] which records a snapshot for each action where the student modifies the source code. The snapshots have a nanosecond level timestamp in addition to keystroke information. Students could turn the data gathering mechanism in the environment off if they chose to – data for this study was provided on a voluntary basis and no incentives were given to students who provided the data.

Preprocessing

For preprocessing the keystroke data, we followed the procedure outlined in the study by Longi et al. [21]. Only digraphs with latencies between 10 ms and 750 ms were included as first done by Dowland and Furnell [7]. The lower bound is necessary to eliminate auto-completion events from the IDE. The upper bound is needed to only capture the subconscious typing rhythm of the student and to remove any breaks they might take while working on an exercise.

Since the typing profiles are built with average latencies, we required that a student should have at least 5 occurrences of any digraph used to build their typing profile. If the student had only typed a digraph under 5 times, the average latency for that digraph was excluded from the student's typing profile. Snapshots where multiple characters were added at the same time were discarded as they were almost exclusively copy-paste events.

After preprocessing, there were 199 students left in the autumn 2014 data set and 153 in the autumn 2015 data set.

Identification

For the identification experiments, we use the acceptance threshold method introduced by Longi et al. [21] where a match in the top k closest training set samples is considered correct for a specific test sample. The idea behind this is that exact identification is not always mandatory. For example, for authentication in online exams, it is sufficient to be quite sure that the students are who they claim to be.

To build the typing profiles, the average latency between two specific characters was calculated for all character pairs, i.e. digraphs, for each student in the data. If a student had not typed a digraph, the missing value was replaced with the student's average typing speed.

For both data sets used in the identification experiments, we chose to build the typing profiles in the training set from the first six weeks of exercises and used the data from exercises of the last week as the test set. To determine if a test sample was correctly identified, we calculated the euclidean distance to each training set sample. We then sorted the training set samples based on the distance from the test sample. We used

an acceptance threshold of $k = 10$, and thus regarded the student to be correctly identified if their typing profile was in the top 10 closest training set matches.

Programming experience inference

Earlier research indicates that the Bayesian Network and Random Forest classifiers have good performance at classifying students in the context of inferring programming experience from typing profiles [20]. Therefore, we classify the students into two groups: those with some programming experience and those with none using the Bayesian Network, Random Forest, and ZeroR classifiers. The ZeroR classifier is a majority class classifier which will classify every sample to the majority class, and is therefore good as a baseline against which the performance of the other two classifiers can be measured. The classification accuracy is evaluated using 10-fold cross-validation.

Anonymization by rounding

We use an anonymization technique similar to generalization [26] where the values in the data are rounded to reduce identification accuracy (RQ1). To investigate how rounding the average latencies in typing profiles affects programmer identification and classification based on programming experience, we modified the latencies using Equation 1. It rounds the latency z to the nearest x, where x is the number of milliseconds given to the anonymization function as a parameter. The resulting value y is then used instead of the original value z in the construction of the typing profile. The aim is to reduce the accuracy of the data, hopefully reducing identification accuracy in the process, which would anonymize the data. We studied how identification accuracy deteriorates when the value of x is increased.

$$y = x * round(z/x) \tag{1}$$

Equation 1 essentially distributes the average latencies into buckets. For example, if x is 100 milliseconds, all latencies will be rounded to the nearest multiple of 100. This leads to all latencies between 0 and 50 ms being rounded to 0 and distributed to the first bucket, all latencies between 50 and 150 ms being rounded to 100 and distributed to the second bucket, and so on.

After rounding the average latencies, the data was normalized to reduce the effect of digraphs with large average latencies on the distance calculations.

Anonymization by distributing the data into even-sized buckets

The buckets that result from the rounding method are not equal in size: the size of the first bucket is half the size of the subsequent buckets. Motivated by this we analyzed whether distributing data into even-sized buckets could be used for anonymizing keystroke data (RQ2). We modified the average latencies in the data by first increasing each latency z by half of the size b of the buckets using Equation 2, and then rounding each latency z_1 to the nearest x, where x is the current bucket size b using Equation 3. The resulting value y is then used instead of the original value z in the construction of the typing profile.

$$z_1 = z + (b/2) \qquad (2)$$

$$y = b * round(z_1/b) \qquad (3)$$

The only difference between this method and the rounding method is that this method distributes the data into even-sized buckets. For example, if we have buckets of 100 milliseconds, we want all latencies between 0 and 100 milliseconds to be in the same bucket. Now, any latency between 0 and 100 ms will first be incremented by 50 ms (half the bucket size), leading to a distribution between 50 and 150 ms. Then, the latencies will be rounded to the nearest multiple of 100 milliseconds (the bucket size), which in the case of values between 50 and 150 milliseconds is 100 milliseconds. The procedure is then repeated for all values between 100 and 200 milliseconds, etc.

Again, after rounding the average latencies, the data was normalized to reduce the effect of digraphs with large average latencies on the distance calculations.

Feature selection

For exploring how identification accuracy suffers when the data is anonymized (RQ1 & RQ2), the 25 most common digraphs were used to construct the typing profiles as first done by Leinonen et al. [19]

In the feature selection for the programming experience data set (RQ3), we followed the procedure outlined by Leinonen et al. [20] for inferring programming experience from typing profiles. Features with no data (e.g. digraphs that no student had typed) were removed. Then, the WEKA Data Mining toolkit [12] was used for feature selection. Out of more than 10000 initial features, less than 50 features were left in each data set after the feature selection.

EXPERIMENTS AND RESULTS

In this section, we describe the experiments we conducted to answer each of the research questions and the results of the experiments.

Identification experiments

To answer the first two research questions *"How does anonymization by rounding keystroke average latencies affect identification accuracy?"* and *"How does anonymization by bucketing affect identification accuracy?"*, we calculated identification accuracies with different degrees of anonymization.

The results of the experiments are presented in Table 1. The millisecond values in the first column represent the rounding for RQ1 and the bucket size for RQ2. The 0 ms row shows the identification accuracy without modifications (rounding or bucketing), i.e. without anonymization.

When using rounding for anonymization, identification accuracies in both data sets deteriorate in the first two 100 ms steps,

Table 1. Identification accuracy percentages with different rounding precisions and bucket sizes between 0 ms (no anonymization) and 600 ms.

Method	Rounding		Buckets	
Data	2014	2015	2014	2015
0 ms	98.0	97.8	98.0	97.8
100 ms	81.7	81.3	26.1	31.7
200 ms	6.5	56.8	12.4	15.8
300 ms	72.5	67.6	6.5	7.2
400 ms	77.1	67.6	6.5	7.2
500 ms	6.5	7.2	6.5	7.2
600 ms	6.5	7.2	6.5	7.2

Table 2. Programming experience classification accuracy percentages with different rounding precisions and bucket sizes.

Method	Rounding		
Classifier	Bayes Net	Random Forest	ZeroR
0 ms	75.4	73.9	58.8
100 ms	73.9	75.4	58.8
200 ms	73.9	72.4	58.8
300 ms	73.9	70.9	58.8
400 ms	68.3	73.4	58.8
500 ms	73.9	73.9	58.8
600 ms	70.4	71.4	58.8
Method	Buckets		
Classifier	Bayes Net	Random Forest	ZeroR
0 ms	75.4	73.9	58.8
100 ms	73.4	73.4	58.8
200 ms	71.4	75.4	58.8
300 ms	70.4	71.4	58.8
400 ms	61.3	69.8	58.8
500 ms	64.3	67.3	58.8
600 ms	58.8	60.3	58.8

but then improve or stay equal in the next two steps. After that they start declining again. The unexpected value of 6.5% in the rounding experiment of the 2014 data set when rounding to 200 ms is studied in further detail later.

Using buckets for anonymization, identification accuracies in both data sets deteriorate with every 100 ms step and reach their lowest values already after three steps. These results are different from the results of the rounding anonymization method, where the lowest values were only attained after 5 steps and at the third step mark the identification accuracies were still quite high at around 70% accuracy compared to around 7% accuracy with the bucket approach.

Inferring programming experience from anonymized data

To answer the third research question, *"How does anonymization affect inferring programming experience from typing profiles?"*, we measured classification accuracies with different amounts of anonymization using both the rounding method and the bucket method and multiple classifiers.

Table 2 shows the classification accuracy results with different amounts of anonymization. With the rounding method, classification accuracies deteriorate slightly with each step, although there are exceptions. We do not observe a similar effect as

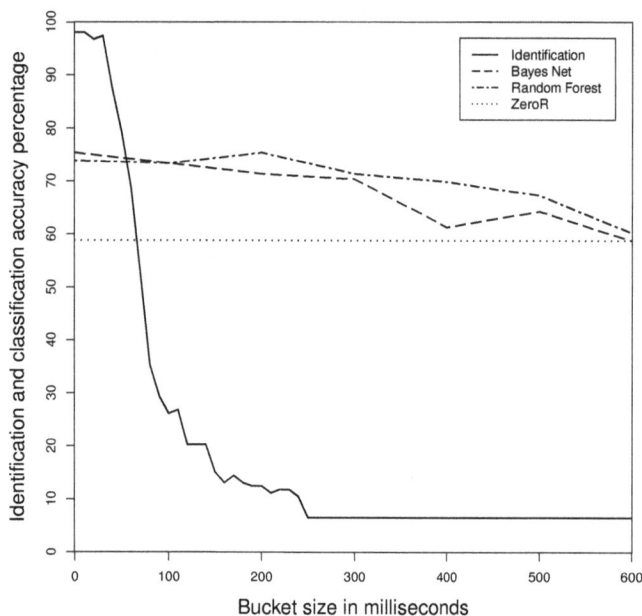

Figure 1. Identification (solid line) and programming experience (dashed lines) classification accuracy compared against increasing bucket size. The data was split into even-sized buckets. Programming experience classification accuracies are shown for three different classifiers: Bayesian Network, Random Forest, and the majority class classifier ZeroR. The x-axis represents bucket size and the y-axis expresses identification and classification accuracy.

with identification, where the accuracy temporarily improved when transitioning from rounding to nearest 200 milliseconds to rounding to nearest 300 milliseconds. Overall, classification accuracy declines more slowly than identification accuracy with the rounding method. Similar to the rounding method, classification accuracies with the bucket method degrade with each step. A clear difference is that with the bucket method the classification accuracies decline faster, nearing the performance of the baseline ZeroR classifier when the bucket size is 600 ms. In contrast, with the rounding method, Bayesian Network and Random Forest outperform ZeroR by over 10 percentage points at the 600 millisecond mark. Nevertheless, classification accuracy does not decline as fast as identification accuracy with the bucket method – for example, with 300 millisecond buckets, reliable identification is no longer possible, but classification accuracy is still significantly better than with the majority class classifier. The decline in identification and classification accuracy is shown in Figure 1.

DISCUSSION AND CONCLUSIONS

In this work, we studied how typing profile data could be anonymized whilst retaining information important to researchers in the data. The motivation for the study is to be able to release open data sets where data that could be used to identify subjects is removed. We explored two different ways of anonymizing data consisting of student typing profiles on programming courses.

The results of our experiments indicate that it is possible to anonymize keystroke data in a way that preserves information relevant to researchers in our context. We showed that typing profiles based on keystroke data can still be used to classify programmers based on their programming experience, even when the data has been sufficiently anonymized so that programmers cannot be identified with reliable accuracy based on keystroke latencies.

For the rounding method, rounding keystroke average latencies to the nearest 500 milliseconds would be optimal in our context. When rounding to the nearest 500 milliseconds, reliable identification is hard. Approximately 7% of the students are correctly identified with a threshold of $k = 10$. This accuracy is very low when compared to the non-anonymized accuracy of around 98.5%. Purely random guessing would yield an identification accuracy of around 5% with our data set, which means that even with the 7% accuracy it is possible that there may still be some information on identity in the data, which might not be acceptable in all scenarios. With the same 500 millisecond rounding, programming experience can be inferred accurately for 73.9% students. With the Random Forest classifier, programming experience classification accuracy has remained the same as without anonymization, and with the Bayesian Network classifier, it declined only by 1.5 percentage points.

For the bucket method, the optimal amount of anonymization is quite different from the rounding method in our context. With even-sized 300 millisecond buckets, identification accuracy has decreased to the lowest value it will reach. At that point, programming experience classification is possible with around 71% accuracy compared to the 58.8% accuracy with the majority classifier. The result indicates that the bucket method is more efficient at anonymizing the data, although more domain-relevant information is lost in the process.

The results of the rounding method are interesting due to the fact that only keystroke latencies between 10 and 750 milliseconds were included in the typing profiles. When rounding to the nearest 500 milliseconds, there are only two possible values for the features – 0 milliseconds or 500 milliseconds – since all values between 0 and 250 milliseconds will be rounded to 0 milliseconds while values between 250 milliseconds and 750 milliseconds (the upper bound) will be rounded to 500 milliseconds. The result means that for inferring programming experience from typing profiles, it is sufficient to categorize all average latencies that the typing profiles include into two buckets based on whether the student is fast or slow at writing the digraph.

Another interesting find is that when the rounding method is used, identification seems quite reliable with an accuracy of around 74% even when rounding to the nearest 300 or 400 milliseconds. To further examine this, we plotted the changes in identification accuracies in 10 millisecond intervals. The resulting plot is in Figure 2. The local maxima for the two courses are at 340 ms with 86.3% accuracy and 360 ms with 90.2% accuracy. When rounding to both 340 and 360 milliseconds, there are only three buckets in our data due to filtering out events that are not between 10 and 750 ms. For exam-

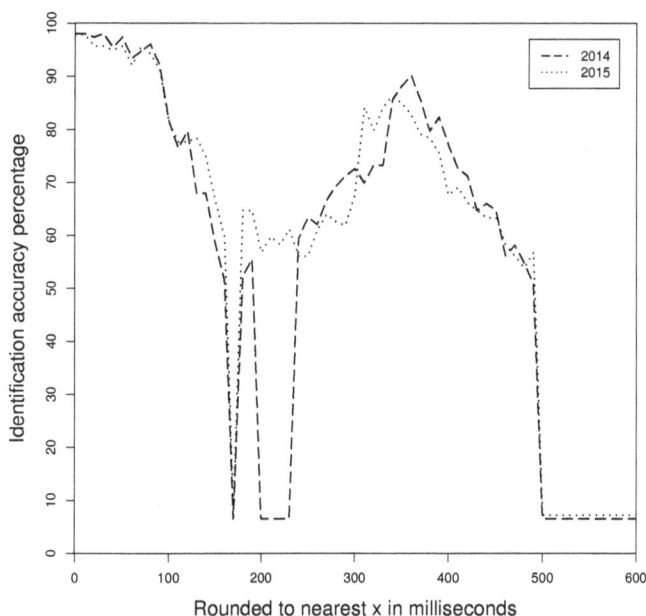

Figure 2. Identification accuracy compared against rounding precision. All values in the data were rounded to a nearest millisecond value. The larger the millisecond value in the x-axis, the lesser the rounding precision. The y-axis expresses identification accuracy.

ple, with 340 milliseconds, values between 0 and 170 ms are rounded to 0 ms, values between 170 and 510 ms are rounded to 340 ms, and values between 510 ms and 850 ms are rounded to 680 ms. This result suggests that fine-grained timestamp data is not actually necessary to identify programmers from their typing patterns. Only categorizing average keystroke latencies into three buckets – slow, mediocre, fast – might be enough for reliable identification.

The effect seen in Figure 2 implies that categorizing data into 3 buckets works better for identification than categorizing data into more buckets, unless the rounding starts to be insignificant (under 100 milliseconds). A potential explanation is that additional buckets beyond three add unnecessary noise to the data. For example, with five buckets – very slow, slow, mediocre, fast, very fast – there might not be enough average latencies in the very slow and very fast buckets. On the other hand, some average latencies that should be categorized to the mediocre bucket for maximal performance might be categorized to the slow or fast buckets.

Moreover, the observed effect is a cautionary result for researchers seeking to anonymize their data. Using a similar method and observing e.g. that the identification accuracies are low enough for sharing the data at the 200 millisecond point, and adding an additional 100 milliseconds "just to be sure", plenty of information that could be used to identify the individuals in the data would be shared accidentally.

The results of our studies show that keystroke timings can be anonymized in a way that retains informative value in data, and thus keystroke timings can be included in open data sets

as long as proper anonymization procedures are followed. A limitation of our study is that there were only 199 and 153 students in our data sets. This is due to a language constraint as the courses were not organized in English. Future work should examine how the methodologies outlined in this work perform when in addition to large-scale data, the amount of students is larger. In addition, further research is needed to investigate whether other information than programming experience can be inferred from obscured data. Furthermore, future work should investigate how removing possible hidden identifiers other than keystroke latencies – such as text content – affect both identification accuracy and inference of valuable information.

ACKNOWLEDGMENTS

We are grateful to the anonymous reviewers whose comments helped us improve the paper. This work was partially funded by Academy of Finland under grant number 303694, *Skills, education and the future of work*.

REFERENCES

1. Ahmed Al-Zubidy, Jeffrey C Carver, Sarah Heckman, and Mark Sherriff. 2016. A (Updated) Review of Empiricism at the SIGCSE Technical Symposium. In *Proceedings of the 47th ACM Technical Symposium on Computing Science Education*. ACM, 120–125.

2. Robert Bixler and Sidney D'Mello. 2013. Detecting Boredom and Engagement During Writing with Keystroke Analysis, Task Appraisals, and Stable Traits. In *Proc. of the 2013 International Conference on Intelligent User Interfaces (IUI '13)*. ACM, New York, NY, USA, 225–234. DOI: http://dx.doi.org/10.1145/2449396.2449426

3. Neil Christopher Charles Brown, Michael Kölling, Davin McCall, and Ian Utting. 2014. Blackbox: a large scale repository of novice programmers' activity. In *Proc. of the 45th ACM technical symposium on Computer science education*. ACM, 223–228.

4. Coursera. 2016. Coursera Signature Track. https://www.coursera.org/signature/. (2016). Accessed: 2016-10-24.

5. Jon P Daries, Justin Reich, Jim Waldo, Elise M Young, Jonathan Whittinghill, Andrew Dean Ho, Daniel Thomas Seaton, and Isaac Chuang. 2014. Privacy, anonymity, and big data in the social sciences. *Commun. ACM* 57, 9 (2014), 56–63.

6. Dataverse. 2016. The Dataverse Project. http://dataverse.org/. (2016). Accessed: 2016-10-24.

7. Paul S. Dowland and Steven M. Furnell. 2004. A Long-Term Trial of Keystroke Profiling Using Digraph, Trigraph and Keyword Latencies. In *Security and Protection in Information Processing Systems*, Yves Deswarte, Frédéric Cuppens, Sushil Jajodia, and Lingyu Wang (Eds.). IFIP - The International Federation for Information Processing, Vol. 147. Springer, 275–289. DOI: http://dx.doi.org/10.1007/1-4020-8143-X_18

8. Cynthia Dwork. 2008. Differential privacy: A survey of results. In *Theory and applications of models of computation*. Springer, 1–19.

9. Clayton Epp, Michael Lippold, and Regan L. Mandryk. 2011. Identifying Emotional States Using Keystroke Dynamics. In *Proc. of the SIGCHI Conference on Human Factors in Computing Systems (CHI '11)*. ACM, New York, NY, USA, 715–724. DOI: http://dx.doi.org/10.1145/1978942.1979046

10. Benjamin C. M. Fung, Ke Wang, Rui Chen, and Philip S. Yu. 2010. Privacy-preserving Data Publishing: A Survey of Recent Developments. *ACM Comput. Surv.* 42, 4, Article 14 (2010), 53 pages. DOI: http://dx.doi.org/10.1145/1749603.1749605

11. R Stockton Gaines, William Lisowski, S James Press, and Norman Shapiro. 1980. *Authentication by keystroke timing: Some preliminary results*. Technical Report.

12. Mark Hall, Eibe Frank, Geoffrey Holmes, Bernhard Pfahringer, Peter Reutemann, and Ian H Witten. 2009. The WEKA data mining software: an update. *ACM SIGKDD explorations newsletter* 11, 1 (2009), 10–18.

13. Yeye He and Jeffrey F Naughton. 2009. Anonymization of set-valued data via top-down, local generalization. *Proc. of the VLDB Endowment* 2, 1 (2009), 934–945.

14. Petri Ihantola, Arto Vihavainen, Alireza Ahadi, Matthew Butler, Jürgen Börstler, Stephen H. Edwards, Essi Isohanni, Ari Korhonen, Andrew Petersen, Kelly Rivers, Miguel Ángel Rubio, Judy Sheard, Bronius Skupas, Jaime Spacco, Claudia Szabo, and Daniel Toll. 2015. Educational Data Mining and Learning Analytics in Programming: Literature Review and Case Studies. In *Proc. of the 2015 ITiCSE on Working Group Reports (ITICSE-WGR '15)*. ACM, New York, NY, USA, 41–63. DOI:http://dx.doi.org/10.1145/2858796.2858798

15. M. Karnan, M. Akila, and N. Krishnaraj. 2011. Biometric personal authentication using keystroke dynamics: A review. *Applied Soft Computing* 11, 2 (2011), 1565 – 1573. DOI: http://dx.doi.org/10.1016/j.asoc.2010.08.003 The Impact of Soft Computing for the Progress of Artificial Intelligence.

16. Georgios Kellaris and Stavros Papadopoulos. 2013. Practical differential privacy via grouping and smoothing. In *Proc. of the 39th international conference on Very Large Data Bases (PVLDB'13)*. VLDB Endowment, 301–312. http://dl.acm.org/citation.cfm?id=2488335.2488337

17. Kevin S. Killourhy and Roy A. Maxion. 2012. Free vs. Transcribed Text for Keystroke-dynamics Evaluations. In *Proc. of the 2012 Workshop on Learning from Authoritative Security Experiment Results (LASER '12)*. ACM, New York, NY, USA, 1–8. DOI: http://dx.doi.org/10.1145/2379616.2379617

18. Kenneth R Koedinger, Ryan SJd Baker, Kyle Cunningham, Alida Skogsholm, Brett Leber, and John Stamper. 2010. A data repository for the EDM community: The PSLC DataShop. *Handbook of educational data mining* 43 (2010).

19. Juho Leinonen, Krista Longi, Arto Klami, Alireza Ahadi, and Arto Vihavainen. 2016a. Typing Patterns and Authentication in Practical Programming Exams. In *Proc. of the 2016 ACM Conference on Innovation and Technology in Computer Science Education*. ACM, 160–165.

20. Juho Leinonen, Krista Longi, Arto Klami, and Arto Vihavainen. 2016b. Automatic Inference of Programming Performance and Experience from Typing Patterns. In *Proc. of the 47th ACM Technical Symposium on Computing Science Education (SIGCSE '16)*. ACM, New York, NY, USA, 132–137. DOI: http://dx.doi.org/10.1145/2839509.2844612

21. Krista Longi, Juho Leinonen, Henrik Nygren, Joni Salmi, Arto Klami, and Arto Vihavainen. 2015. Identification of Programmers from Typing Patterns. In *Proc. of the 15th Koli Calling Conference on Computing Education Research*. ACM, 60–67.

22. J.V. Monaco, J.C. Stewart, Sung-Hyuk Cha, and C.C. Tappert. 2013. Behavioral biometric verification of student identity in online course assessment and authentication of authors in literary works. In *Biometrics: Theory, Applications and Systems (BTAS), 2013 IEEE Sixth International Conference on*. 1–8. DOI: http://dx.doi.org/10.1109/BTAS.2013.6712743

23. John V Monaco and Charles C Tappert. 2016. Obfuscating Keystroke Time Intervals to Avoid Identification and Impersonation. In *The 9th IAPR International Conference on Biometrics (ICB)*. IEEE.

24. Fabian Monrose and Aviel Rubin. 1997. Authentication via Keystroke Dynamics. In *Proc. of the 4th ACM Conference on Computer and Communications Security (CCS '97)*. ACM, New York, NY, USA, 48–56. DOI: http://dx.doi.org/10.1145/266420.266434

25. Ruoming Pang, Mark Allman, Vern Paxson, and Jason Lee. 2006. The Devil and Packet Trace Anonymization. *SIGCOMM Comput. Commun. Rev.* 36, 1 (Jan. 2006), 29–38. DOI:http://dx.doi.org/10.1145/1111322.1111330

26. Pierangela Samarati and Latanya Sweeney. 1998. Generalizing Data to Provide Anonymity when Disclosing Information (Abstract). In *Proc. of the Seventeenth ACM SIGACT-SIGMOD-SIGART Symposium on Principles of Database Systems (PODS '98)*. ACM, New York, NY, USA, 188–. DOI: http://dx.doi.org/10.1145/275487.275508

27. J.C. Stewart, J.V. Monaco, Sung-Hyuk Cha, and C.C. Tappert. 2011. An investigation of keystroke and stylometry traits for authenticating online test takers. In *Biometrics (IJCB), 2011 Int. Joint Conference on*. 1–7. DOI:http://dx.doi.org/10.1109/IJCB.2011.6117480

28. Yan Sun and Shambhu Upadhyaya. 2015. Secure and privacy preserving data processing support for active authentication. *Information Systems Frontiers* 17, 5 (2015), 1007–1015. DOI: http://dx.doi.org/10.1007/s10796-015-9587-9

29. Richard C Thomas, Amela Karahasanovic, and Gregor E Kennedy. 2005. An investigation into keystroke latency metrics as an indicator of programming performance. In *Proceedings of the 7th Australasian conference on Computing education-Volume 42*. Australian Computer Society, Inc., 127–134.

30. Arto Vihavainen, Juha Helminen, and Petri Ihantola. 2014a. How novices tackle their first lines of code in an IDE: analysis of programming session traces. In *Proc. of the 14th Koli Calling International Conference on Computing Education Research*. ACM, 109–116.

31. Arto Vihavainen, Matti Luukkainen, and Petri Ihantola. 2014b. Analysis of Source Code Snapshot Granularity Levels. In *Proc. of the 15th Annual Conference on Information Technology Education (SIGITE '14)*. ACM, New York, NY, USA, 21–26. DOI: http://dx.doi.org/10.1145/2656450.2656473

32. Arto Vihavainen, Thomas Vikberg, Matti Luukkainen, and Martin Pärtel. 2013. Scaffolding students' learning using Test My Code. In *Proc. of the 18th ACM conference on Innovation and technology in computer science education*. ACM, 117–122.

33. Lisa M. Vizer, Lina Zhou, and Andrew Sears. 2009. Automated Stress Detection Using Keystroke and Linguistic Features: An Exploratory Study. *Int. J. Hum.-Comput. Stud.* 67, 10 (Oct. 2009), 870–886. DOI: http://dx.doi.org/10.1016/j.ijhcs.2009.07.005

Do Performance Trends Suggest Wide-spread Collaborative Cheating on Asynchronous Exams?

Binglin Chen, Matthew West, Craig Zilles
University of Illinois at Urbana-Champaign
Urbana, IL 61801, USA
{chen386, mwest, zilles}@illinois.edu

ABSTRACT

Using a data set from 29,492 asynchronous exams in an on-campus proctored computer-based testing facility (CBTF), we observed correlations between when a student chooses to take their exam within the exam period and their score on the exam. Somewhat surprisingly, instead of increasing throughout the exam period, which might be indicative of widespread collaborative cheating, we find that exam scores decrease throughout the exam period. While this could be attributed to weaker students putting off exams, this effect holds even when accounting for student ability as measured by a synchronous exam taken during the same semester. This suggests that precautions can be taken by a CBTF to maintain cheating at a low level (e.g., the level of proctored synchronous exams), in spite of the fact that students are taking their exams over a multi-day period.

Author Keywords

asynchronous exams; student performance; cheating; computerized testing.

INTRODUCTION

Exams are a frequently used method in college education to assess students' understanding of course material. However, running exams for a large class (e.g., 200+ students) can be a logistical nightmare [13, 18, 24]. It has been proposed that computerized exams in a face-to-face proctored environment can greatly reduce the overhead of running exams and broaden the kinds of questions that can be automatically graded [24]. Key to the efficient implementation of computer-based exams for large enrollment classes is running them *asynchronously* (e.g., allowing students to choose their exam time within a given time window), because it allows the testing center where the exams take place to be much smaller than the largest class and gracefully tolerates student conflicts [8, 25].

When faculty are invited to use asynchronous computerized exams in their courses, their almost universal first concern is

L@S 2017, April 20-21, 2017, Cambridge, MA, USA
© 2017 ACM. ISBN 978-1-4503-4450-0/17/04...$15.00
DOI: http://dx.doi.org/10.1145/3051457.3051465

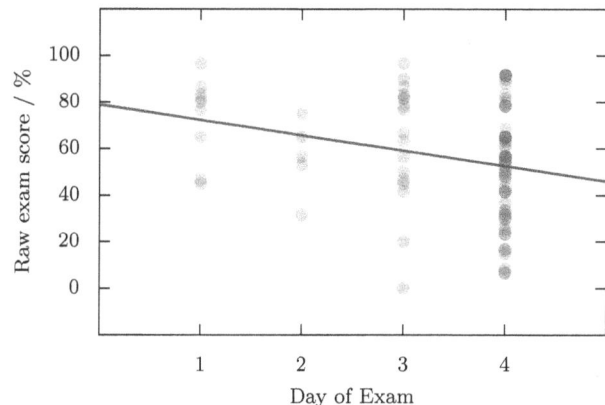

Figure 1. An example data set from one exam (Class D3, Exam 5) that was conducted over a 4 day period. Student raw scores on the exam are plotted against the day on which they took the exam, with each circle being a single student. The straight line is the OLS (ordinary least squares) regression line of the exam score against the day of exam, revealing in this case a large negative association between the day on which the student chose to take the exam and their score. This exam has one of the more negative slopes in our data set, and we chose it here because the highly negative slope is very easy to visualize. For the slopes of all exams, see Figure 6.

the potential for collaborative cheating resulting from the asynchronous nature of the exams. It seems initially reasonable that students taking the exam on the first day would tell their friends about the exam questions, giving students later in the exam period an unfair advantage and resulting in increasing exam scores over the exam period. In fact, in a survey of undergraduate students, the most-reported cheating mechanism was that they had "received answers to a quiz or test from someone who has already taken it" for face-to-face (i.e., non-online) classes [21].

However, when we plot students' exam scores versus the day on which they took the exam (see Figure 1 for an example), we see that on average the scores are actually *decreasing* over the exam period. We characterize this effect by the slope β of the regression line in Figure 1 (for this exam, $\beta = -0.82$ standard deviations per exam period). The questions addressed by this paper are: (1) how robust is this negative-slope effect across courses and across semesters, (2) what factors might explain this phenomenon, and (3) what does this data suggest about cheating during in-person asynchronous exams?

We report on two investigations into the relationship between when students elect to take their exams and their scores on those exams. In **Analysis 1**, we consider the asynchronous exam records of 9 courses over 3 semesters, demonstrating a trend of declining performance throughout the exam period in most of the 93 exams studied. In **Analysis 2**, we demonstrate that this effect remains even if we control for student ability, using a class that offered both a traditional (synchronous) written exam along with computerized exams in the same semester.

ANALYSIS 1 METHOD

The data collection took place in a large public research university during the Spring 2015, Fall 2015, and Spring 2016 semesters. The data was drawn from asynchronous exams that were held in the Computer-Based Testing Facility (CBTF) [24] and administrated via the PrairieLearn system [22]. All of the courses studied were undergraduate engineering subjects, ranging from introductory to advanced classes in computer science, mechanical engineering, and material science & engineering. With IRB approval and the consent from all of the relevant instructors, the CBTF administrators have shared this collection of data with us for this research.

Computer-Based Testing Facility

The CBTF is hosted in a converted computer lab with 49 seats for students and another 4 seats in a reduced distraction environment for students registered with the disability resource center. Each of the computers is outfitted with a privacy screen that prevents test takers from reading off the screens of neighboring computers and the networking and file system are strictly controlled [24]. During the period studied, the facility was open/proctored 10-12 hours a day, 7 days a week to accommodate one to two thousand exams per week [25]. Students were not permitted to take written notes, photos or other records into or out of the exam room.

Exams within the CBTF are typically administered as follows [25]: Courses typically assign a 3-5 day period for the students to take an exam depending on the class size; longer exam periods are used during finals week. Students are free to reserve any time during this exam period, provided that there are slots available at that time. Generally, the exam periods of exams from different classes overlap each other and the CBTF is almost always running a number of distinct exams concurrently. Sign-ups for exams typically begin 2 weeks before the exam period begins. Exam periods are scheduled so that the CBTF doesn't need to run at more than 85% capacity on any given day, to provide students many potential exam times to choose from and to be able to tolerate any operational problems. At their scheduled exam time, students have their identity checked by a proctor and are randomly assigned to a computer (to deter coordinated cheating).

PrairieLearn

PrairieLearn is an online problem posing system that permits the specification of *problem generators*, each of which is capable of generating a range of parameterized problem instances [22]. For exams, PrairieLearn can be configured to select random problem generators from a pool of questions and

Course and semester	Number of students	Number of exams	Average number of questions per exam
Class A2	180	5	22.6
Class A3	335	4	22.5
Class B2	576	5	3.0
Class B3	271	7	8.0
Class C1	482	2	25.0
Class C2	233	7	7.9
Class C3	453	7	9.7
Class D3	91	7	11.0
Class E3	75	5	14.8
Class F2	593	8	16.9
Class F3	587	9	15.4
Class G2	182	1	10.0
Class G3	250	1	15.0
Class H1	329	3	9.7
Class H2	362	4	11.2
Class H3	196	5	17.2
Class I2	246	7	4.7
Class I3	350	6	4.7

Table 1. Summary information for the 93 exams used in Analysis 1. Each course is indicated by a letter (A–I) and a number for the semester (1 = Spring 2015, 2 = Fall 2015, 3 = Spring 2016). Some courses only started using the CBTF/PrairieLearn environment in later semesters.

randomly generate problem instances from those generators to meet instructor-defined coverage and difficulty criteria [25]. Students sitting next to each other in the CBTF will typically be taking exams from different courses, but even if they are taking the same exam, they will generally have different sets of parameterized questions or the same set of questions with different parameters [25]. PrairieLearn also supports allowing students to have multiple attempts at each question with a partial-credit schedule controlled on a per question basis [25].

For each student taking an exam in the CBTF, PrairieLearn logs all the submissions the student makes during the exam period and calculates and stores the final score based on the instructor's multiple-attempts scoring scheme.

ANALYSIS 1 RESULTS

Data overiew

Our data set consists of 29,492 student records from 93 exams in 9 courses over 3 semesters, as listed in Table 1. To obtain this data we took all required exams[1] conducted using the CBTF/PrairieLearn system during these semesters, which yielded 106 exams in total. We then excluded 13 outlier exams with highly unusual score distributions (kurtosis more than 10), for which nearly all students received an identical score

---

[1]By only including required exams we excluded "second chance" exams that allowed students to optionally replace part or all of an exam score by taking a second equivalent exam at a later date [24]. Such optional exams introduce complex selection biases as they are taken by a non-random subset of students, so we excluded them from the analysis.

(e.g., nearly all students received 100%). All of the courses were undergraduate engineering subjects, ranging from introductory to advanced classes in computer science, mechanical engineering, and material science & engineering. The exam questions ranged from multiple choices, fill in the blank, and numerical calculations to vector drawing, finite state machine design, and coding.

For each of these 93 exams we obtained all student records, which are triples of the form (day of exam, hour of exam, raw score). The day of exam ranged from 1 to the exam period length (variable across exams, generally 3 to 4 days, maximum of 8 days), the hour of exam ranged from 1 to 12, and the raw-score was on a 0% to 100% scale.

For each exam we excluded the student records for any student who completed less than 25% of the exams in the class to avoid including course staff members engaged in exam checking and students who dropped early in the semester. We also excluded 313 student records that occurred outside the official exam periods because the student was sick, on travel, or had some other excuse, and which would otherwise exert an artificially high influence on the score slope estimates.

Score standardization and distributions

We standardized each raw score to a **standardized score** on an exam-by-exam basis. That is, the standardized score is computed by subtracting the exam mean and dividing by the exam standard deviation, so the standardized score measures the number of standard deviations above or below the mean.

To understand the exam score distributions we computed the mean raw score, skewness, and kurtosis for each exam, as shown in Figure 2. These plots show that the score distributions are not normal (which would have zero skewness and a kurtosis of 3), but that they deviate from normal in a structured way. While non-normal distributions are pervasive [16], the particular form of non-normality in our score distributions has been observed since the middle of the last century [14, 5, 12]. As described by Lord [14], two key observed features are: (1) exams with mean above 50% generally have negative skew, and (2) exams with near symmetric distributions (skew near zero) generally have negative excess kurtosis (i.e., they are platykurtic, with kurtosis less than the normal distribution kurtosis of 3, so have light tails [23]). For exams with means well above 50%, we see that they are skewed left (negative skew) and have positive excess kurtosis (kurtosis more than 3, heavy tailed, leptokurtic).

The non-normality of exam scores can be explained by regarding the distribution as a limited (or censored) normal distribution, where scores that would be below 0% or above 100% are limited to these values. Figure 3 shows two example normal probability plots (Q-Q plots versus a normal) for representatives exams. We see in both cases that it is the limiting of scores at 0% and 100% that is causing non-normality.

There are many statistical techniques designed to either normalize non-normal data (e.g., the Box-Cox transform [19] or Item Response Theory (IRT) scoring and normalization [15]) before performing regressions or to perform a regression directly with a model designed for the non-normal data (e.g.,

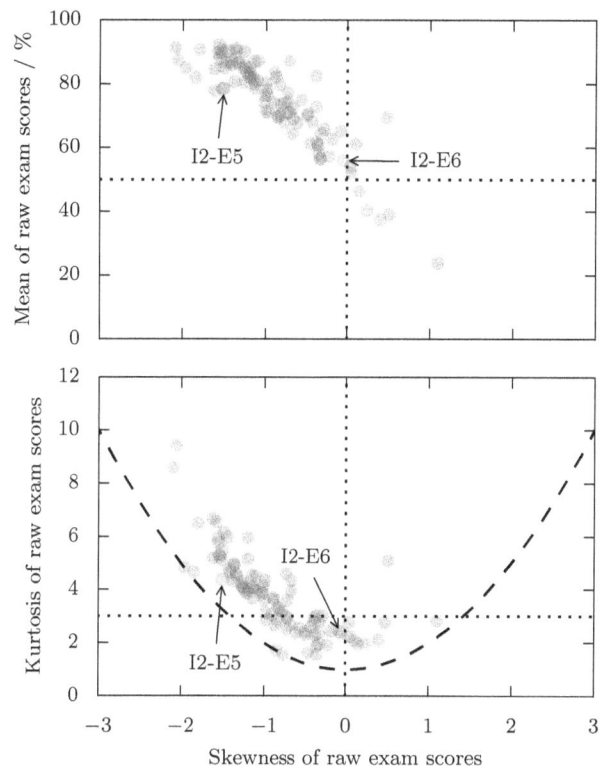

Figure 2. Summary statistics for the exams. Each data point is one exam. The dashed line in the bottom plot is the lower bound for kurtosis in terms of skewness. These plots show that the exam score distributions are non-normal in a way that is consistent with limiting (also called censoring) of the scores at 0% and 100%. Normal probability plots for the two representative labeled exams are shown in Figure 3 and demonstrate this limiting effect.

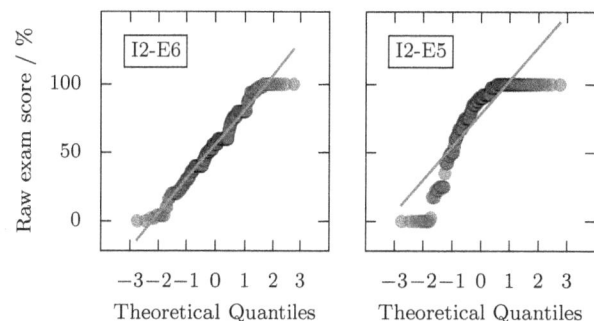

Figure 3. Normal probability plots for two representative exams (see Figure 2 for skew and kurtosis values of these exams). Left: I2-E6 (Class I2, Exam 6) has a nearly symmetric distribution (skew near zero) and negative excess kurtosis (kurtosis less than 3, so lighter-tailed than a normal distribution). Right: I2-E5 (Class I2, Exam 5) has a left-skewed distribution (negative skewness) with positive excess kurtosis (heavy-tailed relative to normal). In both cases we can see that these effects are due to the limiting of the distribution at 0% and 100%.

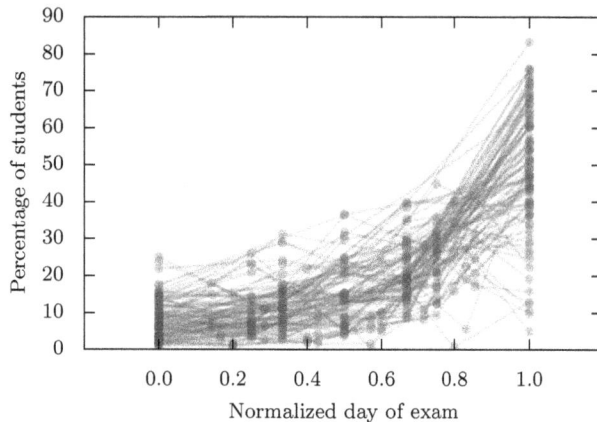

Figure 4. Fraction of students taking the exam on each day. Each exam is a single line on the plot. The horizontal axis shows the normalized day of exam, so 0 is the first day of each exam and 1 is the last day.

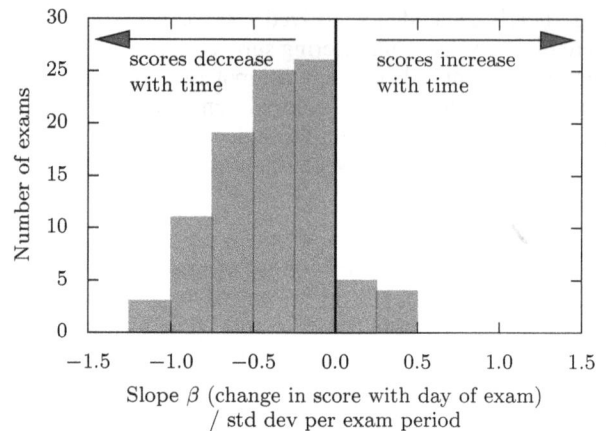

Figure 5. Histogram of exam slopes β_k (change in standardized exam score with normalized day of exam). The units of β are score standard deviations per exam period, so that a value of $\beta = -0.5$ means that scores decline on average by half a standard deviation from the start to the end of the exam.

Tobit models [20]). However, in many situations it may be difficult to avoid introducing other artifacts, such as highly discretized transformed distributions [12].

For this reason and to maintain simplicity of the analysis and clarity of interpretation, we calculate regressions with the standardized exam scores without any extra treatment for non-normality. This will have the effect of systematically underestimating regression slopes [9] because the limited scores have been capped at 0% and 100%, lessening their impact. This means that the effect sizes found in this work are actually underestimates of the true effect.

Day-of-exam student preferences

To compare day-of-exam values between exams of different period lengths, we normalized by dividing the day of exam by the exam period to get the **normalized day of exam** which ranges from 0 on the first day of the exam to 1 on the last day.

Using this scaling we can plot the fraction of students taking the exam on each day for all exams, as shown in Figure 4. Here we see that, when given agency in selecting their exam times, students overwhelmingly prefer to take exams toward the end of the exam period. Each series of connected line segments in Figure 4 represents the distribution of students for a single exam throughout its exam period. The trend in this data is almost exponential, with 40% to 80% of the students taking most exams on the last day of the exam period. While many student motivations could explain this data, two significant hypotheses are: 1) students are delaying their exams so as to have time to gather information from other students that took the exam early in the exam period, and 2) students are self-selecting later exam times so as to give themselves additional preparation time before the exam.

Score as a function of exam day

For each exam we used OLS (ordinary least squares) to fit a regression line of the form

$$z_{ik} = \alpha_k + \beta_k d_{ik}, \qquad (1)$$

where student i took exam k on normalized day of exam d_{ik} (0 to 1 for first day to last day) and received the standardized score z_{ik}. The fitted parameters are the **intercept** α_k and the **slope** β_k for exam k, and we also determine the sampling variance v_k of each slope β_k. Note that the regressions are performed for each exam independently.

The slope β has units of standard deviations per exam period, so a value of $\beta = -0.5$ would mean, roughly speaking, that the student exam scores decline by one half of a standard deviation from the first day to the last day of the exam.

A histogram of the slopes β_k for all exams is shown in Figure 5. The dominant feature is that most exams have negative slopes, meaning that student scores decline over the exam period. While this histogram captures the main effect that slopes are generally negative, it does not allow us to visualize the uncertainty in the slope estimates or to see the relationships between exams for the same class.

Meta-analysis of exam score slopes

To understand the average score trends for asynchronous exams we use the framework of meta-analysis [7] to find the average score slope. We begin by visualizing the slopes β_k together with their 95% confidence intervals on a forest plot in Figure 6. A forest plot is a standard meta-analysis visualization tool [7, Chapter 26] that shows effect sizes for many different studies together with their confidence intervals (horizontal bars) and an indicator of study reliability (area of circles).

The two-tailed significance levels (p-values) for the slope being non-zero are shown on the right hand side of Figure 6. About half of the exam slopes are statistically significantly negative ($p < 0.05$), a majority of the remainder are non-significantly negative, and a small number are non-significantly positive. None of the exams have a slope that is statistically significantly positive ($p < 0.05$).

There is no clear consensus in the meta-analysis community on how to combine regression slopes in the general case [6].

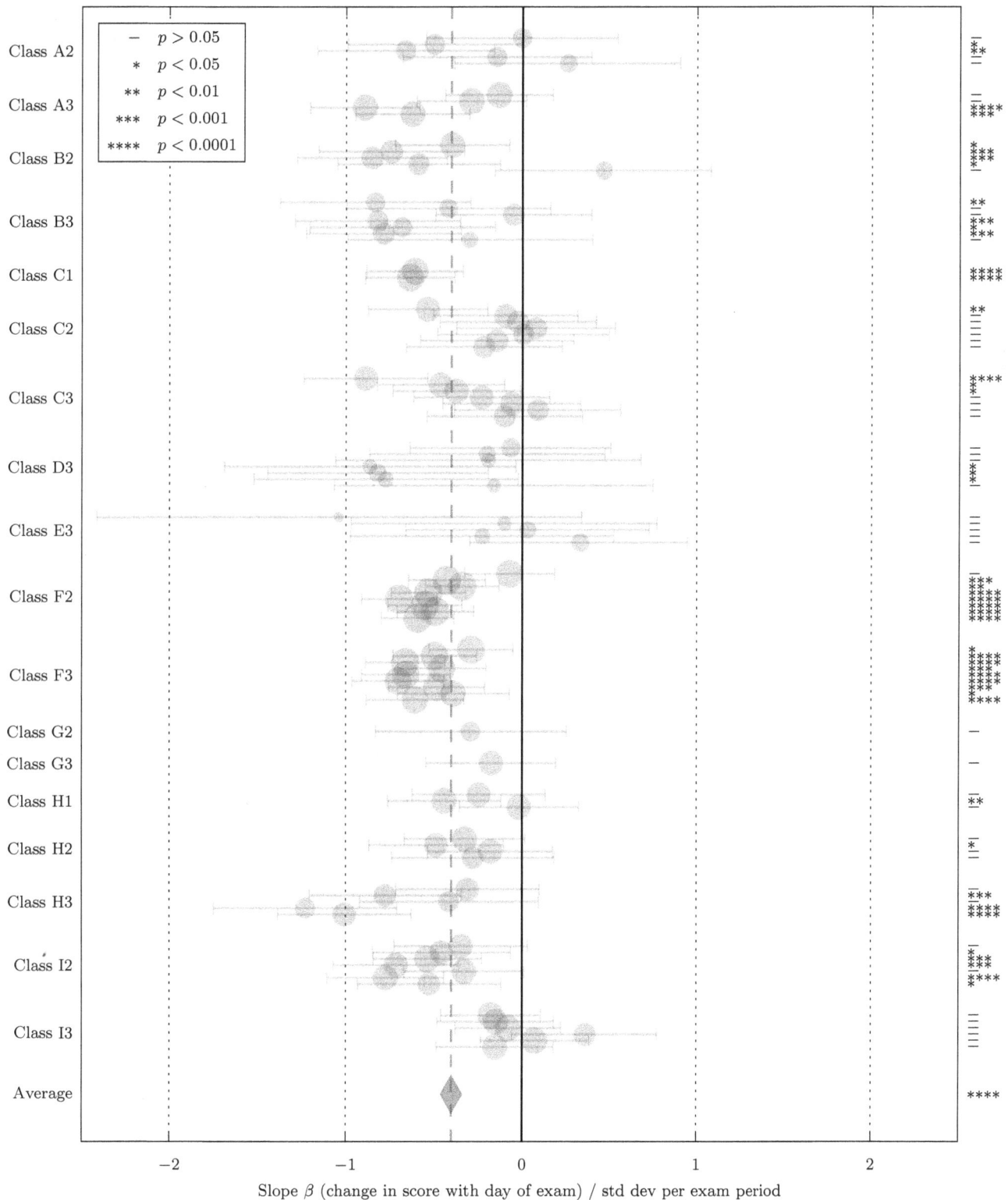

Figure 6. Forest plot shows the slopes β_k of standardized exam score versus normalized day of exam. Each circle represents the slope of one exam and they are grouped by the course and semester as shown on the left. The area of each circle is proportional to the weight $w_k = 1/v_k$ of the exam in the meta-analysis and the horizontal error bar is the 95% confidence interval for the slope. The diamond at the bottom of the figure represents the average population slope $\theta = -0.399$ (**95% CI** $[-0.458, -0.340]$) for all exams and its width specifies the 95% confidence interval (random-effects model, see Eq. (3)). The two-tailed significance levels of the exam slopes away from zero are shown on the right of the figure as a number of stars.

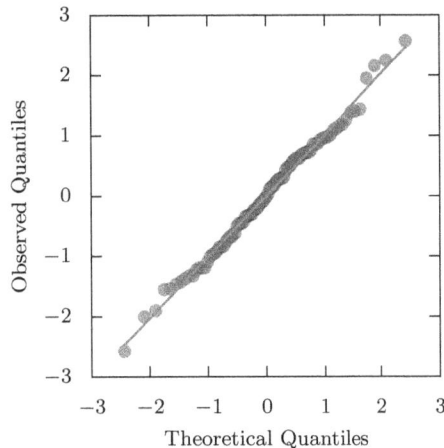

Figure 7. Normal probability plot for the slopes β_k from all exams. This shows that the slopes are approximately normally distributed.

However, both Becker and Wu [2] and Cooper [6] suggested that under the condition when both the response and independent variables are measured similarly across studies, the regression slopes can be safely combined by treating them as a simple effect. This is the approach that we adopted below.

A normal probability plot for the slopes β_k (shown in Figure 7) reveals that they can be regarded as normally distributed. It is thus tempting to use a fixed-effects model of the form

$$\beta_k = \theta + e_k, \qquad (2)$$

where θ is the common slope for all exams and $\text{var}(e_k) = v_k$ is the known sampling variance of the kth slope. We find, however, that such a model fails to account for the heterogeneity in the data. Homogeneity is rejected ($p < 0.0001$, $Q = 216.7$) by the standard homogeneity Q-test (Cochran's χ^2 test) [7, Chapter 14] for a common population effect size, and a more advanced measure of heterogeneity [11] finds that $I^2 = 57.5\%$ of the total variation is due to heterogeneity between exams (a medium degree of heterogeneity).

To account for exam heterogeneity we use a random-effects model of the form

$$\beta_k = \theta + u_k + e_k, \qquad (3)$$

where θ is now the average population slope, $\text{var}(u_k) = \tau^2$ is the heterogeneity between exams, and $\text{var}(e_k)$ is the known sampling variance of the kth slope. Fitting this model yields an average population slope of $\theta = -0.399$ (95% CI $[-0.458, -0.340]$) which is negative ($p < 0.0001$). This average slope is plotted in Figure 6 as the diamond near the bottom.

ANALYSIS 1 DISCUSSION

While many instructors anecdotally expect that exam scores will rise with day of exam over the exam period either because students have longer time to prepare or because they are colluding with students who have taken the exam at an earlier date, our results show that in fact the opposite occurs and on average the exam scores decline by about 0.4 standard deviations over the period of the exam. In fact, we expect that

we have underestimated this effect because we computed per-exam slopes with OLS (ordinary least squares) and ignored the non-normality introduced by the score limits at 0% and 100%.

From Figure 6 there are some indications that the effect size might vary between courses or between semesters. We have not attempted to isolate such variation in the analysis here, but this represents an interesting possibility for future work, perhaps by using three-level (or higher) models [4].

Although the Analysis 1 results do not seem to indicate the existence of widespread collaborative cheating, the possibility exists that stronger students are choosing to take the exam on earlier dates than weaker students. In this case an exam without cheating might actually have a steeper decline (say 1 standard deviation) and collaborative cheating might be assisting the weaker students later in the exam (say by 0.6 standard deviations), resulting in the net decline of 0.4 standard deviations that we observe. We investigate this possibility in Analysis 2 below.

ANALYSIS 2 METHOD

Although the above analysis demonstrated that students' exam scores decrease over time, it does not rule out the possibility that the phenomenon can be explained by good students selecting earlier exam dates while less capable students select later exam dates. To examine the influence of students' ability, we need to calibrate it in some way and take it into account in the regression model. A class that employs both synchronous and asynchronous exams in the same semester can provide such calibration.

In this regard, we exploit a natural experiment resulting from a class that adopted asynchronous computerized exams part way through the semester. In Class C1, a traditional pencil-and-paper synchronous exam (Exam 0) was held before the class changed to hold the remaining two exams (Exams 1 and 2) as asynchronous computerized exams in the CBTF. This exam structure allows us to use Exam 0 as a measure of student ability and investigate how controlling for student ability changes the observed trends of decreasing student performance from the beginning to the end of the exam period on Exams 1 and 2.

Exam Details

The three exams are detailed in Table 2 and the associated score distributions are shown in Figure 8.

Exam 0 was a pencil-and-paper multiple-choice exam in a format that had been traditionally used in Class C, covering material in Homeworks 1–4. All students took the exam at the same time in large classrooms proctored by course staff. The instructor of the course willingly shared the information of the first exam with us for this analysis.

Exams 1 and 2 were computer-based exams administered using PrairieLearn [22] in the CBTF [24], as described above in Analysis 1. Exam 1 was non-comprehensive, covering material from Homeworks 5–7, while Exam 2 was a comprehensive final exam. These exams used a fixed pool of questions for all students, with each student getting different parameterized versions of the same questions, with the question order

	Type	Purpose	Duration	Format	Questions	Mean	Std dev	Skew	Kurtosis
Exam 0	Synchronous	Midterm	2 h	Pencil and paper	20	63.9%	14.0%	−0.083	2.760
Exam 1	Asynchronous	Midterm	2 h	Computerized	20	60.7%	15.1%	−0.260	2.839
Exam 2	Asynchronous	Final	3 h	Computerized	30	73.6%	16.9%	−0.841	3.313

Table 2. Summary information for the three exams used in Analysis 2. Eleven students did not take all three exams during the official exam periods and their records were discarded from the data set. All statistics and analyses use the 469 common students who took all three exams. Exams 1 and 2 are also part of the Analysis 1 data set, where they are the two exams in Class C1. See Figure 8 for score distributions.

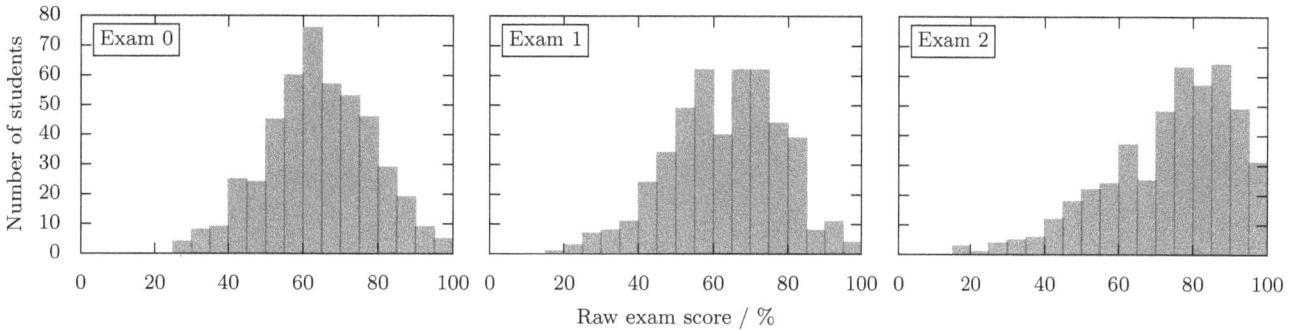

Figure 8. Histograms of exam scores used in Analysis 2. See Table 2 for summary statistics.

randomized. Exam 1 consisted of 10 questions previously assigned as homework and 10 questions that were new for the exam. Exam 2 was drawn exclusively from the pool of 199 PrairieLearn-based homework questions that were assigned throughout the semester. For Exam 1 students were given only one attempt at each question and were graded as correct/incorrect. For Exam 2 students were able to re-attempt questions for partial credit during the exam.

ANALYSIS 2 RESULTS

Slope of exam scores by day of exam

We follow the same procedure as in Analysis 1 and standardize the raw exam scores to standardized scores on an exam-by-exam basis. For Exams 1 and 2, the day of exam is normalized by the exam period to give the normalized day of exam that runs from 0 to 1. The number of students taking the exams on each day is shown in Figure 9, where we see the same general upward trend for Exam 1 as in Figure 4. The drop on the last day was atypical; only 13 out of 93 exams studied in Analysis 1 have this phenomenon. We believe that the behavior observed for this exam is due to the fact that about 40% of the students were enrolled in another class that held an exam immediately after the last day of the exam period. The upward trend was less pronounced for Exam 2 because it was held in the final week of the semester when many students wanted to leave campus early. The drop in the middle is caused by the same co-enrollment class holding a final exam on day 5.

Figure 10 shows the raw exam score distributions by day of exam for Exams 1 and 2 (Exam 0 was held at a single time, so does not have a corresponding plot). The OLS models from Analysis 1 for these standardized exam scores versus the normalized day of exam is shown in Table 4, where the model variables are listed in Table 3. These slopes are shown graphically in the upper half of Figure 11, and an average slope of $\beta_{\text{day}} = -0.607$ (95% CI $[-0.794, -0.419]$) was computed using a fixed-effects model of the form shown in Equation (2).

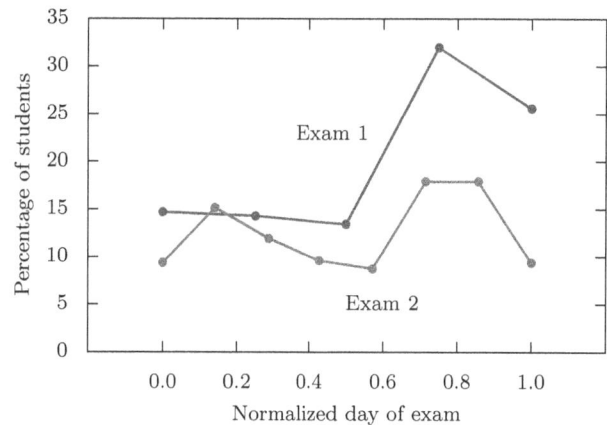

Figure 9. Number of students per exam day for Analysis 2.

Exam scores controlling for Exam 0 score

To investigate the hypothesis that the negative slopes observed in Analysis 1 are due to higher-ability students preferentially taking the exam early, we take Exam 0 scores as a proxy for ability and use it as a control when regressing Exam 1 and 2 scores against the day of exam.

We first checked the correlation of Exam 0 scores with the scores and days of Exams 1 and 2, as shown in Table 5. As expected, Exam 0 scores are significantly positively correlated with both Exam 1 scores and Exam 2 scores. Students who performed well on Exam 0 are also likely to have taken Exam 1 earlier in the exam period (statistically significant negative correlation), but there is no statistically significant relationship between Exam 0 scores and the day of Exam 2. This is consistent with stronger students choosing to take Exam 1 somewhat earlier, but there being no clear preference for scheduling times for Exam 2 which was held at the end of semester.

The lower two models in Table 4 show the regression of the Exam 1 and 2 scores against the day of exam and Exam 0

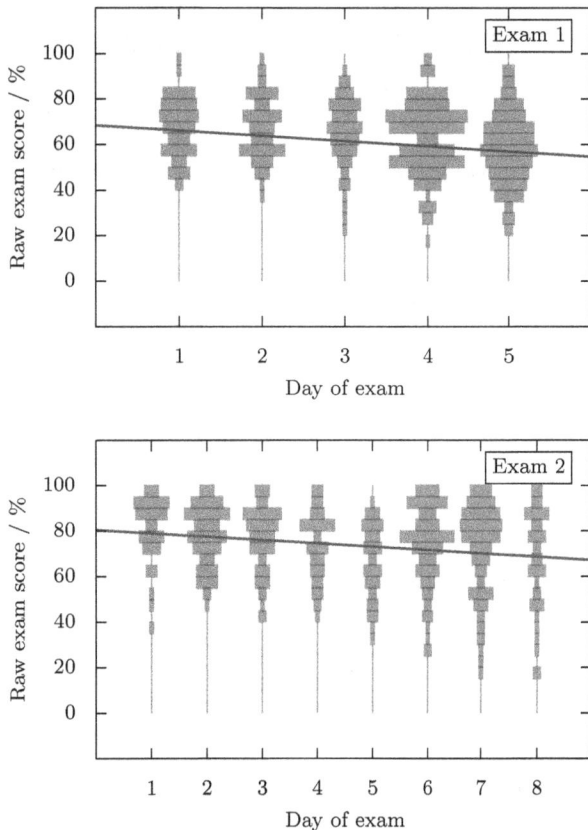

Figure 10. Raw scores versus day of exam for the two asynchronous exams in Analysis 2. The trend line is the OLS regression, as in Analysis 1, and in both cases it shows a negative slope.

Variable	Description
score0	Standardized Exam 0 score
score1	Standardized Exam 1 score
score2	Standardized Exam 2 score
day1	Normalized day of exam for Exam 1
day2	Normalized day of exam for Exam 2

Table 3. Variables used in Tables 4 and 5.

Dep var	Indep	Coef	95% CI		R^2
score1	const	0.364	0.187	0.542	0.045
	day1	−0.609	−0.865	−0.352	
score2	const	0.315	0.145	0.485	0.038
	day2	−0.604	−0.881	−0.327	
score1	const	0.257	0.105	0.409	
	score0	0.513	0.436	0.589	0.303
	day1	−0.429	−0.650	−0.209	
score2	const	0.306	0.157	0.455	
	score0	0.478	0.399	0.556	0.266
	day2	−0.586	−0.829	−0.343	

Table 4. Linear models for Exam 1 and Exam 2 standardized scores in terms of the normalized day of exam (top two model rows), and in terms of the normalized day of exam and the standardized Exam 0 score (bottom two rows). See Table 3 for variable descriptions. Figure 11 shows a graphical representation of the dependence of each model on the day of exam variables.

Correlation	r	p	95% CI	
score0 with score1	0.531	0.000	0.462	0.593
score0 with score2	0.480	0.000	0.407	0.547
score0 with day1	−0.121	0.009	−0.210	−0.031
score0 with day2	−0.012	0.793	−0.103	0.078

Table 5. Correlation coefficients between student scores on Exam 0 and both the scores and the day of exam for Exams 1 and 2. The scores are positively correlated, and there is a weak negative correlation between Exam 0 score and the day of exam for Exam 1. See Table 3 for variable definitions.

scores, where we are regarding the Exam 0 scores as a proxy for student ability. Because the independent variables are correlated, we must be careful of multicollinearity in performing these regressions. We computed the variance inflation factor [1, Chapter 13] and found VIF < 1.02 for all independent variables, indicating that multicollinearity is very low and not a concern. The regression coefficients of Exam 1 and 2 scores with day of exam in the models with Exam 0 as a control are plotted in the lower half of Figure 11, and the average fixed-effects slope is $\beta_{day,Exam0} = -0.500$ (95% CI $[-0.663, -0.337]$).

From Figure 11 we can also see that controlling for student ability via the Exam 0 score reduced the magnitude of the average slope by about 18%, from −0.607 to −0.500 standard deviations per day (not statistically significant, $p = 0.402$).

ANALYSIS 2 DISCUSSION

The magnitude of the negative exam score slope over the exam period is only mildly reduced (about 20%), and not statistically significantly, when controlling for student ability as measured by the synchronous Exam 0 scores. This suggests that the negative slope in scores is not primarily due to stronger students taking the exam earlier, although this does happen to a small extent.

Because Exam 0 is only a proxy for student ability and only moderately correlated with Exam 1 and 2 scores, we cannot rule out the possibility that early exam taking by stronger students is in fact responsible for a larger (or even entire) proportion of the declining-scores effect. One potential approach to more definitively resolve this question might be to use student performance data from other courses as a control.

CONCLUSIONS AND FUTURE WORK

In this paper we examined approximately 30,000 asynchronous exam records from 93 exams in 9 courses over 3 semesters to test the hypothesis that collaborative cheating would inflate student scores in asynchronous exams held in a face-to-face, proctored testing center. We did not find any significant evidence that collaborative cheating was inflating student scores later in the exam period. In fact, we found that student scores decreased substantially over the course of the exam period (by about 0.4 standard deviations), even when controlling for student ability as measured by a synchronous exam scores. In the engineering and computer science courses that formed our data set, 0.4 standard deviations typically corresponds to about half of a letter grade, making this a sizable

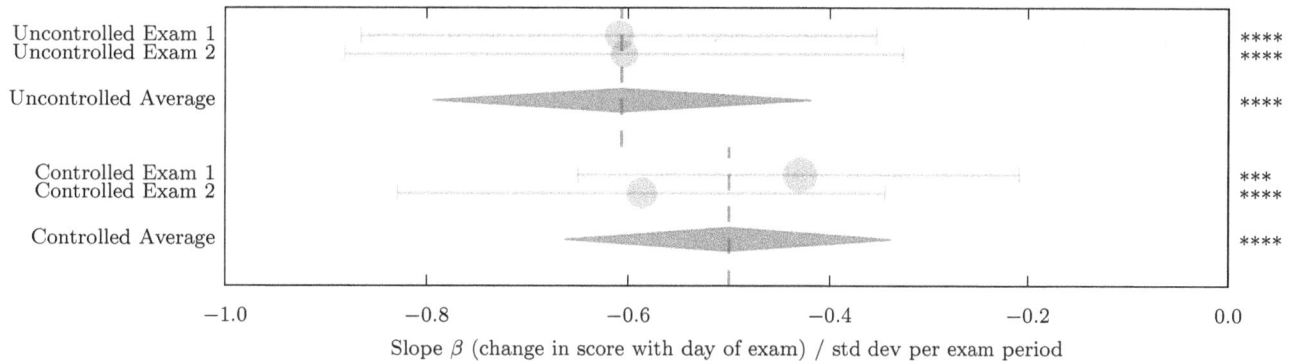

Figure 11. Forest plot for the regressions against day of exam in Analysis 2, as listed in Table 4, with error bars indicating 95% confidence intervals. The "Uncontrolled" regressions fit Exam 1 and 2 scores as functions of the day of exam, while the "Controlled" regressions fit as functions of day of exam and Exam 0 scores, which are a proxy for student ability. The average slope diamonds are the fixed-effects average of the corresponding two exam slopes, and their widths are the 95% confidence interval. We see that controlling for ability reduces the average slope magnitude from -0.607 (95% CI $[-0.794, -0.419]$) to -0.500 (95% CI $[-0.663, -0.337]$) (not statistically significant).

effect. This decline in scores over the exam period seems to indicate that student choice of exam date is revealing additional information about their preparedness or ability level, above and beyond that measured by their scores on the traditional synchronous exam.

In addition, our initial investigations suggest that there also is a time-of-day effect, with similar structure to the day-of-exam effect that is the focus of this paper. Students were able to choose what time they take their exams, and they predominantly preferred exam times later in the day, especially near the end of an exam period. Furthermore, exam scores are negatively associated with the time of day of the exam, although the effect is considerably weaker than the day-of-exam effect. The consistency of these results support the hypothesis that students are signaling their lack of preparation for an exam by selecting later slots in the exam schedule. This observation opens up the possibility that interventions could be targeted to these students.

Our results also support an alternative hypothesis for the study reported by Brothen and Peterson [3]. Their work reports a natural experiment that occurred during a proctored asynchronous computerized final exam where students could elect the day on which to take their exam. Computer problems interrupted the exam in the middle of the first exam period, forcing the faculty to provide the first cohort the opportunity to take the exam online and unproctored later in the week, as some students' travel arrangements prevented them from completing a proctored make-up later in the exam period. When this cohort out-performed the rest of the class by 0.63 standard deviations, the authors found that cheating was the most likely explanation. Our data suggests that a non-trivial portion of this difference can be explained because the experimental cohort was the one that *chose* to sign up for the first time slot. That cheating may not have been the dominant effect is also supported by the partial results from the aborted exams, which actually projected higher average scores than the cohort achieved on their unproctored re-take.

While our findings suggest that collaborative cheating is not the dominant effect in these asynchronous exams, we certainly

cannot conclude that no collaborative cheating is occurring from our results. Nevertheless, it gives some confidence that the precautions taken by the CBTF (e.g., proctoring, question randomization, preventing notes from being brought in or removed from the CBTF) are sufficient to prevent widespread collaborative cheating. Therefore in-person asynchronous environments are encouraged to adopt similar strategies to prevent cheating. Our results, however, offer no direct insight into cheating in the context of unproctored, online exams [10, 17, 21]. Regardless of this, it would be interesting to repeat the analysis with online testing data both for remote-proctored and unproctored online exams, to see whether similar effects are seen in those environments and whether there is evidence of cheating.

The trend of decreasing performance throughout the exam period is well supported by the data, but there is a lot of variation between classes and exams that remains unexplained. Our current hypothesis is that this variation is derived from variations in exam construction (e.g., exam length, exam difficulty, drawing questions from a pool versus using a fixed set of problems for all students). In particular, we believe it is important to understand the degree to which any of these characteristics contribute to deterring collaborative cheating.

Finally, our analysis largely treats each student taking each exam as independent events. We believe that future work that exploits the structure in the data could more clearly elucidate these effects. A few extensions are obvious. First, because our anonymized data set retains the association for all exams taken by a given student, we can study if individual students perform better when they choose to take exams early in the exam period. Second, we can use multi-level models to recognize that, for example, Class H1 Exam 1 is basically the same exam as Class H2 Exam 1 that is taken by a different student cohort. Lastly, we can explore the degree to which our results are being unduly affected by a certain portion of the student distribution, for example the very weakest students choosing to postpone the exam as long as possible.

ACKNOWLEDGEMENTS
This work was partially supported by NSF DUE-1347722, NSF CMMI-1150490, and the College of Engineering at the University of Illinois at Urbana-Champaign under the Strategic Instructional Initiatives Program (SIIP).

REFERENCES

1. R. Azen and D. Budescu (Eds.). 2009. *Applications of Multiple Regression in Psychological Research*. SAGE Publications. DOI: http://dx.doi.org/10.4135/9780857020994

2. B. J. Becker and M.-J. Wu. 2007. The synthesis of regression slopes in meta-analysis. *Statist. Sci.* (2007), 414–429.

3. T. Brothen and G. Peterson. 2012. Online exam cheating: A natural experiment. *International Journal of Instructional Technology and Distance Learning* 9, 2 (2012), 15–20.

4. M. W.-L. Cheung. 2014. Modeling dependent effect sizes with three-level meta-analyses: a structural equation modeling approach. *Psychol. Methods* 19, 2 (2014), 211.

5. D. L. Cook. 1959. A replication of Lord's study of skewness and kurtosis of observed test-score distributions. *Educational and Psychological Measurement* 19, 1 (1959), 81–87. DOI: http://dx.doi.org/10.1177/001316445901900109

6. H. Cooper. 2016. *Research synthesis and meta-analysis: A step-by-step approach*. Vol. 2. SAGE publications.

7. H. Cooper, L. V. Hedges, and J. C. Valentine. 2009. *The handbook of research synthesis and meta-analysis* (2nd ed.). Russell Sage Foundation.

8. R. F. DeMara, N. Khoshavi, S. Pyle, J. Edison, R. Hartshorne, B. Chen, and M. Georgiopoulos. 2016. Redesigning Computer Engineering Gateway Courses Using a Novel Remediation Hierarchy. In *2016 ASEE Annual Conference & Exposition*. ASEE Conferences, New Orleans, Louisiana.

9. W. H. Greene. 1981. On the asymptotic bias of the ordinary least squares estimator of the Tobit model. *Econometrica* 49, 2 (1981), 505–513. DOI: http://dx.doi.org/10.2307/1913323

10. O. R. Harmon and J. Lambrinos. 2008. Are online exams an invitation to cheat? *The Journal of Economic Education* 39, 2 (2008), 116–125.

11. J. P. T. Higgins and S. G. Thompson. 2002. Quantifying heterogeneity in a meta-analysis. *Statistics in Medicine* 21 (2002), 1539–1558. DOI: http://dx.doi.org/10.1002/sim.1186

12. A. D. Ho and C. C. Yu. 2015. Descriptive statistics for modern test score distributions: Skewness, kurtosis, discreteness, and ceiling effects. *Educational and Psychological Measurement* 75, 3 (2015), 365–388. DOI: http://dx.doi.org/10.1177/0013164414548576

13. E. Lee, N. Garg, C. Bygrave, J. Mahar, and V. Mishra. 2015. Can University Exams be Shortened? An Alternative to Problematic Traditional Methodological Approaches. In *Proceedings of the 14th European Conference on Research Methods*. Valletta, Malta.

14. F. M. Lord. 1955. A survey of observed test-score distributions with respect to skewness and kurtosis. *Educational and Psychological Measurement* 15, 4 (1955), 383–389. DOI: http://dx.doi.org/10.1177/001316445501500406

15. F. M. Lord. 1980. *Applications of item response theory to practical testing problems*. Erlbaum.

16. T. Micceri. 1989. The unicorn, the normal curve, and other improbable creatures. *Psychological Bulletin* 105, 1 (1989), 156–166. DOI: http://dx.doi.org/10.1037/0033-2909.105.1.156

17. A. Miller and A. D. Young-Jones. 2012. Academic integrity: Online classes compared to face-to-face classes. *Journal of Instructional Psychology* 39, 3/4 (2012), 138.

18. R. Muldoon. 2012. Is it time to ditch the traditional university exam? *Higher Education Research & Development* 31, 2 (2012), 263–265. DOI: http://dx.doi.org/10.1080/07294360.2012.680249

19. R. M. Sakia. 1992. The Box-Cox Transformation Technique: A Review. *Journal of the Royal Statistical Society. Series D (The Statistician)* 41, 2 (1992), 169–178. DOI:http://dx.doi.org/10.2307/2348250

20. W. Schnedler. 2005. Likelihood Estimation for Censored Random Vectors. *Econometric Reviews* 24, 2 (2005), 195–217. DOI:http://dx.doi.org/10.1081/ETC-200067925

21. G. Watson and J. Sottile. 2010. Cheating in the Digital Age: Do Students Cheat More in Online Courses. *Online Journal of Distance Learning Administration* 13, 1 (2010). http://www.westga.edu/~distance/ojdla/spring131/watson131.html

22. M. West, G. L. Herman, and C. Zilles. 2015. PrairieLearn: Mastery-based Online Problem Solving with Adaptive Scoring and Recommendations Driven by Machine Learning. In *Proceedings of the 2015 ASEE Annual Conference and Exposition (ASEE 2015)*. 26.1238.1–26.1238.14. DOI: http://dx.doi.org/10.18260/p.24575

23. P. H. Westfall. 2014. Kurtosis as Peakedness, 1905–2014. *R.I.P. American Statistician* 68, 3 (2014), 191–195. DOI: http://dx.doi.org/10.1080/00031305.2014.917055

24. C. Zilles, R. T. Deloatch, J. Bailey, B. B. Khattar, W. Fagen, C. Heeren, D. Mussulman, and M. West. 2015. Computerized Testing: A Vision and Initial Experiences. In *Proceedings of the 2015 ASEE Annual Conference and Exposition (ASEE 2015)*. 26.387.1–26.387.13. DOI: http://dx.doi.org/10.18260/p.23726

25. C. Zilles, M. West, and D. Mussulman. 2016. Student Behavior in Selecting an Exam Time in a Computer-Based Testing Facility. In *2016 ASEE Annual Conference & Exposition*. ASEE Conferences, New Orleans, Louisiana. DOI: http://dx.doi.org/10.18260/p.25896

Towards Equal Opportunities in MOOCs: Affirmation Reduces Gender & Social-class Achievement Gaps in China

René F. Kizilcec
Department of Communication
Stanford University
kizilcec@stanford.edu

Glenn M. Davis
Graduate School of Education
Stanford University
gmdavis@stanford.edu

Geoffrey L. Cohen
Graduate School of Education
Stanford University
glc@stanford.edu

ABSTRACT

The presence of achievement gaps in Massive Open Online Courses (MOOCs) implies that not everyone who can gain access to a course shares the same opportunities to succeed. This study advances research on a social psychological barrier to achievement that exists alongside important structural barriers (e.g., Internet access, insufficient prior knowledge). Learners who experience social identity threat (SIT)—a fear of being judged negatively in light of a social group they identify with—are at risk of underperforming. An initial survey identified lower-class men as an at-risk group in an English language learning MOOC for Chinese learners ($N = 1,664$). In a subsequent randomized experiment, an interdependent value relevance affirmation intervention raised grades, persistence, and completion rates exclusively among lower-class men—the lowest performing group in the course ($N = 1,990$). Efforts to establish equal opportunities in online learning should go beyond initiatives that increase access through technology to incorporate strategies that lower psychological barriers to create safe and inclusive learning environments.

ACM Classification Keywords

K.3.1. Computers and Education: E-Learning.

Author Keywords

Social psychology; achievement gaps; randomized experiment; Massive Open Online Course.

INTRODUCTION

Large-scale online learning environments are a technological innovation that can increase access to education by overcoming geographic and financial barriers. In these environments, learning materials such as readings, video lectures, assessments, and interactive simulations can be accessed by many learners simultaneously. Once a set of digital learning materials has been developed, it can in principle serve an unlimited number of interested learners with the appropriate level of prior knowledge. In practice, however, multiple challenges can limit learners' ability to reap the full benefits of online educational resources. Many of these challenges are a by-product of the dominant one-size-fits-all approach to online courses, where the same environment and content are provided to learners from diverse demographic and sociocultural backgrounds. This leaves online learning environments vulnerable to many of the same shortcomings that give rise to educational inequalities in brick-and-mortar settings. In particular, verbal and visual cues can inadvertently communicate values and norms based on the sociocultural context where the environment was created and the learning materials developed. This can lead some learners to feel less welcome and worry about whether they can be successful.

These concerns are especially likely to arise in learning environments that serve a diverse learner population, such as MOOCs, which have attracted over 35 million learners worldwide in over 4,000 different courses [36]. According to edX CEO Anant Agarwal, "MOOCs make education borderless, gender-blind, race-blind, class-blind and bank account-blind." [1]. Barriers to access free-of-charge MOOCs are indeed low. However, in terms of success rates, there are major disparities between learners from different demographic, geographic, and socioeconomic backgrounds. Research has consistently found that learners from less developed parts of the world [24, 22, 25] and poorer neighborhoods in the United States [16] are less likely to complete MOOCs. Moreover, women and less educated learners are less persistent and receive lower grades in a sample of courses in various disciplines [22]. These achievement gaps may be due to technological and language barriers as well as differences in prior levels of education. However, besides structural barriers that are complex and expensive to overcome, there is evidence for a social psychological barrier, which hinders learners from reaching their potential in online environments [25]. In particular, aspects of the environment and learning materials can raise concerns that undermine learners' sense of belonging and threaten their social identity, and lead them to underperform in the course.

Membership in social groups constitutes an essential part of people's identities [4] and people strive to maintain a positive perception of the various social groups they identify with (e.g., gender, race, social class) [42]. The mere concern of being judged negatively in light of a social group that one identifies with—known as social identity threat (SIT) [40]—can impair working memory, learning, and performance [3, 43]. It has been shown that negative stereotypes about African

Figure 1. Screenshot of the English language learning MOOC showing a video lecture by one of the main instructors.

Americans' intellectual abilities and women's abilities in technical subjects can raise concerns about confirming these group stereotypes, and inadvertently cause underperformance [39]. Learners who join a U.S.-based MOOC from a country that is less developed report higher levels of SIT and exhibit lower course completion rates [25]. Individuals who contend with SIT experience greater stress and reduced cognitive capacity, as they become vigilant for cues in the environment that may confirm (or disconfirm) their fears of not belonging and being treated unfairly [46, 33, 35].

The present study tests the role of SIT in contributing to achievement gaps in China in an English language learning MOOC. We hypothesized that male and lower-class learners would be most affected by SIT in this context. First, we conducted a survey to examine how these learners compared with their peers in terms of SIT and subjective social class. Then, we conducted a randomized controlled experiment to test if a social psychological intervention designed to protect against SIT and promote commitment can raise the performance of identity-threatened learners. Our findings show that lower-class men—the most threatened and lowest performing subgroup—exclusively benefited from the intervention, raising their course persistence, grades, and completion rate.

SOURCES OF SOCIAL IDENTITY THREAT
Empirical research on SIT has focused on social issues in the United States and Europe. SIT was found to contribute to the academic underperformance of historically underrepresented minorities (e.g., African American and Latino students) [40], students from low socioeconomic backgrounds [14], and women in STEM (Science, Technology, Engineering, Mathematics) disciplines [8]. However, the implications of SIT are not limited to Western societies. A lab experiment with female students in China found that highlighting negative gender stereotypes reduced subsequent test performance [6]. Nevertheless, SIT has not been investigated in the context of English language learning. We identify two potential sources of SIT for Chinese learners in this context: one based on learners' gender identity, and the other based on their class-based identity in society.

Gender
The first potential source of SIT is gender stereotypes in the context of language learning. Interviews of Chinese students reveal that women are perceived as more talented at language learning [48, 47]. This perception is supported by official records of English achievement in China. A recent study found that while there was no significant gender difference in achievement for the top 10% of students on the English section of the National College Entrance Examination, women outperformed men among students below the 90th percentile [50]. Women also outperformed men in English on the High School Entrance Examination [28]. This gender gap in high school was even greater than the ones observed in elementary and middle school. Learners are likely to be aware of these differences and adopt a stereotype that women are more talented at language learning than men. Situational cues in the MOOC, such as the fact that the main instructors are women, may signal that the stereotype applies in this context (see Fig. 1). We therefore hypothesize that:

Learners are likely to be aware of these differences and internalize a stereotype that women are more talented at language learning than men. Situational cues in the MOOC, such as the fact that the main instructors are women, may signal that the stereotype applies in this context

H1. Men **(a)** experience higher gender identity threat and **(b)** perform lower in the course than women.

Social Class
The second potential source of SIT is differences in social class. We identified two aspects of the course that could raise SIT among learners from a lower social class. First, the course was developed at one of China's most prestigious universities and the course materials discuss topics that are clearly more relevant for members of the upper class. For example, one lesson was about meeting foreigners ("Today we're going to talk about...meeting someone from a different country") and another concerned foreign travel ("Do you like to travel? Yes, of course. Last month I visited..."). Yet people outside of provincial capital cities or the four municipalities (Beijing, Chongqing, Shanghai, Tianjin) are much less likely to encounter foreigners, and people of lower socioeconomic status are less likely to travel to foreign countries. Thus, the lesson materials could reduce their sense of belonging, insinuate outsider status, and raise class-based identity threat.

A second aspect of the course that could raise SIT is that the course employed a highly communicative pedagogical approach. Although the number of classroom hours devoted to learning English may be similar across the country, instructional methods vary widely [20, 15, 29]. In particular, English classes in the more developed capital cities (and municipalities) such as Beijing and Shanghai are more likely to focus on building communicative competence, for instance by using English as the medium of instruction. In contrast, English classes in rural schools are more frequently taught using Chinese as the medium of instruction and with minimal English oral communication, partly due to teachers' lower levels of English proficiency and training [20, 49]. Thus, the communicative pedagogical approach in the course can be challenging and uncomfortable for people from rural areas or smaller cities, raising concerns that they do not belong and that they may be seen as incompetent.

We operationalize social class based on whether a learner is from a capital city or municipality (upper-class) or from a non-capital city (lower-class). This distinction is consistent with the differences in English instruction [20, 29] and expected relevance of course topics noted above. In economic terms, people in capital cities are also better off than those in non-capital cities.[1] We confirm the validity of this operationalization of social status at an individual level using multiple measures. We expect differences in class-based SIT between the two regions to manifest in terms of regional identity threat. Thus, we hypothesize that:

H2. Lower-class learners **(a)** experience higher regional identity threat and **(b)** perform lower in the course than upper-class learners.

Gender-Class Intersectionality

Individuals' social identities defined by gender and social class can overlap to give rise to related systems of disadvantage, as an instance of gender-class "intersectionality" [12]. In the present context, lower-class men are expected to carry the greatest psychological burden, due to both negative gender stereotypes and class-based identity threat. Upper-class women, by contrast, are not expected to face psychological barriers in this context, because they are stereotyped as more capable and better equipped to succeed. The remaining two subgroups (upper-class men and lower-class women) are expected to fall in-between the two extremes in terms of their success in the course. Thus, based on gender-class intersectionality, we hypothesize that:

H3. Lower-class men perform at the lowest level while upper-class women perform at the highest level in the course.

SOCIAL-PSYCHOLOGICAL INTERVENTION

In recent years, social-psychological interventions have been developed to support at-risk students in traditional academic environments. These interventions typically consist of brief reading and writing activities. Nonetheless, they are powerful because they target specific problems at critical points in time (e.g., SIT at the start of a course) [45, 10]. We draw on prior work to develop an intervention that is sensitive to the present educational and cultural context. In a recent set of experiments in MOOCs, a "value relevance affirmation" intervention was found to improve the performance of identity-threatened learners from less developed countries [25].

Value relevance affirmation combines elements of two established intervention approaches: values affirmation [10] and utility-value interventions [21]. First, values affirmation is based on self-affirmation theory [38], which offers an account of how people adapt to threatening information given that they are motivated to maintain their self-integrity. Affirming cherished values, such as relationships with friends and family or sports and athletics, expands people's self-concept and protects them from threats to their sense of belonging and social

identity [10]. Numerous field experiments have demonstrated academic improvements among underperforming students in the U.S. following values affirmation (see [10], for a review). In particular, it was found to reduce gender and social-class achievement gaps in traditional classroom settings [32, 17]. Second, the utility-value intervention aims to increase student motivation by helping them discover connections between the course materials and their lives. To this end, students may write an essay on how the topics covered in class inform their future workout plans. This intervention has also been tested in numerous field experiments; for example, it was found to raise course grades among high school students with low expectations of success [21].

The value relevance intervention is an opportunity for individuals to both affirm cherished values and connect them to the course. This should not be challenging because, unlike in traditional school settings, learners enroll in MOOCs at their own discretion to advance a variety of personal, social, or professional aspirations [26]. The intervention prompts learners to consider how their engagement in the course reflects and serves their most important values. For example, a learner may write that he is taking the course to get a better job, which would allow him to spend more time with his family and friends. A classic values affirmation [38], while supporting achievement in a mandatory school settings, could lead to disengagement in a voluntary online course where the easiest response to psychological threat is often to stop participating. Borrowing from utility-value research [21, 21], the value relevance affirmation recasts the course as instrumental to the fulfillment of learners' most important values. This value-based perspective on their engagement in the course can perpetually strengthen learners' commitment each time they return to the course with a value-driven sense of purpose. Negative experiences are less likely to be interpreted as threats to social identity or belonging if learners are truly ardent. These experiences may be perceived as less consequential or not even noticed at all. Accordingly, we hypothesize that:

H4. Interdependent value relevance affirmation increases the performance of identity-threatened learners in the course.

We further adapted the original value relevance affirmation activity [25] for the highly collectivist culture in China. This culture emphasizes connectedness with family and friends and fosters an *interdependent* self-concept, such that a person's relationships become an integral part of their self [31]. Prior work adapted the standard values affirmation activity for Chinese [6] and Asian Canadian [19] students by prompting them to choose and reflect on values that are not only relevant to themselves but also to close others (e.g., family, friends); the small change in the instructions improved the efficacy of the intervention relative to the standard values affirmation in both studies (see [11] for a similar adaptation for Latino students). Based on this insight, we adapted the activity to have participants select cherished values that they also shared with people close to them. Additionally, we leveraged choice architecture [44] to nudge individuals to affirm their relationships with family and friends by presenting this particular value first in the list (the order of the remaining values was randomized).

---

[1] http://data.stats.gov.cn/english/

Prior work also found that the utility-value intervention is more effective among East Asians if long-term rather than short-term benefits are emphasized [37]. In line with this, the value relevance affirmation focuses on individuals' cherished values, which are not expected to vary much over time. Nevertheless, as it is unknown how affirming the relevance of different values moderates the efficacy of the intervention, we pose the following research question:

RQ1. How does the treatment effect vary depending on whether close relationships are affirmed as a value?

PRELIMINARY SURVEY

Prior to the intervention experiment, we fielded a survey in an earlier offering of the same English language MOOC featured in our main study. The purpose of the survey was to identify the at-risk group of learners. We evaluated gender differences in SIT and differences in social status between participants from capital versus non-capital cities. The survey was administered in Mandarin. Respondents were 1,664 learners located in (and originally from) China. They were enrolled in an English language learning MOOC offered by Tsinghua University on the Chinese XuetangX platform. In this sample, 50% of respondents were women and 37% were from capital cities. It was not possible to connect survey responses with course outcomes.

Gender identity threat was assessed by rating agreement with a single item: "In the course, I worry that people will draw conclusions about my gender, based on my performance" (adapted from [9]). As predicted, men's ratings of gender-based identity threat were 11% higher than women's (H1a; $z = 5.07, p < 0.001, d = 0.25$). Regional identity threat was assessed by rating two items: "In the course, I worry that people will draw conclusions about my hometown, based on my performance," and "In the course, I worry that people will draw conclusions about me, based on what they think about my hometown." Against our prediction, lower-class respondents (i.e. those from non-capital cities) did not report higher regional identity threat (H2a; $z = -0.55, p = 0.58$). The statements may have been too specific to capture class-based identity threat. Nevertheless, subjective social status in terms of the MacArthur Scale ("Where do you place yourself on a ladder representing where people stand in your country?") was lower for lower-class than upper-class respondents ($z = 3.78, p < 0.001, d = 0.19$). Moreover, lower-class respondents reported lower levels of parental education: only 10% of parents of lower-class respondents held a bachelor's degree, compared with 18% among upper-class respondents ($z = 4.53, p < 0.001$). Overall, the data tend to support our hypotheses that men experience higher SIT than women and that lower-class learners experience lower social status, though no differences in regional identity threat were detected.

METHODS

Participants and Context

Participants were enrolled in a beginners' English language learning MOOC targeted at Mandarin speakers. The course was offered for free by Tsinghua University for the second time on the openly accessible XuetangX platform. The course materials encompassed lecture videos, a large number of low-stakes assessments, and a final exam. Participants were recruited with an optional survey at the start of the course.

The survey was started 3,117 times and in 2,864 cases a learner progressed far enough in the survey to be randomly assigned and exposed to the control or treatment activity. We only consider the 2,772 learners who reported that their hometown was located in mainland China (i.e., not Hong Kong, Macau, or a region outside of China) and who were located in China based on their IP address. We excluded duplicate responses by discarding all responses if a learner was exposed to both conditions, and maintaining only the initial response if a learner was repeatedly exposed to the same condition. Of the remaining 2,460 unique responses, we were able to match 2,164 to course outcome records, due to technical problems with passing anonymous user IDs. Finally, we only considered responses that occurred at least one week before the official end of the course, as learners who began after that cutoff date were unlikely to be able to complete the course. The final sample included $N = 1,973$ learners. Importantly, despite these exclusions, random assignment to conditions remained balanced on all available pre-treatment measures ($ps > 0.13$).

Participants were 64% women and 40% were from a capital city. The average age was 23.9 ($SD = 6.95$) and the level of education was varied: 8.2% held a master's or doctoral degree; 69% held a bachelor's, associate, or professional degree, and 23% had only completed high school or less schooling. For 42%, this was their first open online course. Most participants intended to complete all course materials (83%) and reported that it was very or extremely important to them to possess good English skills (89%).

Procedure

The survey was implemented at the start of the course as the first activity in the materials (with reminders also added before each of the first four videos). Most learners in MOOCs complete course materials in the specified order, though some may take the survey at a later time, which we could not verify as this data was unavailable. The intervention activity was embedded at the end of the survey. Following a number of demographic questions and pre-treatment measures (see Measures), participants were randomly assigned to receive either a study skills activity (control) or an interdependent value relevance affirmation (treatment). Both activities, which were translated into Mandarin, asked participants to read prompts and write responses. Participants spent twice as long on the affirmation activity as on the study skills activity (median = 3.4 vs. 1.6 minutes), but they were equally likely to complete each activity (94% proceeded to the following survey page; $\chi_1^2 = 0.18, p = 0.67$).

Study skills control: Participants read four brief testimonials from previous students describing strategies and tips for taking the course. For example, one testimonial stated, "When there's a lot on your mind it helps to make a list. I found writing down a bunch of personal due dates in my planner really helped, even though there were no deadlines in the course." Participants then wrote about their own strategies and insights about how

Table 1. Descriptive statistics (means and SDs) by participant gender and social class across both experimental conditions.

Gender	Social Class	N	Completion Rate	Gender Identity Threat	Regional Identity Threat	Self-Esteem	English Importance	English Anxiety	English Skill	GDP/capita (CNY)
Men	Low	461	30.6%	3.49 (1.41)	3.72 (1.45)	3.30 (0.69)	4.26 (0.78)	3.19 (1.10)	2.66 (0.85)	52,087 (18,542)
Men	High	243	34.6%	3.68 (1.45)	3.91 (1.45)	3.29 (0.69)	4.27 (0.81)	3.16 (1.06)	2.75 (0.78)	74,925 (29,081)
Women	Low	730	47.5%	3.17 (1.22)	3.56 (1.34)	3.18 (0.63)	4.40 (0.70)	3.38 (1.04)	2.82 (0.73)	49,600 (17,844)
Women	High	539	55.8%	3.30 (1.32)	3.57 (1.39)	3.28 (0.61)	4.48 (0.67)	3.32 (1.10)	2.91 (0.75)	83,342 (30,258)

to learn best, and how they compare to the ones they just read. This type of activity showed no effect on learners in another MOOC [23].

Interdependent value relevance affirmation: Participants selected from a list of twelve values and qualities (adapted from [10]) the 2 or 3 most important ones that they shared with people who were close to them, such as friends and family.[2] Then, participants wrote about why their chosen values were the most important ones to them, and how taking this course might reflect and reinforce their values. To amplify the impact of the affirmation, participants also wrote a message to their future self about how they can gain strength from the fact that taking this course reinforces their most important values.

Measures

The primary outcome measure was course completion (binary), which required earning an overall course grade above 50%. Two secondary outcome measures were the overall course grade (between 0 and 100) and the number of attempted assessments (between 0 and 47), a measure of persistence with course materials. The secondary outcome measures were highly correlated with course completion (Spearman's $rs > 0.87$) and featured bimodal distributions with point masses at the extremes.

Multiple self-report measures were included in the survey prior to the experimental activities. There were a small number of missing values (~1% missing for most questions), which were imputed with predictive mean matching using the *R mice* package [5]. The following self-report measures were included as covariates in regression analyses: age (normalized), education level (in three bins as reported above), number of prior open online courses started (normalized), and intent to complete all course materials (binary). Additionally, we determined participants' regional GDP/capita based on their self-reported home province/region to include it as another covariate. These covariates are largely objective measures expected to reduce unexplained variance in outcomes.

Additionally, we assessed regional identity threat ($M = 3.6, SD = 1.4, range = [1,7], \alpha = 0.86$) as in the preliminary survey. Gender identity threat ($M = 3.3, SD = 1.3, range = [1,7], \alpha = 0.86$) was assessed with agreement/disagreement on two items mirroring the regional identity threat items (adding a second item to the measure used in the preliminary survey). Self-esteem ($M = 3.7, SD = 0.75, range = [1,5], \alpha = 0.73$)

was measured with three questions: "How good or bad do you feel about yourself?", "How confident are you in your abilities?", and "How much do you feel that others respect and admire you?" English skill ($M = 2.8, SD = 0.78, range = [1,5], \alpha = 0.82$) was measured by rating writing, speaking, and understanding, each on a scale from very poor to very good. English anxiety ($M = 3.3, SD = 1.1, range = [1,5]$) was measured by "How anxious do you feel about speaking English with a native speaker without preparation?"

Open Science and Analytic Approach

The de-identified dataset, analysis script, and intervention materials for this study are available online at osf.io/s5pwv. Intervention effects were tested using linear regression with robust standard errors and z-tests. The regression models included multiple pre-treatment covariates (specified above) to reduce unexplained variance.

RESULTS

Gender and Social-Class Differences

Descriptive statistics for subgroups defined by gender and social class (pooling across experimental conditions) are provided in Table 1. As hypothesized, men again experienced more gender identity threat than women (H1a; $z = 5.20, p < 0.001, d = 0.25$). Men also reported lower English skills ($z = -4.53, p < 0.001, d = 0.22$), assigned less importance to knowing English ($z = -4.68, p < 0.001, d = 0.23$), and reported lower English speaking anxiety than women ($z = -3.37, p < 0.001, d = 0.16$). This could be a sign of psychological disengagement to cope with identity threat (i.e., "I am not good at it and I don't really care"; [39]). Men performed lower than women in terms of completion rates, as hypothesized (H1b; 32% vs. 51%, $z = 8.49, p < 0.001$).

We confirmed that participants from capital cities showed clear signs of higher social status compared with those from non-capital cities. Upper-class learners were 56% more likely to hold advanced academic degrees (master/Ph.D.; $z = -2.87, p = 0.004$), reported having better English skills ($z = -2.88, p = 0.004, d = 0.13$), and came from 60% richer regions/provinces ($z = -25.2, p < 0.001$). They also reported higher self-esteem ($t = -1.97, p = 0.049, d = 0.09$). However, we found no difference in regional identity threat between upper- and lower-class participants (H2a; $z = 0.83, p = 0.41$). Yet upper-class participants were significantly more likely to complete the course (H2b; 49% vs. 41%, $z = 3.61, p < 0.001$).

At the intersection of gender and social class, consistent with our hypothesis, we found that the course completion rate pooling across conditions was lowest for lower-class men and highest for upper-class women, yielding a 25.3 percentage point gap in average completion rates (H3; $z = 8.34, p < 0.001$).

---

[2]Twelve values and qualities: Relationships with family or friends; Artistic skills/aesthetic appreciation; Sense of humor; Spontaneity/living life in the moment; Learning for the sake of learning; Religious/spiritual values; Sports and athletics; Musical ability/appreciation; Physical attractiveness; Creativity; Business/managerial skills; Romantic values.

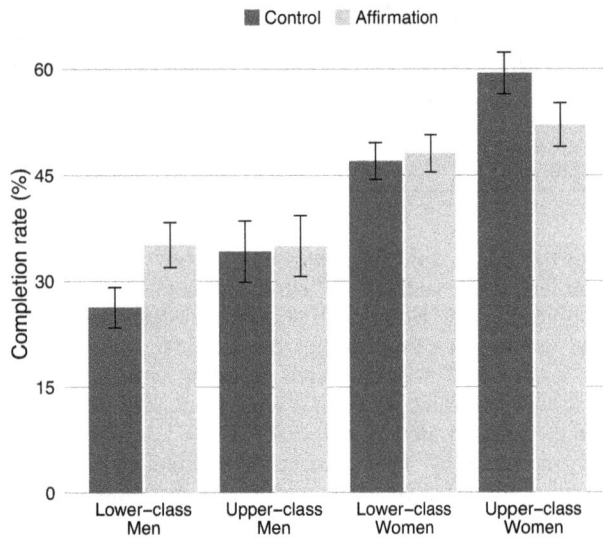

Figure 2. Mean course completion rate in each experimental condition by participant gender and social class. Affirmation raised completion rates exclusively for lower-class men. The drop in completion for upper-class women was not statistically significant. Error bars are ±1SE.

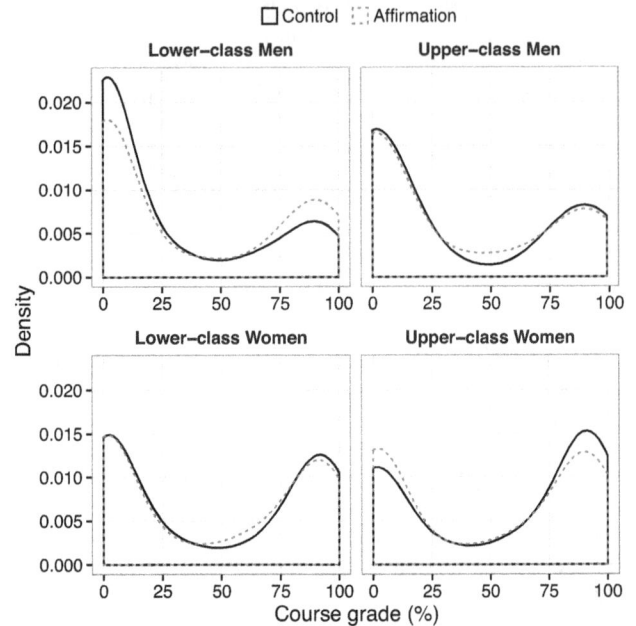

Figure 3. Grade distribution in each experimental condition by participant gender and social class.

Intervention Effects: Completion, Grades, & Persistence

The affirmation intervention significantly increased the completion rate among the lowest performing group, lower-class men, from 24.6% to 34.6% (H4; $z = 2.47, p = 0.013$), adjusting for covariates ($p = 0.039$ unadjusted; Fig. 2). Women in capital cities saw a small and not statistically significant decrease in completion from the affirmation intervention ($z = -1.66, p = 0.098$). The achievement gap (unadjusted) between lower-class men and upper-class women was cut in half, from 33 to 17 percentage points. No change in the completion rate was detected for the remaining two groups: lower-class women and upper-class men ($|zs| < 0.85, ps > 0.39$).

An identical pattern of intervention effects was observed for course grades (Fig. 3). Among lower-class men there was a visible shift in density from grades below 25 to grades above 60. Indeed, the affirmation intervention significantly raised average course grades for this group (H4; $z = 2.86, p = 0.004$, adjusting for covariates; $p = 0.017$ unadjusted). A slight negative shift in grades occurred for upper-class women, but this shift was not significant ($z = -1.78, p = 0.075$). As with completion rates, no major changes in the grade distribution occurred in the remaining two groups ($|zs| < 1.1, ps > 0.30$).

We conducted a survival analysis to test effects on persistence, measured by the number of assessments attempted throughout the course (data on video watching and other behaviors were unavailable). Kaplan-Maier survival curves show that the affirmation intervention improved the trajectory of persistence for lower-class men early in the course (Fig. 4). The intervention reduced the drop-out risk by 24% (H4; $e^{coef} = 0.76, z = -2.88, p = 0.004$, according to a covariate-adjusted Cox regression ($p = 0.048$ unadjusted; proportional hazards assumption not violated, all $p > 0.12$). Consistent with the results for completion rates and grades, the survival

analysis yielded no significant effect on the other subgroups ($|zs| < 1.8, ps > 0.087$).

Heterogeneity in Affirmed Values

In the value relevance affirmation activity, 88% of participants selected three values to affirm, while others selected one or two. The most frequently selected values were relationships with family/friends (69%), physical attractiveness (56%), creativity (39%), sense of humor (34%), and spontaneity/living life in the moment (30%). To test if affirming certain values was associated with stronger or weaker intervention effects, we compared the average completion rate in the control condition (c) with the average rate in the affirmation condition when a specific value was affirmed (a_1) and when it was not affirmed (a_0). Group differences in completion rates were tested using z-tests with robust standard errors (c, a_1, a_0 represent means).

We found significant heterogeneity in the effect of the affirmation for lower-class men (RQ1). The increase in completion rates was exclusively observed for the 65% of participants who affirmed their relationships with family/friends ($c = 26\%$; $a_0 = 24\%$; $a_1 = 41\%$; $z = 2.93, p = 0.003$). Repeating the analysis for upper-class women, we again found heterogeneity. While the 70% of upper-class women who affirmed their relationships with family/friends exhibited no change from control levels, those who did not affirm this value performed significantly worse ($c = 59\%$; $a_0 = 36\%$; $a_1 = 59\%$; $z = -3.80, p < 0.001$). These correlational findings suggest that affirming close relationships is important for the intervention to support identity-threatened individuals in China. For non-threatened individuals, however, the intervention may lead them to invest their efforts outside of the course, unless they connect the course to their close relationships (e.g., learning English to make their parents proud). This raises questions

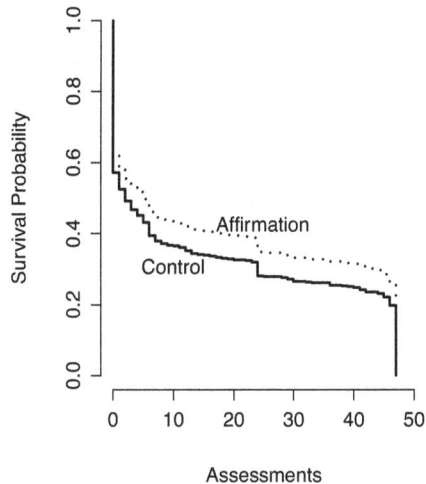

Figure 4. Course persistence for lower-class men in each experimental condition. Kaplan-Meier survival curves are based on the number of attempted course assessments.

for future research on strategies to encourage individuals to affirm values that may be culturally most relevant.

For completeness, we report additional associations between treatment effects and commonly affirmed values (chosen by at least 10%). For lower-class men, intervention effects were detected only when sports/athletics and learning for the sake of learning were not affirmed (e.g., sports: $c = 26\%$; $a_0 = 37\%$; $a_1 = 26\%$; $z = 2.38, p = 0.017$). Upper-class women exhibited lower completion rates relative to the control condition ($c = 59\%$) if they affirmed physical attractiveness ($a_0 = 56\%$; $a_1 = 48\%$; $z = -2.17, p = 0.030$) and if they did not affirm spontaneity/living life in moment ($a_0 = 49\%$; $a_1 = 57\%$; $z = -2.06, p = 0.039$). These exploratory findings are tentative and invite future research into which values are most conducive to achievement.

DISCUSSION

This research advances the social-psychological account of achievement gaps in online learning [25]. We provide new evidence that psychological barriers can undermine academic learning and achievement not only in brick-and-mortar settings but also in online learning environments. An intervention in the form of a brief writing activity, which did not remove any structural barriers, reduced gender and social-class achievement gaps. This suggests that social and cultural cues in the environment, such as the instructor's gender and references in the learning materials, raised SIT by conveying that group stereotypes apply in this setting or by insinuating outsider status [33].

We found that men experienced higher gender SIT and performed lower than women in an English language learning MOOC (H1), and lower-class learners reported lower self-esteem and subjective social status and performed lower than upper-class learners (H2b), even though no difference in regional SIT was found (H2a). Consistent with research on

intersectionality [12], lower-class men performed the lowest, while upper-class women performed the highest (H3). To test the psychological basis of this achievement gap, we used an intervention designed to support identity-threatened online learners from a collectivist culture. The interdependent value relevance affirmation substantially improved persistence, grades, and completion rates for the most disadvantaged group in this context, lower-class men (H4). Other groups of learners remained unaffected, except for a negative trend ($p = 0.098$) for upper-class women, the highest performing group. A slight reduction in completion rates in the highest performing group due to a value relevance affirmation was also observed in prior work [25]. We shed new light on this phenomenon by revealing that this tendency to disengage depends on which values high-achievers affirm. The intervention may lead non-threatened individuals in a collectivist context to disengage from the course unless they affirm the relevance of the course to their close relationships.

Limitations

The current research demonstrates both pre-treatment differences in SIT and social status, and the behavioral and performance impact of a value relevance affirmation on identity-threatened individuals; however, it leaves a closer investigation into the psychological mechanisms for future research. Building on psychological theory and prior empirical work, the value relevance affirmation was designed to foster motivation and buffer against SIT, but without follow-up self-report data we cannot examine the mechanism by which the intervention improved outcomes among lower-class men. An attempt to collect relevant data in a follow-up survey was unsuccessful due to very low response rates. While open learning environments lend themselves to collecting longitudinal behavioral data, the same cannot be said for self-report data, as surveys are optional and attrition rates are high and often differential across conditions.

We found converging evidence that learners from capital cities and municipalities are on average from a higher social class than learners from non-capital cities. However, this geographic operationalization of social class is relatively coarse—clearly not everyone from a capital city is in the upper-class of society and vice versa. It is also unclear whether learners from non-capital cities experienced class-based identity threat, because we only assessed regional identity threat and found no difference. The communicative pedagogical approach in the course in combination with gender cues may have raised SIT specifically among men who were aware of gender stereotypes in language learning and who additionally felt unprepared—even intimidated—by the course format because they attended schools in lower-class regions with less emphasis on English communication. Further research should disentangle potential sources of SIT and evaluate how they relate to social class identity using individual-level data.

Theoretical Contributions

How psychological processes tied to identity, belonging, and threat unfold in computer-mediated learning environments is a largely unexplored theoretical frontier. The present findings demonstrate the influence of social-psychological processes on academic achievement in a novel context—large-scale online learning environments—and in a novel population—Chinese English language learners. This extends prior work focusing on social inequalities that arise in in-person settings, but it remained unclear how threats to social belonging and identity arise in online environments that afford low levels of social presence and interaction. These environments present numerous social and cultural cues through the design of the environment and the content and format of learning materials. Learners who are conscious of a stigma associated with their group identity (e.g., women being more talented at language learning than men) tend to respond more strongly to identity-relevant cues (e.g., both course instructors being women) [34], especially in novel situations that bear greater uncertainty about one's ability to be successful [13]. Thus, online learning environments can serve as a research site to investigate the impact of different cues and the psychological mechanisms that give rise to achievement gaps.

Another theoretical contribution of this work arises from the study sample, which was collected in a highly interdependent cultural context [31]. We expected that relationships with family and friends would be an important value to affirm in China [19, 6], though prior work has not tested how the choice of affirmed values relates to the efficacy of the value relevance affirmation. Affirming close relationships turned out to be vital for supporting lower-class men and preventing affirmation-induced disengagement among upper-class women (RQ1). This initial correlational evidence suggests that it matters which values people affirm, though it is unclear how the choice of affirmed values moderates the intervention effects in other cultural contexts, such to the U.S., where people tend to have highly independent self-concepts [31]. Perhaps affirming certain values requires less effort and is more effective at protecting people's sense of self-integrity depending on the cultural context. Another interpretation of the finding is that people who affirm close relationships are more likely to benefit from the intervention. Further research could examine heterogeneity in affirmed values across demographic and sociocultural contexts, and test the effects of strategically presenting different sets of values to affirm.

From a disciplinary education perspective, there is a large body of literature on foreign language classroom anxiety [18], but this phenomenon has not been examined in online classrooms. We therefore included a question to assess this type of anxiety and found that, consistent with prior work in in-person environments [2, 27], women reported higher anxiety than men ($p < 0.001$). While we cannot evaluate the effect of affirmation on anxiety because this variable was assessed before treatment, we also found no evidence that anxiety moderated the intervention effect. This suggests that men's underperformance is not due to foreign language classroom anxiety. The pattern that men underperform despite reporting lower levels of anxiety may be interpreted as a symptom of psychological disengagement from the English course, a context in which they feel stigmatized [30]; future research could investigate the relationship between SIT and foreign language classroom anxiety.

Practical Implications

Despite increasing access to higher education content, MOOCs have fallen short of providing equal opportunities to success, especially for members of social groups that underperform in traditional academic settings, as evidenced by systematic differences in course outcomes [16, 22, 25]. We demonstrate the role of a social-psychological barrier to achievement and introduce a theory-based intervention approach to reduce educational disparities. This intervention can be scaled to any number of learners; it takes them just minutes to complete; and the implementation of the activities is fast and does not incur any costs. Additionally, the intervention can be targeted to just those (identity-threatened) learners expected to benefit from the activity. More research is needed to understand when and for whom the intervention is most effective. Points of transition (e.g., entering a new course) and before a threatening interaction (e.g., taking a test, receiving critical feedback) are critical times when an affirmation can support at-risk learners [10]. Moreover, it may be important to tailor the intervention activity and its framing to fit the cultural context, as was done here for Chinese learners.

Another practical implication of this work concerns the importance of social and cultural cues in learning environments. Prior work identifies multiple cues that can raise SIT, including numeric underrepresentation and stereotypical classroom decorations (e.g., gaming posters in a computer science classroom) [7, 33]. However, instructional designers can also plant cues in an environment to forestall experiences of SIT and fears of non-belonging, for example, by designing the virtual classroom with warm colors and by explicitly communicating that diversity is valued in the community [7, 35]. In a "neutral" environment, the absence of cues may not be sufficient to alleviate stress and vigilance, which depletes valuable cognitive resources that could be otherwise invested in learning [46, 33, 35]. It may therefore be necessary to embed affirming experiences in the learning environment to lift the threat that at-risk learners experience by default in such settings. It may also be necessary to adapt learning materials to different cultural contexts to avoid perceptions of cultural mismatch [41].

CONCLUSION
Social-psychological factors can limit academic achievement in online learning environments, especially among learners who are already disadvantaged in brick-and-mortar settings. To move beyond providing equal access and fulfill the promise of providing equal learning opportunities, MOOCs and other learning environments need to provide a psychologically safe climate for all learners. In no way does this lessen the critical need to address persistent structural sources of educational inequality. Instead, it is a reminder that even if structural barriers were overcome and universal access to education were available, there would still be a need to address social-psychological barriers to achievement.

ACKNOWLEDGEMENTS
We thank Yi Yan for help translating the study materials. This work benefited from feedback by Michael Schwalbe and three anonymous reviewers.

REFERENCES

1. Anant Agarwal. 2013. Online universities: It's time for teachers to join the revolution. *The Observer* June (2013).

2. Yukie Aida. 1994. Examination of Horwitz, Horwitz, and Cope's construct of foreign language anxiety: The case of students of Japanese. *The Modern Language Journal* 78, 2 (1994), 155–168.

3. Roy F Baumeister, C Nathan DeWall, Natalie J Ciarocco, and Jean M Twenge. 2005. Social exclusion impairs self-regulation. *Journal of personality and social psychology* 88, 4 (2005), 589–604.

4. Roy F Baumeister and M R Leary. 1995. The need to belong: desire for interpersonal attachments as a fundamental human motivation. *Psychological Bulletin* 117, 3 (may 1995), 497–529.

5. S Buuren and K Groothuis-Oudshoorn. 2011. Mice: multivariate imputation by chained equations in R. *Journal of Statistical Software* 45, 3 (2011).

6. Huajian Cai, Constantine Sedikides, and Lixin Jiang. 2013. Familial self as a potent source of affirmation: Evidence from China. *Social Psychological and Personality Science* 4, 5 (2013), 529–537.

7. Sapna Cheryan, Andrew N. Meltzoff, and Saenam Kim. 2011. Classrooms matter: The design of virtual classrooms influences gender disparities in computer science classes. *Computers & Education* 57, 2 (2011), 1825–1835.

8. Sapna Cheryan, Sianna A. Ziegler, Amanda Montoya, and Lily Jiang. 2016. Why are some STEM field more gender balanced than others? *Psychological Bulletin* 206 (2016).

9. Geoffrey L Cohen and Julio Garcia. 2005. "I am us": negative stereotypes as collective threats. *Journal of personality and social psychology* 89, 4 (2005), 566–582.

10. Geoffrey L Cohen and David K Sherman. 2014. The psychology of change: self-affirmation and social psychological intervention. *Annual review of psychology* 65 (jan 2014), 333–71.

11. Rebecca Covarrubias, Sarah D Herrmann, and Stephanie A Fryberg. 2016. Affirming the interdependent self: Implications for Latino student performance. *Basic and Applied Social Psychology* 38, 1 (2016), 47–57.

12. Kimberle Crenshaw. 1991. Mapping the margins: Intersectionality, identity politics, and violence against women of color. *Stanford Law Review* (1991), 1241–1299.

13. Jennifer Crocker and Brenda Major. 1989. Social stigma and self-esteem: The self-protective properties of stigma. *Psychological Review* 96, 4 (1989), 608–630.

14. J.-C. Croizet and Theresa Claire. 1998. Extending the Concept of Stereotype Threat to Social Class: The Intellectual Underperformance of Students from Low Socioeconomic Backgrounds. *Personality and Social Psychology Bulletin* 24, 6 (1998), 588–594.

15. Anwei Feng. 2009. English in China: Convergence and divergence in policy and practice. *AILA Review* 22 (2009), 85–102.

16. J. D. Hansen and J. Reich. 2015. Democratizing education? Examining access and usage patterns in massive open online courses. *Science (New York, N.Y.)* 350, 6265 (2015), 1245–1248.

17. Judith M Harackiewicz, Elizabeth A Canning, Yoi Tibbetts, Cynthia J Giffen, Seth S Blair, Douglas I. Rouse, and Janet S Hyde. 2014. Closing the social class achievement gap for first-generation students in undergraduate biology. *Journal of Educational Psychology* 106, 2 (2014), 375–389.

18. Elaine K. Horwitz, Michael B. Horwitz, and Joann Cope. 1986. Foreign language classroom anxiety. *The Modern Language Journal* 70, 2 (1986), 125–132.

19. Etsuko Hoshino-Browne, Adam S Zanna, Steven J Spencer, Mark P Zanna, Shinobu Kitayama, and Sandra Lackenbauer. 2005. On the cultural guises of cognitive dissonance: the case of easterners and westerners. *Journal of personality and social psychology* 89, 3 (2005), 294–310.

20. Guangwei Hu. 2005. Contextual influences on instructional practices: A Chinese case for an ecological approach to ELT. *TESOL Quarterly* 39, 4 (2005), 635–660.

21. Chris S Hulleman and Judith M Harackiewicz. 2009. Promoting interest and performance in high school science classes. *Science (New York, N.Y.)* 326 (2009), 1410–1412.

22. René F. Kizilcec and Sherif Halawa. 2015. Attrition and Achievement Gaps in Online Learning. In *Proceedings of the Second ACM Conference on Learning@Scale*. ACM, 57–66.

23. René F Kizilcec, Mar Pérez-Sanagustín, and Jorge J Maldonado. 2016. Recommending Self-Regulated Learning Strategies Does Not Improve Performance in a MOOC. In *Proceedings of the Third ACM Conference on Learning@Scale*. ACM, 101–104.

24. René F Kizilcec, Chris Piech, and Emily Schneider. 2013. Deconstructing Disengagement: Analyzing Learner Subpopulations in Massive Open Online Courses. In *Proceedings of the International Conference on Learning Analytics and Knowledge*.

25. René F Kizilcec, Andrew J Saltarelli, Justin Reich, and Geoffrey L Cohen. 2017. Closing global achievement gaps in MOOCs. *Science (New York, N.Y.)* 355, 6322 (2017), 251–252.

26. René F Kizilcec and Emily Schneider. 2015. Motivation as a Lens to Understand Online Learners: Toward Data-Driven Design with the OLEI Scale. *Transactions on Human-Computer Interaction* 22, 2 (2015).

27. Ravinder Koul, Laura Roy, Sittichai Kaewkuekool, and Suthee Ploisawaschai. 2009. Multiple goal orientations and foreign language anxiety. *System* 37 (2009), 676–688.

28. Fang Lai. 2010. Are boys left behind? The evolution of the gender achievement gap in Beijing's middle schools. *Economics of Education Review* 29 (2010), 383–399.

29. Jinjin Lu and Han Jiang. 2016. Chinese education and learning activities outside of class: What lies beyong basic education? *International Education Studies* 9, 4 (2016), 54–68.

30. Brenda Major, Steven J Spencer, Toni Schmader, Connie Wolfe, and Jennifer Crocker. 1998. Coping with Negative Stereotypes About Intellectual Performance: The Role of Psychological Disengagement. *Journal of Composite Materials* 24, 1 (1998), 34–50.

31. Hazel Rose Markus and Shinobu Kitayama. 1991. Culture and the self: Implications for cognition, emotion, and motivation. *Psychological Review* 98, 2 (1991), 224–253.

32. Akira Miyake, Lauren E Kost-Smith, Noah D Finkelstein, Steven J Pollock, Geoffrey L Cohen, and Tiffany a Ito. 2010. Reducing the gender achievement gap in college science: a classroom study of values affirmation. *Science (New York, N.Y.)* 330, 6008 (2010), 1234–1237.

33. Mary C Murphy, Claude M. Steele, and James J Gross. 2007. Signaling Threat. *Psychological science* 18, 10 (2007), 879–885.

34. Elizabeth C Pinel. 1999. Stigma consciousness: The psychological legacy of social stereotypes. *Journal of Personality and Social Psychology* 76, 1 (1999), 114–128.

35. Valerie Purdie-Vaughns, Claude M. Steele, Paul G Davies, Ruth Ditlmann, and Jennifer Randall Crosby. 2008. Social identity contingencies: How diversity cues signal threat or safety for African Americans in mainstream institutions. *Journal of Personality and Social Psychology* 94, 4 (2008), 615–630.

36. Dhawal Shah. 2015. MOOCs in 2015: Breaking Down the Numbers. *EdSurge* (December 2015).

37. Olga G Shechter, Amanda M Durik, Yuri Miyamoto, and Judith M Harackiewicz. 2011. The role of utility value in achievement behavior: The importance of culture. *Personality and Social Psychology Bulletin* 37, 3 (2011), 303–317.

38. Claude M. Steele. 1988. The psychology of self-affirmation: Sustaining the integrity of the self. *Advances in Experimental Social Psychology* 21, 2 (1988), 261–302.

39. Claude M. Steele. 1997. A threat in the air. How stereotypes shape intellectual identity and performance. *The American Psychologist* 52, 6 (1997), 613–629.

40. Claude M. Steele, Steven J Spencer, and Joshua Aronson. 2002. Contending with group image: The psychology of stereotype and identity threat. *Advances in Experimental Social Psychology* 34 (2002), 379–440.

41. Nicole M. Stephens, Stephanie A. Fryberg, Hazel Rose Markus, Camille S. Johnson, and Rebecca Covarrubias. 2012. Unseen disadvantage: How American universities' focus on independence undermines the academic performance of first-generation college students. *Journal of Personality and Social Psychology* 102, 6 (2012), 1178–1197.

42. H Tajfel and JC Turner. 1986. The Social Identity Theory of Intergroup Behavior. In *Psychology of Intergroup Relations*, S. Worchel and WG Austin (Eds.). Nelson-Hall Publishers, Chicago, I.L., 7–24.

43. Valerie Jones Taylor and Gregory M Walton. 2011. Stereotype threat undermines academic learning. *Personality and social psychology bulletin* 37, 8 (2011), 1055–1067.

44. Richard H. Thaler and Cass R. Sunstein. 2008. *Nudge: Improving Decisions About Health, Wealth, and Happiness*. Yale University Press, New Haven, C.T. 293 pages.

45. Gregory M Walton. 2014. The New Science of Wise Psychological Interventions. *Current Directions in Psychological Science* 23, 1 (2014), 73–82.

46. Gregory M Walton and Geoffrey L Cohen. 2007. A question of belonging: Race, social fit, and achievement. *Journal of Personality and Social Psychology* 92, 1 (2007), 82–96.

47. Jackie Xiu Yan and Elaine Kolker Horwitz. 2008. Learners' perceptions of how anxiety interacts with personal and instructional factors to influence their achievement in English: A qualitative analysis of EFL learners in China. *Language Learning* 58, 1 (2008), 151–183.

48. Lawrence Zhang. 2000. Uncovering Chinese ESL students' reading anxiety in a study-abroad context. *Asia Pacific Journal of Language in Education* 3, 3 (2000), 31–56.

49. Lawrence Jun Zhang. 2001. Exploring variability in language anxiety: Two groups of PRC students learning ESL in Singapore. *RELC Journal* 32, 1 (2001), 73–91.

50. Yu Zhang and Mun Tsang. 2015. Gender gap in the National College Entrance Exam performance in China: A case study of a typical Chinese municipality. *Asia Pacific Education Review* 16 (2015), 27–36.

Learning about Learning at Scale: Methodological Challenges and Recommendations

Frans van der Sluis[*]
Online Learning Lab
Leiden University
The Hague, The Netherlands

Tim van der Zee[†]
Graduate School of Teaching
Leiden University
Leiden, The Netherlands

Jasper Ginn[‡]
Online Learning Lab
Leiden University
The Hague, The Netherlands

ABSTRACT

Learning at scale opens up a new frontier to learn about learning. Massive Online Open Courses (MOOCs) and similar large-scale online learning platforms give an unprecedented view of learners' behavior whilst learning. In this paper, we argue that the abundance of data that results from such platforms not only brings novel opportunities to the study of learning, but also bears novel methodological challenges. We show that the resulting data comes with various challenges with respect to the granular, observational, and large nature of these data. Additionally, we discuss a series of potential solutions, such as sharing validated models and performing pre-registered confirmatory research. With these contributions, this paper aims to increase awareness and understanding of both the strengths and challenges of research on learning at scale.

ACM Classification Keywords

K.3.1 Computer Uses in Education: Distance learning; G.3
G.3 Probability and Statistics: Experimental design

Author Keywords

Learning analytics; research validity; research methodology; big data; behavioral traces; online learning

INTRODUCTION

Online learning at scale opens up a new frontier for research on learning. MOOCs and similar large-scale online learning environments do not only offer a nearly unconstrained environment to learners, they also offer an abundance of data with which to monitor the learning process. This provides us with an unprecedented view of learner behavior whilst they are learning, and positions large-scale online learning environments as new platforms for research on learning behaviour. In particular, research in online learning environments can bridge the realism of classroom studies with the control of laboratory research. In online learning research, the setting

[*]f.vandersluis@fgga.leidenuniv.nl [†]t.van.der.zee@iclon.leidenuniv.nl
and [‡] j.h.ginn@fgga.leidenuniv.nl

L@S 2017, April 20-21, 2017, Cambridge, MA, USA
© 2017 ACM. ISBN 978-1-4503-4450-0/17/04 ...$15.00
DOI: http://dx.doi.org/10.1145/3051457.3051461

in which the data is measured is not just an approximation of, but *equals* the world under examination. This is in contrast with laboratory research on learning, which has to simulate an educational setting. However, similar to laboratory research, online learning studies suffer little from variability in treatment delivery [20] and allow for detailed measurements. It is this mixture that permits the researcher to address questions that were previously difficult to answer.

Online learning platforms offer new techniques for experimental and correlational studies of online learning. Opportunities for experimental studies arise from the large number of students, which makes it easy to test and compare numerous stimuli simultaneously. This is more commonly known as A/B or split testing. It provides an excellent testing ground to compare many variations of different instructional designs and educational interventions. Opportunities for correlational studies arise from the abundance and large variety of data, which allows researchers to look for associations between naturally occurring variables. In combination, these types of studies do not only allow us to verify which stimuli and interventions are optimal for learning, but they also allow us to discover the conditions under which learning is optimal.

What enables these new types of studies is the richness of the gathered data. This is unlike traditional field research, which often suffers from the limitation that only a few varieties of data can be gathered. Digital environments enable us to track every mouse click, every page a student visits, and how long educational videos are being watched. Furthermore, they allow us to examine detailed information about student responses to quizzes and assignments. This adds a plethora of behavioral traces to the study of learning that form the basis of the experimental and correlational studies at scale. In the case of experimental studies, certain stimulus characteristics are often evaluated by using a trace measure as a scalable evaluation criterion. For example, this happens when evaluating video characteristics by the relative time that students watch a video [14, 18]. In the case of correlational studies, numerous trace measures are often used to predict processes and outcomes related to learning, such as learning gains, experienced comprehension, student knowledge [5], and whether and when students drop out from a course [48].

In this paper we will explore the characteristics of research on learning at scale. We argue that these characteristics do not only feature strengths, but also numerous pitfalls that threaten the scientific validity of online learning research. Specifically, research on online learning can benefit from having *i)* very rich, or varied, data, *ii)* strong ecological validity, and *iii)* large numbers of students. As we will argue next, these strengths come with various challenges resulting from the *i)* granular, *ii)* observational, and *iii)* large nature of these data, respectively.

Granular data refers to measuring small grains of data, like a mouse click, for which it is theoretically unclear to what construct it is associated with. When the measured variables become too granular, it becomes more difficult to unambiguously assign meaning to them [39]. Behavioral trace measures in particular tend to stem from one or a few underlying subjective constructs [44], where such a subjective construct - if measured - can explain the effects found for the trace measures. For example, the amount of time spent on watching a video can be a proxy of engagement, difficulty, or even boredom [14, 18, 42]. The ambiguity surrounding what a certain trace measure means troubles the *interpretation* of observations and, consequently, the validity of using granular data to explain and understand learning [33].

Observational data describes naturally occurring behaviors from students whilst studying in a realistic, online setting. This realism is what makes the data valuable to study learning behaviour, but at the same time hinders control over students' behavior. In online learning environments such as MOOCs the student enjoys a great amount of freedom, which partly explains the high drop-out rates and unstructured learning paths. However, this freedom leads to the exclusion of students that do not portray the behaviors being studied. This exclusion does not only result in missing data, but also affects whether a student is subjected to an intervention or completes a questionnaire or test. A student might drop out before receiving an intervention or simply not partake in a test [19]. Since students behave autonomously, this exclusion is non-random and possibly affects the validity of *generalisations* made from studies on online learning.

Big data is a characterization of scale, describing the large amounts of data collected from the behavioral measurements in online learning platforms. These data are big in two dimensions: the number of samples (e.g. students) as well as the number of features per sample (i.e. different variables). Both dimensions affect the correct application of statistical tests and the correct interpretation of its statistical conclusions. Due to the increase in sample size the p values resulting from frequentist tests decrease for any non-zero effect, easily leading to undesirable conclusions such as significant but practically non-existent relations and incorrect interpretations of the p value [23]. Similarly, due to the increase in the number of features per construct the chance of obtaining false positive findings increases, which is further amplified by greater freedom in analysis methods [10]. Both effects potentially lead to type I statistical errors, inflating the *confidence* of statistical tests and consequently overestimating a relation where none exists [17].

Studies about online learning tend to have an excellent ecological validity due to the setting in which the data is measured,

which is not just an approximation of but equals part of the real world under examination. However, the tripartite of potential issues of over-generalisation, over-interpretation, and over-confidence each affect the validity of a study, in particular its internal, external, construct, and statistical conclusion validity. When the goal of a study is to understand, evaluate, or predict learning, validity is a prerequisite to drawing any conclusion from the findings. This positions this tripartite as essential to studies on online learning.

In this paper, we seek to elaborate in which cases granular, observational, and big data lead to over-interpretation, over-generalisation, or over-confidence. In the remainder of this paper, we will discuss: *i)* how behavioral trace data are used in studies on online learning, *ii)* the tripartite of interpretation, generalisation, and confidence, *iii)* the potential solutions of triangulation, replication, and alternative approaches to statistics, and finally, *iv)* our contributions.

ON BEHAVIORAL DATA

A broad range of data sources are used in studies on online learning. Firstly, these include data sources with behavioral traces like event logs (clickstream, page views), forum data (posts, likes, reads), in-game data (moves, steps), social data (relationships, messages), and communication data (emails, chats) [6]. Secondly, these include data sources consisting of subjective measures entered by students, such as student profiles (demographics), quizzes and tests, surveys and psychological questionnaires. These potentially reflect certain traits, states, and experiences of a student, like curiosity, knowledge, and engagement. And thirdly, we identify data sources that contain information on the objective properties of stimuli and environments, such as video characteristics, textual content, and so forth. Of these three types of data, the new opportunities for learning about learning at scale lay in the behavioral trace data [31, 39].

The relevance of the tripartite of potential issues depends on how behavioral trace data are used. The fact that behavioral trace data are common to online learning environments, coupled with the particular characteristics of granular, observational, and big datasets highlights the need to look closely at how these data are used to study online learning behaviour. We propose to distinguish between three ways in which behavioral trace data are used; *i)* explanatory, *ii)* predictive, *iii)* and normative use, and highlight the key data characteristics for these uses.

Firstly, behavioral trace data is to explain or be explained by other phenomena. Here, the scientific goal is to increase theoretical understanding of a phenomenon of interest. An example in which behavior is explained is [42], who show how the proportion of a video that students watch (a trace measure) is statistically explained in part by the complexity of the video (an objective property). An example in which behavior is used to explain is [6], who shows how a sense of community (a subjective measure) is influenced by communicative behaviour of students such as calling and emailing with university staff (trace measures). This explanatory approach is particularly successful when the phenomenon of interest has a workable causal structure. That is, when it has the potential to be explained from a number of general laws or rules [32]. The behavioral trace data used for these type of studies tends to be of a smaller scale because it is used in conjunction with other validated, non-observational measures and it is less granular, allowing the researcher to assign meaning to trace measures.

Secondly, behavioral trace data often function, possibly in combination with other data sources, as a proxy to predict a phenomenon of interest. Here, the scientific goal is to optimize prediction accuracy. Some examples are the prediction of subjective measures of video comprehension [22] and in-video dropouts [41] through click-stream events. This predictive approach is particularly successful when the phenomenon of interest has a complex causal structure. That is, when it is difficult to understand how certain conditions interact to explain a phenomenon. The behavioral trace data used for these type of studies needs to contain all possible combinations of potentially causally relevant conditions for a phenomenon [32]. Consequently, good prediction accuracy often necessitates big, observational data sets with granular, detailed features.

Thirdly, behavioral trace data are often applied as a normative proxy in studies about online learning, either to be optimized for its intrinsic goodness (e.g., course retention) or to be applied as a scalable evaluation criteria (e.g., time on task). Here, the scientific goal is to evaluate interventions and optimize objective properties. An example is the evaluation of objective properties of a video by proxies of student engagement, such as time on task, post-video quiz participation [14], and in-video dropouts [18]. This normative use presupposes a particular pattern of 'good' behavior that is closely linked to a phenomenon of interest. In order to draw causal conclusions, this approach depends on the validity of the proxies used and on having a representative set of observations. Consequently, such conclusions often necessitate big, even all-encompassing observational data sets with few, meaningful measures.

The preceding overview shows the potential of behavioral trace data to explain, predict, and evaluate. Each of these uses has a different pattern of requirements for interpretation, generalisation, and confidence for drawing valid conclusions. The next sections will further elaborate in detail on each.

ON INTERPRETATION

Interpretation refers to the process of assigning meaning to measurements. This captures a certain level of understanding which in turn allows us to draw conclusions from the measurements, such as causal relationships and theoretical explanations.

The prevalence of issues with interpretation is a result of the granular measurements typical to studies about online learning. Granularity makes it difficult to interpret measurements in two related ways: *i)* The measured variables tend to be ambiguous in their meaning, because *ii)* they can have various underlying causes. For example, variables such as mouse clicks and video pauses are too fine-grained to unambiguously assign meaning. Other variables, such as time-on-task, are less granular and better understood in terms of causes. Nonetheless, they

too confound causal inferences due to the multiple potential causes, as we will argue in the next section.

Ambiguous meaning

Common phrases such as "voting with your feet" suggest that meaning can be given to certain observable behaviors. In online courses, students' (granularly observed) behavior can similarly convey meaning (i.e., its message or "vote") [1]. For example, when students finish watching a video, this (presumptively) tells us that the video is well designed [14]. Or, when students show more communicative behavior, we may assume that they are more likely to experience a higher sense of community with their peers [6]. However, more granularity complicates such conclusions, since granular observations can imply many things and cannot be linked to one or even a small number of possible conclusions once observed [44]. This affects a the construct validity of a study: the degree to which a measurement (the operational concept) actually means what the researcher seeks to measure (the theoretical concept).

For example, it might be reasonable to assume that students who are highly engaged with a course will typically watch educational videos for a longer period of time [14, 18]. However, if we only have data on the video dwelling time this does not - by itself - allow us to assume that more viewing time means higher engagement. That is, higher dwelling times have at least several plausible reasons, only one of which is higher engagement. Such behaviour could also be caused by the video characteristics such as the complexity or difficulty [42], or other student characteristics such as motivation, confusion, or perhaps even boredom. When a latent construct (like engagement) leads to a certain behavior (like video dwelling time), it is a logical fallacy to conclude that the latent construct (engagement) occurred when we have only observed the behavior (video dwelling time). Put formally, if A leads to B, observing B does *not* allow us to conclude A.

Whether ambiguity leads to over-interpretation depends on the extent to which a study appeals to theory. This makes the issue of ambiguity particularly relevant to explanatory studies that aim to explain phenomena related to learning, such as comprehension [22] and information processing [41] by looking at observed behaviors. The ambiguity surrounding the meaning of behavioral traces complicates the interpretation of observations and, consequently, of using granular data to explain and understand learning [33]. For example, if students show learning transfer by applying the concepts they learned in online repositories, then this implies that they have learned those concepts [2]. Nonetheless, this measure is still a proxy of learning as it does not measure learning directly. Furthermore, ambiguity troubles normative studies which attempt to evaluate phenomena (e.g., the design quality of a video) based on an assumed unambiguous interpretation of a trace measure (e.g., dwelling time).

To draw theoretical or normative conclusions from behavioral traces requires us to either derive meaning from other validated measures or to validate the trace measures themselves. In the former case, the meaning of behavioral traces can be derived from a subjective measure. For example, [34] explains differences in forum activity and content by comparing these trace measures to the political ideology of the poster(s). In the latter case, meaning can be derived from a predictive model. Predictive studies can model the relation between (a combination of) measures and a particular phenomenon of interest. For example, [22] models the way in which comprehension ratings can be predicted using in-video click-stream data. In both cases, the meaning of behavioral traces is established in comparison with other validated measures. These possibilities will further be explored in Section *Triangulation*.

Confounding explanations

Behavior reflects, or is related to, conscious or unconscious mental processes [1]. This makes it a mirror of mental activity, as illustrated in the previous section. However, this also implies difficulty in using behavior alone to explain and understand certain outcomes, as behavioral traces in particular tend to stem from one or several underlying latent constructs, where such a latent construct - if measured - can explain the effects found for the trace measures. Consequently, if we only have trace measures then this prevents us from drawing the underlying causal structure. This affects the internal validity of a study: The extent to which a causal conclusion based on a study is warranted.

One example is a finding that students who finish watching a video learn more. This finding in itself would be enough to justify normative studies that aim to optimize videos for this measure. However, it would not be enough to conclude that finishing a video is causal to learning. Instead, there is likely to be another latent construct, such as engagement, that causes both the viewing behavior and the learning outcome. Put formally, if A explains B, this does not allow us to conclude that A causes B. Especially for behavioral traces, there is high likelihood that there is a latent construct C underlying both A and B.

Because behavioral traces share few underlying latent constructs they can be expected to be closely related to each other. To illustrate this, Figure 1 presents a small case study on the correlations that exist between trace measures. For this study, we explore 19 measures for 51,100 students on 18 months of observations from our Coursera course "Terrorism and Counterterrorism: Comparing Theory and Practice". The trace measures come from various data sources, including forum, quiz, video viewing, peer review, and certificate data. The data has been summed over various observations (e.g., quiz attempts) unless otherwise indicated (e.g., mean quiz score). Missing values were treated as 0. Figure 1 shows a 10-bin histogram of the absolute Pearson's correlation coefficient for each unique pair-wise comparison between the 19 trace measures, 171 comparisons in total. Applying Cohen's rule of thumb [3] for categorising the strength of the correlations, the results show that the majority of the correlations are small ($.100 <= r < .300$, $n = 94$, 54.97%). Followed by a medium sized correlations ($.300 <= r < .500$, $n = 30$, 17.54%), large correlations ($r >= .500$, $n = 25$, 14.62%), and finally very weak to no correlations ($r < .100$, $n = 22$, 12.87%).

The results show at least a small correlation for the large majority of comparisons (87.14%), and suggests that most of the behavioral traces we measured are at least statistically

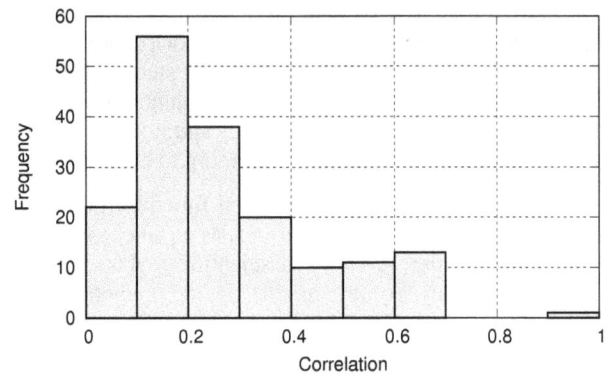

Figure 1. Histogram of Pearson's inter-correlations between 19 trace measures.
Note. The correlated measures are: *1)* Received financial aid; *2)* Bought certificate; *3)* Lecture weeks started and *4)* stopped; *5)* Peer reviews started and *6)* completed; *7)* Quizes started and *8)* completed; *9)* Supplements started and *10)* completed; *11)* Mean quiz and *12)* peer review scores; *13)* Quiz and *14)* in-video question attempts; *15)* Forum threads started and *16)* responded; *17)* Average answer, *18)* thread, and *19)* title length.

related to one another. However, this case study does not show whether there are latent constructs underlying the behavioral traces. Such a conclusion requires further investigation into the shared causes of this relatedness.

Whether confounds lead to over-interpretation depends on the extent to which a study aims for an understanding of the causal structure of a phenomenon. This makes confounds not *necessarily* an issue for predictive or normative studies. Predictive studies can even benefit from indirectly including confounds through measures that are: "*potentially causally relevant to the phenomenon or are at least symptoms or proxies of other variables that might be causally relevant*" (p. 140) [32]. Normative studies do not necessitate understanding the causes of an evaluation. A normative proxy can cover multiple causes through multiple confounding variables which might all be troublesome to a certain outcome.

Even though it is not necessary to know the actual reason for a prediction or normative evaluation, knowledge about the causes is needed to intervene and improve on such outcomes. Only when the causal structure of a phenomenon is clear the correct actions can be taken to improve on the outcome. To explain the causal structure of a phenomenon, potential confounds need to be measured directly; this endeavor will be further explored in the section *Triangulation*.

ON GENERALIZATION

Generalization refers to drawing broad conclusions from particular observations. This allows us to use the findings from empirical studies outside of the studied context.

The prevalence of issues with generalisation depends on which observations are made. Yet, the widespread use of observational data makes it difficult to control what exactly is observed. Since such data describes naturally occurring behaviors and events, this can limit generalisations when the studied observations: *i)* Tend to be a non-random sample of the population about which conclusions are drawn (i.e., a selection bias), and; *ii)* Include a homogeneous set of students, materials, and courses or when differences within the included samples go unnoticed (i.e., a homogeneity bias). In this section we identify when generalisation becomes over-generalisation, illustrating this for both the selection and homogeneity biases.

Selection bias

The random selection of samples from a population is essential to the validity of statistical tests. Yet, using random sampling generally does not result in a purely random selection. A very large number of samples is needed to assure that the samples are similar to the larger population on key aspects [9]. Studies on online learning have the potential to measure the whole population of interest (N=all) rather than sampling from them [32]. However, even when all students are included in a study, generalizations also refer to future students in future iterations of a course, such that a true N=all is never obtained. And, the observational nature of the data used in studies on online learning tends to lead to the use of samples from less than all available students. Students self-select by portraying the behaviors under observation or by partaking in experiments [19], leading to non-random exclusions of students and a weakening on the 'N=all' criterion. This affects a study's internal validity: The extent to which findings can be generalised to the wider population.

An example would be the finding that students who write a summary (intervention) learn more than students who read a summary (control) after watching a lecture video. This conclusion is based on those students that portray the behaviors of interest (writing or reading a summary) and auxiliary behaviors (video watching and test participation). Consequentially, whether the intervention (writing) benefits learning can only be concluded for the group of students that are willing or capable of partaking, restricting the resulting sample to a non-random group. This potentially inflates positive conclusions, since a higher willingness likely leads to a higher chance of engaging with the writing activity, creating an over-representation of highly engaged students in the intervention group. Put formally, the population about which inferences can be made is restricted from 'students of course X' to 'students of course X that show behavior Y and auxillary behavior Z', which increases the likelihood of confounds: interactions between reasons for attrition and characteristics of the behaviors under observation.

Even though a selection bias is common to most scientific studies [9], it only leads to over-generalization if the bias is not acknowledged by the researcher. Whether the goal is explanatory, normative, or predictive; it is possible to limit rather than broaden the population about which inferences are made and to understand how a possible bias in selection might have affected the outcomes. For example, rather than applying to 'online students', findings typically need to be limited to 'active students' that show the behaviors under observation. The population of interest can subsequently be expanded again by replicating studies with different selection procedures. The balance between populations and replications is further explored in Section *Replication*.

Homogeniety bias

The robustness of a study's findings across variations in populations (e.g., student characteristics) and situations (e.g., course characteristics) is key to analytical generalisation [35]. Analytical generalisation involves making projections about the likely transferability of models, theories, and evaluations [9]. Understanding and representing the diversity in the phenomena of interest and the setting or people studied is key to make analytical generalisations [27]. It allows us to identify the key factors in producing an outcome and the conditions under which they hold. Particularly in the case of studies about online learning the observational nature of the data assures a rich variety in observations. Yet, an over-emphasis on similarities or common features, such as the assumption that students are alike, leads to an over-generalisation. This affects the external validity: The extent to which the results of a study can be generalized to other situations and to other people.

Consider the finding that 'active' students, those who show the behaviors under observation, benefit from writing summaries (P)[1] (see Section *Selection bias*). Since we are not only interested in just those students and videos that are part of the study, we can make several analytical generalisations. For example, we can hypothesize that: *a)* Similar learning benefits (P') will be found for different (D) videos with similarly (S) active students, and that; *b)* Higher learning benefits (P') will be found for students who show more activity (D), other things equal (S). These generalisations require knowledge about influential characteristics of students and videos. If these insights are not available, this potentially leads to an over-emphasis based on similarities, which results in a situation in which the analytical generalisation *a)* might be drawn falsely because differences between videos are ignored and *b)* cannot be drawn because differences between students are ignored. Each of these analytical generalisations can be seen as a theory by itself for which variation and representation on key factors and conditions are needed to be falsified or confirmed. Put formally, a target finding P' can be hypothesized given a finding P and the similarities S and differences D between study and target population and situation [47].

In general, a homogeniety bias restricts analytical generalisations from those students that portrayed the behaviors of interest to other, new groups and other, new situations: *i)* Predictive models might show different accuracies when validated in new situations; *ii)* Normative evaluations might come to different conclusions with other samples, and; *iii)* Explanatory studies might lead to non confirmatory or opposing inferences during replications. To make sound analytical generalisations requires an understanding and representation of diversity. A generalisation can be supported during exploratory studies by representing the variations within the selected group of students and within the used stimuli and context. A generalisation can further be supported during subsequent confirmatory studies that aim to confirm whether a model, theory, or evaluation holds under different conditions, either making the findings more robust or adding to the scope conditions for those findings. Together, representation and replication are

---

[1]The formalizations in this paragraph are adopted from [47], p. 208.

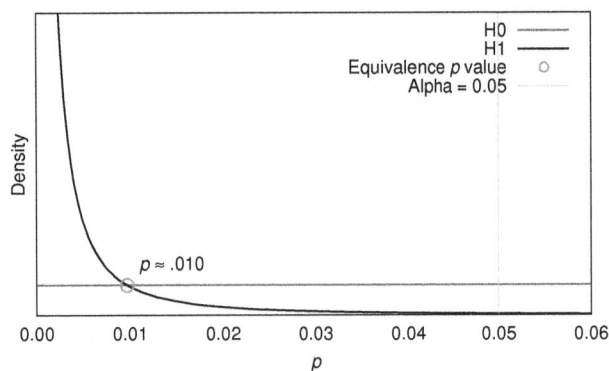

Figure 2. Distribution of *p*-values under H0 and H1.
Note. Parameters: N = 100, Cohen's d = 0.5

key to hypothesize and confirm analytical generalisations; the possibility of each will be discussed in sections *Triangulation* and *Replication*, respectively.

ON CONFIDENCE

With 'confidence' we refer to the strength of any statistical evidence provided to support conclusions. The strength of claims, such as interpretations and generalizations, must be proportional to the strength of the provided evidence, which makes assessing this strength vital to theory building.

The prevalent method to assess statistical strength is through frequentist statistics with *p* values. However, *p* values can be difficult to interpret, which leads to common misconceptions even among experienced researchers, statisticians, and professors [15]. The true meaning of a *p* value is the probability of the observed result, and more extreme results, assuming that the null hypothesis is true, or $P(D \geq d|H_0)$. Whether the null or alternative hypothesis are true or false, or supported by the data, is *not* quantified by a *p* value. That is, a *p* value of .04 does not mean that the null hypothesis has a 4% probability of being true, or $P(H_0|d)$, or that the false-positive error probability is 4%, or that the data supports the alternative hypothesis [12]. In addition, *p* values interact with scale in two ways: *i)* *p* values decrease with an increase in the number of samples when the null hypothesis is false (leading to the Lindley Paradox), and; *ii)* the false-positive error probability increases with the number of variables (the Forking Paths problem). In this section we will identify how these effects can lead to over-confidence and consequentially affect the statistical conclusion validity: Whether conclusions about the relationship between variables are reasonable.

Lindley Paradox

P values have a peculiar relationship with sample size. Assuming that the true difference between two groups is not exactly zero, *p* values become smaller as sample size increases. Notably, this is true even if the actual difference is very small and of no practical importance. As such, a result can be *statistically significant* without being of *practical significance*. With large sample sizes, which often occur in research on learning at scale, the common significance threshold of .05 is so easily reached that it does not aid interpreting effects. In

fact, when we consider the probability of finding a specific *p* value given either the null or alternative hypothesis (instead of only considering the null hypothesis), all but very small *p* values are more likely under the null hypothesis than under the alternative hypothesis with sufficiently large sample sizes. This is commonly referred to as the "Lindley Paradox" [23].

To illustrate this paradox, we simulate a small study with 100 participants and a true effect size of Cohen's d of 0.5. Figure 2[2] shows the distribution of *p* values under the null hypothesis (d = 0) and when d = 0.5. If the null hypothesis is true, the distribution of *p* values is uniform and independent of sample size. With every *p* value being equally likely, this makes the probability of obtaining a *p* value between 0.01 and 0.05 exactly 4%. If the alternative hypothesis is true, the distribution of *p* values is highly skewed towards zero, and 99.07% of the *p* values are smaller than 0.01. Only 0.79% of the *p* values are found between 0.01 and 0.05, which is much less than when the null hypothesis is true. In other words, obtaining a *p* between 0.01 and 0.05 is much more likely under the null hypothesis (4%) than under the alternative hypothesis (0.79%), *even though it is significant*. Figure 2 shows the threshold ($p \approx .010$) at which there is an equal support for either H_0 or H_1. All larger *p* values provide more evidence for the null, despite being below the significance threshold of 0.05. All values above this threshold indicate a higher probability of the data under the null hypothesis, or put formally $P(D \geq d|H_0) > P(D \geq d|H_1)$.

Whether *p* values lead to over-confidence and incorrect conclusions depends on how they are interpreted. The preceding case study shows that the paradox occurs when we consider not only the probability of the data under the null hypothesis, but also under the alternative hypothesis. The larger the sample size, the bigger the resulting over-confidence becomes when adhering to the standard significance threshold of $p < .05$. The Lindley Paradox does not signify a problem inherent to *p* values, but should serve as a warning that *p* values should not be interpreted as if they allow claims about the probability of hypotheses. A true interpretation of *p* values is only concerned with the probability of data, but never of theories. To make such statements about the probability of hypotheses and theories, other statistical tools are required. The possibilities for such alternatives are further discussed in Section *Statistical solutions*.

Forking paths

A second issue with big data sets and statistical inference is that the large amount of variables increases the chance of finding significant correlations by chance alone. That is, if no true relationships exist (H_0 is true) we will on average still obtain a maximum of *alpha%* significant false positives per analysis. Performing multiple comparisons is one possible fork of so-called 'forking paths' - the sequence of possible decisions or forks that influence the obtained results. The 'forking paths' do not only include different statistical analyses, but also include decisions such as which participants to include or exclude, which measures to use, what interactions to consider, which cut-off points to use, outlier detection, and

---

[2]Based on `http://rpubs.com/richarddmorey/t-pvalues`

many other decisions [40]. The alpha value or false positive error rate is only controlled under the assumption that exactly one path is followed, which is decided upon a priori and is not conditional on the data. Otherwise a *"dataset can be analyzed in so many different ways [...], that very little information is provided by the statement that a study came up with a p < .05 result."* [10].

For example, imagine someone is exploring a dataset and decides to run 20 hypothesis tests, out of the, say, 200 possible comparisons which can be made. If 10 of these tests turn out significant, we cannot state that 10 out of 20 tests are successful. Rather, we should state that 10 out of 200 tests are successful. The number of possible comparisons strongly inflates the family-wise type I error probability. With an alpha of .05, 10 possible comparisons leads to an error probability of over 40.13%, and with 200 possible comparisons to nearly 100.00%. Readers of published scientific work rarely know the circumstances in which the results were obtained, thus making it nearly impossible to estimate whether a finding is the result of noise mining. Described formally, the chance of a false-positive finding is $1 - (1 - alpha)^k$ where k is the number of possible analyses.

Big data can quickly lead to over-confidence as the total amount of tests which could be done becomes extremely large, and what is worse, unspecified. This inhibits the valid interpretation of p values, that is, in their relation to the alpha. These issues have been highlighted repeatedly in the last few decades [7, 17] but deserve to be carefully reconsidered in the era of big data. Essentially, by exploring the data the researcher makes decisions which are conditional on the data at hand. Had the data been different, the researcher would have made other decisions. Even though this is a vital aspect of exploratory research, it troubles the use of inferential statistics to the point where their validity is nil. For these inferential statistics to be useful, the degrees of freedom for the researcher to adjust the analysis to the findings need to be limited. The next section discusses several possible solutions to this conundrum between inferential statistics and forking paths.

PROPOSED SOLUTIONS

In this section, we propose several solutions that seek to mitigate over-interpretation, over-generalisation, and over-confidence. These are all suggestions which need to be evaluated within the context of a study.

Triangulation

Triangulation is a well-known research methodology in which multiple perspectives on the same phenomenon are studied simultaneously. The traditional definition [46] focuses on an intuitive understanding of triangulation, in which multiple measures are expected to converge on a singular outcome, such as by measuring the distance to a point in space from two other distinct points. Convergence increases the confidence in the outcome. However, the value of triangulation lies not only in the (often unlikely) perfect convergence of measures but rather in their degree of divergence [26]. Different methods tap into different aspects of a phenomenon, which together

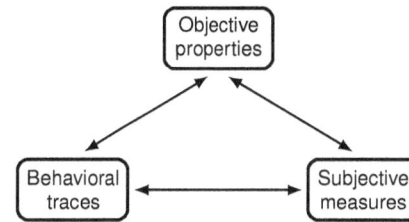

Figure 3. Triangulation using multiple data types

provide a rich and complex view on the phenomenon of interest. Divergence increases the understanding of the outcome. Here, we will apply this type of triangulation as illustrated in Figure 3: The ability to draw a complete picture about a phenomenon from multiple perspectives through gathering multiple types of data. Three suggestions will be given on how one can utilize triangulation to enhance the evidential value of studies on online learning.

Suggestion 1: Combine multiple measurements of the studied phenomenon and of related aspects.

Multiple measurements create a broad and rich view on a phenomenon of interest. On the one hand, measuring two or more different types of data on the same phenomenon creates overlapping yet distinct views. As illustrated in Figure 3, such distinct measurements add complementary information in comparison to each other. This alleviates ambiguity by giving a more detailed record of the phenomenon studied. On the other hand, measuring aspects of a phenomenon that are theoretically related creates a complementary view. When such measures influence an outcome, they suggest potential covariates of and conditions for the outcome which strengthen subsequent generalisations. When such measures even explain an outcome, they measure potential confounds which contribute to understanding the causal structure of the outcome. This makes a diversity in measurements not only a solution for potential ambiguity and confounds troubling interpretations, but also a contributor to the diversity needed for generalisations.

Suggestion 2: Develop, share, and use validated models.

Meaning is not inherent to behavioral traces or objective properties, even though any interpretation and subsequent conclusion depends on such meaning. Instead, meaning can be assigned and validated in comparison with other, validated, measures using the triangulation principles shown in Figure 3. In particular existing, validated instruments that measure subjective constructs are a likely starting point of explanatory and predictive studies. They allow us to compare behavioral traces and objective properties with their hypothesized subjective counterparts. Either to explain observed relations or to create predictive models. Examples are a model that predicts engagement based on click-stream data [41] and a model that predicts human interest based on textual analyses [43]. Such studies result in models and theories that allow other studies to interpret otherwise ambiguous traces or properties. An important requirement for the re-use of the resulting models is that they are shared in a standardized way, such as through the Predictive Model Markup Language [13].

Suggestion 3: Vary on time, courses, and stimuli.

So-called data triangulation [8] aims for enough diversity within the data to cover the width of conditions relevant to the studied phenomenon. To measure a wide variety of conditions, Denzin [8] suggests to triangulate between time, place, and people. Applied to an online learning context, measurements need to cover multiple moments in time and multiple courses. In particular, different types of courses, such as combining both courses from engineering and social sciences, will cover multiple virtual 'places' as well as presumably different types of students. Diversity can further be fostered by developing and using standardized sets of stimuli that cover a broad range of properties and of expected responses by students (e.g., [21]). By applying such methods for data triangulation, the resulting data allows studies to identify possible covariates to and conditions for its findings, strengthening generalisations.

Replication

Replication is at the heart of the scientific process. It is part of scientific scrutiny that aims to strengthen the evidence of claims and is required for theory building. When replications fail, this can identify false positives or an incomplete theoretical understanding of the necessary and sufficient conditions for reproduction [4]. Besides this direct form of replication, which aims to fully reproduce a study, an equally important form is conceptual replication. Here, hypotheses or results from earlier research are tested with a different experimental setup [37]. When a finding has been shown to replicate in similar settings, (not) confirming a finding in a different context is particularly informative. These kind of studies are key to show the scope of a finding: the conditions within which a finding holds. Applying the notion of replication to studies on online learning leads us to the following two suggestions:

Suggestion 4: Perform pre-registered, confirmatory studies.

Confirmatory studies aim to verify findings from earlier (exploratory) studies. Confirmatory studies are essential for assessing the validity of evaluations, models, and theories and for strengthening generalisations. Pre-registration is an important method to distinguish confirmatory from exploratory work. Through pre-registering hypotheses and analyses this guarantees a well-specified methodology before the results are known. This ensures that these choices are not conditional on the data, ensuring that one 'forking path' is laid out a priori, and, with that, ensuring the validity of inferential statistics [17, 7]. Independent pre-registration can be done by authors themselves at platforms like the Open Science Framework at `https://osf.io`. In addition, more and more journals and conferences have started offering Registered Reports tracks, in which the main peer-review phase is done before the data has been gathered in order to verify the methodology prior to data analysis.

Suggestion 5: Balance interpretation, generalisation, and confidence over replications.

No single study can combine immaculate interpretation, generalisation, and confidence. Every study needs to choose measurement types and research designs that strike a balance over this tripartite. Nonetheless, all three properties can be covered

through multiple replications. Initially, exploratory studies can use more measurements from the right side of Figure 3 in finding and explaining an effect (see Suggestion 1). These subjective measures leave the least ambiguity but tend to ask the most from students. Their obtrusiveness inadversibly leads to a selection bias due to students that do not participate. At a later point in time, confirmatory studies can use more measurements from the left side of Figure 3 in replicating such findings at scale. These behavioral traces are inherently more ambiguous, but their unobtrusiveness allows researchers to scale to nearly all students. And finally, confirmatory studies can be setup as traditional laboratory studies for maximum experimental control [19]. By using replication with different measurement types and research designs, the validity of any findings increases with different combinations of width (number of features) and of scale (number of samples).

Statistical solutions

We highlighted two issues related to statistical confidence when making inferences: the Lindley Paradox and forking paths. These problems are aggravated by the scale of the data. However, their effects are not uniform and affect exploratory and confirmatory studies differently. In the former case, one can argue that inferential statistics are not needed nor appropriate. In the latter case, one can either adjust the *alpha*-threshold or apply different statistical techniques. We will further elaborate on each of these possible solutions.

Suggestion 6: Correct the alpha.

The effects of number of samples and number of variables on statistical (over-)confidence can partially be resolved by corrected alpha levels or p values, as long as the researchers' degrees of freedom is known. First, the alpha threshold can be lowered to, say, .01 or .001, or to a variable level (e.g., an equivalence level). Second, it is possible to correct p values based on sample size, to ensure that p values for analyses with different sample sizes can be interpreted in a similar manner (cf. [11, 30]). Third, the alpha level can be corrected for multiple hypothesis testing. When the number of possible comparisons for a hypothesis is known (cf. pre-registration, Suggestion 4), a Holm-Bonferonni correction can be applied, which guarantees that the family-wise error probability of the set of tests is maintained at a desires alpha level [16]. However, in cases when it is less clear to what extent the error probability is inflated (e.g., forking paths), it is not feasible to attempt to correct this statistically. In any case, we suggest to report the exact p value such that readers can apply other thresholds for significance and/or directly estimate statistical confidence from it.

Suggestion 7: Focus on parameter estimation.

Another possible solution to over-confidence of p values with big data is to move from hypothesis testing to focus on parameter estimation. In this approach, one does not care about inferential statistics but about obtaining accurate parameter estimations, such as correlations and other types of effect sizes. Even though it is not a trivial matter to present and interpret effect sizes [24], this can be relevant in two specific cases in which generalisations are not appropriate. First, parameter estimation (but not inferential statistics) can be done in exploratory studies, which can subsequently be used for hypotheses tests in pre-registered confirmatory research. Second, studies with large samples are especially suitable for a focus on parameter estimation, as they will give stable and accurate estimations [38]. However, focusing on parameter estimation and foregoing hypothesis testing is not so much a way to increase the validity of claims, but simply avoids these issues by not making claims in the first place.

Suggestion 8: Use Bayesian statistics.

Another possible statistical solution is to use a different set of statistical operations: Bayesian statistics. Using so-called Bayes Factors it is possible to calculate the relative amount of evidence for one hypothesis compared to another hypothesis [28]. This has several useful properties, such as being able to quantify (relative) evidence, being able to support a null hypothesis (unlike p values), and being directly interpretable as a continuous variable without reference to a threshold such as alpha. This circumvents the issues caused by Lindley's paradox, as Bayesian statistics directly compute the relative amount of evidence of the two hypotheses irrespective of sample size. Bayesian equivalents of traditional tests such as t-tests, ANOVAs, and regressions have already been proposed [36]. Furthermore, Bayesian statistics can be applied to accurately estimate population parameters such as effect sizes and other variables of interest [45]. Software such as JASP [25] and BayesFactor for R [29] allows researchers to explore the benefits of Bayesian statistics for their own research.

CONCLUSION

In the preceding paragraphs, we have outlined methodological problems and solutions that are important to the way in which we research learning at scale. We started out by making explicit the three considerations relevant to any empirical research paper that concerns learning at scale:

1. **Interpretation** concerns the way in which we assign meaning to measurements.

2. **Generalization** concerns the way in which research applies to a wider - or different - context.

3. **Confidence** concerns the degree to which the strength of your evidence supports the strength of your conclusions.

We discussed the existence of several threats to the preceding considerations, which affect the validity of studies on learning at scale. Finally, we offered a series of solutions and tools that help the researcher avoid the pitfalls of over-interpretation, over-generalization, and over-confidence.

While the indicated threats are not novel, nor unique to learning at scale research (e.g., [39]), this paper contributes by reconceptualizing these problems specifically in relation to the data typical to research on online learning. This paper contributes by identifying three core properties of these data - being granular, observational, and big - which influence the validity of research on online learning. As such, we aid the researcher in understanding the impact of methodological choices on the validity of their conclusions, specifically with

regards to the issues of over-interpretation, over-generalization and over-confidence.

This article has several implications for the way in which we conduct research, as well as the way in which we interpret the validity of that research. Firstly, this article provides researchers with the key considerations to assess the strengths and weaknesses of their research, and to address those weaknesses accordingly. Researchers are strongly encouraged to be transparent about the degree to which their research may suffer from over-interpretation, over-generalization or over-confidence, and are provided with a toolbox with which they can identify and prevent the pitfalls of such issues. Secondly, this article provides readers of scientific publications with a list of threats which signal issues of over-interpretation, over-generalization and over-confidence, regardless of whether this is discussed or not by the researcher. These implications apply primarily to online learning research, but also generally to research that uses granular, observational, and big data.

Online learning platforms offer a previously unseen potential for learning about learning. As we've shown, they offer a new platform for explanatory, predictive, and normative studies. As a hybrid between realism and experimental control, they can help us learn, predict, and evaluate what works when and for who. This potential arises from the nature of the behavioral data collected on such platforms. We believe that, through understanding the specifics of these data and their impact on study validity, we can fully embrace their potential for learning about learning.

REFERENCES

1. Raymond M. Bergner. 2011. What is behavior? And so what? *New Ideas in Psychology* 29, 2 (2011), 147 – 155.

2. Guanliang Chen, Dan Davis, Claudia Hauff, and Geert-Jan Houben. 2016. Learning Transfer: Does It Take Place in MOOCs? An Investigation into the Uptake of Functional Programming in Practice. In *Proceedings of the Third (2016) ACM Conference on Learning @ Scale (L@S '16)*. ACM, New York, NY, USA, 409–418.

3. J. Cohen. 1992. A Power Primer. *Psychological Bulletin* 112, 1 (1992), 155–159.

4. "Open Science Collaboration". 2015. Estimating the reproducibility of psychological science. *Science* 349, 6251 (2015).

5. AlbertT. Corbett and JohnR. Anderson. 1994. Knowledge tracing: Modeling the acquisition of procedural knowledge. *User Modeling and User-Adapted Interaction* 4, 4 (1994), 253–278.

6. Shane Dawson. 2006. A study of the relationship between student communication interaction and sense of community. *The Internet and Higher Education* 9, 3 (2006), 153 – 162.

7. AD De Groot. 2014. The meaning of "significance" for different types of research. *Acta psychologica* 148 (2014), 188–194.

8. Norman K Denzin. 1978. The research act: A theoretical orientation to sociological methods. (1978).

9. William A Firestone. 1993. Alternative arguments for generalizing from data as applied to qualitative research. *Educational researcher* 22, 4 (1993), 16–23.

10. Andrew Gelman and Eric Loken. 2013. The garden of forking paths: Why multiple comparisons can be a problem, even when there is no "fishing expedition" or "p-hacking" and the research hypothesis was posited ahead of time. *Department of Statistics, Columbia University* (2013).

11. IJ Good. 1992. The Bayes/non-Bayes compromise: A brief review. *J. Amer. Statist. Assoc.* 87, 419 (1992), 597–606.

12. Steven Goodman. 2008. A dirty dozen: twelve p-value misconceptions. In *Seminars in hematology*, Vol. 45. Elsevier, 135–140.

13. Alex Guazzelli, Michael Zeller, Wen-Ching Lin, and Graham Williams. 2009. PMML: An open standard for sharing models. *The R Journal* 1, 1 (2009), 60–65.

14. Philip J. Guo, Juho Kim, and Rob Rubin. 2014. How Video Production Affects Student Engagement: An Empirical Study of MOOC Videos. In *Proceedings of the First ACM Conference on Learning @ Scale Conference (L@S '14)*. ACM, New York, NY, USA, 41–50.

15. Heiko Haller and Stefan Krauss. 2002. Misinterpretations of significance: A problem students share with their teachers. *Methods of Psychological Research* 7, 1 (2002), 1–20.

16. Sture Holm. 1979. A simple sequentially rejective multiple test procedure. *Scandinavian journal of statistics* (1979), 65–70.

17. John P. A. Ioannidis. 2005. Why most published research findings are false. *PLoS Med* 2, 8 (2005), e124.

18. Juho Kim, Philip J. Guo, Daniel T. Seaton, Piotr Mitros, Krzysztof Z. Gajos, and Robert C. Miller. 2014. Understanding In-video Dropouts and Interaction Peaks Inonline Lecture Videos. In *Proceedings of the First ACM Conference on Learning @ Scale Conference (L@S '14)*. ACM, New York, NY, USA, 31–40.

19. Anne Lamb, Jascha Smilack, Andrew Ho, and Justin Reich. 2015. Addressing Common Analytic Challenges to Randomized Experiments in MOOCs: Attrition and Zero-Inflation. In *Proceedings of the Second (2015) ACM Conference on Learning @ Scale (L@S '15)*. ACM, New York, NY, USA, 21–30.

20. Kathleen L. Lane, Kathleen M. Bocian, Donald L. MacMillan, and Frank M. Gresham. 2004. Treatment Integrity: An Essential But Often Forgotten Component of School-Based Interventions. *Preventing School Failure: Alternative Education for Children and Youth* 48, 3 (2004), 36–43.

21. Margaret M. Bradley Lang, Peter J. and Bruce N. Cuthbert. 2008. *International affective picture system (IAPS): Affective ratings of pictures and instruction manual*. Technical Report. University of Florida, Gainesville, FL.

22. Nan Li, Łukasz Kidziński, Patrick Jermann, and Pierre Dillenbourg. 2015. MOOC Video Interaction Patterns: What Do They Tell Us? In *Design for Teaching and Learning in a Networked World*. Lecture Notes in Computer Science, Vol. 9307. Springer International Publishing, 197–210.

23. Dennis V. Lindley. 1957. A statistical paradox. *Biometrika* 44, 1/2 (1957), 187–192.

24. Mark W Lipsey, Kelly Puzio, Cathy Yun, Michael A Hebert, Kasia Steinka-Fry, Mikel W Cole, Megan Roberts, Karen S Anthony, and Matthew D Busick. 2012. Translating the Statistical Representation of the Effects of Education Interventions into More Readily Interpretable Forms. *National Center for Special Education Research* (2012).

25. J. Love, R. Selker, M. Marsman, T. Jamil, D. Dropmann, A. J. Verhagen, and E. J. Wagenmakers. 2015. JASP (Version 0.7)[Computer software]. (2015).

26. Sandra Mathison. 1988. Why Triangulate? *Educational Researcher* 17, 2 (1988), 13–17.

27. Joseph A. Maxwell. 1995. Diversity and methodology in a changing world. *Pedagogia* 30 (1995), 32–40.

28. Richard D. Morey and Jeffrey N. Rouder. 2011. Bayes factor approaches for testing interval null hypotheses. *Psychological methods* 16, 4 (2011), 406.

29. Richard D. Morey and Jeffrey N. Rouder. 2014. *BayesFactor: Computation of Bayes Factors for Common Designs*.

30. Michael Naaman. 2016. Almost sure hypothesis testing and a resolution of the Jeffreys-Lindley paradox. *Electronic Journal of Statistics* 10, 1 (2016), 1526–1550.

31. Nancy E. Perry and Philip H. Winne. 2006. Learning from Learning Kits: gStudy Traces of Students' Self-Regulated Engagements with Computerized Content. *Educational Psychology Review* 18, 3 (2006), 211–228.

32. Wolfgang Pietsch. 2016. The Causal Nature of Modeling with Big Data. *Philosophy & Technology* 29, 2 (2016), 137–171.

33. Justin Reich. 2015. Rebooting MOOC Research. *Science* 347, 6217 (2015), 34–35.

34. Justin Reich, Brandon Stewart, Kimia Mavon, and Dustin Tingley. 2016. The Civic Mission of MOOCs: Measuring Engagement Across Political Differences in Forums. In *Proceedings of the Third (2016) ACM Conference on Learning @ Scale (L@S '16)*. ACM, New York, NY, USA, 1–10.

35. William S. Robinson. 1951. The Logical Structure of Analytic Induction. *American Sociological Review* 16, 6 (1951), 812–818.

36. Jeffrey N. Rouder, Paul L. Speckman, Dongchu Sun, Richard D. Morey, and Geoffrey Iverson. 2009. Bayesian t tests for accepting and rejecting the null hypothesis. *Psychonomic bulletin & review* 16, 2 (2009), 225–237.

37. Stefan Schmidt. 2009. Shall we really do it again? The powerful concept of replication is neglected in the social sciences. *Review of General Psychology* 13, 2 (2009), 90–100.

38. Felix D. Schönbrodt and Marco Perugini. 2013. At what sample size do correlations stabilize? *Journal of Research in Personality* 47, 5 (2013), 609 – 612.

39. Neil Selwyn. 2015. Data entry: towards the critical study of digital data and education. *Learning, Media and Technology* 40, 1 (2015), 64–82.

40. Joseph P. Simmons, Leif D. Nelson, and Uri Simonsohn. 2011. False-positive psychology undisclosed flexibility in data collection and analysis allows presenting anything as significant. *Psychological science* (2011), 1359–1366.

41. Tanmay Sinha, Patrick Jermann, Nan Li, and Pierre Dillenbourg. 2014. Your click decides your fate: Inferring Information Processing and Attrition Behavior from MOOC Video Clickstream Interactions. In *Empirical Methods in Natural Language Processing Workshop on Modeling Large Scale Social Interaction in Massively Open Online Courses*. Doha, Qatar.

42. Frans van der Sluis, Jasper Ginn, and Tim van der Zee. 2016. Explaining Student Behavior at Scale: The Influence of Video Complexity on Student Dwelling Time. In *Proceedings of the Third (2016) ACM Conference on Learning @ Scale (L@S '16)*. ACM, New York, NY, USA, 51–60.

43. Frans van der Sluis, Egon L. van den Broek, Richard J. Glassey, Elisabeth M. A. G. van Dijk, and Franciska M. G. de Jong. 2014. When Complexity becomes Interesting. *Journal of the American Society for Information Science and Technology* 65, 7 (2014), 1478–1500.

44. George Veletsianos, Justin Reich, and Laura A Pasquini. 2016. The Life Between Big Data Log Events: Learners' Strategies to Overcome Challenges in MOOCs. *AERA Open* 2, 3 (2016).

45. Eric-Jan Wagenmakers, Richard D Morey, and Michael D Lee. 2016. Bayesian benefits for the pragmatic researcher. *Current Directions in Psychological Science* 25, 3 (2016), 169–176.

46. Eugene J. Webb, Donald Thomas Campbell, Richard D. Schwartz, and Lee Sechrest. 1966. *Unobtrusive measures: nonreactive research in the social sciences*. Rand McNally sociology series, Vol. 111. Rand McNally.

47. Roel J. Wieringa. 2014. *Design Science Methodology for Information Systems and Software Engineering*. Springer Berlin Heidelberg, Berlin, Heidelberg, Chapter Analogic Inference Design, 201–211.

48. Diyi Yang, Tanmay Sinha, David Adamson, and Carolyn P. Rose. 2013. Turn on, tune in, drop out: Anticipating student dropouts in massive open online courses. In *Proceedings of the 2013 NIPS Data-Driven Education Workshop*, Vol. 10. Lake Tahoe, NV, USA, 13–20.

Discourse: MOOC Discussion Forum Analysis at Scale

Alexander Kindel[1], Michael Yeomans[2], Justin Reich[3], Brandon Stewart[1], Dustin Tingley[2]
[1]Princeton University, [2]Harvard University, [3]MIT
akindel@princeton.edu, myeomans@fas.harvard.edu, jreich@mit.edu,
bms4@princeton.edu, dtingley@gov.harvard.edu

ABSTRACT

We present *Discourse*, a tool for coding and annotating MOOC discussion forum data. Despite the centrality of discussion forums to learning in online courses, few tools are available for analyzing these discussions in a context-aware way. Discourse scaffolds the process of coding forum data by enabling multiple coders to work with large amounts of forum data. Our demonstration will enable attendees to experience, explore, and critique key features of the app.

Author Keywords

Discussions; content analysis; reply mapping; MOOCs

INTRODUCTION

Many kinds of social interactions are now mediated through technology — online forums, chatrooms, social media, and other collaborative platforms. These discussions produce rich datasets that can help researchers discover new answers to fundamental questions about the nature of communication. For example, online courses bring together large, diverse groups of students to discuss political or controversial topics, and record a wealth of forum data from their discussions [1,2].

Discussion data pose unique challenges for qualitative data analysis, because the meaning of individual posts are dependent on the posts that came before. However, the tools most commonly used for qualitative coding do not take this context into account. Some tools only show one document at a time (e.g. NVivo), which hides the necessary context of the focal post. Other tools display all of the data at once (e.g. Excel), which puts the burden of parsing context on the coder.

Here we present a tool that was built for efficient, context-sensitive qualitative coding of discussion data at scale. Our system allows many discussions to be simultaneously coded by many coders. Furthermore, the posts are automatically embedded in the relevant context of the discussion, so that coders can more easily understand the posters' intent.

DESIGN AND ADVANTAGES

Discourse is a specialized tool for the qualitative analysis of discussion data that offers two key advances over existing content analysis software. First, Discourse is aware of the structure of discussion data, rather than treating each post as an atomic document. Specifically, each post is presented along with its "parents" - the posts to which it replies, which are higher up in the thread structure and posted before the focal post. This allows each coder to efficiently understand the context in which the focal post was made, to more accurately label the content of the post (see Fig 1).

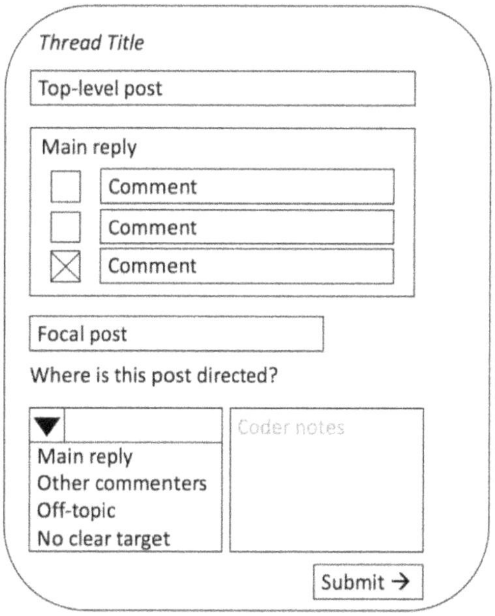

Figure 1. Coder-level view (schematic). Focal post is presented below the parent posts that preceded, along with a menu of coding choices and optional text box for coder notes.

Second, Discourse automates the management of coding. Coders select from a researcher-defined set of codes in a drop-down menu, which minimize the possibility of typos or mis-targeted entries. The app automatically provides coders only the data they need to code, and each code is logged in a relational database immediately upon submission. Coding tasks can be dynamically assigned to coders based on workflow and availability, increasing potential throughput for large coding tasks. The app also simplifies the task of merging and exporting data at the conclusion of coding. Rather than collecting and collating multiple spreadsheets or retrieving data from proprietary analysis software, data can be selected and exported directly from the app's database.

USE CASE

Discourse is currently supporting data analysis on discussion forum data from two edX MOOCs: *Introduction to American Government* and *Saving Schools*. To date, coders have generated approximately 40,000 codes on 140 discussion threads from these two courses. Discourse is compatible with forum data from any edX course, facilitating cross-course analyses and comparisons.

So far, coders have been focused on a task we call "reply mapping." This task is built to circumvent a limitation in edX (and other) forum data: forum participation is recorded in threads with finite (i.e. 3-level) depth. These metadata do not necessarily reflect the true reply structure of discussions. Comments at level 3 can (and often do) talk to one another rather than each responding to the level 2 post (see Fig. 2). This ambiguity makes it difficult to use the forum metadata to identify which users are interacting with one another.

For reply mapping, coders are tasked with identifying the previous posts (if any) towards which the focal post is directed. Discourse streamlines this task by displaying only those posts to which a comment could plausibly have responded. Preliminary results based in part on these codes have been submitted for publication [2].

FUTURE DIRECTIONS

At the time of submission, we have planned a number of features for the tool designed to make it easier to manage and reconcile results from multiple coders working on the same corpus of forum data. Dashboards for automatically calculating coder progress, reliability measures and agreement statistics provide research managers with a synoptic overview of data analysis as it progresses. Where a single canonical coding is needed, "reconciliation" or "tiebreaking" tasks permit managers to assign a third coder to only those forum posts where a pair of coders disagreed. By reducing the manual labor associated with merging and

comparing codes, these features will simplify the task of managing qualitative data analysis on forum data.

In the future, we also plan to extend the app to handle any kind of discussion data. The unique advantages of our analysis tool—sensitivity to document context and automation of routine research management tasks—are applicable to a broad range of structured discussion data, including group meetings, chat logs, or forum data with infinite depth (e.g. Reddit). We look forward to seeking feedback from conference attendees on these planned features, as well as suggestions for other desirable analytic tools for forum data.

DEMONSTRATION

To demonstrate the app, we plan to briefly show the app's basic features. Additionally, a number of guest accounts on Discourse will be made available throughout the conference so that attendees may test out the app on their own devices. We also plan to seek user feedback through the demonstration in order to improve the usability and functionality of the app.

ACKNOWLEDGMENTS

We gratefully acknowledge grant support from the Spencer Foundation's New Civics initiative and the Hewlett Foundation. We also thank the course teams from *Saving Schools* and *American Government*, and the Harvard VPAL-Research Group for research support. Finally, we appreciate the research assistance from our coders: Ben Schenck, Elise Lee, Jenny Sanford, Holly Howe, Jazmine Henderson & Nikayah Etienne.

REFERENCES

1. Justin Reich, Brandon Stewart, Kimia Mavon, and Dustin Tingley. 2016. "The Civic Mission of MOOCs: Measuring Engagement across Political Differences in Forums." *Proceedings of the Third Annual ACM Conference on Learning at Scale, L@S 2016.* Edinburgh, UK.

2. Michael Yeomans, Justin Reich, Brandon Stewart, Kimia Mavon, Alex Kindel, and Dustin Tingley. 2016. "The Civic Mission of MOOCs: Engagement across Political Differences in Online Forums." *Under review.*

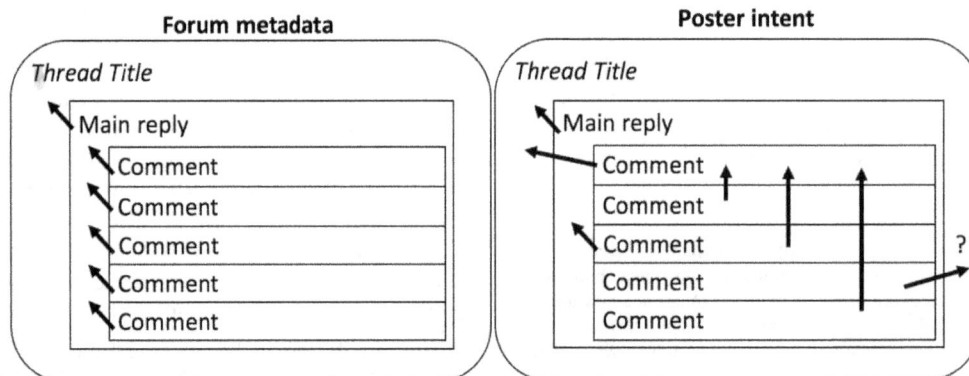

Figure 2. Recorded forum metadata (left) vs. true poster intent (right) structure of edX MOOC forum discussions. Arrows indicate comment target. Replies may skip earlier replies, respond directly to a top-level post, or be completely off-topic.

Demo of Orchestration Graph Engine: Enabling Rich Social Pedagogical Scenarios in MOOCs

Louis Faucon
Ecole Polytechnique Fédérale
de Lausanne
louis.faucon@epfl.ch

Stian Håklev
Ecole Polytechnique Fédérale
de Lausanne
stian.haklev@epfl.ch

Thanasis Hadzilacos
Open University of Cyprus and
Ecole Polytechnique Fédérale
de Lausanne
thanasis.hadzilacos@ouc.ac.cy

Pierre Dillenbourg
Ecole Polytechnique Fédérale
de Lausanne
pierre.dillenbourg@epfl.ch

ABSTRACT

This demo submission is associated with the Work-in-Progress submission "Orchestration Graphs: enabling rich social pedagogical scenarios in MOOCs".

We present our implementation of a web application for designing, running and orchestrating social pedagogical scenarios. The application is based on Orchestration Graphs, an educational modeling language. We plan to demonstrate our technology by automatically simulating user activity, and offering visitors the opportunity to interact with the graph editor.

Author Keywords
MOOCs; Scripting; Orchestration.

INTRODUCTION
The gathering of students with very different backgrounds and origins in MOOCs has the potential to provide a rich setting for collaborative learning and exchange. However, current MOOC platforms provide only rudimentary social features, which offer little space for exploration of rich collaborative scripts. Often, the only social interaction in MOOCs is the discussion forums and peer-review of assignments.

We show our implementation of a web learning platform allowing the creation, editing, and running of complex social scenarios as Orchestration Graphs (described in our Work in Progress paper). We believe this technology offers new opportunities for richer collaboration and orchestration in MOOCs, and can support a broad research agenda for learning at scale.

L@S 2017 April 20-21, 2017, Cambridge, MA, USA

© 2017 Copyright held by the owner/author(s).

ACM ISBN 978-1-4503-4450-0/17/04.

DOI: http://dx.doi.org/10.1145/3051457.3053968

PLATFORM

Graph Editor
The first interface of our application is the graph editor (shown in Figure 1). It allows teachers or instructional designers to design their own pedagogical scenarios.

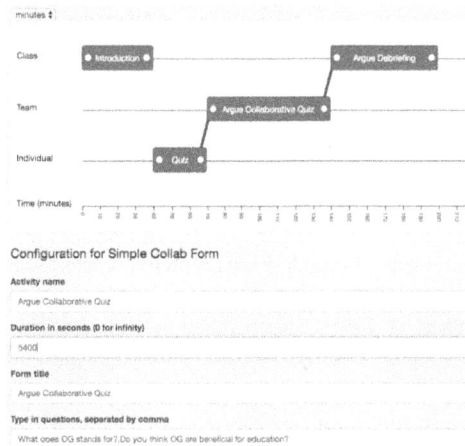

Figure 1. Orchestration Graph Editor (top) with the activity configuration interface (bottom).

The main functionality includes:

- Creating learning activities as nodes, and moving and resizing them to change their starting time and duration
- Creating operators to generate social structures or send the student product from one activity as input for another activity
- Creating edges to depict the pedagogical relationship between activities
- Configuring learning activities and operators

Learning Activities
Once the teacher starts a session based on a specific Orchestration Graph, registered students are able to join the session

and are presented with the current learning activity. We have implemented several simple types of learning activities in the prototype, such as Quiz, Video, Collaborative Quiz with a chat, and Visual Brainstorming. The activity API enables the design of new rich collaborative activities with little code.

For example, Figure 2 shows two students answering a quiz collaboratively. Their answers are synchronised and they can use a chat to reach agreement. The students would have been matched in a group by an operator based on some criteria, which could range from very simple, like generating random pairs, to very complex, like calculating the maximum divergence in opinion (from a previous questionnaire) to form teams.

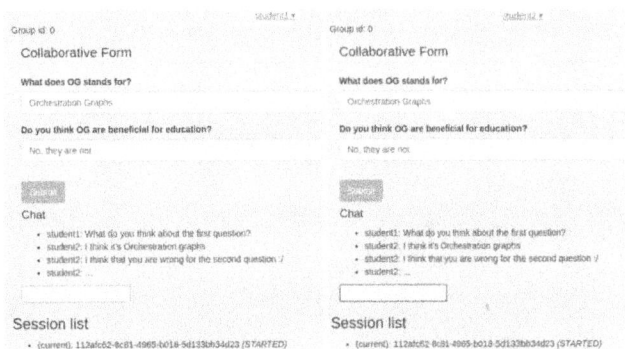

Figure 2. Two students participating in a collaborative learning activity.

Orchestration and analytics dashboard

One of the main strengths of our implementation is the ability for the teacher to orchestrate a learning session. We provide a live-streaming learning analytics dashboard for the teacher to access information needed to make decisions for his course. The teacher can also update the graph to orchestrate the session while it is running, within integrity constraints (as an example of an integrity constraint, a group activity cannot run if the groups have not been previously defined through an operator).

Figure 3 shows a custom teacher dashboard displaying the progress of individual students' video watching. This dashboard is only an example on a small classroom, but we are currently in the process of implementing new visualisations for monitoring larger groups of students.

The aim of this dashboard is to allow the teacher to decide whether he needs to intervene with the script or if it is running satisfactorily. An ongoing line of research focuses on effective representations of student state at scale, allowing teachers to see at a glance how the whole class is performing, identify outliers, and zoom in or sub-select based on various criteria to study student progress in more detail.

As well as utilizing the stream of learning traces to update the live dashboard, details are also captured for future study, using the xAPI standard [1].

EXECUTION OF THE DEMONSTRATION

Our demonstration will aim at showing the main features of our technology. As our application is hosted on a server, we

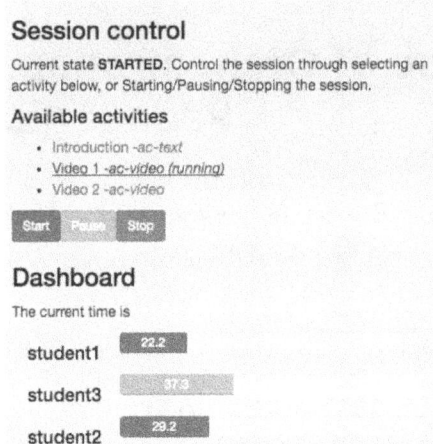

Figure 3. The teacher's analytics dashboard and orchestration controls.

will only require to use the web browser of 3 to 4 computers with Internet connection.

As the design of a non-trivial orchestration graph or the completion of a sequence of learning activities are processes that can last several hours, we plan to automatically simulate the interaction of a teacher and a group of students within our application. The simulation will first show the teacher designing a collaborative scenario using our orchestration graph editor, then the students following the pedagogical script, including individual and collaborative activities and finally the teacher monitoring and orchestrating student learning with the help of the analytics dashboard.

Visitors willing to spend more time with us will be able to explore our application, either by designing their own pedagogical scripts with the graph editor or by testing as a student one of some well-known collaborative learning scenarios such as ArgueGraph and Jigsaw [2].

CONCLUSION

We will present a web learning platform using the concepts of Orchestration Graphs to build and run rich social pedagogical scenarios with the goal of bringing collaborative learning in MOOCs. We expect to collect new ideas about scripts, learning activities and operators.

REFERENCES

1. Aneesha Bakharia, Kirsty Kitto, Abelardo Pardo, Dragan Gašević, and Shane Dawson. 2016. Recipe for success: lessons learnt from using xAPI within the connected learning analytics toolkit. In *Proceedings of the Sixth International Conference on Learning Analytics & Knowledge*. ACM, 378–382.

2. Pierre Dillenbourg and Patrick Jermann. 2007. Designing Integrative Scripts. In *Scripting Computer-Supported Collaborative Learning*, Frank Fischer, Ingo Kollar, Heinz Mandl, and Jörg M. Haake (Eds.). Vol. 6. Springer US, Boston, MA, 275–301.

Full Engagement Educational Framework: A Practical Experience for a MicroMaster

Rocael Hernández Rizzardini
Universidad Galileo
Guatemala, Guatemala
roc@galileo.edu

Hector R. Amado-Salvatierra
Universidad Galileo
Guatemala, Guatemala
hr_amado@galileo.edu

ABSTRACT

This work presents an innovative framework with the aim to create full engagement for the learners on massive open online learning environments. The proposed framework was prepared with the aim to increase the engagement and motivation of the student from the enrollment step to the start of the course, but the most important objective is to extend the interaction beyond the end of the course, the post-MOOC phase. This work explores the experience from two "MicroMaster" specializations in the edX platform: "Professional Android Developer" and one specialization taught in Spanish: "E-Learning for teachers: create innovative activities and content".

Author Keywords

MOOC; engagement; motivation; community

ACM Classification Keywords

K.3.1 Computer Uses in Education - Distance learning.

INTRODUCTION

For the particular case of massive online open courses MOOCs, there are interesting studies in literature [1-3] about the high drop-out and low approval rates from students. In general, it is possible to identify three phases related to the participation cycle for a student in a MOOC: pre-MOOC, MOOC and post-MOOC. In order to identify each of the aforementioned phases, the use case of a participant enrolled in a course is presented. In the pre-MOOC phase, the student was enrolled to the course two months before the beginning of the learning experience. During this waiting time several scenarios can happen, including a loss of interest from the student in the course topics or the incursion of new time-consuming tasks that will hinder the participation of the student in the course, leading to a potential drop-out. In this sense, it is important to mention the high amount of students that enroll on a course and actually never log-in to start the learning

experience. The second phase of the participation cycle is the learning experience within the MOOC, this phase involves the specific duration of the course and the different activities planned by the teaching staff.

The post-MOOC phase begins after the end of the course and it is important to highlight that nowadays a good part of the students that are enrolled in MOOC courses are looking to improve their careers or learn new competencies to apply to a new job. It is interesting to mention that Jennings and Wargnier [4] explored on the so-called 70:20:10 rule [5]. This rule states that only 10% of relevant knowledge and expertise is acquired through formal training and education (e.g., MOOC courses), 20% through coaching and mentoring (e.g., from team-workers and bosses), and 70% via on-the-job learning, learning by doing, and other actual experience-building activities. This rule is well-accepted and used in the corporate training world, at the same time this could be interpreted that students need to continue learning, apply the content of the courses in their jobs and get feedback from peers. This fact gives a potential opportunity to create a community from the participants of a course interested in a common subject. At the same time the idea to be part of a long-lasting and active community could engage participants after the end of a course.

FRAMEWORK PROPOSAL

This work explores the experiences from two "MicroMaster" specializations. The experiences were prepared by Galileo University within the edX platform.

In terms of engaging content, the work by Malthouse & Peck [7], highlights that the most engaging experiences in media content, that can be applied to a learning scenario, are related to prepare content that fulfills some of the following characteristics: "The content makes me smarter", "It looks out for my interests", "It is convenient" and "It gives me something to talk about". Complementarily, it is useful to highlight the term "communities of practice" that was introduced by Wenger as: "… *are groups of people who share a concern or a passion for something they do and learn how to do it better as they interact regularly*" [8]. This concept is particularly important in MOOCs because in general, a good amount of the participants of MOOC courses are professionals that are looking to update their knowledge and improve their career.

For the proposed innovative framework two engaging communities for each of the aforementioned specializations were prepared. The communities, part of the full engagement educational framework, were prepared following the principles proposed by Wenger et al. [8]:

1. The communities are designed for evolution with dynamic and updated content.
2. There are facilities for an open dialogue between inside and outside perspectives.
3. Participation is encouraged at all levels, from starters to professionals in the specific topic.
4. The interaction was developed with public and private community spaces.
5. The communities have a focus on value.
6. There is a combination of familiarity and excitement.
7. The communities have a rhythm related to the publication of contents and interaction.

For this innovative framework, specific engaging actions were identified for each of the three phases: pre-MOOC, MOOC and post-MOOC. The proposed engaging experiences are intended to take the participants from a very low interest in pursuing the course at a specific time, to an increased level of engagement that will enable the learner to gain real interest in the topic and invest more time to learn in the near future. Related to the three phases, the teaching staff prepared engaging and informative content to periodically send e-mail messages to keep the students interested and informed even if they enrolled in the course three months before the start of the course.

For this full engagement educational framework a real community is built around each MOOC specialization. The aim is to create a community that persists after the learner finished the course through the post-MOOC phase. While nurturing a sense of belonging, sharing knowledge and increase skills, the community also serves as a place where participants can ask for help with real job questions and problems, while at the same time giving the student the opportunity to be part of a strong and long-lasting community. The discussion forums are the heart of the community, thus all questions and answers are done through the community. The communities provide blogs, high quality content and videos related to the topic of the courses. It is important to mention that the community resides outside of the MOOC platform, but is fully integrated with it.

Additionally, the discussion forums that are used during the MOOC course provide enhanced and easy tools to foster collaboration, and increase visibility of community leaders and major contributors, providing means for community recognition. Gamification instruments are introduced as part of this process. An important fact is that the community is fully open, and will remain open after the end of the course so the students are able to browse through it without login, and also is possible to participate into it without being member of a MOOC in order to create a live and growing community to enhance the post-MOOC phase.

The proposed framework is composed by three communication channels: Blogs, Social Networks and Mailing Engagement. The first results show that in the case of blog visits, the bounce rate from Email Marketing is lower than 2%. Complementarily, related to the Mailing Engagement, the average open rate is over 25%.

CONCLUSIONS

Nowadays the MOOC movement brings together thousands of students around a common topic for a short period of time. However, the student's experience may last up to three to four months since the enrollment, creating a long waiting time that should be filled with engaging content. This work presents a thought-provoking work to evolve the MOOC conception to a wider scope through the use of engaging experiences within an external community.

As a future work, the first results of the running experience will be presented on how the students perceived, interacted and engaged with the community, serving as a motivation mean to conclude the courses and being part of a learning community. Then, the full engagement educational framework will be expanded as a showcase for Portfolios and Job Market Place to be evolved into a strong professional network for the post-MOOC phase.

REFERENCES

1. Daniel Onah, Jane Sinclair and Russell Boyatt. 2014. Dropout rates of massive open online courses: behavioural patterns. In *Proceedings EDULEARN14* 5825-5834.

2. Christian Guetl, Rocael Hernández, Vanessa Chang and Miguel Morales. 2014. Attrition in MOOC: Lessons learned from drop-out students. In *International Workshop on Learning Technology for Education in Cloud*. 37-48. Springer.

3. Rocael Hernández, Miguel Morales and Christian Guetl. 2016. An Attrition Model for MOOCs: Evaluating the Learning Strategies of Gamification. In: *Formative Assessment, Learning Data Analytics and Gamification*. 295-310. Elservier.

4. Charles Jennings and Jerome Wargnier. 2011. *Effective learning with 70:20:10. The new frontier for the extended enterprise*. CrossKnowledge.

5. Michael Lombardo and Robert W. Eichinger. 1996. *The career architect development planner*. Lominger Limited.

6. Etienne Wenger. 1998. *Communities of practice: Learning, meaning and identity*. Cambridge Univ Press

7. Abe Peck and Edward C. Malthouse. 2011. *Medill on media engagement*. Hampton Press.

8. Etienne Wenger, Richard McDermott and William Snyder. 2002. *Cultivating Communities of Practice: a guide to managing knowledge*. Harvard Busin. Press.

CODECAST: An Innovative Technology to Facilitate Teaching and Learning Computer Programming in a C Language Online Course

Rémi Sharrock
Ella Hamonic
Telecom ParisTech
LTCI, IMT, Paris Saclay
Paris, France
first.last@imt.fr

Mathias Hiron
France-IOI
Paris, France
mathias.hiron@gmail.com

Sebastien Carlier
Epixode
Paris, France
s.carlier@epixode.fr

ABSTRACT

This paper introduces the CODECAST tool: an in-browser C language interpreter, paired with an event and voice recorder and player that facilitates teaching and learning to program by synchronizing audio with source code edition, visualization, step by step execution and testing.

Author Keywords

teaching; programming; code edition; audio; code visualization; code execution; code testing; mooc; online learning.

INTRODUCTION

The CODECAST tool offers an innovative approach to teaching and learning C programming using an online code editor and interpreter that runs in the browser and doesn't require any software installation. The teacher is able to orally explain the entire code creation process while his interaction with a code editor and interpreter is recorded. He can also explain different aspects of the coding process like testing, running, debugging and optimising, with the help of several data and algorithms visualization modules. The learner can play back the explanation and can take control over it anytime he wishes. This means the learner can interact directly with the code and try different ideas he may have while listening to the teacher's explanation: making his own changes to the code, testing with his own inputs, running the code step-by-step to better understand its behaviour, visualizing other parts of the algorithm or the data. CODECAST lets learners go back and forth between the teacher's explanation and their own ideas at any point during the explanation. This facilitates the understanding by easily switching from the teacher's contexts and examples to the learner's ones.

L@S 2017, April 20-21, 2017, Cambridge, MA, USA.
ACM 978-1-4503-4450-0/17/04.
http://dx.doi.org/10.1145/3051457.3053970

CODECAST: MOOC USE CASES

This tool has been created for MOOCs with the help of France-ioi, a french non-profit that offers online contents and tools to teach programming to young students and prepares students for the international Olympiads in Informatics. It has been successfully used with more than 30.000 learners within two MOOCs (Massive Online Open Courses) dedicated to the C Language, available in French on the FUN platform (France Université Numérique) in 2016. Designed for early beginners in computer programming, the *C Language ABC* MOOC made it easier for learners to get onboard with computer programming. It is worth noting that this MOOC had a remarkable completion rate: 16,7% of enrolled learners got an "Honor Certificate". Through a facilitated process of self-appropriation of code uses logic and autonomous testing, the CODECAST tool may be a significant explanatory factor.

CODECAST: THE FEATURES

While developing this tool, the team aimed to combine a "tutorial style video" and an Integrated Development Environment. If online tutorials are traditionally made with screencast technologies, video content has many limitations for the students (e.g.impossibility to copy-paste parts of the code). CODECAST enables online tutorials to be fully interactive.

The CODECAST tool consists of a C language interpreter, integrated with visualization tools, a code editor and an event and voice recorder for the teacher and a player for the learner, all directly accessible on the web within a browser.

The recorder: recording audio and coding events simultaneously.

The recorder is accessible on a single web page that displays, in its most simple configuration, a record/stop button and a source code editor as seen in Figure 1. Other configurations may include a display of some specific programming teaching modules like algorithm and data structure visualizations, a variable inspector, a memory monitor, compilation and step-by-step execution controls, a program input editor and program output display. The default code editor supports source code color syntax highlighting and is also configurable (text font, color, background, line numbering…)

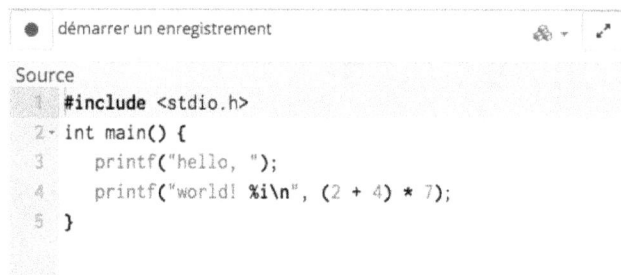

```
●  démarrer un enregistrement                              ⚙ ▾   ↗
Source
 1  #include <stdio.h>
 2▾ int main() {
 3      printf("hello, ");
 4      printf("world! %i\n", (2 + 4) * 7);
 5  }
```

Figure 1. The CODECAST tool in its most simple configurable interface: a recording button and a code editor area.

Clicking the record button starts the capture of audio as well as keyboard and mouse interactions with the active modules, including key presses, mouse clicks, drag-and-drops and text selection. The teacher is able to explain a complete "coding from scratch" process by starting the recording with a blank source code editor and typing the code one letter at a time. He may also copy/paste some existing code then modify it, and orally explain his changes while he is performing them. Another approach is for the teacher to pre-fill the code before starting the recording, then focus his explanation on the step-by-step execution of this code. Portions of the code may be highlighted to point out some of its aspects, and multiple visualization modules may be activated to help the teacher introduce specific concepts, algorithms or other relevant runtime information.

Once the teacher stops the recording, the recorded files are compressed and uploaded to a cloud service. A unique URL link is then generated for the recording to be shared or integrated in online learning platforms.

The player: playing audio and coding events and interacting with code.

The player is accessed or displayed integrated in a website, using the URL link generated during the recording process. It presents exactly the same graphical user interface as was configured during the recording (enabled modules, colors) except that the record/stop button becomes a play/pause button and a timeline appears right next to the play button. When the play button is pressed, the playback starts and the audio is played in synchronisation with all the keyboard and mouse events. The CODECAST player shows every action performed by the teacher during the recording, and displays the same screen. By dragging the timeline cursor, the learner may rapidly seek a relevant part of the recording;

the state of the interface is updated instantaneously while the cursor is moved. The learner may also pause and take control of CODECAST at any time, then modify the code, test it with his own use cases, run it step-by-step, change the inputs or the code itself or use all the modules in the same conditions as the teacher. When the learner clicks the play button again, all the modifications made are discarded and the screen goes back to the state it was in when the pause button was previously clicked.

CODECAST: TECHNICAL DETAILS

The CODECAST tool is developed mostly in Javascript. The code is open source and available on the github platform. It has to be installed on a web server and a cloud service has to be configured to upload the recordings (such as Amazon Web Services). When compiling a C program, a server-side service uses clang to generate an abstract tree, which is then used for the in-browser interpretation of the code. During the recording process, both the audio and the events are stored in the browser memory. The audio is recorded using specific browser audio APIs (Application Programming Interfaces) that interfaces with the system audio and enables to use the computer's external or integrated microphones. When the recording is finished, the audio is compressed to the MP3 format inside the browser, and uploaded to a server. All the events are stored using a JSON based format [1] and uploaded to a server. The player only needs a unique identifier to download the MP3 and the corresponding JSON file from the server before playing then in sync.

CODECAST: THE DEMO

The audience will be able to test the CODECAST tool, directly on their own computer, loading both the recorder and the player within a browser. To test the recorder, the computer has to have a microphone. Many existing "CODECASTS" were created for MOOCs and will be directly accessible from a page of collected URLs. A website will be available to centralize the demonstrations.

ACKNOWLEDGMENTS

We thank France-ioi and Epixode for helping us designing and developing the CODECAST tool. We acknowledge the Patrick and Linda Drahi foundation for providing the funding.

REFERENCES

1. France-IOI website Retrieved January, 2, 2017 from
    http://www.france-ioi.org/

Taking Informed Action on Student Activity in MOOCs

Ralf Teusner, Kai-Adrian Rollmann, Jan Renz
Hasso Plattner Institute, Potsdam, Germany
{firstname.lastname}@hpi.de

ABSTRACT

This paper presents a novel approach to understand specific student behavior in MOOCs. Instructors currently perceive participants only as one homogeneous group. In order to improve learning outcomes, they encourage students to get active in the discussion forum and remind them of approaching deadlines. While these actions are most likely helpful, their actual impact is often not measured. Additionally, it is uncertain whether such generic approaches sometimes cause the opposite effect, as some participants are bothered with irrelevant information. On the basis of fine granular events emitted by our learning platform, we derive metrics and enable teachers to employ clustering, in order to divide the vast field of participants into meaningful subgroups to be addressed individually.

Author Keywords

MOOC; Learning Analytics; Cluster; Survey; Metrics

INTRODUCTION

The most striking differences when comparing MOOCs with in-class courses are the mere amount of participants enrolled in MOOCs and the absence of direct personal communication. These differences make it difficult to gain an intuitive perception of how well a MOOC is currently running. While a holistic view might present that the overall quiz scores are at about 80% and the number of support tickets is on average, it would not show that there is a specific group that issued support tickets and achieved low scores due, for example due to wording problems.

Uncovering specific groups in MOOCs is difficult. Several previous works have labelled student groups [11, 5, 7, 2, 8], but there are no best practices yet on how to separate the participants. Additionally, it is highly debatable whether there is a common separation criteria that holds for all MOOCs with respect to their strongly varying topics, requirements and settings. Necessary steps are therefore the distinction of potential events to separate users, combine those to relevant metrics and to provide a framework that allows real-time exploration of the course status, progress and interaction.

RELATED WORK

This paper contributes to the research area Learning Analytics in MOOCs. Recent work investigates learner motivation and activity, finding and labelling characteristic groups.

Learner Activity

Part of Learning Analytics research skips motivational factors and starts at learner activity, which is represented by website usage in form of clickstream events.

Whitehill et al. [10] have the goal to react automatically to student stopout. In order to predict a good time to intervene, they include metrics such as the time since the last student activity, a measure for the regularity of the events, and the total number of different event types produced by a user.

Taylor et al.[9] analyze event stream data from edX[1] courses and aim to predict stopout one week in advance. Among their metrics are the total number and the average length of forum posts, the total time spent on all resources, and a correctness percentage for homework assignments.

Another approach by Halawa et al. [4] uses binary features to predict student dropout. Their features include whether an assignment or a video was skipped, whether a student is lagging behind by more than two weeks, as well as whether the average quiz score fell below 50%.

Kizilcec et al. [7] examine learner disengagement. They use engagement trajectories of students, based on assignment completion and video consumption. They argue, that for their feature choice, favoring trends of engagement over student scores was a deciding factor in finding meaningful groups. As a second step, they test these activity groups for correlations with another set of features. Among these features are survey results, such as enrollment intentions and overall course experience, and the number of forum posts per student.

Characteristic Groups

Previous work has derived several characteristic groups from student activity. All of the regarded works describe their groups as mutually exclusive for a given point in time, but students may move between groups during the time of the course. Wilkowski et al. [11] identify four groups of students based on their stated intentions. Hill [5] describes five types of student activity. Regarding groups with less activity, they both agree on: *No-shows*, who enroll for the course, but never log in or engage with the content; *Observers*, who drop in, only to see how the course is taught. Within more active learners,

---

[1] https://www.edx.org/

Wilkowski et al. describe two groups: *Casual learners*, who engage with the content to learn a few new things related to school, work, or simply curiosity, and *Completers*, who complete all necessary tasks and earn a certificate of completion. Here, Hill sees three additional groups, *Drop-ins*, who watch videos for selected topics, browse or participate in the forum, but do not attempt to complete the course; *Passive Participants*, who view the course as content to consume, participate, but do not engage with the assignments; *Active Participants*, who take part in discussion forums and finish the majority of the assignments.

Knowing these findings, similarities can be observed in the 4 groups found by Kizilcec et al. [7] through clustering engagement trajectories. *Auditing* and *Completing* users seem to closely resemble the *Passive Participants* and *Active Participants* by Hill. The group of *Sampling* users is similar to *Observers*. Kizilcec's *Disengaging* group is not examined extensively in the descriptions of Wilkowski et al. and Hill, probably because they did not focus on changes in activity over time.

Coffrin et al. [2] define three groups on a weekly basis depending on student participation and success: *Auditors* watched videos but did not participate in assessments for a particular week; *Active* participated in assessments for a particular week; *Qualified* watched a video or participated in an assessment for a particular week and obtained marks above the 60th percentile, leading to the assumption that these students have the capabilities to complete the course. *Auditors* and *Active* are similarly defined to Kizilcec's *Auditing* and *Completing* groups. In their work, Coffrin et al. also consider visualizing state changes between these groups and argue that those visualizations may benefit course instructors.

Lingras et al. [8] analyze data from an online course offered internally to students of a particular university (non-MOOC). They define three student groups: *Studious* download current reading material for a week as they usually study using class notes; *Crammers* download a large set of reading material, indicating their plan for a pre-test cramming; *Workers* continuously work on assignments and access the discussion forum.

Some efforts focus on single specific groups. Beaudoin [1] suggests that learning often happens on course absence and names this student group *Invisible*, who do not show visibility on the platform in form of written contributions in the forums. In contrast, Huang et al. [6] look at characteristics and influence of very active forum participants and label those *Superposters*, who are among the top 5% of students based on the number of forum contributions.

The various terms coined in the different works all describe related behavior and are based on similar observations and metrics. However, there are no standardized definitions yet, thus it is helpful to compare and align the existing terms. Clustering users should be done starting from the actual platform data instead of an artificial metric defined beforehand. Thus we describe the verbs used on our platform and the actions they reflect in fine granularity, in order to ease portability and reproducability of the underlying concepts.

To illustrate the relation between the cited groups, the diagram in Figure 1 was created. Non-overlapping ovals indicate groups that were distinctly or differently defined, overlapping ovals signal similar definitions, and groups in the same oval were likely to be merely differently labeled. While the width of the ovals has no further meaning, the Y-axis describes the degree of course activeness for a group.

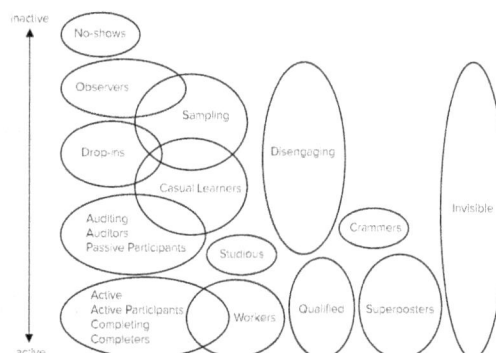

Figure 1. Approximate relations between the characteristic groups discovered by previous works.

Previous work supports course instructors and researchers in finding previously described and partly defined student groups in MOOCs. Currently lacking is support and tooling to tailor and discover previously unknown groups. This work presents concepts as well as an implementation to fill this current gap.

CONCEPT

This paper presents a concept that enables instructors of online courses to take informed action based on student activity.

On the most abstract level, our concept consists of two motivations: (1) To find a reason for action, instructors need to be able to understand their students. (2) After gaining a detailed understanding, instructors need to be able to take action that is as targeted and as measurable as possible. We refer to this kind of action as *informed action*. With the first goal in mind - understanding students - we introduce metrics that reflect student activity, some of which have also been found in previous work. These metrics are sorted into five categories and set in relation to each other. To approach the second goal - taking informed action - we define three categories of instructor actions and allow the instructors to *encourage* students on an informed basis.

Metrics

In order to understand characteristic student activity, we collect platform usage data in the form of events triggered when users perform tracked actions. The structure of the gathered events is similar to the definitions in the Experience API[2] [3]. On the gathered events, aggregations can be performed.

Yet, combining information inherent in events into possibly more meaningful metrics could provide a more abstract understanding of the underlying activity. Therefore, we derive 17 metrics from the events and grouped them into five categories

---
[2]https://github.com/adlnet/xAPI-Spec/blob/master/xAPI.md

(Fig. 2). All metrics are computed for each individual user and specific to a particular course. In addition to the verb counts, we allow these metrics to be used as the basis for discovering characteristic groups of students.

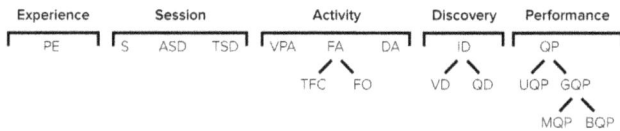

Figure 2. Overview of the metrics and their relation to higher-level platform usage categories.

Platform Exploration (PE) measures the number of distinct verbs per user. Since most actions are possible in various courses, this metric expresses the experience a user has with the platform.

Sessions (S) is the number of consecutive event streams (events per user have no wider gap than 30 minutes).

Total Session Duration (TSD) is the duration of all sessions.

Average Session Duration (ASD) is the total duration of all sessions divided by the amount of sessions.

Forum Activity (FA) represents the sum of textual forum contribution (TFC, questions, comments, and answers) and forum observation (FO, visits and subscriptions).

Video Player Activity (VPA) represents the sum of video player-related events (video played, paused, resized, fullscreen triggered, speed changed).

Download Activity (DA) represents the sum of downloads.

Item Discovery (ID) measures the share of visited items (quizzes (QD) and videos (VD)).

Quiz Performance (QP) measures the average percentage of correct answers over all graded (GQP) and ungraded (UQP) quizzes taken. Graded quizzes are further divided into main quizzes (MQP, mandatory) and bonus quizzes (BQP, optional).

Group Discovery

Once computed, the previously described metrics can be used to create characteristic student groups. The aim is to minimize the number of groups to be able to digest the clustering results, such as group sizes, coherencies and attributes, but to maximize a group's expressivity. We suggest a group is very expressive when teachers can easily understand who is part of the group and are able to assign the group a label that describes their activity. Simply assigning and labelling groups based on multiples of standard deviations from the mean for a particular metric, is not expressive, while groupings with labels like *frequent video downloaders* or *moderate quiz performers* would be. The task of finding groups can be approached by classification algorithms. While many machine learning algorithms for classification need a ground truth or other prior knowledge about expected classes (supervised learning), cluster analysis is one way to perform classification when there is little known about the data or the resulting groups (unsupervised learning). As we do not have prior understanding about distributions or possible correlations of our metrics we decided to use clustering algorithms.

Informed Action

When course instructors have gained enough understanding about individual learner activity, they should be able to react to specific activity groups and take interventions to increase student success. Given all options that came up, we found three action categories: *Encouragement* (i.e. personalized emails), *Rewarding* (i.e. badges) and *Material Improvement* (i.e. add reading material, re-record videos). From the three action categories, we focus on enabling the *Encouragement* actions, since we consider them most promising to potentially influence student success. Thus, we enable teachers to save discovered student groups and send targeted emails to members of a specific group.

Visualization

Instructors are free to choose any metrics and events the system has to offer to be included into the clustering process. To give them a starting point, the interface also suggests several common clustering tasks to have a look into. After the clustering has finished, several visualizations are presented, including a representation of the cluster sizes and qualities (Figure 3), the centroids, several scatter plots (Figure 4) and distribution charts. Colors, indicating the clusters, are coherent across all visualizations, so that the graphs support each other and instructors can get a quick glimpse whether their chosen input parameters result in a meaningful distribution. If they are confident with their findings and believe they understand the students, they can assign names to the found clusters and perform an informed action on users in the clusters afterwards.

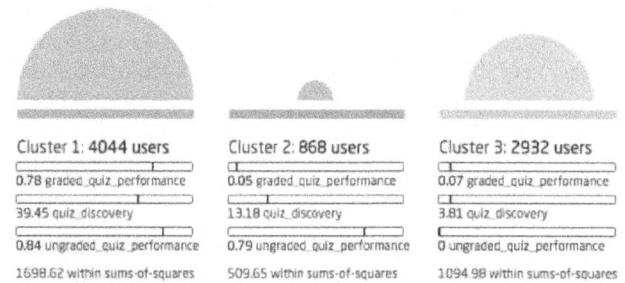

Figure 3. Cluster centers for quiz metrics measured in our MOOC.

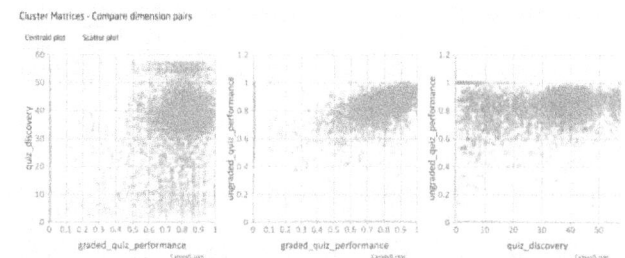

Figure 4. Scatter plot visualization.

Performing Actions

From the mentioned possibilities to react to student behavior, our tool Cluster Viewer allows to send targeted emails to found clusters, or half of the cluster for A/B testing. Changes in the metrics can be compared on the respective group pages to track the effects.

EVALUATION

We evaluated our concepts and tool with two interview series, ensuring we covered instructors' needs and provided a helpful tool. The first interviews conducted were aimed to validate the acceptance of our tool and used an early stage prototype of the Cluster Viewer, allowing us to adapt the software and process if necessary. For this series, we interviewed eight instructors from five different MOOCs, about 30 minutes each. Regardless of knowing the cited publications concerning the different student groups, most instructors had encountered and were able to name groups as "no-shows", students who finish but don't show up in the forum (we coined them "private passers") and individuals that contribute extensive and helpful forum posts ("thoughtful thread starters"). When offering instructors the possibility to uncover and react to students with specific behavior, they were most interested in students who: are likely to drop out (stopouts), behave malicious in the forum (trolls), are most active (actives), have questions but don't ask in the forum (reluctants), are active but don't perform well (effortlers) and those who perform best (high-performers).

A second series of interviews was conducted with five different instructors of a german course about internet security at course mid to evaluate the final implementation of the prototype. Four of five rated the tool as helpful, while the one expressing that it did not help was confident that his existing experience was enough to support and steer a MOOC. The four instructors were able to find interesting student groups and wanted to react to them: Students endangered of stopout after they performed worse in graded quizzes than in ungraded quizzes should be encouraged to ask their questions in the forum prior to the next assignments. Students performing below average and learning in few very long session should be encouraged to try another studying schedule consisting of more but shorter sessions.

FUTURE WORK

The methods targeting both aspects of our initial motivation - understanding students and taking informed action - can be improved individually. The metrics could be expanded to cover aspects such as peer assessments to determine social behavior and learning styles. They could also be computed for specific weeks to reveal student trajectories. Incorporating user optional profile data (age, gender, educational background) also adds further potential. The exploratory data analysis can be extended to allow filtering on discovered groups and to add additional metrics to be tracked. To further improve performance, sampling and selective rendering could provide faster feedback for the instructors. To reproduce the findings of related work, a direct next step is to use our metrics and attempt to find previously discovered groups by others (see Subsection 2.2). As soon as experience with typical student activity has been gathered across several courses, it will be possible to highlight activity out of the norm in a running course and suggest actions for course instructors.

CONCLUSION

This paper presented a concept to take informed action on student activity in MOOCs. We related our work to recent research and contributed a holistic overview of characteristics groups discovered in previous works. Based on individual events and 17 combined metrics that may be used in any online learning platform, our prototype Cluster Viewer allows to explore student behavior within courses. We showcased parts of our visualization and explained how instructors can send targeted emails to groups, based on their findings. The acceptance and perceived usefulness of our tool was validated with several interviews. A first test in a live course revealed an effect on our conducted informed action, but requires further re-evaluations in order to show statistic significance.

REFERENCES

1. Michael F Beaudoin. 2002. Learning or lurking?: Tracking the "invisible" online student. *The internet and higher education* 5, 2 (2002), 147–155.

2. Carleton Coffrin, Linda Corrin, Paula de Barba, and Gregor Kennedy. 2014. Visualizing patterns of student engagement and performance in MOOCs. In *Proceedings of the fourth international conference on learning analytics and knowledge*. ACM, 83–92.

3. Ángel Del Blanco, Ángel Serrano, Manuel Freire, Iván Martínez-Ortiz, and Baltasar Fernández-Manjón. 2013. E-Learning standards and learning analytics. Can data collection be improved by using standard data models?. In *EDUCON*. IEEE, 1255–1261.

4. Sherif Halawa, Daniel Greene, and John Mitchell. 2014. Dropout prediction in MOOCs using learner activity features. *Experiences and best practices in and around MOOCs* 7 (2014).

5. Phil Hill. 2013. Emerging Student Patterns in MOOCs: A (Revised) Graphical View. (2013). `http://mfeldstein.com/emerging-student-patterns-in-moocs-a-revised-graphical-view/` [Online; Accessed: 2016-04-04].

6. Jonathan Huang, Anirban Dasgupta, Arpita Ghosh, Jane Manning, and Marc Sanders. 2014. Superposter behavior in MOOC forums. In *Proc. First ACM conference on Learning@Scale conference*. ACM, 117–126.

7. René F Kizilcec, Chris Piech, and Emily Schneider. 2013. Deconstructing disengagement: analyzing learner subpopulations in massive open online courses. In *Proceedings of the third international conference on learning analytics and knowledge*. ACM, 170–179.

8. Pawan Lingras and Chad West. 2004. Interval set clustering of web users with rough k-means. *Journal of Intelligent Information Systems* 23, 1 (2004), 5–16.

9. Colin Taylor, Kalyan Veeramachaneni, and Una-May O'Reilly. 2014. Likely to stop? predicting stopout in massive open online courses. *arXiv preprint arXiv:1408.3382* (2014).

10. Jacob Whitehill et al. 2015. Beyond prediction: First steps toward automatic intervention in MOOC student stopout. *Available at SSRN 2611750* (2015).

11. Julia Wilkowski, Amit Deutsch, and Daniel M Russell. 2014. Student skill and goal achievement in the mapping with Google MOOC. In *Proceedings of the first ACM conference on Learning@ scale conference*. ACM, 3–10.

In-Video Reuse of Discussion Threads in MOOCs

Qian Zhao
Computer Science
University of Minnesota
Minneapolis, United States
qian@cs.umn.edu

Sashank Varma
Educational Psychology
University of Minnesota
Minneapolis, United States
sashank@umn.edu

Joseph A. Konstan
Computer Science
University of Minnesota
Minneapolis, United States
konstan@cs.umn.edu

ABSTRACT

In MOOCs, both instructors and students invest substantial effort into discussion forums. However, those discussions are abandoned when instructors start a new session in session-based courses. In an observational field study through a popular online Coursera course, we evaluate an approach that directly embeds high-value past discussion threads into future lecture videos to reuse them. Survey feedback shows that this approach can be useful to a large proportion of learners. We find that instructor involvement increases learners' chance of reading the threads, reduces learners' negative reactions, but is not associated with more perceived usefulness. Learners perceive enhancing threads embedded in the middle of videos less enhancing but more explanatory compared with at the end. Embedding explanatory threads at the end is rated less distracting and more helpful to understand the video compared with in the middle, right after the related content is lectured.

Author Keywords

MOOCs; Computer Supported Collaborative Learning.

INTRODUCTION

In Massively Open Online courses (MOOCs), discussion forums are the basic media for students and instructors to interact with each other. Discussion threads enable students to socially co-construct knowledge with peers, which prior research shows is essential for learning [7]. Both instructors and learners invest substantial effort into these discussions. We believe that these highly-voted threads are potentially re-usable learning assets that can be incorporated into future sessions of courses to address known questions and stimulate deeper learning. However, these discussions are not generally indexed by search engines because of the signing-up barrier and because of proprietary concerns. Transferring the knowledge in these discussions to future course offerings is especially difficult for session-based courses, where sequential cohorts of learners attend, leaving previously offered sessions almost abandoned.

L@S 2017, April 20-21, 2017, Cambridge, MA, USA
© 2017 ACM. ISBN 978-1-4503-4450-0/17/04 $15.00
DOI: http://dx.doi.org/10.1145/3051457.3053972

In this paper, we explore directly embedding high-value past discussion threads into the lecture videos for future course sessions. We think this approach might be useful because of two reasons. First, previous research in learning and education shows that in-classroom question-and-answer interactions between the instructor and students, or among students, are important to learning [4]. The proposed approach might be able to mimic that interactive learning experience to some extent. Second, in-time help or feedback might reduce learners' cognitive load – either extrinsic load because of unclear instruction or intrinsic load inherent in the difficulty of the content to be learned [3]. Previous research in intelligent tutoring systems also shows that the best tutoring style is one which gives immediate feedback [1].

We are facing two challenges in implementing the embedding approach in the current MOOCs. First, it is not obvious how to decide which threads to use. Unlike annotated discussions studied in previous research [2], these threads are wide open discussions and there are no direct links between the threads and videos. Second, the embedded threads are not designed together with the lecture videos. As a result, embedding threads into videos might interrupt the flow of instruction. Given (1) high quality threads that are (2) well-matched with lecture videos, we still need to decide on a time point to display the thread. Therefore, we adopted the Wizard of Oz [5] approach by manually selecting high-value threads and matching them with time points in the lecture videos. We answer two research questions in our study.

RQ1: *Is directly embedding peer discussion threads into lecture videos useful to learners?*

RQ2: *How do different design factors for embedding threads affect learner reactions?* We identify three design factors (two involving thread selection, one involving the embedding itself) that are particularly interesting and generalizable to different courses:

- *instructor-involvement* (whether instructors replied to the thread)

- *explanatory vs. enhancing thread type* (whether the thread explains a lecture point or provides enhancing content beyond the lecture)

- *timing of the interruption* (at a relevant point in the middle vs. at the end of the lecture).

RESEARCH DESIGN

We conduct an observational field study in an online course *Introduction to Recommender Systems* (one of the authors is the instructor of this course) offered through Coursera. Our design depends on utilizing threads as they naturally occurred to maintain ecological validity. We selected 24 threads from the discussion forums in the session-based offering of the course and embedded them into 24 lecture videos (one thread for each video) in the on-demand version in a pop-up format similarly to in-video quizzes as shown in Figure 1[1]. The threads were selected to balance conditions of *instructor-involvement (yes vs. no)* and *thread type (explanatory vs. enhancing)* and then assigned to one *timing condition (in the middle vs. at the end of the lecture video)*. In total, three threads were present in each of the eight (2x2x2) conditions. The study followed a *within-subjects* design: if a learner taking the on-demand offering went through all the lecture videos, then they saw three discussion threads in each of the eight conditions.

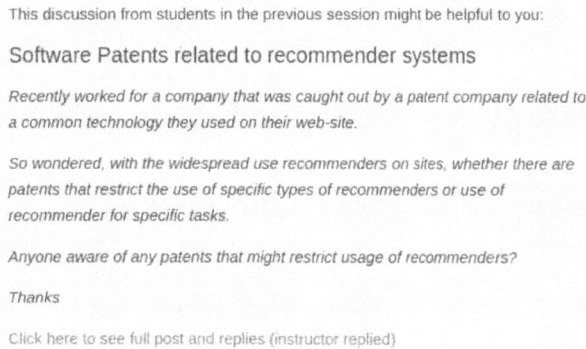

This discussion from students in the previous session might be helpful to you:

Software Patents related to recommender systems

Recently worked for a company that was caught out by a patent company related to a common technology they used on their web-site.

So wondered, with the widespread use recommenders on sites, whether there are patents that restrict the use of specific types of recommenders or use of recommender for specific tasks.

Anyone aware of any patents that might restrict usage of recommenders?

Thanks

Click here to see full post and replies (instructor replied)

Figure 1. The in-video quiz pop-up interface in Coursera with our selected discussion thread.

We used three types of measurements in this study. The first one measures engagement with the lecture video. Specifically, we used the metric of **Completion Rate** defined as the percentage of learners watching to the end of a lecture video out of those who started watching it. We compared the completion rates of two time periods: *three weeks before* and *three weeks after* the embedded threads were taken off. Time can be a confounding factor here, but since there are no other changes to this on-demand course during the two periods, we think that this is a reasonable comparison. The second measurement is **Click-Through Rate (CTR)**, i.e. the probability of learners clicking the displayed thread link given that they see the question text of the thread.

In addition, we directly embedded a survey into the video lecture associated with each thread and displayed it immediately after the thread pop-up was dismissed. We show learners six options of which they could select zero or more, grouped in one survey pop-up as shown in Table 1.

---

[1] See http://tinyurl.com/jo74fkc for the selected threads.

Option Label	Full Text in the Survey
helpful to video	I found it helpful to me in understanding the video
useful extra	I found it useful extra information beyond the video
unwanted	I did not need/want this
distracting	Interrupting me with the discussion was distracting
didn't read	I did not read the discussion thread
helpful but distracting	I found it interesting or useful, but would prefer not as an interruption in the video

Table 1. The survey options to collect feedback from learners. The order of the options is shuffled randomly each time the survey is displayed.

The order of the options was shuffled randomly each time. After making their choices, learners were shown the responses of their peers aggregated in a poll. By considering all possible cases of checking the six options, we classified each survey response into six exclusive categories: **unknown** (checking none of the six options), **strong negative** (only checking "unwanted" or "distracting"), **strong positive** (only checking "helpful to video" or "useful extra"), **mixed** (only checking "helpful but distracting" or "didn't read"; Otherwise, checking both strong positive and strong negative), **weak negative** (checking both strong negative and mixed but not strong positive), **weak positive** (checking both strong positive and mixed but not strong negative).

RESULTS

The study lasted from August 16, 2015 until March 15, 2016. During the study period, 4,593 learners saw the embedded threads. In total, the thread pop-ups (Figure 1) were displayed 21,164 times and the survey pop-ups were displayed 16,953 times. We collected 15,407 survey responses in total.

RQ1. First of all, we analyze the effect of embedding discussion threads in the middle of lecture videos on completion rate. During the two periods (three weeks before and after the threads were taken off), 1227 learners started watching the relevant lecture videos 3666 times and completed watching them 2190 times (i.e. *completion rate=59.7%*). These data only include *in-the-middle* embedding conditions because in *at-the-end* condition learners had by definition already completed the lecture video. We employ a *mixed-effect logistic regression analysis*, in which we model having embedded threads as a fixed effect and model learners as a random intercept. The fitted coefficient of having embedded threads is 0.1680 ($p=0.301$; associated odd-ratio change is 18.2%), i.e. there is no significant negative effect on completion rate by

Model		helpful to video	useful extra	unwanted	distracting	didn't read	helpful but distracting
Designed Factors	instructor involvement=yes	0.120 (0.073)	-0.023 (0.071)	-0.326 (0.095) ***	0.079 (0.130)	-0.248 (0.075) **	0.425 (0.098) ***
	thread type=explanatory	1.168 (0.131) ***	-0.708 (0.115) ***	0.049 (0.158)	0.324 (0.234)	0.204 (0.122)	0.023 (0.165)
	timing=in the middle	0.556 (0.109) ***	-0.306 (0.092) ***	-0.209 (0.130)	1.54 (0.179) ***	-0.211 (0.101) *	0.611 (0.128) ***
	thread type=explanatory & timing=in the middle	-0.783 (0.171) ***	0.077 (0.155)	0.409 (0.211)	-0.499 (0.299)	-0.032 (0.164)	-0.332 (0.217)
Covariates	log(#thread-views)	0.169 (0.087)	0.054 (0.083)	0.131 (0.111)	0.188 (0.151)	-0.042 (0.088)	0.173 (0.116)
	log(#question-upvotes)	0.110 (0.099)	-0.029 (0.097)	-0.149 (0.130)	-0.407 (0.180) *	0.111 (0.104)	-0.105 (0.134)
	log(#question-replies)	-0.207 (0.085) *	0.247 (0.084) **	0.169 (0.115)	1.02 (0.157) ***	-0.132 (0.090)	0.664 (0.115) ***
	log(#reply-upvotes)	0.187 (0.052) ***	-0.121 (0.051) *	-0.057 (0.067)	-0.206 (0.092) *	0.093 (0.053)	-0.209 (0.071) **
	log(video-length)	0.173 (0.097)	0.599 (0.093) ***	-0.066 (0.120)	0.477 (0.164) **	-0.243 (0.096) *	0.0008 (0.123)
	video-completion-rate	2.26 (0.750) **	1.29 (0.757)	3.51 (1.01)***	2.52 (1.33)	-2.138 (0.787) **	-0.702 (0.999)

Table 2. The coefficients of logistic regression models for the six survey options with std. in the parentheses. Significance Code: $p<0.05*$, $p<0.01**$, $p<0.001***$.

embedding threads in the middle of a lecture video. Instead, there is a trend suggesting that embedding threads might increase completion rate.

Options	% in 21,164 thread pop-ups	% in 15,407 responses
not-seen-survey	19.8%	n/a
checked-none	7.30%	9.11%
helpful-to-video	19.5%	26.8%
useful-extra	23.3%	32.1%
unwanted	9.24%	12.7%
distracting	7.38%	10.1%
didn't-read	18.5%	25.4%
useful-but-interrupting	11.9%	16.4%
strong-negative	9.90%	13.5%
weak-negative	4.01%	5.51%
mixed	23.0%	31.6%
weak-positive	2.91%	3.99%
strong-positive	32.9%	45.2%

Table 3. Response distribution, i.e. out of all the thread pop-ups we displayed or survey pop-ups learners responded, what is the ratio of learner's reaction in those categories?

Learners on average saw 4.6 threads, and each thread on average was displayed to 962 learners. From Table 3, in all survey response, 45.2% of them rated strong positive, 3.99% weak positive, 13.5% strong negative and 5.51% weak negative. In summary, to a large proportion of learners, the embedded threads are rated to be useful.

Lastly, our data show that aggregating across all of the thread pop-ups, the mean CTR is 66.0%, i.e. the probability of clicking through the displayed link to see more details about a discussion thread. The minimum CTR across all the threads is 37.8% and the maximum is 82.7%. We believe these high CTRs suggest that learners are interested by those discussion threads which reflects the usefulness of the embedding from learners' behaviors. This is also consistent with the self-reported survey response that to a large proportion of learners, the embedded threads are useful.

RQ2. We build six mixed-effect logistic regression models with the six survey options as binary responses (*checking vs. not checking*) respectively, modeling embedding factors and covariates as fixed effects and learners as a random intercept (shown in Table 2). The embedding factors are the three design conditions plus an interaction term between *thread type* and *timing*. The covariates are *the number of thread views*, *the number of up-votes* on the question in the thread, *the number of replies* for the question in the thread, *the number of up-votes* on the replies in the thread, *length of the video* in minutes and *the video completion rate*.

In terms of "*helpful to video*", instructor involvement is not a significant factor. We find a significant interaction between *thread-type=explanatory* and *timing=in-the-middle* (*coef=-0.783, p<0.001*). Specifically, for enhancing threads, there is an increase in perceived helpfulness when they are embedded in the middle versus at the end, whereas for explanatory threads there is a significant decrease. In terms of "*useful extra*", we find embedding threads in the middle is associated with a decrease in being perceived as useful extra information (*coef=-0.306, p<0.001*) and this is true for both explanatory and enhancing threads (i.e. there is no significant interaction effect). It suggests that, for educational goals of enhancement, presenting enhancing content in the middle might reduce its effectiveness. In addition, we find that there is an associated decrease in the probability of checking the "*unwanted*" option if the threads are replied by instructors than if they are not (*coef=-0.326, p<0.001*). Embedding in the middle is more distracting than embedding at the end of the video (*coef=1.54, p<0.001*). Learners are more likely to read the threads if the threads have instructor involvement (*coef=0.248, p<0.01*) and if the threads are embedded in the middle (*coef=0.211, p<0.05*).

DISCUSSION

The above results show that embedding peer discussion threads directly into lecture videos is rated to be useful by a large proportion of learners. Learners are more interested in viewing discussion threads with instructor replies (i.e., there was a lower probability of checking "*didn't read*" if there is instructor involvement), although this did not affect their perceived helpfulness. However, learners seem to be able to identify the relevance or quality of the thread by themselves, and hence rate threads with higher numbers of previous votes to be more helpful and less distracting as shown in Table 2.

Confirming our definition of the two types of discussion threads, we find that explanatory threads are more helpful for understanding the video itself, whereas enhancing threads are more useful as extra information. However, the interaction between thread type and timing is surprising and has important implications for future design. First, embedding enhancing threads in the middle is perceived to be more helpful to understanding the video itself, which we call the *construction effect of contextual relevance*. It suggests that learners tend to think of the embedded threads (even though they are enhancing content) in a narrower context and seem to create more contextual relevance between the threads and the content currently being lectured. It is not ideal for the educational goals of enhancement but also suggests that we may underestimate the usefulness of certain information in helping learners understand other related knowledge. On the other hand, contrary to the hypothesis that explanatory threads might be better being embedded in the middle to achieve the benefits of in-time help or feedback, learners perceive explanatory threads as more helpful for understanding the video itself if they are placed at the end. One benefit of this finding is reducing negative distraction because embedding at the end is perceived less distracting. Another benefit is the potential learning gain suggested by research on the delay of confusion resolution [6] which shows that delaying resolving learners' confusion might result in deeper learning later.

CONCLUSION

We propose and evaluate a reusing approach of directly embedding past high-value discussion threads into future lecture videos through an observational field study in a popular online Coursera course. We find that this approach is rated to be useful by a large proportion of learners. Our study provides guidance on three design factors of the embedding approach for future implementations, i.e. we find that instructor involvement increases learners' chance of reading the threads and reduces learners' negative reactions – but is not associated with higher perceived usefulness. Learners perceive enhancing threads embedded in the middle of videos less enhancing but more explanatory compared with at the end. Embedding explanatory threads at the end of the lecture video is less distracting and reported to be more useful in helping understand the video itself compared with embedding in the middle. Therefore, we generally propose embedding at the end of lecture videos is better both for explanatory threads which seek clarification on the lecture content and for enhancing threads which introduce useful extra information beyond the lecture. Limited by the access to Coursera platform, we leave it as future work to evaluate this approach through fully controlled experiments and thorough learning measurements.

ACKNOWLEDGEMENT

This work was supported by NSF IIS-1319382. We thank all Coursera learners who participated in our study.

REFERENCES

1. J.R. Anderson, A.T. Corbett, K.R. Koedinger, and R. Pelletier. 1995. Cognitive tutors: Lessons learned. *The journal of the learning sciences*, 4(2), pp.167-207.

2. D. Bargeron, A. Gupta, J. Grudin, and E. Sanocki. 1999. Annotations for streaming video on the Web: system design and usage studies. *Computer Networks*, 31(11), pp.1139-1153.

3. R.H. Bruning, G.J. Schraw, and R.R. Ronning. 1999. Cognitive psychology and instruction. *Prentice-Hall, Inc.*, One Lake Street, Upper Saddle River, NJ 07458.

4. M.D. Gall. 1970. The use of questions in teaching. *Review of educational research*, 40(5), pp.707-721.

5. J.D. Gould, J. Conti, and T. Hovanyecz. 1983. Composing letters with a simulated listening typewriter. *Communications of the ACM*, 26(4), pp.295-308.

6. B. Lehman, and A. Graesser. 2015. To Resolve or not to Resolve? that is the Big Question About Confusion. In *AIED* (pp. 216-225). Springer International Publishing.

7. L. Vygotsky. 1978. Interaction between learning and development. *Readings on the development of children*, 23(3), pp.34-41.

A Crowdsourcing Approach to Collecting Tutorial Videos – Toward Personalized Learning-at-Scale

Jacob Whitehill
Worcester Polytechnic Institute
Worcester, MA, USA
jrwhitehill@wpi.edu

Margo Seltzer
Harvard University
Cambridge, MA, USA
margo@eecs.harvard.edu

ABSTRACT

We investigated the feasibility of crowdsourcing full-fledged tutorial videos from ordinary people on the Web on how to solve math problems related to logarithms. This kind of approach (a form of *learnersourcing* [9, 11]) to efficiently collecting tutorial videos and other learning resources could be useful for realizing *personalized learning-at-scale*, whereby students receive specific learning resources – drawn from a large and diverse set – that are tailored to their individual and time-varying needs. Results of our study, in which we collected 399 videos from 66 unique "teachers" on Mechanical Turk, suggest that (1) approximately 100 videos – over 80% of which are mathematically fully correct – can be crowdsourced per week for $5/video; (2) the average learning gains (posttest minus pretest score) associated with watching the videos was stat. sig. higher than for a control video (0.105 versus 0.045); and (3) the average learning gains (0.1416) from watching the best tested crowdsourced videos was comparable to the learning gains (0.1506) from watching a popular Khan Academy video on logarithms.

INTRODUCTION & RELATED WORK

The goal of *personalized learning*, in which students' learning experiences are tailored to their individual and time-varying needs, has been been pursued by psychologists, computer scientists, and educational researchers for over five decades [15, 2, 17, 4, 8, 5]. A key challenge when developing personalized learning systems is *how to efficiently collect a set of learning resources* – e.g., illuminating tutorials of key concepts, edifying practice problems, helpful explanations of how to solve them, etc. – that are used to personalize instruction [1]. Without a sufficiently large and diverse set of resources from which to draw, personalized learning may not offer much advantage over traditional, single-path instruction.

One recently proposed and promising approach to collecting and curating large volumes of educational resources is to *crowdsource* data from learners themselves. This process, sometimes known as *learnersourcing*, has been used, for example, to identify which parts of lecture videos are confusing [9], and to describe the key instructional steps [11] and subgoals [10] of "how-to" videos. More recently, learnersourcing has been used not only to annotate existing educational content, but also to create novel content itself [6, 12, 16].

In this paper, we too explore a crowdsourcing approach to efficiently collecting a large and diverse set of learning resources. However, in contrast to previous work, which thus far has focused on text-based content, our work is concerned with asking ordinary people from a crowdsourcing web site to take on the role of a teacher ("teachersourcing" [7]) and to create *novel, full-fledged, video-based explanations* that provide worked examples [3] of how to solve math problems. In contrast to static text, multimedia videos such as whiteboard animations can help to focus students' attention on the most salient parts of an explanation – e.g., by pointing to a specific mathematical expression with the mouse pointer while talking. Moreover, some students may find video to be more engaging than text, and there is preliminary evidence from the education literature that multimedia presentations lead to greater knowledge retention compared to static text-based presentations [14]. We note that the effort involved for the "teachers" in creating these videos is considerable – often an hour or more according to self-reports by the participants in our study. It is thus unclear how many people on crowdsourcing websites such as Mechanical Turk would even respond to such a task, and even less clear how useful such crowdsourced explanations might be for helping students to learn.

This paper describes what we believe to be the first investigation into crowdsourcing entire tutorial videos from ordinary people on the Web. In particular, the rest of the paper investigates two main research questions: (1) How feasible is it to attempt to crowdsource novel (i.e., not just a link to an existing video), full-fledged tutorial videos of math concepts from ordinary people on a crowdsourcing website (e.g., Mechanical Turk)? (2) How effective are these videos in helping students to learn? Further results and analyses are available at https://arxiv.org/pdf/1606.09610.pdf.

EXPERIMENT 1: CROWDSOURCING VIDEOS

We focused on crowdsourcing tutorial videos that explain how to simplify mathematical expressions and solve equations involving *logarithms*. Logarithms are well-suited for this study because (1) many people know what they are; (2) many other people – even those who once learned them many years ago – do not; and (3) people who are not familiar with logarithms can still learn something useful about them in a small (< 10 minutes) amount of time. In particular, we chose 18 math problems related to logarithms – e.g., "Simplify $\log_3 81$", or "Solve for x: $\log_3(x-1) = 4$" – that were given as part of a pre-test from another research project [13] on how math tutors interact with their students in traditional classroom settings.

Participants: The "teachers" in our study were adult (18 years or older) workers on Amazon Mechanical Turk. All participants were first required to give informed consent (Harvard IRB15-0867) and also sign a video recording release form so that their video explanations could be used in subsequent experiments on learning. Participants who completed the experiment received a payment of $5. **Procedure**: In order to give the participant an idea of what we were looking for, we asked her/him to watch several examples of what a good video explanation might look like; the examples we chose were popular videos from YouTube about long division and quadratic equations. For the benefit of participants who chose to record their own handwriting, we also provided explicit guidelines on handwriting quality and showed good and bad examples of each. After presenting these guidelines, we showed a particular math problem – e.g., "Simplify $\log_3 81$" – and asked them to create and upload a video explaining how to solve it. **Dependent variables** were (1) the number of participants who created a tutorial video, (2) the average number of tutorial videos created by each participant, and (3) the fraction of submitted videos that were mathematically correct.

Results

Over 2 data collection periods consisting of approximately 2 weeks each, we collected 399 videos from 66 unique teachers (17% female; minimum reported age of 18, maximum reported age of 55) – approximately 6 videos per participant. This corresponds to approximately 100 videos per week of active data collection. The duration of most videos was between 1 and 3 minutes. Interestingly, several of the participants in our study expressed to us via email their enjoyment in completing the HIT, and many of them created explanations for several different problems. See Figure 1 for a small sample of the crowdsourced videos.

Analysis of correctness

To-date, we have manually annotated 145 out of the 399 submissions for mathematical correctness. Of the 145 annotated videos, 117 (81% of 145) were judged to be fully correct (i.e., contained no objectively false assertions); 16 videos (11%) contained at least one mathe-

Figure 1. Snapshots of 3 representative examples of 399 total crowdsourced explanatory videos on logarithms.

matical error; 7 (5%) were judged as "borderline" (contained minor missteps such as when the teacher referred to a mathematical *expression* (e.g., $\log_2 1$) as an *equation*); and 5 (3%) were not proper submissions (e.g., the submission was not a math video at all).

EXPERIMENT 2: FINDING THE BEST VIDEOS

After crowdsourcing the videos, we next explored whether the videos show any promise for actually helping students to learn. Because this study is about crowdsourcing novel explanations from ordinary people around the world who may have varying mathematical skill and pedagogical expertise, we do not expect *all* the videos to be effective in helping students to learn. Rather, we assessed whether the *average* learning effectiveness of the videos – quantified by posttest-minus-pretest score of participants who watched the videos in a separate experiment – was statistically significantly higher than the learning effectiveness of a "control" video about a math topic unrelated to logarithms (specifically, a historical tutorial about the number π).

With this goal in mind, we randomly sampled 40 videos from the 117 that were confirmed (out of the 145 total that were annotated) to be mathematically correct. We then used these videos to conduct the experiment described below. In contrast to Experiment 1, the participants in this experiment were not expected to know anything *a priori* about logarithms.

Participants: We recruited $N = 200$ participants from Amazon Mechanical Turk. Each participant who completed the experiment received $0.40 payment. **Apparatus**: We created a Web-based pretest and posttest on logarithms based on the materials in [13]. **Procedure**: After taking a pretest, each participant watched a randomly assigned video – with probability 0.2, the participant was assigned the control video, and with uniform probability of $0.8/40 = 0.02$, the participant was assigned to watch one of the 40 crowdsourced videos. Then the participant took a posttest. The **dependent variables** in this experiment were the average learning gains

$$G_k \doteq \frac{1}{|V(k)|} \sum_{i \in V(k)} (\text{post}_i - \text{pre}_i)$$

for each video k, where pre_i and post_i are the pretest and posttest scores (each between 0 and 1) for participant i, and $V(k)$ is the set of participants who were assigned to watch video k.

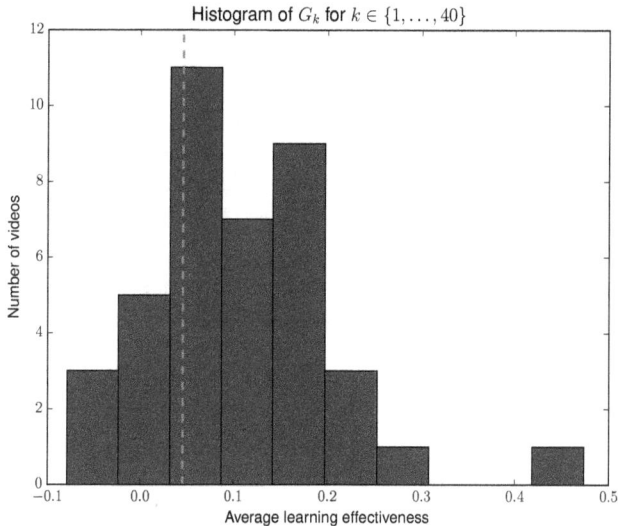

Figure 2. Histogram of the average learning gains G_k (average posttest minus pretest score across all subjects who watched video k) for 40 ($k \in \{1, \ldots, 40\}$) crowdsourced videos. The red dashed line shows the average learning gains for the "control" video.

Video	Participants	G_k
1	58	0.1416
2	42	0.1140
3	57	0.0942
4	35	0.0932
Khan	58	0.1506

Table 1. Average learning gains G_k as measured in Experiment 3, for the 4 videos were estimated to be highest in Experiment 2, compared to the average learning gains of a popular Khan Academy video on logarithms.

EXPERIMENT 3: COMPARING TO KHAN ACADEMY

In our third experiment, we compared the learning gains of the best 4 videos as estimated in Experiment 2, to the learning gains of a popular tutorial video on logarithms produced by Khan Academy (https://www.youtube.com/embed/Z5myJ8dg_rM, with 924,520 views as of October 20, 2016). **Participants:** We recruited $N = 250$ participants from Amazon Mechanical Turk. Each participant who completed the experiment received $0.40 payment. **Apparatus:** Same as in Experiment 2. **Procedures:** Same as in Experiment 2 except that each participant was assigned uniformly at random to watch one of five different tutorial videos: 4 of these videos were crowdsourced videos, and 1 was the Khan Academy video. The **dependent variables** were the same as in Experiment 2.

Results

As shown in Table 1, the learning gains associated with the Khan Academy video compared to the best of the 4 crowdsourced videos were very similar – 0.1506 versus 0.1416, respectively. The difference between them was not statistically significant ($t(114) = 0.2277, p = 0.82$, two-tailed).

We note the following issues when comparing the crowdsourced math videos to the Khan Academy video: On the one hand, the Khan Academy video was substantially longer (7 minutes and 2 seconds) than the 4 crowdsourced videos (maximum length 2 minutes and 16 seconds) and hence can contain subtantially more potentially useful math content. On the other hand, the content presented in the crowdsourced videos was arguably more closely aligned to the post-test (though none of the questions explained in the video was exactly the same as any problem on the post-test) than was the Khan Academy video. Nonetheless, the results suggest that math tutorials crowdsourced from ordinary people on the Web can, at least sometimes, produce high-quality educational content.

SUMMARY & CONCLUSIONS

We explored how to devise a crowdsourcing task for use on Amazon Mechanical Turk in which ordinary people are asked to take on the role of a "teacher" and create novel tutorial videos that explain how to solve specific math problems related to logarithms. Results of three experiments suggest that crowdsourcing of full-fledged tutorial videos from ordinary people is feasible, provided

Results

The histogram of the G_k for $k \in \{1, \ldots, 40\}$ is shown in Figure 2. The average learning gains (0.105) for the 40 crowdsourced videos that were tested was higher than for the control video (0.045); the difference was statistically significant ($t(39) = 3.715$, $p < 0.001$, two-tailed).

Differential Drop-out

Since some subjects started but did not complete the experiment, the number of subjects collected per video varied. This issue of differential drop-out can lead to distorted estimates: for example, if one tutorial video is particularly bad and only those students who are highly engaged decide to persist through the bad video and complete the HIT, then the estimated learning gains for that video might be positively biased. Unfortunately, Mechanical Turk does not provide an easy mechanism to track which workers started, but did not complete, the experiment – data are available only for participants who finished the entire HIT. However, since we do know how many participants completed the HIT for each video, and since we know the prior probability of assigning each participant to each video, we can assess whether some videos resulted in drop out more often than others. Specifically, we conducted a Pearson's χ^2 test where the vector of probabilities for the 41 videos (1 control plus 40 crowdsourced videos) was $[0.2 \ \frac{0.8}{40} \ \ldots \ \frac{0.8}{40}]$. The result of the test ($\chi^2(40) = 34$, $p = 0.7363$) indicate that the *completion* rates for the videos were not statistically significantly different from the *assignment* rates. Though this result does not mean that the estimates of learning effectiveness in Figure 2 are completely unbiased, it provides some evidence that they are not to be completely discounted.

that appropriate guidelines (e.g., about using clear hand-writing) on how to craft the explanations are provided. In fact, several of the crowdsourced workers expressed enthusiasm for the task, which likely requires more creativity than the kinds of tasks that are typically crowdsourced (e.g., image tagging). Although a few of the crowdsourced tutorial videos – which would need to be filtered out – contained important mathematical errors, the best of these videos were statistically significantly more effective, in terms of helping students to learn, than what would be expected from a "control" video on an irrelevant math topic. In fact, in terms of associated learning gains, the very best crowdsourced videos were comparable – and statistically indistinguishable from – a popular tutorial video on logarithms produced produced by Khan Academy. In sum, these findings provide support for the hypothesis that crowdsourcing can play an important role in collecting large, rich, and diverse sets of educational resources that enable personalized learning at scale.

Acknowledgement

The authors gratefully acknowledge a Spark grant (Spring 2015) from the Harvard Institute of Learning and Teaching (HILT) that partially funded this research.

REFERENCES

1. T. Aleahmad, V. Aleven, and R. Kraut. Creating a corpus of targeted learning resources with a web-based open authoring tool. *IEEE Transactions on Learning Technologies*, 2(1):3–9, 2009.

2. J. R. Anderson, C. F. Boyle, and B. J. Reiser. Intelligent tutoring systems. *Science*, 228(4698):456–462, 1985.

3. J. L. Booth, K. E. Lange, K. R. Koedinger, and K. J. Newton. Using example problems to improve student learning in algebra: Differentiating between correct and incorrect examples. *Learning and Instruction*, 25:24–34, 2013.

4. P. Brusilovsky and C. Peylo. Adaptive and intelligent web-based educational systems. *International Journal of Artificial Intelligence in Education (IJAIED)*, 13:159–172, 2003.

5. C.-M. Chen. Intelligent web-based learning system with personalized learning path guidance. *Computers & Education*, 51(2):787–814, 2008.

6. Y. Chen, T. Mandel, Y.-E. Liu, and Z. Popovic. Crowdsourcing accurate and creative word problems and hints. 2016.

7. N. T. Heffernan, K. S. Ostrow, K. Kelly, D. Selent, E. G. Inwegen, X. Xiong, and J. J. Williams. The future of adaptive learning: Does the crowd hold the key? *International Journal of Artificial Intelligence in Education*, pages 1–30, 2016.

8. G.-J. Hwang, F.-R. Kuo, P.-Y. Yin, and K.-H. Chuang. A heuristic algorithm for planning personalized learning paths for context-aware ubiquitous learning. *Computers & Education*, 54(2):404–415, 2010.

9. J. Kim, P. J. Guo, D. T. Seaton, P. Mitros, K. Z. Gajos, and R. C. Miller. Understanding in-video dropouts and interaction peaks inonline lecture videos. In *Proceedings of Learning at Scale*, pages 31–40. ACM, 2014.

10. J. Kim, R. C. Miller, and K. Z. Gajos. Learnersourcing subgoal labeling to support learning from how-to videos. In *CHI'13 Extended Abstracts on Human Factors in Computing Systems*, pages 685–690. ACM, 2013.

11. J. Kim, P. T. Nguyen, S. Weir, P. J. Guo, R. C. Miller, and K. Z. Gajos. Crowdsourcing step-by-step information extraction to enhance existing how-to videos. In *Proceedings of the 32nd annual ACM conference on Human factors in computing systems*, pages 4017–4026. ACM, 2014.

12. O. Polozov, E. O'Rourke, A. M. Smith, L. Zettlemoyer, S. Gulwani, and Z. Popovic. Personalized mathematical word problem generation. In *IJCAI*, pages 381–388, 2015.

13. L. P. Salamanca, A. R. Carini, M. A. Lee, K. Dykstra, J. Whitehill, D. Angus, J. Wiles, J. S. Reilly, and M. S. Bartlett. Characterizing the temporal dynamics of student-teacher discourse. In *International conference on Development and Learning*, pages 1–2, 2012.

14. S. Türkay. The effects of whiteboard animations on retention and subjective experiences when learning advanced physics topics. *Computers & Education*, 98:102–114, 2016.

15. K. VanLehn, C. Lynch, K. Schulze, J. A. Shapiro, R. Shelby, L. Taylor, D. Treacy, A. Weinstein, and M. Wintersgill. The andes physics tutoring system: Lessons learned. *International Journal of Artificial Intelligence in Education*, 15(3):147–204, 2005.

16. J. J. Williams, J. Kim, A. Rafferty, S. Maldonado, W. Lasecki, K. Gajos, and N. Heffernan. Axis: Generating explanations at scale with learnersourcing and machine learning. In *ACM Learning at Scale*, 2016.

17. B. Woolf, W. Burleson, I. Arroyo, T. Dragon, D. Cooper, and R. Picard. Affect-aware tutors: recognising and responding to student affect. *International Journal of Learning Technology*, 4(3-4):129–164, 2009.

MOOC Dropout Prediction: How to Measure Accuracy?

Jacob Whitehill
Worcester Polytechnic Institute
Worcester, MA, USA
jrwhitehill@wpi.edu

Kiran Mohan
Worcester Polytechnic Institute
Worcester, MA, USA
kmohan@wpi.edu

Daniel Seaton
Harvard University
Cambridge, MA, USA
daniel_seaton@harvard.edu

Yigal Rosen
Harvard University
yigal_rosen@harvard.edu

Dustin Tingley
Harvard University
dtingley@gov.harvard.edu

ABSTRACT

In order to obtain reliable accuracy estimates for automatic MOOC dropout predictors, it is important to train and test them in a manner consistent with how they will be used in practice. Yet most prior research on MOOC dropout prediction has measured test accuracy on the same course used for training, which can lead to overly optimistic accuracy estimates. In order to understand better how accuracy is affected by the training+testing regime, we compared the accuracy of a standard dropout prediction architecture (clickstream features + logistic regression) across 4 different training paradigms. Results suggest that (1) training and testing on the same course ("post-hoc") can significantly overestimate accuracy. Moreover, (2) training dropout classifiers using proxy labels based on students' *persistence* – which are available *before* a MOOC finishes – is surprisingly competitive with post-hoc training (87.33% v. 90.20% AUC averaged over 8 weeks of 40 HarvardX MOOCs) and can support real-time MOOC interventions.

INTRODUCTION

Within the fields of learning analytics and educational data mining, the possibility of creating automatic MOOC "dropout detectors" has generated considerable interest within the past few years. Such detectors could facilitate automated interventions designed to improve the persistence and performance of those MOOC learners who are at-risk of dropping out. Existing research on dropout prediction (see Table 1) has varied across several dimensions including the **features** (clickstream, social network measures, etc.) used for prediction as well as the machine learning **classifier** (logistic regression, survival analysis models, neural networks, etc.) used for training and testing.

More subtle, but important for real-time deployment in an actual course, is the **training paradigm** that describes how the *source* of the training data – e.g., the same course, a prior instance of the same course, or a different course altogether – relates to the *target use* of the classifier once it has been trained. To-date, most research on MOOC dropout prediction has focused on training and testing on data sampled from the same MOOC, likely because it is simplest to implement in simulation. Live interventions, on the other hand, require dropout predictors that are operational near the *start* of a MOOC when students can still benefit from receiving an intervention. But producing such a predictor can be difficult because the target values which indicate whether each student dropped out or completed the MOOC, and which are usually required by supervised learning algorithms, become available only at the *end* of a MOOC – at which point any intervention is moot.

In this paper, we seek to fill a methodological gap in MOOC dropout prediction research and to investigate how the training paradigm affects the accuracy of the trained predictors. In particular, we conduct machine learning experiments on 40 HarvardX MOOCs using a standard architecture – clickstream features classified by L_2-regularized logistic regression – and compare performance across 4 different training paradigms as well as 2 simple baseline prediction approaches. Our greater goal is to increase awareness of the trade-offs across different training paradigms in terms of accuracy, ease of implementation, and applicability to new courses, so that researchers and practitioners can make better decisions about how to implement real-time MOOC interventions.

DATASET

The analyses in this paper are based on data from 40 MOOCs from HarvardX; due to space constraints, these courses are summarized in Table 2 of [16]. The binary **target labels** used for training and testing were whether (1) or not (0) each student accrued enough points during the MOOC to earn a certificate. The grade threshold for certification differed across the MOOCs but is typically around 70%. Note that, starting in late 2015, some HarvardX MOOCs required students to pay a fee (to have

Survey of Prior Research on MOOC Dropout Prediction

Study	#MOOCs	Features	Architecture	Training paradigm
Balakrishnan & Coetzee [1]	1	Clickstream	HMM + SVM	Same course
Boyer & Veeramachaneni [2]	3	Clickstream	TL+LR	Different offering In-situ
Coleman et al. [3]	1	Clickstream	LDA+LR	Same course
Crossley et al. [4]	1	Clickstream; NLP	DFA	Same course
Fei & Yeung [5]	2	Clickstream	RNN	Same course
He et al. [7]	2	Clickstream	Smoothed LR	Different offering
Jiang et al. [8]	1	Social network; grades	LR	Same course
Kizilcec et al. [9, 6]	20	Clickstream	LR	Different course Same course
Kloft et al. [10]	1	Clickstream	SVM	Same course
Koedinger et al. [11]	1	Clickstream; grades	LR	Same course
Robinson et al. [12]	1	Survey; NLP	LR	Same course
Rose et al. [19, 13]	1	Forum; social network	SA	Same course
Stein & Allione [14]	1	Clickstream; survey	SA	Same course
Taylor et al. [15]	1	Clickstream	LR	Same course
Whitehill et al. [17]	10	Clickstream	LR	Different course
Xing et al. [18]	1	Clickstream; social network	PCA+{BN,DT}	Same course
Ye & Biswas [20]	1	Clickstream	LR	Same course
Our work	40	Clickstream	{LR, DNN}	Same course In-situ Different course

Table 1. Survey of prior literature on MOOC dropout prediction. For the architecture, we use the following abbreviations: Bayesian network (BN), decision tree (DT), deep neural network (DNN), discriminant function analysis (DFA), hidden Markov model (HMM), latent Dirichlet allocation (LDA), logistic regression (LR), principal component analysis (PCA), recurrent neural network (RNN), support vector machine (SVM), survival analysis (SA), and transfer learning (TL). Architecture $a + b$ means methods a and b were used in conjunction; $\{a, b\}$ means that a or b were used as alternatives. Note that our full paper [16] describes our experiments using DNN.

their identity verified) in order to receive a certificate. For these courses, we still considered the target label for a student to be 1 as long as her/his point total exceeded the verification threshold – in other words, we ignored whether or not the student paid the fee.

EXPERIMENTS

We conducted experiments to compare the accuracies of different MOOC dropout predictors. All the predictors that we trained were based on clickstream **features**; these are computed from the clickstream log describing interaction events between the student and the MOOC courseware, e.g., answers to quiz questions, play/pause/rewind events on lecture videos, etc. When predicting at week w whether a learner will drop out, clickstream features only up until w are extracted. For the **classifier**, we used L_2-regularized logistic regression and optimized the regularization strength. See [16] for more details on the feature representation and classifier design.

The key independent variable that we manipulated in our experiments was the **training paradigm**. Specifically, for each week w of each of the 40 MOOCs, we trained one classifier for each of the following paradigms:

1. *Train on same course (post-hoc)*: When predicting which students from course c will drop out, train using features and target labels from the exact same course c. **Assumptions**: since target labels for c become available only *after* c has ended, this approach essentially would require either that (a) the practitioner go "back

in time" to when the MOOC first started, or (b) that a new MOOC with the exact same distribution of students (demographics, prior knowledge, etc.) and with the exact same content and structure is offered in the future, and that no exogenous factors cause students to behave differently during the later incarnation of the course.

2. *Train on other course from same field*: When predicting which students from course c will drop out, train using features and target labels from a different course c' that has already completed, and for which the target labels are thus already available. Although it is difficult to know *which* prior course should be used for training, a reasonable choice is a different course from within the same discipline (social sciences, humanities, etc.). We chose to use the *largest* such course in order to maximize the number of data available for training.

3. *Train on many other courses*: When predicting which students will drop out, train using features and target labels from *many* different courses (not necessarily within the same discipline). Specifically, for each course c, we trained a dropout classifier from each of the 39 other courses (recall that our dataset includes 40 MOOCs) and then averaged the classifiers' hyperplanes together.

4. *Train using proxy labels (in-situ)*: When predicting at week w which students from course c will drop out, train using *proxy labels* corresponding to whether each student *persisted* – i.e., interacted with the MOOC courseware at least once – within the previous week $w-1$ (see Figure 1). This approach (similar to [2]) can be implemented for any MOOC. Because it does not require "seeing into the

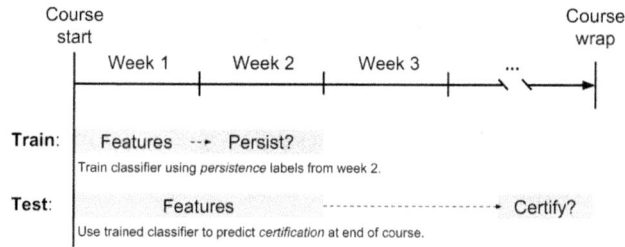

Figure 1. Schematic representing how to train using proxy labels (in-situ): At each week w, proxy labels of whether the student *persisted* during week $w-1$ are used to predict whether or not the student will certify or drop out by the end of the course.

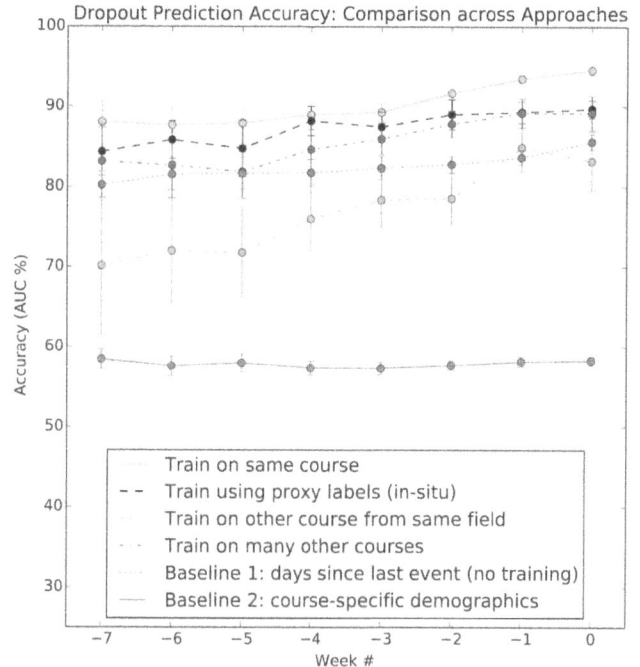

Figure 2. Results comparing different approaches.

future" to obtain target labels, it can deliver a dropout predictor that can be deployed during a *live* MOOC, not just after it has finished. There is, however, a mismatch between the *training* target labels (based on persistence) and the *testing* target labels (based on certification), and this mismatch may degrade performance.

Baseline Approaches

In order to gauge how much "added value" is brought by machine learning approaches to MOOC dropout prediction that utilize detailed clickstream information, we also assessed the accuracy of two simple baseline heuristics. *Baseline 1* uses only demographic information – consisting of self-reported year of birth, continent of origin (Africa, North America, etc.), level of education (primary/elementary school, high/secondary school, college, etc.), and gender – to make predictions. This information is available for each student as soon as she/he registers for the course. We also compared against an even simpler *Baseline 2* which requires no machine learning (and hence no training data) at all; rather, the predictor makes predictions based on the number of days since the student last interacted with the courseware. This variable alone has previously been shown to be highly predictive of dropout [17, 9].

When to Measure Accuracy

When using MOOC dropout detectors to facilitate real-time interventions, it is more useful to be able to predict early in the course, rather than later, which students will eventually drop out. Moreover, near the end of the MOOC, some students may have already accrued enough points to earn a certificate. A dropout detector that predicts that such students will not drop out is not so much "predicting" these students' future performance as it is reporting what they have already achieved; hence, accuracy statistics computed over such students may overestimate the performance of the predictor. For both these reasons, we decided to compute accuracy over all weeks of each MOOC between the course start date (which we call $T_{0\%}$, when instruction begins) and the earliest date by which students could possibly have earned enough points to earn a certificate ($T_{100\%}$).

RESULTS

Dropout prediction accuracy (AUC) for all training approaches are shown in Figure 2. The horizontal axis indexes the week in the MOOC, where week 0 is defined for each course to be $T_{100\%}$. (Week -3 corresponds to 3 weeks prior to $T_{100\%}$, etc.) Error bars show standard errors. Since the lengths of the courses varied, the accuracy statistics for each week w were computed using only those MOOCs for which data were available at week w.

The most accurate training paradigm was *Train on same course (post-hoc)*, which is the predominant training paradigm used in the dropout prediction literature. It achieved an accuracy (averaged over all 8 weeks, and all MOOCs within each week) of 90.20%. As explained above, the assumptions made by this training paradigm are unrealistic for most intervention scenarios.

Perhaps more surprising is that the second most accurate approach was *Train using proxy labels (in-situ)*. This approach does not require any MOOC – similar or dissimilar – to have been offered previously. Despite the inherent mismatch between the labels of persistence (did the student participate during the previous week?) and labels of certification (will the student earn enough points to earn a certificate?), this approach attained an accuracy (averaged over 40 MOOCs and 8 weeks) of 87.33%.

The third most accurate approach was *Train on many other courses*, with an accuracy of 85.56%. This training paradigm attained a higher accuracy than did *Train on other course from same field* (76.85%), suggesting that, if it is not possible to exploit course-specific structure via either *Train on same course (post-hoc)* or *Train using proxy labels (in-situ)*, then it is better to harness prior data from a large variety of courses than from just a single course (even from within the same discipline).

Comparison to Baseline Approaches: *Baseline 1* achieved an average prediction accuracy of 58.85%, suggesting that only a small amount of information about dropout is contained in the demographics. *Baseline 2* performed remarkably well: It attained an average dropout prediction accuracy of 82.45%, which corroborates previous findings [17, 9] that this variable is highly salient for prediction. Nonetheless, *Baseline 2* was still substantially less accurate than either *Train on same course (post-hoc)* or *Train using proxy labels (in-situ)*, suggesting that harnessing more detailed clickstream features does bring a substantial accuracy boost.

SUMMARY

We explored, on data from 40 HarvardX MOOCs, how MOOC dropout prediction accuracy varies as a function of the **training paradigm**. Results suggest that accuracy estimates obtained by training on the same course (post-hoc) as the target course for deployment – which is generally not possible in real-world intervention scenarios – can be significantly overly optimistic. In addition, we explored a new training paradigm, similar to *in-situ* training [2], based on the idea of *proxy labels* – labels that approximate the quantity of interest (dropout versus certification) but that can be collected *before* a course has completed. Surprisingly, the accuracy of this approach – which is suitable for live interventions in a large variety of MOOCs – is very similar to when classifiers are trained *post-hoc* on courses that have already finished.

REFERENCES

1. G. Balakrishnan and D. Coetzee. Predicting student retention in massive open online courses using hidden markov models. Technical report, UC Berkeley, 2013.

2. S. Boyer and K. Veeramachaneni. Transfer learning for predictive models in massive open online courses. In *International Conference on Artificial Intelligence in Education*, 2015.

3. C. Coleman, D. Seaton, and I. Chuang. Probabilistic use cases: Discovering behavioral patterns for predicting certification. In *Learning at Scale*, 2015.

4. S. Crossley, L. Paquette, M. Dascalu, D. S. McNamara, and R. S. Baker. Combining click-stream data with nlp tools to better understand MOOC completion. In *Learning Analytics & Knowledge*, pages 6–14. ACM, 2016.

5. M. Fei and D.-Y. Yeung. Temporal models for predicting student dropout in massive open online courses. In *International Conference on Data Mining Workshop (ICDMW)*, 2015.

6. S. Halawa, D. Greene, and J. Mitchell. Dropout prediction in MOOCs using learner activity features. In *European MOOC Summit*, 2014.

7. J. He, J. Bailey, Benjamin, I. Rubinstein, and R. Zhang. Identifying at-risk students in massive open online courses. In *AAAI*, 2015.

8. S. Jiang, A. Williams, K. Schenke, M. Warschauer, and D. O'Dowd. Predicting MOOC performance with week 1 behavior. In *Educational Data Mining*, 2014.

9. R. Kizilcec and S. Halawa. Attrition and achievement gaps in online learning. In *Learning at Scale*, 2015.

10. M. Kloft, F. Stiehler, Z. Zheng, and N. Pinkwart. Predicting MOOC dropout over weeks using machine learning methods. In *Proceedings of the EMNLP 2014 Workshop on Analysis of Large Scale Social Interaction in MOOCs*, pages 60–65, 2014.

11. K. R. Koedinger, J. Kim, J. Z. Jia, E. A. McLaughlin, and N. L. Bier. Learning is not a spectator sport: Doing is better than watching for learning from a MOOC. In *Learning at Scale*, 2015.

12. C. Robinson, M. Yeomans, J. Reich, C. Hulleman, and H. Gehlbach. Forecasting student achievement in MOOCs with natural language processing. In *Learning Analytics & Knowledge*, 2016.

13. C. P. Rosé, R. Carlson, D. Yang, M. Wen, L. Resnick, P. Goldman, and J. Sherer. Social factors that contribute to attrition in MOOCs. In *Learning at Scale*, pages 197–198. ACM, 2014.

14. R. Stein and G. Allione. Mass attrition: An analysis of drop out from a principles of microeconomics MOOC. *PIER Working Paper*, 14(031), 2014.

15. C. Taylor, K. Veeramachaneni, and U.-M. O'Reilly. Likely to stop? Predicting stopout in massive open online courses. *arXiv*, 2014. http://arxiv.org/abs/1408.3382.

16. J. Whitehill, K. Mohan, D. Seaton, Y. Rosen, and D. Tingley. Delving deeper into MOOC student dropout prediction. *arXiv*, 2017. http://arxiv.org/abs/1702.06404.

17. J. Whitehill, J. Williams, G. Lopez, C. Coleman, and J. Reich. Beyond prediction: Toward automatic intervention to reduce MOOC student stopout. In *Educational Data Mining*, 2015.

18. W. Xing, X. Chen, J. Stein, and M. Marcinkowski. Temporal predication of dropouts in MOOCs: Reaching the low hanging fruit through stacking generalization. *Computers in Human Behavior*, 58:119–129, 2016.

19. D. Yang, T. Sinha, D. Adamson, and C. P. Rose. "Turn on, tune in, drop out": Anticipating student dropouts in massive open online courses. In *NIPS Workshop on Data-Driven Education*, 2014.

20. C. Ye and G. Biswas. Early prediction of student dropout and performance in MOOCs using higher granularity temporal information. *Journal of Learning Analytics*, 1(3), 2014.

Collaboration and Teamwork on a MOOC Platform
A Toolset

Thomas Staubitz, Christoph Meinel
Hasso Plattner Institute, University of Potsdam, Potsdam, Germany
{firstname.lastname}@hpi.de

ABSTRACT

Teamwork is an an important topic in education. It fosters deep learning and allows educators to assign interesting tasks, which would be too complex to be solved by single participants due to the time restrictions defined by the context of a course. Furthermore, today's jobs require an increasing amount of team skills. On the other hand, teamwork comes with a variety of issues of its own. Particularly in large scale settings, such as MOOCs, teamwork is challenging. Courses often end with dysfunctional teams due to drop-outs or insufficient matching. The paper at hand presents a set of three tools that we have recently added to our system to enable teamwork in our courses. The presented tools are evaluated in terms of success rates of the created teams and workload reduction for the courses' teaching teams.

Author Keywords

Teamwork; Collaboration; MOOC; Massive Open Online Courses; PeerAssessment.

INTRODUCTION

Based on the result of experimental courses on our platform with small numbers (200-500) of participants, we identified three major issues that hinder real teamwork in our MOOCs:

1. The formation of teams needs to be supported, satisfactory self-organization is not to be expected.

2. The teams need to be enabled to jointly edit common task related documents and they need proper communication tools.

3. The teams need a tool to jointly hand-in their solution, which allows the assessment of their work.

In this paper we introduce a toolset, which allows us to employ and assess teamwork exercises in large scale settings and provides solutions for the challenges listed above.

L@S 2017, April 20 - 21, 2017, Cambridge, MA, USA

© 2017 Copyright held by the owner/author(s). Publication rights licensed to ACM.
ISBN 978-1-4503-4450-0/17/04. . . $15.00

DOI: http://dx.doi.org/10.1145/3051457.3053975

- The *TeamBuilder*—is a standalone web application to form teams out of a given pool of participants, based on a variable set of parameters. It allows to limit the number of participants that will be admitted to attend the teamwork assignments. The limiter can be applied either on a *first-come/first-serve* basis or on the participants' previous course performance.

- The *TeamCollabSpaces*—provide teams with an area of their own within the course and offer a set of communication and collaboration tools.

- The *TeamPeerAssessment*—extends our built-in PeerAssessment tool and allows teams to jointly submit digital artifacts. The submissions of each team are reviewed and assessed individually by members of other teams. It additionally allows team members to rate the work of their team mates in terms of contribution, organization, and social skills.

THE TOOLSET

TeamBuilder

The term *team building* describes either the process of selecting the members of the future team or the process of transforming a collection of individuals (following their own agenda) to a successful team with a common goal. In the paper at hand the term is used in the meaning of selecting or matching the members for the future team. The *TeamBuilder*, a standalone tool that can be connected to any Learning Management System (LMS) that supports the Learning Tools Interoperability (LTI) interface (see Figure 1), provides a limited set of parameters to be used for the team matching process:

- The participant's preferred language—a limited set of languages is provided. If deactivated, the course language is assumed to be the "lingua franca".

- The participant's location—clustering based on the participants' location to allow face-to-face meetings.

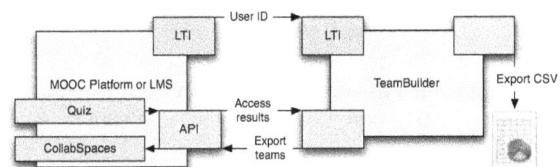

Figure 1. The TeamBuilder can be connected to any LMS that provides an LTI interface.

- The timezone in which the participant prefers to work.

- The participant's area of expertise—options are provided.

- The participant's preferred task—any number of tasks can be defined by the teaching team.

A missing, but yet important parameter is the participant's commitment in terms of time.

The *TeamBuilder* allows educators to activate the parameters that are suited best for their ideas on matching teams. One teaching team's major requirement was to form local teams that are able to meet physically. Another teaching team, in contrary, tried to team up participants with a diverse cultural background. They also required, however, that the participants were able to collaborate synchronously so they had to live at least in the same range of timezones. The example illustrates that the criteria differ significantly between the courses.

Next to the possibility of activating and deactivating certain matching criteria, the tool provides the option to choose if a parameter is to be employed homogeneously or heterogeneously. The *TeamBuilder's* strategy is to build as many as possible teams with a **good** heterogeneous distribution of a certain parameter instead of few teams with a **perfect** heterogeneous distribution and the rest getting more and more homogeneous (depending on the available features of the participants).

The data we gather from the participants is deliberately kept simple and does not include sophisticated and more personal criteria, such as personality traits, or Belbin tests, etc. Our intention is to keep things simple and not to confront our participants with a multi-page survey that asks them to share detailed, fine-grained personal information. On the other hand, all data that we ask from the participants is mandatory. Those who refuse to provide a relevant piece of information will not be considered for the team assignments. The findings of Zheng et al. [4] show that participants that have at least partially answered surveys before joining a team were less likely to drop-out than those who did not take the surveys at all. This supports our idea of requiring the participants to show some commitment before they are allowed to participate in the team assignments.

Next to the selection of matching criteria, the tool allows to define a range for the desired team size. It attempts to build the teams as close as possible to the given upper limit. Finally, the tool allows to limit the total number of participants for the team assignments within a course. This limiter can be employed either in first come/first serve mode, or it can be employed in combination with the results of the assignments that have been handed-in before the team building item is published in the course. First come/first serve simply allows the teaching teams to select the first N participants that have applied for the teamwork assignment(s). In case the teaching team decides to employ the results of one or more assignments to decide which participants will be admitted to take the teamwork assignments, the tool allows two different settings:

1. Set a maximum amount N of students to be admitted for teamwork—The N participants that performed best so far will be admitted.

2. Set a lower boundary for the results in the exams that has to be achieved—In addition to the total maximum amount of participants, a lower limit for the results can be set. Only participants that have achieved at least $X\%$ of the points in the relevant exams–but no more participants than the total maximum–will be admitted.

While the *TeamBuilder* attempts to build teams fully automated, it still allows manual corrections. The final decisions are made by the teaching team. Participants can be moved from one team to another, new teams can be created and existing ones can be removed, etc. To assist the teaching team, the UI provides meta-information about the created teams, such as the max. local distance between team members or the team's state of heterogeneity concerning a given parameter. The teaching team can flag teams as finalized to override these indicators when they decide that the current state might not be perfect but is as good as it will get. If it becomes obvious that with the requested parameters, a proper matching is not possible, each of the requested parameters can be deactivated for the actual matching process.

Finally, there are two options to export the created teams. The *TeamBuilder* can either create an Excel sheet for further usage, or it can directly create *CollabSpaces* on our platform and add the team members to their respective *CollabSpace*.

CollabSpaces

We have introduced the concept of the *CollabSpaces* in [3]. Basically, the *CollabSpaces* provide synchronous and asynchronous communication tools as well as some co-creation tools to jointly work on digital artifacts. To keep the *CollabSpace* feature flexible, we defined two different collaboration concepts: *Groups* and *Teams*.

Groups—are loosely coupled and have a self-set goal or a common interest. Groups are self-organized, the participant who creates the *CollabSpace* has administration privileges and decides if it is public or private (invitation only). Group members can come and go as they want.

Teams—are tightly coupled and have a common task on which they are collaborating. The task is an essential element of the course and part of the grading scheme. Teams are formed by the teaching team using the *TeamBuilder*. In case teams become dysfunctional, the teaching teams have the possibility to merge teams or to move remaining members to other teams.

In the *TeamCollabSpaces*, the forums have received a slight upgrade. Emails are sent to each team member whenever a new question, answer, or comment is posted. Grade relevant team assignments are enabled by the possibility to add *TeamPeerAssessments*.

TeamPeerAssessment

In all courses that featured teamwork assignments, the teams were provided with a mentor, mostly volunteers. As the platform by then did not provide proper tools to enable graded team assignments, an improvised workaround had to be employed. It soon became obvious, however, that we need a better tool to hand-in team assignments.

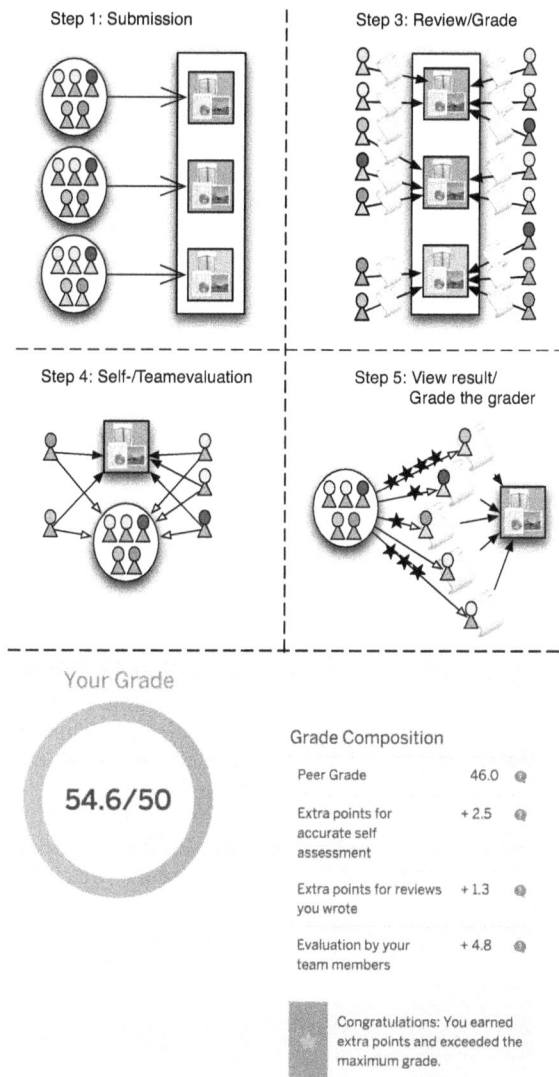

Figure 2. TeamPeerAssessment—Top/down, left/right. Step 1: The team jointly submits a solution for the given challenge. (Step 2: the training step has been omitted for simplicity.) Step 3: individual members of the teams review the work of the other teams. Step 4: individual members of a team assess the solution of their own team and rate the contribution of their fellow team members. Step 5: the team reviews and discusses the results and rewards helpful reviewers with stars. Bottom: screenshot of a participant's results view. The "Peer Grade" component contains the credits that the team received together. The other components contain credits that have been achieved for individual work, which can differ between team members.

A tool that allows...

- ...one team member to hand-in a solution for all.
- ...to review and grade the team work in a scalable manner.
- ...great flexibility in the type of assignments.

We already have a sophisticated peer assessment tool tightly integrated in our platform, which covers two of the three major requirements. We decided to modify this tool in a way that allows teams to jointly hand-in their work. In our original peer assessment tool, the process consists of 3-5 steps:

submission, training (optional), peer review and assessment, self-evaluation (optional), results view and reviews rating.

For more details about the single user peer assessment system see [2].

To allow the assessment of teamwork, first of all we had to decide "who grades whom". Should the teams grade the other teams, should individual team members grade the other teams, or should the members of a team grade their team mates?

We decided to go for the second option. This way submissions receive more reviews, while the workload for the team members is kept low. Managing the review process is easier, as the team members do not have to be coordinated and no versioning is required. Participants have less opportunities for free-riding. Even if they manage not to contribute to the actual work, they still have to write their own reviews if they intend to receive credits. Additionally, each team member can rate her team mates in terms of contribution, organization, and social skills. The combination of these two aspects allows us to grade the team members individually. With this we're following established best practices, e.g. Carnegie Mellon's *Eberly Center for Teaching Excellence* suggests to compose grades based on the several components, including the team's final product but also the team processes and the functioning of the team. They also recommend to translate the team's overall performance into individual grades [1]. Just as in the single user peer assessment, participants can report submissions and reviews, whereas reporting submissions is an individual effort, while reporting reviews is a team effort. The team can also reward reviewers that wrote helpful reviews with additional points. Figure 2 gives an impression of the tool's abilities and shows how an exemplary result might be displayed to a participant.

EVALUATION

The tools that have been introduced in the previous sections, so far have been employed in various combinations and stages of completion in five courses on one of our platforms.

- Three iterations of the course *Developing Software Using Design Thinking*—all pilots with a limited amount of participants
- *Designing Business Models for the Digital Economy (BMI)*
- *Enabling Entrepreneurs to Shape a Better World (SBW)*

We focus the evaluation of the toolset on the SBW course here, as this was the first full scale course, which made use of the complete toolset. 12025 participants were enrolled for this course. The course employed the *TeamBuilder's* limiter feature to select the course's best performing participants for the teamwork exercises. 240 participants were admitted for the teamwork as the number of available mentors did not allow for more than 40 teams. The teams had to complete five tasks throughout the course, on which they received feedback from their team mentors. Finally, the teams created a document based on their preliminary work and submitted it to the *TeamPeerAssessment* system, where it was reviewed and graded by members of the other teams. While 32 of 39 teams (80%) submitted their completed work, only 40% of the team

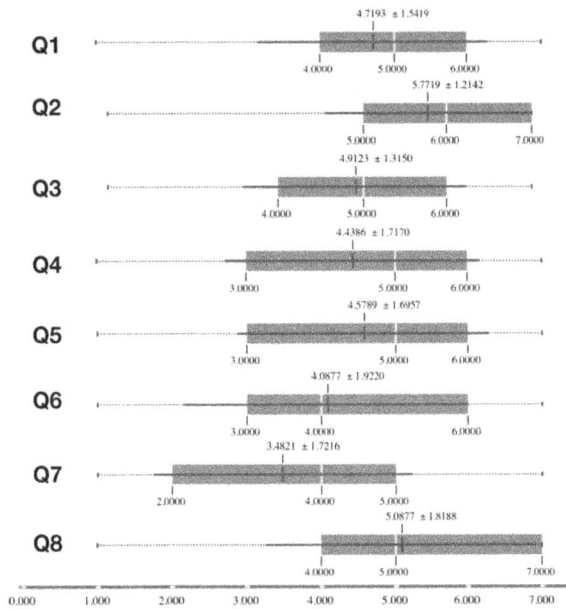

Figure 4. Participants' satisfaction with team challenge. Answers on a seven point Likert scale: Q1: How satisfied have you been with the Team Challenge? Q2: Have the tasks been relevant? Q3: Have the tasks been manageable? Q4: Have the tasks been suitable for virtual teamwork? Q5: Did you enjoy working in your team? Q6: Did you receive valuable support from your mentor? Q7: Did your mentor spent sufficient time with your team? Q8: Did you acquire important know-how through the tasks? 60 out of 240 participants have answered the survey.

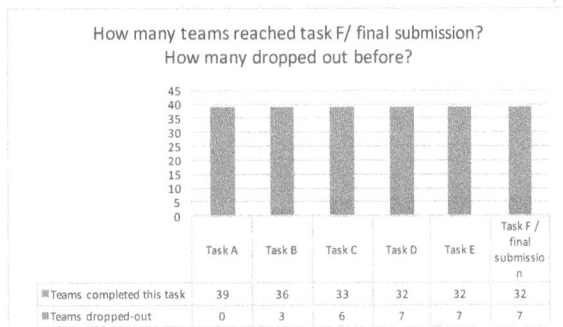

Figure 3. Dropped-out teams

members arrived at that point. Figure 3 shows that most of the teams dropped out during tasks two and three. Having a closer look at the teams, we found that 20 of the 32 teams that went till the end still were functional teams with 3 to 7 members. 8 teams still had two members left and 4 were dysfunctional with only one member left. If we have a look at the submission rates of the intermediate team tasks, we can see that only 228 of the 240 participants of the team challenge actually started by handing in the first assignment. A survey conducted at the end of the course among the participants of the team assignment, shows that the overall perception was

rather positive (Figure 4). Mentor support and particularly the time the mentors spent supporting their teams need to be improved however.

FUTURE WORK

Next to optimizations in the tools implementation and features, such as e.g. adding a participant's time commitment for the team work task as a matching criterium, we need to support the mentors with a toolset that enables them to coach teams more efficiently. Even if there was no lack of volunteers to mentor teams in the examined courses, this resource is the major bottleneck to scale up teamwork assignments to full-size courses. From our experience, we doubt that automating the role of the mentors is a feasible option. We still have to prove these assumptions by extending our research in this direction.

CONCLUSION

We presented a toolset to enable teamwork on our MOOC platforms. We have evaluated our work in various stages during four pilots and one regular course on one of our platforms. The results show that our approach has been successful as a majority of teams has succeeded with their tasks. For MOOCs it is a reasonable approach to set high entrance barriers for teamwork assignments. Allowing only those participants, who have already shown a certain amount of commitment to engage in the teamwork assignments reduces the dropout problem in teams, however it does not eliminate it. The introduced toolset provides a good foundation for larger scale teamwork assignments. We have identified the weak points that need to be fixed and see the future of teamwork assignments on our platform with confidence.

REFERENCES

1. Eberly Center for Teaching Excellence & Educational Innovation. 2008. How can I assess group work? https://www.cmu.edu/teaching/ designteach/ design/instructionalstrategies/ groupprojects/ assess.html. (2008). [Online; accessed 16-10-2016].

2. T. Staubitz, D. Petrick, M. Bauer, J. Renz, and C. Meinel. 2016. Improving the Peer Assessment Experience on MOOC Platforms. In *Proceedings of the Third (2016) ACM Conference on Learning Scale (LS '16)*. ACM, New York, NY, USA, 389–398.

3. T. Staubitz, T. Pfeiffer, J. Renz, C. Willems, and C. Meinel. 2015. Collaborative Learning in a MOOC Environment. In *Proceedings of the 8th International Conference of Education, Research and Innovation (ICERI '15)*. IATED, 8237–8246.

4. Z. Zheng, T. Vogelsang, and N. Pinkwart. 2015. The Impact of Small Learning Group Composition on Student Engagement and Success in a MOOC. In *Proceedings of the 8th International Conference on Educational Data Mining (EDM 2015)*. Madrid, Spain, 500–503.

Incorporating Rich Features into Deep Knowledge Tracing

Liang Zhang
Worcester Polytechnic
Institute
Worcester, MA 01609 USA
lzhang6@wpi.edu

Xiaolu Xiong
Worcester Polytechnic
Institute
Worcester, MA 01609 USA
xxiong@wpi.edu

Siyuan Zhao
Worcester Polytechnic
Institute
Worcester, MA 01609 USA
szhao@wpi.edu

Anthony Botelho
Worcester Polytechnic
Institute
Worcester, MA 01609 USA
abotelho@wpi.edu

Neil T. Heffernan
Worcester Polytechnic
Institute
Worcester, MA 01609 USA
nth@wpi.edu

ABSTRACT

The desire to follow student learning within intelligent tutoring systems in near real time has led to the development of several models anticipating the correctness of the next item as students work through an assignment. Such models have included Bayesian Knowledge Tracing (BKT), Performance Factors Analysis (PFA), and more recently with developments in deep learning, Deep Knowledge Tracing (DKT). This DKT model, based on the use of a recurrent neural network, exhibited promising results. Thus far, however, the model has only considered the knowledge components of the problems and correctness as input, neglecting the breadth of other features collected by computer-based learning platforms. This work seeks to improve upon the DKT model by incorporating more features at the problem-level. With this higher dimensional input, an adaption to the original DKT model structure is also proposed, incorporating an auto-encoder network layer to convert the input into a low dimensional feature vector to reduce both the resource requirement and time needed to train. Experiment results show that our adapted DKT model, observing more combinations of features, can effectively improve accuracy.

ACM Classification Keywords

H.5.m Information interfaces and presentation: Miscellaneous

Author Keywords

Knowledge Tracing, Deep Learning, Deep Knowledge Tracing (DKT), Recurrent Neural Networks (RNN), Auto Encoder

1. INTRODUCTION

Models that attempt to follow the progression of student learning often represent student knowledge as a latent variable. As

students work on new problems, these models update their estimates of student knowledge based on the correctness of responses. The problem emerges to be time series prediction, as student performance on previous items is indicative of future performance. Models then use the series of questions a student has attempted previously and the correctness of each question to predict the student's performance on a new problem.

Two well-known models, Bayesian Knowledge tracing (BKT) [2] and performance factor analysis (PFA) [5] have been widely explored due to their ability to capture this progression of knowledge with reliable accuracy. Both of these models, exhibiting success in terms of predictive accuracy, use differing algorithms to estimate student knowledge. BKT uses a Bayesian network to learn four parameters per knowledge component, or skill, while the PFA model uses a logistic regression over aggregated performance to determine performance for each skill.

Deep learning is an emerging approach which has proved to yield promising results in a range of areas including pattern recognition, natural language processing and image classification. The *deep* aspect of deep learning refers to the multiple levels of transformation that occur between input nodes and output nodes; these levels are usually referred to as layers, with each layer consisting of numerous nodes. The hidden nodes are used to extract high level features from previous layers and pass that information on to the next layer. However, the features extracted by deep learning are largely uninterpretable due to the complexity. This complexity makes it infeasible to explain the meaning behind every parameter learned by the model, unlike BKT and PFA which attempt to incorporate interpretability with its estimates.

Many deep learning algorithms like Recurrent Neural Network (RNN) and Convolutional Neural Networks (CNN) have been proposed in recent years to benefit machine learning systems with complex, yet more accurate representative models. Such an attempt in the field of learning analytics is that of Deep Knowledge Tracing (DKT) [6]. Building from the promising results of that model, this work seeks to make better use of the complex nature of deep learning models to incorporate more features to improve predictive accuracy. We also explore how other deep learning structures can help reduce these high dimensional inputs into smaller representative feature vectors.

2. DEEP LEARNING IN EDUCATION

Deep knowledge tracing (DKT), introduced in paper [6], applies a RNN for this educational data mining task of following the progression of student knowledge. Similar to BKT, this adaptation observes knowledge at both the skill level, observing which knowledge component is involved in the task, and the problem level, observing correctness of each problem. The input layer of the DKT model is described as an exercise-performance pair of a student. In other words, the skill and correctness of each item is used to predict the correctness of the next item, given that problem's skill.

The DKT algorithm uses a RNN to represent latent knowledge state, along with its temporal dynamics. As a student progresses through an assignment, it attempts to utilize information from previous timesteps, or problems, to make better inferences regarding future performance. Specifically, the DKT model implements a popular variant of RNN, Long Short-Term Memory (LSTM), that employs cell states and three *gates* to determine how much information to remember from previous timesteps and also how to combine that memory with information from the current timestep.

Due to the recency of the DKT model, it is not as deeply researched as other established methods. We believe that DKT is a promising approach due to its comparable performance, and with the emergence of new neural network optimization algorithms, the structure has space for improvement. Thus far, only question (or skill) and correctness are considered as input to the model, but the neural network can easily consider more features. In this paper, we explore the inclusion of more features to improve the predictive accuracy of the model. In addition to these added features, we explore the usage of an Undercomplete Auto Encoder that incorporates a small central layer to convert high dimensional data to low dimensional representative encodings in order to increase the feasibility of implementing feature vectors of larger dimensionalities.

3. IMPROVING DKT WITH MORE FEATURES

Intelligent tutoring systems (ITS) often collect numerous features as students work, including information pertaining to problems, instructional aid, and time spent on individual tasks. Models and algorithms that make use of these additional information have been proposed. For example, students response time, hint request and number of attempts are added to make better student model [3]. In this paper, we do something similar using these extra features. In our experiment, students response time, attempt number, and first action are selected for consideration as these are recorded by almost all such learning platforms. All input information is converted into a sequence of fixed-length input vectors in the RNN model, representing problem-level covariates while working through a possible multitude of assignments.

3.1 Feature process

Feature engineering plays a vital role in representing features effectively. The goal of this process, as it pertains to this

work and coincides with how input is represented in the DKT model, is to convert the features to categorical data to simplify the input without losing much information. This process is described briefly for each considered feature as follows:

- *Exercise tag* exhibits differing representations described by either a numeric skill id or the name of the knowledge component in different dataset. Regardless of representation in the data, this is strictly categorical and is handled as such.

- *Correctness* is represented as a binary value where 1 indicates correctness and 0 represents an incorrect response.

- *First Response Time* is z-scored within skill and discretized based on its relationship with correctness as shown in Figure 1.

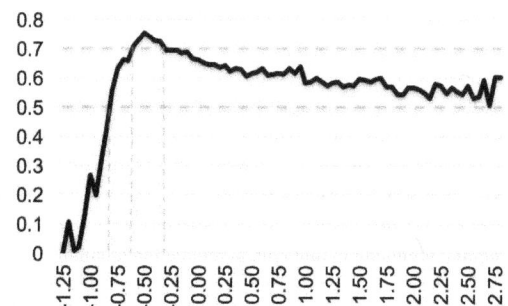

Figure 1. ASSISTments 2009 dataset z-scored time feature (*X axis*) and problem correctness (*Y axis*). Two reference lines of correctness, 50% and 70%, are selected to form the discretized boundaries.

- *Attempt count* is the number of attempts needed to correctly answer each item and are discretized as $[0, 1, other]$ in ASSISTments and $[== 1, 1 < and <= 5, > 5, other]$ in Open Learning Initiative as described further in a later section.

- *First action* is strictly categorical, representing if a student makes an attempt or requests help within the system as a first action.

After converting to categorical data, features are represented as a sparse vector by a one-hot encoding. These form cross features, where, for example, correctness is expressed as two values (correct and incorrect) for each skill. The combination of some features into cross features can improve model accuracy. The cross features of exercise and correctness, as well as time and correctness are selected in our model. All the ecodeed features are concatenated to construct the input vector in Figure 2.

Using cross features leads to a rapid increase of the dimensionality of the input vector. RNNs are considerably more computationally expensive due to the comparatively larger number of parameters. For example, training a LSTM DKT model with 50 skills and 200 hidden nodes, which needs to learn 250,850 parameters, takes 3.5 minutes per epoch, equating to more than 14 hours when using a 5 fold cross validation run over 50 epochs. To this extent, the network structure of DKT may benefit from reduced dimensionality, particularly if this can be achieved without sacrificing performance. Auto Encoder[4] is one such approach to this problem. It is a multilayer neural network with a small central layer that can convert

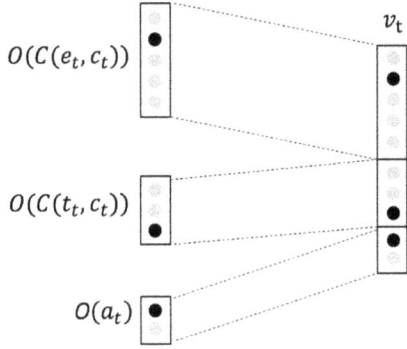

Figure 2. Concatenated encoded features to input layer

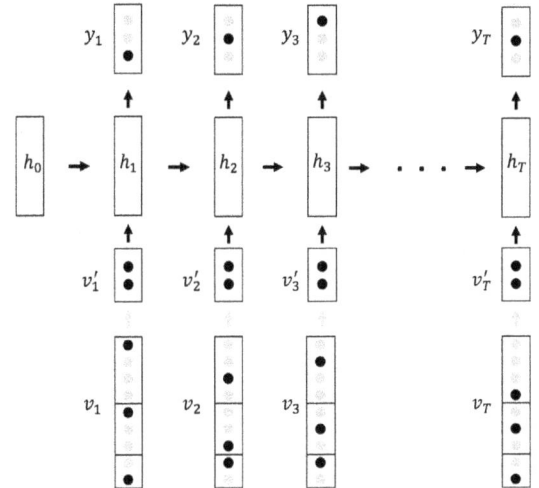

Figure 4. New DKT LSTM Model to incorporate more featuers with fixed Auto Encoder weights

high dimensional data to low dimensional representative encodings that can be used to reconstruct the high dimensional input vectors; in this way dimensionality is reduced without the loss of too much important information.3 Once trained, the output layer can be removed, and the hidden layer can connect to another network layer. Auto Encoder may be stacked in this way but each layer must be trained one at a time. Like other neural network, the gradient descent method is used to train the weight values of the parameters. In our experiment, the dimension is reduced to a half of the input size.

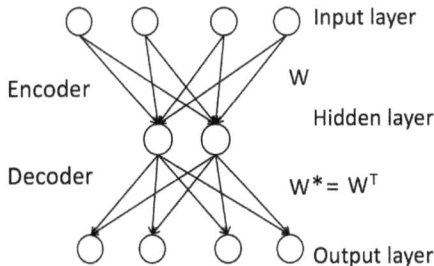

Figure 3. Representation of an Auto Encoder that reconstructs its input layer from a hidden layer of smaller dimensionality.

3.2 Model

[1] The input vector is constructed by concatenating one-hot encodings for separate features as illustrated in Figure 2, where v_t represents the resulting input vector of each student exercise. e_t refers to the exercise tag, while c_t refers to correctness, and t_t represents time.

$$C(e_t, c_t) = e_t + (max(e) + 1) * c_t \qquad (1)$$

$$v_t = O(C(e_t, c_t)) \frown O(C(t_t, c_t)) \frown O(t_t) \qquad (2)$$

$$v'_t = tanh(W_{ae} * v_t + b_{ae}) \qquad (3)$$

$C()$ is the cross feature, $O()$ is the one-hot encoder format, and the $\frown$ operator is used to denote concatenation. In Equation 1, 1 is added to represent the unincluded exercise. Figure 4 depicts the resulting model representation utilizing an Encoder layer to support the added features. v'_t represents the feature vector extracted by Auto Encoder according to Equation 3.

The gray arrows mean that weights between the two layers are held constant, meaning the encoder weights are trained separately in advance. h_t represents the LSTM hidden nodes while y_t represents output layers nodes. The performance of every exercise is predicted but just one is supervised because only one label exists at each time step. We use a loss function of binary cross entropy. Only one LSTM layer with 200 hidden nodes is used and a dropout probability of 0.4 is applied during training.

4. DATASETS

ASSISTments and Open Learning Initiative (OLI) are computer-based learning platforms which embed practice and assessment throughout the learning process. Table 1 show running hyperparamters and information on the two data sets.

	ASSISTments 2009-2010	OLI Statics F2011
Student	3,866	332
Skill	124	82
Record	303k	257k
TimeStep	1,218	1,500
BatchSize	30	10
Epoch	40	40

Table 1. ASSISTments 2009-2010 and Statics 2011 dataset statistics and running hyper parameter setting

ASSISTments 2009-2010[2] dataset was gathered from mastery-based, skill builder problem sets. Three issues discovered [7] had unintentionally inflated the performance of DKT in initial reported results, so the updated version is utilized here.

[1] https://github.com/lzhang6/DKT-extension

[2] https://sites.google.com/site/assistmentsdata/home/assistment-2009-2010-data/skill-builder-data-2009-2010

Model	Auto Encoder	ASSISTments		OLI Statics	
		AUC(%)	R^2	*AUC(%)*	R^2
Baseline: skill/correct	No	83.1 ± 0.6	0.324 ± 0.012	70.6 ± 0.7	0.105 ± 0.009
Baseline⌒time/correct	No	$\mathbf{85.8} \pm 0.7$	$\mathbf{0.391} \pm 0.015$	$\mathbf{73.1} \pm 0.5$	$\mathbf{0.135} \pm 0.010$
Baseline⌒time/correct	Yes	86.7 ± 0.4	0.410 ± 0.008	73.5 ± 0.9	0.142 ± 0.012
Baseline⌒time/correct⌒time⌒action⌒attempt	No	86.1 ± 0.4	0.398 ± 0.011	73.2 ± 0.5	0.140 ± 0.011
Baseline⌒time/correct⌒time⌒action⌒attempt	Yes	86.7 ± 0.2	0.411 ± 0.005	74.0 ± 0.5	0.148 ± 0.009
Baseline⌒time/correct⌒time/skill⌒time⌒action⌒attempt	Yes	$\mathbf{86.7} \pm 0.5$	$\mathbf{0.412} \pm 0.012$	$\mathbf{74.0} \pm 0.9$	$\mathbf{0.147} \pm 0.016$

Table 2. Test Result

OLI Statics F2011[3] dataset was from a college-level engineering statics course in OLI. The exercise tag is a numerated knowledge component derived from the text description.

Since it is a time-series algorithm, students whose records contain less than 2 time steps are not considered.

5. RESULTS

We use a 5-fold student level cross validation and the result is evaluated by *AUC* and square of Pearson correlation (R^2). Many possible feature combinations exist, but only a select few are explored here.

On both datasets in Table 2, models with incorporated features outperform the original DKT model. In the ASSISTments 2009 dataset, *AUC* value is improved to 85.8 from 83.1 and R^2 value increases to 0.391 from 0.342 after adding the cross feature of skill and correctness. In the Statics 2011 dataset, the *AUC* value increases to 73.1 from 70.6 and R^2 value is from 0.105 to 0.135 if only add cross feature of skill and correctness. Actually, if only incorporating cross feature of skill and correctness, the dimension of input layer dimension just increases $8, 4(time) * 2(correctness)$ so that it almost has smiliar running efficiency as original DKT model. However, it exhibits only a marginal increase to this upon adding time, first action, and attempt count into the input vectors.

The adoption of Auto Encoder when compared to models using the same features also shows increased performance, supporting its usage for reducing dimensionality. In the ASSISTments 2009 dataset, *AUC* value is improved to to 86.7 from 85.8 and R^2 value increases from 0.391 to 0.410. While in OLI Statics dataset, *AUC* value is from 73.1 to 73.5 while R^2 value is from 0.135 to 0.142. In our analyses, the model incorporating all features in the last record in Table 2 was not even feasible without the use of this auto encoder, deeming it necessary to use when given large dimensional inputs.

6. DISCUSSION

Extending this model encompasses several potential directions to pursue. One such direction can explore even more student features like class-level features and school-level features, engineered in different manners, such as tokening the words of knowledge components for different exercise representations. Similarly, a wide and deep approach can be explored in how the features are represented within model training. The numerical data like time and hint usage can also be revisited

in future work. Another direction is the usage of differnet dimensionality reduction methods like Principal Component Analysis (PCA) and Locally Linear Embedding (LLE), or different Auto Encoder methods, like adding noise, stacking layers or using RBM for initial weights. Because of flexible structure of deep learning, another research direction is to use similar RNN model structures to multi-task predictions in education data mining such as wheel spinning [1], student dropout, or hint usage.

ACKNOWLEDGMENTS

We acknowledge funding from multiple NSF grants (ACI-1440753, DRL-1252297, DRL-1109483, DRL-1316736 & DRL-1031398), the U.S. Department of Education (IES R305A120125 & R305C100024 and GAANN), the ONR, and the Gates Foundation.

REFERENCES

1. J. E. Beck and Y. Gong. 2013. Wheel-spinning: Students who fail to master a skill. In *International Conference on Artificial Intelligence in Education*. Springer, 431–440.

2. A. T. Corbett and J. R. Anderson. 1994. Knowledge tracing: Modeling the acquisition of procedural knowledge. *User Modeling and User-Adapted Interaction* 4, 4 (1994), 253–278.

3. M. Feng, N.T. Heffernan, and K. R. Koedinger. 2009. Addressing the assessment challenge with an online system that tutors as it assesses. *User Modeling and User-Adapted Interaction* 19, 3 (2009), 243–266.

4. G. E. Hinton and R. R. Salakhutdinov. 2006. Reducing the dimensionality of data with neural networks. *Science* 313, 5786 (2006), 504–507.

5. P.I. PAVLIK JRa, H. Cen, and K. R. Koedinger. 2009. Performance Factors Analysis–A New Alternative to Knowledge Tracing. *Online Submission* (2009).

6. C. Piech, J. Bassen, J. Huang, M. Sahami S. Ganguli, L. Guibas, and J. Sohl-Dickstein. 2015. Deep knowledge tracing. In *Advances in Neural Information Processing Systems*. 505–513.

7. X. Xiong, S. Zhao, E.G. VanInwege, and J. E. Beck. 2016. Going deeper with deep knowledge tracing. In *Proceedings of the 9th International Conference on Educational Data Mining (EDM 2016)*. 545–550.

---

[3]https://pslcdatashop.web.cmu.edu/Project?id=48

Formal Forum Triage: Towards the Strategic Selection of Responses to Student Discussion Forums

Nickolas Falkner, Claudia Szabo, and Katrina Falkner
The University of Adelaide
{nickolas.falkner,claudia.szabo,katrina.falkner}@adelaide.edu.au

ABSTRACT
It can be difficult for educators with limited resources to decide which queries need immediate attention when a high volume of questions arises on the discussion forum. This becomes increasingly complex as the educator aims to obtain the best outcome across all threads in a timely fashion. Existing approaches to automated forum analysis provide a useful grouping of messages and identify common discussions, but require additional attention towards effective intervention. Research has shown that the timing of messages relative to associated deadlines is a key indicator of priority. In this paper, we propose the formal representation of events within a discussion forum to facilitate the definition of potential and existing intervention strategies. We enhance forum events with information about teaching activities, such as assignment deadlines, and discuss intervention strategies.

INTRODUCTION
Forums are a vital resource if educators wish to know when to intervene to address misconceptions, concerns, and weaknesses in learning. As student forums are increasing in size in the context of Massive Open Online Courses (MOOC) [1], where tens of thousands of students contribute to a similar scale of discussions, the effort required for a successful, on-time, educational intervention increases dramatically [11]. There is a need for automated approaches that facilitate educators in understanding when, where, and how to intervene effectively.

Successful interventions to improve the educational experience and outcome, rely on good on-line discussion forum data, comprised of the collection of textual student posts, and other context information, such as forum structure. However, existing text-based analysis approaches are computationally intensive and often require initial manual classification [5, 9, 12, 16]. Further, they do not provide an order in which the educator could act to address student issues in the most timely or pedagogically effective manner.

Deep analysis of the content of a forum can reveal a great deal about student levels of engagement, the roles that students are playing in the discussion, and how students feel about the course in terms of sentiment analysis [13]. Such detailed analysis, although very useful, is often beyond the resources of educators [3] or is carried out after the completion of the course, when no intervention can be undertaken [10]. Many mechanisms and tools exist for the automated classification of discussion contents at a range of scales [5, 9, 10, 12, 16], but have limits in their application, as they are often restricted to a specific domain or course context and require manual assistance.

Approaches such as sentiment analysis [15] and social network analysis [18] provide useful information, in that they assist educators in determining relationships between forum participants, and the tone, or emotion, expressed in these discussions but can scale poorly.

There is a need for representation that allows for the discussion of *strategic approaches* to intervening in and responding to discussions. Traditional approaches to the analysis of social media discussions do not necessarily work here because individual forum discussions implicitly integrate within the overall course discussion.

RELATED WORK
Collaborative learning, where learners work jointly to construct understanding, is a well-studied field [3] and practitioners now seek those methods and approaches to collaborative learning that lead to the best outcomes. The discussion conducted in a collaborative space will be of the most benefit if it is sustained, has broad participation and is focused on course topics.

The primary advantage of an on-line forum is the ability to carry out *asynchronous* exchanges, when both parties have the time and focus to communicate effectively [17]. Instructor responses must, however, go beyond mere immediacy or platitude if these interventions are to be seen as valuable by students. Additionally, students must value the interaction if there is to be the potential to change student behaviour or support desirable practice. The type of contribution makes a difference: well-chosen anchoring statements can serve as prompts and guides [6]. The issue is the construction of interventions and the timeline of their implementation [6].

Data-mining of discussion forums is an active and promising area of research, however it requires the instructor to interpret the extracted information [4], and thus the requirement to form an intervention strategy still rests firmly with the instructor. Moreover, data-mining allows us to expose and analyse the process but it does not automatically tell us how to proceed. Existing text-based techniques for automated analysis of discussion forum content include coarse-grained categorisation of posts (e.g. pedagogy, social, technical), dialog act classification of posts for activities (brainstorming, reacting, organising)[19] or structural type (question, answer, opinion) and fine-grained topic analysis, designed to facilitate both educators and learners in navigating discussion forum content at-scale. Stump *et al.* [20] introduce a coding framework to manually classify discussion posts into eight categories such as content, other course work, and social/affective classifications. Ezen-Can *et al.* [5] analyse discussion forum data within a single MOOC, incorporating clustering techniques to group each post into clusters (e.g. agreement, personal viewpoints, and questions and disagreements) and topic modeling techniques (i.e. LDA) to obtain a deeper understanding of the post.

Existing work has sought to understand how discussion threads grow and wither, with simulation models [7] showing that, in order to have a sustained learning community, participants must have a reason to participate that is valuable within their personal temporal window. Instrumentality, the capacity to associate the completion of tasks now with successful achievement of goals in the future, strongly influences whether a participant will stay task-focused and thus participate [8]. These studies further reinforce the role of the instructor, as summarisation, response, probing, prompting and providing feedback to participants are essential components in keeping a forum active. However, the amount and timing of interventions, and the optimum use of limited instructor resources remain open questions.

EXAMPLE

Ideally, we wish to construct a total order of our on-line student queries, for a given moment, to clearly identify the post that we should respond to first. Then, having addressed that post, we should have a clear idea of the next intervention. In the absence of formal structure, we cannot embed this total order into a computational frame and thus we have to apply the mechanisms manually. This move away from a more objective ranking is prone to error as we may start to confuse active threads with important threads, e.g., a simple time analysis might reveal that we have weeks to respond to the 'busy' thread but only hours or days to make a difference to a much quieter thread.

We illustrate this with a sample third year course's forum evolution over a semester from the University of X. The on-line discussion augmented traditional face-to-face learning and comprised of 945 individual posts. The lecturer took an active role in the course, contributing 105 of these posts. The dataset was analysed for time of post, proximity to the associated landmark (assignment deadline) for a given post, word count per post, and post density related to time.

Student activity increases dramatically as the deadline approaches, but the lecturer activity increases only slightly. This is understandable as the course staff, in this case, is a single person with limited scaling ability.

Further complicating matters, the average word count for student posts in this course is 66 words, with the mean lecturer response being 50 words. Thus, the lecturer will take approximately three minutes to read and respond to a post. (We assume 200 WPM for reading English and 25 WPM for composing responses that require thought, after [14].)

Student effort increases as deadlines approach [8] and the resources of the teaching staff do not expand to meet this. To illustrate the problem, there are four separate occasions in this course where large blocks of messages arrive at a rate faster than the lecturer can read them, across a range of topics and deadlines.

The above analysis was not performed for a large course as there are fewer than 100 students, with only half active on the forums. Yet we have clearly shown resource starvation that requires a reliable strategy for classification which will not overwhelm the lecturer. The production rate for this course was 945 messages over 14 weeks, an average rate of 68 messages per week. We note the expected increase in activity as the deadline approaches but also observed other behaviours that are less expected, such as a high volume of posts that are 20-60 days late.

REPRESENTING FORUM STRUCTURE

The first step in providing an ordering mechanism for forum discussion is identifying and representing the aspects of forum structure that contribute to it. The overall context of a course discussion forum is one where questions may be asked on a given topic. For ease of management and to reduce cognitive load and decision making overheads, we often provide a thread-based mechanism where students can start a new *thread of discussion* for each problem that they face. These discussion threads are usually presented first-to-last (in time order) or by order of reply to given posts (threaded).

We have constructed the decision problem for a given set of events as "Should the educator intervene" to capture the key decision that has to be made in a limited resource environment. We assume that once the decision to intervene has been established potentially through an automated decision-making tool, contextual information from the forum will allow the educator to determine the appropriate action.

We define a decision rule, r, as a function from the set of complete sequences E^* to the decision set $\{0, 1\}$, where 0 represents no intervention ("NO: Do not intervene")

E	Landmark	Text	User	Time
1	A1-1	I think I understand...	1612	10:21PM
2	A1-1	Refer here: http://f...	5542	10:22PM
3	A1-1	tl.hd to be exact.	5542	10:23PM
4	A1-2	To do the list the r...	1612	10:39PM
5	L1-1	Actually, I just tes...	5542	10:39PM
6	A1-3	\<p>Hi,\</p>\<p>If yo...	3582	11:28PM
7	A1-2	???? must be whateve...	2747	11:29PM
8	A1-2	yeah the '????' shou...	1612	11:31PM
9	L1-2	Thanks guys all good...	2553	11:33PM

Table 1. Focus events in Case Study 1

and 1 represents an intervention ("YES: Intervene"):
$$r : E^* \to \{0, 1\}$$

Thus, $r(E_1) + r(E_2) = r(E_1 + E_2), \forall E_1, E_2 \in E^*$, where $+$ refers to the addition of all events from E_2 to E_1, and their subsequent ordering based on timestamps.

A partial event sequence is the key motivator of our scenario, where a number of events have arrived at the educator as the students are posting, and the decision problem must decide on intervention immediately, rather than wait for the termination of the course or the main timeout of the thread. The result of the decision problem is provided by a number of strategies.The temporal order of arrival is useful information but is not automatically the order in which we should handle the events. The final ordering of events should be in a sequence where the educator can process the most posts effectively.

Any instructor working with students is faced with an optimisation problem where finite resources are to be distributed between students fairly and equitably. Within the context of on-line discussion fora, we assume that a *resource unit* is the *average* amount of time or attention required to conduct a single effective student intervention activity within the on-line space. There are a number of strategies that can be employed here, from a naive 'respond to all' to a 'respond to nothing', with many alternatives between them. The choice of response strategy becomes more important as resources become more limited but a strategic approach requires us to be objective and methodical in our analysis of fora, if we are to choose the correct strategy for a situation.

Our observations of forum data show that the urgency of escalation is dependent upon how close an escalation event is to a critical time point such as an assignment deadline, in agreement with the landmarks mentioned in [2]. We extend the timestamp model of events to include landmarks. This motivates an "escalation focus" strategy, where resources are prioritised to escalated events.

From student data collected previously, we focus on the arrival of 17 events, with nine shown in Table 1, and will illustrate another strategy, an ordered immediate intervention model, where priority is associated with proximity to course landmarks. Because of the arrival time, these events are unlikely to be a strictly sequential de-

velopment of one topic, as there is not enough time for students to be reading and writing responses. These events are parallel developments inside a topic. The first 3 events (E1, E2, and E3) are all in a topic associated with Assignment 1 (A1-1), and the next event (E4) is on a separate topic, also within Assignment 1 (A1-2). Event E5 arrives less than a minute later, and is associated with the landmark for Lecture 1 (L1-1). E5 was generated by the author of E1 but is on a different topic, with a different landmark.

When E1 arrives, we would process it if resources were available and similar for E2 and E3. However, E2 and E3 arrive inside E1's processing window. E3 is an follow-up to E1, from another student, and is thus an escalating event (and thus in σ_ξ and this raises its priority. The order of processing is now E1, E3, E2.

E4 arrives after the processing window has (temporarily) cleared and refers to a topic that was last discussed 90 minutes earlier. E5 arrives a second later. E5's identified landmark shows it as being over two weeks late for the deadline. If we define E5 as a necro-thread, this sudden interest in a long sleeping thread would reverse the order of processing to E5, E4.

Looking further along in this chain of events, four more events E6, E7, E8, and E9 arrive over five minutes. E6 is a new topic for Assignment 1 (A1-3), E7 and E8 are related to a previous Assignment 1 topic (A1-2) and E9 refers to the same delayed Lecture thread but is a different question (L1-2). If we are treating awakening dormant threads as an intervention opportunity, our order would be E6, E9, E7, and E8. If necro-threads are last to be addressed, then the order would remain E6, E7, E8 and E9 but would be, by our definition, the most efficient processing order that happens to be in the same time order. As noted in the mathematical underpinnings for this, the time at which we observe the events can make a difference. If the lecturer was still answering E4 when events E7 and E8 arrive, the most efficient order would potentially be E4, E5, E9, E7, E8 and E9 if we are prioritising awakened threads, or E4, E7, E8, E6, E5 and E9 otherwise. By implementing the formalism, this ordering can take place during the processing time for the first event and the movement to process the second.

CONCLUSION

Targeted intervention through the automated analysis of discussion forums has the potential to drastically reduce instructors' load, especially under resource constraints. In this paper, we propose the formal representation of discussion forum events as a basis for defining several intervention strategies. We advance primitive strategies that are formalisations of current practice, but also propose the use of course and instructor information in extended intervention models. Our formal approach can be easily automated as it relies heavily on structural forum event information, which can be augmented with more resource-intensive and complex techniques such as sentiment analysis or social network analysis. Our strategies also provide a clear outcome for educators, in the form of YES/NO answers describing whether interventions or summaries are needed for a particular thread or forum respectively. This allows a resource-constrained instructor to focus on learning and teaching outcomes, and not on forum mechanics. But it also allows us to look backwards at our decisions and be able to say that, with the same knowledge and at the same time, we made the best decision that we could. Our work represents a first step towards automated intervention analysis, with several immediate extensions. Firstly, while our strategies were derived from the manual analysis of existing discussion forums, the analysis needs to be extended with several small and large-scale case studies of other educational fora, employing our prototype implementation. Secondly, more complex strategies than the proposed will require the classification of events beyond our proposed categories, and into the defined specific types. Finally, the model can be used to estimate the resources required to support a pre-determined level of intervention, combined with existing work in queueing theory.

REFERENCES

1. S. Bayne and J. Ross. The pedagogy of the massive open online course: the uk views. *The Higher Education Academy*, 2014.

2. S. Chaturvedi, D. Goldwasser, and H. Daumé. Predicting instructor's intervention in mooc forums. In *Proceedings of the Annual Meeting of the Association for Computational Linguistics*, pages 1501–1511, 2014.

3. B. De Wever, H. Van Keer, T. Schellens, and M. Valcke. Structuring asynchronous discussion groups: Comparing scripting by assigning roles with regulation by cross-age peer tutors. *Learning and Instruction*, 20(5):349 – 360, 2010.

4. L. P. Dringus and T. Ellis. Using data mining as a strategy for assessing asynchronous discussion forums. *Computers & Education*, 45(1):141–160, 2005.

5. A. Ezen-Can, K. E. Boyer, S. Kellogg, and S. Booth. Unsupervised modelling for understanding mooc discussion forums: a learning analytics approach. In *Proceedings of the Conference on Learning Analytics and Knowledge*, pages 146–150, 2015.

6. M. Guzdial and J. Turns. Effective discussion through a computer-mediated anchored forum. *The journal of the learning sciences*, 9(4):437–469, 2000.

7. J. Hewitt. Toward an understanding of how threads die in asynchronous computer conferences. *The journal of the learning sciences*, 14(4):567–589, 2005.

8. J. Husman, E. McCann, and H. M. Crowson. Volitional strategies and future time perspective: embracing the complexity of dynamic interactions.

International Journal of Educational Research, 33(7):777–799, 2000.

9. S. Joksimović, V. Kavonavić, J. Javonović, A. Zouaq, D. Gašević, and M. Hatala. What do cmooc participants talk about in social media?: a topic analysis of discourse in a cmooc. In *Proceedings of the Fifth International Conference on Learning Analytics and Knowledge*, pages 156–165, 2015.

10. R. F. Kizilcec, C. Piech, and E. Schneider. Deconstructing disengagement: Analyzing learner subpopulations in massive open online courses. In *Proc. of the International Conference on Learning Analytics and Knowledge*, pages 170–179, 2013.

11. R. Kop. The challenges to connectivist learning in open online networks: Learning experiences during a massive open online course. *International Review of Research in Open and Distance Learning*, 12(3):19–38, 2011.

12. A. Liddo, S. Shum, I. Quinto, M. Bachler, and Cannavacciuolo. Discourse-centric learning analytics. In *Proceedings of the 1st International Conference on Learning Analytics and Knowledge*, pages 23–33, 2011.

13. R. M. Marra, J. L. Moore, and A. K. Klimczak. Content analysis of online discussion forums: A comparative analysis of protocols. *Educational Technology Research and Development*, 52(2):23–40, 2004.

14. J. M. Noyes and K. J. Garland. Computer-vs. paper-based tasks: Are they equivalent? *Ergonomics*, 51(9):1352–1375, 2008.

15. B. Pang and L. Lee. Opinion mining and sentiment analysis. *Foundations and Trends in Information Retrieval*, 2(1-2):1–135, Jan. 2008.

16. J. Reich, D. Tingley, J. Leder-Luis, M. E. Roberts, and B. M. Stewart. Computer assisted reading and discovery for student generated text in massive open online courses. *Journal of Learning Analytics*, 2(1), 2015.

17. M. H. Rossman. Successful online teaching using an asynchronous learner discussion forum. *Journal of Asynchronous Learning Networks*, 3(2):91–97, 1999.

18. R. F. Simon Buckingham Shum. Social learning analytics. *Journal of Educational Technology & Society*, 15(3):3–26, 2012.

19. E. K. Sorensen and E. S. Takle. Collaborative knowledge building in web-based learning: Assessing the quality of dialogue. 2001.

20. G. S. Stump, J. DeBoer, J. Whittinghill, and L. Breslow. Development of a framework to classify mooc discussion forum posts: Methodology and challenges. In *Proceedings of the NIPS Workshop on Data Driven Education*, 2013.

A Novel Self-Paced Model for Teaching Programming

Jeff Offutt, Paul Ammann, Kinga Dobolyi, Chris Kauffmann, Jaime Lester,
Upsorn Praphamontripong, Huzefa Rangwala, Sanjeev Setia, Pearl Wang,
and Liz White

George Mason University, Fairfax VA, USA

{offutt,pammann,kdobolyi,jlester2,uprapham,setia,pwang,white}@gmu.edu {kauffman,rangwala}@cs.gmu.edu

ABSTRACT

The Self-Paced Learning Increases Retention and Capacity (SPARC) project is responding to the well-documented surge in CS enrollment by creating a self-paced learning environment that blends online learning, automated assessment, collaborative practice, and peer-supported learning. SPARC delivers educational material online, encourages students to practice programming in groups, frees them to learn material at their own pace, and allows them to demonstrate proficiency at any time. This model contrasts with traditional course offerings, which impose a single schedule of due dates and exams for all students. SPARC allows students to complete courses faster or slower at a pace tailored to the individual, thereby allowing universities to teach more students with the same or fewer resources. This paper describes the goals and elements of the SPARC model as applied to CS1. We present results so far and discuss the future of the project.

ACM Classification Keywords

K.3.2 Computer and Information Science Education: Computer science education

Author Keywords

Scaling CS1; Active learning; Gender and diversity; Self-pacing; Online learning; Collaboration; Peer learning

1. INTRODUCTION

This paper introduces a project that is attempting to significantly scale our ability to teach introductory programming to more students with the same or fewer resources by re-inventing the way we teach CS1 (CS 112 at George Mason). In addition to responding to the recent enrollment surge [?] by increasing the capacity of our CS1 courses, we have additional goals of retaining more students, increasing learning with less effort, and reducing or eliminating cheating. The Self-Paced Learning Increases Retention and Capacity (SPARC[1]) project blends self-pacing, separation of practice and assessment, collaborative and peer learning, automated grading, and flipped classrooms to create a more efficient and effective way to teach introductory computer science.

---

[1] http://sparc.cs.gmu.edu/

L@S'17, April 20-21, 2017, Cambridge, MA, USA

© 2017 Copyright held by the owner/author(s). Publication rights licensed to ACM. ISBN ???.

DOI: ???

George Mason University is a 34,000-student state-supported university. As at many universities, our introductory computing courses are under great stress. Explosive enrollment growth has doubled our undergraduate enrollment in the last five years, with our introductory classes tripling since 2012. Mason also accepts significant numbers of transfer students, mostly from community colleges, including 80 transfer CS majors in fall 2016. Although great news for the labor shortage in the software industry, this dramatic national enrollment increase puts enormous stress on universities in a time of declining state funding.

The increase in enrollment in CS1 and CS2 has not been matched by increased TA support, so current TAs are overloaded. Some TAs report spending as much as 50% more hours per week than they are officially required to work. Furthermore, there is a ripple effect—more TAs are being pulled into our introductory classes every semester, leaving less support for upper-level and graduate courses.

A particular concern is when students fail. From fall 2009 through summer 2015, 37.7% of our students failed CS1 at least once. We consider a failure to be a C- or below, since students must have a C or better to take the follow-on course (CS2). This includes most students who are accused of plagiarism. National studies report that average six-year graduation rates across higher-education institutions is only 59% and have remained relatively stable over the last 15 years [?]. Requiring students to repeat classes, or worse, leave college without graduating, has high human and monetary costs. It can even deprive students of the economic benefits of a college degree, which can exceed $1 million lifetime and even higher in STEM fields [?].

In a pure economic sense, failing students are also expensive to the system as they consume extra resources. If they change majors, leave the university, or otherwise do not re-take the course, then the resources they used when taking the course are lost with little benefit. If they repeat the course, then they consume course resources twice. Worse, most students who fail learned part of the course material the first time, so they are in effect required to learn that material twice, at a cost to both students and the university.

Computer Science majors at our university are a diverse group comprised in fall 2015 of 46% European-Americans and 26% Asian-Americans. Several other ethnicities constitute the remainder. Although the number of female students is increasing, only 15% of Mason's CS student majors are female. Worse, the percentage of female and minority students decreases through the four years of college.

Mason's CS1 instructors catch up to 20% of students cheating. Most are copying programs from classmates or other sources. This is only what we find—it is impossible to know how many cheating students are not caught. Cheating imposes huge costs. Although alerts are raised through automatic similarity checking programs, instructors still have to deal with each case individually, spending time and emotional energy. As enrollment continues to increase, these costs are becoming unsustainable.

Our novel educational pedagogy is being designed and implemented by a diverse team of faculty and students. The team includes CS1 instructors, an educational specialist, a programmer, our department chair and undergraduate studies associate chair, and very experienced instructors.

Challenges

The overarching goal of the project is to improve the capacity of CS1 while maintaining, and hopefully improving, educational quality. For the purposes of this paper, we define a *traditional* introductory CS course as CS1 that lasts for a term (usually semester or quarter); assigns for-credit programs that are done out-of-class with specific deadlines, while allowing little or no collaboration; have class sizes dictated by resources including classroom size and instructors; and uses most of the class time for instructor presentations. We present several challenges faced when using this traditional pedagogy, each of which leads to unnecessary use of student time and university resources.

Challenge 1: Using practice problems for assessment wastes instructor and TA resources. Students need a lot of programming practice, and they need to be assessed on their programming skills. Traditional pedagogy mix practice and assessments by giving students programming assignments that are used for practice as well as for grades (assessment). Many students learn programming best collaboratively, where students work together and help each other develop those skills [?]. Using the same assignments for both practice and assessment forces students to choose between working alone (which can lead to unnecessary struggles and less learning) and working together (cheating). The traditional pedagogy requires instructors and TAs to spend time searching for and penalizing such cheating. Besides wasting time, this inhibits student learning, and can discourage some from pursuing a CS major, especially under-represented minority and female students, who have been found to learn better with collaborative approaches [?, ?].

Challenge 2: Traditional introductory CS courses do not adequately support students with diverse learning styles. It is well known that students learn material at widely varying paces: some faster than the traditional curriculum and some slower. However, the traditional pedagogy requires all students to move at exactly the same pace. This puts slower learners at a severe disadvantage while making classes painfully slow and unchallenging for faster learners.

Challenge 3: Traditional introductory CS courses do not adequately support students with diverse backgrounds. Students start these courses with dramatically different amounts of computing knowledge, programming skills, and general academic knowledge. Because of prior preparation, fewer students every year need all the material in these courses. While many students test out of one or both courses completely, every year hundreds of moderately-prepared students are required to take an entire introductory course, even though they only need part of it. Repeating material is not only a poor use of their time, it is a poor use of university resources. In contrast, less prepared students rarely receive enough instruction, hands-on teaching, and skills practice to master the course material. These students often fail CS1, not because they cannot learn it, but because they cannot keep up. Neither student population is well served by the traditional *one-size-fits-none* approach to early CS education.

The traditional model of 3-hour, semester-long, lock-step courses forces students into boxes that all move at the same speed, regardless of how fast the students master course material. This has been called a "conveyor-belt" or "factory" education model [?, ?]. The conveyor-belt model often drives talented students away, and we suggest that it reduces capacity and throughput in introductory CS classes.

Pedagogical Elements

Our overall goal in this project is to address these challenges with an approach that reduces overall costs without sacrificing educational quality. This is accomplished through several major elements:

1. Separating individual assessment activities from collaborative practice activities (*challenge 1*).
2. Permitting students to demonstrate mastery of skills at any time (*challenge 2 & 3*).
3. Allowing students to pace their own learning, decreasing the need to retake courses (*challenge 2 & 3*).
4. Moving lectures online and using contact hours for interactive teaching (*challenge 2 & 3*).
5. Automating, as much as possible, evaluations of students' programming skills and computing knowledge (*challenge 1*).

2. THE SPARC MODEL

We are creating an innovative teaching model of **self-paced** introductory programming courses. Students periodically demonstrate competency with skills, similar to earning martial arts black-belts. While the self-pacing aspect of martial arts studies are important, we explicitly downplay competition to encourage retention and diversity. Flipped learning [?] has been used successfully in prior introductory CS courses. Our self-paced learning model adapts best practices from these different learning paradigms.

The rest of this section describes the major elements in the SPARC model for teaching.

Practice assignments: The courses is divided into 10 *stages*. For each stage, students are given many practice assignments to be done collaboratively, at their own pace, and using any resources desired. Students are not just **allowed**, they are **strongly encouraged** to help each other. Instructors, GTAs, and undergraduate TAs are in classrooms, hold office hours in public places, and are available through online discussion boards (we use *piazza.com*).

Assessments: Since our students learn in a less rigid schedule, we replace the traditional assessments such as out-of-class individual programs with anytime assessments. When ready, students appear in scheduled labs to attempt an assessment. Our automated system contains about 10 versions of each assessment (a mix of programming assignments and concept questions), and on each attempt, a student is presented with one version chosen randomly and without replacement. The assessments are supervised and use locked-down computers (no access to the web or other materials unless explicitly authorized). The results are graded immediately with automated tests and an automated coding style assessment. Students have up to five chances to pass each assessment, and are not penalized for repeated attempts. To pass the class, students must eventually pass all assessments with a score of 70% or higher.

Classroom activities: We free instructor resources to teach more students by using the *flipped classroom* model [?]. Most knowledge is delivered online through self-recorded lectures, tutorials, and other resources. Class time is primarily used to practice programming, which has three elements. (1) Students collaboratively practice programming skills with help from peers, the teacher, and TAs. When possible, we prefer rooms that have multiple whiteboards, movable chairs, and desks that facilitate group-work. (2) The teacher and TAs work directly with students to solve problems, answer questions, and offer advice. (3) Students work on material and programs related to their individual current stage, forming groups dynamically of students at the same stage.

Small group discussions are led by instructors and TAs. Discussions are often in the form of *mini-lectures* where the instructor or TAs explain core concepts needed to solve the programming problems. Mini-lectures usually take 10 to 15 minutes and involve small groups—a type of *just-in-time* learning [?]. Instructors and TAs sometimes start discussions based on student questions. Students then collaborate to design algorithms to solve the problems. As students become familiar with the teaching model, they form study groups by themselves.

Assessment labs: Students use our software to register for assessments weekly, where they get a new, random assignment for their current stage. TAs are present to help students understand the assignment, solve syntax problems, understand the language, and facilitate record keeping, but **not** to solve the problem. After completing an assessment, the automatic grading program gives immediate feedback in the form of which automated tests pass and which fail. Students may resubmit the assignment during lab until they pass it. If a student fails to pass that assessment during the lab, the instructor or a TA helps the student understand what was wrong to improve for the next attempt.

Grading: The overall grade is 70% assessment scores, 20% final exam, and 10% participation. Students who do not finish by the end of the term are given an *in-progress* grade, and have 10 weeks after the end of the term to complete.

Software: To support our educational model, the SPARC team is developing custom software that will be shared with the community in an open source model.

3. RESULTS AND PLANS

This project started with a grant in spring 2015 and the team has developed over 100 practice problems and 75 assessment problems with corresponding automated tests for CS 112. At Mason, CS 112 is taught in Python, and includes programming, problem solving, testing and debugging, and the use of program documentation[2]. We have taught four sections to a total of 344 students, including 78 CS majors. CS1 is required by most STEM majors at Mason, and most CS majors took the equivalent course in high school. To demonstrate scalability, we have progressively taught more students and sections with the same instructor. The SPARC model is allowing her to teach more students with less effort.

Our most dramatic result thus far is that the number of students caught cheating has gone from 10% on average, and up to 20%, down to zero. **We have not caught a single student cheating.** Collaboration is encouraged rather than proscribed, and assessments are done individually in an environment engineered to make undetected cheating extremely difficult. This is not just a huge savings in time and effort, we also eliminate the hugely destructive "false positives," that is, we do not erroneously accuse students of cheating.

Our completion rates have been at least the same as, and sometimes dramatically more than, the pass rates in non-SPARC sections. This is partly because of the self-pacing, which is allowing 10% to 25% of students to finish after the end of the semester, and partly because the class environment puts students in a more positive frame of mind. By comparing final exam scores among courses, we have also verified that students who pass SPARC sections are learning at least as much as students who pass non-SPARC sections.

Anecdotally, the instructor reports much more pleasant interactions with students in SPARC sections. She feels more effective as a teacher, and reports higher job satisfaction. She feels this model is more stimulating as she was interacting with students directly rather then talking to them. The TAs report similar views, and said they enjoy working for a SPARC class more than other CS 112 classes, and had better interactions with the students.

We are starting to extend the SPARC model to CS2 (CS 211 at Mason).

We are also computing longitudinal data to assess how the SPARC teaching model affects students as they progress into subsequent courses. We are measuring effort by the instructors, scalability, performance of students, number of students who finish early and late, and retention to compare with students who did not participate in SPARC courses. This will be used to evaluate several experimental hypotheses: (1) SPARC students learn at least as much as students in our regular courses; (2) this model allows us to teach more students with less effort;

---

[2]A SPARC CS 112 course website can be found at https://cs.gmu.edu/~kdobolyi/sparc/.

(3) this model helps retain more students; and (4) this model helps retain more female and minority students.

4. DISCUSSION AND LESSONS LEARNED

We believe the this model of teaching introductory CS courses has potential to increase capacity, retention, and learning. A major effect is that it frees instructors and TAs to be *teachers*, instead of talkers, graders, cops, judges, and managers.

The effect of the undergraduate teaching assistants (UTAs) has been enormous and helpful beyond expectations. They learned, the CS1 students enjoyed having knowledgeable peers to work with, and they all developed useful collaborative skills. UTAs are significantly cheaper than instructors and GTAs, so this is a major accelerator for our goal of scaling our ability to teach more students with fewer resources.

The SPARC model is increasing our capacity to teach more students in several ways. Eliminating cheating frees up substantial instructor time to teach more students. It also means fewer students have to repeat the course, freeing up even more resources. Many students can learn CS1 material, but need more than a semester. In past years, such students failed the course the first time, and either took it again (expensive for them and us!), or gave up (also expensive). Every student who completes past the end of the semester saves money for the university, saves instructor time, saves their time, and increases their confidence. Another savings in instructor time comes from the collaboration, which in effect lets students teach each other. Finally, the automatic grading frees up instructor and TA time. Every hour saved allows the SPARC model to scale to teaching more students.

We continue to face challenges. We need more classrooms that facilitate group work, which our university is slowly creating. Hiring lots of great UTAs is also a challenge that we are still learning how to solve. We are also staffing labs between terms (winter and summer break). This is currently funded out of our grant, but will eventually need to be funded internally.

5. CONCLUSIONS

Ultimate success of this project depends not just on these innovations working for us, but whether this model is used successfully elsewhere.

The effect that we are most happy about is that this approach has completely changed classroom atmosphere and student-teacher relationships. The students feel the teacher wants them to learn, and they believe that they can. When students believe the system is designed to make learning difficult, they become discouraged, lose confidence, and are more likely to quit or cheat. The SPARC teaching model disrupts this dynamic in such a way that we hope will lead to greater retention, especially among female students and under-represented minorities.

The SPARC model also dramatically decreases instructor's workload. We are currently increasing class sizes without making instructors suffer or impacting learning. This effort is already indicating that the SPARC model of teaching can go a long way towards reaching the goal of learning at scale.

ACKNOWLEDGMENTS

We want to thank all of the UTAs for making this course possible. We also want to acknowledge support from our entire department, especially the other CS1 instructors for allowing us to intrude on their classrooms as observers. This project is supported by Google through a CS Capacity Award.

Google BigQuery for Education: Framework for Parsing and Analyzing edX MOOC Data

Glenn Lopez
Harvard
Cambridge, MA
glenn_lopez@harvard.edu

Daniel T. Seaton
Harvard
Cambridge, MA
daniel_seaton@harvard.edu

Andrew Ang
Harvard
Cambridge, MA
andrew_ang@harvard.edu

Dustin Tingley
Harvard
Cambridge, MA
dtingley@gov.harvard.edu

Isaac Chuang
MIT
Cambridge, MA
ichuang@MIT.EDU

ABSTRACT

The size and complexity of MOOC data present overwhelming challenges to many institutions. This paper details the functionality of edx2bigquery – an open source Python package developed by Harvard and MIT to ingest and report on hundreds of MITx and HarvardX course datasets from edX, making use of Google BigQuery to handle multiple terabytes of learner data. For this application, we find that Google BigQuery provides ease of use in loading the multi-faceted MOOC datasets and near real-time interactive querying of data, including large clickstream datasets; moreover, we are able to provide flexible research and reporting dashboards, visualizing and aggregating data, by interfacing services associated with BigQuery. This framework makes it feasible for edx2bigquery to be open source, following standards which emphasize the importance of data products that transcend a particular data science platform and allow teams with diverse backgrounds to interact with data. edx2bigquery is being adopted by other institutions with an aim toward future collaboration.

ACM Classification Keywords

K.3.1. Computers and Education: Computer Use in Education.

Author Keywords

MOOC; learning analytics; big data; BigQuery; educational data mining.

INTRODUCTION

Applications found in the Learning at Scale community require efficient and pliable data infrastructure capable of processing millions of user interactions in order to study the learning process. Massive Open Online Courses (MOOCs) are one

L@S 2017, April 20-21, 2017, Cambridge, MA, USA
© 2017 ACM. ISBN 978-1-4503-4450-0/17/04. . . $15.00
DOI: http://dx.doi.org/10.1145/3051457.3053980

such example where data sizes and the complexity of learning environments present challenges to institutional analyses. To date, HarvardX and MIT have well over 300 total courses launched on edX.org, and the overall number of courses and learners, and dataset sizes, continue to grow.

The data generated from MOOCs are easily some of the largest and most complex educational course data institutions have encountered. The majority of course user interactions have a unique record indicating when and with which resource an interaction occurred. Each record takes up storage space, often leading to data sizes of tens of gigabytes per course. In addition to individual interaction data, there are often contextual data that must be merged with interaction data in order to interpret an action. Processing these data has been the responsibility of diverse teams, often extending to some combination of institutional analysts and academic researchers.

Harvard and MIT recently turned to the cloud – Google's BigQuery – for processing MOOC data. Google BigQuery combined with custom Python libraries offers an efficient and pliable analytics pipeline whose features satisfy stakeholders hoping to glean insights from MOOC data. And although HarvardX and MITx data are continuously growing in size and complexity, the data pipeline used to parse and aggregate MOOC data is stable to share openly with other institutions.

In this paper, we describe the primary open source package responsible for the Harvard and MIT MOOC data pipeline: edx2bigquery [7]. The edx2bigquery framework has facilitated the majority of external reporting on HarvardX and MITx MOOCs. Institutions working with edX data are encouraged to clone edx2bigquery for standing up their own data pipeline.

EDX DATA

edX is a provider of Massive Open Online Courses (MOOCs) and the unifying body for roughly 90 partner organizations from higher education, government, and industrial settings (e.g., HarvardX and MITx are both edX consortium members). edX partners create MOOC content while edX develops the open-source platform and handles distribution of courses. edX as an organization provides regular data exports to partners whose courses are running on edX.org, allowing partner organizations to prioritize their own research interests around MOOC learners and their behavior.

edX provides partners with regular research data exports [3] from courses run on edX.org and the piloting site edge.edx.org. These exports include the majority of user-interactions and arrive in two formats: 1) *Database Data* - snapshots of the platform's backend tables delivered weekly and 2) *Event Data* - all user click interactions across a partner's courses delivered nightly. Database data (also called SQL) contain all user information required to maintain a current state of a user's learning experience in a given course, such as, self-reported demographics, course enrollments, problem submissions for grading, etc. Event data (also called clickstream) contains a complete history of user interactions in the courseware. Clickstream data are generally quite complex containing a semi-structured format to allow data to evolve over time as new tools and features are developed. Events are generally the largest source of data recorded by the edX platform – often gigabytes per course – and by far the most challenging to work with pragmatically.

External data sources may also be required to better understand edX data. edx2bigquery has integrated data from the YouTube API, and geolocation via external libraries like Maxmind GeoIP2 City Database [11]. Each of these external sources has played a role in reporting from Harvard and MIT.

Finally, there are a number of stakeholder groups that have specific needs with regard to extracting insights from MOOC data. Although not discussed in detail here, data requests from Harvard and MIT come from one of four stakeholders: faculty, course teams, researchers, and administrators.

GOOGLE BIGQUERY: A POSITIVE HARVARDX AND MITX EXPERIENCE

Prior to the development of edx2bigquery, teams at Harvard and MIT developed a processing pipeline using a MongoDB database, hosted on a small computing cluster at the Office of Digital Learning at MIT. After roughly 2 years of MOOC data, processing times soon exceeded the limits of practical wait time for aggregating data, with some aggregate data taking longer than 48 hours to generate. Harvard / MIT decided to try Google BigQuery - a fully managed cloud service that enables storage and fast querying of large and multi-faceted datasets.

BigQuery is fast, returning results in seconds even when running queries on terabyte scale data; behind the scenes, the vital key making this speed uniform and easily obtained is that BigQuery does not require creation (or even specification) of indexes – any field can be queried rapidly. This is a huge advantage, compared with MongoDB, and traditional SQL systems like MySQL and Postgres, all for which queries are quick only on fields with existing indexes.

At the time of this writing, BigQuery's storage charge is $0.01-0.02 / GB stored per month, and query charges are $5 per TB processed per month. For MOOC data analysis, this per-query pricing model turns out to be remarkably affordable. As an example, Harvard spends in the range of $20-$50 / month to process 130+ courses, containing over 700 million click

events generated by almost 3 million unique learners. These costs also include custom queries from an active research team. Davidson College – which processes data from a small handful of MOOCs and has fewer researchers interacting with BigQuery – spends typically under $1 / month.

Summarizing the BigQuery Choice

Summarizing the advantages provided by Google BigQuery over our previous on-premise MongoDB solution, we find:

1. No technical overhead costs for maintaining infrastructure;

2. Scalability of processing research data products across a growing number of courses and users;

3. Quick interactive data analysis, no database indexes needed;

4. Perform ad-hoc query across any and all courses, allowing joins across thousands of tables;

5. Affordable relative to many on-premise solutions.

EDX2BIGQUERY FRAMEWORK

The edx2bigquery framework provides an efficient, optimized solution for processing massive amounts of learner event data (billions of rows) per course efficiently using Google BigQuery while minimizing querying costs given a daily update frequency of event log data from edX. The framework can be used generically to process all events for a single course, or group(s) of courses, and a time interval can be specified with a custom start and end time (for the purposes of generating landmark annual reports). Figure 1 provides an illustration of how the edx2bigquery framework handles processing of edX database data and daily event data.

The dataflow for canonical daily datasets (green), begins with the stacked tables in the top left corner, representing multiple event tables in BigQuery, one table for each day. The table in the top right corner represents a generic Canonical Daily table (e.g., Person-Course-Day) produced in BigQuery as the result of the aggregate SQL query passed. Processing time in Google BigQuery takes the longest the first time the query is executed since millions of rows of event data are queried from the beginning of the course. Daily updates thereafter require performing a query only on new daily events data for each course and consequently provide quicker incremental updates by appending data to the end of the BigQuery table. As a real world example, a query to generate the Person Course Day for our largest and most popular course CS50X over a period of 73 days containing 13.4 million events took BigQuery 21.17 seconds. The results of that query created a Person Course Day table containing 1.15 million rows. New events for the next day took 7.57 seconds to process 165K events.

The dataflow for canonical datasets are highlighted in blue in Fig. 1. New database tables are delivered to each institution once a week representing a snapshot in time from edX's database. In the bottom right of the figure, canonical dataset (e.g., Person Course) in BigQuery is replaced when this occurs instead of updating and modifying each row. For efficiency, the SQL that generates a new canonical dataset (e.g., Person Course table) should simply aggregate the results of the latest

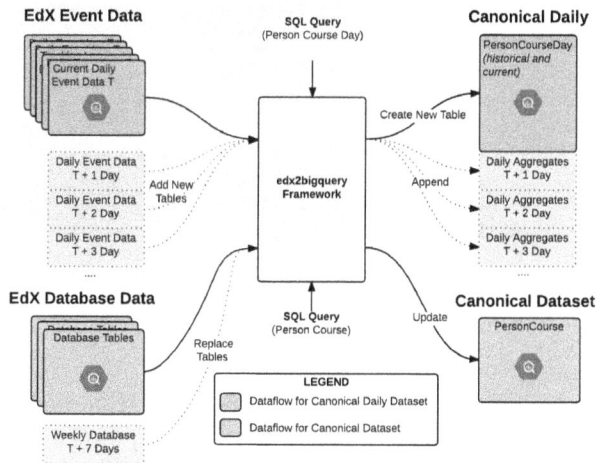

Figure 1. The edx2bigquery framework for processing event and database data to generate Person-Course-Day and Person-Course datasets. Solid lines represent up-to-date BigQuery tables. Dotted lines represent future edX data refreshed daily/weekly. Events are added as new BigQuery tables, while database tables are replaced weekly.

canonical daily dataset(s) (e.g., Person Course Day). As an example, loading for one our biggest courses took a total of 13.73 minutes to update 312K rows of data, 60+ columns wide.

Person-Course Dataset

The Person-Course dataset summarizes learning activity of a particular learner enrolled in an individual course. The key identifiers are a unique user ID and course ID. The dataset comprises enrollment time and mode, demographics, resources accessed, progression through a course, and time spent in the course. Currently, the Person-Course dataset contains 60+ variables centered on learner backgrounds and their behavior in a specific course. The Person-Course dataset is created for each MOOC run on edX and the dataset can be appended for multiple courses without duplicating data. A machine-readable Person-Course Schema in JSON format is defined, along with a Harvard VPAL Private Datasets Documentation record, maintained on Dataverse with version control by the Harvard Vice Provost for Advances in Learning (VPAL) Research Team [4]. We note that the majority of visualizations and analyses presented in the yearly reporting from Harvard and MIT are generated using the Person-Course dataset.

XANALYTICS

We have taken advantage of how Google BigQuery makes it straightforward to create dashboards. Reporting is largely handled by XAnalytics [8] – an open-source dashboard application hosted on Google's App-Engine [6] – which provides stakeholders with interactive graphics and tables based on aggregate datasets created using edx2bigquery. Dashboards can be created for every course at Harvard and MIT, as well as, for groups of many courses. XAnalytics was built around visualizing the various data products generated by edx2bigquery, hence, there are numerous interactive visualizations available. Figure 2 also contains visualizations directly available in XAnalytics (A1, B1, B2). The HarvardX and MITx administrative

offices have also made significant use of data connectors offered by BigQuery, to flexibly extract, analyze, and visualize HarvardX and MITx data using external applications, in particular with Tableau, Python Jupyter Notebooks, and R Shiny.

DISCUSSION AND CONCLUSION

In summer 2016, Harvard and MIT hosted an edX data workshop that brought a number of universities together to explore using edx2bigquery [5]. Colgate University, Davidson College, Hamilton College, University of British Columbia, and Wellesley College now all have a working instance of edx2bigquery and others are working to deploy the framework. Cross-institutional use opens numerous opportunities to explore MOOC metrics across institution. Our hope is that collaborating with a diverse group of organizations will lead to richer insights into the MOOC movement.

Although we greatly value the edx2bigquery framework, we are also aware that data standards and canonical data products are the most important aspect of the Harvard and MIT data pipeline. Shared standards for data aggregation and reporting mean that institutions can readily compare metrics in a common format. Such sharing takes place in the realm of institutional research through organizations like the Association of American Universities Data Exchange (http://aaude.org/).

Cross-institutional sharing also brings up serious legal concerns related to IRB and regulations such as FERPA [13]. Open communication with policy makers is essential before committing to research and data sharing of any kind. In the very early days of the MOOC movement, Harvard and MIT setup a data use agreement to allow cross-institutional analysis of MOOC data. The Liberal Arts Collaborative – Colgate University, Davidson College, Hamilton College, and Wellesley University – modeled a similar agreement and are in the process of comparing their respective MOOC data [2].

Lastly, we note the existence of other MOOC data frameworks, e.g. MOOCdb and MOOC Czar. MOOC DB was an early framework whose focus was similar to our own in creating standards that can be shared between institutions [12]. MOOC Czar focused more on getting from raw data to dashboards with interactive visualizations [14]. We emphasize that data products (e.g., Person-Course) are the most meaningful basis for comparison. Institutions could remain platform agnostic and still share insights given common canonical datasets.

Institutionally, edx2bigquery, and its set of canonical datasets, continue to be immensely valuable for the multi-level reporting framework provided, embodying the research methodologies developed by Harvard and MIT [10] [9] [1].

ACKNOWLEDGMENTS
We are grateful for the support from Harvard University and MIT, specifically, the Office of the Vice Provost for Advances in Learning at Harvard, the Office of Digital Learning at MIT, and the VPAL-Research group. Special thanks to Professor Jim Waldo for early contributions and the many others contributing to the open source code base. Above all, we are thankful for the tireless efforts of HarvardX and MITx course designers whose MOOCs make this project possible.

Sample Visualization

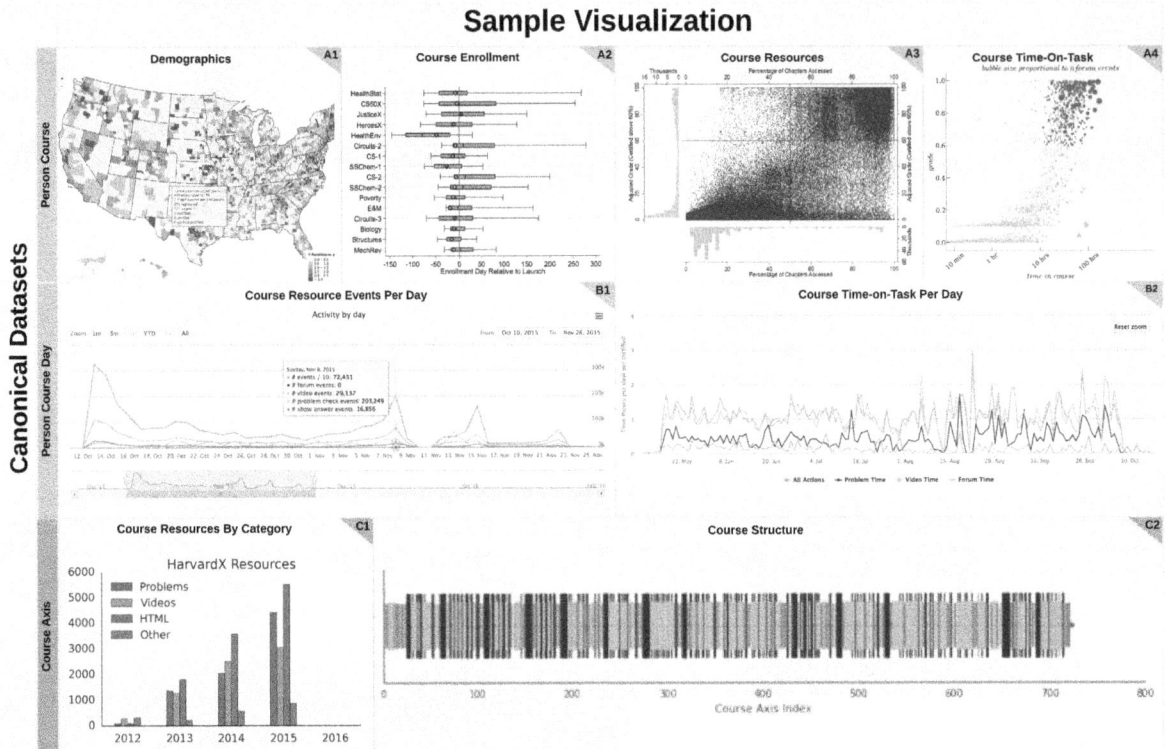

Figure 2. Visualization mosaic produced from canonical datasets generated by edx2bigquery; many are directly available with the dashboard application XAnalytics. Top row provides visualizations based on the Person-Course data product: left to right, geolocation as an example of demographic data, course enrollments across multiple HarvardX courses, performance versus amount of course accessed, and final grade versus time-on-task. Middle row provides visualizations for Person-Course-Day: left to right, number of daily events by event type and daily time on task by behavior (problem time, video time, forum time). Bottom row visualizes the course-axis data product: left to right, counts of total amount of HarvardX content created by year and a course structure visualization where bars and colors indicate course ordering for videos (orange), problems (navy), and text pages (light blue).

REFERENCES

1. Isaac Chuang and Andrew Dean Ho. 2016. Harvardx and MITx: Four Years of Open Online Courses – Fall 2012-Summer 2016. *Available at SSRN 2889436* (2016).

2. Davidson College. 2015. A Liberal Arts Take on Tech. `https://www.davidson.edu/news/news-stories/150512-davidson-co-founds-online-learning-consortium-.` (12 May 2015).

3. edX Documentation. 2016. Research Guide. (2016). `http://edx.readthedocs.io/projects/devdata/en/latest/.`

4. Harvard Vice Provost for Advances in Learning Research. 2016. Harvard VPAL Private Datasets Documentation. (2016). `http://dx.doi.org/10.7910/DVN/RTVIEM.`

5. Harvard Gazette. 2016. MOOCS Ahead. (2016). `http://news.harvard.edu/gazette/story/2016/07/moocs-ahead/.`

6. Google. 2016. Google App Engine. (25 October 2016). `https://cloud.google.com/appengine/docs.`

7. Harvard and MIT. 2016a. edx2bigquery. (25 October 2016). `https://github.com/mitodl/edx2bigquery.`

8. Harvard and MIT. 2016b. xanalytics. (25 October 2016). `https://github.com/mitodl/xanalytics.`

9. Andrew Dean Ho, Isaac Chuang, Justin Reich, Cody Austun Coleman, Jacob Whitehill, Curtis G Northcutt, Joseph Jay Williams, John D Hansen, Glenn Lopez, and Rebecca Petersen. 2015. Harvardx and MITx: Two years of Open Online Courses, Fall 2012 - Summer 2014. *Available at SSRN 2586847* (2015).

10. Andrew Dean Ho, Justin Reich, Sergiy O Nesterko, Daniel Thomas Seaton, Tommy Mullaney, Jim Waldo, and Isaac Chuang. 2014. HarvardX and MITx: The First Year of Open Online Courses, Fall 2012 - Summer 2013. *Available at SSRN 2381263* (2014).

11. Maxmind. 2016. GeoIP2 City Database. (2016). `https://www.maxmind.com/en/geoip2-city.`

12. Kalyan Veeramachaneni, Franck Dernoncourt, Colin Taylor, Zachary Pardos, and Una-May O'Reilly. 2013. Moocdb: Developing data standards for mooc data science. In *AIED 2013 Workshops Proceedings Volume*. Citeseer, 17.

13. Elise Young. 2015. Educational privacy in the online classroom: FERPA, MOOCs, and the big data conundrum. *Harv. J. Law & Tec* 28 (2015), 549–593.

14. John Zornig. 2016. MOOCczar. (25 October 2016). `https://github.com/UQ-UQx/MOOCczar.`

Characterizing ELL Students' Behavior During MOOC Videos Using Content Type

Judith Uchidiuno, Jessica Hammer, Evelyn Yarzebinski, Kenneth R. Koedinger,
Amy Ogan
Carnegie Mellon University, Human-Computer Interaction Institute
Pittsburgh, USA
{jio; hammerj; eey2; krk; aeo}@cs.cmu.edu

ABSTRACT

Making MOOCs accessible to English Language Learners (ELLs) requires that students understand the language of instruction, and that instructional strategies address their unique learning challenges. Through the analysis of clickstream log data gathered from two MOOC courses deployed on Coursera, Introduction to Psychology and Statistical Thermodynamics, we show that ELL students exhibit distinct struggle behaviors in video portions without visual aids e.g., narrations without slides. Our findings challenge widely accepted multimedia design principles such as the *split attention effect*, provide insights into designing MOOC videos, and emphasize the need for adaptivity to increase MOOC access for ELLs.

Author Keywords

MOOCs; English Language Learners; MOOC Behavioral Analysis; ELL Student Identification; Language Support Interventions.

ACM Classification Keywords

K.3.1; Miscellaneous.

INTRODUCTION AND RELATED WORK

Researchers are increasingly aware that MOOCs may not be supporting all students effectively, including English Language Learners (ELLs). Studies show that a substantial percentage of MOOC enrollees originate from non-English speaking countries [2], but MOOCs are predominantly deployed in English [15]. ELLS face the dual challenges of learning course content and learning in a non-native language, which can potentially increase their cognitive load and decrease their overall learning.

Translating MOOCs into local languages is costly, and not scalable given the diversity of languages that MOOC enrollees speak. Also, research studies show that some ELL students intentionally opt to take MOOCs in English for several reasons including improving their career prospects, connecting to other English speakers, and preparing for geographic mobility [14]. Rather than translating MOOCs to their local languages, students with these goals need language support interventions that help them satisfy their learning goals in English-language MOOCs.

ELL students can be identified using proxies such as the default language of their web browsers [13]. These methods may infer students' native or preferred language, however, they do not indicate whether a given student actually needs language support while navigating the course. Many language interventions, such as captions, support ELL students' learning needs without harming the performance of other students; however, other interventions may be distracting to native speakers [12]. Additionally, ELLs exhibit distinct behavioral patterns while interacting with MOOC video content, which may require different support [6]. Given that students spend much of their time watching and interacting with MOOC videos [7], a potential area for research is to investigate how MOOC video design can support students who speak a variety of languages.

Mayer et al. [8-10] have published a significant and widely accepted body of research that guide how learning multimedia including videos should be designed to reduce the cognitive load on students. One major principle, the *split attention effect* [1] shows how a learner's attention is split between animations and reading on-screen texts. For example, Mayer et al. [8] recommend narrations instead of text to reduce the cognitive load of processing different channels.

There are valid reasons to question whether these findings are applicable for ELLs in MOOCs. ELL students face greater difficulties understanding spoken language – these difficulties are more pronounced when they are unable to interact with the speaker [11]. Another problem ELLs face with comprehending spoken English is the speech rate [11]. Researchers have attempted to alleviate this problem by slowing down multimedia listening materials but have had little success with improving comprehension [5]. One explanation for these findings is that native speakers of a language may unintentionally alter, remove, add sounds, or blend words together, increasing ELLs' difficulty in identifying and differentiating word boundaries [11]. This

L@S 2017, April 20-21, 2017, Cambridge, MA, USA.
© 2017 ACM. ISBN 978-1-4503-4450-0/17/04...$15.00.
DOI: http://dx.doi.org/10.1145/3051457.3053981

problem is apparent even among English dialects; research shows that matching the English dialect of recorded instructions to the student's own dialect increases learning [3]. ELL students can also be affected by the difficulties inherent in processing speech, which has been shown to hurt learning in contrast to other channels like reading [9]. Because instructional videos in MOOCs also make heavy use of spoken language, they are likely a struggle for ELLs.

Given the evidence that student behavior can be inferred by analyzing clickstream logs in MOOCs [4,13], we analyzed clickstream logs from two MOOCs: an Introduction to Psychology ("Psych") course of 47 videos, taken by 13,887 students, and a Statistical Thermodynamics ("Stat. Therm.") course of 26 videos, taken by 2971 students. The Psych course featured the instructor lecturing over text-based slides. The Stat. Therm. course, on the other hand, incorporated many different instructional strategies, including the instructor speaking with and without slides, displaying equations and charts, and conducting hands-on experiments. Using this data, we identified differences in clickstream behavior patterns when ELL students were presented with narrations only versus multiple simultaneous sources of information. These patterns reveal how ELL students behave in the presence and absence of text information in addition to other learning channels, and contribute to the literature on how multimedia design principles should be applied in MOOCS to meet the needs of ELLs and native English speakers alike.

METHODOLOGY

We analyzed clickstream data for two MOOCs deployed on Coursera, focusing on interactions with video. The Psych MOOC has been studied previously in [7]. Approximately 33% of the 13,887 students enrolled since March 25, 2013 were categorized as ELL based on their browser language preferences [21]. 3372 students (35% ELL) volunteered to participate in Coursera's demographic survey (see Table 1). The top five English-speaking countries represented in the data were United States (31%), India (14%), Canada (5%), United Kingdom (5%), and Singapore (3%), while the top five countries categorized as ELL were Brazil (9%), Russia (7%), Greece (7%), China (6%), and Spain (6%).

The Stat. Therm. course ran from April 1 to June 30, 2015. We analyzed data from all 2971 participants, of whom 32% were categorized as ELL based on browser language preference [21]. Coursera's demographic survey was removed in March 2015, therefore students who created a new account on Coursera after that date (such as the students in Stat. Therm.) were not presented with the survey. As a result, we do not have demographic information for the students enrolled in this course.

To understand how student behavior varied across different content with text and narrations, and those that contained narrations only, we coded the videos for content type (see Table 2). Two researchers independently coded 5% of the videos. In an initial coding pass, they achieved 93%

		ELL	English
Profession	Student	45%	39%
	Industry Professional	13%	16%
	Research Scientist	5%	3%
	Academic/Professor	7%	4%
	Hobbyist	19%	19%
	None of the Above	11%	19%
Education	High School	10%	13%
	Bachelors	16%	17%
	Masters	15%	11%
	PhD	3%	2%
	Other	4%	8%
	Not Indicated	52%	49%
Age	Under 18	2%	4%
	18-29	60%	51%
	30-39	22%	21%
	40-49	10%	11%
	50-59	4%	8%
	60+	1%	3%
Gender	Female	63%	63%
	Male	37%	37%

Table 1: Demographic Information for Psych MOOC Students

agreement on the codes; they discussed and iterated on the codes until 100% agreement was reached. Coding of the remaining videos was split among the coders.

Code	Meaning	Stat. Therm. MOOC	Psych MOOC
Narration	Instructor talking, no support materials displayed	48%	7.41%
Text	Text content was displayed in addition to narration	11%	71.91%

Table 2: Video content type codes

Variables of Interest

For each MOOC, we computed a number of video interaction behavioral variables (see Table 3). While most of these computations were straightforward, seeking required additional analysis.

Play	Play button is pressed on content type
Pause	Pause button is pressed on content type
Seek Back From	Student seeks back from content type
Seek Forward From	Student seeks forward from content type
Seek Back To	Student seeks back to content type
Seek Forward To	Student seeks forward to content type
Slow Down	Student reduces play rate on content type
Speed Up	Student increases play rate on content type

Table 3: Behavioral variables of interaction with a video

Coursera logs only indicate where students seek *to*. If a student presses 'play' at the 2 second mark, watches until 22 secs, and seeks back to 15 secs, the clickstream logs only indicate the 'play' event at 2 secs, and 'seek' at 15 secs. In order to determine where the students seeked *from*, as well as whether the seek was backward or forward, the difference in clock time (adjusted by the play rate) was compared to the seek time. For the example given above, the student's watch time of 20 secs on the clock is added to the 'play' time at 2 secs, to determine that the student was at the 22 sec before they seeked, and compared to the 15 sec 'seek' point to determine that the student seeked backward 7 seconds.

Using timestamps, we connected interaction events to what content type was present in the video at the time. For example, for a seek event, we identified the video codes associated with the start point and end point, allowing us to create seeking sequences, such as a student seeking back from Text to Narration, from Text to Text, etc.

FINDINGS AND DISCUSSION

To understand how learner behaviors differed by their ELL status, for both courses, we ran a cumulative odds ordinal logistic regression with proportional odds to assess whether the frequency of each video behavior (play, pause, speed up, slow down, seek forward to/from and seek backward to/from) during each content type (text and narration), increased or reduced the probability of a student being classified as ELL. In the logistic regression models for each course, the video ID was included as a random effect, because our exploratory data analysis revealed that students' behavior appeared to depend on the specific content of the video being watched. Our results (Table 4) confirm previous findings [13] that ELLs exhibit distinct behavioral patterns compared to native English speakers in MOOCs. However, our results also show that these behavioral patterns vary depending on whether there is text displayed on the screen.

In portions of the video that had text as well as narration, ELLs paused significantly more, slowed down the play rate significantly more, and sped up the play rate significantly less than native English speakers. Although slowing down the pace of listening materials is a popular ELL strategy, there is little evidence of it improving ELL listening comprehension [5]. It might seem like ELL students pause more because they struggle to understand the content, but our results suggest that while ELL students may require more time to process text information, more pausing may

indicate that the content is accessible enough for them to apply learning strategies such as looking up unfamiliar words. Figure 1 shows the average play rates of English students and ELLs.

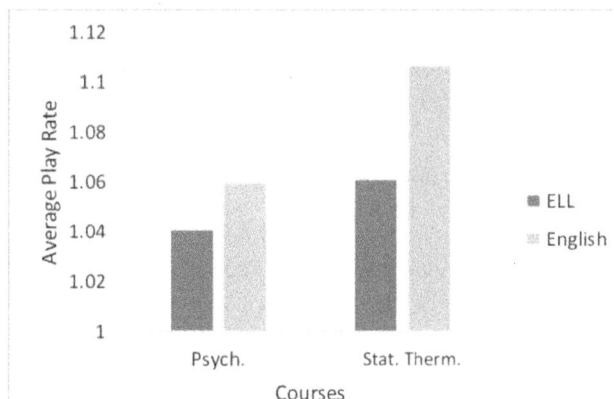

Figure 1: Average play rate between English and ELL students on both courses

In portions where narration was unaccompanied by text, ELL students interacted with the materials differently. Results from the Stat. Therm. MOOC show that ELLs seek from these video sections significantly more, and seek to these sections significantly less than English speakers. We hypothesize that ELL students are not spending time with 'narration' portions of the videos but rather seeking towards other parts of the video to help in their comprehension of the subject matter. Similar behavior was observed in the Psych MOOC, though since only 11% of video segments fell into this category (compared to 48% for the Stat. Therm. MOOC), the effects were not consistently significant.

Our results not only emphasize the importance of text

		PSYCHOLOGY			THERMODYNAMICS		
		Estimate	*Pr(>|z|)*	*sig*	*Estimate*	*Pr(>|z|)*	*sig*
	English (Intercept)	-0.712789	<0.001	***	-1.16281	5.97E-16	***
TEXT	Play	-0.012341	0.089794	.	-0.05069	0.2978	
	Pause	0.036714	1.63E-07	***	0.0625	0.1989	
	Seek Back From	-0.010742	0.430722		-0.02116	0.51	
	Seek Forward From	-0.015503	0.472654		-0.03773	0.458	
	Seek Back To	0.003389	0.804601		0.02465	0.4477	
	Seek Forward To	0.020637	0.338705		0.05727	0.238	
	Slow Down	0.083446	8.63E-05	***	0.2575	0.0118	*
	Speed Up	-0.078578	0.00012	***	-0.06991	0.4646	
	English (Intercept)	-0.704774	<0.001	***	-1.14157	3.36E-15	***
TALKING	Play	0.006573	0.749386		0.02871	0.41477	
	Pause	0.05863	0.002031	**	-0.03639	0.29641	
	Seek Back From	0.016352	0.532178		0.06224	0.00874	**
	Seek Forward From	0.111759	3.49E-05	***	0.11585	0.00161	**
	Seek Back To	-0.039965	0.132454		-0.06416	0.00853	**
	Seek Forward To	-0.06081	0.030004	*	-0.10387	0.00801	**
	Slow Down	0.057648	0.096838	.	0.07129	0.1698	
	Speed Up	-0.056824	0.132279		-0.07757	0.15618	

Table 4: Summary of logistic regression of video behaviors/content type, probability of being categorized as ELL

content for ELL students in MOOCs, but also have direct implications for the implementation of multimedia design principles such as those proposed by Chandler, Mayer, and Plass in [1,8,10]. Mayer et al. [8] specifically recommend that one solution to the problem of cognitive overload is to "present words as narration," so that "the words are processed in the verbal channel." However, we show that presenting words as narration may have detrimental effects for ELL students in MOOCs.

Our results do not discount the validity of existing multimedia design principles, but emphasize that course video designers should consider the language needs of their students to decide what video design principles are appropriate to apply. However, it is important to remember that there are also native English speakers whose needs also must be met in these courses, and who benefit from the implementation of these principles. We also note that these findings are currently limited to text displayed in the video, rather than visual aids or other video content. Plass et al. [10] found that visual annotations on foreign language content negatively impacted translation recall for learners with low verbal ability compared to their high-ability peers, and reduced comprehension for all learners compared to verbal annotations. For this reason, we conclude that further study of specific video content types is needed.

These findings suggest that rather than engaging in the futile task of trying to design MOOCs to meet the needs of all students, adaptive techniques can be used to apply the correct strategies for students' language and learning needs.

CONCLUSION
In this paper, we use clickstream data from two MOOCs to identify behavioral differences between ELL students and native English speakers in their interactions with course videos. Additionally, we have shown that ELL students use coherent strategies, namely, heavy use of slowed play rate and pausing, or seeking through the video in the absence of text. Our data suggests that widely accepted multimedia design principles may be detrimental when applied to online learning environments where students speak different native languages, and argues for the transformation of MOOCs into adaptive platforms that customize content based on the learning needs of its diverse student body.

REFERENCES
1. Paul Chandler and John Sweller. 1992. The split-attention effect as a factor in the design of instruction. *British Journal of Educational Psychology* 62, 2: 233–246.
2. Jennifer DeBoer, Glenda S. Stump, Daniel Seaton, and Lori Breslow. 2013. Diversity in MOOC students' backgrounds and behaviors in relationship to performance in 6.002 x. In *Proceedings of the Sixth Learning International Networks Consortium Conference.*
3. Samantha Finkelstein, Evelyn Yarzebinski, Callie Vaughn, Amy Ogan, and Justine Cassell. 2013. The effects of culturally congruent educational technologies on student achievement. In *Artificial Intelligence in Education*, 493–502.
4. Philip J. Guo, Juho Kim, and Rob Rubin. 2014. How Video Production Affects Student Engagement: An Empirical Study of MOOC Videos. In *Proceedings of the First ACM Conference on Learning @ Scale Conference* (L@S '14), 41–50. https://doi.org/10.1145/2556325.2566239
5. Abdolmajid Hayati. 2010. The Effect of Speech Rate on Listening Comprehension of EFL learners. *Creative Education* 01, 02: 107–114. https://doi.org/10.4236/ce.2010.12016
6. Juho Kim, Philip J. Guo, Daniel T. Seaton, Piotr Mitros, Krzysztof Z. Gajos, and Robert C. Miller. 2014. Understanding in-video dropouts and interaction peaks inonline lecture videos. In *Proceedings of the first ACM conference on Learning@ scale conference*, 31–40.
7. Kenneth R. Koedinger, Jihee Kim, Julianna Zhuxin Jia, Elizabeth A. McLaughlin, and Norman L. Bier. 2015. Learning is Not a Spectator Sport: Doing is Better Than Watching for Learning from a MOOC. In *Proceedings of the Second (2015) ACM Conference on Learning @ Scale* (L@S '15), 111–120. https://doi.org/10.1145/2724660.2724681
8. Richard E. Mayer and Roxana Moreno. 2003. Nine ways to reduce cognitive load in multimedia learning. *Educational psychologist* 38, 1: 43–52.
9. Richard E. Mayer, Kristina Sobko, and Patricia D. Mautone. 2003. Social cues in multimedia learning: Role of speaker's voice. *Journal of Educational Psychology* 95, 2: 419.
10. Jan L. Plass, Dorothy M. Chun, Richard E. Mayer, and Detlev Leutner. 2003. Cognitive load in reading a foreign language text with multimedia aids and the influence of verbal and spatial abilities. *Computers in Human Behavior* 19, 2: 221–243.
11. Willy A. Renandya and Thomas SC Farrell. 2010. "Teacher, the tape is too fast!"Extensive listening in ELT. *ELT journal*: ccq015.
12. Rebecca Silverman and Sara Hines. 2009. The effects of multimedia-enhanced instruction on the vocabulary of English-language learners and non-English-language learners in pre-kindergarten through second grade. *Journal of Educational Psychology* 101, 2: 305.
13. Judith Uchidiuno, Amy Ogan, Kenneth R. Koedinger, Evelyn Yarzebinski, and Jessica Hammer. 2016. Browser Language Preferences as a Metric for Identifying ESL Speakers in MOOCs. In *Proceedings of the Third (2016) ACM Conference on Learning@ Scale*, 277–280.
14. Judith Uchidiuno, Amy Ogan, Evelyn Yarzebinski, and Jessica Hammer. 2016. Understanding ESL Students' Motivations to Increase MOOC Accessibility. In *Proceedings of the Third (2016) ACM Conference on Learning@ Scale*, 169–172.
15. Find MOOCs By Languages. *MOOC List*. Retrieved October 23, 2015 from https://www.mooc-list.com/languages?static=tru

A Memory-Augmented Neural Model for Automated Grading

Siyuan Zhao
Worcester Polytechnic
Institute
Worcester, MA 01609, USA
szhao@wpi.edu

Yaqiong Zhang
Worcester Polytechnic
Institute
Worcester, MA 01609, USA
yzhang19@wpi.edu

Xiaolu Xiong
Worcester Polytechnic
Institute
Worcester, MA 01609, USA
xxiong@wpi.edu

Anthony Botelho
Worcester Polytechnic
Institute
Worcester, MA 01609, USA
abotelho@wpi.edu

Neil Heffernan
Worcester Polytechnic
Institute
Worcester, MA 01609, USA
nth@wpi.edu

ABSTRACT

The need for automated grading tools for essay writing and open-ended assignments has received increasing attention due to the unprecedented scale of Massive Online Courses (MOOCs) and the fact that more and more students are relying on computers to complete and submit their school work. In this paper, we propose an efficient memory networks-powered automated grading model. The idea of our model stems from the philosophy that with enough graded samples for each score in the rubric, such samples can be used to grade future work that is found to be similar. For each possible score in the rubric, a student response graded with the same score is collected. These selected responses represent the grading criteria specified in the rubric and are stored in the memory component. Our model learns to predict a score for an ungraded response by computing the relevance between the ungraded response and each selected response in memory. The evaluation was conducted on the Kaggle Automated Student Assessment Prize (ASAP) dataset. The results show that our model achieves state-of-the-art performance in 7 out of 8 essay sets.

Author Keywords

Automated grading; neural networks; memory networks; word embeddings; natural language processing

INTRODUCTION

Automated grading is a critical part of Massive Open Online Courses (MOOCs) system and any intelligent tutoring systems (ITS) at scale. Some standard tests, such as Test of English as a Foreign Language (TOEFL) and Graduate Record Examination (GRE), assess student writing skills. Manually grading these essay will be time-consuming. Moreover, as massive

open online courses (MOOCs) become widespread and the number of students enrolled in one course increases, the need for grading and providing feedback on written assignments are ever critical.

As part of the automated grading system, AES has employed numerous efforts to improving its performance. AES uses statistical and Natural Language Processing (NLP) techniques to automatically predict a score for an essay based on the essay prompt and rubric. Most existing AES systems are built on the basis of predefined features, e.g. number of words, average word length, and number of spelling errors, and a machine learning algorithm [1]. It is normally a heavy burden to find out effective features for AES. Moreover, the performance of the AES systems is constrained by the effectiveness of the predefined features. Recently another kind of approach has emerged, employing neural network models to learn the features automatically in an end-to-end manner [5]. By this means, a direct prediction of essay scores can be achieved without performing any feature extraction. The model based on long short-term memory (LSTM) networks in [5] has demonstrated promise in accomplishing multiple types of automated grading tasks.

Memory Networks (MN) [6, 4] have been recently introduced to deal with complex reasoning and inferencing NLP tasks and have been shown to outperform LSTM on some complex reasoning tasks [4]. MN is a class of models which contains an external scalable memory and a controller to read from and write to that memory.

To our knowledge, no study has been conducted to investigate the feasibility and effectiveness of MN applied in automated grading tasks. In this study, we develop a generic model for such tasks using Memory Networks inspired by their capability to store rich representations of data and reason over that data in memory. For each essay score, we select one essay exhibiting the same score from student responses as a sample for that grade. All collected sample responses are loaded into the memory of the model. The model is trained with the rest of student responses in a supervised learning manner on these

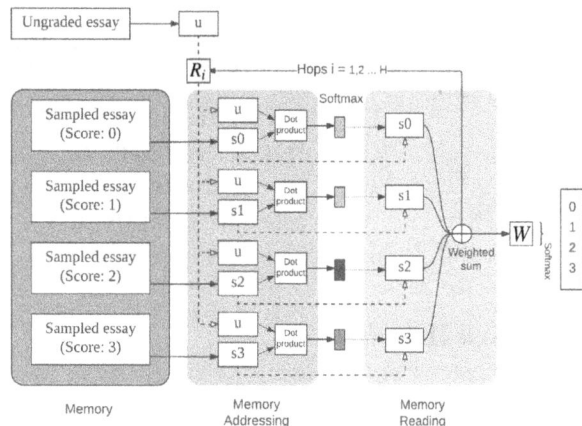

Figure 1. An illustration of memory networks for AES. The score range is 0 - 3. For each score, only one sample with the same score is selected from student responses. There are 4 samples in total in memory. Input representation layer is not included.

data to compute the relevance between the representation of an ungraded response and that of each sample. The intuition is that as a part of a scoring rubric, a number of sample responses of variable quality are usually provided to students and graders to help them better understand the rubric. These collected responses are characterized with expectations of quality described in the rubric. The model is expected to learn the grading criteria from these responses. We evaluate our model on a publicly available essay grading data set from the Kaggle Automated Student Assessment Prize (ASAP) competition (https://www.kaggle.com/c/asap-aes). Our experiments show that our model achieves state-of-the-art results on this dataset.

MODEL
An illustration of our model is given in Figure 1, which is inspired by the work of memory networks applied in question answering [4]. Our model consists of four layers: input representation layer, memory addressing layer, memory reading layer, and output layer. Input representation layer is responsible for generating a vector representation for a student response. Memory addressing layer loads selected samples of student responses to memory, and assigns a weight to each memory piece. Afterward memory reading layer gathers the content from memory by taking weighted sum of each memory piece based on the weights calculated from previous layer, and produces a resulting state. Finally the output layer makes the prediction on the basis of the resulting state. Neural networks models are usually featured with multiple computational layers to learn a more abstract representation of the input. Our model is extended to have the structure of multiple layers (hops) by stacking memory addressing layer and memory reading layer repeatedly.

Input Representation
Each student response is represented as a vector in our model. Given a student response $x = \{x_1, x_2, x_3, ..., x_n\}$, where n is the length of the response, we map each word into a word

vector $w_i = Wx_i$. All word vectors come from a word embedding matrix $W \in R^{d \times V}$, where d is the dimension of word vector and V is the vocabulary size. To represent an essay in a vector, we selected position encoding (PE) described in [4]. By the scheme of PE, the vector representation of a response is calculated by $m = \sum_j l_j \cdot Wx_{ij}$, where $\cdot$ is an element-wise multiplication. l_j is a column vector with the structure $l_{kj} = (1 - j/J) - (k/d)(1 - 2j/J)$ (assuming 1-based indexing), where J is the total number of words in the response, d is the dimension of word vector, and k is the embedding index. PE is a simple and efficient way to represent a response, and does not need to learn extra parameters.

Memory Addressing
After generating the representation of the responses, we select a sample from student response for every possible score, which is graded with the same score. The selected samples work as a representation of the criteria in the rubric for all possible scores. Expert knowledge can be used here to choose most representative sample for each score or even generate a number of ideal samples. For our experiment, we randomly pick a sample from student responses for each score, which is graded with that score.

All sampled responses are loaded into the memory as an array of vectors $m_1, m_2, ..., m_h$, where h is the total number of sampled essays. An ungraded response is denoted as x. The basic idea of memory addressing is that it assigns a weight/importance to each sampled response m_i by calculating a dot product between x and m_i followed by a softmax.

$$p_i = Softmax(xA^T \cdot m_i B^T) \qquad (1)$$

where $Softmax(y_i) = e^{y_i} / \sum_j e^{y_j}$, A is a $k \times d$ matrix and so is B. Defined in this way p is a weight vector over all sampled responses. A and B are learned matrices used to transfer the response representation to a d-dimensional features space.

Memory Reading
After weight vector p is calculated, the output of the memory is computed as a weighted sum of each piece of memory in m:

$$o = \sum_i p_i m_i C^T \qquad (2)$$

where C is a $k \times d$ matrix used to transfer the response representation to the feature space. The $k \times d$ matrix C may be identical to A, but from our experiment, we found that training a separate C leads to a better performance. From the equation, we can see that weight vector p controls the amount of content that is read from each memory piece.

Multiple Hops
The success of neural networks is due to its ability of learning multiple layers of neurons and each layer can transform the representation at previous level into a higher level of abstract representation. Inspired by this idea, we stack multiple memory addressing steps and memory reading steps together to handle multiple hops operations.

Set	# Essays	Avg len	Max len	Min score	Max score
1	1,783	350	911	2	12
2	1,800	350	118	1	6
3	1,726	150	395	0	3
4	1,772	150	383	0	3
5	1,805	150	452	0	4
6	1,800	150	489	0	4
7	1,569	250	659	0	30
8	723	650	983	0	60

Table 1. Selected Details of ASAP dataset

After receiving the output o from equation 2, the ungraded response u is updated with:

$$u_2 = Relu(R_1(u+o)) \qquad (3)$$

where R_1 is a $k \times k$ matrix, $u = xA^T$ and $Relu(y) = max(0,y)$. Then memory addressing step and reading memory step are repeated, using a different matrix R_j on each hop j. The memory addressing step is modified accordingly to use the updated representation of the ungraded response.

$$p_i = Softmax(u_j \cdot m_i B) \qquad (4)$$

Output Layer

After a fixed number H hops, the resulting state u_H is used to predict a final score over the possible scores:

$$\hat{s} = Softmax(u_H W + b) \qquad (5)$$

where W is $k \times r$ matrix, r is the number of possible scores and b is the bias value. Note that the number of output nodes equals to the length of score range. We calculate a distribution over all possible scores and select most probable score as the prediction. The matrices A, B, C, W and $R_1, ..., R_H$ are learned through backpropagation and stochastic gradient descent by minimizing a standard cross entropy loss between the predicted score $\hat{s}$ and the actual score s.

EXPERIMENTAL SETUP

Dataset

Dataset used in this study comes from Kaggle Automated Student Assessment Prize (ASAP) competition sponsored by William and Flora Hewlett Foundation (Hewlett). There are 8 sets of essays and each set is generated from a single prompt. All responses collected in the dataset were written by students ranging from grade 7 to grade 10. Score range varies on essay sets. All essays were graded by at least 2 human graders. The average length of the essays differs for each essay set, ranging from 150 words to 650 words. Selected details for each essay set is shown in Table 1.

Evaluation Metric

Quadratic weighted Kappa (QWK) is used to measure the agreement between the human grader and the model. We choose to use this metric because it is the official evaluation metric of the ASAP competition. Other work such as [1, 5, 3] that uses the ASAP dataset also uses this evaluation metric.

QWK is calculated using

$$k = 1 - \frac{\sum_{i,j} w_{i,j} O_{i,j}}{\sum_{i,j} w_{i,j} E_{i,j}} \qquad (6)$$

where matrices O, w and E are the matrices of observed scores, weights, and expected scores respectively. Matrix $O_{i,j}$ corresponds to the number of student responses that receive a score i by the first grader and a score j by the second grader (the model in our experiment). The weight matrix are $w_{i,j} = (i-j)^2/(N-1)^2$, where N is the number of possible scores. Matrix E is calculated by taking the outer product between the score vectors of the two graders, which are then normalized to have the same sum as O.

Implementation Details

We used the publicly available pre-trained Glove word embeddings [2], which was trained on 42 billion tokens of web data, from Common Crawl (http://commoncrawl.org/). The dimension of each word vector is 300.

5-fold cross validation was used to evaluate our model. For each fold, the data was split into two parts: 80% of the data as the training data and 20% as the testing data. The sampled response for each score is randomly selected from the training data. A model was trained on each essay set due to the fact that score range varies among 8 essay sets.

Baselines

Similarly to [5], our model is compared with Enhanced AI Scoring Engine (EASE), an open-source AES system, to demonstrate the improvements on performance. The reason we use this system as baseline is that it achieved best QWK scores among all open-source systems participated in ASAP competition. [3] described a set of reliable features and reported the results of two models using these features: support vector regression (SVR) and Bayesian linear ridge regression (BLRR).

[5] examined several neural networks models, e.g. RNN and Convolutional Neural Networks (CNN), on ASAP dataset. We also compared our model with their models

To verify the efficacy of GloVe word embeddings and external memory, we developed a simple multi-layer forward neural networks (FNN) model, which is similar to our model with respect to the model structure, but without an external memory. We refer this model as FNN for the rest of paper for convenience. As shown in Figure 2, each word of a student response is first converted to a continuous vector using GloVe word embeddings and the vector representation for the response is obtained by applying PE on all word vectors. Afterward the representation is fed into 4 hidden layers, each of which has 100 hidden nodes. FNN is properly defined by the equations below:

$$h_0 = Relu(A^T x) \qquad (7)$$
$$h_i = Relu(R_i h_{i-1}), \ for \ i \geq 1 \qquad (8)$$
$$\hat{s} = Softmax(h_H W) \qquad (9)$$

where x is the representation generated by GloVe with PE for a student response. h_i is the output of hidden layer i. H is

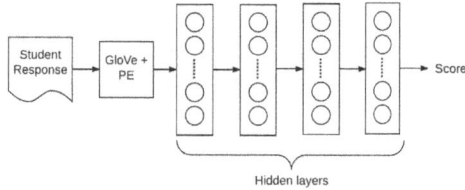

Figure 2. An illustration of baseline FNN. Use GloVe with PE to represent a student response. The representation is fed into 4-layer networks and each layer has 100 hidden nodes.

Set	MN	FNN	EASE	LSTM
1	**0.83**	0.75	0.76	0.78
2	**0.72**	0.7	0.61	0.69
3	**0.72**	0.7	0.62	0.68
4	**0.82**	0.8	0.74	0.8
5	**0.83**	0.8	0.78	0.82
6	**0.83**	0.79	0.78	0.81
7	0.79	0.73	0.73	**0.81**
8	**0.68**	0.63	0.62	0.59
Avg	**0.78**	0.74	0.71	0.75

Table 2. QWK scores on ASAP dataset.

the total number of hidden layers. A, R_i, and W are weight matrices. The bias vectors are omitted in the equations.

RESULTS

In this section, we describe the results of our experiments on the ASAP dataset and compare these results with baselines mentioned above. Column MN of Table 2 presents the QWK scores of our model. Column EASE contains the results from EASE. We also compare our model to other neural models in [5] and pick the best performance achieved by a single model (LSTM) from their paper. The results are listed in Column LSTM of Table 2.

As indicated in Table 2, our model outperforms in 7 out of 8 sets (except for set 7) and improves the average QWK score by 4.0% compared to the baseline LSTM. As expected, our model surpasses EASE in all 8 sets and improves average QWK score by 10%.

The results from the FNN model mentioned above is presented in column FNN of Table 2. When comparing these results to the best results from EASE, we find that this basic model outperforms EASE in 7 out of 8 sets of essays (except for essay set 1) and is even comparable with the complex model (LSTM). This proves that using Glove word embeddings with PE to represent a student response is able to capture important features useful for grading the response. The effectiveness of the external memory is demonstrated by the fact that MN accomplishes better performance on 7 sets (set 4 is equal) than FNN does.

DISCUSSION AND CONCLUSION

In this study, we develop a generic model for automated grading tasks using memory networks. To our best knowledge this is the first study that memory networks are applied for this kind of task. Our model is tested on ASAP dataset and achieves state-of-the-art performance in 7 out of 8 essay sets.

Our model can be generalized to automatically grade assignments from other subjects. As shown above, there are two key factors to the performance: reliable representation and memory component. In order to apply our model to other kinds of assignment, learning a good vector representation for the assignment is the first step. The next step is to select characterized samples and store these samples to memory. The purpose of this step is to teach the model to understand the grading strategy and eventually associate a vector representation to a score.

However, we only test our model on one dataset. There is a need to explore our model with more datasets that contain various formats of assignments. Furthermore, the representation of the assignment and the mechanism for measuring relevance among assignments is still elementary. Future work should therefore focus on these two areas to improve the generalizability of the model.

ACKNOWLEDGMENTS

We acknowledge funding from multiple NSF grants (ACI-1440753, DRL-1252297, DRL-1109483, DRL-1316736 & DRL-1031398), the U.S. Department of Education (IES R305A120125 & R305C100024 and GAANN), the ONR, and the Gates Foundation.

REFERENCES

1. Hongbo Chen and Ben He. 2013. Automated Essay Scoring by Maximizing Human-Machine Agreement. In *EMNLP*.

2. Jeffrey Pennington, Richard Socher, and Christopher D Manning. 2014. Glove: Global Vectors for Word Representation. In *EMNLP*, Vol. 14. 1532–1543.

3. Peter Phandi, Kian Ming Adam Chai, and Hwee Tou Ng. 2015. Flexible Domain Adaptation for Automated Essay Scoring Using Correlated Linear Regression. In *EMNLP*.

4. Sainbayar Sukhbaatar, Arthur Szlam, Jason Weston, and Rob Fergus. 2015. End-To-End Memory Networks. In *Advances in Neural Information Processing Systems 28*, C Cortes, N D Lawrence, D D Lee, M Sugiyama, and R Garnett (Eds.). Curran Associates, Inc., 2440–2448.

5. Kaveh Taghipour and Hwee Tou Ng. 2016. A Neural Approach to Automated Essay Scoring. In *EMNLP*.

6. Jason Weston, Sumit Chopra, and Antoine Bordes. 2014. Memory Networks. *CoRR* abs/1410.3916 (2014).

One Decision Tree is Enough to Make Customization

Hao Wan
Worcester Polytechnic Institute
Worcester, USA
hale@wpi.edu

Joseph E. Beck
Worcester Polytechnic Institute
Worcester, USA
josephbeck@wpi.edu

ABSTRACT

The ability to customize instruction to individuals is a great potential for adaptive educational software. Unfortunately, beyond mastery learning and learner control, there has not been much work with adapting instruction to individuals. This paper provides an approach to determine what type of learner does best with a different intervention. We focused on constructing a decision tree that discriminated difference between tutoring interventions, and thus to make customization for each student. We evaluated our model on simulated and on real data. In the simulated data set, it outperformed other methods and the constructed models captured a pre-defined customization structure. With the real data, the customized learning approach achieved stronger learning gains than simply picking the best overall teaching option. Surprisingly, it was difficult to outperform a decision tree that simply used how quickly students tended to learn a skill. That is, more features and more complex models did not result in a more effective system.

Author Keywords

Decision tree; customization; treatment effect

ACM Classification Keywords

Algorithms

INTRODUCTION

Even since Bloom's paper showing a 2 standard deviation effect size of individual tutoring [1], computer's ability to adapt instruction has been pitched as a solution. However, most educational software does little adaption to the individual beyond mastery learning and learner control. Each student (largely) sees the same help messages and the same instruction. Mastery learning enables students to keep practicing a skill until they have mastered it. Learners maintain a degree of control, such as selecting which story to read next or which type of help to receive (e.g., [2]). Those two approaches overlook the fact that students' learning outcomes might differ in tutoring interventions, because they have different learning styles [3, 4], prior knowledge [5, 6],

L@S 2017, April 20-21, 2017, Cambridge, MA, USA
© 2017 ACM. ISBN 978-1-4503-4450-0/17/04…$15.00
DOI: http://dx.doi.org/10.1145/3051457.3053983

or other factors that affect which type of instruction is most effective for *this* learner.

In this paper, we explore finding which intervention works best for what type of learners. This can be divided into two sub-problems: identify the different "types" of learners; estimate the outcome for a type of learner in each intervention. In the work [4], the authors state that the tutorial methods are effective if and only if the optimal tutorial method differs in different types of learners, which is called "acceptable evidence". Likely, given a set of students, we separate them into groups, such that the optimal intervention differs in the groups. In this work, we use decision tree algorithm to solve the two sub-problems. In a constructed decision tree, we consider the students fall into a leaf node are in the same group.

Unlike traditional classification problem, where every student is marked with which option is optimal for him/her, we focus the problem where we do not know *a priori* how each student best learns. Even worse, we only know how a student would perform with one of the possible options, this is very likely to happen in the randomized control experiments. Therefore, we must find commonalities in what types of students learn better from one intervention vs. another. Consequently, we need to employ the decision tree to determine difference of outcome between options for each student, based on the corresponding features, and then output the best option for this student.

One possible approach to solve the problem is to build a model to estimate the effect of each possible option, and then select the one with the best estimated outcome for this student [3, 7]. However, it has three disadvantages.

1. The mechanism would be very complicated if the size of possible options is large, like in course recommendation systems [8, 9], each course could be considered as an option, and there might be tens of different options.

2. It would be hard to extract rules from the decision trees if they are constructed on different set of features or nodes are split with different values.

3. The constructed models might be meaningless, and learn about what is termed "unacceptable evidence" [4] of a meaningful interaction. Like in Figure 1, the optimal option for students, no matter with high or low knowledge level, is always option 1. This conclusion does not need a decision tree. This is because traditional decision tree algorithms use criteria such as information gain, Gini

index, and impurity, to construct a tree with the least error in prediction [10-12]. However, in this problem, we should focus on building decision trees to find splits that would alter which option works best. As a result, the decision tree is an "acceptable evidence", i.e., the best option differs for different types of students.

To overcome those disadvantages, we will introduce a new decision tree algorithm in this paper that constructs a decision tree for all possible tutoring options. In this manner, we address our research question: which option is optimal for a particular type of student? Moreover, many studies focus on investigating the effect of **an** intervention. However, this paper explores a set of 22 experiments to find a mechanism for customizing instruction to an individual student.

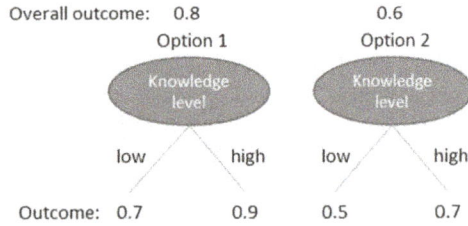

Figure 1. Example of decision trees based on Pashler et al.'s framework of "unacceptable evidence" [4]. These two decision trees are useless, because students would always have a better outcome with option 1 with or without the decision trees.

METHODOLOGY

Split Criterion

We define the cross effect as the improvement of target value from picking the overall best option to picking the best option for each group. If there is no cross effect, then there is no difference with disaggregated by the feature, like the sample decision tree in Figure 1, and thus the improvement is 0. In this work, we focus on dealing with the continuous target variable, so the leaf node in the decision tree constructed by our method represents the mean target value of instances in that node. The cross effect of a feature f in a data space D is computed as:

$$CE = \sum_{g_i \in G} \frac{mean\left(D_{g_i, a=\hat{a}\left(D_{g_i}\right)}\right) * |D_{g_i}|}{|D|} - mean(D_{a=\hat{a}(D)})$$

$$\hat{a}(D) = argmax_{a_j}\left(mean\left(D_{a=a_j}\right)\right)$$

Where G is the set of all groups disaggregated by the feature f, a is the option variable, $mean(D)$ is the mean target value of all instances in D, and $\hat{a}(D)$ represents the best option in the data space D.

Discretization

In this work, we deploy binary split in decision tree induction. To evaluate a discrete feature f, for each possible value f_i, we consider the data space is divided into two groups, the one with "$f = f_i$" and the other with "$f \neq f_i$", and then we compute cross effect according to this division. Finally, the best one is marked as the cross effect of f.

```
PROCEDURE split(D, R, n, l):
1:    best_feature ← '', cut ← −∞, best_effect ← −∞
2:    FOR each feature f in R:
3:        (f_i, e) ← pickBestCutpoint(D, f, n)
4:        p ← computePValue(D, f, f_i)
5:        IF p ≤ l AND e > best_effect:
6:            best_effect ← e, best_feature ← f, cut ← f_i
7:    IF best_feature ≠ '':
8:        root ← createInternalNode(D, best_feature, cut)
9:        R ← R − f
10:       (D_1, D_2) ← divide(D, best_feature, cut)
11:       root.left = split(D_1, R, n, l)
12:       root.right = split(D_2, R, n, l)
13:   ELSE
14:       root ← createLeafNode(D)
15:   RETURN root
```

Figure 2. The split process in decision tree induction. It takes current data set, a set of features, and other two parameters as inputs, and it outputs the root node of the tree constructed based on the input data set.

To discretize a continuous feature f, as its values are denoted in order as $\{f_1, f_2, ..., f_m\}$, each value will be considered as a cut point, so that a value, f_i, will divide the data into two groups, one containing the instances with $f \leq f_i$, and the other with $f > f_i$. The cross effect according to this division will be computed. Therefore, we need to examine $m - 1$ possible values.

After computing the cross effect for all possible values of a continuous feature, we are not going to pick the value with the best cross effect as the cut point for this feature. To reduce the effect of noise, we smooth the result by replacing the cross effect of each value with the average of its 5 neighbors, including itself. Finally, we pick the value with the best smoothed effect as the cut point for a continuous feature. We also use factorial ANOVA on the resulted disaggregation to compute p-value for both continuous feature and discrete feature. This p-value will be used in decision tree induction.

Decision Tree Induction

Our method is a top-down induction method, starting with the whole data set, it keeps splitting the data set into two sub data sets, until all possible splits meet one or both of following stop criteria:

Stop criterion 1: in one of the two sub data sets, there is an option, such that the number of instances with the option is less than n, a parameter of minimum size used in the induction.

Stop criterion 2: in a split, the corresponding p-value > l, where l is another parameter in the induction, which indicates the significant level of splitting.

The split procedure is shown in Figure 2, line 1 is initialization; line 2-6 picks the feature alone with its corresponding cut point that produces the best significant split. A significant split means the corresponding p-value is less than or equal to a pre-defined significant level l; line 7-12 constructs an internal node with the feature and cut point, and then recursively runs the split procedure on the two split sub data sets; if stop criterion 2 has been reached, then the tree stop growing, so line 14 creates a leaf node. Finally, this procedure outputs either an internal node or leaf node.

EXPERIMENTS AND RESULTS

Experiments Setup

We use 5-fold cross validation to evaluate our method on two types of data sets, one is the simulated data set that is generated with pre-defined distributions, and the other is collected from real experiments. The process of evaluating trained model in this work is different from in the traditional classification problems, since we going to evaluate how well students would have done by given the customized options, not how well the model predicts. After a model is trained by the training set, each separated group, according to the model, is marked with an option which brings the best mean target values. To evaluate the trained model in the testing set, first, the testing set is also assigned into corresponding groups based on the model structure. And then for each group, the mean target value of the instances in the testing group with the marked option is the estimated value. Finally, how well a model is making customization is computed by taking the average target value of all groups.

Simulated Data

Data Generation

This simulated data set contains 6 features, 2 options, and 1 continuous target variable. The 6 features are generated with uniform distribution $U(0,1)$, and the target variable with normal distributions, of which parameters are defined in the Table 1. We generated 200 instances for each group, 100 for each option. According to these distributions, the optimal option for group 1 and group 4 is option 0, while option 1 for group 2 and group 3. With picking the optimal option for each group, the upper bound of this data set that the best method can achieve is 0.708.

Results

We use the method described in previous section to construct decision trees on this simulated data with different significant levels, 0.05, 0.1, 0.2, 0.3, 0.5, and 0.9, the other parameter, minimum size, is set to be 20 in all trees. We also compared the constructed decision trees with two methods, random selection and always pick the option that has the best overall mean target value in the training set. As shown in Figure 3, the results of decision trees are very closed to the upper bound, and they are much better than random selection and method of picking the best. Moreover, the decision tree with parameter 0.05 is better than the other models, and it is statistical significantly ($\alpha < 0.001$) better than the method of picking the overall best, the reason could be that it is less overfitting to the training set.

Another issue we want to focus on is the structure of the decision trees. The constructed trees have the same structure on the top 2 levels: the feature f1 is used in the root node, and f2 is used in both of nodes in the 2nd level. The mean of all cut points of f1 is 0.491, the mean of cut points of f2 in the

left node is 0.665, and 0.685 in the right node. The trees have the structure that is similar with the pre-defined one, except that they have more levels since we impute the data with some noise – the other four features.

			option 0		option 1	
	f1	f2	μ	σ	μ	σ
group 1	≤0.5	≤0.8	0.5	0.2	0.4	0.2
group 2		>0.8	0.3	0.2	0.8	0.2
group 3	>0.5	≤0.8	0.4	0.2	0.6	0.2
group 4		>0.8	0.9	0.2	0.2	0.2

Table 1. Parameters of the distributions used to generate simulated data set.

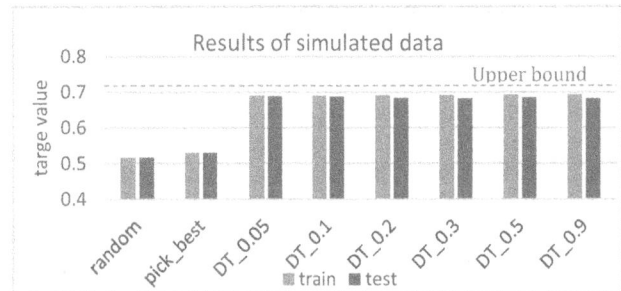

Figure 3. Results of running our decision tree algorithm with different significant levels on the simulated data, compared with random selection method and the method of picking the overall best option.

Real Data

Data Description

This data set is collected from 22 ASSISTments experiments. In each experiment, a student is randomly assign into one of two groups, and the two groups are associated with different tutoring conditions, such as video feedback and text feedback. And each experiment has a unique pair of conditions. The experiment with minimum size has 121 students, 1640 of maximum, and 10690 students in total.

In each experiment, students are learning a specific skill by practicing related problems, and they are required to obtain 3 correct in a row to complete the experiment. To investigate which condition is optimal for each student, we defined $target = (3/\#practices)^{0.7}$, if complete; otherwise, 0. And we use 6 student features in decision tree induction: prior completion rate, prior percent of correctness, prior average mastery speed, guessed gender, learning rate in previous 3 days, and percent of correctness in previous 3 days.

Results

In this experiment, we run our decision tree algorithm on the 6 features with different significant levels, 0.05, 0.1, 0.2, 0.3, 0.5, and 0.9. We also use only one feature, prior mastery speed, to build decision trees with significant level 0.9 on this data. The parameter of minimum size is also set to 20 in the decision tree induction. These methods are also compared with random selection and picking the overall best option.

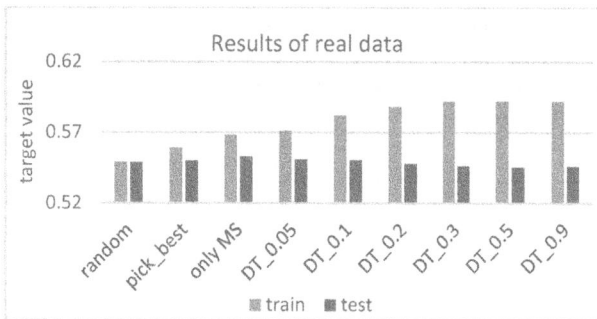

Figure 4. Results of running our decision tree algorithm on 6 features with different significant levels on real data, compared with the decision tree constructed with only one feature, prior master speed, and another two methods, random selection and picking the overall best option.

The average of the 22 results is shown in Figure 4. In the training set, the decision tree with larger significant level performs better, but this also could result in more likely to be overfitting. Such as in the testing set, the decision tree with parameter of significant level 0.05 is better than the other decision trees that are constructed on the same set of features. This might be one reason that no remarkable improvement is obtained from decision trees. Another reason might be no treatment effect exists in some experiments, which results in the "faked" patterns of cross effect captured in the decision trees. Therefore, we examined the test results in each individual experiment, and found that in some experiments, the decision tree algorithm had poor performance, while in other experiments, it performed reliably better than the other methods.

More interesting, the decision tree based on only one feature, prior master speed, is even better than the ones built with more features, but it is not statistical-significantly ($\alpha = 0.9$) better than picking the overall best. Finally, we can conclude that even though some decision trees might be overfitting, if we use appropriate features and parameters, we could get a better result, at least as well as, than just picking the overall best option for all students.

CONCLUSIONS AND FUTURE WORK

In this paper, we proposed an algorithm that constructs a decision tree to predict the optimal tutoring option for each student. We demonstrated our algorithm could capture the pre-defined customization structure in a simulated data set. We also illustrated how to use the constructed decision tree to make customization in real experimental data sets, and compute the how many learning gains we could obtain with the customized options. Although there have been many A/B to evaluate the effect of individual interventions in the learning process, little effort has been done on searching for educationally useful aptitude-treatment interactions. This work represents a step in that direction.

It is interesting to use our method to explore other tutoring systems, such as Reading Tutor [2]. The challenge is to obtain a good data set that are large with a lot of

interventions. Are we able to find interesting patterns, and what are the potential gains for customization?

REFERENCES

1. Benjamin S Bloom, *The 2 sigma problem: The search for methods of group instruction as effective as one-to-one tutoring.* Educational researcher, 1984. **13**(6): p. 4-16.

2. Jack Mostow and Joseph Beck, *When the rubber meets the road: Lessons from the in-school adventures of an automated Reading Tutor that listens.* Scale-Up in Education, 2006. **2**: p. 183-200.

3. Hyun Jin Cha, Yong Se Kim, Seon Hee Park, Tae Bok Yoon, Young Mo Jung, and Jee-Hyong Lee. *Learning styles diagnosis based on user interface behaviors for the customization of learning interfaces in an intelligent tutoring system.* in *International Conference on Intelligent Tutoring Systems.* 2006. Springer.

4. Harold Pashler, Mark McDaniel, Doug Rohrer, and Robert Bjork, *Learning styles concepts and evidence.* Psychological science in the public interest, 2008. **9**(3): p. 105-119.

5. Anthony Botelho, Hao Wan, and Neil Heffernan. *The prediction of student first response using prerequisite skills.* in *Proceedings of the Second (2015) ACM Conference on Learning@ Scale.* 2015. ACM.

6. Hao Wan and Joseph Barbosa Beck, *Considering the Influence of Prerequisite Performance on Wheel Spinning.* International Educational Data Mining Society, 2015.

7. Jong Woo Kim, Byung Hun Lee, Michael J Shaw, Hsin-Lu Chang, and Matthew Nelson, *Application of decision-tree induction techniques to personalized advertisements on internet storefronts.* International Journal of Electronic Commerce, 2001. **5**(3): p. 45-62.

8. Gerhard Weber, Hans-Christian Kuhl, and Stephan Weibelzahl. *Developing adaptive internet based courses with the authoring system NetCoach.* in *Workshop on Adaptive Hypermedia.* 2001. Springer.

9. Joseph Jay Williams, Na Li, Juho Kim, Jacob Whitehill, Samuel Maldonado, Mykola Pechenizkiy, Larry Chu, and Neil Heffernan, *The MOOClet framework: Improving online education through experimentation and personalization of modules.* Available at SSRN 2523265, 2014.

10. Hendrik Blockeel and Luc De Raedt, *Top-down induction of first-order logical decision trees.* Artificial intelligence, 1998. **101**(1): p. 285-297.

11. Leo Breiman, Jerome Friedman, Charles J Stone, and Richard A Olshen, *Classification and regression trees.* 1984: CRC press.

12. J Ross Quinlan, *C4. 5: programs for machine learning.* 2014: Elsevier.

Factor Analysis Reveals Student Thinking using the Mechanics Reasoning Inventory

Sunbok Lee[1]
sunbok@mit.edu
Alex Kimn[1]
akimn@mit.edu

Zhengzhou Chen[2]
Zhongzhou.Chen@ucf.edu
Andrew Paul[3]
pawla@uwplatt.edu

David Pritchard[1]
dpritch@mit.edu

ABSTRACT

The Mechanics Reasoning Inventory (MRI) [1] is an assessment instrument specifically designed to assess strategic reasoning skills involving core concepts in introductory Newtonian mechanics. Being an assessment of higher order thinking (as opposed to declarative or rule-based procedural thinking), it is necessary to check whether or not the mental constructs underlying actual student responses correlate with the authors' domain classification, which is the subject of this paper. The instrument consists of three types of problems: whether momentum or energy is conserved in a given situation and why, (partly inspired by the paired what/why questions in Lawson's Classroom Test of Scientific Reasoning), application of Newton's 2nd and 3rd law, and decomposing problems into parts (inspired by Van Domelen [2]'s Problem Decomposition Diagnostic). It has been administered 183 times in two MIT courses since 2009. Exploratory Factor Analysis (EFA) revealed that each Lawson pair of questions should be considered as one item, after which it identified four factors among the 21 questions that correspond reasonably well with the intended physics topics, and a fifth factor correlated with the concept of circular motion, a difficult topic for students (even though not viewed as a core principle by the designers). We discuss why 6 of the items classified under factors that differed from the expert assignments. There was no strong indication that the students answered each of different problem types similarly, which is a hallmark of students using novice heuristics rather than reasoning based on physical principles to answer the questions.

Author Keywords

mechanical reasoning inventory; exploratory factor analysis

ACM Classification Keywords

I.2.4 Knowledge Representation Formalisms and Methods

L@S 2017, April 20–21, 2017, Cambridge, MA, USA.
ACM ISBN 978-1-4503-4450-0/17/04.
DOI: http://dx.doi.org/10.1145/3051457.3053984

INTRODUCTION

As the emphases of both online education and this conference turn more toward learning, and as the goals of learning turn toward "higher" level cognitive skills such as critical thinking and problem solving [p21.org], it is important to develop assessments that can be deployed at scale to measure whether these goals have been met. This paper analyzes a large data set of students' responses to an assessment designed to probe strategic knowledge of introductory Newtonian Mechanics; the Mechanics Reasoning Inventory (MRI) [1]. While experts can perform cognitive task analysis to find the knowledge components necessary in a simple domain like arithmetic, the mental constructs that underlie something like strategic thinking are harder to determine. (Note: In this paper we use mental constructs, familiar from psychometrics, which is somewhat broader than a knowledge component.) Mental constructs are often determined by observing people actually doing the target task – for example, Tuminaro and Redish [8] found students applying several different "epistemic games" while solving physics problems. Observation is important because several lines of research show that novice students do not use the same mental constructs as experts when solving the same problem [3,4]

The MRI was designed from an expert's point of view with the objective of measuring students' ability to determine and explain which core physics principle applies in a given problem situation. In light of the previous concerns, we must therefore address two research questions:

1. What mental constructs do the students actually use to answer the questions?

2. Are these the same constructs that the assessment authors' designed the assessment to measure?

These questions are of concern in: psychometrics, data mining, machine learning, and physics education research. We discuss below why we selected Exploratory Factor Analysis (EFA) for this study, and how large an educational data set is required to make it work. Of pedagogical interest, our study demonstrates one route to developing assessments of higher level mental constructs– in this case of strategic knowledge (as opposed to the more usually assessed declarative or procedural knowledge).

METHODS

Data Collection and Selection

WE analyze data only from the latest version (MRI.v5), which was used as pre or post test in two MIT remedial physics courses: 8.IAP and 8.011. The former is a three-week remedial course administered to students who had earned a D in their introductory physics course (8.01) the previous semester, while the latter was a semester long remedial course for those who failed 8.01.

Altogether 185 test instances were collected from 8 different classes (one class used MRI for both pre and post test), all taught by author DEP. Two of the 8.011 classes had pre-test data, for a total of 60 administrations, and a different two had post-test data, for a total of 49 post test instances.

Applying exploratory factor analysis to the MRI data

Basically, identifying the underlying mental constructs of students requires dimension reduction techniques that reduce the number of variables necessary to explain the data below the number of items. Among many dimension reduction techniques for item response data, we used EFA to identify the underlying factor structure of the MRI. In EFA, the covariance structures of observed variables are assumed to be explained by a small number of underlying latent variables, which is usually called *factors*. EFA has been widely used to explore underlying factor structures of educational tests and psychological assessments, and has some advantages over other methods. First, EFA is the model that reflects our theoretical assumption about the relationship between underlying mental constructs and observed items responses because factors are formulated as the causes or predictors of correlated item responses. Second, EFA explicitly models measurement errors by

separating common and unique sources of variance in item responses. It is known that ignoring measurement errors can cause bias [5]. We used the Mplus software package [7] to handle binary responses (right or wrong) from the MRI.

Initial factor analysis and data processing

In our initial EFA analysis, we treated each question in the MRI as an item. This approach identified factors that consisted largely of the statement/justification pairs in the first and last section of the instrument, which is an unsurprising but uninformative result. Furthermore, treating the paired problems as separate items clearly violates the premises of FA that the solution to each item is independent. Therefore, each statement/justification pair was treated as one item, judging the combined item correct only when both statement and justification are answered correctly (using a less strict criteria resulted in non-converging FA result). Furthermore, author AP identified from student interviews that the wording of problems 5 and 6 caused some students to incorrectly interpret the problems. Therefore, those two problems were discarded from the FA analysis. The resulting data now comprise 14 items, 5 of them consisting of a pair of questions.

Determining the Number of Factors

One of the key decisions in EFA is to decide the number of meaningful factors. Several criteria have been proposed in literature [5]. First, factors with eigenvalues greater than 1 can be considered to be meaningful factors. Second, factors can also be retained based on the scree plot in which the eigenvalues are plotted against their corresponding factors. In the scree plot, the number of meaningful factors can be determined by the number of eigenvalues above the breakpoint of the scree plot, or the point between the steep slope and the leveling-off. Third, the optimal number of factors can be determined based on the model comparison.

	I1-2	I7	I16-17	I18-19	I20-21	I3-4	I8	I13	I11	I15	I9	I10	I14	I12
Cluster	1	1	1	1	1	2	2	3	3	3	4	4	5	5
F1	0.92*	0.73*	0.57*	0.47*	0.45*	-0.05	0.35*	-0.22	0.05	0.09	0.00	0.05	0.03	0.02
F2	-0.05	0.06	0.20	0.41*	-0.07	0.90*	0.37*	0.01	-0.22	0.23	0.04	-0.03	0.00	-0.08
F3	0.03	0.03	0.06	-0.06	0.02	0.16	-0.14	1.10*	0.78*	0.47*	0.03	-0.03	0.56*	0.20
F4	0.01	0.20	-0.07	-0.06	0.15	0.04	0.14	0.04	0.00	-0.07	0.96*	0.53	-0.01	0.12
F5	-0.55*	0.02	0.04	0.19	0.28	0.01	-0.23	-0.02	0.08	-0.13	-0.04	0.14	0.74*	0.36
Disc	0.99	1.50	0.99	0.80	1.18	0.43	0.54	1.21	1.29	0.73	0.86	0.81	1.39	0.80
Diff	-0.40	-1.01	-0.42	1.98	1.83	-1.82	2.22	-1.57	-1.02	-1.70	0.44	2.46	-1.35	-3.26

Note. * indicates that a factor loading is statistically significantly different from zero at 5% level of significance. Bold fonts are used to represent factor loadings greater than 0.3. The numbers in the row named cluster indicate the cluster identified by the hierarchical cluster analysis. F1-F5 represent factor 1 through 5.

Table 2. Factor loadings from EFA.

Mplus provides us a series of tests for comparing the Chi-square model fit indices between two consecutive models.

RESULTS

In this study, we adopt the criteria that factors with eigenvalues greater than 1 can be considered to be meaningful factors. As shown in Figure 1, this eigenvalue criterion supports a 5-factors model.

A simple loading structure for the five-factor model is produced by the Mplus software and presented in Table 2. We adopted three different criteria to interpret this loading matrix. First, the relationship between an observed variable and a factor can be considered to be meaningful when the corresponding loading is greater than .3. Second, items can be clustered to give maximum interpretability using the hierarchical cluster analysis [6]. The row named cluster in Table 2 represents the clusters obtained from the hierarchical cluster analysis using R package psych. Third, Mplus provides the results of statistical tests for checking whether each loading is statistically significantly different from zero. All three criteria are displayed in Table 2 (see Note in Table 2).

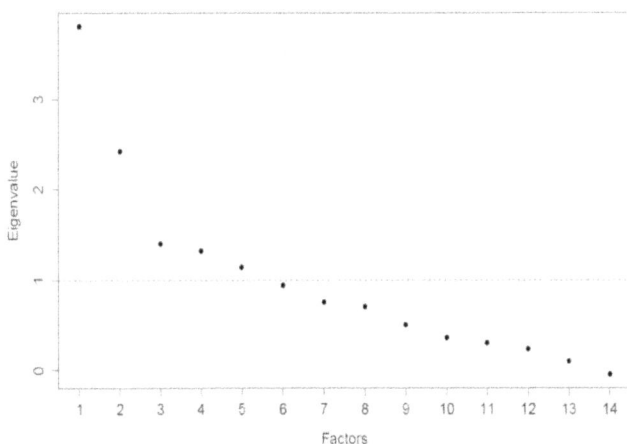

Figure 1.The scree plot representing eigenvalues against factor number. The dotted line represents eigenvalue equal to 1.

DISCUSSION AND FUTURE DIRECTIONS

If a fine-grained assessment is to be used to guide instruction – and especially to guide remediation of a particular student's weak points – it must provide ratings aligned with how the target audience organizes its domain knowledge. For example, if a student approaches physics problems using a plug and chug method (which is agnostic to physical concepts) remediation for that student needs to start at a very basic level. But if statistical errors or extra difficulties for plug and chug resulted in more mistakes on those questions dealing with mechanical energy, then analysis based on the expert domain map will guide us to clarifying the concept of mechanical energy for that student – something that is foreign to that student's thinking and won't address that student's fundamental misunderstanding.

Unlike many concept inventories that focus on probing one or two topics at a time, the MRI involves multiple topics from introductory mechanics. It is intended to assess four different concepts (Newton's Law #2, Newton's Law #3, Momentum, and Energy) in three different problem formats. Therefore, factor analysis is particularly informative for MRI, as it can illuminate our research questions:

1. What mental constructs do the students actually use to answer the questions?

2. Are these the same constructs that the assessment authors' designed the assessment to measure?

Factor analysis might also reveal clusters corresponding to different problem formats – an indication that students may be using heuristic methods to answer questions on the MRI. And by comparing with final exam scores, we might infer the importance of the strategic knowledge required for the MIR for overall problem solving ability.

Interpretation of the five-factor model

The outstanding result of the analysis (see Table 1 and 2) is that five significant factors were discovered whereas the instrument was designed with 4. Examining Table 2 shows that factor 4 is measured heavily only by items 9 and 10, and that these items load far more heavily on factor 4 than on the other factors. These questions are unique wrt the MRI because both involve "circular motion" in addition to (the designed) concepts of energy and momentum. The fact that these items have very light loadings on other factors indicates that students find that understanding circular motion is the most significant concept in the problem in spite of the presence of other important concepts (to the experts). Both factors 3 and 5 belong to the middle section involving Newton's laws. Interestingly, the two factors do not correspond to second law vs. third law as intended. Upon a closer look at the problems, we noticed that in problems 11 and 13, the problem body shares a common structure of "force on A from B and force on A from C are:" whereas the correct answer is "newton's second law applied to A." Problem 15 asks which pair of forces remain equal when the safe is accelerating, and the correct choice, "force from person on safe and force from safe on person", has a similar symmetric grammatical structure emphasizing the word which is key to the correct answer. Such grammatical cues towards the correct answer are absent from problems 12 and 14. Therefore, a plausible interpretation of the factors may be that a significant fraction of students employed (novice) heuristic methods based on verbal analysis to solve the problem. We plan to rewrite these items in a way that such heuristic methods will not work.

Granting the reclassification of the circular motion questions and the two of the 5 Newton's Law questions, the factor analysis and the expert assignments differ only for the two question pairs 16-17 and 17-18. The reasons for this are not clear to us. Although 16-17 might be classified as kinematics, there seems to be no reason to think that either this problem or 18-19 is a momentum problem. This suggests that perhaps factor 1 is not purely momentum. We plan to investigate this further.

In summary, we regard the application of EFA to the MRI.v5 as generally successful. It clearly revealed that the two questions on circular motion were mis-classified by the experts due to student difficulties with the concept of circular motion. This left only 6 of the 21 questions where the expert classification disagreed with the factors revealed by the EFA. We hope that careful investigation of the particular patterns of wrong answers will give insight into what is going on in the minds of the students and allow us to revise the items to get clearer factor loadings. Beyond that, we can write and analyze new questions or seek to interview students on these questions.

One final qualification: the relative consistency between expert classification and EFA is somewhat unusual in physics. However, it might be due to the fact that most conceptual inventories focus on one general topic and one problem type, whereas the MRI spans multiple topics and problem formats. College students are in the early stages of the novice to expert transition process, and therefore they may have learned the expert categorization on the topic level (helpful here), but not at the subtopic level required for most concept tests.

Implications for Future Development

The FA results imply a certain level of validity of the MRI. Notably, the second and third sections of the instrument seem to be each testing its own underlying skill, whereas the first section is more related to students' topical understanding.

The results also provide important information for the continuous improvement of the instrument. For example, the wording of problems 11-15 needs to be improved to prevent the use of heuristic methods. In fact, interviews conducted at University of Wisconsin Platteville suggested that many students believe the pair of forces given weren't equal to each other. The absence of this option in the current version could have driven students towards heuristic methods.

It would also be wise to add some energy and momentum questions involving the situation in the middle section. Finding a way to collect more data more quickly would also be helpful.

Authors' Affiliation

1= Massachusetts Institute of Technology, Cambridge MA; 2=University of Central Florida, Orlando FL; 3=University of Wisconsin, Platteville WI.

REFERENCE

1. Andrew Pawl, Analia Barrantes, Carolin Cardamone, Saif Rayyan, David E. Pritchard, N. Sanjay Rebello, Paula V. Engelhardt, and Chandralekha Singh. 2011. Development of a mechanics reasoning inventory. In *Physics Education Research Conference*, 287–290. https://doi.org/10.1063/1.3680051

2. David Van Domelen. 2000. The development of the problem decomposition diagnostic.

3. Michelene T.H. Chi, Paul J Feltovich, and Robert Glaser. 1981. Categorization and representation of physics problems by experts and novices. *Cognitive Science* 5: 121–152. Retrieved from papers2://publication/uuid/66AFC0DE-6DB6-4276-8C3A-C90185B1064F

4. Jonathan Tuminaro and Edward Redish. 2007. Elements of a cognitive model of physics problem solving: Epistemic games. *Physical Review Special Topics - Physics Education Research* 3, 2: 1–22. https://doi.org/10.1103/PhysRevSTPER.3.020101

5. Jum C Nunnally, Ira H Bernstein, and Jos M F ten Berge. 1967. *Psychometric theory*. JSTOR.

6. William Revelle. 1979. HIERARCHICAL CLUSTER ANALYSIS AND TIHE INTERNAL STRUCTURE O F TESTS. *Multivariate Behavwral Research* 14: 57–74.

7. Linda K Muthén and Bengt O Muthén. 2010. *Mplus User's Guide: Statistical Analysis with Latent Variables: User'ss Guide*. Muthen & Muthen.

8. Jonathan Tuminaro and Edward Redish. 2007. Elements of a cognitive model of physics problem solving: Epistemic games. *Physical Review Special Topics - Physics Education Research* 3, 2: 1–22. https://doi.org/10.1103/PhysRevSTPER.3.020101

Deep Knowledge Tracing On Programming Exercises

Lisa Wang
Stanford University
Stanford, USA
lisa1010@cs.stanford.edu

Angela Sy
Stanford University
Stanford, USA
angelasy@stanford.edu

Larry Liu
Stanford University
Stanford, USA
hrlarry@stanford.edu

Chris Piech
Stanford University
Stanford, USA
piech@cs.stanford.edu

ABSTRACT

Modeling a student's knowledge state while she is solving exercises is a crucial stepping stone towards providing better personalized learning experiences at scale. This task, also referred to as "knowledge tracing", has been explored extensively on exercises where student submissions fall into a finite discrete solution space, e.g. a multiple-choice answer. However, we believe that rich information about a student's learning is captured within their responses to open-ended problems with unbounded solution spaces, such as programming exercises. In addition, sequential snapshots of a student's progress while she is solving a single exercise can provide valuable insights into her learning behavior. In this setting, creating representations for a student's knowledge state is a challenging task, but with recent advances in machine learning, there are more promising techniques to learn representations for complex entities. In our work, we feed the embedded program submissions into a recurrent neural network and train it on the task of predicting the student's success on the subsequent programming exercise. By training on this task, the model learns nuanced representations of a student's knowledge, and reliably predicts future student performance.

Author Keywords

Educational data mining; Online education; Personalized Learning; Knowledge tracing; Machine learning; Deep learning, Representation learning; Sequential modeling.

INTRODUCTION

With the inception of online learning platforms, educators around the world can reach millions of students by disseminating course content through virtual classrooms.

However, in these online environments, teachers' ability to observe students is lost. Understanding a student's incremental progress is invaluable. For instance, if a teacher watches a student work through an exercise, she can observe the student's strengths, knowledge gaps as well as motivation. Hence, the process by which the student reaches the final solution is as important as the solution itself. We attempt to encode these markers of progress.

We performed representation learning with recurrent neural networks to understand a student's learning trajectory as they solve open-ended programming exercises from the *Hour of Code* course, a Massive Open Online Course (MOOC) on *Code.org*. The deep learning model trains on a student's history of past code submissions and predicts the student's performance on the next exercise. The model is able to learn meaningful feature representations for a student's series of submissions and hence does not require manual feature selection, which would be very difficult for open-ended exercises. Furthermore, the learned representations can be used for other related tasks, such as predicting an intervention.

RELATED WORK

Representation Learning with Recurrent Neural Networks

In the field of machine learning, representation learning is the task of learning a model to create meaningful representations from low-level raw data inputs. The goal of representation learning is to reduce the amount of human input and expert knowledge needed to preprocess data before feeding it into machine learning algorithms [1].

In contrast to manually selecting high-level features, representation learning algorithms are trained to extract features directly from raw input, e.g. from words in a document.

The learned representations can be used for other related tasks as well. E.g. In *word2vec* [6], word representations were trained on predicting context words but were then used for document classification and translation.

In recent years, representations learned by Deep Neural Networks (DNNs) have outperformed other methods in many tasks including image classification [1]. Empirically, DNNs do particularly well when the raw data has high semantic complexity and manually choosing features is not only tedious, but often insufficient.

Recurrent neural networks (RNNs) are a subtype of neural networks that takes inputs over multiple timesteps, which makes them particularly suited for learning representations on sequential data. RNNs have been successfully applied to modeling and translating natural language sentences, performing speech recognition, and completing other tasks on data with temporal relationships.

Knowledge Tracing

The task of knowledge tracing can be formalized as: given observations of interactions $x_0 \ldots x_t$ taken by a student on a particular learning task, predict aspects of their next interaction x_{t+1} [2].

RNNs have been applied to the knowledge tracing task in the past to understand how students progress through different problems. Piech et al. applied RNNs to data from Khan Academy's online courses to predict student performance [8]. The authors found that RNNs can robustly predict whether or not a student will solve a particular problem correctly given the accuracy of historic solutions. More recent answers are a more accurate representation of students' current state, hence our DKT models use RNNs with long short-term memory (LSTM) to weight recent inputs more heavily while still taking into account historic inputs, a method developed in Hochreiter and Schmidhuber's paper [4]. Other models that are designed to take low dimensional inputs, such as IRT and modifications of Bayesian Knowledge Tracing [13] [7], sometimes outperform the initial version of Deep Knowledge Tracing (DKT) [12] [5]. However, DKT does not require student interactions to be manually labeled with relevant concepts and the RNN paradigm was designed to take vectorized inputs, hence it can utilize inputs that extend beyond the discrete inputs of traditional models [3]. These properties make the model an appropriate fit to understand trajectories of open-ended student responses.

A limitation with the work of Piech et al. is that it does not fully leverage the promise of using neural networks to trace knowledge. The dataset used only contained binary correct/incorrect information about a student's final answer. In contrast, the *Hour of Code* dataset offers richly structured data in the form of program submissions.

Previous work in deep knowledge tracing has looked at student responses over multiple exercises, but not within an exercise. Our method focuses on a student's sequence of submissions within a *single* programming exercise to predict future achievement. We model student learning and progress by capturing representations of the current state of a student's program as they work through the exercise. When focusing exclusively on the final submission, these steps are ignored.

TASK DEFINITION

In order to create representations of a student's current state of knowledge, we chose the following training task:

> Based on a student's sequence of code submission attempts **over time** (hereby, their "trajectory") on a programming exercise, predict whether the student will successfully complete the next programming exercise within the same course.

DATASET: HOUR OF CODE EXERCISE 18

The *Hour of Code* course consists of twenty introductory programming exercises aimed at teaching beginners fundamental concepts in programming. Students build their programs in a drag-and-drop interface that pieces together blocks of code. The number of possible programs a student can write is infinite since submissions can include any number of block types in any combination. A student can run their code multiple times for any exercise. These submissions provide temporal snapshots to track the student's learning progress. The student submission data for Exercises 4 and 18 from this course are publicly available on `code.org/research`.

For our experiments, we focus on the sequences of intermediate submissions on Exercise 18. It covers multiple concepts such as loops, if-else statements, and nested statements. This Exercise 18 data set contains 1,263,360 code submissions, of which 79,553 are unique, made by 263,569 students. 81.0% of these students arrived at the correct solution in their last submission.

Student Trajectory Within A Single Exercise

For each student, we focus on her sequence of code submissions for Exercise 18 and her success on Exercise 19. Each code submission is represented as an abstract syntax tree (AST). Given a student's trajectory on Exercise 18, our task is to predict their success on the next coding challenge. We believe success on the next exercise is a good indicator of the student's learning progress since succeeding challenges add new concepts incrementally.

Since the *Hour of Code* exercises do not have a bounded solution space (open-ended solutions), students could produce an infinitely long trajectory of submissions. We noted that the accuracy of student submissions have a high correlation with trajectory lengths. For instance, the vast majority of students with trajectory length 1 solved the problem with their very first submission. Hence, we chose to control for trajectory length and train our models independently for each trajectory length. We ran experiments on 9 data subsets with trajectory lengths ranging from 2 to 10, including submissions from 81,880 students.

MODEL

Recurrent Neural Network Model for Student Trajectories

For our model, we used a Long Short Term Memory (LSTM) RNN architecture, which is a popular extension to plain RNNs since it reduces the effect of vanishing gradients [4].

For our task, x_t is the program embedding vector of a student's trajectory at time step t. E.g., assume that a student's trajectory consists of k submissions. These are converted into program embeddings which form a sequence of k embeddings. This sequence is fed into an RNN, whose final hidden state is passed through a fully connected layer and a subsequent softmax layer. The output $\hat{y}$ of the softmax layer is a probability distribution over two binary classes, indicating whether the student successfully solved the next exercise.

Recursive Neural Network for Program Embeddings

In order to expand DKT to understand students as they produce rich responses over time within an exercise, a necessary task is to create meaningful embeddings of their responses. Based on Piech et al.'s previous work on creating program embeddings for student code[9], we trained a *recursive* neural network which allowed us to vectorize the AST representation of student programs. Recursive neural networks that learn embeddings on trees were developed by the NLP community to vectorize sentence parse trees [11]. We extended this idea to coding programs.

In our program embedding based model, a subtree of the AST rooted at a node j is represented by a vector which is computed by a linear combination of subtree representations rooted at the children of j. Representation of leaf nodes in the AST are parameters learned by the model. The hidden activations at the root of the AST are used as embeddings.

Baseline Model

For the baseline, we chose two features for each student's trajectory $T = trajectory(s)$, which is the published state of the art at predicting completion of the next exercise on this dataset, shown to be highly correlated with learning outcome and performance on the next exercise.

- The Poisson path score of the trajectory T as defined in [10]. Intuitively, the path score is an estimate of the time it will take a student to complete the trajectory series. The path score of a student trajectory has previously been related to student retention in sequential challenges [10].

$$pathScore(T) = \sum_{x \in T} \frac{1}{\lambda_x}$$

where λ_x is the number of times AST x appears in student submissions.

- Indicator feature of student success on current exercise 18. A student succeeded if they ended the trajectory

with the solution AST. (In *Hour of Code*, there is a unique solution to the exercises, since the solution has to satisfy both functionality and count requirements.)

To summarize, the two-dimensional feature vector $\phi(s)$ for a student s is built as follows:

$$\phi(s)[0] = pathScore(trajectory(s))$$

$$\phi(s)[1] = \begin{cases} 1 \text{ if } s \text{ solved current exercise,} \\ 0 \text{ otherwise .} \end{cases}$$

Using the features $\phi(s)$ as input and $successNextChallenge(s)$ as a binary label, we trained a simple logistic regression model. A separate model for each data subset of trajectory length.

PRELIMINARY RESULTS

To compare our proposed model to the baseline model, we trained and evaluated each model on each data subset separately. Each data subset contains student trajectories of the same length. For both the baseline model and the LSTM model, we used 90% of the data set to perform training and the remaining 10% for testing.

Figure 1 illustrates test accuracies of both the baseline model and the LSTM model on the 9 data subsets. We can observe that the LSTM model consistently outperforms the state of the art baseline by around 5%.

This result is significant since the input we feed into the LSTM model consists of program embeddings, and not handpicked features like success on current problem. Our model identified trajectories that show more promise and improved student learning.

The ability to understand trajectories suggests that the representations used for the programs within the trajectories were also meaningful. The program embeddings were trained to predict the output of any given student program. Our program embedding model was able to correctly predict the output for 96% of the programs in a hold out set, compared to a 54% accuracy from always predicting the most common output.

FUTURE WORK

Further Analysis of Representations

Since our model is able to predict future student success reliably purely based on a sequence of program submissions, it learned representations for the trajectories that are meaningful at least for this particular task. We have noticed a distinct clustering of trajectory representations, and will further investigate whether these clusters are indicative of certain types of learning behaviors or knowledge states. These trajectory representations of students could potentially be used for subsequent decision making, e.g. choosing the next exercise or intervention.

Extending to Multiple Exercises

Subject to data availability, we would like to extend our analysis to cover a series of exercises in the *Hour of*

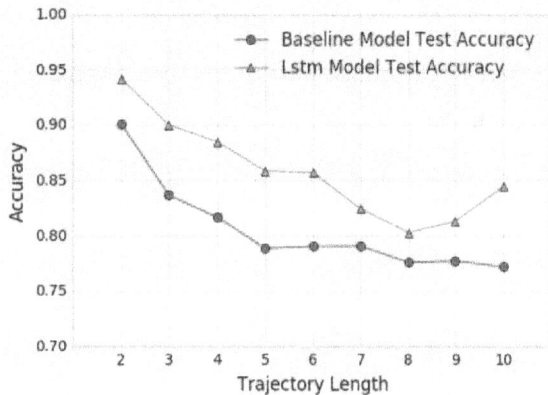

Figure 1. Test accuracies of baseline model and LSTM model.

Code course. By tracing a students' progress not just over submissions to multiple related exercises, we hope to learn a more accurate picture of the student's knowledge state. In addition, by jointly training our model over multiple exercises, the model could potentially learn more general representations of student knowledge and behavior that are not exercise specific.

CONCLUSION

We have shared a preliminary investigation into knowledge tracing over richly structured data with the goal of gaining a deeper understanding of a student's current knowledge and the progression of their learning while she is progressing through a complex exercise. The only input we use to trace a student's knowledge are the raw code submissions. The model we proposed is generalized, reducing the need for handpicked features by leveraging the power of internal feature learning in deep neural networks.

Our results suggest that our model can reliably predict a student's success on the next problem purely based on their sequence of code submissions. Thus, the learned trajectory representations contain meaningful information about a student's learning and could be potentially used for making decisions about interventions, e.g. giving a hint, providing feedback or suggesting a new exercise. Not just if, but how a student arrives at a solution, is crucial to understanding a student's knowledge acquisition and could improve the effectiveness of intelligent tutoring systems.

ACKNOWLEDGEMENTS
We thank *Code.org* for providing the *Hour of Code* data set to the research community.

REFERENCES
1. Yoshua Bengio, Aaron Courville, and Pascal Vincent. 2013. Representation learning: A review and new perspectives. *IEEE transactions on pattern analysis and machine intelligence* 35, 8 (2013), 1798–1828.

2. Albert T Corbett and John R Anderson. 1994. Knowledge tracing: Modeling the acquisition of procedural knowledge. *User modeling and user-adapted interaction* 4, 4 (1994), 253–278.

3. Geoffrey E Hinton and Ruslan R Salakhutdinov. 2006. Reducing the dimensionality of data with neural networks. *Science* 313, 5786 (2006), 504–507.

4. Sepp Hochreiter and Jürgen Schmidhuber. 1997. Long short-term memory. *Neural computation* 9, 8 (1997), 1735–1780.

5. Mohammad Khajah, Robert V Lindsey, and Michael C Mozer. 2016. How deep is knowledge tracing? *arXiv preprint arXiv:1604.02416* (2016).

6. Tomas Mikolov, Kai Chen, Greg Corrado, and Jeffrey Dean. 2013. Efficient estimation of word representations in vector space. *arXiv preprint arXiv:1301.3781* (2013).

7. Zachary A Pardos and Neil T Heffernan. 2010. Modeling individualization in a bayesian networks implementation of knowledge tracing. In *International Conference on User Modeling, Adaptation, and Personalization.* Springer, 255–266.

8. Chris Piech, Jonathan Bassen, Jonathan Huang, Surya Ganguli, Mehran Sahami, Leonidas J Guibas, and Jascha Sohl-Dickstein. 2015a. Deep knowledge tracing. In *Advances in Neural Information Processing Systems.* 505–513.

9. Chris Piech, Jonathan Huang, Andy Nguyen, Mike Phulsuksombati, Mehran Sahami, and Leonidas J Guibas. 2015b. Learning program embeddings to propagate feedback on student code. *CoRR abs/1505.05969* (2015).

10. Chris Piech, Mehran Sahami, Jonathan Huang, and Leonidas Guibas. 2015c. Autonomously generating hints by inferring problem solving policies. In *Proceedings of the Second (2015) ACM Conference on Learning@ Scale.* ACM, 195–204.

11. Richard Socher, Alex Perelygin, Jean Y Wu, Jason Chuang, Christopher D Manning, Andrew Y Ng, and Christopher Potts. 2013. Recursive deep models for semantic compositionality over a sentiment treebank. In *Proceedings of the conference on empirical methods in natural language processing (EMNLP)*, Vol. 1631. Citeseer, 1642.

12. Kevin H Wilson, Yan Karklin, Bojian Han, and Chaitanya Ekanadham. 2016. Back to the Basics: Bayesian extensions of IRT outperform neural networks for proficiency estimation. *arXiv preprint arXiv:1604.02336* (2016).

13. Michael V Yudelson, Kenneth R Koedinger, and Geoffrey J Gordon. 2013. Individualized bayesian knowledge tracing models. In *International Conference on Artificial Intelligence in Education.* Springer, 171–180.

Modeling MOOC Student Behavior With Two-Layer Hidden Markov Models

Chase Geigle[1]   ChengXiang Zhai[1]

[1]Department of Computer Science
University of Illinois at Urbana-Champaign
Urbana, Illinois, USA
{geigle1, czhai}@illinois.edu

ABSTRACT

Massive open online courses (MOOCs) provide educators with an abundance of data describing how students interact with the platform, but this data is highly underutilized today. This is in part due to the lack of sophisticated tools to provide interpretable and actionable summaries of huge amounts of MOOC activity present in log data. In this paper, we propose a method for automatically discovering student behavior patterns by leveraging the click log data that can be obtained from the MOOC platform itself in a completely unsupervised manner.

Author Keywords

MOOC log analysis; student behavior modeling; Markov models; hidden Markov models

CCS CONCEPTS

•**Mathematics of computing → Kalman filters and hidden Markov models;** •**Computing methodologies → Mixture modeling;**

INTRODUCTION

The proliferation of massive open online courses (MOOCs) has resulted in a profound impact on education. As more and more learners turn to MOOCs to educate themselves on various topics, more and more behavioral data is being collected as part of the system on which the MOOC is offered. The data present in these logs has the power to aid us in understanding the behavior of students who take our MOOCs, which is mostly undetectable for instructors of these MOOCs today due to its vast scale. As a result, the rich data available through these MOOC logs is highly underutilized today.

What stands in the way? Clearly, intelligent systems to create concise and digestible summaries of the massive amount of interaction data collected are needed in order to empower the instructors of these courses. If we can understand how users are interacting with our MOOCs, we are much more likely to be able to make changes to these courses that positively impact learners. While we can easily observe the changes in behavior of students in real classrooms, MOOCs present

a challenge due to their hands-off nature and sometimes irregular schedule due to being a full-time worker. We view this paper as attempting to bridge this gap. Specifically, in this paper we propose unsupervised learning methods for automatically discovering and characterizing student learning behavior patterns or profiles from large collections of click logs associated with MOOCs.

Our work is motivated by the following observations:

1. Student behavior is complicated and cannot necessarily be captured sufficiently by rule-based methods such as those explored by Kizilcec et al. [5] and Davis et al. [1]. We instead propose to treat student behavior patterns as being characterized (represented) via a sequence of *latent states*. This allows us to automatically capture patterns that we might not have been able to articulate clearly a priori via a series of rules, and also allows us to model the inherent uncertainty in assigning a student's behavior to a particular pattern or group.

2. Student behavior can vary over time. Previous models that treat students as exhibiting only one behavioral pattern over time [2] miss out on the opportunity to understand student behavior dynamics in a course. We propose a latent space model with *latent state transitions* to flexibly model the dynamics.

3. Analysis of student behavior can and should be performed at varying levels of granularity. This requires us to aggregate data over time with *different levels of resolution*; existing models tend to come with a particular assumption about the resolution of time they consider [2, 5, 8]. We propose a more flexible model to accommodate different levels of resolution.

Thus, what we propose is a *latent variable approach* to mining student behavior patterns that is *probabilistic* for inference and *flexible to model state changes over different time resolutions*. More specifically, we propose a novel two-layer hidden Markov model (TL-HMM) to discover latent student behavior patterns via unsupervised learning on large collections of student behavior observation sequences. Evaluation results on a MOOC data set on Coursera demonstrate that TL-HMM can effectively discover a variety of interesting interpretable student behavior patterns at different levels of resolution, many of which are beyond what existing approaches can discover. TL-HMM further enables easy use of the discovered patterns for discriminative analysis such as prediction of learning outcome. Since our proposed methods are unsupervised, they can potentially be applied to any MOOC data without

L@S 2017, April 20-21, 2017, Cambridge, MA, USA.
Copyright is held by the owner/author(s). Publication rights licensed to ACM.
ACM 978-1-4503-4450-0/17/04. . . $15.00.
DOI: http://dx.doi.org/10.1145/3051457.3053986

requiring any manual work to facilitate understanding of student behaviors and their variations, opening up many possibilities for developing intelligent tutoring systems that can adaptive to student behavior.

A TWO-LAYER HMM FOR MOOC LOG ANALYSIS

Our general idea is to use a probabilistic generative model to model the student activities as recorded in a MOOC log, which means we will assume that all the observed student activities are samples drawn (i.e., "generated") from a parameterized probabilistic model. We can then estimate the parameter values of the probabilistic model by fitting the model to a specific MOOC log data set. The estimated parameter values could then be treated as the latent "knowledge" discovered from the data. Because such a generative model attempts to fit *all* the data, it enables us to discover interesting patterns that can explain the *overall* behavior of a student or the *common* behavior patterns shared by many students.

An HMM is a specific probabilistic generative model with a "built-in" state transition system that would control the data to be generated by the model, thus it is especially suitable for modeling sequence data [7]. At any moment, the HMM would be in one of k states $U = \{u_1, ..., u_k\}$, and at the next moment, the HMM would move to another state stochastically according to a transition matrix that specifies the probability of going to state u_i when the HMM is currently in state u_j, i.e., $p(u_i|u_j)$. When the HMM is in state u, the HMM can generate an observable data point x according to an output probabilistic model $p(x|u)$. Thus if we "run" an HMM for N time points denoted by $t = 1, ..., N$, the HMM could "generate" a sequence of observations $x_1...x_N$, where each x_i is an output symbol by going through a sequence of *hidden states* $w_1...w_N$ where $w_i \in U$ is a state. The association of such a latent sequence of state transitions with the observed symbols makes it possible to use HMM to "decode" the latent behavior of students behind the surface behavior we directly observe in the log data, allowing for understanding student behavior more deeply than a model with no latent state variables.

In many ways, the generation process behind an HMM is meant to simulate the actual behavior of a student. We may say that students transition through different "task states" (or "behavior states") in the process of study. One such task state may be to learn about a topic by mostly watching lecture videos, another task state may be to work on quizzes, and yet another may be to participate in forum discussions. While in each of these different states, the student would tend to exhibit different surface "micro" behaviors. For example, in the lecture study state, the student would tend to have many video-watching related behaviors and occasionally forum activities, while in the quiz-taking state (in order to pass each module), the student would tend to show many quiz-related "micro" activities as well as asking questions or checking discussions on the forum. Note that due to the complexity of the student behavior, it is very difficult to accurately *prescribe* the specific surface "micro" behavior patterns for each state in advance, especially without prior knowledge about the students. For example, forum activities are likely interleaved with other activities in every task state and the interleaving pattern can

be somewhat irregular with potentially many variations. The major motivations for using an HMM are that (1) it uses a probabilistic model (i.e., the output probability distribution $p(x|u)$ conditioned on each state) to directly capture the inevitable uncertainty in the association of surface "micro" activities with their corresponding latent task/behavior state, which is often our main target to discover and characterize, and (2) it does not make any assumption about which latent task/behavior state must be associated with which observed activities or how a student would move from one state to another, but instead allows our data to "tell" us what kind of associations are most likely, what kind of transitions are most probable, and which states tend to be more long-lasting for any particular set of students.

However, if we use an ordinary HMM to analyze our data, we would treat each observed "micro" activity (e.g., video watching, or forum post reading) as an output symbol, and thus the output distribution $p(x|u)$ for each discovered latent state would be a simple distribution over all kinds of observable micro activities recorded in our log data (e.g., 50% lecture watching, 8% quiz taking, 7% quiz submission, 2% course wiki reading, ...). While such a distribution is meaningful and can already help us interpret the corresponding latent state, it only gives us a rather superficial characterization of student behavior.

Ideally, we want $p(x|u)$ to characterize the directly observable "micro" behavior in more detail to further capture the relations and dependencies of these micro activities. To this end, we would treat an *entire sequence* of micro activities (e.g., one session of activities) as an observed "symbol" from a latent state, and further model the generation of such a sequence with another Markov model where we treat each micro activity as an *observable* state, and model the transitions between these activity states in very much the same way as the state transitions in HMM.

Adding this second layer would allow us to characterize a latent task state in much more detail, as it would reveal not only what activities are most common to a task state, but also the transition patterns between these "micro" activities (e.g., it can reveal frequent back-and-forth transitions between quiz-taking and quiz-submission, which would suggest a concentrated period of taking quizzes). Combining this "surface" Markov model over the "micro" actions with the "deep" hidden Markov model over the latent task states gives us a fairly general and powerful two-layer HMM (TL-HMM) that can simultaneously learn "deeply" the latent task/behavior states and their transitions as well as the corresponding "micro" activity transition patterns associated with each latent state to facilitate interpretation and analysis of the discovered latent state patterns. Our implementation of the learning algorithm for TL-HMMs is included as part of the META toolkit [6].

EXPERIMENT RESULTS

As an analysis tool, the TL-HMM model provides with us the following two patterns to characterize student behavior: (1) the latent state representations, and (2) the latent state transitions. Thus to evaluate the proposed model, we conduct experiments to qualitatively analyze both types of patterns discovered from empirical MOOC log data.

Specifically, we looked at the MOOC logs associated with the textretrieval-001 Coursera MOOC offered by UIUC and extracted a dataset consisting of 18,941 students who produced 85,240 sequences with an average length of 7.31. We used the following ten actions as our action set **A**: (1) quiz start, (2) quiz submit, (3) wiki (course material), (4) forum list (view the list of all forums), (5) forum thread list (view the list of all threads in a specific forum), (6) forum thread view (view the list of posts within a specific thread), (7) forum search (a search query issued against the forum), (8) forum post thread (a new thread was posted), (9) forum post reply (a new post was created within an existing thread), and (10) view lecture (defined as either streaming or downloading a lecture video).

Latent State Representations

To visualize these Markov models that represent our latent states, we plot them as a directed graph where we set the size of a node to be proportional to its probability of being visited during a random walk. We let the thickness of a directed edge (u, v) reflect the probability of taking that edge given that a random walk is currently at note u (as indicated by the transition matrix)[1].

Figure 1 shows the latent state representations learned by fitting a 4-state TL-HMM to the textretrieval-001 sequence dataset. Our interpretations of the states is as follows: (a) **state 0** likely captures all sequences where a student logged in to the platform and did nothing else (likely just checking for updates); (b) **state 1** seems to capture a more engaged browsing session, where there is non-negligible probability associated with different activities such as quiz taking and forum browsing and, importantly, these activities have high probability symmetric edges (so students are taking quizzes one after the other, or viewing forum threads in succession); (c) **state 2** captures a "forum browsing" state, with most weight being placed on consecutive thread views; and (d) **state 3** seems to capture a more passive student, with negligible probability mass associated with forum activity (with low symmetry in the edges). The link between "quiz submit" and "quiz start" (indicating quiz repetition) is also significantly lower than state 1.

Transitions Between Latent States

A unique property of our model is its ability to capture transitions between the *behavior patterns themselves* that are captured by the latent states. In Figure 2a we show the latent state transition diagram for a 4-state TL-HMM fit on textretrieval-001. We can immediately observe two things: (1) each latent state has a very high "staying" probability, and (2) the prevalence of each latent state matches our intuition. In particular, we can see that the forum browsing state (state 2) has relatively lower probability than the other states as we might expect. It also makes sense that state 0 (low activity) has rather high probability. If we look at state 1 and state 3,

their relative probabilities match our intuition as well: there should be more students exhibiting more passive behaviors (state 3) than very active behaviors (state 1).

Thus, we might expect to see students that perform well in the course preferring states 1 and 2 over states 0 and 3. To verify this, we took the model we learned on the full training data and retrofit it to training data consisting only of sequences produced by students in textretrieval-001 that had perfect marks. To prevent the latent state meanings from drifting, we forced the model parameters associated with their Markov model representations to be fixed, in effect only learning initial and transition probabilities for the top layer of our TL-HMM. We show the updated latent state transition diagram in Figure 2b. We can clearly see that the probability of state 2 has increased dramatically, consistent with previous observations of the positive correlation between forum activity and grades [3], while the probability of states 0 and 3 has decreased. State 1 had its probability increase very slightly.

In Figure 2c we plot the latent state transition diagram for a second group of "low" students. These students were selected so that they attempted all required quizzes in the course, but such that their average quiz score was $\leq 70\%$. Here, we see that *state 1* has a large increase in size, where we might have expected state 3 to grow instead. However, there is an alternative explanation for this phenomenon. Since state 1 seems to indicate a highly engaged student, it is a perfectly reasonable explanation for the "low" student group as they are going to be working hard to try to fill in the gaps in their knowledge. By contrast, the "perfect" student group likely has many members who can take the quiz more passively and get perfect marks, perhaps because they already know much of the material being presented, or are just naturally strong and do not require much background review to perform well. This also explains why state 1 did not increase in size for the "perfect" group like we were anticipating. Kizilcec et al. [4] observe similar phenomena with the courses they studied where they find that certificate earning is negatively correlated with help seeking behavior. Our model enables data-driven discovery of potentially counter-intuitive insights like this.

CONCLUSION

We proposed a two-layer hidden Markov model for MOOC student behavior modeling in an unsupervised learning framework on large collections of actions extracted from MOOC log data. This model is different from existing methods in that it treats behavior patterns as a sequence of *latent states*, rather than assigning these states in a rule-based manner. It captures the variable behaviors of students over time, and allows analysis at different levels of granularity.

We showed that such a model does in fact capture meaningful behavior patterns and produces descriptions of these behavior patterns that are easy to interpret. We argued that it is important to capture student behavior patterns with more sophisticated models than simple discrete distributions over actions in order to capture information present in bigrams of actions (or above). Finally, we investigated whether we can detect differences in student behavior patterns as they correlate with course performance. Specifically, we demonstrated

---

[1]We do not plot the transition probabilities directly within the figure to ease readability; we instead will mention relevant transition probabilities in the text as we discuss the plots. The plots were created using python-igraph: http://igraph.org/python/.

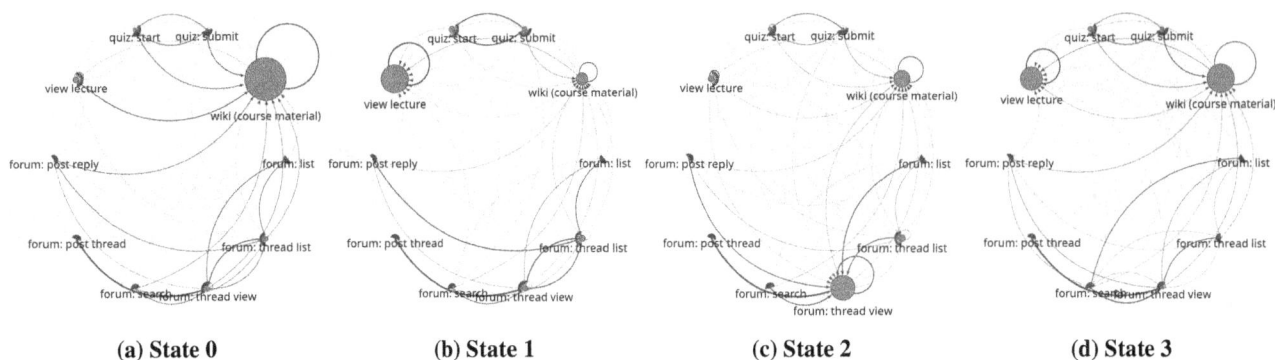

(a) State 0 (b) State 1 (c) State 2 (d) State 3

Figure 1. Example states learned by a 4-state TL-HMM.

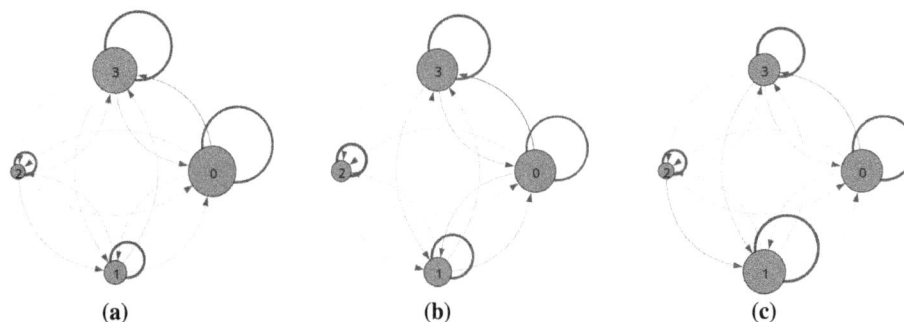

(a) (b) (c)

Figure 2. The latent state transition diagrams for a 4-state TL-HMM fit to textretrieval-001 for all students (a) compared to only "perfect" students (b) and only "low" students (c).

that high-performing students produce substantially different HMM transition diagrams that tend to show longer concentration span in quiz-taking and more active forum participation as compared with the average students.

Future Work

Although we only experimented with our model on one MOOC, the model is completely general and can be easily applied to analyze the log of any other course to enable deep understanding of student behaviors as well as the coorrelations of such behaviors as other variables such as grades. We plan to develop a MOOC log analysis system based on the proposed model to both facilitate education research and help instructors improve course design.

Specifically, our model can be used to produce an ordered list of latent states for each student over time. Given these labeled sequences, we could correlate course-wide drifts in these latent states with events in a course. For example, we might be able to automatically discover difficult or confusing parts of a course by noticing spikes in the distribution of students over latent states over time.

ACKNOWLEDGMENTS

This material is based upon work supported by the National Science Foundation under Grant Number DGE-1144245 (GRFP) and Grant Number 1629161.

REFERENCES

1. Dan Davis, Guanliang Chen, Claudia Hauff, and Geert-Jan Houben. 2016. Gauging MOOC Learners' Adherence to the Designed Learning Path. In *Proc. EDM*. 54–61.

2. Louis Faucon, Lukasz Kidzinski, and Pierre Dillenbourg. 2016. Semi-Markov model for simulating MOOC students. In *Proc. EDM*. 358–363.

3. Jonathan Huang, Anirban Dasgupta, Arpita Ghosh, Jane Manning, and Marc Sanders. 2014. Superposter Behavior in MOOC Forums. In *Proc. L@S*. 117–126.

4. René F. Kizilcec, Mar Pérez-Sanagustín, and Jorge J. Maldonado. 2017. Self-regulated learning strategies predict learner behavior and goal attainment in Massive Open Online Courses. *Computers & Education* 104 (2017), 18 – 33.

5. René F. Kizilcec, Chris Piech, and Emily Schneider. 2013. Deconstructing Disengagement: Analyzing Learner Subpopulations in Massive Open Online Courses. In *Proc. LAK*. 170–179.

6. Sean Massung, Chase Geigle, and ChengXiang Zhai. 2016. MeTA: A Unified Toolkit for Text Retrieval and Analysis. In *Proc. ACL Sys. Demo*. 91–96.

7. Lawrence R. Rabiner. 1990. Readings in Speech Recognition. Chapter A Tutorial on Hidden Markov Models and Selected Applications in Speech Recognition, 267–296.

8. Benjamin Shih, Kenneth R Koedinger, and Richard Scheines. 2010. Unsupervied Discovery of Student Strategies. In *Proc. EDM*. 201–210.

Getting to know English Language Learners in MOOCs: Their Motivations, Behaviors and Outcomes

Selen Türkay
Harvard University
Cambridge, MA, USA
selen_turkay@harvard.edu

Hadas Eidelman
Harvard University
Cambridge, MA, USA
hadas_eidelman@harvard.edu

Yigal Rosen
Harvard University
Cambridge, MA, USA
yigal_rosen@harvard.edu

Daniel Seaton
Harvard University
Cambridge, MA, USA
daniel_seaton@harvard.edu

Glenn Lopez
Harvard University
Cambridge, MA, USA
glenn_lopez@harvard.edu

Jacob Whitehill
Worcester Polytechnic Institute
Worcester, MA, USA
jrwhitehill@wpi.edu

ABSTRACT

Massive Open Online Courses (MOOCs) promise to engage a global audience and emphasize the democratic achievement of free, university-level education. While such open access enables participation, it is unclear how learners who are not fluent in English (ELLs) engage with MOOC content. After all, the language of MOOCs is English. In order to improve accessibility for ELLs in digital learning environments, we must first have a clear understanding of the educational landscape: who are the non-native English speakers enrolled in MOOCs? Where are they located geographically? What are their current online learning behaviors, motivations and outcomes? In this paper we start answering some of these questions by analyzing data from 100 HarvardX courses, using self-report and log data. Preliminary analysis show evidence that ELLs are motivated by more utilitarian goals compared to non-ELLs.

Author Keywords

MOOCs; English language learners; motivations; behaviors; outcomes

ACM Classification Keywords

K.3.1. Computers and Education: Computer Use in Education

INTRODUCTION

MOOCs have the potential to promote equity in educational opportunity for traditionally underserved learners worldwide. Often, the most underserved learners are those in less economically developed nations, where the native language is not English. However, because English is the primary language for MOOCs, for learners with beginning and intermediate English language ability, authentic materials are often beyond their language proficiency and may become incomprehensible without help [12]. A recent survey by Guokr [4] with Chinese learners (n=13,526) presented dire language barriers in online learning. 82% of the respondents said that they wouldn't be able to follow the course unless Chinese close caption is provided. Consequently, more than half of the participants have not taken an online course (n=7809) and 31% of them pinpointed the language barrier as the main reason. For those who have taken online courses, 11% reported that they failed to complete the course because they could not follow the content in English.

In this paper, we aim to learn more about ELLs, their motivations, behaviors, and outcomes in HarvardX MOOCs by analyzing data from 100 courses which is a subset of 150 courses that includes only those learners who filled out pre-course surveys self-reporting their English proficiency and motivations for enrolling in the MOOC (11.35% of all use cases, representing 521221 unique users). Finally, we use recent data from one course, CS50, to produce analysis of transcript usage. CS50 has twelve languages available to learners to use as transcripts.

Opportunities and Challenges for English Language Learners in Online Learning and MOOCs

The education of non-native English speakers in MOOCs is a critical issue both within the United States and abroad. On a domestic level, the U.S. Census Bureau [10] indicates 59.5 million people aged 5 and over spoke a language other than English at home. Only 58% of this population reported speaking English "very well" whereas 7% did not speak English at all. ELLs' educational outcomes, including high school graduation rates (57% versus 79%), tend to be lower compared to native English speakers [5, 11]. Outside of the U.S. context, one of the promising features of MOOCs is the ability to deliver high-quality educational content to learners in disadvantaged portions of the globe. As it was

L@S 2017, April 20-21, 2017, Cambridge, MA, USA.
© 2017 ACM. ISBN 978-1-4503-4450-0/17/04...$15.00.
DOI: http://dx.doi.org/10.1145/3051457.3053987

noted earlier, ironically, the geographic areas that could most benefit from MOOC content are often those where English is not the main language of communication. Therefore, both within and outside of the American education system, the issue of access to MOOC curricula for students who are non-native English speakers is critical from the perspective of equalizing opportunity for underserved learners.

There are several reasons why MOOCs represent learning environments offering a unique opportunity to educate learners from vulnerable populations. Compared to traditional classroom-based learning environments, online learning and MOOCs in particular offer the potential to (a) cross geographic and educational boundaries to deliver high-quality content; (b) give students agency to learn when and where they want; and (c) provide educational content in multiple modalities (e.g., audio, video, text) to suit students' differing needs or preferences (e.g., closed captioning, adjustable playback speed) [5]. The asynchronous nature of MOOCs provides ELLs more privacy and preparation time by lowering barriers [12]. For ELLs, these advantages can facilitate subject matter comprehension while simultaneously promoting learning of the language of instruction itself [7,8].

However, without deliberate design for accessibility, online education risks broadening the gap between advantaged and disadvantaged learners [5]. The digital divide in online education has two fronts: content access driven by economic status and students' capability to benefit from that content [2]. The latter prevents many ELLs from accessing courses developed in English-speaking countries [3]. Considering the large number of students with low English proficiency in the US and around the world, only 20% of the world population can fully benefit from English-only educational content [1], highlighting the need for implementing various accommodations to increase access for these students to digital learning environments. Some most common accommodations are video captions and subtitles. Lecture transcripts are beneficial by-products of these accommodations. ELLs can download the transcripts to aid their language comprehension.

A previous interview study showed evidence that ELLs may have different motivations than non-ELLs [9]. In this paper, we will investigate ELLs' motivation to take MOOCs, using self-reported survey questions, and how learners' motivations may differ based on their level of engagement in the course. We will also compare ELLs' motivations to non-ELLs' motivations to find potential differences between these learner groups.

DATA

HarvardX enrollment data and events data generated by participants across all HarvardX courses were analyzed using the HarvardX/MITx edx2bigquery canonical dataset Person-Course-Survey. This comprehensive dataset includes all the common standard Qualtrics pre-course survey questions (including English proficiency), and merges together the edX user data and learning metrics including course enrollment and registration information, demographics, resource access, course progression and time-on-task for all HarvardX courses.

By the time we wrote this paper, HarvardX pre-course survey included four questions on learners' English fluency in reading, writing, speaking, and listening (e.g., How fluent are you in English, the language of this course - reading?), and users rated their English fluency on a 5-point Likert scale (0=Weak; 1=Basic; 2=Intermediate; 3=Proficient; 4=Fluent). Here, we define ELLs as learners who answer in the fluency questions *not fluent*. If a learner answers one of these language skills as not fluent, we categorize this learner as an ELL. If s/he answers all four items as "fluent", we categorize these learners as non-ELLs.

RESULTS

Geographic Locations

The top five countries with most ELLs in HarvardX MOOCs are India, USA, Brazil, China, and Spain. The fact that USA is among these top five countries with ELL MOOC users strengthens our emphasis on national dimension of ELL user population. From USA, California, New York and Massachusetts have the most number of ELL registrants in HarvardX courses.

Certification Rates

For this portion of our analysis, in order to avoid wildly imprecise estimates of certification rates that might occur in particularly small courses, we restricted our sample of MOOCs to only those that had 100 or more ELLs enrolled and 100 or more students who received certification (n=64). In these 64 courses, using the operationalization for ELLs that we presented above, we found that the proportion of ELLs by course ranged from 6.0-29.6%. Similarly, restricting the data to only those UN geographic regions that had 100 or more ELLs and 100 or more learners who received certification (n=17), we found that the proportion of ELLs ranged from 3.9% in Northern America to 56.5% in Northern Africa. At the course level, certification rates for ELLs ranged from 0.33-35.6% for ELLs and 0.32-56.3% for non-ELLs. We fit logistic regression models estimating students' probability of certification by ELL status, controlling for age, gender, geography, developing nation status, and online behaviors. Preliminary modeling in the full sample suggests the odds of ELLs certifying are roughly 0.6 times the odds for non-ELLs (p<0.001), accounting for the nesting of students in courses and in different configurations of covariates. We conclude with sensitivity analyses using our two alternate versions of the language-proficiency measure.

Transcript Use

Our dataset included a transcript variable: *ntrancript*, which describes the number of video transcript events from tracking logs. These transcript events include download transcript, and toggle on and off closed captions. We found that ELL users, on average, create significantly more transcript events than non-ELL users ($t(279720) = -21.82$, *cohen's d* = 0.07, M_{ELL}=14.36, $M_{non-ELL}$=11.15).

Comparison of ELL and non-ELL users' behavior of transcript download show that ELLs downloaded transcripts more than non-ELLs did ($t(239560)$=-15.9, $p<.0001$, *cohen's d*=0.05). (Reader should keep in mind that we are able to track transcript downloads only since May 2016.) Another transcript related video player feature is the running transcripts on the right side of the video. Learners can choose to view these or close it by clicking on the "CC" button. This event is registered as *show_transcript* in our data. Considerable numbers of ELLs used this function (n=59518). However we are unable to conclude whether their goals were to show or close running transcripts.

The HarvardX course with the highest number of ELL registrants is CS50: Introduction to Computer Science course, which is also the largest course offered at HarvardX. CS50 also offers 12 different transcript languages to assist learners. When investigating further, approximately 38% (n=8790) of CS50 learners who filled out the pre-survey are ELLs. Examining log event data related to transcripts, we find that 32% (n=2851) of these learners use transcripts other than English as their modal transcript language, and 2771 learners have downloaded the video transcripts to aid their comprehension.

Video Events and Forum Participation

We analyzed video and forum interaction events for ELL and non-ELL users based on the cumulative data on each type of interaction (i.e., video play, pause, forum threads, forum comments). On average, we found that ELLs take significantly more video play ($t(247930) = -25.11$, *Cohen's d* = 0.03), video pause ($t(304220) = -10.31$, *Cohen's d* = 0.08), and seek actions ($t(354200) = -6.75$, *Cohen's d* = 0.02) compared to non-ELL users (see Figure 1). Forum participation metrics revealed that compared to ELLs, non-ELL users start more forum threads ($t(52269) = 3.06$, *Cohen's d* = 0.02, p=.002), make more comments($t(61398) = 11.05$, *Cohen's d* =0.08, p < 2.2e-16), and votes more on other learners' posts (t(67943)=13.52, *Cohen's d* =0.10, p < 2.2e-16) (see Figure 2).

Comparison of ELL and non-ELL Users' Motivations to Take MOOCs

In pre-course surveys, learners answer questions on their motivations to take the course that they signed up for. They are asked to rate their motivation to take a MOOC on ten dimensions (How important were the following reasons in choosing to register for this course?) These dimensions are: Engaging in lifelong learning; learn from the best professors and universities; advancing learners' formal education; participate in an online community; curiosity about online learning; career advancement; access learning opportunities not otherwise available to them; learn about course content; earn a certificate; better serve their

community. See Table 1 for ratings by learners where Cohen's d is larger than 0.2 (a small effect size).

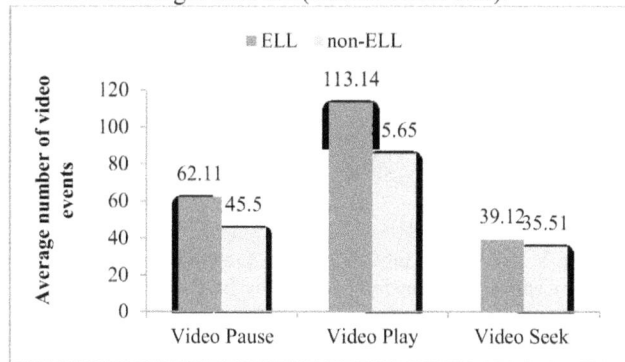

Figure 1. Average number of video events per person by language proficiency.

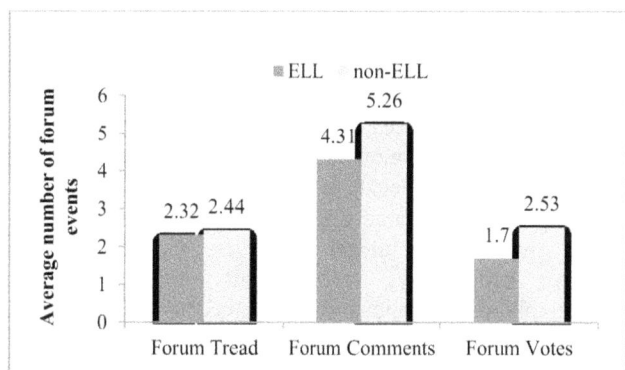

Figure 2. Average number of forum events per person by language proficiency.

	t	$M_{(non-ELL)}$	$M_{(ELL)}$	Cohen's d
Lifelong learning	69.3	3.37	3.17	0.23
Best professors	-64.98	3.19	3.39	0.21
Education advan.	-92.55	2.55	2.93	0.30
Participate	-89.65	1.57	1.94	0.29
Career advance.	-84.76	2.48	2.85	0.27
Certification	-82.15	1.57	1.94	0.27
Community	-69.83	2.14	2.43	0.23

Table 1. Two sample t-test statistics and effect sizes, comparing ELL and non-ELL users' motivations.

Results show evidence that ELL and non-ELL users may be motivated by different goals to take MOOCs. When we further compare ELL and non-ELL registrants' motivations by course progress (i.e., certified, explored, viewed), the differences across motivations become even more salient. In Figure 3, we can see that ELL and non-ELL users tend to view courses if their motivation is to engage in life long learning. For all other levels of engagement, the differences between ELLs and non-ELLs remain statistically significant.

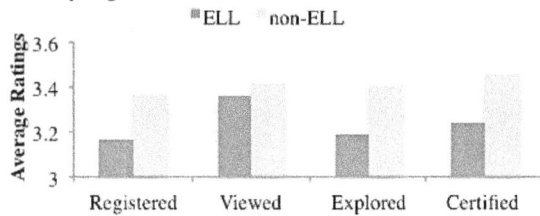

Figure 3. Average ratings on *lifelong learning* motivation item by course progression grouped by language fluency.

DISCUSSION

This study explored differences and similarities in motivation, behaviors and outcomes between ELL and non-ELLs in HarvardX courses. We hope the results will inspire L@S community to look closer at sub-learner groups in MOOCs and their potentially differing needs, as one-size-fits-all approach is not the ideal model of education.

Results showed that ELL and non-ELL registrants have somewhat different motivations on various dimensions. Although it is expected to find significant differences among groups with large sample sizes, this finding is still telling: users' motivations may differ based on their language proficiency, which usually relates to other demographics and socioeconomic status. It is evident that learners who are ELLs have more utilitarian goals when signing up for these courses. For instance, previous studies found that many learners do not seek credit toward any credential [6]. Our findings not only confirm this for non-ELLs, but also show that ELL users might be more motivated toward earning certificate than non-ELLs. This implies potential focus on helping ELLs attain certification and devising tracks similar to ID verification to give certificates more utility for ELL users. We also found that although ELL users were more motivated to participate in community than non-ELLs, their forum participation is lower than non-ELLs. This may indicate that ELLs need more support to encourage their participation in forums and other online learning communities.

While we recognize the importance of encouraging universities and colleges in non-English speaking counties to develop their own culturally targeted content in their own languages, we believe that goal driven interventions to make high quality instructional materials, which are usually developed in English, available to ELLs will lower barriers to democratize education through MOOCs.

We acknowledge generalizability issues for the sample we used for this paper, such as underestimated ELL prevalence (learners with especially-low English proficiency are less likely to fill out the survey) and inflated rates of course certification (learners who complete the survey are likely more committed to persistence), by comparing them to the full sample.

CONCLUSION

This work contributes to practical and scholarly knowledge of online instruction and learning environments. Results illuminate successes and challenges for ELLs in MOOCs, descriptively and through modeling statistically the relationships between learners' likelihood of certification and student-level behaviors and region-level characteristics. We hope that findings will inform future research and experimentation in digital learning environments to benefit both ELLs and non-ELLs globally and within the U.S.

REFERENCES

1. Tita Beaven, Anna Comas-Quinn, Mirjam Hauck, Beatriz De los Arcos, and Timothy Lewis. 2013. The Open Translation MOOC: creating online communities to transcend linguistic barriers. *Journal of Interactive Media in Education* 2013, 3, 18.

2. Sheryl Burgstahler. 2002. Distance learning: Universal design, universal access. *Educational Technology Review* 10, 1, 32–61.

3. Rainbow Tsai-Hung Chen, Sue Bennett, and Karl Maton. 2008. The adaptation of Chinese international students to online flexible learning: two case studies. *Distance Education* 29, 3, 307–323.

4. GuoKr. 2015. Available online: http://mooc.guokr.com

5. Grace Kena et al. 2015. The condition of education 2015. NCES 2015-144. *National Center for Education Statistics* (2015).

6. Steve Kolowich. 2013. The professors who make the MOOCs. *The Chronicle of Higher Education* 18.

7. Deborah L. Linebarger. 2001. Learning to read from television: The effects of using captions and narration. *Journal of Educational Psychology* 93, 2, 288–298.

8. Peter Shea. 2000. Leveling the playing field: A study of captioned interactive video for second language learning. *Journal of Educational Computing Research* 22, 3, 243–263.

9. Judith Uchidiuno, Amy Ogan, Kenneth R. Koedinger, Evelyn Yarzebinski, and Jessica Hammer. 2016. Browser Language Preferences as a Metric for Identifying ESL Speakers in MOOCs. In ACM Press, 277–280.

10. U.S. Census Bureau, 2011. Changes in Population Controls, American Community Survey Research Note.

11. Evelien Van Laere, Orhan Agirdag, and Johan van Braak. 2016. Supporting science learning in linguistically diverse classrooms: Factors related to the use of bilingual content in a computer-based learning environment. *Computers in Human Behavior*, 57, 428–441.

12. Yi (Leaf) Zhang. 2013. Power distance in online learning: Experience of Chinese learners in U.S. higher education. *The International Review of Research in Open and Distributed Learning* 14, 4.

Generating Language Activities in Real-Time for English Learners using Language Muse

Jill Burstein
Educational Testing Service
Princeton, USA
jburstein@ets.org

Nitin Madnani
Educational Testing Service
Princeton, USA
nmadnani@ets.org

John Sabatini
Educational Testing Service
Princeton, USA
jsabatini@ets.org

Dan McCaffrey
Educational Testing Service
Princeton, USA
dmccaffrey@ets.org

Kietha Biggers
Educational Testing Service
Princeton, USA
kbiggers@ets.org

Kelsey Dreier
Educational Testing Service
Princeton, USA
kdreier@ets.org

ABSTRACT

K-12 education standards in the U.S. require all students to read complex texts across many subject areas. The *Language Muse*[TM] *Activity Palette* is a web-based language-instruction application that uses NLP algorithms and lexical resources to automatically generate language activities and support English language learners' content comprehension and language skills development. The system's online platform for activity generation, scoring, and feedback is scalable for MOOCs, as well as for other online learning settings.

INTRODUCTION

The Common Core State Standards adopted by most U.S states explicitly emphasize the need for students to read complex subject area texts to prepare for college and careers [6]. Classroom texts may contain language unfamiliar to English language learners (ELLs), e.g. figurative language. ELLs could be disadvantaged without scaffolding to aid in comprehension of unfamiliar language [8]. One way to help is through the use of linguistic activities designed to get ELLs familiar with the language used in the subject area texts [7].

We present the Language Muse Activity Palette (*LM* heretofore), an open-access, web-based tool [1], and discuss a small-scale instructional pilot intervention that has shown promise with regard to addressing ELL content comprehension and language learning needs. Teachers can input their own classroom texts into LM to automatically generate language activities in real-time which can then be assigned to students online. The activities are generated using several existing NLP algorithms and lexical resources designed to help ELLs with multiple

[1]available at http://languagemuse.10clouds.com.

L@S 2017, April 20 - 21, 2017, Cambridge, MA, USA

© 2017 Copyright held by the owner/author(s). Publication rights licensed to ACM.
ISBN 978-1-4503-4450-0/17/04. . . $15.00

DOI: http://dx.doi.org/10.1145/3051457.3053988

aspects of language learning needed to support content comprehension: vocabulary, syntactic structures, and discourse structure.

LM is related to existing NLP work on automatic question generation [2, 12, 14]. In contrast to previous work, it can generate over 20 activity types for any given classroom text, covering a large set of language constructs, and offers activity customizability. In addition, many activities can be automatically scored. Analytics can also be generated for students' language proficiency from both automatically-scored and teacher-scored activities.

Below, we describe the LM NLP backend, the teacher and student interactions, findings from a small-scale instructional intervention, and future work.

NLP BACKEND

LM relies on a backend that uses NLP algorithms to identify linguistic features contained in an input text [5]. These features include: (a) lexical entities (single word and multi-word expressions), (b) syntactic structures, and (c) discourse relations. LM also relies on a few manually-crafted resources either directly, or indirectly as a filter for statistical NLP algorithms that may yield somewhat noisier outputs. This limits the teachers' need to edit over-generated, incorrect options.

Lexical resources are used for activities related to these language elements: homonyms [3], cognates [5], academic words [9], and antonyms [10]. Synonym-based activities are powered using a thresholded combination of WordNet, a distributional thesaurus [13], and statistically extracted paraphrases [1]. Multiword expression activities are generated using a rank-ratio based collocation detection algorithm trained on the Google Web1T *n*-gram corpus [11]. Regular expressions defined on constituency parses generate phrasal and sentential structures for activities related to contractions, complex verb, noun phrases, relative clauses, and multi-clause sentences. A morphological analyzer and word-form database are used to generate activities related to derivational and inflectional word forms. Discourse relations related to cause-effect, compare-

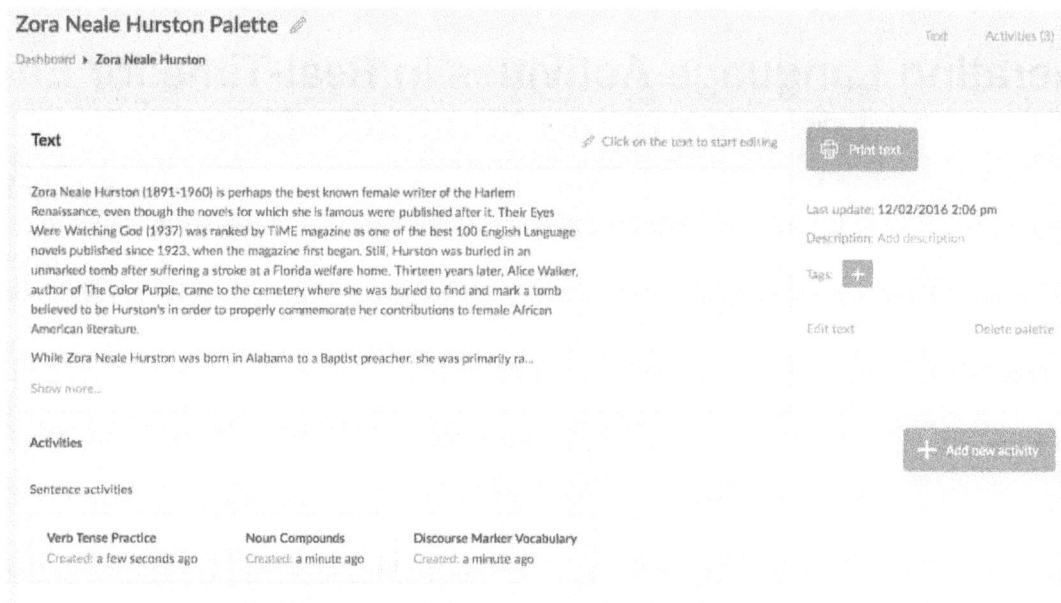

Figure 1. An example activity palette generated using Language Muse.

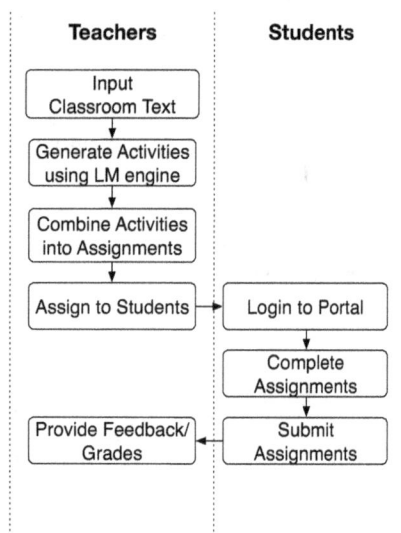

Figure 2. A flowchart illustrating the complete Language Muse instructional workflow from activity generation to students receiving feedback on their work.

contrast, and evidence draw from an adapted rule-based, discourse analyzer [4].

PALETTE & ASSIGNMENT CREATION, AND SCORING
Teachers upload a classroom text into LM. The engine automatically generates over 20 activities based on linguistic features identified in the text. Teachers then select activities to create an "activity palette" (Figure 1) — a set of text-specific activities — to support one or more learning objectives, such as "practice with derivational word forms".

Full palettes, or specific activities in a palette, can be used to create assignments targeting the learning objective. Assignments can be administered to and completed online by students. Multiple choice, and cloze activities are automatically scored. For activities requiring open-ended responses, teachers provide scores and written feedback. Teachers and students may view scores and feedback at any time. See Figure 2 for a high-level overview of this workflow.

INSTRUCTIONAL INTERVENTION
In Spring 2016, a 6-week instructional intervention study was conducted to examine the promise and feasibility of LM use in a classroom setting, in preparation for a large-scale randomized control trial (RCT) in Spring 2017.

- **Teacher & Student Participants**. Results are based on 12 English Language Arts (ELA), Science, and Social Studies teachers from two participating middle schools where ELL populations were over 33%. 167 students who completed pre- and post-tests were included in the analysis presented here.

- **Instruments**. The RISE reading assessment [15] was administered to students pre- and post-intervention to examine intervention outcomes. The test contains 6 component measures related to reading proficiency, e.g., vocabulary and morphology. An observational protocol [5] was used to collect teacher observation data pre-, during and post-intervention. Teacher perception surveys were administered post-intervention.

- **Preliminary Findings**. The pre-post assessment outcomes were difficult to interpret, especially outside of an RCT. Gains were observed in some components, but there were also score losses – potentially due to motivation, since the assessments were no-stakes. Observational data suggested

Activity Type	Count
Academic Vocabulary	19
Antonyms	9
Cognates (Spanish)	17
Compare/Contrast	6
Finding Homonyms	17
Multiple Clauses	16
Phrasal Verbs	3
Referential Terms	5
Summary Practice	3
Synonyms	18
Variant Word Forms	21
Verb Tenses	12
Word Stems	9

Table 1. Teachers' self-reported usage showing counts of activities during the instructional intervention.

that teachers productively integrated LM into classroom instruction. A positive survey finding showed that all teachers successfully completed the intervention, and reported that activities completely (47%) or mostly (39%) fulfilled intended learning objectives. See Table 1 for activity usage during the intervention.

FUTURE WORK
In Spring 2017, an instructional intervention will be conducted with LM in an RCT with approx. 20 U.S. middle schools with high EL populations. Outcomes showing promising use of and positive reactions to LM, and pre-post assessment gains would suggest promise of LM as a classroom tool, with potential applications in language learning MOOCs and other online classrooms to support learning at scale. Currently, Paper Airplanes[2] is also exploring LM use for one-on-one online English tutoring for Syrian students.

ACKNOWLEDGMENTS
Research presented in this paper was supported by the Institute of Education Science, U.S. Department of Education, Award Number R305A140472, and by the 10Clouds front-end development team.

REFERENCES
1. Colin Bannard and Chris Callison-Burch. 2005. Paraphrasing with Bilingual Parallel Corpora. In *Proceedings of ACL*.

2. Jonathan C Brown, Gwen A Frishkoff, and Maxine Eskenazi. 2005. Automatic Question Generation for Vocabulary Assessment. In *Proceedings of EMNLP*.

3. Jill Burstein, Martin Chodorow, and Claudia Leacock. 2004. Automated Essay Evaluation: The Criterion Online Writing Service. *AI Magazine* 25, 3 (2004), 27.

4. Jill Burstein, Karen Kukich, Susanne Wolff, Chi Lu, and Martin Chodorow. 1998. Enriching Automated Scoring using Discourse Marking. In *Proceedings of the ACL Workshop on Discourse Relations and Discourse Marking*.

5. J. Burstein, J. Shore, J. Sabatini, B. Moulder, J. Lentini, K. Biggers, and S. Holtzman. 2014. From Teacher Professional Development to the Classroom. *Journal of Educational Computing Research* 51, 1 (2014), 119–144.

6. CCSSO. 2010. *Common Core State Standards for English language Arts & Literacy in History/Social Studies, Science, and Technical Subjects. Appendix A: Research supporting key elements of the Standards*. Washington, DC.

7. Frances Christie. 1989. *Language Education*. Oxford University Press, Oxford, UK.

8. Rhonda Coleman and Claude Goldenberg. 2012. The Common Core Challenge for English Language Learners. *Principal Leadership* (2012), 46–51.

9. A. Coxhead. 2000. The Academic Word List. Retrieved from `http://www.victoria.ac.nz/lals/resources/academicwordlist/`. (2000).

10. Christiane Fellbaum. 1998. *WordNet*. Blackwell Publishing Ltd.

11. Yoko Futagi, Paul Deane, Martin Chodorow, and Joel Tetreault. 2008. A Computational Approach to Detecting Collocation Errors in the Writing of Non-native Speakers of English. *Computer Assisted Language Learning* 21, 4 (2008).

12. Michael Heilman and Noah A Smith. 2010. Good question! Statistical Ranking for Question Generation. In *Proceedings of NAACL*.

13. Dekang Lin. 1998. Automatic Retrieval and Clustering of Similar Words. In *Proceedings of COLING*.

14. Ruslan Mitkov and Le An Ha. 2003. Computer-aided Generation of Multiple-choice Tests. In *Proceedings of the Workshop on Building Educational Applications*.

15. John Sabatini, Kelly Bruce, Jonathan Steinberg, and Jonathan Weeks. 2015. *SARA Reading Components Tests, RISE Forms: Technical Adequacy and Test Design, 2nd Edition*. Technical Report ETS-RR-15-32.

[2] `http://www.paper-airplanes.org/`

Humans and Machines Together: Improving Characterization of Large Scale Online Discussions through Dynamic Interrelated Post and Thread Categorization (DIPTiC)

Yi Cui
Simon Fraser University
Surrey, B.C. V3T OA3 Canada
yca231@sfu.ca

Wan Qi Jin
Simon Fraser University
Surrey, B.C. V3T OA3 Canada
wanqij@sfu.ca

Alyssa Friend Wise
New York University
New York, NY 10003 USA
alyssa.wise@nyu.edu

ABSTRACT
This paper presents a thread characterization method that compares categorization results for thread starters and replies made by a previously-developed natural language model, using human judgment to resolve discrepancies. In an example application using the complete discussion forum data from a MOOC on medical statistics, the method increased the estimation of classification accuracy from .81 to .88 with the addition of a minimal number of human hours.

Author Keywords
Massive open online courses; discussion forum; thread categorization.

MOOC DISCUSSION CATEGORIZATION PROBLEMS
Due to the great variety of type, topics and styles present, characterization of online discussions in MOOCs and other large scale online discussions can be useful to both practitioners and researchers [1; 2]. While historically much post characterization has been done manually, the rise of large-scale environments creates a need to automate the process. One common approach is to manually code a portion of the posts and then train a classifier based on extracted linguistic features [3]. However, there are two critical issues related to discussion forum data that make the task distinct from standard text classification. First, there is the issue of the appropriate unit of analysis. Individual posts do not exist in a vacuum but have meaning in the context of those that come before and after it. Thus a model that returns classification results for individual posts devoid of context is not as useful as one which returns a collection of related posts. Second, threaded discussions evolve as new participants join the conversation, thus it is not possible to

L@S 2017, April 20-21, 2017, Cambridge, MA, USA
© 2017 ACM. ISBN 978-1-4503-4450-0/17/04...$15.00
DOI: http://dx.doi.org/10.1145/3051457.3053989

characterize a thread simply by its starting post. These two challenges present a novel opportunity to use the *collection of posts* that make up a thread as the characterization unit in a way that both takes into account co-thread post interdependencies and offers an efficient approach to the human checking of machine classification.

PROPOSED SOLUTION: DYNAMIC INTERRELATED POST AND THREAD CATEGORIZATION (DIPTIC)
In this section we describe and demonstrate a method for dynamic interrelated post and thread categorization (DIPTiC) in which each discussion thread is categorized twice based on model-based classification of its (a) starting post and (b) reply posts. Mismatches in categorization (which may indicate model error or shifting trends in conversation) are identified for manual checking. The steps in the approach are described below with an example application using the complete discussion corpus (3129 posts in 817 threads made by 568 forum users) from a MOOC on Medical Statistics offered in 2014. For a further description and analysis of the data, see [6]. Usefulness is evaluated as the extent to which mismatch examination results in changes in categorization that improve accuracy.

Step 1: Articulate categorization purpose, classifier(s) for starter and reply posts, and the operational definitions of the relationships between the two
For the example application, the goal of thread characterization was to make a binary distinction between threads that were substantively related to course-content and those which were not [4]. Thus, a single classifier, which identified a post as content-related or not, was used on both thread starters and replies [5]. In this case, the alignment between the thread categorization target and the classifier used made for a straightforward mapping (see Figure 1a). In other situations the mapping between classifier and characterization purpose may not be as direct and different classifiers may be required to categorize starter and reply posts. For example, if the purpose is to identify threads containing controversy, the starter classifier might be targeted at posts which take a forceful position, while the reply classifier may focus on the presence of sentiments such as confusion and disagreement. Classifiers which result in more than two categories can also be used.

In addition, rules are needed for how to characterize threads when the verified categorizations based on the starter and replies differ. In the current case, priority was given to the presence of content-relatedness of any form (see Figure 1b). That is, if a starter was truly content-related but the proportion of replies did not meet the threshold, or if a starter was non-content but the proportion of content-related replies exceeded the threshold then the entire thread was considered to be content-related. In other cases, a standard could be set that requires the presence of certain categories in *both* the starter and replies to achieve the characterization, or a third characterization could be created to uniquely designate such mixed situations.

$$S = C \rightarrow T_{(Starter)} = C$$
$$S = NC \rightarrow T_{(Starter)} = NC$$
$$\Sigma R_x / \Sigma x \geq P \rightarrow T_{x(Reply)} = C$$
$$\Sigma R_x / \Sigma x < P \rightarrow T_{x(Reply)} = NC$$

(a)

	$T_{(Reply)} = C$	$T_{(Reply)} = NC$
$T_{(Starter)} = C$	$T_{(Final)} = C$	$T_{(Final)} = C$
$T_{(Starter)} = NC$	$T_{(Final)} = C$	$T_{(Final)} = NC$

(b)

Key: S = Starter's classification; R_x = Reply's classification; C = Content-related; NC = Non-content; $T_{(Starter)}$ = Thread's categorization based on starter's classification; $T_{(Reply)}$ = Thread's categorization based on the aggregation of reply-post classifications (in this case if the proportion of replies that are content-related is above a certain threshold P where 0 < P < 1); $T_{(Final)}$ = Thread's final categorization.

Figure 1 (a) Classifier to categorization mappings for threads (b) Thread categorization matrix based on verified $T_{(Starter)}$ and $T_{(Reply)}$.

Step 2: Prepare the data and assess the base reliability of the classifier(s)

Cleaning data for DIPTiC includes removing any empty or duplicate posts and posts which do not fit the classifiers' working parameters (e.g. foreign language etc., 5 removed here). Depending on the research purpose, starters without replies can be removed from the dataset entirely (done here for 117 starters without replies) or segregated for simple classification. Establishing the base reliability of the classifier with the data is done by manually coding a randomly chosen subset. In this case, annotation of 304 starters and 402 reply posts by two researchers ($\kappa_{Starters} = .81$, $\kappa_{Replies} = .79$) produced evidence of acceptable reliability of the model to proceed ($\alpha_{Starters} = .81$, $\alpha_{Replies} = .85$).

Step 3: Apply the classifier, establish cut-off point(s), and calculate reply based categorization

The 700 thread starters with 2307 associated replies were classified by the model as content-related or non-content (see Table 1). The proportion of content-related replies in each thread was then calculated (see Figure 2). The

majority of threads had either no or all content-related replies while a large number had exactly half. This distribution was in part influenced by the high presence of threads with only one (N=230) or two (N=194) replies.

	Content-Related	Non-Content
# of Starters	385	315
% of Starters	55%	45%
# of Replies	897	1410
% of Replies	39%	61%

Table 1: Model-based classification of starters and replies.

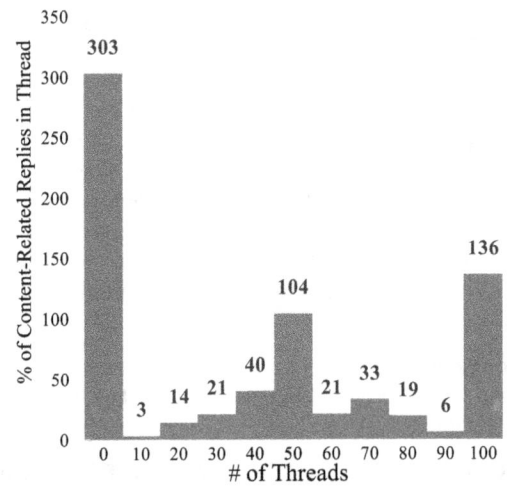

Figure 2: Distribution of percentage of content-related replies per thread.

To categorize threads based on the proportion of content-related replies in them, a threshold level P is needed. This determination should take into consideration the base-rates of the classification across all replies. Here, 39% of all replies were content-related, suggesting a threshold of around one-third. P was thus set to be ≥ 0.33, resulting in a reply-based categorization of 359 threads (51%) as content-related and 341 (49%) as non-content.

Step 4: Identify mismatches, examine and recategorize as appropriate

Of the 700 threads, 301 (43%) had double content-related categorization, 257 (37%) had double non-content categorization and 142 (20%) had mismatches between starter and reply categorizations (this matches expected model error rate of 19%).

To examine the mismatches (see Figure 3), starters in all 142 threads were hand coded by two researchers ($\kappa = .73$). A total of 65 starters were verified as content-related and an additional 31 which the model had labelled as non-content were reclassified as content-related. Following the previously established priority rules (Figure 1b) all of these threads were characterized as content-related. Of the remaining starters, 19 which the model had labelled as content-related were recategorized as non-content. For these 19 both the starter and reply categorizations now matched, thus the threads were categorized as non-content. The remaining 27 threads were verified as having non-content starters, but were above the threshold of content-related replies based on the model classification. Thus the 133 replies in these 27 threads were hand coded by two researchers ($\kappa = .78$). 25% of replies were recategorized (see Table 2) and the proportion of content-related replies in these 27 threads were recalculated. Thirteen of the reply-chains still surpassed the $P \geq 0.33$ threshold and were thus verified as content-related threads. With the reclassifications 14 threads dropped below 0.33 replies and thus were characterized as non-content threads.

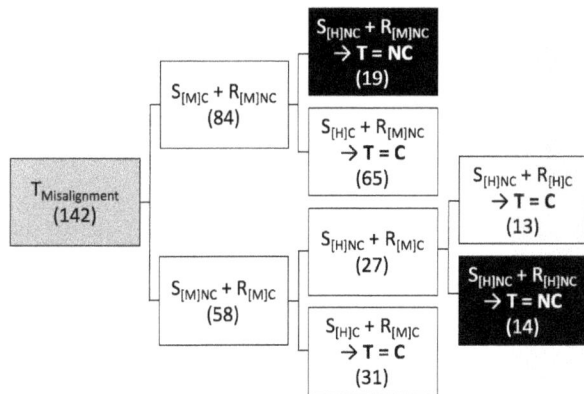

Key: S = Starter's classification; R = Reply's classification; T = Thread's classification; C = Content-related; NC = Non-content; [M] = Classified by model; [H] = Classified by humans.

Figure 3: Mismatch examination.

	$R_{[M]C}$	$R_{[M]N}$
$R_{[H]C}$	42	11
$R_{[H]N}$	22	58

Key: R = Reply's classification; [M] = Classified by model; [H] = Classified by humans; C = Content-related; NC = Non-content.

Table 2: Comparison of manual and model-based reply post classifications.

DISCUSSION AND IMPLICATIONS
The impact of the DIPTiC method can be evaluated by examining the changes to thread characterization in comparison to the expected error rate. The data set used had a total of 700 starters with replies. Based on the .81 model accuracy on a sample of 304 starters, the number of misclassified starters would be expected to be 133. The DIPTiC approach recharacterized 50 starters, leading to an estimate that ~38% (50/133) of the expected classification errors were addressed and allowing for an estimated new accuracy of starter classification of .88 (.81+(50/700)). Thus the DIPTiC method provides an efficient way to improve model results. In addition, reclassifications can be fed back to further improve the model for future use.

In addition, another 13 threads were identified in which the starter was verified as non-content but an evolution of the discussion led to a (verified) substantial proportion of content-based replies and thus a content-related characterization, indicating that including reply-based categorization allows for capturing such changes in discussion topic that would be lost otherwise.

The discussion forum dataset used for this example application is typical in terms of the number of posts for MOOCs of its scale. In total manual examination of the 142 threads which led to 63 recategorizations (44%) took 16 person-hours (using only a single coder this time would be halved). The DIPTiC method showcases a way that humans and machines can work together to improve characterization accuracy and efficiency.

ACKNOWLEDGEMENTS
We thank Stanford University and the MOOCPosts team for their assistance in accessing and working with the data.

REFERENCES
1. Akshay Agrawal, Jagadish Venkatraman, Shane Leonard, and Andreas Paepcke. 2015. YouEDU: addressing confusion in MOOC discussion forums by recommending instructional video clips. In *Proceedings of the 8th International Conference on Education Data Mining*, 297-304.

2. Aneesha Bakharia. 2016. Towards cross-domain MOOC forum post classification. In *Proceedings of the 3rd ACM Conference on Learning@ Scale*, 253-256.

3. Miaomiao Wen, Diyi Yang, and Carolyn Penstein Rosé. 2014. Linguistic reflections of student engagement in massive open online courses. In *proceedings of the International Conference on Weblogs and Social Media*.

4. Alyssa Friend Wise, Yi Cui, and Jovita Vytasek. 2016. Bringing order to chaos in MOOC discussion forums with content-related thread identification. In *Proceedings of the 6th International Conference on Learning Analytics & Knowledge*, 188-197.

5. Alyssa Friend Wise, Yi Cui, Wanqi Jin, and Jovita Vytasek. 2017. Mining for gold: identifying content-related MOOC discussion threads across domains through linguistic modeling. *The Internet and Higher Education*, 32: 11-28.

6. Alyssa Friend Wise, Yi Cui, and Wanqi Jin. 2017. Honing in on social learning networks in MOOC forums: examining critical network definition decisions. In *Proceedings of the 7th International Conference on Learning Analytics & Knowledge*.

CROWDLEARNING: Towards Collaborative Problem-Posing at Scale

Alireza Farasat
Department of Industrial and
Systems Engineering
University at Buffalo
afarasat@buffalo.edu

Alexander Nikolaev
Department of Industrial and
Systems Engineering
University at Buffalo
anikolae@buffalo.edu

Suzanne Miller
Graduate School of Education
University at Buffalo
smiller@buffalo.edu

Rahul Gopalsamy
Department of Industrial and
Systems Engineering
University at Buffalo
rahulgop@buffalo.edu

ABSTRACT

This paper presents a new pedagogical paradigm "Crowdlearning", where students experience deeper learning through collaboratively creating learning materials for each other. Crowdlearning practice is envisioned to produce large "banks" of subject matter problems generated by students themselves, in a crowdsourced way, as the students learn new subjects; these problems can then serve as learning and assessment materials usable at scale. This paper overviews the motivation for the development of Crowdlearning as a teaching practice and the theoretical drivers behind it. The paper then reports on preliminary field studies and experiences suggesting that Crowdlearning has a solid potential for adoption in STEM.

CCS Concepts

•**Social and professional topics** → **Socio-technical systems;** Student assessment; •**Applied computing** → **Computer-assisted instruction; Collaborative learning;** *E-learning;*

Author Keywords

Crowdlearning; problem posing; collaborative learning; intelligent tutoring systems; learning technologies; massive open online courses.

INTRODUCTION

This paper presents the socio-technical pedagogical paradigm "Crowdlearning", aimed at engaging students in physical and virtual classrooms in creative problem-posing and problem-solving. The objective of Crowdlearning is to help learners gain new perspectives on the use of subject-matter concepts

L@S 2017, April 20-21, 2017, Cambridge, MA, USA

© 2017 ACM. ISBN 978-1-4503-4450-0/17/04…$15.00

DOI: http://dx.doi.org/10.1145/3051457.3053990

and let them learn with and from each other. The vision of Crowdlearning is that of a self-sustaining problem-posing and problem-solving environment, where the students of a given subject intermittently take on roles as (A) the creators of subject-focused problems (problem statements/formulations with answer alternatives, hints, correct answers with explanations, etc.); (B) evaluators of problem quality; and (C) problem solvers. The activities that the students perform in roles (A) and (B) are consensus-driven, wherein students create and "vote" in the problems that help them learn, thereby building "banks" of subject matter problems to use for learning and assessment. While Crowdlearning can be adopted as an in-class practice, it is expected to be most useful when implemented as an online platform that will direct collaborative activities across classrooms, campuses and colleges, thus enabling an organized growth and refinement of problem banks for individual academic subjects. Such question banks are primed to become ideal companions for classes around the world and MOOCs, enabling deeper learning and automated assessment [8] and potentially triggering the formation of MOOC-based knowledge building communities [6].

This paper discusses the motivation of Crowdlearning as a teaching practice, the theoretical drivers behind it, and challenges to its implementation and adoption. The paper then reports on exploratory investigations that assessed STEM students' abilities to competently pose problems and engage in Crowdlearning, shedding empirical insights into the associations between student performance in class and in Crowdlearning. Finally, it discusses the immediate plans and long-term goals of the ongoing crowdlearning research.

MOTIVATION AND PROMISE OF CROWDLEARNING

Postsecondary STEM education often lacks research-based foundations, with curricula being grounded in basic science models, rather than in models for learning. Further, while addressing education justice concerns, the current practices undermine such strong motivational drivers in learning as competitive spirit and sense of unity in achieving common goals. Crowdlearning brings "peer learning" [7] and "learning-by-teaching" [5, 11] ideas into the online learning world, in particular in STEM.

The following challenges are characteristic of higher STEM education. First, instructors find it hard to assess the level of conceptual understanding of the material by their audience prior to exams, as students may be hesitant to provide live in-class feedback when the material is technically challenging. Second, the example/quiz/exam problems tend to be re-used for instruction and assessment each year because formulating new problems at higher cognitive levels takes much time. Third, "curves," i.e., distributions of test scores over all students in the same course, are commonly used for assigning grades, yet over the course of a semester, students might not know where they are in the "curve."

The above challenges played the major roles in the conceptualization of Crowdlearning, which targets several objectives. The first one is to enable students to *collaborate in a new capacity* – as teachers. The premise here is that deeper learning can be achieved once students recognize that, having acquired some skill, they can immediately start helping peers to master the same skill [7]. In Crowdlearning, they do it by posing problems – not as open-ended questions but as statements/formulations with answer alternatives (including designated correct one(s)), solutions, hints, etc., – which the peers can then try to solve. Posed problems are collaboratively improved relying on the principles of crowdwork, where the assignment of the tasks to multiple workers allows even non-experts to collectively produce quality outputs [16]. The second objective of Crowdlearning is to increase the number/diversity of assessment materials for any subject to the point where posed problems can be used for learning by themselves (with the learning materials attached to or referenced within them). The third objective is for Crowdlearning to offer a new means to form knowledge-building communities [6].

THEORETICAL BASES OF CROWDLEARNING

Postsecondary STEM education often lacks sufficient research-based foundations [2]. The historical approach to curricula has been grounded in basic science models, rather than on models for learning. New approaches to STEM teaching demonstrate that students' learning can be stimulated by engaging in the processes of problem posing, peer assessment, and metacognition-developing activities [9].

The cornerstone of Crowdlearning is crowdsourced, collaborative problem posing. Problem posing is the process of creating or reformulating problems/questions based on given conceptual content [12]. The assumption of this theoretical approach is that students learn the science content and processes in the context of creating/investigating a problem, and attempt to apply their knowledge to do so. Note that problem-posing has been widely utilized as a teaching strategy mainly in mathematics, but has seen only very limited use in physics, nursing, biochemistry, and computer science and engineering [12].

A second theoretical basis for Crowdlearning is peer assessment as a learning tool, which has been increasingly emphasized in education. Palmero and Rodrigues described several

advantages of peer assessment activity: evaluating peer works (1) contributes to student learning processes, (2) increases their motivation to learn, (3) improves their perception of their work quality, and (4) increases their responsibility and satisfaction in the learning process [14]. Peer assessment generally includes an activity that students evaluate, and/or is evaluated by their peers. Van Zundert et al. reviewed published studies on peer assessment, and found that most studies on this subject reported positive effects on students' domain-specific skills - such as science activities, autobiographical writing, and writing a research proposal - from enabling students to revise their own work based on peer feedback [15].

The third basis for Crowdlearning is the adoption of the learning-by-teaching paradigm, to both engage students and help them develop metacognitive abilities. STEM knowledge theorists claim that students' conceptual understanding is composed of many elements of knowledge, which are spontaneously and unconsciously activated when explaining different phenomena (e.g., [4]). Conceptual change is theorized as a process of knowledge integration, based on accumulation, linking, connecting, and structuring of isolated elements of knowledge and concepts [10]. However, the transition to scientific understanding of content does not occur autonomously, since students often do not have metacognitive awareness of their own understanding. Developing metacognition – the ability to monitor one's own understanding [3] – in students is one of key goals of learning science professionals.

Taken together, the works on metacognition, learning-by-teaching, peer evaluation, and problem posing suggest that deeper learning can be achieved through Crowdlearning.

CROWDLEARNING PLATFORM DEVELOPMENT AT UNIVERSITY AT BUFFALO

To assess the potential of crowdlearning to accelerate learning, the authors set out to conduct an exploratory feasibility study aimed to establish the students' ability to competently act in roles (A) and (B) in crowdlearning, i.e., collaboratively initiate the creation of problems and refine them to the point where the instructor would approve their entry into a problem bank.

To this end, an online platform was designed. The platform back-end is supported by MySQL database and PHP, and front-end is written in JavaScript and HTML5 using Laravel API. In the platform, the registered students can propose new problems, revise them, and upon approval, see the aggregate peer performance in those problems. The module where students collaboratively evaluate and help improve each other's creations is currently in testing. Each approved problem is automatically added to the problem bank for the corresponding subject; the problems in the bank can then be randomly selected by the platform to be offered to someone to solve, ensuring anonymity. The platform provides real-time feedback to students about how their performance on attempted problems compares against that of their peers (in aggregate). Figure 1 illustrates the problem-posing functionality of the described Crowdlearning platform.

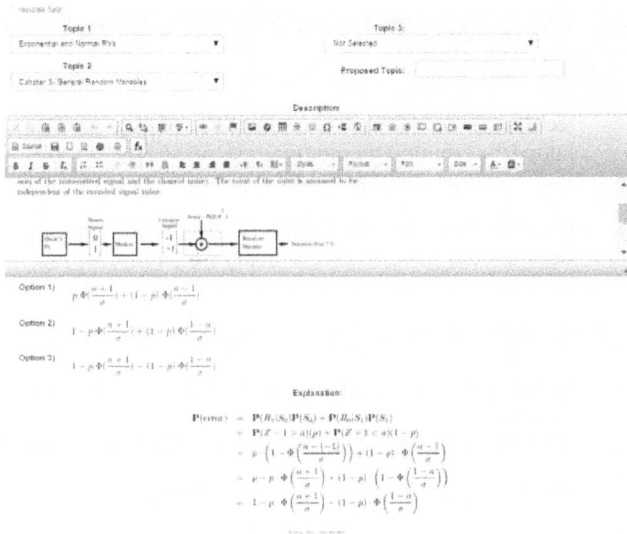

Figure 1. Crowdlearning allows students to pose their own problems, which are then given to their peers to solve.

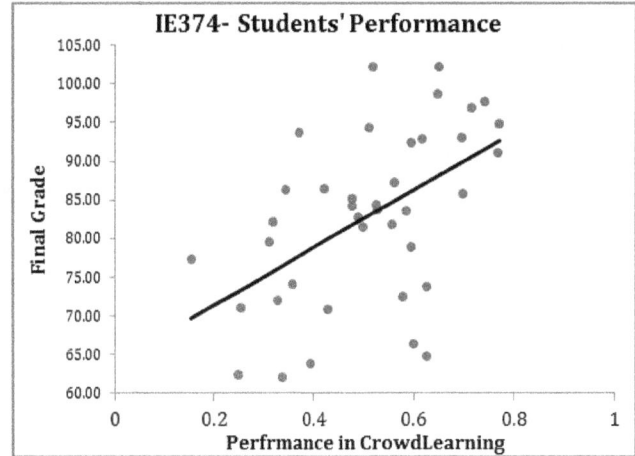

Figure 2. A positive correlation is observed between students' performance in problem solving activities.

Course	Students	Questions	Created by students
IE 551	29	195	192
IE 500	13	37	36
IE 374	42	99	43
IE 320	12	59	0
IE 575	27	46	0
IE 320*	18	37	5

Table 1. A summary of students' participation in crowdlearning for the students in six courses, among which IE 320* was an long-distance (on-line) course, as one of xxxxxxxxx courses. Columns 2 to 4 report the number of students, the number of questions and the number of questions created by the students, respectively.

CROWDLEARNING EXPERIENCES IN STEM

The feasibility studies, assessing the potential for an adoption of Crowdlearning, were conducted in the STEM setting, within the curricula of Industrial Engineering, where the use of technological innovations and new instructional practices is rare.

The 2015 problem-posing module of Crowdlearning was tested in several Industrial Engineering courses (see Table 1). Seeded by the material given in certain course modules, the students were asked to contribute problems on the respective topic to a problem bank as part of their homework assignments. The completed problems, with the authors anonymized, were made available to all the students to try and solve in preparation for quizzes and exams. The regression analyses with IE 320 and IE 374 data revealed a positive, statistically significant correlation between the student problem solving performance in Crowdlearning and their final course grades, albeit with a low R-squared (see Figure 2). This can be in part explained by the observation that, while looking to learn, some students did not try hard to solve problems correctly, because they knew they would benefit from seeing the problems' solutions and

explanations anyway. While clearly exposing intent to "game the system", this observation gives reasons to believe that students will enjoy and benefit from evaluating peers' problems, wherein they see both the problem statements and solutions.

In 2016, the students of "IE 551: Simulation" students were asked to work in teams (formed at their preference) to pose problems, which, upon the instructor's review and revision, were combined into quizzes for the same student teams to take - each team earned points if they solved a quiz problem right, and also, if their created problem(s) were challenging for the other teams. The instructors contributed 77 problems to seed the problem bank; the student teams then added 81 more problems, of which 41 entered the problem bank, after being iteratively refined to reach a very high quality with the instructor's formative feedback. The interview-based feedback on in-class Crowdlearning activities was positive, with the vast majority of the students voicing support of this practice as a learning aid. It was discovered that teamwork leads to both the higher problem quality and higher excitement about the platform use. Many students praised the Crowdlearning activity in their anonymous post-course feedback reports, e.g., writing that "...Crowdlearning assignments really added to understanding of the course material." According to students' feedback, team-based problem-solving contests were engaging: students worked to do well, often accessing and discussing lecture notes, and communicating frequently. This finding speaks in favor of the positive influence of the community-building activities [6], and perhaps, the competitive incentives of the Crowdlearning contests.

In summary, the described studies established that a majority of college students were capable of posing quality problems on specified subject topics after limited dedicated in-class instruction and with the offline advice provided by the instructors and teaching assistants. This finding is in contrast to the experience of Beal and Cohen who did a similar study with middle school students and reported that the students demanded more flexibility in choosing problem topics and required more guidance [1], but in line with the experience of Mitros who observed students in an online electronics course to competently create quality problems. The Crowdlearning students were also found to be particularly effective in contributing good problem content when working in teams [13].

FUTURE RESEARCH AND USE AT SCALE

Connecting the Crowdlearning problem bank use with educational materials will allow learners to access these materials with a purpose – to learn to solve problems of specific types or clear specific misconceptions. In particular, Crowdlearning can be used with e-learning tools. Its dissemination is likely to snowball, as new adopters will be benefitting from all the products (problems bank refinements) contributed by prior adopters; moreover, the problems most helpful to learners will be automatically recognized as such. Crowdlearning immediately opens possibilities for deeper learning in any field where multiple-choice questions can be used for assessment, not limited to the university setting or STEM (e.g., it can be used for SAT preparation). The Crowdlearning idea can be expanded to the crowdsourced creation of study "cases" (to be used in business and law), and later, perhaps to more open-ended problem formulations (to be used in arts and education).

The future Crowdlearning platforms will benefit from the advances in intelligent tutoring systems to assign tasks to students and guide problem generation in an organized, "smart" manner. The machine learning and data mining algorithms can help us understand how good problems tend to be created. ITS can also be useful to explain the dynamics of knowledge acquisition and identifying knowledge gaps [17], predict student performance on not-yet-taken problems, identify optimal sequences of roles/activities to assign to each student, and direct crowdsourced evaluation and refinement of new problems.

Future online learning platforms are primed to benefit from the new ITS tools and Crowdlearning-specific algorithms, e.g., for enabling and improving organized problem assessment. The authors of this paper also envision growing a community of teachers and researchers interested in adopting and developing Crowdlearning. Such individuals can serve on voted-in Editorial Boards of instructors who will oversee the formation of publicly accessible problem banks in respective subjects.

ACKNOWLEDGMENTS

This research was supported by UB Center of Educational Innovation and SUNY IITG Program grants.

REFERENCES

1. Carole R Beal, Paul R Cohen, and others. 2012. Teach ourselves: Technology to support problem posing in the STEM classroom. *Creative Education* 3, 04 (2012), 513.

2. Dan Braha and Oded Maimon. 1997. The design process: properties, paradigms, and structure. *IEEE Transactions on Systems, Man, and Cybernetics-Part A: Systems and Humans* 27, 2 (1997), 146–166.

3. John D Bransford, Ann L Brown, and Rodney R Cocking. 1999. *How people learn: Brain, mind, experience, and school*. National Academy Press.

4. Andrea A diSessa. 2002. Students' criteria for representational adequacy. *Symbolizing, modeling and tool use in mathematics education* (2002), 105–129.

5. Stanley Frager and Carolyn Stern. 1970. Learning by teaching. *The Reading Teacher* 23, 5 (1970), 403–417.

6. Christopher M Hoadley and Peter G Kilner. 2005. Using technology to transform communities of practice into knowledge-building communities. *ACM SIGGROUP Bulletin* 25, 1 (2005), 31–40.

7. Diane M Hogan and Jonathan RH Tudge. 1999. Implications of Vygotsky's theory for peer learning. (1999).

8. Kenneth R Koedinger, Jihee Kim, Julianna Zhuxin Jia, Elizabeth A McLaughlin, and Norman L Bier. 2015. Learning is not a spectator sport: Doing is better than watching for learning from a MOOC. In *Proceedings of the Second (2015) ACM Conference on Learning@ Scale*. ACM, 111–120.

9. Ming-Chaun Li and Chin-Chung Tsai. 2013. Game-based learning in science education: A review of relevant research. *Journal of Science Education and Technology* 22, 6 (2013), 877–898.

10. Marcia C Linn, Douglas Clark, and James D Slotta. 2003. WISE design for knowledge integration. *Science education* 87, 4 (2003), 517–538.

11. Noboru Matsuda, Evelyn Yarzebinski, Victoria Keiser, Rohan Raizada, Gabriel J Stylianides, and Kenneth R Koedinger. 2013. Studying the effect of a competitive game show in a learning by teaching environment. *International Journal of Artificial Intelligence in Education* 23, 1-4 (2013), 1–21.

12. Shitanshu Mishra and Sridhar Iyer. 2015. An exploration of problem posing-based activities as an assessment tool and as an instructional strategy. *Research and Practice in Technology Enhanced Learning* 10, 1 (2015), 1.

13. Piotr Mitros. 2015. Learnersourcing of complex assessments. In *Proceedings of the Second (2015) ACM Conference on Learning@ Scale*. ACM, 317–320.

14. Julio Ruiz Palmero and Jose Sanches Rodriguez. 2012. Peer Assessment in Higher Education. A Case Study. *New Educational Review* 27, 1 (2012), 247–255.

15. Marjo Van Zundert, Dominique Sluijsmans, and Jeroen Van Merriënboer. 2010. Effective peer assessment processes: Research findings and future directions. *Learning and Instruction* 20, 4 (2010), 270–279.

16. Joseph Jay Williams, Juho Kim, Anna Rafferty, Samuel Maldonado, Krzysztof Z Gajos, Walter S Lasecki, and Neil Heffernan. 2016. AXIS: Generating Explanations at Scale with Learnersourcing and Machine Learning. In *Proceedings of the Third (2016) ACM Conference on Learning@ Scale*. ACM, 379–388.

17. Michael V Yudelson, Kenneth R Koedinger, and Geoffrey J Gordon. 2013. Individualized bayesian knowledge tracing models. In *International Conference on Artificial Intelligence in Education*. Springer, 171–180.

What are the Expectations of Disabled Learners when Participating in a MOOC?

Francisco Iniesto, Patrick McAndrew, Shailey Minocha and Tim Coughlan
The Open University
Milton Keynes, MK7 6AA, United Kingdom
{francisco.iniesto, patrick.mcandrew, shailey.minocha, tim.coughlan} @open.ac.uk

ABSTRACT

Massive Online Open Courses (MOOCs) are making low cost learning opportunities available at large scale to diverse groups of learners. For that reason, MOOCs need to be accessible so that they can offer flexibility of learning and benefits to all. In order to direct efforts towards developing accessible MOOCs, it is important to understand the current expectations of disabled learners. Analysis of data from MOOC surveys that support disclosure of disability provide quantitative information such as the proportions participating in MOOCs; their reasons for participating, and the types of MOOCs they prefer. This paper presents analysis of pre- and post-study survey data from eight MOOCs offered by the UK's Open University on the FutureLearn platform. Results from disabled learners are compared with those of other learners and preliminary findings are used to frame an agenda for our further work.

Author Keywords

MOOC; instructional design; eLearning; universal design; accessibility

INTRODUCTION

Open education can provide opportunities at scale for lifelong learning amongst currently underserved populations, such as those with disabilities [13]. In comparison to other online learning opportunities [1] MOOCs have potentially beneficial characteristics such as: open access within a structured learning framework, low cost of learning, flexibility to allow individual planning in terms of the learner's time and preferred pace and place, opportunities for social learning, as well as scope to gain knowledge.

Despite this potential suitability as an approach to support

disabled learners, there is limited research to understand accessibility and MOOCs, and also on the expectations of disabled MOOC learners. This paper outlines a preliminary study to analyse existing MOOC survey data, in order to understand the expectations of disabled learners participating in MOOCs. We provide a brief background to research in disability and open learning, introduce the aims and methodology of the research project and the study described here, and then describe preliminary findings and directions for future work.

OPEN LEARNING AND DISABILITY

The changing attitude of society to disability is shown in the growing proportion of learners who declare disabilities. With more disabled students than any other university in Europe, data from The Open University (OU) provides an illustration of the changes. Analysis shows a rise in students declaring a disability from 6.8% in 2010/11 to 16.4% in 2014/15 [9]. This is close to a World Health Organization (WHO) estimate that disability affects approximately 15% of the world population [14]. The OU is also a major provider of Open Educational Resources (OER), and the proportion of declared disability amongst OER users has been found to be higher than in the registered student population, comprising 19% of users of the OpenLearn Platform[1] [6].

Analysis has shown complex differences between disabled and non-disabled learners. For example, Richardson identifies variable levels of lower achievement in distance education for groups with specific disabilities [11], and Perryman & de los Arcos find that a larger proportion of disabled users of OER report problems with technology and digital skills [10].

Research that considers MOOCs and accessibility directly is limited, and more needs to be done to understand disabled learner perspectives [5]. Learner analytics and survey data have been explored as a means to identify accessibility problems in online distance courses [3], but such approaches have yet to be applied to MOOCs. Few quantitative studies have explored the accessibility of MOOCs or the expectations of disabled learners. Rizzardini et al. [12] developed a MOOC that incorporated

---

[1] OpenLearn, http://www.open.edu/openlearn/

accessibility features and got feedback from disabled learners via online surveys. Liyanagunawardena and Williams [7] analysed data via a pre-course survey for 10 MOOCs to show evidence that learners in their old age, who require accessible content, are participating in MOOCs. However, studies reporting demographic data may miss disability as a factor (e.g. [2]) and there are no published studies relating to the number of disabled learners taking up MOOCs, and their interests and expectations from MOOCs.

RESEARCH AIMS AND METHOD

The quantitative study reported in this paper is a part of a wider research programme to investigate the current accessibility of MOOCs, the processes through which this accessibility is achieved, and the potential use of data to improve MOOC accessibility [4,5]. This particular study aims to understand the current expectations of disabled learners when taking part in MOOCs. To explore this, data is analysed from surveys conducted with a set of FutureLearn MOOCs that were designed and supported by the OU. FutureLearn[2] is a MOOC provider with 109 partners from around the world and over 5 million registered users. A sample of eight MOOC presentations from 2015 were selected to cover a range of subjects. Table 1 shows the MOOCs in the sample, with subject coverage according to Higher Education Statistics Agency (HESA) classifications.

Subject	Name of the MOOC	Start-date
Medicine & dentistry	The Science of Nutrition	Sep 2015
Physical sciences	Elements of Renewable Energy	Jan 2015
Computer sciences	Learn to code for data analysis	Oct 2015
Architecture, building & planning	Smart Cities	Sep 2015
Business & administrative studies	The Business of film	Oct 2015
Historical & philosophical studies	The Lottery of Birth	Aug 2015
Creative arts & design	Understanding Musical Scores	Aug 2015
Education	Get Started with Online learning	Aug 2015

Table 1. MOOCs selected for the study

Responses to the same pre- and post-course surveys were requested from learners across all eight MOOCs. Those completing these surveys are asked to indicate if they consider themselves to have a disability. Our preliminary study uses this to allow comparison focussed on three key questions in the survey that can be used to understand the expectations of disabled learners from MOOCs: Why are you interested in studying this course?, Which of the following subject areas are you interested in?; and, What sort of online course have you taken?

---

2 FutureLearn, https://www.futurelearn.com

PRELIMINARY FINDINGS

The total number of learners who completed the pre-course survey is 14,396. Of these, 752 respondents declined to answer the question "Do you consider yourself to have a disability" reducing the total replies to 13644. The number of learners who consider themselves as disabled are 1468 (10.8%). A smaller number completed the post-course surveys where the total number is 2564, of which 2259 provided a response, and the number of disabled learners was 255 (11.3%).

Table 2 shows the information disaggregated by MOOC. In all courses, the number of learners who completed the post-course survey is smaller than the pre-course survey. The MOOCs 'The Science of Nutrition', 'The Business of Film', 'Understanding Musical Scores' and 'Get Started with Online Learning' show a bigger proportion of disabled learners in the post-course survey than the pre-course one. 'Get Started with Online Learning' has the biggest percentage of disabled learners with 15.2% (pre) and 15.7% (post) in the sample.

Name of course	Pre-Course Survey		Post-Course Survey	
	Total	% Disabled Learners	Total	% Disabled Learners
The Science of Nutrition	2812	10.5%	702	11.9%
Elements of Renewable Energy	655	12.7%	175	10.5%
Learn to code for data analysis	3454	8.8%	158	7.6%
Smart Cities	1020	5.0%	137	2.9%
The Business of film	977	8.3%	240	9.6%
The Lottery of Birth	1427	13.5%	116	7.3%
Understanding Musical Scores	1631	12.8%	435	14.0
Get Started with Online learning	1668	15.2%	280	15.7%
Total	13644	10.75%	2259	11.28%

Table 2. Pre-and post-course survey participation

The following tables show the percentage positive responses for all learners, then non-disabled and disabled, and compares the response levels in percentage terms between non-disabled and disabled learners. (Significance is indicated in these tables by * at p<0.01 using z-test.) Table 3 considers the various reasons for interest when taking part in a MOOC. The highest relative percentage response levels for disabled learners are: 'Relevant to voluntary work' (146.4%), and 'To find out if I can study at this level' (165.9%). On the other hand the sub questions 'Relevant to my work' (70%) and 'To improve my English' (49%) show least relative interest.

Sub question	Percentages in each category indicating 'Yes'.			
	Total	Non-Disabled	Disabled	Disabled /Non-disabled
Personal Interest	80.6%	82.9%	86.2%	104.0%*
Relevant to my work	27.7%	29.7%	20.8%	70.0%*
Relevant to my current studies	13.7%	14.0%	15.1%	108.4%
To prepare me for future study	21.3%	21.4%	25.5%	119.1%*
For the purpose of teaching others	9.6%	10.2%	8.3%	81.6%
For the purpose of sharing with others	15.1%	15.4%	17.3%	112.5%
Relevant to voluntary work	6.1%	6.0%	8.8%	146.4%*
To improve my English	11.9%	12.8%	6.3%	49.0%*
To find out if I can study at this level	9.3%	8.8%	14.6%	165.9%*
To find out more about FutureLearn or MOOCs in general	9.1%	9.1%	10.9%	119.8%
The course was free	34.0%	34.0%	42.4%	124.7%*
To try out learning online	20.5%	20.5%	25.1%	122.0%*

Table 3. Interest in the MOOC from response to 'Why are you interested in studying this course?'

Table 4 shows the subjects areas of interest in MOOCs. While many subjects show similar or higher interest there is low interest in Business (81.6%) and in Languages (83.8%).

Sub question	Percentages in each category indicating 'Yes'.			
	Total	Non-Disabled	Disabled	Disabled/Non-disabled
Health, Sports and Psychology	42.0%	43.0%	46.3%	107.7%
Nature and Environment	40.7%	41.3%	48.5%	117.4%*
Science, Technology, Engineering and Maths	54.6%	56.5%	55.5%	98.2%
Business and Management	28.3%	29.9%	24.4%	81.6%*
Education	29.1%	30.5%	32.9%	108.0%
History and the Arts	40.6%	40.6%	51.2%	126.1%*
Languages	33.7%	35.3%	29.6%	83.8%*
Society	31.1%	31.1%	39.4%	126.9%*

Table 4. Subject areas of interest from response to 'Which of the following subject areas are you interested in?'

Previous experiences in taking online courses is similar for professional development and MOOCs, however noticeably higher for open educational resource (138.6%) and for university credit (140.9%), (Table 5).

Sub question	Percentages in each category indicating 'Yes'.			
	Total	Non-Disabled	Disabled	Disabled /Non-disabled
An online course for continuing professional development	22.6%	23.5%	22.4%	95.4%
A MOOC	49.7%	51.4%	50.6%	98.4%
An online course for university credit	14.0%	13.8%	19.5%	140.9%*
An online course based around open educational resource	14.1%	13.9%	19.2%	138.6%*

Table 5. Previous experience with online courses from response to 'What sort of online course have you taken?'

CONCLUSIONS AND FUTURE WORK

Limitations to this analysis are that it was undertaken with a small number of MOOC presentations, and that a simple disability marker may not reflect diversity within the population. It should not be assumed that these results generalise to the whole of the disabled learner population, or that this population is homogenous in nature. Nevertheless, some preliminary findings can be drawn for further investigation:

- The proportions of disabled learners taking part in MOOCs and responding to these surveys are lower than the disabled population in general, and also below current proportions found in OU registered students and in the OER repository OpenLearn.
- In comparison with other learners, disabled learners are particularly interested in taking up MOOCs to determine if they can study at a higher educational level and to link to voluntary work. They are less interested in the relevance of the MOOC to their work, or in using MOOCs to improve their English.
- Based on this initial analysis, disabled learners appear to be more interested in these subject areas: Society, History and Arts and Nature and Environment. Languages seem to be of least interest.
- Finally, disabled learners have previous experience in online courses that allows them to get university credit, which is related to their interest in studying at a higher educational level. They have less experience of participating in online courses for continuing professional development. They have more previous experience using OERs than MOOCs, which has also been outlined in the statistics from Table 1.

These findings will inform our future direction with this work. Planned further work with this data includes the following aspects:

- It would appear fruitful from other work [3, 8] to include related data in the analysis, such as demographics, completion rate and satisfaction.

- Including categories of disability, (e.g. Visual impairment, hard of hearing or learning difficulties) will provide greater insight into differences within the population of disabled learners.
- Extensions to the analysis approach to include clustering of responses, and identification of correlations.
- Increase the sample to more MOOCs and their survey data to form a more comprehensive picture. Look to introduce and utilise comparable survey approaches across platforms
- Analyse further sources of data that describe the activity of learners inside the MOOC.
- Undertake a qualitative interview study of learners, building on a recent interview study of providers and stakeholders [5], to capture the disabled learners' experiences with MOOCs in depth. This study will be useful to understand in detail the accessibility issues learners may be facing in MOOCs.

ACKNOWLEDGEMENT

This work is supported by a Leverhulme Trust Doctoral Scholarship in Open World Learning based in the Centre for Research in Education and Educational Technology at The Open University. Francisco would like to thank the Global OER Graduate Network (GO-GN) which is supported by the William and Flora Hewlett Foundation.

REFERENCES

1. Christian Bühler and Björn Fisseler. 2007. Accessible e-learning and educational technology-extending learning opportunities for people with disabilities. In *Proceedings of ICL2007*. Kassel University Press.

2. Gayle Christensen, Andrew Steinmetz, Brandon Alcorn, Amy Bennett, Deirdre Woods, and Ezekiel J. Emanuel. 2013. The MOOC phenomenon: who takes massive open online courses and why? *Working Paper*. Retrieved from: https://papers.ssrn.com/sol3/papers.cfm?abstract_id=2350964

3. Martyn Cooper, Rebecca Ferguson and Annika Wolff. 2016. What Can Analytics Contribute to Accessibility in e-Learning Systems and to Disabled Students' Learning? *In: 6th International Learning Analytics and Knowledge (LAK) Conference*, ACM. 99-103.

4. Francisco Iniesto, Patrick McAndrew, Shailey Minocha, Tim Coughlan. 2016. The current state of accessibility of MOOCs: What are the next steps? *In Proceedings of Open Education Global 2016: Convergence Through Collaboration*.

5. Francisco Iniesto, Patrick McAndrew, Shailey Minocha and Tim Coughlan. 2016. Accessibility of MOOCs: Understanding the Provider Perspective. *Journal of Interactive Media in Education*, 2016(1): 20, 1–10

6. Patrina Law, Leigh-Anne Perryman, and Andrew Law. 2013. Open educational resources for all? Comparing user motivations and characteristics across The Open University's iTunes U channel and OpenLearn platform. *In Proceedings of Open and Flexible Higher Education Conference*. EADTU. 204-219.

7. Tharindu Rekha Liyanagunawardena and Shirley Ann Williams. 2016. Elderly Learners and Massive Open Online Courses: A Review. *Interactive J. Med Res.* 5(1)

8. Neil Peter Morris, Stephanie Hotchkiss and Bronwen Swinnerton. 2015. Can demographic information predict MOOC learner outcomes? *Proceedings of European MOOC Stakeholder Summit*, 199-206.

9. The Open University Equality and Diversity Monitoring Report: Students. 2016. pg. 54. Retrieved from: http://www.open.ac.uk/equality-diversity/content/monitoring-reports

10. Leigh-Anne Perryman and Beatriz de los Arcos. 2016. Meeting the needs of disabled learners through OER and OEP: insights from the OE Research Hub dataset. *OER16: Open Culture*. Retrieved from: https://oer16.oerconf.org/programme/#/day2

11. John TE Richardson. 2014. Academic attainment of students with disabilities in distance education. *Journal of Postsecondary Education and Disability*, 27(3), 291-305.

12. Rocael Hernández Rizzardini, Vanessa Chang, Christian Gütl and Hector Amado-Salvatierra. 2013. An Open Online Course with Accessibility Features. *Proceedings of World Conference on Educational Multimedia, Hypermedia and Telecommunications*, 635–643.

13. Eileen Scanlon, Patrick McAndrew, and Tim O'Shea. 2015. Designing for educational technology to enhance the experience of learners in distance education: How open educational resources, learning design and MOOCs are influencing learning. *Journal of Interactive Media in Education*, 2015(1). Art. 6.

14. World Health Organization. 2011.World report on disability. Retrieved from: http://www.who.int/disabilities/world_report/2011/report.pdf

Applying and Exploring Bayesian Hypothesis Testing for Large Scale Experimentation in Online Tutoring Systems

Vijaya Dommeti
Rivier University
Nashua, NH 03060, USA
vdommeti@rivier.edu

Douglas Selent
Rivier University
Nashua, NH 03060, USA
dselent@rivier.edu

ABSTRACT

This paper demonstrates the viability of using Bayesian hypothesis testing for statistical analysis of experiments run in online learning systems. An empirical Bayesian method for learning a genuine prior from past historical experiment data is applied to a dataset consisting of twenty-two randomized controlled A/B experiments collected from the ASSISTments online learning platform. We show that using only twenty-two experiments results in a learned genuine prior with poor confidence interval estimates, and that roughly 200 experiments are required for a reasonable estimate of the true probability of an experiment having differences between experiment groups. We also conducted a leave-one-experiment-out cross-validation experiment, where a genuine prior is learned from twenty-one of the randomized controlled experiments provided in the dataset and then used to evaluate the remaining experiment. From this experiment we show that Bayesian hypothesis testing performs similar to Frequentist hypothesis testing and both methods were in agreement.

Author Keywords

Bayesian Hypothesis Testing, ASSISTments, Large Scale Experimentation, Randomized Controlled Trials

INTRODUCTION

Within the last decade, online experimentation is becoming more popular in the area of learning sciences and educational research. Several intelligent tutoring systems and online learning platforms are now running randomized controlled experiments on a regular basis. A common reason for the growing popularity of these systems is grounded in research done by Bloom [2]. Bloom showed that a small student-teacher ratio has a large impact on the effect size for improving student learning (two standard deviations). This is now commonly known as "Bloom's 2 Sigma Problem". Many online tutoring systems attempt to achieve

L@S 2017, April 20-21, 2017, Cambridge, MA, USA
© 2017 ACM. ISBN 978-1-4503-4450-0/17/04...$15.00
DOI: http://dx.doi.org/10.1145/3051457.3053992

the same result as Bloom with a reduced cost, by having the computer tutor mimic the functionality of a one-to-one tutoring scenario with a teacher/tutor.

As a result of the increased popularity of online tutoring systems, there are a growing number of randomized controlled experiments being run in these systems. Online experimentation at large scale is an area initially studied by various web-facing companies such as Google, Microsoft, Facebook and others [7]. Many of these companies are moving toward using Bayesian hypothesis testing (as opposed to the traditional frequentist null hypothesis statistical testing) to analyze the results of their experiments.

There are several advantages to using Bayesian hypothesis testing over Frequentist hypothesis testing. One advantage of using Bayesian hypothesis testing is that it produces a probability of a null result in addition to probabilities for positive and negative effects [4]. This is contrary to frequentist statistics where we can only fail to reject the null hypothesis. As a result, a large number of scientific experiments are not reported or published because of the lack of ground-breaking findings. Most experiments do not result in conclusive results. Kohavi discusses in some cases up to 90% of experiments do not result in any changes in companies such as Google and Netflix [7]. This contributes to the "File Drawer" problem, where a large number of null results fail to be published due to publication bias, which favors positive results [10].

Using Bayesian statistics will also help alleviate the reproducibility problem, where the reported results of many research findings cannot be reproduced. Ioannidis has demonstrated this in the medical field by analyzing 49 clinical research studies reported in the top three medical journals. He has shown that out of the 49 studies, 45 reported that the intervention was effective. Out of these 45 interventions, 16% were contradicted by subsequent studies, 16% had found effects that were originally stronger than the effects of subsequent studies, 44% were replicated, and 24% remained unchallenged [8].

Ioannidis has stated that one of several reasons for the lack of reproducibility is because of a low prior probability of the research findings being true [9]. Standard statistical methods do not consider this piece of information, which results in a large number of false positive (Type-I error) results.

In order to conduct Bayesian hypothesis testing, a *genuine prior* must be known or learned from data. This genuine prior represents the prior probability of an event being true. For example, a coin flip has a prior probability of 0.5 for the coin to land on heads. Those who are using Bayesian hypothesis testing for online controlled experiments are using historical data on thousands of previously run experiments to accurately learn a prior from those previously run experiments when such prior is not known.

In the context of this paper, the genuine prior will represent the prior probability of an A/B experiment having a difference in Mastery Speed between the control group and experiment group. Mastery Speed is the total number of problems a student attempted before reaching mastery and completing the assignment [12].

This paper demonstrates the viability and advantages of applying Bayesian hypothesis testing to analyze randomized controlled experiments being run in online tutoring systems. First we apply the objective Bayesian A/B testing framework described by Alex Deng to learn a Bayesian genuine prior from an unbiased collection of experiment data on twenty-two randomized controlled A/B tests obtained from the ASSISTments online learning platform [4, 11]. We then run a separate experiment, where we learn a genuine prior from twenty-one experiments and use that prior to perform Bayesian hypothesis testing on the twenty-second experiment in a leave-one-experiment-out cross-validation format. This is done for each of the twenty-two experiments, where one experiment is evaluated using the genuine prior learned from the other twenty-one experiments. We compare the results between the two statistical methods.

DATA DESCRIPTION

The dataset[1] we use in our experiments comes from 22 randomized controlled A/B tests run inside the ASSISTments online learning platform [11]. A total of 6,819 unique students participated in these experiments. All of the experiments were created by either internal or external researchers working with ASSISTments. There are two major characteristics of this dataset that make it ideal for conducting our experiments.

Firstly all of the 22 experiments are in a canonical format with the same dependent measure. All experiments were mathematic assignments with a control group and an experiment group. Students were randomly assigned into one of the two groups. Students continued to receive problems in the tutoring system until they had reached mastery of the content. Mastery occurs after a student has answered *n* problems correctly in a row, where *n* is typically set to three. The logarithm base ten of Mastery Speed is used as the dependent measure for the experiments in this dataset to reduce the effect of outliers on the mean.

Secondly these experiments represent an unbiased collection of experiments with positive, negative, and null results. Due to publication bias, it is hard to obtain such a dataset because positive results are reported more often than negative or null results. These two characteristics are important in order to learn a genuine prior, which requires an unbiased sample estimate of the population of experiment outcomes.

LEARNING A GENUINE PRIOR

We implemented the method described by Alex Deng to learn a genuine prior from the dataset [4]. This method works by first calculating effect sizes for each experiment. Since it is unknown whether these effect sizes were generated from experiments with a true difference between conditions (alternate hypothesis), expectation maximization is used to calculate the posterior odds of a given effect size belonging to the alternate hypothesis against the null hypothesis. The final learned posterior odds are then converted to a probability which is used as the genuine prior in Bayesian analysis. The details of this algorithm are described by Deng [4].

We calculate confidence intervals for the learned prior using the bootstrap method described in Basford et al [1]. We also simulate having a larger number of experiments to see how many experiments are required for reasonable confidence on the learned prior. To do this we vary the sample size of the bootstrap samples, where the sample size is equivalent to the number of experiments.

Figure 1 shows the confidence intervals for a varying number of experiments with 10,000 bootstrap samples for each sample size. The mean probability (for a given experiment to have an effect on Mastery Speed) learned back is roughly 0.39 for all numbers of experiments with varying confidence intervals. We acknowledge that the confidence intervals for the prior learned on twenty-two experiments are quite poor [0.001, 0.86]. The number of experiments required for a reasonable confidence interval is somewhat subjective; however it appears that there would need to be roughly 200 experiments of historical data to learn from.

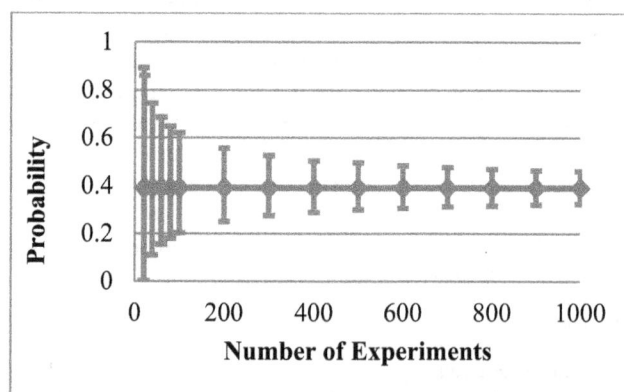

Figure 1. Confidence interval estimates on learned probability

---

[1]https://sites.google.com/site/las2016data/data

APPLYING BAYESIAN HYPOTHESIS TESTING

To apply Bayesian hypothesis testing we use leave-one-experiment-out cross-validation, using the methodology previously described to learn a prior with data from all of the experiments except one. We then use that learned prior to evaluate the last experiment. This repeats until all twenty-two experiments have been evaluated. We compare the results for both the Bayesian and Frequentist (T-Test) analysis methods.

Table 1 summarizes the results for all experiments. For the Frequentist results we report the p-value and the effect size (Cohen's D). In Bayesian statistics there are three probabilities that are reported. P(flat) is the probability of the result being zero, P(positive) is the probability of the result being positive, and P(negative) is the probability of the

result being negative [4]. In our context P(flat) represents the probability of the treatment having no impact on student learning, P(positive) represents the probability of the treatment having a positive impact on student learning, and P(negative) represents the probability of the treatment having a negative impact on student learning.

In addition to the three probabilities, it is common to report the Bayes Factor. The Bayes factor is the ratio of the posterior odds of the alternate hypothesis being true to the prior odds of the alternate hypothesis being true [6]. For example, if the Bayes factor is ten, then this can be interpreted as the data is ten times more likely to occur under the alternate hypothesis. Kass & Raftery give general benchmarks on interpreting the Bayes Factor [6].

Experiment Number	Bayesian						Frequentist	
	Learned Prior	Learned Variance	Bayes Factor	P(positive)	P(flat)	P(negative)	p	Effect Size
1	0.445	0.199	0.348	0.218	0.782	0.000	0.812	0.017
2	0.362	0.215	4.383	0.713	0.287	0.000	0.016	0.186
3	0.367	0.192	414.230	0.996	0.004	0.000	0.000	0.464
4	0.336	0.200	44.597	0.958	0.042	0.000	0.001	0.290
5	0.359	0.199	0.303	0.000	0.855	0.145	0.606	-0.029
6	0.370	0.200	0.483	0.206	0.779	0.015	0.871	0.018
7	0.378	0.201	0.484	0.000	0.773	0.227	0.745	-0.034
8	0.384	0.201	0.439	0.000	0.785	0.215	0.768	-0.028
9	0.389	0.201	0.468	0.008	0.771	0.222	0.8475	-0.020
10	0.381	0.203	2.491	0.606	0.394	0.000	0.038	0.200
11	0.384	0.204	0.594	0.000	0.730	0.270	0.799	-0.085
12	0.387	0.204	0.528	0.000	0.750	0.250	0.663	-0.050
13	0.382	0.204	3.016	0.651	0.349	0.000	0.029	0.277
14	0.382	0.205	0.962	0.000	0.627	0.373	0.136	-0.120
15	0.382	0.205	0.844	0.000	0.657	0.343	0.2244	-0.135
16	0.382	0.206	0.948	0.370	0.630	0.000	0.261	0.207
17	0.383	0.206	0.762	0.321	0.679	0.000	0.245	0.118
18	0.386	0.206	0.367	0.004	0.813	0.183	0.8727	-0.013
19	0.386	0.206	0.746	0.320	0.680	0.000	0.146	0.088
20	0.390	0.205	0.225	0.082	0.874	0.044	0.985	0.001
21	0.392	0.205	0.471	0.000	0.767	0.233	0.654	-0.044
22	0.389	0.206	1.745	0.000	0.473	0.527	0.0653	-0.187

Table 1. The results comparing both Bayesian and Frequentist hypothesis testing. The Bayesian method used an initial prior learned from EM as well as an initial variance. All three probabilities are reported for Bayesian statistics as well as the Bayes factor. The p value and effect size (Cohen's D) are reported for the Frequentist statistics.

Overall the results reported in Table 1 are fairly standard results that would be expected from an unbiased collection of randomized controlled A/B experiments run in an online tutoring system. Both Bayesian and Frequentist methods report a null result for most of the experiments. Most effect sizes and Bayes Factors are small, which is expected in this area of research. Bayesian methods perform similar to Frequentist methods.

When comparing both the Bayesian and Frequentist methods we look to see if there are any differences and where those differences are. There are five experiments (2-4, 10, 13) with reported p-values < 0.05. Out of these five experiments only two (2, 3) had a P(positive) > 0.95 with the Bayesian method. Those two experiments were the only two experiments with either a P(positive) or P(negative) greater than 0.95. Without knowing the ground truth values it is not possible to say which method is more accurate. It is also worth pointing out that although Bayesian methods can accept the null hypothesis, none of the experiments had a P(flat) > 0.95. Fortunately there was only one experiment with a P(negative) of greater than 0.5, which was experiment 22.

There are several P(flat) probabilities between 0.7 and 0.9. Although these probabilities are not yet large enough to accept the null, they provide promise that with possibly a few more samples the probabilities would be large enough to accept the null hypothesis; Thus turning a null result by Frequentist methods into a conclusive result by using Bayesian methods.

FUTURE WORK

The work described in this paper applies Bayesian hypothesis testing on existing experiment data. Since it was shown that Bayesian hypothesis testing can be used, given enough historical experiments, it is future work to continue to implement this framework into online tutoring systems to better manage the randomized controlled experiments. It is expected that as the number of historical experiments increase, Bayesian hypothesis testing will be a superior alternative to traditional methods. Several Bayesian advantages can then be gained, such as continuous monitoring and optional stopping. There already exists a template to implement these methods described in [3]. It is future work to continue to integrate Bayesian hypothesis testing into online tutoring systems for better experiment methodology that could ultimately benefit thousands of students using these systems.

CONTRIBUTIONS AND CONCLUSIONS

This paper makes a first attempt at applying Bayesian hypothesis testing to randomized controlled A/B experiments run inside online tutoring systems. We show that the methods can be applied in this context and extended the existing methodology to do so. We report on how to calculate confidence intervals on the prior probability learned from using expectation maximization on the effect sizes of treatments in experiments. We also show how many experiments would be required to have reasonable confidence estimates on the genuine prior learned from historical experiment data. We show that using Bayesian hypothesis testing generates results consistent with the Frequentist methods in addition to having a more intuitive probability interpretation.

REFERENCES

1. Basford, K. E., Greenway, D. R., McLachlan, G. J., & Peel, D. (1997). Standard Errors of Fitted Component Means of Normal Mixtures. Computational Statistics, 12(1), 1-18.

2. Bloom, B. S. (1984). The 2 Sigma Problem: The Search for Methods of Group Instruction as Effective as One-to-One Tutoring. Educational researcher, 13(6), 4-16.

3. Deng, A. Lu, J., Chen, S. (2016) Continuous Monitoring of A/B Tests Without Pain: Optional Stopping in Bayesian Testing (ArXiv ver.)

4. Deng, A. (2015, May). Objective Bayesian Two Sample Hypothesis Testing for Online Controlled Experiments. In Proceedings of the 24th International Conference on World Wide Web (pp. 923-928). ACM.

5. Efron, B. (2013). A 250-year argument: Belief, Behavior, and the Bootstrap. Bulletin of the American Mathematical Society, 50(1), 129-146.

6. Kass, R. E., & Raftery, A. E. (1995). Bayes factors. Journal of the American Statistical Association, 90(430), 773-795.

7. Kohavi, R., Deng, A., Frasca, B., Walker, T., Xu, Y., & Pohlmann, N. (2013, August). Online Controlled Experiments at Large Scale. In Proceedings of the 19th ACM SIGKDD International Conference on Knowledge Discovery and Data Mining (pp. 1168-1176). ACM.

8. Ioannidis, J. P. A. (2005). Contradicted and Initially Stronger Effects in Highly Cited Clinical Research. JAMA: the Journal of the American Medical Association 294 (2): 218–228. doi:10.1001/jama.294.2.218.

9. Ioannidis J. P.A. (2005). Why Most Published Research Findings Are False. PLoS Med 2(8): e124. doi:10.1371/journal.pmed.0020124.

10. Rosenthal, R. (1979). The File Drawer Problem and Tolerance for Null Results. Psychological Bulletin, 86(3), 638.

11. Selent, D., Patikorn, T., & Heffernan, N. (2016, April). ASSISTments Dataset from Multiple Randomized Controlled Experiments. In Proceedings of the Third (2016) ACM Conference on Learning@ Scale (pp. 181-184). ACM.

12. Xiong, X., Li, S., & Beck, J. E. (2013, May). Will You Get It Right Next Week: Predict Delayed Performance in Enhanced ITS Mastery Cycle. In FLAIRS Conference.

Designing Adaptive Assessments in MOOCs

Yigal Rosen
Harvard University
Cambridge, USA
yigal_rosen@harvard.edu

Ilia Rushkin
Harvard University
Cambridge, USA
ilia_rushkin@harvard.edu

Andrew Ang
Harvard University
Cambridge, USA
andrew_ang@harvard.edu

Colin Fredericks
Harvard University
Cambridge, USA
colin_fredericks@harvard.edu

Dustin Tingley
Harvard University
Cambridge, USA
dtingley@gov.harvard.edu

Mary Jean Blink
TutorGen, Inc.
Fort Thomas, USA
mjblink@tutorgen.com

ABSTRACT

There is an indisputable need for evidence-based instructional designs that create the optimal conditions for learners with different knowledge, skills and motivations to succeed in MOOCs. The study explores the technological feasibility and implications of adaptive functionality to course (re)design in the edX platform. Additionally, the study aims to establish the foundation for future study of adaptive functionality in MOOCs on learning outcomes, engagement and course drop-out rates. Preliminary findings suggest that the adaptivity of this kind leads to a higher efficiency of learning: students go through the course faster and attempt fewer problems, since the problems are served to them in a targeted way. And yet there is no evidence that the students' overall performance in the course suffers. Further research is needed to explore additional facets of adaptive assessment in different contexts of MOOCs and the effects on learning outcomes.

Author Keywords

MOOCs; assessment; adaptive assessment; adaptive learning.

INTRODUCTION

Digital learning systems are considered adaptive when they can dynamically change to enhance learning in response to student interactions within the MOOC rather than on the basis of preexisting information such as a learner's gender, age, or achievement test score. Adaptive learning systems use information gained as the learner works with them to vary such features as the way a concept is represented, its difficulty, the sequencing of problems or tasks, and the nature of hints and feedback provided. Adaptive

technologies build on decades of research in intelligent tutoring systems, psychometrics, cognitive learning theory and data science [1, 3, 4]. These capabilities result in the ability to pinpoint the optimal pieces of content for learners (e.g., video, reading, discussion post, assessment item) across all educational domains based on growing evidence from the learner's performance and associated learning progression (i.e, learning objectives map). Harvard University partnered with TutorGen to explore the feasibility of adaptive learning and assessment technology implications of adaptive functionality to course (re)design in HarvardX, and examine the effects on learning outcomes, engagement and course drop-out rates. As the collaboration evolved, the following two strategic decisions have been made: (1) Adaptivity will be limited to assessments in four out of 16 graded sub-sections of the course. Extra problems will be developed to allow adaptive paths; and (2) Development efforts will be focused on Harvard-developed Learning Tool Interoperability (LTI) tool to support assessment adaptivity on edX platform. Therefore, in the current prototype phase of this project, adaptive functionality is limited to altering the sequence of problems. The order is determined by a personalized learning progression , using learners' real-time performance and statistical inferences on sub-topics they have mastered. The inferences are continuously updated based on each learners' performance.

While the prototype will enable us to explore the feasibility of adaptive assessment technology and implications of adaptive functionality to course (re)design in HarvardX, it will be challenging to anticipate its effects on learning outcomes, engagement and course drop-out rates due to the prototype limitations. However, we believe that the study will help to establish a solid foundation for future research on the effects of adaptive learning and assessment on outcomes such as, learning gains and engagement.

METHOD

A number of subsections in the course contain homework assessment pages, each made of several problems. The course users were randomly split 50%-50% into an experimental group and into a control group. When arriving on a homework page, users in the control group see a predetermined, non-adaptive set of problems on a page. In the experimental group, the experience is the same in all homework assessments except the four used in this study, where the adaptive tool was deployed. In those four assessments a user from the experimental group is served problems sequentially, one by one, in the order that is determined on-the-fly based on the user's prior performance. To enable adaptivity, all problems in the course were manually tagged with one or several learning objectives. Moreover, all problems in the 4 adaptive assessments were tagged with one of three difficulty levels: advanced, regular and easy. The adaptive engine (a variety of Bayesian Knowledge Tracing algorithm) decides which problem to serve next based on the list of learning objectives covered by the homework and course material. It estimates the user's mastery of a learning objective each time the user gives an answer to a problem tagged with this learning objective (even if this problem is outside of the adaptive assessments). If the problem served is advanced, the engine serves the instructional system advanced materials covering the necessary learning objectives, providing the students with an option to study these before attempting the problem. A given user in the experimental group does not necessarily see all of these problems. The user may stop working on the homework after reaching the required score (higher score does not give extra credit), or indeed for any other reason. In addition, the engine may stop serving problems if the user's mastery level for a learning objective becomes sufficiently high that it needs no further verification. Students in the control group also have access to these materials in an optional part of the course.

In order to explore possible effects of adaptive experiences on learners' mastery of content knowledge competence-based pre- and post-assessment were added to the course and administered to study participants in both experimental and control groups. Typical HarvardX course clickstream time-stamped data and pre-post course surveys data will also be collected and analyzed.

Course Design Considerations

Adaptive learning techniques require the development of additional course materials, so that different students can be provided with different content. For our prototype, tripling the existing content in the four adaptive subsections was considered a minimum to provide a genuine adaptive experience. This was achieved by work from the project lead and by hiring an outside content expert. The total time outlay was ~200 hours. Keeping the problems housed within the edX platform avoided substantial amounts of software development.

LTI Tool Development

To enable the use of an adaptive engine in an edX course, Harvard developed the Bridge for Adaptivity (BFA) tool. BFA is a web application that uses the LTI specification to integrate with learning management systems such as edX. BFA acts as the interface between the edX course platform and the TutorGen SCALE (Student Centered Adaptive

Learning Engine) system, and handles the display of problems recommended by the adaptive engine.

This LTI functionality allows BFA to be embedded in one or more locations in the course. The user interface seen by a learner when they encounter an installed tool instance is shown below:

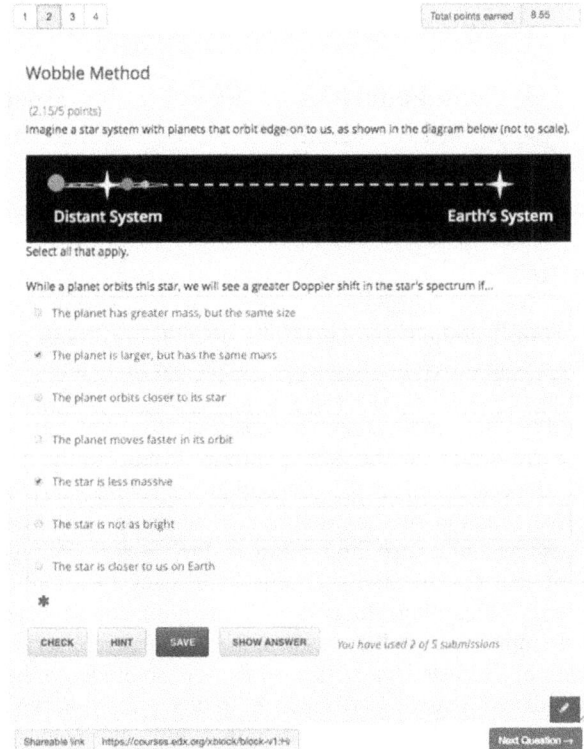

Figure 1. Adaptive assessment user interface

Problems from the edX course are displayed one at a time in a center activity window, with a surrounding toolbar that provides features such as navigation, a score display, and a shareable link for the current problem (that the learner can use to post to a forum for help). When a learner completes a problem in the activity window, embedded Javascript in the edX content sends data about the learner and their response to BFA. This data is then processed and sent to SCALE. When the learner chooses to advance to the next problem, BFA makes a query in real-time to SCALE for the next recommended activity for that learner, then serves the appropriate edX content in the activity window via xBlock URL.

TutorGen Adaptive Engine

TutorGen SCALE, is focused on improving learning outcomes using data collected from existing and emerging educational technology systems combined with the core technology to automatically generate adaptive capabilities. Key features that SCALE provides include knowledge tracing, skill modeling, student modeling, adaptive problem selection, and automated hint generation for multi-step problems. SCALE engine it improves over time with additional data and/or with the help of human input by providing machine learning using a human centered approach The algorithms have been tested on various data sets in a wide range of domains. For successful implementation and optimized adaptive operations, it is important that the knowledge components / skills (KC) be tagged at the right level of granularity. The system will provide opportunity to refine the tagging of these KCs after data has been collected from actual student interactions.

SCALE has been used in the intelligent tutoring system environment, providing adaptive capabilities during the formative learning stages. SCALE with HarvardX for this course is being used more as in the assessment stage of the the student experience. In order to accomplish the goals of the prototype for this pilot study, we extended our algorithms to consider not only the learning objectives, identified as the KCs, but also to consider problem difficulty and problem selection within the modules or groupings of concepts and problems. This will accommodate the needs for this course by providing an adaptive experience for students while still supporting the logical flow of the course. Further, the flexible nature of the course, having all content available and open to students for the duration of the course, presents some additional requirements to ensure that students are presented with problems based on their current state and not necessarily where the system believes they should navigate.

PRELIMINARY FINDINGS

The course was launched on Oct 19, 2016. The data for the analysis presented in this paper were accessed on Jan 04, 2017 (plus or minus a few days, since different parts of the data were extracted at different times), about two and a half months later.

	Experimental group	Control group
Regular level only	68	99
Easy level only	0	0
Advanced level only	1	1
(Regular ∪ Easy) levels only	2	41
(Regular ∪ Advanced) levels only	121	0
(Easy ∪ Advanced) levels only	0	1
(Regular ∪ Easy ∪ Advanced) levels	84	144
Total students attempting new problems	276	286

Table 1. Number of students attempting assessment items of different difficulty level

More students are registering for the course on a daily basis, so the results of the analysis are preliminary. We will refer to the list of problems from which problems were served adaptively to the experimental group as "new problems". The control group may have interacted with these as well, although not adaptively. There were 39 new problems, out of which 13 were regular difficulty (these formed the assessments for the control group of students), 14 were advanced and 12 were easy. For the control group, the advanced and easy problems were offered as extra material after assessment, with no credit toward the course grade. The numbers of students attempting assessment problems of different difficulty levels are given in Table 1.

To get a sense of how the two groups of students performed in the course, we compared the group averages of the differences in scores in the pre-test and post-test (Figure 2). We included only the scores from the test questions tagged with the learning objectives that are encountered among the new problems. Each question was graded on the scale 0-1, and we took the average question score for each student in each test.

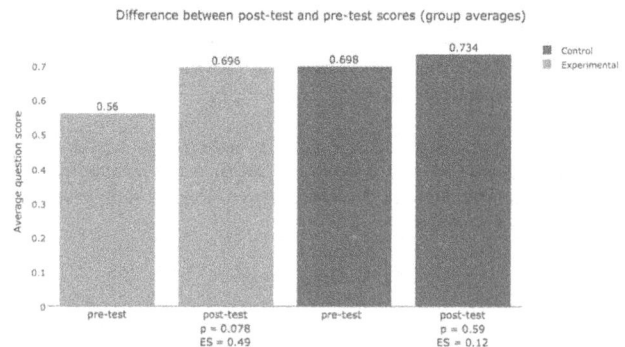

Figure 2. Comparison of post-test and pre-test scores. The population of users is subset to only those who attempted the pre-test, the new problems, and the post-test. Here and everywhere below, the p-values are two-tailed from the Welch two-sample t-test, and the effect size is the Cohen's d.

There is a noticeable between-group difference in the pre-test scores (p-value 0.066, effect size 0.46). This is due to subsetting to those users who attempted new problems and the post-test (in the absence of this subsetting, the effect size drops to 0.00028, meaning that initially the two populations have virtually no difference, as expected), Therefore, Figure 2 shows two patterns: 1) the experimental group achieves a larger knowledge gain, even with less prior knowledge; 2) in the experimental group students with low prior knowledge are more likely not to drop out and reach the post-test.

We did not see a difference in the final grade of the course: the mean grade was 84.3% in the experimental group vs. 85.77% in the control group, which is not significant at all (p-value 0.63, effect size −0.12).

Students in the experimental group tended to make more attempts at a problem (Figure 3). they tried fewer problems (Figure 4) most strikingly among the easy new problems: for these we have 1,122 recorded scores in the control group and only 325 in the experimental group. The interpretation emerges that the students who experienced adaptivity showed more persistence by giving more attempts per problem (presumably, because adaptively served problems are more likely to be on the appropriate current mastery level for a student), while taking a faster track through the course materials. Corroborating this last interpretation, we observe that the experimental group students tended to have a lower net time on task in the course: an average of 4.37 hours vs. 4.80 in the control group (in this comparison, p-value 0.11, effect size −0.14).

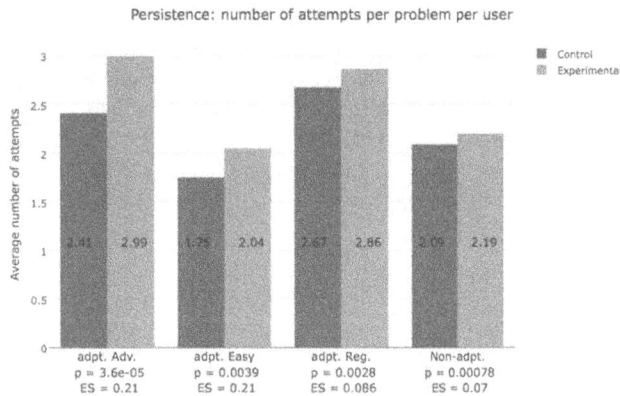

Figure 3. Comparison of attempt numbers between the experimental and control groups in the modules (chapters) where adaptivity was implemented. The attempt numbers are averaged both over the problems and over the users.

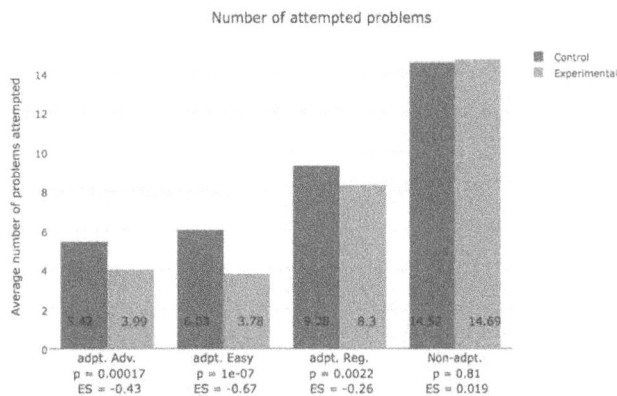

Figure 4. Comparison of attempt numbers between the experimental and control groups in the modules (chapters) where adaptivity was implemented.

No significant between-group difference was found in the rates of course completion and certification, or in demographics of students who did not drop out.

Thus, we propose that the adaptivity of this kind leads to a higher efficiency of learning: students go through the course faster and attempt fewer problems, since the problems are served to them in a targeted way. And yet there is no evidence that the students' overall performance in the course suffers: in fact, Figure 2 tentatively suggests a benefit. Given the limited implementation of adaptivity in this course, it is not surprising that we cannot find a statistically significant effect on student overall performance in the course. We expect to refine these conclusions in the future courses with a greater scope of adaptivity.

FUTURE WORK

There appear to be extensive opportunities to expand adaptive learning and assessment in MOOCs. Ideally, larger sets of questions that are tagged to the learning objectives for a module could provide a more adaptive learning experience for students, while also providing a higher degree of certainty of assessment results. Given the structure of many MOOCs, more integration between learning content and assessment could provide an adaptive experience that would guide students to content that could improve their understanding based on how they perform on integrated assessments. Affective factors, such as boredom and frustration, as well as behaviors like gaming the system, are areas where, if detected, the system could provide a more personalized learning experience. Finally, this work could lead to improved MOOC platform features that would contribute to improved student experiences, such as optimized group selection [2]. In addition, we anticipate expanding this adaptive assessment system to work with other LTI-compliant course platforms. Enabling use in a platform such as Canvas, the learning management system used university-wide at Harvard (and many other schools), would enable adaptivity for residential courses on a large scale. An adjustment to the current system architecture would be the use of OpenEdX as the platform for creating and hosting problems.

ACKNOWLEDGEMENTS

We are grateful for the support from the Office of the Vice Provost for Advances in Learning at Harvard University for thoughtful leadership and support to HarvardX and the VPAL-Research group. Special thanks to Professor Dimitar Sasselov from the Department of Astronomy whose SuperEarths and Life MOOC make this project possible.

REFERENCES

1. Koedinger, K., and Stamper, J. 2010. A Data Driven Approach to the Discovery of Better Cognitive Models. In Baker, R.S.J.d., Merceron, A., Pavlik, P.I. Jr. (Eds.) *Proceedings of the 3rd International Conference on Educational Data Mining.* (EDM 2010), 325-326. Pittsburgh, PA.

2. Rosen, Y. in press. Assessing students in human-to-agent settings to inform collaborative problem-solving learning. *Journal of Educational Measurement.*

3. Rosen, Y. 2015. Computer-based assessment of collaborative problem solving: Exploring the feasibility of human-to-agent approach. *International Journal of Artificial Intelligence in Education* 25, 3: 98-129.

4. Stamper, J., Barnes, T., and Croy, M. 2011. Experimental Evaluation of Automatic Hint Generation for a Logic Tutor. In Kay, J., Bull, S. and Biswas, G. eds. *Proceeding of the 15th International Conference on Artificial Intelligence in Education (AIED2011).* 345-352. Berlin Germany: Springer.

Authentic Science Inquiry Learning at Scale Enabled by an Interactive Biology Cloud Experimentation Lab

Zahid Hossain [1,2,*] , Engin Bumbacher [3], Paulo Blikstein [2,3], Ingmar Riedel-Kruse [1,*]

[1]Bioengineering, [2]Computer Science, [3]Education
Stanford University
*{zhossain@cs.stanford.edu, ingmar@stanford.edu}

ABSTRACT

National guidelines advocate for a more sophisticated STEM education that integrates complex and authentic scientific practices, e.g., experimentation, data collection, data analysis, and modeling. How to achieve that is currently unclear for both presential and distance education. We recently developed a scalable cloud lab that enables many online users to perform phototaxis experiment with real, living Euglena cells (opposed to just simulations). Here we iteratively designed and deployed an open course on the edX platform including suitable user interfaces that facilitates inquiry-based learning on this cloud lab: Online students (>300) run real experiments (>2,300), performed data analysis, explored models, and even formulated and experimentally tested their own hypotheses. Platform and course content are now suited for global adaptation in formal K-16 education. We will demo our cloud lab at the conference.

ACM Classification Keywords

C.2.4 Computer-Communication Networks: Distributed Systems; K.3.1 Computers and Education: Computer Uses in Education; I.6.7 Simulation and Modeling: Simulation Support Systems; H.5.2 Information Interfaces and Presentation (e.g. HCI): User Interfaces; I.4.7 Image Processing and Computer Vision: Feature Measurement

Author Keywords

inquiry-based learning; cloud lab; remote experimentation; life science; biology; interactive biotechnology; Euglena; phototaxis; modeling; data analysis; user interface; user studies; learning analytics; MOOC; edX; education

INTRODUCTION

An unsolved challenge for presential and distance learning is the proper design and integration of tools that enable authentic scientific practices [2], especially with real experimentation [4], e.g., living organisms, as opposed to mere simulations.

Inquiry-based practices in which students construct knowledge like professional scientists [9] are at the core of national

guidelines such as the Next Generation Science Standards of the United States [10, 3], and the benefits of these approaches for science education have been demonstrated [9]. Many *remote labs* [4] with real experimentation have been developed but these labs are usually not suitable for large scale deployment due to lack of concurrent access design, and none of them includes living matter. We recently developed a *cloud lab* that allows remote users to perform real biology experiments (with live organisms, opposed to just simulations) at high-throughput with concurrent user access (akin to cloud computation, Fig. 1) [6]. The contributions of this paper are: (1) We developed and deployed an open online course that enables for the first time inquiry-based learning at scale over the Internet that combines real experimentation, augmented data analytics and modeling tools (in line with bifocal modeling [1]). (2) We report on how to scaffold authentic inquiry tasks online and at scale with such cloud labs.

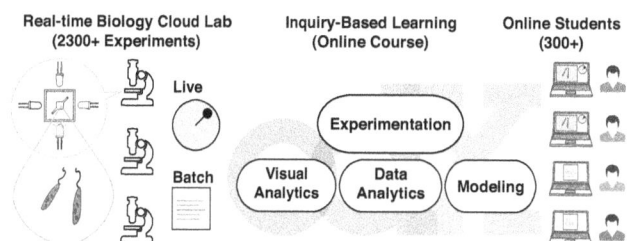

Figure 1. We integrated a scalable biology cloud lab, designed as a distributed system, into an open online course to enable authentic science practices. Real biology experiment (with live organism) can be executed in real-time interactive manner (*live*) as well as with offline (*batch*) processing. We explored the general affordances and design rules of online experimentation science labs to enable inquiry-based learning.

RESEARCH AND ONLINE COURSE DESIGN

We adopted an iterative design-based research approach building on our previous pilot studies [6]. We converged on a mini-course ($\sim$ 4h over 1 week) on the Open edX platform that is suitable for a diverse MOOC audience (middle school and university students, science teachers). The course theme centered on the core scientific practices (Fig. 2A), which the students executed while investigating the phototactic behavior of the single-celled organism *Euglena gracilis* (Fig. 2B,C). Importantly, our fully automated cloud lab technology enables students to execute real experiments with living cells from across the world 24/7 (Fig. 3).

The course had six highly scaffolded units [5]. Each unit introduced a new *scientific practice*, a new *biological target concept*, and a new *UI tool* as described below:

A

Figure 3. Number of experiments run over 24 h period over the 6 weeks of deployment. The inset map shows the distribution of incoming traffic from different geographic locations.

B

C

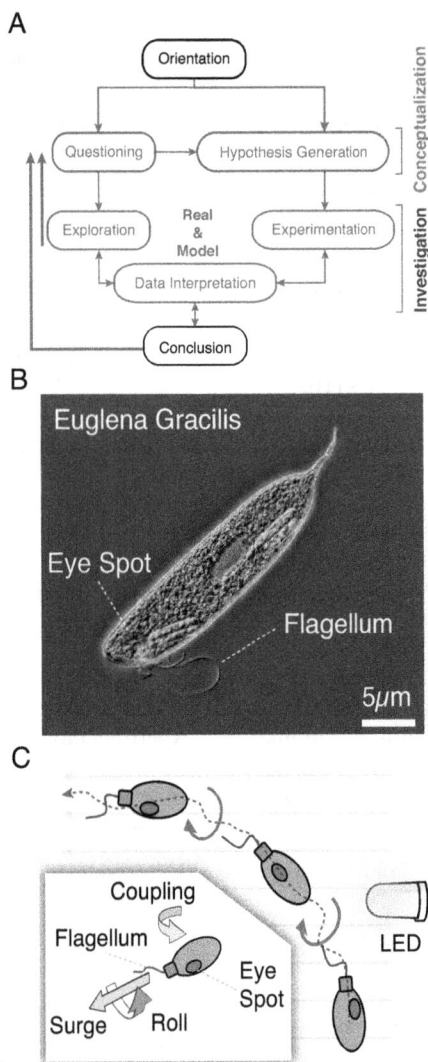

Figure 2. Cloud-based biology experimentation with living cells. (A) Inquiry-based learning emphasizing exploration and experimentation with real specimen and models (adapted from [9]). (B) Single-celled *Euglena gracilis*. (C) Negative phototaxis mechanism of Euglena.

Unit 1: Observation (online microscope)
Students were introduced to the cloud lab dashboard interface (Fig. 4A), i.e., how to select an online microscope, how to observe the Euglena cells in real time, and how to watch the resulting experimental video afterwards either directly on the website via streaming or after downloading. Students were tasked to describe their observations in a free form manner. We deliberately started scaffolding with a passive observation, rather than asking students to already explore the light responses because our earlier pilot studies have shown that premature interactivity without the proper foundation being established could overwhelm students, especially when working with a noisy biological system. This passive observation was then followed by a short description on the basic biology of Euglena: they are photosynthetic organisms that detect light using an eye-spot; there was no mention of phototaxis yet.

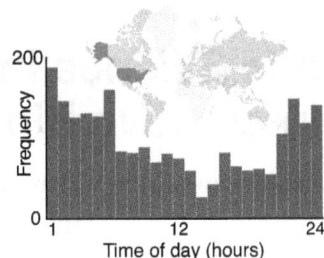

Unit 2: Experimentation (interactive live and scripted batch)
Students were introduced to the virtual joystick to actuate directional light stimuli on the interactive online microscope (*live* mode) (Fig. 4B). Students were prompted to then run experiments to explore how Euglena reacts to light stimuli. In order to eradicate misinterpretation of the instrument usage early on, we primed students with simple test questions, e.g., *"In which direction does the light shine when you pull the joystick in this direction?"* We also introduced the *batch* mode (Fig. 4C), which is suitable for scripting controlled and repetitive experimentation, but importantly also counters low Internet bandwidth that is unsuitable for the *live* mode.

Unit 3: Visual analytics and qualitative data interpretation
Students were instructed to analyze and explain their movie data more closely (Fig. 4D), where Euglena exhibit a wobbling, meandering motion as apparent via the overlaid tracks. Students then performed simple, direct measurements regarding speed and rolling frequency - solely based on visual analytics using these overlaid tracks, the timer and the scale bar.

Unit 4: Model exploration and evaluation
Students explored models (Fig. 4E) that provide a mechanistic explanation of the phototaxis phenomena in the absence of real-life noise. Students were tasked to find the best parameter values that fit the model to a real Euglena path and then explore how to accomplish both positive and negative phototaxis. Students were introduced to the relevant sub-cellular structure of Euglena and the mechanistic explanation of Euglena phototaxis, i.e., the coupling of the eye spot with the flagellum (Fig. 2B,C), which causes rolling around the long axis and side way turning. These activities then also provided a deeper explanation for the wobbling motion analyzed in the previous unit. Students were also asked to go back to the real experimentation and compare.

Unit 5: Quantitative data processing and analysis
Students engaged in the process of exporting the numerical data into a google spreadsheet, graphing that data, and interpreting the graphs. Students first worked through a highly scaffolded example to analyze how the Euglena speed depends on Light-On versus Light-Off, which typically has a weak effect. Then the students were asked to perform a similar analysis on their own, but now to determine graphically whether the average velocity vectors changed with directional light stimulus from the LEDs (Fig. 4F). Here the students received

A. Landing Page/Routing
B. Live Real-time Experiment
C. Script for Batch Experiment
D. Visual Analytics
E. Modeling
F. Data Analytics

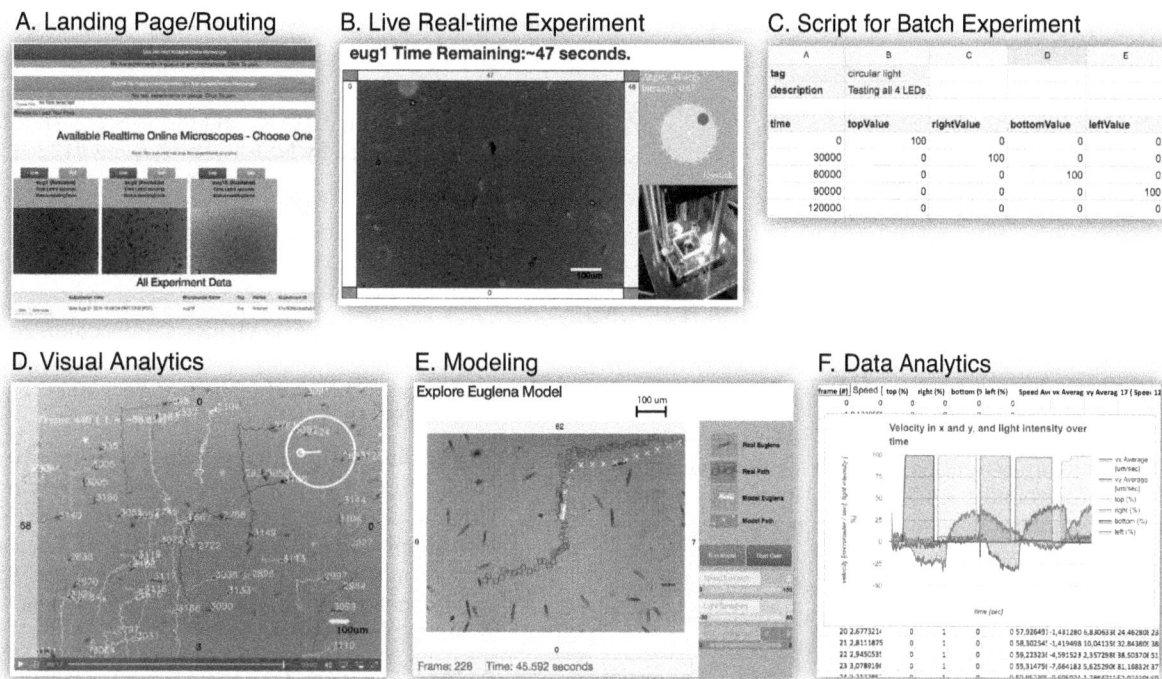

Figure 4. Enabling the key components of inquiry-based learning at scale. (A) Landing page to route students to a suite of online microscopes. (B) Real-time Euglena biology lab in *live* interactive mode. (C) Experiment script in CSV format for *batch* mode. (D) A playback movie viewer for automatic tracking of Euglena cells. (E) Modeling applet simulating Euglena overlaid on a pre-recorded video. (F) Google Sheets for data analytics.

the data in a format where the velocity of each cell was already decomposed into its cardinal directions (x and y). Depending on the direction of the light origin, one velocity component would average to zero, and the other would be either negative or positive. Students had to design and run a new set of experiments to generate the data for this analysis. During pilot studies we had offered units 4 and 5 in reverse order, but user feedback revealed that it is more effective to do the interactive modeling activity before the comlex data analysis.

Unit 6: Open and self-guided investigations
Students were prompted to carry out a self-guided research activity, where they proceeded through the main parts of the inquiry cycle (Fig. 2A) while applying all or most of the previously used tools (Fig. 4). They were asked to make an observation (specifically one that had not been stated by the course material previously), and transform this observation into a testable hypothesis with experimental designs. Students were then encouraged (optionally) to pursue the actual experimentation, analysis, and interpretation.

COURSE DEPLOYMENT AND RESULTS
The course (3.5 ± 1.1 h to finish on avg.) was offered six times with minor updates between successive offerings. Students (N=325, active) came from 46 countries (Fig. 3) with 47% female and a median age of 32 years (IRQ=19). A total of $\sim 2,300$ experiments were executed (*live* and *batch*) with little wait time (median: 4.8 s, IRQ=1.55 s) for *live* experimentation due to distributed geographic timezones (Fig. 3). The capacity of the cloud lab would have enabled >500 students/week.

As a case study, we consider the work flow of a single student. This student ran a total of 13 experiments (nine *live*,

four *batch*) and completed the course in ~ 3 h. She ran five experiments, including one *batch*, before noting that Euglena moves faster upon light stimulus but without a clear direction of motion. Later, she executed three experiments on different online microscopes and thereby experienced biological and system variabilities. She then ran three experiments before formulating her hypothesis that *"Euglena respond when light intensity is above the threshold of 50%."* To test this hypothesis, she ran two carefully designed *batch* experiments. Her data analysis in google sheets revealed that the vertical velocity component of the cells increased with increasing light intensity, while the horizontal component remained at 0 μm/s (Fig. 5). Hence instead of the hypothesized discrete threshold, she found a more gradual response. Thus, our cloud lab platform and the associated online course enabled students to perform realistic science-practices including self-formulating and experimentally testing hypotheses, and where the various interaction modalities (Fig. 4) brought forward the nuances and natural variability of real biology.

Our logged data from all participants revealed a $\sim 51\%$ completion rate, which is high even for a 1-week course. Here our user interfaces and inquiry activities appeared to have been effective, e.g., *"The tangibility that lab provided was one important reason that carried me on...[sic]"*, *"The way we could conduct experiments remotely was very cool!"*, *"Feeling like I was part of real research"*. Crucially, the course changed student attitudes toward science, e.g., 15 voluntarily responded on a scale of 1-9 (*"not at all"* to *"totally"*), before and after participating in our course, to the statements *"Ordinary people can be scientists"* ($8.7 \pm 0.6 \rightarrow 7.5 \pm 2.0, p < 0.05$) and *"I can imagine myself as a scientist"* ($6.7 \pm 1.8 \rightarrow 8.5 \pm 1.3, p <$

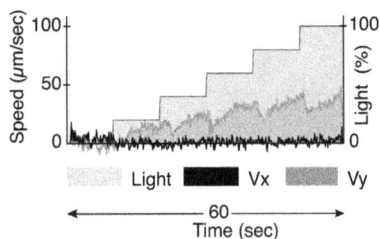

Figure 5. Students formulated and experimentally tested their own hypotheses. Here this student expected an intensity threshold for light responsiveness, instead a more complex relationship between the light intensity (increased by 20% every 10s) and the Euglena swarm velocity was found (Vx/Vy: average horizontal/vertical velocity components).

0.005). The majority of students, $\sim 72\%$, indicated great value in having real living organisms (opposed to pure simulations), e.g., to capture ground truth details that simulations would miss. Overall, students rated their experience between *"very"* and *"extremely"* positive (6.3 ± 0.6 on a 1-7 scale, N=34); difficulty was rated as between *"neutral"* and *"somewhat easy"* (4.6 ± 1.1 on a 1-7 scale, N=31). A detailed analysis of all student activities and data will be published elsewhere.

DISCUSSION

Achievements and implications: We demonstrated, that our cloud lab enables concurrent online users at scale to experiment with real biological materials, which is a key technological advancement for online learning including MOOCs. We augmented this cloud lab with data analytics and modeling components, which enabled inquiry-based learning with authentic, high-dimensional, "interactive biology" experiments [7, 8]. The key design features of our platform not only mitigate non-deterministic and noisy biological behavior but actually exploit its educational value. Recognizing the inherent variability in biological systems empowers students to recognize differences between a determinist model and real biology (bifocal modeling [1]). The science practices that this cloud lab affords are a paradigm shift of what students currently can do in either presential or online life-science education. Multiple K-12 science teachers who took this course expressed interest to use these and related activities with their own students, the corresponding deployment studies are currently under way.

Future work: There are multiple important avenues for future research and development with cloud-based experimentation and pedagogy. (1) Utilizing platform data for learning analytics. (2) Refining and testing course content for specific learner groups. (3) Including other relevant scientific practices such as collaborative teamwork and model building. (4) Extending the platform to other experiment types.

Conclusion: We successfully deployed an open online course with an integrated biology cloud lab (with real live organism) in a scalable manner. Students could engage in the core activities of scientific inquiry while interacting with living cells, which goes significantly beyond current educational practices of passive observation through a microscope or using computer simulations or animations. Instead, the lab automation and ease of data collection and analysis leads to easier logistics and extended lab time for students, also when working from home. Ultimately, this approach could bring authentic science practices to millions of students annually across the globe.

Acknowledgements: We would like to thank A. Brauneis, M. Diaz, A. Saltarelli, J. Cash, and the Riedel-Kruse lab. This work was supported by NSF Cyberlearning #1324753.

REFERENCES

1. P. Blikstein. Bifocal Modeling: Comparing Physical and Computational Models Linked in Real Time. *Playful Learning Interfaces*, pages 317–352, 2014.

2. C. A. Chinn and B. A. Malhotra. Epistemologically authentic inquiry in schools: A theoretical framework for evaluating inquiry tasks. *Science Education*, 86(2):175–218, 2002.

3. N. R. Council. Guide to Implementing the Next Generation Science Standards. Technical report, Committee on Guidance on Implementing the Next Generation Science Standards, Board on Science Education, Division of Behavioral and Social Sciences and Education, Washington, DC: The National Academies Press, 2015.

4. R. Heradio, L. d. l. Torre, D. Galan, F. J. Cabrerizo, E. Herrera-Viedma, and S. Dormido. Virtual and remote labs in education: A bibliometric analysis. *Computers & Education*, 98:14 – 38, 2016.

5. C. E. Hmelo-Silver, R. G. Duncan, and C. A. Chinn. Scaffolding and achievement in problem-based and inquiry learning: A response to kirschner, sweller, and clark (2006). *Educational psychologist*, 42(2):99–107, 2007.

6. Z. Hossain, E. W. Bumbacher, A. M. Chung, H. Kim, C. Litton, A. D. Walter, S. N. Pradhan, K. Jona, P. Blikstein, and I. H. Riedel-Kruse. Interactive and scalable biology cloud experimentation for scientific inquiry and education. *Nat Biotech*, 34(12):1293–1298, Dec. 2016.

7. Z. Hossain, X. Jin, E. W. Bumbacher, A. M. Chung, S. Koo, J. D. Shapiro, C. Y. Truong, S. Choi, N. D. Orloff, P. Blikstein, et al. Interactive cloud experimentation for biology: An online education case study. In *Proceedings of the 33rd Annual ACM Conference on Human Factors in Computing Systems*, pages 3681–3690. ACM, 2015.

8. S. A. Lee, A. M. Chung, N. Cira, and I. H. Riedel-Kruse. Tangible interactive microbiology for informal science education. In *Proceedings of the Ninth International Conference on Tangible, Embedded, and Embodied Interaction*, pages 273–280. ACM, 2015.

9. M. Pedaste, M. Mäeots, L. A. Siiman, T. De Jong, S. A. Van Riesen, E. T. Kamp, C. C. Manoli, Z. C. Zacharia, and E. Tsourlidaki. Phases of inquiry-based learning: Definitions and the inquiry cycle. *Educational research review*, 14:47–61, 2015.

10. H. Quinn, H. Schweingruber, T. Keller, et al. *A framework for K-12 science education: Practices, crosscutting concepts, and core ideas*. National Academies Press, 2012.

Intelligent Math Tutor: Problem-Based Approach to Create Cognizance

Monika Gupta
IBM Research, India
monikgup@in.ibm.com

Neelamadhav Gantayat
IBM Research, India
neelamadhav@in.ibm.com

Renuka Sindhgatta
IBM Research, India
renuka.sr@in.ibm.com

ABSTRACT

Mathematical word problems (or story problems) allow students to apply their mathematical problem solving ability to other subjects and real-world situations. Word problems build higher-order thinking, critical problem-solving, and reasoning skills. Generally solving a word problem is associated with mathematical modeling of a real word situation or a concept of another subject which is embedded in the problem. Manually creating word problems require knowledge of other topics a student is learning in parallel. Besides this, modeling mathematics with some other dissociated concept is a time-consuming and labor-intensive task. Due to lack of this integrated knowledge of other topics being taught, the substantive breadth of word problems is often very narrow and is limited to very few concepts. To address this limitation, we built a tool called *Intelligent Math Tutor (IMT)*, which automatically generates mathematical word problems such that teachings from other subjects from a given curriculum can also be incorporated. Our tool thus widens the scope of word problems and uses this problem-solving based approach to indirectly create cognizance in its students. To the best of our knowledge, our tool is the first of its kind tool which explicitly blends knowledge from multiple dissociated subjects and uses it to enhance the cognizance of its learners.

Author Keywords

Intelligent Math Tutor; Mathematical Word Problems; Concept Mapping; Integrated Curriculum

INTRODUCTION

One of the fundamental challenges in contemporary education system is the *separate subject* or *layer cake* approach to knowledge and skills [1, 2, 3]. Rather than having a strict divergence between subjects, using an interdisciplinary or integrated curriculum provides

L@S 2017, April 20-21, 2017, Cambridge, MA, USA.
© 2017 ACM. ISBN 978-1-4503-4450-0/17/04…$15.00.
DOI: http://dx.doi.org/10.1145/3051457.3053995

opportunities for more relevant, less fragmented, and more stimulating experiences for students. Problem-based learning invokes process skills instead of rote learning and has thus become a classroom norm in integrated science and mathematics. As an example, mathematical word problems frequently integrate math and science concepts, and this problem-based learning approach have always been a preferred tool used to enforce learning of math/science concepts, especially at primary and secondary school level. Manually creating word problems can be a time-consuming and laborious task. Further, manual creation restricts the scope of word problems in terms of concepts and subject-breadth, as it requires availability of experts from multiple domains and knowledge of other topics a student is learning in parallel.

To overcome this challenge, we built a tool called *Intelligent Math Tutor (IMT)*, which automatically generates mathematical word problems using teachings from other subjects and concepts without expert intervention. Importantly, students usually have inclination/dis-inclination towards specific subjects. Intelligent Math Tutor can generate mathematical word problems drawn from one or more focused subjects (for example, subjects that a given student is not excelling), so as to introduce the given student to concepts from the one or more subjects. For example, using facts from geography to compose math word problem, will familiarize the student to concepts from both math and geography. Our tool thus not only widens the scope of math word problems but also uses this problem-solving based approach to indirectly create cognizance in its students.

To the best of our knowledge, Intelligent Math Tutor is the first of its kind tool to explicitly combine knowledge from multiple, possibly dissociated subjects and use this problem-solving based approach to enhance the cognizance of the learners.

ILLUSTRATIVE EXAMPLES

In this section we present two scenarios through illustrative examples showcasing the strength and capabilities of our IMT tool. Figure 1 presents the first scenario where two concepts, drawn from primary school math and science curriculums are shown. The math problem is based on the topic of *Percentage*, while the science sample is from basic natural science subject which explains about *human body*. As such there is no apparent commonality between the two concepts. Both of these are fed as inputs to our IMT tool, which now uses the math concept as a template to generate a new similar math word problem which incorporates the teachings from the given science concept as well. Figure 1 shows the output word problem as generated by IMT. It is evident that when students solve this blended problem, they are simultaneously exposed to the given science concept as well, highlighting the importance of this tool.

Figure 1. An illustrative example showing two concepts, one from math, other from natural science, and the output math word problem as generated by our tool. Phrases in color are information points which are automatically picked up by the tool to generate new word problem.

Figure 2 presents another scenario where only one science concept on *Chemical Elements*, again drawn from primary school curriculum is given as the input. In this case, IMT matches the given concept with some predefined math templates (which are managed grade and topic wise) and generates a new math word problem which incorporates the teachings from the given science concept. As aforementioned, when a student attempts to solve such a blended math word problem, he/she is simultaneously exposed to the given science concept as well.

Figure 2. An illustrative example showing the input science concept and an output math word problem as generated by our tool.

ARCHITECTURE AND DESIGN

In this section, the technical implementation details of the Intelligent Math Tutor system are described. Figure 5 shows the architecture diagram of the tool. There are three main modules of the system: (1) *Concept Map Generation Module*, (2) *Concept Map Matching Module*, and, (3) *Problem Generation Module*.

Concept Map Generation Module

The aim of this module is to generate *concept maps* for the given input samples. We define a concept map as a graph

representing the conceptual entities and the relationships between the entities. Figure 3A and 4 show the concept maps for the two example inputs shown in Figure 1. For each input concept, an *Entity Relationship Extractor* first extracts the conceptual entities (shown in red color in Figure 1 and 2) and the relationships between them (shown in brown color in Figure 1 and 2), and then creates a graphical representation of concept maps. A *Numerical Property Extractor* augments the entities and relationships in the map with numerical values wherever applicable.

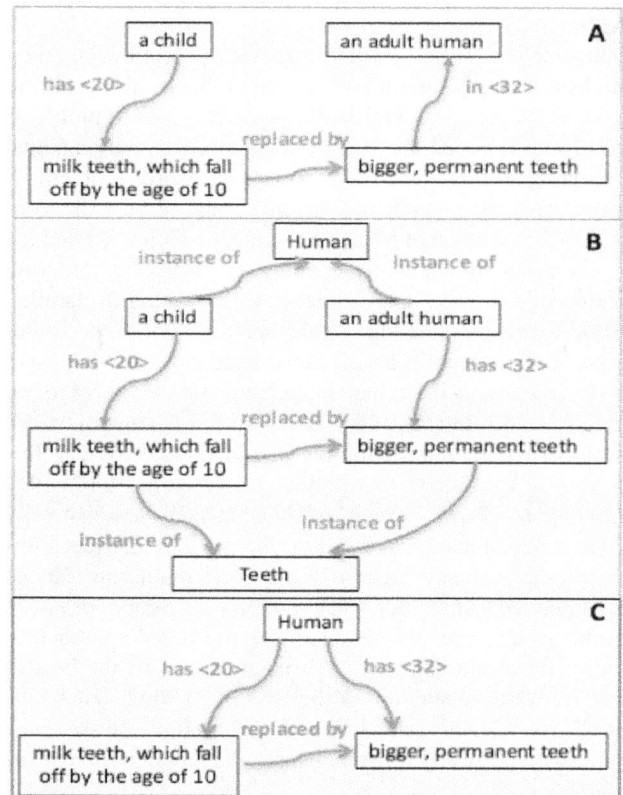

Figure 3. A. Concept Map for the Science sampler in Figure 1, B. Augmented Concept Map, C. Matching subgraph for the example in Figure 1.

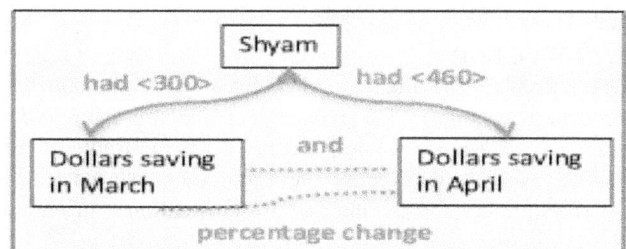

Figure 4. Concept Map for the Math sampler in Figure 1

Conceptual text statements are first parsed using *Stanford NLP dependency parser* [6] and the resultant dependency tree is used to generate concept maps. Stanford NLP parser tags each word with one of the Stanford dependencies [8], which refers to a grammatical relation between words in a sentence. Output of dependency parser is an array of tuples containing head and dependent. Stanford dependency parser ensures that each word has a unique head, which ensures

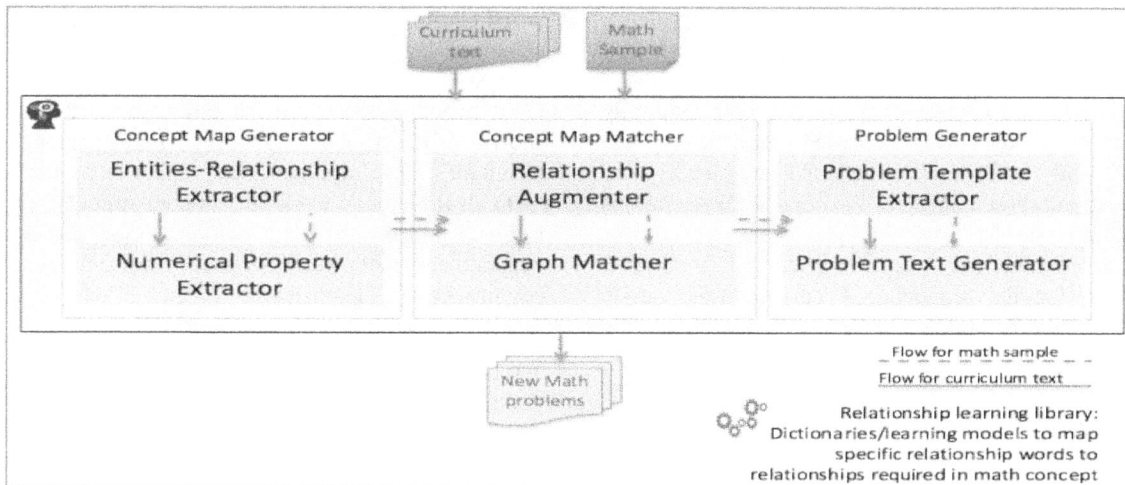

Figure 5. Architecture of Intelligent Math Tutor System

unambiguous relation between two words. Figure 6 shows *dependency parser output tree of the phrase, "A child has 20 milk teeth"*, where *child* and *milk teeth* are extracted as *entities*, and *has* is considered as the *relationship* between them. A *nummod* is used to identify the number quantity.

Figure 6. Output of Stanford dependency parser

Concept Map Matching Module

A *Relationship Augmenter* now augments the concept map with more generic relationships like *"instanceOf"*, *"typeOf"* etc. It also explicitly identifies mathematical relationships in the math samples, for example, *"percentage change"* in this case. For the same, it uses an explicit *Relationship Learning Library* that maps discrete relationship words to a class in the relationship taxonomy. Figure 3B shows the augmented concept map for the science concept in Figure 1. Note the two new generic entities, *human* and *teeth* as introduced in the map and that they are associated with the existing entities using the generic *instanceOf* relationship. A *Graph Matcher* now finds structurally matching sub-graphs in these augmented concept maps. In our implementation of the method, we store the concept graph in *Titan (a Graph DB)* and use graph queries to find matching sub-graphs. Figure 3C shows the portion of the science concept map that gets matched with the corresponding math concept map in Figure 4.

Problem Generation Module

The final step in the process is to generate a new math word problem. A *Problem Template Extractor* uses an NLP parser and the matched concept maps from previous steps to extract out a problem template from the input math sample. For the example in Figure 1, the Problem Template Extractor extracts the following template –

What is the percentage change in *<root-entity>* from *<entity-1>* to *<entity-2>*?

The *Problem Text Generator* finally replaces variable portions in the template with matched subgraph entities and relationships to generate a new math word problem as shown in Figure 1.

PILOT STUDY

We conducted a very basic preliminary study to investigate the usefulness of our Intelligent Math Tutor tool in relation to existing tools and manual approaches for doing the same and to discover the possible hurdles in its adoption.

Participants

Twenty-five participants which included 8 teachers, 5 parents, and 12 students participated in the survey. Half of the teachers were from primary school (grade 4-5), and other half were from secondary school (grade 6-8). Three out of 8 teachers taught math subject, 2 taught history, 1 taught geography, and the remaining 2 taught science. All the 5 parents had children going to primary school. Seven out of the 12 students were from primary school and remaining 5 were from secondary school. Further, each student spent an average of 5 hours in a week to practice math problems. We used a combination of word-of-mouth, and snowball sampling to select our participants. The survey was conducted as a special session during a math lab event in a reputed high school.

Method and Results

The first part of the study was to figure out what topics students usually find too hard or too boring to learn. We developed a questionnaire with free-form questions about (1) the subjects they find boring, (2) specific examples of the concepts in that subject which they find difficulty in, and, (3) the reasons why that particular concept is so difficult/boring. The questionnaire was filled by all teachers, students, and parents. From the survey results, it was clearly evident that the students usually find concepts which involve lots of rote learning as either too boring or too difficult. Some examples given were chemical valence numbers in chemistry, reigning periods and dynasty hierarchies in history, and mining/crop production related information within a country in geography. We randomly took 10 of these concepts, and passed them through our Intelligent Math Tutor tool to generate new math word problems around these concepts. Two distinct observations were - (1) for 6 out of 10 given input concepts, our tool was able to generate new math word problems with good level of accuracy; for the remaining 4 concepts, the newly generated math word problem lacked desired structure and had to be manually tuned, and, (2) the more the exposure the students would have to these concepts in one or the other form (as an example in word problem form since students spend a considerable number of hours per work to solve math assignments), the lesser the requirement there would be to rote learn them.

For the second part of the study, we presented a list of 8 such word problems to each participant, and asked them to fill a questionnaire with questions rated on a 5-point Likert scale. The questions were around the usefulness and helpfulness of these blended word problems in the student's learning process, and on their excitement level in solving the same. We asked the participants to rate the answers on a scale of 1 to 5. All the participants rated the problems as 3 or more (mean=3.75, sd=0.622) in terms of usefulness and excitement level. In general, the excitement and helpfulness level ratings were higher in primary school participants than in secondary school participants.

Another set of questions asked specifically from teacher and parent participants were around how easy or difficult it would be to generate such blended word problems manually and some free-form questions on why it would be difficult if that is the case. It came out that it would not be very difficult to generate these word problems manually also, however the main issues would be to identify other topics a student is learning in parallel, and that it would be a time-consuming and labor-intensive task.

As a key take away from these studies, we observed that the real strength of Intelligent Math Tutor would be when it is plugged-in as a component of a bigger online intelligent tutor framework which constantly monitors each student's performance on various subjects and topics. As a cognitive component of such a framework, Intelligent Math Tutor can use some of the concepts where the student is not doing good to automatically generate math problem worksheets for him.

RELATED WORK

Many tools like Microsoft Math Worksheet Generator and Wolfram Problem Generator, exist which automatically generate math worksheets by analyzing existing samples. Automated question generation has been identified as a desirable requirement, to reduce the labor intensive task of generating questions for intelligent tutoring systems [4]. Heilman et. Al [5] present their work on generating fact-based questions about the content in an article. The problem of natural language generation of math word problems has been studied earlier. Frame Semantics has been explored [7] to generate new test items and math word problems are shown to be tractable targets for natural language general techniques. Our Intelligent Math Tutor steps further ahead from all these prior work and its core strength is its ability to blend information from multiple dissociated concepts to generate new math word problems and use it to enhance the cognizance of its learners.

CONCLUSIONS AND FUTURE WORK

We built a tool, called Intelligent Math Tutor, which automatically generates mathematical word problems using concepts from other subjects in a given curriculum. Our study showed that all participants unanimously agreed to the usefulness and relevance of the tool. We believe that the real strength of Intelligent Math Tutor would be when it is plugged-in as a component of a bigger online intelligent tutor framework which constantly monitors each student's performance on various subjects and topics. In future, we plan to work on the scalability of our tool We also plan to work on its integration with other student performance monitoring tools.

REFERENCES

1. Joseph M. Furner and David D. Kumar. The Mathematics and Science Integration Argument: A Stand for Teacher Education. Eurasia Journal of Mathematics, Science & Technology Education.

2. Frykholm, J., & Glasson, G. (2005). Connecting science and mathematics instruction: Pedagogical context knowledge for teachers. School Science and Mathematics, 105 (3), 127-141.

3. Koirala, H. P., & Bowman, J. K. (2003). Preparing middle level preservice teachers to integrate mathematics and science: Problems and possibilities. School Science and Mathematics, 145(10), 145-154.

4. Andrew McGregor Olney, Arthur C. Graesser, Natalie K. Person: Question Generation from Concept Maps. Dialogs and Discourse, Vol 3(2): 75-99 (2012)

5. Heilman, M. and Smith, N. A. (2010b). Good Question! Statistical Ranking for Question Generation. In HLT-NAACL 2010, pages 609–617

6. Danqi Chen and Christopher Manning. 2014. A Fast and Accurate Dependency Parser Using Neural Networks. In Proceedings of EMNLP 2014.

7. Deane, Paul; Sheehan, Kathleen. Automatic Item Generation via Frame Semantics: Natural Language Generation of Math Word Problems. Annual Meeting of the National Council on Measurement in Education (Chicago, IL, April 22-24, 2003).

8. De Marneffe, Marie-Catherine, and Christopher D. Manning. Stanford typed dependencies manual. Technical report, Stanford University, 2008.

D.TRUMP: Data-mining Textual Responses to Uncover Misconception Patterns

Joshua Michalenko[1], Andrew S. Lan[2], Richard G. Baraniuk[1]
[1]Rice University, [2]Princeton University
{jjm7@rice.edu, andrew.lan@princeton.edu, richb@rice.edu}

ABSTRACT

An important, yet largely unstudied, problem in student data analysis is to detect misconceptions from students' responses to *open-response* questions. Misconception detection enables instructors to deliver more targeted feedback on the misconceptions exhibited by many students in their class, thus improving the quality of instruction. In this paper, we propose D.TRUMP, a new natural language processing (NLP) framework to detect the common misconceptions among students' textual responses to open-response, short-answer questions. We introduce a probabilistic model for students' textual responses involving misconceptions and experimentally validate it on a real-world student-response dataset. Preliminary experimental results show that D.TRUMP excels at classifying whether a response exhibits one or more misconceptions. More importantly, it can also automatically detect the common misconceptions exhibited across responses from multiple students to multiple questions; this is especially important at large scale, since instructors will no longer need to manually specify all possible misconceptions that students might exhibit.

Author Keywords

Learning analytics, Misconception detection, Natural language processing

INTRODUCTION

The rapid developments of large-scale learning platforms (e.g., MOOCs (edx.org, coursera.org) and OpenStax Tutor (openstaxtutor.org)) have enabled not only access to high-quality learning resources to a large number of students, but also the collection of student data at very large scale. The scale of this data presents a great opportunity to revolutionize education by using machine learning algorithms to *automatically* deliver personalized analytics and feedback to students and instructors in order to dramatically improve the quality of teaching and learning.

Detecting misconceptions from student-response data

The predominant form of student data, their *responses* to assessment questions, contain rich information on their knowledge states. Analyzing why a student answers a question incorrectly is of crucial importance to deliver timely and effective feedback. Among the possible causes for a student to answer a question incorrectly, exhibiting one or more *misconceptions* is critical, since upon detection of a misconception, it is very important to provide targeted feedback to a student to correct their misconception in a timely manner. Examples of using misconceptions to improve instruction include incorporating misconceptions to design better distractors for multiple-choice questions [8], implementing a dialogue-based tutor to detect misconceptions and provide corresponding feedback to help students self-practice [16], preparing prospective instructors by examining the causes of common misconceptions among students [15], and incorporating misconceptions into item response theory (IRT) for learning analytics [14].

The conventional way of leveraging misconceptions is to rely on a set of pre-defined misconceptions provided by domain experts [4, 8, 15, 16]. However, this approach is not scalable, since it requires a large amount of human effort and is domain-specific. With the large scale of student data at our disposal, a more scalable approach is to automatically detect misconceptions from data.

Recently, researchers have developed approaches for data-driven misconception detection; most of these approaches analyze students' response to *multiple-choice* questions. Examples of these approaches include detecting misconceptions in mathematics and modeling students' progress in correcting them [7] via the additive factor model [2], detecting misconceptions in chemistry by monitoring group discussions [12], and clustering students' responses across a number of multiple-choice physics questions [17]. However, multiple-choice questions have been shown to be inferior to open-response questions in terms of pedagogical value [6]. Indeed, students' responses to open-response questions can offer deeper insights into their knowledge.

To date, detecting misconceptions from students' responses to open-response questions has largely remained an unexplored problem. A few recent developments work exclusively with *structured* responses, e.g., sketches [13], short mathematical expressions [9], and algebra with simple syntax [3].

Contributions

In this paper, we propose D.TRUMP (Data-mining Textual Responses to Uncover Misconception Patterns), a NLP framework that detects students' common misconceptions from their *textual* responses to open-response, short-answer questions. This problem is very difficult, since the responses are, in general, *unstructured*.

D.TRUMP consists of the following steps. First, we transform students' textual responses to a number of short-answer questions into low-dimensional feature vectors using well-known word-vector embedding tools. The embedding is then input to a new statistical model that jointly models both the textual feature vectors and expert labels on whether a response exhibits one or more misconceptions; these labels identify only *whether or not* a response exhibits one or more misconceptions but not *which* misconception it exhibits. Our model uses a series of latent variables: the feature vectors corresponding to the correct response to each question, the feature vectors corresponding to each misconception, the tendency of each student to exhibit each misconception, and the confusion level of each question on each misconception. We develop a Markov Chain Monte Carlo (MCMC) algorithm for parameter inference under the D.TRUMP statistical model; details regarding this algorithm are omitted due to space constraints.

We experimentally validate D.TRUMP on two real-world educational datasets collected from two high-school classes, one on AP biology and one on high school Physics. Our experimental results show that D.TRUMP excels at classifying whether a response exhibits one or more misconceptions compared to standard classification algorithms. More importantly, we show an example of a common misconception detected from our datasets and discuss how this information can be used to deliver targeted feedback to help students correct their misconceptions.

THE D.TRUMP STATISTICAL MODEL

We now detail the D.TRUMP statistical model; its graphical model is visualized in Figure 1. Concretely, let there be a total of N students, Q questions, and K misconceptions. Let $M_{i,j} \in \{0, 1\}$ denote the binary-valued misconception label on the response of student j to question i provided by an expert grader, with $j \in \{1, \ldots, N\}$ and $i \in \{1, \ldots, Q\}$, where 1 represents the presence of (one or more) misconceptions, and 0 represents no misconceptions.

We transform the raw text of student j's response to question i into a D-dimensional real-valued feature vector, denoted by $\mathbf{f}_{i,j} \in \mathbb{R}^D$, via a pre-processing step (detailed later in the experimental setup section). Let $\Omega \subseteq \{1, \ldots, Q\} \times \{1, \ldots, N\}$ denote the subset of student responses that are labeled, since every student only responds to a subset of the questions.

We denote the *tendency* of student j to exhibit misconception k, with $k \in \{1, \ldots, K\}$ as $c_{k,j} \in \mathbb{R}$, and the *confusion level* of question i on misconception k, as $d_{i,k} \in \mathbb{R}$. Then, let $P_{i,j,k} \in \{0, 1\}$ denote the binary-valued latent variable that represents whether student j exhibits misconception k in their response to question i, with 1 denoting that the mis-

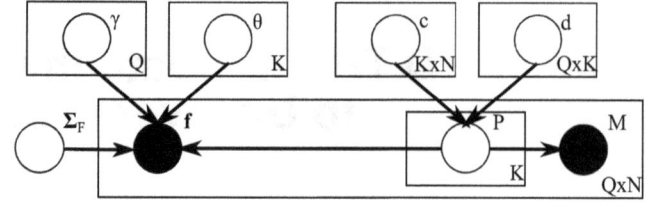

Figure 1: Visualization of the D.TRUMP statistical model. Black nodes denote observed data; white nodes denote latent variables to be inferred.

conception is present and 0 otherwise. We model $P_{i,j,k}$ as a Bernoulli random variable

$$p(P_{i,j,k} = 1) = \Phi(c_{k,j} + d_{i,k}), \quad (i, j) \in \Omega,$$

where $\Phi(x) = \int_{-\infty}^{x} \mathcal{N}(t; 0, 1) dt$ denotes the inverse probit link function (the cumulative distribution function of the standard normal random variable). Given $P_{i,j,k}$ $\forall k$, we model the observed misconception label $M_{i,j}$ as

$$M_{i,j} = \begin{cases} 0 & \text{if } P_{i,j,k} = 0 \ \forall k, \\ 1 & \text{otherwise,} \end{cases} \quad (i, j) \in \Omega.$$

In words, a response is labeled as having a misconception if one or more misconceptions is present (given by the latent misconception exhibition variables $P_{i,j,k}$). Given $P_{i,j,k}$ $\forall k$, the textual response feature vector that corresponds to student j's response to question i, $\mathbf{f}_{i,j}$, is modeled as

$$\mathbf{f}_{i,j} \sim \mathcal{N}(\boldsymbol{\gamma}_i + \sum_k P_{i,j,k} \boldsymbol{\theta}_k, \boldsymbol{\Sigma}_F), \quad \forall (i, j) \in \Omega,$$

where $\boldsymbol{\gamma}_i$ denotes the feature vector that corresponds to the correct response to question i, $\boldsymbol{\theta}_k$ denotes the feature vector that corresponds to misconception k, and $\boldsymbol{\Sigma}_F$ denotes the covariance matrix of the multivariate normal distribution characterizing the feature vectors. In other words, the feature vector of each response is a *mixture* of the feature vectors corresponding to the correct response to the question and each misconception the student exhibits.

EXPERIMENTS

We experimentally validate the efficacy of D.TRUMP using two real-world educational datasets. We first detail the datasets, then compare D.TRUMP against a baseline random forest (RF) classifier that classifies whether a student response exhibits one or more misconceptions. We conclude by showing a common misconception detected in our datasets and discuss how D.TRUMP can use this information to deliver meaningful targeted feedback to students that helps them correct their misconceptions.

Dataset

Our two datasets consist of students' textual responses to short-answer questions in high-school classes administered on OpenStax Tutor [11] on two subjects: AP biology and Physics. For AP biology, $N = 113$ students responded to a total of 798 questions, and for Physics, $N = 208$ and $Q = 99$. Not every student responded to every question, which resulted in a total of 13131 responses in AP biology and 1177 responses in Physics. Every response was labeled by an expert grader as to whether it exhibited one or more misconceptions.

Experimental setup

We first perform a pre-processing step by transforming each textual student response into a corresponding real-valued vector via word-vector embeddings. We train a standard skip-gram Word2Vec model [10] over the Openstax Biology and Physics textbooks (an approach also mentioned in [1]), to learn embeddings that put more emphasis on the technical vocabulary specific to each subject. We create the feature vector for each response by mapping each individual word in the response to its corresponding feature vector, and then adding them together. Concretely, denote the textual response of student j to question i, $\mathbf{x}_{i,j} = \{w_1, w_2, ..., w_{T_{i,j}}\}$ as the collection of words in the response, where $T_{i,j}$ denotes the total number of words in this response (excluding common stopwords). We then map each word w_t to its corresponding D-dimensional feature vector $r(w_t) \in \mathbb{R}^D$ using the trained Word2Vec model. We use $D = 10$ in our experiments. We then compute the student response feature vector as $\mathbf{f}_{i,j} = \sum_{t=1}^{T_{i,j}} r(w_t)$.

The assessment questions in AP Biology and Physics draw questions from the OpenStax textbooks; we divide the full AP Biology dataset into smaller subsets corresponding to each of the first four units of the Biology textbook , since different units correspond to entirely different sub-areas in biology. We do not further divide the Physics dataset since it is too small. We also trim each dataset by filtering out students who respond to less than 10 questions and questions with less than 10 responses in every dataset. We run D.TRUMP with $K = 2$ latent misconceptions.[1] We compare D.TRUMP against a baseline random forest (RF) classifier[2] using the textual response feature vectors $\mathbf{f}_{i,j}$ to classify the binary-valued misconception label $M_{i,j}$, with 100 decision trees.

We randomly partition each dataset into 5 folds and use 4 folds as the training set and the other fold as the test set. We then train D.TRUMP and RF on the training set and evaluate their performance on the test set, using two metrics: i) prediction accuracy (ACC), i.e., the portion of correct predictions, and ii) area under curve (AUC), i.e., the area under the receiver operating characteristic (ROC) curve of the resulting binary classifier [5]. Both metrics take values in $[0, 1]$, with larger values corresponding to better prediction performance. We repeat our experiments for 20 random partitions of the folds.

Results and discussion

We compare the performance of D.TRUMP against RF on misconception label classification in Table 1 and Table 2.

---

[1] We omit experimental results with other values of K due to spatial constraints.

[2] The RF classifier achieves the best performance among a number of off-the-shelf baseline classifiers, e.g., logistic regression, support vector machines, etc. Therefore, we do not compare D.TRUMP against other baseline classifiers.

D.TRUMP significantly outperforms RF (1–4% using the ACC metric and 4-17% using the AUC metric). The performance gain of D.TRUMP over RF is larger for the AP Biology datasets, in which students write longer textual responses and smaller in the Physics dataset due to the fact that most responses therein only contain a few words.

We emphasize that, in addition to D.TRUMP's significant improvement over RF in terms of misconception label classification, it features great interpretability since it identifies common misconceptions from data. For example, the following responses from multiple students across two questions are identified to exhibit the same misconception in the AP Biology Unit 4 dataset:

Question 1: People who breed domesticated animals try to avoid inbreeding even though most domesticated animals are indiscriminate. Evaluate why this is a good practice.
Correct Response: A breeder would not allow close relatives to mate, because inbreeding can bring together deleterious recessive mutations that can cause abnormalities and susceptibility to disease.
Student Response 1: Inbreeding can cause a rise in unfavorable or detrimental traits such as genes that cause individuals to be prone to disease or have unfavorable mutations.
Student Response 2: Interbreeding can lead to harmful mutations.

Question 2: When closely related individuals mate with each other, or inbreed, the offspring are often not as fit as the offspring of two unrelated individuals. Why?
Correct Response: Inbreeding can bring together rare, deleterious mutations that lead to harmful phenotypes.
Student Response 3: Leads to more homozygous recessive genes thus leading to mutation or disease.
Student Response 4: When related individuals mate it can lead to harmful mutations.

Although these responses are from different students to different questions, they exhibit one common misconception, that inbreeding leads to harmful mutations. Once this misconception is identified, course instructors can deliver the targeted feedback that inbreeding only brings together harmful mutations, leading to issues like abnormalities, rather than directly leading to harmful mutations.

Moreover, D.TRUMP can automatically discover common misconceptions that students exhibit without input from domain experts, especially when the number of students and questions are very large. Specifically, in the example above, D.TRUMP is able to detect such a common misconception that 4 responses exhibit by analyzing the 2278 responses in the AP Biology Unit 4 dataset; however, it would not likely be detected if the number of responses was smaller and fewer students exhibited the misconception. This feature makes D.TRUMP an attractive data-driven aid to domain experts in designing content to address student misconceptions.

Table 1: Performance comparison on misconception label classification of a textual response in terms of the prediction accuracy (ACC) of D.TRUMP against a random forest (RF) classifier.

	AP Biology unit 1	AP Biology unit 2	AP Biology unit 3	AP Biology unit 4	Physics
D.TRUMP	0.789±0.014	0.774±0.015	0.779±0.019	0.887±0.011	0.756±0.034
RF	0.762±0.019	0.735±0.011	0.758±0.017	0.873±0.009	0.745±0.031

Table 2: Performance comparison on misconception label classification of a textual response in terms of the area under the receiver operating characteristic curve (AUC) of D.TRUMP against RF.

	AP Biology unit 1	AP Biology unit 2	AP Biology unit 3	AP Biology unit 4	Physics
D.TRUMP	0.762±0.027	0.758±0.023	0.752±0.020	0.774±0.029	0.782±0.045
RF	0.645±0.025	0.676±0.014	0.630±0.024	0.604±0.034	0.746±0.042

CONCLUSIONS AND FUTURE WORK
In this paper, we have proposed D.TRUMP, a NLP framework for detecting and classifying common misconceptions in students' textual responses. Our experiments on two real-world educational datasets consisting of students' textual responses to short-answer questions show that D.TRUMP excels at classifying whether a response exhibits one or more misconceptions. Moreover, the D.TRUMP model is also able to group responses with the same misconceptions into clusters, enabling the data-driven discovery of common misconceptions without input from domain experts. Possible avenues of future work include i) test other word-vector embeddings that take word ordering into account, i.e., embeddings that map responses "If X then Y" and "If Y then X" to different feature vectors, and ii) automatically generate the appropriate feedback to correct each misconception.

REFERENCES
1. Bhatnagar, S., Desmarais, M., Lasry, N., and Charles, E. S. Text classification of student self-explanations in college physics questions. In *Proc. 9th Intl. Conf. Educ. Data Min.* (July 2016), 571–572.

2. Cen, H., Koedinger, K. R., and Junker, B. Learning factors analysis – A general method for cognitive model evaluation and improvement. In *Proc. 8th. Intl. Conf. Intell. Tutoring Syst.* (June 2006), 164–175.

3. Elmadani, M., Mathews, M., Mitrovic, A., Biswas, G., Wong, L. H., and Hirashima, T. Data-driven misconception discovery in constraint-based intelligent tutoring systems. In *Proc. 20th Int. Conf. Comput. in Educ.* (Nov. 2012), 1–8.

4. Griffiths, A. K., and Preston, K. R. Grade-12 students' misconceptions relating to fundamental characteristics of atoms and molecules. *J. Res. in Sci. Teaching 29*, 6 (Aug. 1992), 611–628.

5. Jin, H., and Ling, C. X. Using AUC and accuracy in evaluating learning algorithms. *IEEE Trans. Knowl. Data Eng. 17*, 3 (Mar. 2005), 299–310.

6. Kang, S., McDermott, K., and Roediger III, H. Test format and corrective feedback modify the effect of testing on long-term retention. *Eur. J. Cogn. Psychol. 19*, 4-5 (July 2007), 528–558.

7. Liu, R., Patel, R., and Koedinger, K. R. Modeling common misconceptions in learning process data. In *Proc. 6th Intl. Conf. on Learn. Analyt. & Knowl.* (Apr. 2016), 369–377.

8. Maass, J. K., and Pavlik Jr, P. I. Modeling the influence of format and depth during effortful retrieval practice. In *Proc. 9th Intl. Conf. Educ. Data Min.* (July 2016), 143–149.

9. McTavish, T., and Larusson, J. Discovering and describing types of mathematical errors. In *Proc. 7th Intl. Conf. Educ. Data Min.* (July 2014), 353–354.

10. Mikolov, T., Chen, K., Corrado, G., and Dean, J. Efficient estimation of word representations in vector space. *arXiv preprint arXiv:1301.3781* (Sep. 2013).

11. OpenStax Tutor. https://openstaxtutor.org/, 2016.

12. Schmidt, H. J. Students' misconceptions—Looking for a pattern. *Sci. Educ. 81*, 2 (Apr. 1997), 123–135.

13. Smith, A., Wiebe, E. N., Mott, B. W., and Lester, J. C. SketchMiner: Mining learner-generated science drawings with topological abstraction. In *Proc. 7th Intl. Conf. Educ. Data Min.* (July 2014), 288–291.

14. Tatsuoka, K. K. Rule space: An approach for dealing with misconceptions based on item response theory. *J. Educ. Meas. 20*, 4 (Dec. 1983), 345–354.

15. Tirosh, D. Enhancing prospective teachers' knowledge of children's conceptions: The case of division of fractions. *J. Res. Math. Educ. 31*, 1 (Jan. 2000), 5–25.

16. VanLehn, K., Jordan, P. W., Rosé, C. P., Bhembe, D., Böttner, M., Gaydos, A., Makatchev, M., Pappuswamy, U., Ringenberg, M., Roque, A., Siler, S., and Srivastava, R. The architecture of Why2-Atlas: A coach for qualitative physics essay writing. In *Proc. 6th Intl. Conf. on Intelligent Tutoring Systems* (June 2002), 158–167.

17. Zheng, G., Kim, S., Tan, Y., and Galyardt, A. Soft clustering of physics misconceptions using a mixed membership model. In *Proc. 9th Intl. Conf. Educ. Data Min.* (July 2016), 658–659.

Teamscope: Scalable Team Evaluation via Automated Metric Mining for Communication, Organization, Execution, and Evolution

An Ju
University of California
Berkeley, USA
an_ju@berkeley.edu

Elena Glassman
University of California
Berkeley, USA
eglassman@berkeley.edu

Armando Fox
University of California
Berkeley, USA
fox@cs.berkeley.edu

ABSTRACT

Teaching software development teams can be difficult to scale. Based on various cloud-based software development tools, Teamscope provides automated or semi-automated metrics to improve the scalability of a course with team projects. Metrics developed in Teamscope provide a synthesized view of a student team. Our preliminary results have shown the validity of these metrics. We also present a case study of applying metrics to teaching software development course in this paper.

Author Keywords

process conformance; software engineering; education; massive courses

INTRODUCTION

There is an increasing number of cloud-based tools that can be used to support certain best practices of software development: branch-oriented source code control (GitHub), effort estimation/division of labor/progress tracking (Pivotal Tracker), frequent informal communication (Slack), and so on. We believe the emergence of these cloud-based tools has provided us with new perspectives for team projects.

The broad goal of Teamscope is to identify and eliminate violations of practices in project teams when not all team members consistently follow the best practices prescribed by the methodology they've presumably adopted. Specifically, the goals of Teamscope are as follows:

- Infer the collaborative-development behaviors of a team and a team member via analytics from such tools;

- Detect both "soft" and "hard" violations of known best practices;

- Determine which processes are most critical to project success and personal learning;

- Study the application of process metrics to teaching software development teams.

The result can be used to measure the learning of students and provide instructions accordingly. Furthermore, instructions can be prepared automatically or semi-automatically, which will greatly enhance the scalability of a course.

RELATED WORK

Our project is inspired by the study presented in 2016 by Matthies et al., in which they studied several aspects of teaching software development[5], including a software that analyzes conformance of processes based on software development artifacts. The focus of their study is process conformance, which has a long history in software development community. For example, in 1998 and 1999, Cook et al. presented models that discover and validate a process model based on software development artifacts[2][3].

Data available on software development tools provides us with opportunities beyond process conformance. For example, it can be used to help novice programmers[1], and make defect predictions[6]. We believe those information is equally important in guiding team projects.

Our case study is focused on teaching Agile methods. There has been several studies on teaching Agile methods, and more on the application of Agile methods in general[4]. We borrowed some ideas from the survey in [7] to build our metrics.

METRICS DEVELOPMENT

In this section, we will present some examples of metrics that can be used to evaluate student teams, and preliminary results showing the validity of some metrics.

Process Conformance Template

Metrics are selected and improved based on a standard development process. Following the protocol introduced in [7], each process is represented by a process conformance template. A process template gives information about a standard process, data to be collected, and measurements. Detailed information of process conformance template can be found in [7]. Table 1 shows an example[1].

L@S 2017, April 20-21, 2017, Cambridge, MA, USA

© 2017 ACM. ISBN 978-1-4503-4450-0/17/04. . . $15.00

DOI: http://dx.doi.org/10.1145/3051457.3053997

---

[1]A Pivotal Tracker story represents a new feature/functionality planned for the project. Each story has a point, which is an estimation of workload required to deliver the story.

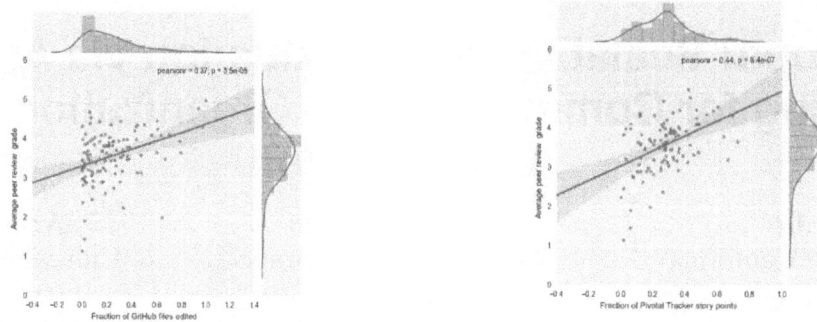

(a) The correlation between fraction of files edited and average peer review grades. The number of files edited is defined as a weighted sum of number of commits of a student, where the weight is the number of files.

(b) The correlation between fraction of Pivotal Tracker points and average peer review grades. Fraction of Pivotal Tracker points is defined as the total number of points assigned to a student over the total number of points of the project.

Figure 1: Correlation between average peer review grades (a) fraction of files edited and (b) fraction of Pivotal Tracker points. Peer review grade is the average grade of a student. Only students appear in both sets are considered.

Process Name	Consistent Velocity
Process Focus	Development
Process Description	A team should have a consistent velocity, since a consistent velocity means a good estimation of work and a consistent delivery of new features.
Collected Data (Automated)	Pivotal Tracker story points delivered.
Collected Data (Manual)	None.
Process Violations	An unstable velocity graph. A velocity graph is a line graph of points finished per iteration (velocity per iteration). A unstable velocity graph also means a large standard error.

Table 1: A process conformance template

Abbreviated conformance templates for some metrics are shown in Table 2.

Preliminary Results

In this section, we will show some preliminary results from a real software development course to support the use of metrics for measuring student performance.

Course information

The experiment is based on course data of CS169 in Fall 2016 semester. There are 142 students enrolled in the course, divided into 29 teams. Each team is assigned to a software development project, developing a web service with Ruby on Rails architecture. Development process follows Agile method, and is divided into four iterations.

Peer review grade as performance measurement

Peer review grades are used as a performance measurement for students. Peer review is a compulsory component at the end of each iteration.

Correlation between Estimated Workload and Average Peer Review Grades

We use two metrics for workload estimation: 1) fraction of number of files edited within a team, 2) fraction of user story points assigned within a team. The definition of both metrics are listed below.

Fraction of Files Edited is defined as a fraction of weighted sum of number of commits within a team. The weight is the number of files of a commit.

Fraction of Pivotal Tracker Story Points is defined as fraction of total number of pivotal story points a student is assigned to within a team.

Results are shown in Figure 1a and 1b respectively. Both metrics have a moderate correlation (with a Pearson's $r = 0.37$ and $r = 0.44$ respectively, $p < 0.01$) with average peer review grades.

To further show the correlation, we built a linear regression model to predict the peer review grade. Figure 2 shows the result. X-axis shows how many iterations are used for training and y-axis shows the mean squared error between predicted and real peer review grades. The best result is given by training with first 3 iterations, which is 0.21. For comparison, a linear model based on peer review grades of first 3 iterations gives a MSE of 0.52, and a prediction model based on average peer review grades of first 3 iterations gives a MSE of 0.25. A detailed list is shown in Table 3. So with GitHub and Pivotal Tracker data, we can capture more information underlying average peer review grades.

Process Name	Data Collected	Description
Consistent Velocity	Pivotal Tracker Story Points	Teams should deliver new features with a consistent velocity.
Clearly Defined Product Owner	Pivotal Tracker Story Information	Each team should have only one manager for each iteration, who manages all stories of the iteration.
Even Contribution	GitHub Commits. Pivotal Tracker Story Points.	Work should be distributed evenly among team members.
Reasonable Workload Estimation	GitHub Commits. Pivotal Tracker Story Points.	The estimation of story points should be proportional to the actual workload.
Pull Requests Review	GitHub Pull Requests Information.	A pull request should be reviewed by other members before merged.
Test Driven Design	GitHub Commits.	Tests should be implemented first before the actual implementation.
Communication Frequency	Slack data.	Communication should follow a daily pattern prescribed by the development method.
Code Quality	Code Climate Score	Teams should keep a healthy code quality score.

Table 2: Metrics

CASE STUDY

We built a system integrating some metrics. The system presents project information to instructors so that they can provide instructions accordingly. The system is highly extendable in that a new metric can be easily plugged in. We plan to extend this system further to serve as a platform that facilitates the design, management, instruction, and grading of team projects.

As is shown in Figure 3, metrics are shown on the website directly. Together with the number, a figure is also shown to

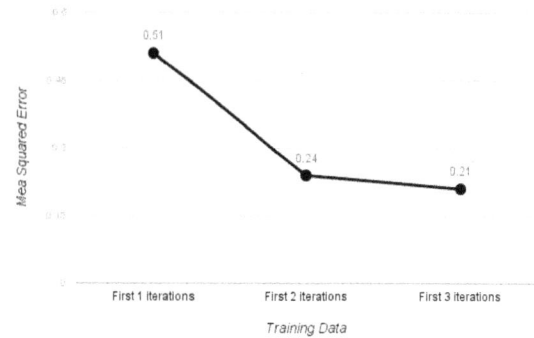

Figure 2: Mean squared error of linear prediction model based on fraction of pivotal tracker points and fraction of files edited. The x-axis shows the number of iterations used for training. Remaining iterations are used for prediction.

Models	MSE
Linear Regression (peer review grades of first 3 iterations)	0.52
Average (first 2 iterations)	0.66
Average (first 3 iterations)	0.25
Linear Regression (first 2 iterations)	0.24
Linear Regression (first 3 iterations)	0.21

Table 3: Results of different prediction models.

users so that more detailed information can be accessed. Furthermore, the system supports the view-by-time functionality, which enables instructors to see the information for a specific time.

The system has been used in CS169 at UC Berkeley in Fall 2016 semester. The system is used by instructors to grade and track team projects.

FUTURE WORK
Process conformance
There are two parts in process conformance analysis: process mining and conformance analysis. Both have a rich collection of literature in software engineering research community. However, most studies are about professional development teams, which are different from student development teams. One major difference is the assumption of a single process model (or several concurrent process models). However, in a classroom scenario, since students are learning, the process model changes over time, and understanding the change is important for understanding the learning. So new techniques are needed to study process conformance under an educational setting.

Metrics in more detail
It is natural to ask questions about the validity, reliability, scalability of metrics. Furthermore, those metrics are mostly designed out of intuition. Is it possible to build a theory of

Project List

Preference

Current date: ‹ **2017-01-07** ›

Project Name	Code climate	Github	Slack	Pivotal tracker	Slack trends
Project 1	2.41	3.54	0.07	1.92	
Project 10	3.31	3.77	3.38	3.25	
Project 11	1.70	3.56	0.46	1.40	

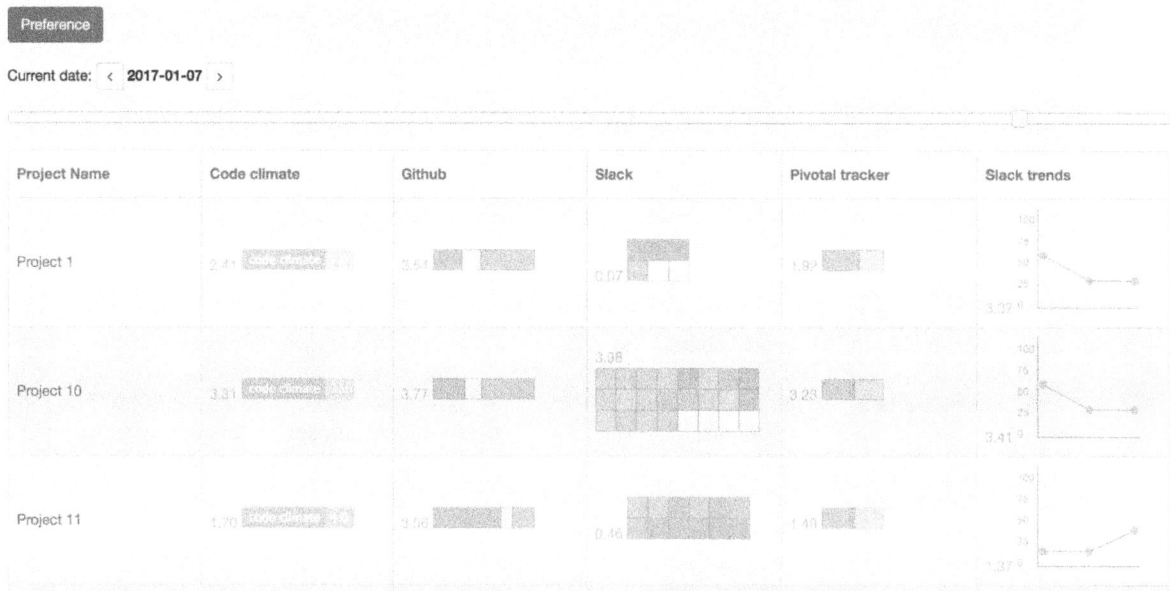

Figure 3: The system interface. Each column is a metric, and each row is a project.

metric design? A theory can provide a structure to study the importance of different metrics and also the role each metric plays.

The application of metrics

It is interesting to study the gap between knowing the status of teams and providing instructions to students. Our system presenting the information is the first step towards a more intelligent and comprehensive team project learning center.

CONCLUSION

In this work, we presented our vision and preliminary results towards a scalable team evaluation system. Team projects are important components of modern computer science education. Our work can help extend large-scale computer science courses with broader contents and forms.

The key point of our system is analysis on artifacts from various software development tools, which are accessible only in recent years. We believe those artifacts provide a detailed record of software development processes, which can be used to track, evaluate and improve student teams. We presented our way of designing, managing, executing and improving metrics, and some preliminary results showing the validity of metrics. Our work is mainly focused on teaching scenario. However, it can be used for general software development teams, or for tutoring new software development teams.

REFERENCES

1. Rachel Cardell-Oliver. 2011. How can software metrics help novice programmers?. In *Proceedings of the Thirteenth Australasian Computing Education Conference-Volume 114*. Australian Computer Society, Inc., 55–62.

2. Jonathan E Cook and Alexander L Wolf. 1998. Discovering models of software processes from event-based data. *ACM Transactions on Software Engineering and Methodology (TOSEM)* 7, 3 (1998), 215–249.

3. Jonathan E Cook and Alexander L Wolf. 1999. Software process validation: quantitatively measuring the correspondence of a process to a model. *ACM Transactions on Software Engineering and Methodology (TOSEM)* 8, 2 (1999), 147–176.

4. Tore Dybå and Torgeir Dingsøyr. 2008. Empirical studies of agile software development: A systematic review. *Information and software technology* 50, 9 (2008), 833–859.

5. Christoph Matthies, Thomas Kowark, Keven Richly, Matthias Uflacker, and Hasso Plattner. 2016. How surveys, tutors, and software help to assess Scrum adoption in a classroom software engineering project. In *Proceedings of the 38th International Conference on Software Engineering Companion*. ACM, 313–322.

6. Raimund Moser, Witold Pedrycz, and Giancarlo Succi. 2008. A comparative analysis of the efficiency of change metrics and static code attributes for defect prediction. In *2008 ACM/IEEE 30th International Conference on Software Engineering*. IEEE, 181–190.

7. Nico Zazworka, Kai Stapel, Eric Knauss, Forrest Shull, Victor R Basili, and Kurt Schneider. 2010. Are developers complying with the process: an XP study. In *Proceedings of the 2010 ACM-IEEE International Symposium on Empirical Software Engineering and Measurement*. ACM, 14.

ProjectLens: Supporting Project-based Collaborative Learning on MOOCs

Hao Fei Cheng , Bowen Yu , Yeong Hoon Park , and Haiyi Zhu

GroupLens Research
University of Minnesota
{cheng635, yuxxx856, park1779, zhux0449}@umn.edu

ABSTRACT

Team project, which emphasizes collaborative learning in a project-based context, is one of the most commonly-used teaching and learning methods in higher education classrooms, but is not well-supported on existing Massive Open Online Course (MOOC) platforms. In this paper, we present ProjectLens, a MOOC supplement tool that supports team projects building and collaborative learning on MOOC platforms like Coursera and edX. In addition, ProjectLens is a research tool that provides opportunities to conduct large-scale field experiments to study how different factors influence the effectiveness of collaborative learning. We illustrate how ProjectLens can achieve these two goals in a case example.

Author Keywords

Massive Open Online Courses; MOOCs; Collaborative Learning; Group Collaboration

INTRODUCTION

Massive Open Online Courses (MOOCs) have steadily gained popularity in recent years because of their ability to provide easily-accessible and high quality education to students all over the world. Many current MOOC platforms (e.g. Coursera and edX) provide good support for individual learning activities, such as watching pre-recorded lecture videos, reading documents, and completing individual assignments, quizzes and exams, but have very limited support for collaborative learning among students.

Collaborative learning is defined as two or more people learning together [3]. Prior research has demonstrated that collaborative learning is an effective learning technique, because it can generate extra activities (e.g., explanation, disagreement and mutual regulation), trigger learning mechanisms (e.g, knowledge elicitation, internalisation, reduced cognitive

L@S 2017, April 20 - 21, 2017, Cambridge, MA, USA

© 2017 Copyright held by the owner/author(s). Publication rights licensed to ACM.
ISBN 978-1-4503-4450-0/17/04. . . $15.00

DOI: http://dx.doi.org/10.1145/3051457.3053998

load, and critical thinking), and therefore improve learning outcomes [4][3]. However, current collaborative learning activities on MOOCs, such as forum discussion and peer-grading do not have the necessary collaboration depth to generate such learning activities and trigger important learning mechanisms.

Team projects emphasize collaborative learning in a problem-based context, and are one of the most commonly-used teaching and learning methods in higher education classrooms [14][8]. When teams of students spend tens or hundreds of hours together to solve real and meaningful problems, they gain a deeper understanding of course materials. This helps them acquire higher learning skills including cooperative ability, critical reasoning, creative thinking, responsibility, and communication [9]. To the best of our knowledge, there is no system-level support for team projects on existing MOOC platforms.

In this paper, we present ProjectLens, a tool that aims to support project-based collaborative learning for teams on existing MOOC platforms, including Coursera and edX. In addition, we believe that ProjectLens will also allow researchers to access interesting data to examine important research questions related to computer-supported collaborative learning.

OVERVIEW OF PROJECTLENS

ProjectLens has two primary goals:

1. ProjectLens is a MOOC supplement tool that supports team projects and collaborative learning on the existing MOOC platforms. ProjectLens can be integrated quickly with MOOCs that involve collaborative learning.

2. ProjectLens is a research tool that provides new opportunities to conduct field experiment and answer important research questions on online group learning.

AS A SUPPORT TOOL

ProjectLens provides the following key features that allow instructors to easily set up team projects which are not well supported by the current MOOC platforms. The most important function that ProjectLens supports is team formation, which assigns students into groups. Figure 2 shows how the instructors can select which attributes (e.g., gender, age, time

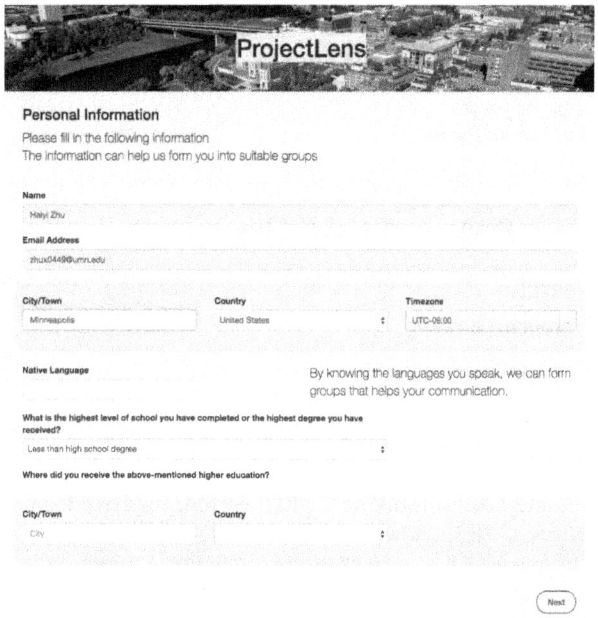

(a) During the signup stage, students fill out a survey about their demographic information and attributes. ProjectLens will put students into suitable groups based on the algorithm selected by the instructor.

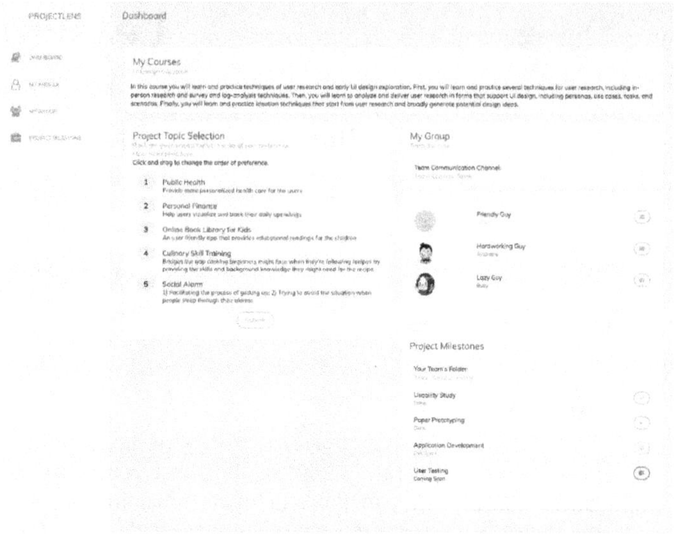

(b) The main dashboard helps students collaborate with their group members and motivates their group communication. Students can interact with their group members, discuss and vote on project ideas, and update their project progress using the platform.

Figure 1: The user interfaces of the ProjectLens student platform.

zone, country, prior experience) they want to use to group the students with. Additionally, instructors are required to decide the team size. Moreover, ProjectLens recommends the instructor to upload detailed instructions for the team project, set up a time window for students to register for team projects, and provide a deadline for uploading deliverables (e.g. project report).

As shown in Figure 1, students will have to navigate to ProjectLens to sign up for a team project and fill out a survey (i.e. reporting their demographic information, geography information, prior research experience, and contact information) during the signup period. After the end of the signup period, ProjectLens will analyze the survey data and group students into different teams based on the criteria the instructors set up. Students will be notified of the grouping information and have access to their team members' information on the ProjectLens page. They are encouraged to start communicating and working with their team members using the communication channels provided by ProjectLens.

ProjectLens can be integrated with Coursera and other MOOC platforms through the Learning Technologies Interoperability (LTI). LTI is a specification developed by IMS Global Learning Consortium to establish a standard way of integrating external learning applications with learning platforms [1]. Students can directly access ProjectLens pages from the MOOC interface. In other words, students do not need to navigate to an external website.

---
[1] https://www.imsglobal.org/activity/learning-tools-interoperability

AS A RESEARCH TOOL

For over twenty years, researchers have been studying under what circumstances collaborative learning is more or less effective [13]. Potential variables that could influence the effectiveness of collaborative learning include size of the group, composition of the group, nature of the task, communication media, and so on. Moreover, these variables often interacted with one another on affecting the interaction between people and the collaboration outcomes [3]. Drawing a comprehensive picture of the effects of these factors requires a very large sample size that is difficult to obtain in traditional context.

ProjectLens provides a unique opportunity to access a large participant pool, given the success and popularity of the current MOOC platforms. Since its launch in 2012 to September 2015, Coursera has accumulated 15 million registered learners [6]. From Summer 2012 to Fall 2016, HarvardX and MITx attracted 2.4 million unique learners. On average 1,554 unique new participants enroll each day [2]. ProjectLens has the potential to run field experiments on hundreds of thousands of students.

CASE EXAMPLE

Supporting "UI Design Capstone" on Coursera

ProjectLens will be used to support Coursera class "UI Design Capstone". "UI Design Capstone" is the final course of the UI Design Specialization on Coursera, provided by the University of Minnesota. In the eight weeks, students engage in a team project which requires them to apply and combine the skills they have learned in the previous courses in the specialization.

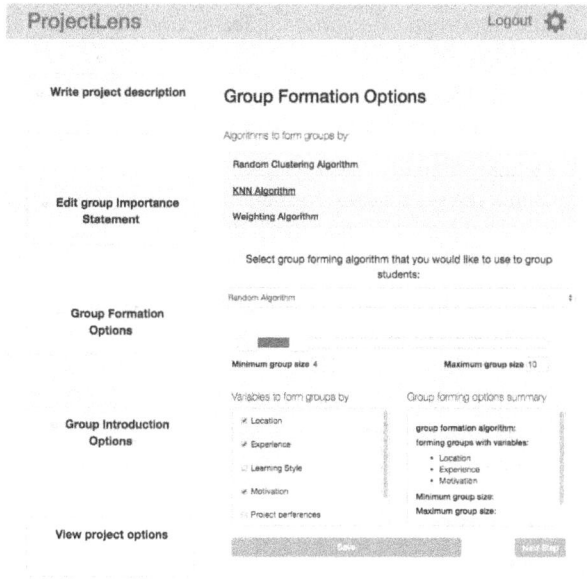

Figure 2: The user interface of the ProjectLens instructor platform. Instructors can customize the group formation process, which includes tweaking the clustering algorithm, group size and group formation variables.

Students will work in groups in designing the UI solution to a selected project.

Studying the effects of geographical locations

As MOOCs are providing education at a global scale, students come from all over the world. For example, in the class "Circuits and Electronics" on edX, 155,000 students come from 194 countries spanning multiple time zones [1]. This demonstrates a huge diversity in the geographical locations of the students on MOOCs.

The geographical location is an important factor that can influence the team formation and team composition, and thus can affect the performance of team collaboration. However, geographical location is less studied in prior research examining team work and team formation in education setting [10] [7], as these studies often examine co-located students in the traditional classroom environment.

The geographical location of team members has two functional dimensions that could influence the effectiveness of collaborative learning — *culture* and *timezone*. Both factors affect how well a MOOC team could collaborate. Research has shown that cultural diversity had a positive influence on the group decision-making, but had a negative influence on effective communication [12][11]. Similarly, time zone differences could be a problem for communication, but could also be an asset — projects could literally zip around the globe with work being completed 24 hours a day [5].

We designed a 2 X 2 experiment (shown in table 1) to examine how culture and timezone affects the effectiveness of collaborative learning. We will recruit students from the "UI design capstone" class to participate in the study. Students can

Table 1: Experimental design to examine the effects of geographical location on collaborative learning.

		Timezone	
		Same - 0	Different - 1
Culture	Uniform - 0	00	01
	Diverse - 1	10	11

voluntarily join the research study, when they sign up their team projects on ProjectLens.

We will collect the location information (including the culture and timezone) of the students who joined the research study. These students will be assigned into one of four types of groups: 1) diverse culture and same timezone, 2) uniform culture and same timezone, 3) diverse culture and different timezone, or 4) uniform culture and different timezone. We define a group with members from more than two cultures as "diverse culture" and otherwise as "uniform culture". We define "different timezone" as a group with timezones difference between two members greater than 3 hours, otherwise as the "same timezone".

We will regularly monitor the performance of each group and evaluate the effectiveness of collaborative learning on the following four aspects:

1. The learning outcome of the group: we will evaluate the final milestone of the group.

2. The communication frequency and effectiveness: we will monitor how often each team member communicates in a group and use semantic analysis to analyze whether the team communication environment has been positive or negative.

3. The dropout rate and free-rider rate: we will monitor if any group member does not contribute to the group project or does not participate in the group communication.

4. The satisfaction of each group member: we will have each group member rate their satisfaction with the project experience and evaluate their teammates after the project.

DISCUSSION AND FUTURE DEVELOPMENTS

We will complete the case study on the effects of geographical locations on collaborative learning. Data will be collected from March 2017 to July 2017, in a span of five months. A new session of the class starts every two weeks and we are expecting to collect data from around 1000 students and 200 student groups.

The future development involves providing more data visualization for analysis. We plan to release ProjectLens as an open source platform to help other MOOCs incorporate collaborative learning into their courses.

REFERENCES
1. Lori Breslow, David E Pritchard, Jennifer DeBoer, Glenda S Stump, Andrew D Ho, and Daniel T Seaton.

2013. Studying learning in the worldwide classroom: Research into edX's first MOOC. *Research & Practice in Assessment* 8 (2013).

2. Isaac Chuang and Andrew Dean Ho. 2016. HarvardX and MITx: Four Years of Open Online Courses–Fall 2012-Summer 2016. (2016).

3. Pierre Dillenbourg. 1999. *Collaborative Learning: Cognitive and Computational Approaches. Advances in Learning and Instruction Series.* ERIC.

4. Anuradha A Gokhale. 1995. Collaborative learning enhances critical thinking. (1995).

5. Matthew Guay. 2015. How to Work in Different Timezones. (2015). `https://zapier.com/learn/remote-work/remote-work-time-shift/`

6. Daphne Koller, Nicholas Eriksson, and C Zhenghao. 2015. Impact revealed: learner outcomes in open online courses. (2015).

7. David L Largent and Chris Lüer. 2010. You mean we have to work together!?!: a study of the formation and interaction of programming teams in a college course setting. In *Proceedings of the Sixth international workshop on Computing education research.* ACM, 41–50.

8. Hye-Jung Lee and Cheolil Lim. 2012. Peer evaluation in blended team project-based learning: what do students find important? *Educational Technology & Society* 15, 4 (2012), 214–224.

9. David G Moursund. 2003. Project-based learning using information technology. (2003).

10. Debbie Richards. 2009. Designing project-based courses with a focus on group formation and assessment. *ACM Transactions on Computing Education (TOCE)* 9, 1 (2009), 2.

11. Rebecca H Rutherfoord. 2001. Using personality inventories to help form teams for software engineering class projects. In *ACM Sigcse Bulletin*, Vol. 33. ACM, 73–76.

12. Pnina Shachaf. 2008. Cultural diversity and information and communication technology impacts on global virtual teams: An exploratory study. *Information & Management* 45, 2 (2008), 131–142.

13. Gerry Stahl, Timothy Koschmann, and Dan Suthers. 2006. Computer-supported collaborative learning: An historical perspective. In *The Cambridge handbook of the learning sciences*, R Keith Sawyer (Ed.). Cambridge University Press, 409–426.

14. Astrid Von Kotze and Linda Cooper. 2000. Exploring the transformative potential of project-based learning in university adult education. *Studies in the Education of Adults* 32, 2 (2000), 212–228.

Data-Driven Feedback Generator for Online Programing Courses

Ke Wang
University of California, Davis
Davis, USA
kbwang@ucdavis.edu

Benjamin Lin
Microsoft
Redmond, USA
benjlin@microsoft.com

Bjorn Rettig
Microsoft
Redmond, USA
bjoernr@microsoft.com

Paul Pardi
Microsoft
Redmond, USA
paul.pardi@microsoft.com

Rishabh Singh
Microsoft
Redmond, USA
risin@microsoft.com

ABSTRACT

Manually providing feedback for programming assignments is a tedious task in traditional classroom education. The challenge increases drastically in Massive open online courses (MOOCs), where the student-teacher ratio can reach thousands to one or even millions to one. Despite the necessity, the current automated feedback approaches suffer from significant weaknesses: inability to scale to larger programs, manual involvement of teacher effort, and lack of precision for pinpointing errors. We present a technique to tackle these challenges by developing a data-driven automated grader, iGrader, capable of generating instant and precise feedback for programming assignments.

INTRODUCTION

The current nascent paradigm shift in education towards Massive Open Online Courses (MOOCs) increases the accessibility of higher education substantially. Despite the profound impact, it presents several new challenges, particularly on the scalability aspect. In this paper, we target one specific challenge of providing personalized feedback for programming assignments in introductory programming language courses. Unfortunately, the traditional approach of providing manual instructor feedback for programming assignment is no longer feasible in MOOCs. As a counter-measure, online course vendors adopt the following approaches: 1) customize the style of questions to have multiple-choice or those of similar forms for which the hard-coded answer can be easily provided; 2) peer-review each other's answer to the same question [5]; 3)

L@S 2017, April 20-21, 2017, Cambridge, MA, USA
© 2017 ACM. ISBN 978-1-4503-4450-0/17/04. . . $15.00
DOI: http://dx.doi.org/10.1145/3051457.3053999

```
 9        class Program
10        {
11  public static void Main()
12        {
13            for (int i = 0; i < 8; i++)
14            {
15                string query = string.Empty;
16                for (int j = 0; j < 8; j++)
17                {
18                    if (j%2==0)
19                    {
20                        query += "X";
21                    }
22                    else
23                    {
24                        query += "O";
25                    }
26                }
27                Console.WriteLine(query);
28            }
```

Your program has errors in the following lines:
Line 17, change: j --> (i + j)

Figure 1. An example feedback generated by iGrader.

execute students' program submissions through a set of predefined tests. Even though the existing feedback generation mechanisms are valuable, they are far from ideal solutions.

Background and Related Work

There has been two broad lines of research proposed for personalized feedback generation: program synthesis based [7] and machine learning based [4, 6]. The idea behind the former is to first generate a collection of candidate programs based on the error rules manually provided by the instructor, and then use SAT-based synthesis algorithm to find minimal repairs to correct the student programs. There are two major drawbacks of this approach. First, an instructor must manually provide error models for each problem. Second, scalability is a big issue especially with larger programs. There has also been some promising machine learning based approaches developed for personalized feedback generation [3,4], but their focus is to establish a mechanism that allows for fast searches into large dataset of student submissions. Thus, teachers can leverage

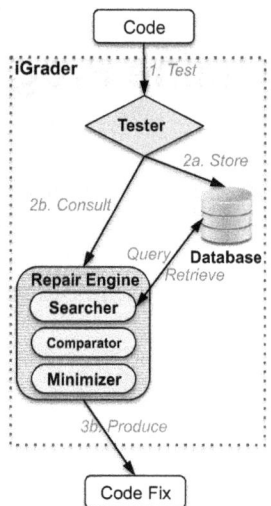

Figure 2. An example feedback generated by iGrader.

the redundancy of student homework to force-multiply their effort [3].

In this paper, we introduce a data-driven approach for automatically generating feedback for programming assignments. Our key insight is given the large amount of student submissions; the sub-parts of vast majority of incorrect attempts should have correct counterparts that can be used for correcting incorrect submissions.Given an incorrect submission, iGrader first finds closely related submission (both syntactically and semantically) to compute corresponding expression discrepancies and then finds a minimal set of repairs from the discrepancies to correct the student program. We have implemented our technique in a new feedback generator system, iGrader, and preliminarily evaluated it on student submissions for Microsoft C# online course on Edx [2] and CodeHunt [1]. The results show iGrader is very effective — repairing more than 70% of the submission with correct control flow and requiring less than three fixes, within few seconds.

OVERVIEW OF THE APPROACH

In this section, we give a high-level algorithm of how iGrader takes student submissions and produces automatic fixes. Figure 2 depicts the architecture of iGrader and Figure 1 depicts an example feedback generated by iGrader. We discuss the key components in this section, and defer the discussion of the core componen — the "Repair Engine" — to later section. We next give a description of iGrader's workflow:

1. **Testing**: iGrader first tests programs for functional correctness using a set of predefined test cases.

2. **Test Outcome**: Two cases:

    (a) **Storing**: If the program passed all the test cases, iGrader stores it in an internal database.

    (b) **Consulting**: Otherwise, iGrader calls Repair Engine into action, which

   i. **Querying and Retrieving**: automatically queries the database and retrieves a set of correct programs that are most similar to the student program.
   ii. **Comparing**: compare the programs in a pair-wise way to collect potential fixes.
   iii. **Minimizing**: minimize the set of fixes that the student program needed for repair.

3. **Feedback Generation**: Finally, iGrader produces the minimal set of fixes back to students

REPAIR ENGINE

In this section, we give a detailed presentation on the repair engine — the centerpiece of iGrader that consists of three components: *Searcher*, *Comparator* and *Minimizer*.

Searcher

Given a database of correct solutions, iGrader performs a hierarchical search to find the programs that are similar to the student submission. The first level targets the control-flow structure. Specifically, iGrader only looks for programs that have the same control flow graph as the student program. iGrader then proceeds to the next level of non-control statement/expression. At this level, iGrader defines the similarity to be the maximum number of matching nodes in the two ASTs of the respective non-control statement/expression over the total number of nodes in the two ASTs. iGrader considers two non-leaf nodes to be a match if they represent identical type of expression such as parenthesis, binary op, method invocation, etc., and leaf nodes to be a match if they are the same identifier, operator, literals, etc. Furthermore, matching two nodes in the context of trees necessitates two additional constraints: 1). Any node in one tree can match one and only one node in the other and vice versa. 2) Any two nodes in an ancestral relationship in one tree must match two nodes in the same relationship in the other and vice versa. Now we introduce an algorithm that computes the maximum number of matching nodes in two ASTs under the two structural constraints.

Given the two ASTs (T_1 and T_2 rooted at α and β) to be matched, we split the problem into three separate scenarios:

i α is directly matched with β in which case the maximum number of matching nodes will be equal to total maximum number of matching nodes from each of the subtrees rooted at the each of the children nodes of α and α in order plus 1 if α is indeed matched to β.

ii α is matched with γ, one descendent nodes of β, in which case the maximum number of matching nodes will be equal to that between T_1 and the tree rooted at γ.

iii α's descendent node, ε, is matched with β in which case the maximum number of matching nodes will be equal to that T_2 and the tree rooted at ε.

We use a dynamic programming algorithm to compute the maximum number of matching nodes between the two trees.

Step	Subtree in T$_1$ (Root)	Subtree in T$_2$ (Root)	Best Score	Best Score Scenario
1	a	a	1	(i)
2	a	+	0	(i)
3	a	c	0	(i)
4	a	a+c	1	(ii)
5	a	(a+c)	1	(ii)
6	a	(a+c)*b	1	(ii)
...	...	...	...	...
24	a*b	a	1	(iii)
...	...	...	...	...
32	a*b	(a+c)*b	3	(i)

Table 1. The table shows the matching procedure between the subtree in T$_1$ and T$_2$ in order.

Because in any of the three scenarios, the maximum number of matching nodes between the two trees will depend on that of the subtrees. Hence we can start by finding the maximum matching nodes for the atomic trees rooted at the leaf nodes and then propagate in a bottom-up fashion until we reach the root. Any two subtrees in the process for which we compute the maximum matching nodes, we compare the three scenarios and find the one yielding the best score. For instance, given the two ASTs depicted in Figure 3, we show a truncated version of computation procedure in Table 1.

Comparator

After the *Searcher* finds a set of most similar programs to what student submitted, it's up to *Comparator* to produce the operations (edit/delete/insert) that can transform the student program to different counterparts. In other words, *Comparator* outputs the set of all fixes that can repair the student program. Given the matching between the two ASTs from *Searcher*, *Comparator* recursively traces the roots of the subtrees on the optimal path and produces the operations based on the matching scenarios in a top-down manner. For example, in T$_1$ and T$_2$, the matching between $a*b$ and $(a+c)*b$ suggests an edit operation, specifically changing $a*b$ to $(a+c)*b$. In addition, the matching scenario also entails that a in T$_1$ and $(a+c)$ in T$_2$ will become the subsequent roots for consideration. This time their matching indicates an insertion operation — adding $(a+c)$ in between $a*b$ and a in T$_1$. Finally, a in T$_1$ will be matched with a in T$_2$, meaning $a+c$, $+$ and c will all be added into T$_1$.

Minimizer

We can fix the student program using the set of fixes obtained from *Comparator*, but that will not result in good repairs, because: 1) the number of fixes *Comparator* produces will typically be large; 2) not all of them are necessary to repair the program. The *Minimizer* module discovers the minimum set of fixes a program needs. We use an enumerative algorithm to apply the set of fixes in increasing number of fixes to output the minimum set of fixes.

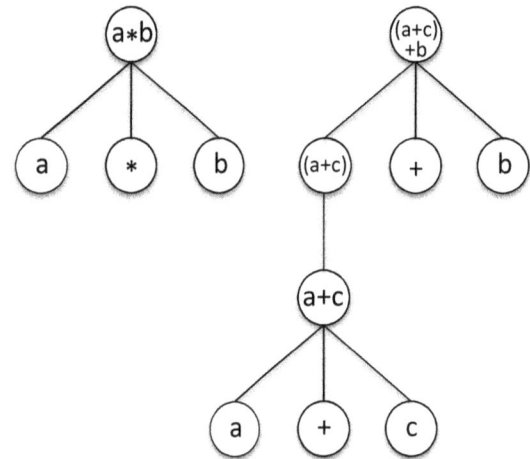

Figure 3. AST T$_1$ (left) and T$_2$ (right).

PRELIMINARY EVALUATION

We collected submissions from the Microsoft C# online course Module Two programming assignment on *Edx* (3,361 student submissions). We used Microsoft's Roslyn compiler framework for static parsing and dynamic execution of the C# programs. The current results are as follow:

- 46% of student submissions failed to match with any reference solution at the control flow level.

- Among the submission that succeeded at the control flow matching, 72% of them can be corrected with less then three fixes.

- iGrader generates feedback within 2-5 seconds for each program (depending on the number of fixes).

To further demonstrate the generality of iGrader's, we have also used two other programming problems[1] from Code-Hunt [1]. The iGrader system is already capable of repairing 95%, 61% of the student submissions with less than three fixes.

FUTURE WORK

There are several directions we want to pursue. 1) Feedback generation for performance issues. 2) A sophisticated user interface on the instructor side which control how the feedback will be provided to the students. 3) We would also like to extend iGrader to other online courses to benefit more students.

REFERENCES

1. 2013. Code Hunt. `https://www.codehunt.com/`. (2013). Accessed: 2017-01-10.

2. 2014. Programming with C# | edx. `https://www.edx.org/course/programming-c-microsoft-dev204x-2`. (2014). Accessed: 2017-01-10.

---

[1]One problem was to find the difference between the minimum and maximum values from an array and the other was to write a parenthesis-matching algorithm for a given string.

3. Elena L Glassman, Rishabh Singh, and Robert C Miller. 2014. Feature engineering for clustering student solutions. In *Proceedings of the first ACM conference on Learning@ scale conference*. ACM, 171–172.

4. Jonathan Huang, Chris Piech, Andy Nguyen, and Leonidas Guibas. 2013. Syntactic and functional variability of a million code submissions in a machine learning mooc. In *AIED 2013 Workshops Proceedings Volume*. Citeseer, 25.

5. Chinmay E Kulkarni, Michael S Bernstein, and Scott R Klemmer. 2015. PeerStudio: rapid peer feedback emphasizes revision and improves performance. In

Proceedings of the Second (2015) ACM Conference on Learning@ Scale. ACM, 75–84.

6. Andy Nguyen, Christopher Piech, Jonathan Huang, and Leonidas Guibas. 2014. Codewebs: scalable homework search for massive open online programming courses. In *Proceedings of the 23rd international conference on World wide web*. ACM, 491–502.

7. Rishabh Singh, Sumit Gulwani, and Armando Solar-Lezama. 2013. Automated feedback generation for introductory programming assignments. *ACM SIGPLAN Notices* 48, 6 (2013), 15–26.

Orchestration Graphs: Enabling Rich Social Pedagogical Scenarios in MOOCs

Stian Håklev
Ecole Polytechnique Fédérale
de Lausanne
stian.haklev@epfl.ch

Louis Faucon
Ecole Polytechnique Fédérale
de Lausanne
louis.faucon@epfl.ch

Thanasis Hadzilacos
Open University of Cyprus and
Ecole Polytechnique Fédérale
de Lausanne
thanasis.hadzilacos@ouc.ac.cy

Pierre Dillenbourg
Ecole Polytechnique Fédérale
de Lausanne
pierre.dillenbourg@epfl.ch

ABSTRACT

One of the initial promises of MOOCs was to enable participants from around the world to learn and build knowledge together, however existing MOOC platforms are very limited in their collaborative functionality. Using a recent educational modeling language which can express a broad diversity of educational scenarios, we present a technical infrastructure design and prototype which enables instructors to design and run pedagogically rich and therefore complex scenarios. We present this as a theoretical and technical contribution to support a broad program of research and innovation related to collaborative learning at scale.

Author Keywords

MOOCs; Scripting; Orchestration.

INTRODUCTION

Globally distributed MOOCs are characterized by large numbers of learners, and significant student diversity, in terms of geographical location, life experience, culture and language. Ideally, we would treat the number of learners, and their diversity, as an astounding opportunity for rich learning and communal knowledge building, rather than as an obstacle to be overcome.

However, several studies show that simply asking students to solve a task or discuss a problem is unlikely to engage them in a productive process of collaborative knowledge construction [1]. A key question, which has guided much of the research in the field of Learning Sciences, is how this process can best be supported and guided by an instructor or learning designer, through the careful design of the physical and digital learning context and its affordances.

L@S 2017, April 20 - 21, 2017, Cambridge, MA, USA
© 2017 Copyright held by the owner/author(s). Publication rights licensed to ACM.
ISBN 978-1-4503-4450-0/17/04...$15.00
DOI: http://dx.doi.org/10.1145/3051457.3054000

To help support such learning, Fischer and his colleagues [4] proposed a form of scaffold, which they call an "external collaboration script", that specifies the roles and goals of the participants, allocates material and tasks, and coordinates student grouping and learning activities. Once scripts have been designed, they need to be implemented or enacted. Dillenbourg, et al. call this process "orchestration", defined as "how a teacher manages, in real time, multi-layered activities in a multi-constraints context" [3].

CHALLENGE

Despite a long history of research on pedagogical scripts for small groups and school classes, there has been very little research on appropriate pedagogical scripts that take advantage of very large numbers of heterogeneous learners. One example is Håklev, who has suggested design principles for pedagogical scripts for collaborative MOOCs that use a matrix of weekly thematic scripts which feed into a set of interdependent longer running scripts [5].

We need more creativity and sharing in this area, and to enable this, a common notation, or educational modeling language, as well as tools for editing and sharing educational scenarios, could help. However, our largest challenge is how to implement these scripts in very large settings. A school teacher can fall back to using sticky notes and "talk to your neighbour" strategies, but currently implementing even a very simple script on a MOOC platform (for example wanting to set up a peer-review session, but in a different way than the built-in approach) requires significant software development resources not available to most groups.

This paper will present a suggested common educational modeling language called Orchestration Graphs; our prototype framework for authoring and sharing Orchestration Graphs; as well as the design of an ecosystem of activities and operators which can be "run" by an Orchestration Engine. We posit that this is an innovation which has the potential to promote development and research around rich collaborative activities and scenarios at scale.

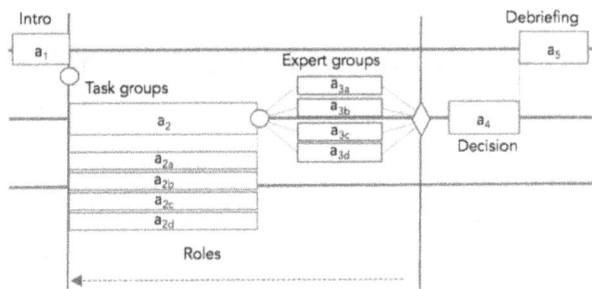

Figure 1. Example of an Orchestration Graph. From Orchestration Graphs by Pierre Dillenbourg, Lausanne: EPFL Press. Copyright 2015 by Pierre Dillenbourg. Reprinted with permission.

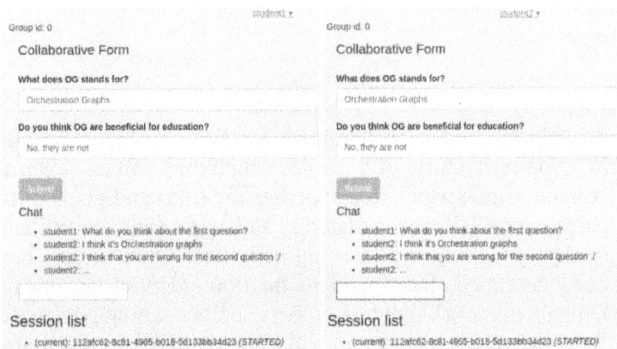

Figure 2. Two students participating in a collaborative learning activity.

ORCHESTRATION GRAPHS

An Orchestration Graph (such as the example in Figure 1) is a structured view of a learning scenario, consisting of learning activities (nodes) [2]. These nodes have a start and an end-time. The X-axis of the graph denotes time, and the placement and width of activities on it denote start and duration. In short synchronous scripts, these time cut-offs might be absolute, to enable students to "sync up" (e.g., after five minutes, everyone has to switch groups), whereas in long-running asynchronous scripts, activities might be open for several days, and students can choose when to engage with them.

Planes

Activities take place at different social planes (Y axis), the three key ones being individual activities, team activities, and whole class activities.

Activities

Activities range from reading a text or watching a video, to contributing ideas in a brainstorm, or experimenting with a simulation. They can take input data and social structures from previous activities and operators, and produce student products (such as students answers and designs), as well as detailed student trace data. See an example of a running activity in Figure 2.

Edges

Activities (nodes) are connected through edges. These can contain pedagogical justifications (e.g., activity 1 is an advanced

organiser for activity 2), learning analytics information (e.g., student success is activity 1 is 34% correlated with/predictive of success in activity 2), and operators.

Operators

Operators receive data from student activities (products), and generate input for subsequent activities. Operations can include aggregation, disaggregation, assignment, translation and transformation of the student product. Operators are also used to generate social structures based on input data, such as organizing students into groups based on their previous answers.

PRIOR ART

The idea of an educational modelling language (EML) has a long history. Several of these languages also come with their own software for editing, and sometimes executing the graphs. LAMS [9] offers a graphical editor of learning workflows, which can be executed by the system. Collage [7] proposes richer design patterns, which can be executed within GLUE!-PS [10].

Two recent platforms, ILDE [6] and Learning Designer[8] build upon a community of designers. The latter provides feedback to designers, for instance the proportion of various learning activity types (investigation, practice, etc.). However, the designed scenarios are not runnable on the platform.

EXAMPLE

Orchestration Graphs can describe orchestrated live interactions, such as a "jigsaw script" centred around earthquake mitigation in San Francisco (depicted in Figure 1). Each team comprises four roles: the mayor of San Francisco (a_{2a}), a seismology expert (a_{2b}), a security officer (a_{2c}), and an insurance agent (a_{2d}). Students begin by discussing the task in groups composed of all four roles, but are then interrupted by "expert group meetings", where all mayors meet with each other separately. This cycle can be repeated several times, before the teams conclude (a_4) and meet as a whole class.

Scripts can also move across much larger granularities and time frames. For example, Håklev [5] describes a script which begins by thousands of students (in-service teachers) contributing individual educational resources that they find useful. Students are then presented with relevant resources to their own teaching (based on semantic tags), and tag, vote and add comments. The curated and annotated list of resources feed into the small (3-6 person) groups which work on developing a lesson plan using technology. Their work in progress is cycled back to the community for constructive peer-review on a weekly basis. Thus we see overlapping scripts that last over several weeks, and which distribute input from thousands of students, to small teams, and back to larger "communities of interest".

Repair/orchestration

All of the individual activities, and the graph as a whole, have a standardised interface for live-streaming learning traces (log data) from learners, and a well-defined API for the teacher to interface with the execution (re-ordering groups, modifying the configuration or order of activities, etc). This can allow

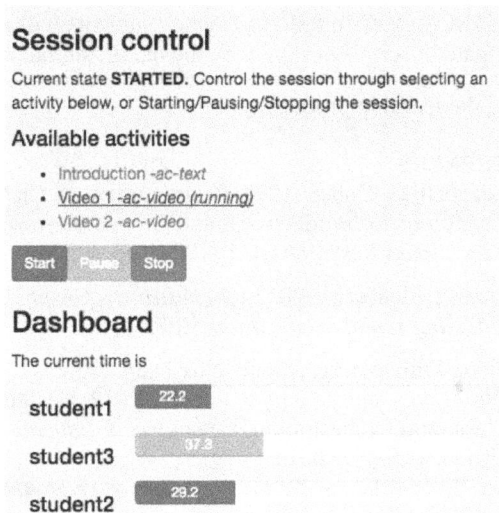

Figure 3. The teacher's analytics dashboard and orchestration controls

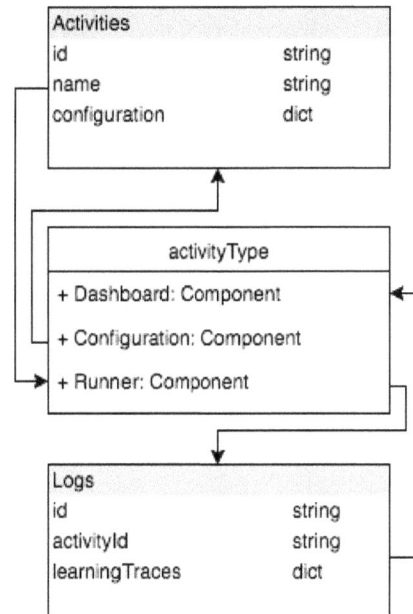

Figure 4. API of activity types

an instructional team to monitor the progress of thousands of students through innovative visualisations and alerting systems, and intervene where groups are not working well, or the community is not moving forwards as planned (see an example of a dashboard in Figure 3).

Given this standardised interface, it would also be feasible to construct intelligent agents that use machine learning to "act on the teacher's behalf" (perhaps even trained on a history of teacher actions), automatically monitoring group and individual student progress, and intervening when necessary.

ECOSYSTEM OF ACTIVITIES AND OPERATORS

The online education space has a long history of plugins, widgets and protocols for integrating external learning activities into Learning Management Systems, and now MOOCs. However, existing standards do not satisfy several of our requirements: the ability to have an artefact generated in one activity used as an input in another activity, the access to a live stream of learning analytics data, class reorganisation into teams, and the ability for a teacher to "orchestrate"/intervene in an ongoing activity.

We have defined an API (shown in Figure 4) to enable rich integration with highly modular activities. Activities are currently distributed as separate packages; in the future we will allow for activities which run on separate servers. Activities provide their own metadata, configuration function (e.g., a video player requires a URL, a quiz requires questions and alternatives), and a "runner", which receives the configuration data, the input data from any previous activities, and a social structure. Activities also implement a live analytics dashboard using the learning traces sent as logs by the "runner".

Operators are located on the edge between two nodes, and receive the student products from the source node, and either transform the product, or generate new social structures based on the student products. Operators are also separate packages (and will be able to run on remote servers as APIs), providing

a configuration function, and a "runner", which receives it's own configuration, as well the data to process, returning the output data or social structure.

INTEGRATION IN MOOC PLATFORMS

The first version of the Orchestration Engine is being developed as a stand-alone tool, but there are several possible ways in which it can be integrated into traditional MOOC platforms. One possibility is to offer several synchronous sessions within a MOOC. Students could be asked to log on at a certain time and date, and visit a specific section in any platform supporting the Learning Tools Integration (LTI) API[11].

This activity would function as a "window" to the Orchestration Engine, and within this window, an entire learning scenario could play out. While the script were running, the instructional staff would be monitoring the live learning analytics, and have the ability to intervene to repair or improve the script.

We could also imagine that each separate activity in an Orchestration Graph could be given a unique LTI URL. A course designer working within the EdX platform (as an example) who wanted to implement something similar to the macro script described above [5], could add an "Individual survey" activity in Week 1 of the MOOC. In the graph, this activity would be connected to an operator that would generate group structures based on the responses, and further to a group activity that would rely on this group structure. The designer could then insert the group activity as a separate LTI component in Week 2 of the EdX course, and the Engine would take care of all the data flow and social structure behind the scenes (see an example in Figure 5).

FUTURE POSSIBILITIES

Our work on the educational modelling language Orchestration Graphs, and the technical infrastructure/architecture for

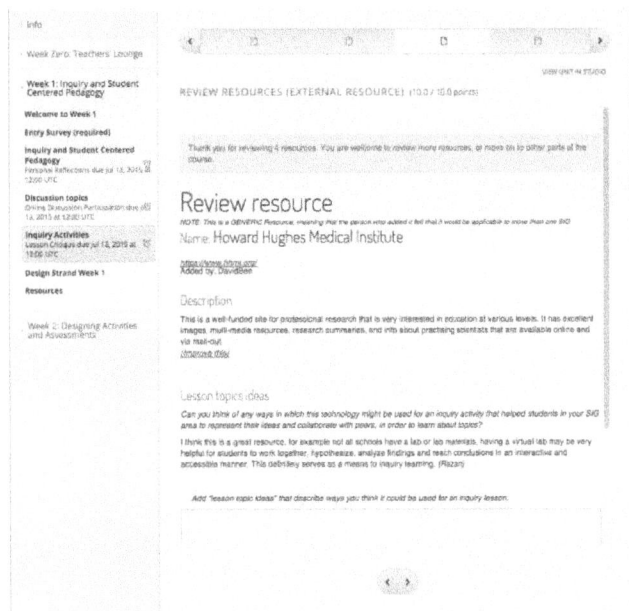

Figure 5. Example of an external activity from the Orchestration Graph seamlessly embedded in an EdX MOOC

editing and running these graphs, form part of a larger research program to empirically investigate and improve our understanding of large-scale collaborative learning scripts. Typical learning analytics research with MOOCs has generated large amounts of data points, but the analysis has rarely taken into account the instructional design or the pedagogical role of each activity.

If we begin with a computer legible description of the pedagogical design, and can automatically map rich learning analytics (both general, and activity-specific) onto the graphs, we can begin to develop models of student learning in the form of transition matrices (predicting the success of a student on an activity from his observed behaviour, his performance on the previous activity and the performance of other students on the current activity).

CURRENT STATUS AND CONCLUSION

We currently have a working prototype system, which allows users to edit scripts by adding and configuring activities and operators. We have a set of activities and operators, which are all completely isolated code-bases connected to the Engine through the public API, and we are able to run scripts generated by the editor, with learning analytics and teacher orchestration capabilities.

We are in the process of refining the design of the API, and expanding the collection of activities and operators, as well as rebuilding the architecture to be more scaleable (distributed across multiple servers). We plan a number of smaller experiments in the spring of 2017 aimed at testing UI/UX with instructional designers/teachers, and running scripts with actual students. The platform will then become an integral part

of an EdX MOOC in fall 2017, when students will not only participate in scripts designed by the instructor, but will also get the opportunity to themselves design and run scripts as part of the learning process.

REFERENCES

1. Elizabeth G. Cohen. 1994. Restructuring the Classroom: Conditions for Productive Small Groups. *Review of Educational Research* 64, 1 (1994), pp. 1–35.

2. Pierre Dillenbourg. 2015. *Orchestration Graphs: Modeling scalable education*. EPFL Press.

3. Pierre Dillenbourg, Miguel Nussbaum, Yannis Dimitriadis, and Jeremy Roschelle. 2012. Design for Classroom Orchestration. *Computers & Education* 69 (2012), 485–492. DOI: http://dx.doi.org/10.1016/j.compedu.2012.10.026

4. Frank Fischer, Ingo Kollar, Karsten Stegmann, and Christof Wecker. 2012. Toward a Script Theory of Guidance in Computer-Supported Collaborative Learning. *Educational Technologist* 48, 1 (2012), 56–66.

5. Stian Håklev. 2016. *From seminar to lecture to MOOC: Scripting and orchestration at scale*. Ph.D. Dissertation. University of Toronto.

6. Davinia Hernández-Leo, Juan I Asensio-Pérez, Michael Derntl, Luis P Prieto, and Jonathan Chacón. 2014. ILDE: community environment for conceptualizing, authoring and deploying learning activities. In *European Conference on Technology Enhanced Learning*. Springer, 490–493.

7. Davinia Hernández-Leo, Eloy D. Villasclaras-Fernández, Juan I. Asensio-Pérez, Yannis Dimitriadis, Inés Ruiz-Requies, Bartolomé Rubia-Avi, and Iván Jorrín-Abellán. 2006. COLLAGE: A collaborative Learning Design editor based on patterns. *Journal of Educational Technology & Society* 9, 1 (2006), 58.

8. Diana Laurillard. 2013. *Teaching as a Design Science: Building Pedagogical Patterns for Learning and Technology*. Routledge.

9. Patrick McAndrew, Peter Goodyear, and James Dalziel. 2006. Patterns, designs and activities: unifying descriptions of learning structures. *International Journal of Learning Technology* 2, 2-3 (2006), 216–242.

10. Luis Pablo Prieto, Juan Alberto Muñoz-Cristóbal, Juan Ignacio Asensio-Pérez, and Yannis Dimitriadis. 2012. Making learning designs happen in distributed learning environments with GLUE!-PS. In *21st Century Learning for 21st Century Skills*. Springer, 489–494.

11. Charles Severance, Ted Hanss, and Joseph Hardin. 2010. Ims learning tools interoperability: Enabling a mash-up approach to teaching and learning tools. *Technology, Instruction, Cognition and Learning* 7, 3-4 (2010), 245–262.

Enhancing the Experience Application Program Interface (xAPI) to Improve Domain Competency Modeling for Adaptive Instruction

Robert A. Sottilare
US Army Research Laboratory
Orlando, FL, USA
robert.a.sottilare.civ@mail.mil

Rodney A. Long
US Army Research Laboratory
Orlando, FL, USA
rodney.a.long3.civ@mail.mil

Benjamin S. Goldberg
US Army Research Laboratory
Orlando, FL, USA
benjamin.s.goldberg.civ@mail.mil

ABSTRACT

This paper describes methods for enhancing the experience application program interface (xAPI) to improve the assessment of domain competency modeling for adaptive instruction. xAPI is an e-learning software specification which allows individual learning experiences and achievements to be amassed in a Learning Record Store (LRS). Adaptive instruction includes tailored training or educational experiences usually delivered and guided by Intelligent Tutoring Systems (ITSs). ITSs can more effectively tailor or adapt instruction when they have more accurate models of the learner's prior knowledge or competency. This paper examines the potential effect of methods to more accurately model learner experiences and domain competency in an LRS. Specifically, we recommend five methods to improve xAPI statements by documenting: 1) achievement types; 2) experience duration; 3) experience source information; 4) domain learning and forgetting; and 5) assessment within learning experiences.

Author Keywords

distributed learning; distance learning; mobile learning; eXperience application program interface (xAPI); learning record store (LRS); intelligent tutoring system (ITS); adaptive instruction; competency modeling

INTRODUCTION

Modeling user experience has long been part of the fabric of Intelligent Tutoring Systems (ITSs) as primary tools for adaptive instruction. Kalyuga, Chandler & Sweller [1] suggested that differing levels of learner experience should be considered when selecting an appropriate user-adapted instructional design. These findings are intended to guide ITS design and multimedia course design through the selection of content (e.g., diagrams, audio, or text) and management of each learner's cognitive load.

L@S 2017, April 20 - 21, 2017, Cambridge, MA, USA
ACM 978-1-4503-4450-0/17/04
DOI: http://dx.doi.org/10.1145/3051457.3054001

Under the auspices of the Advanced Distributed Learning Initiative, the US Department of Defense defined the Shareable Content Object Reference Model (SCORM) as an interoperability standard for online learning [4]. Since SCORM was established prior to the widespread adoption of mobile devices, it was necessary to update the standard to support smartphones, tablets, and other mobile devices.

The experience application program interface (xAPI) is a specification which can be used by a wide variety of instructional technologies (e.g., mobile learning, Intelligent Tutoring Systems (ITSs) or distributed simulations for training) as well as traditional online learning systems to capture data about a broad range of individual learning experiences (e.g., online or offline instruction, reading, or on-the-job training). This includes both formal (e.g., education or training) and informal learning experiences (e.g., reading or games).

Just as SCORM was quickly adopted by the online learning community, xAPI has been rapidly adopted by the mobile learning community as an international standard. The ADL Initiative now has plans to make xAPI the centerpiece of its training and learning architecture (TLA), a collaborative landscape of content providers and consumers. In TLA, providers will be responsible for populating learner achievements in a record store through xAPI statements. The completeness of those statements will form the basis of a long term learner model that can be accessed to populate domain competency just prior to new learning experiences.

xAPI statements format data about a person or group's activities from various sources in a consistent manner and include an actor, a verb, an object, a result, and context [9]. These xAPI components are briefly defined in the next section [9, 10]. xAPI statements may support the modeling of domain competency, an individual's level of proficiency at performing tasks successfully or efficiently in a particular area of expertise (e.g., mathematics). Competency may be viewed as the expectation or potential to perform in the future based on knowledge and skill accumulated in the past (e.g., an expert is expected to perform at a high level while there are lower performance expectations for novices).

Adaptive instruction is the tailored delivery of computer-based training or educational content to learners according to their personal learning needs/gaps. The learner's level of domain competency may be one of the factors considered by an Intelligent Tutoring System (ITS) when adapting instruction, but most ITSs (e.g., AutoTutor or Cognitive Tutor) tailor the instruction based on the learner's recent previous performance rather than long term states like competency.

The level of competency influences adaptation (instructional decisions and actions) by artificially-intelligent tutoring systems. We are specifically examining opportunities to expand the competency assessment capabilities of the Generalized Intelligent Framework for Tutoring (GIFT), a computer based architecture with design goals to improve ITS adaptation and effectiveness [7]. For example, an individual (or group's) level of competency may be used to set expectations for learning and performance during subsequent tutoring experiences so it is important to understand and measure domain competency more precisely than it has been in the past when the primary driver of adaption in tutors was near term modeling of performance.

xAPI statements may help in defining individual or team competency, but could be improved to provide a more accurate picture of both individual and group domain knowledge and skill. The authors are recommending a set of additions/modifications to the existing xAPI specification with this goal in mind. Next we present rationale for what might be needed to fully and accurately define domain competency for computer-based adaptive instruction. Some of these attributes discussed below are already represented within the xAPI specification, while others are not. Before discussing the elements of a competency model, we review the basic elements of an xAPI statement.

Elements of an xAPI Statement
The following are the five components of an xAPI statement [10]:

- Actor: an individual or a group that does something. An actor is required for each xAPI statement. In the statement, "Bob completed the algebra course", "Bob" is the actor.
- Verb: identify the actions of the actor(s). In the statement, "Rodney created a webpage", created is the verb.
- Object: is the thing that is acted upon by the actor. The object can be an activity, agent or group, or a sub-statement. In the statement, "Ben completed the boating course", the object is "boating course" (an activity). In the statement, "The course manager assessed Bob", the object is "Bob" (an agent). In the statement, "Rodney reviewed Ben's final exam", the object is "Ben's final exam" (a sub-statement).
- Result: a measured outcome (completion, success, response or duration). Results are optional. In the

statement "Bob scored 92% on the final exam", the result is "92% on the final exam."
- Context: the conditions under which the activities took place. Context is optional. In the statement "Rodney and Ben completed a flying lesson in rainy conditions", the context is "rainy conditions."

ELEMENTS OF A COMPETENCY MODEL
Werkenthin [9] argues "you should always try to use built-in properties of an xAPI statement before creating extensions. Otherwise, you may sacrifice the analytical abilities of your Learning Record Store (LRS). For example, if you created an extension for *score* instead of using the built-in score property of *result*, your extension for *score* may not be included in reports." For this reason, we annotated the competency model schema discussed below as to whether they are an existing part of the xAPI specification or a new recommended extension. Our goal here is to identify and argue the merit of changes to be included in the xAPI specification. So, what is needed to fully understand/measure a learner domain competency at any given time over the course of a career?

We identified five information classes in the literature associated with domain competence: 1) achievement types; 2) experience duration; 3) experience source information; 4) domain learning and forgetting; and 5) assessment within learning experiences. Each of these classes and their associated subclasses is discussed below.

Documenting Achievement Types
The ability to capture a variety of learning achievements based on domain experiences (e.g., instruction, reading or practice) is at the core of the xAPI specification and contributes to the assessment of domain competence. While there are no recommended changes with respect to domain achievements, there are design considerations for implementation in ITS architectures like GIFT. The first consideration is how GIFT will generate xAPI statements for achievements accomplished in GIFT-based tutors. The second consideration is how GIFT will be enabled to consume xAPI statements and use them to adapt instruction.

GIFT is currently enabled to generate xAPI statements when lessons or courses are completed. It might be useful to generate statements for more fine grained achievements (e.g., correct answers to individual questions or problems). Future versions of GIFT will be designed to consume xAPI statements from an LRS to determine domain competency prior to instruction in that domain. GIFT will require mechanisms to read the statements and conduct competency assessments to determine course flow, options to skip course lessons, and selection of strategies to optimize the learning experience.

Documenting Experience Duration

Currently, the xAPI specification supports the generation and storage of domain achievements including a completion date and time. While the specification provides the ability to generate information about the duration of domain experiences, it is critical to be able to sum contact hours (time in the learning experience) over a series of separate events. In other words, we need to be able to track cumulative participation in a learning experience. For example, the contribution of a one hour tutorial on algebra toward mathematics competency is much different than a one week course involving 5 one hour sessions, or a semester long course with 45 one hour sessions, or a four year degree program in mathematics involving thousands of class sessions, lab sessions, and homework sessions. This function might be enabled by adding two elements called "session completion" and "part of" to the result specification. In the example below, the learner completed a one hour session of a semester long math course with no assigned score for the session.

```
"result": {
    "session completion": true,
    "duration": 1 hour,
    "part of": semester math course,
    "success": true,
    "score": {
    "not applicable"
```

This result might be used in conjunction with an xAPI object denoting the topic studied during the session (e.g., quadratic equations). GIFT-based tutors would use this information and information in the subsequent sections to determine an overall domain competency (e.g., low, moderate, or high).

Documenting Source and Quality of Domain Experiences

Just as the varying duration of a learning experience has varying influence on domain competency so does the source of learning experiences. Currently, the xAPI specification generates and stores messages which identify the source of domain experiences, but has no mechanism for assessing the quality of the experience. While it is possible for external systems to act on the xAPI source information to make a determination of quality, it would be convenient to have the each source rate the learner's experience based on the effectiveness of its curriculum, the duration of the experience and the level of assessment inherent to the system providing the experience. A standard method for generating this assessment is desirable for consistency.

Modeling of Domain Learning and Forgetting

As discussed above, assessed domain experiences have quantifiable contributions to domain learning and competency. During learning experiences, memory of domain information is strengthened, but once the last

learning experience in a particular domain ends, forgetting begins (Figure 1) [8].

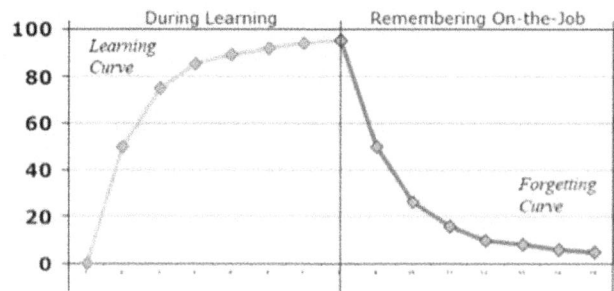

Figure 1. Typical Learning and Forgetting Curve: during learning events (e.g., instruction, reading, practice), memory for domain information is strengthened [8].

For example, a learner completes a course in calculus at age 20. The learner's performance at 30 is likely to be much lower without any intervening practice.

Also the highest level of learning achieved in a domain may result in differing rates of forgetting. For example, a learner who did not reach full competency has less knowledge and skill than someone who is fully competent. While forgetting rates may be the same, the level of forgetting is different at any given time because each individual began the forgetting process with different levels of learning.

For this reason, the level of knowledge and skill decay is critical to assessing domain competency and is not currently represented in the xAPI specification. Also important to learning and forgetting is the understanding of when learning decays to a point where refresher training is needed. This could be part of the result specification in xAPI statements as follows:

```
"result": {
    "completion": true,
    "duration": 1 hour,
    "success": true,
    "score": 92
    "refresher needed": one year after completion
```

Modeling Assessment of Domain Experiences

What is assessment and why should it be represented in xAPI statements? Assessments are methods used to understand the nature, quality, or ability of someone or something. Assessments may include oral or written tests (also called checks on learning). The quality of learning may be different for experiences that are assessed versus those that are not assessed, but learning can still occur during unassessed/informal experiences (e.g., reading). The accuracy of the understanding of a learner's domain competency may also be affected by the validity of the assessment used. Assessment is an activity type that is part of the xAPI specification and may be used to determine domain competency. The use of unassessed experiences, however, may require some generalized rules to determine their influence on domain competency. For example, an hour of unassessed reading in a domain is recognized as a learning experience and contributes "X" to domain competency. Each of these generalized rules could be updated based on their effect on learners leading into future assessed learning experiences.

NEXT STEPS IN THE APPLICATION OF XAPI IN GIFT

As noted earlier, GIFT is already enabled to generate xAPI statements, but will require specifications to generate statements at various levels of granularity (e.g., course completion, lesson completion, or action completion). Mechanisms must also be developed to consume xAPI statements and to use them for both pre-course recommendations and real-time adaptations for the selection of content, feedback, and interactions with the tutor. Pre-course recommendations might include future learning opportunities based on the learning in previous experiences.

Data analytic capabilities in GIFT should also be targeted to continuously evaluate the effect of decisions based on xAPI statements leading to future design changes and improvements. For example, as GIFT transitions from a rule-based to an agent-based framework, tutor decision will be improved over time through reinforcement machine learning techniques.

We also want to expand the diversity of training domains to which xAPI statements are applied [3]. Most ITSs are currently focused on well-defined, procedural tasks predominately teaching mathematics, physics, and computer programming. The ability to apply ITS technologies to psychomotor and social/collaborative task will increase their relevance as instructional tools.

In particular, the ability to assess learners and adapt instruction for teams will make ITSs useful as tools for self-regulated learning in large organizations (e.g., corporations and military organizations) where teams are the common denominator for pursuing goals and executing missions. The application of ITSs to team training domains will require the assessment of achievements at the team level as well as the individual learner level both in the near term (within a training session) and the long term (across multiple training experiences).

Finally, we have a goal to standardize the assessment of competency levels based on achievement statements instantiated via xAPI statements. The development of a competency index to assess long term modeling of skills in a variety of domains would be useful complement to the real-time behavioral analysis used to assess performance levels in cognitive, psychomotor, and social taxonomies [2, 5, 6].

ACKNOWLEDGEMENTS

The research described herein has been sponsored by the U.S. Army Research Laboratory. The statements and opinions expressed in this article do not necessarily reflect the position or the policy of the United States Government, and no official endorsement should be inferred.

REFERENCES

[1] Kalyuga S, Chandler P, Sweller J. Incorporating learner experience into the design of multimedia instruction. Journal of educational psychology. 2000 Mar; 92(1):126.

[2] Krathwohl DR. A revision of Bloom's taxonomy: An overview. Theory into practice. 2002 Nov 1;41(4):212-8.

[3] Long R, Hruska M, Medford AL, Murphy JS, Newton C, Kilcullen T, Harvey Jr RL, Port Orange FL. Adapting Gunnery Training Using the Experience API. InProceedings of the Interservice/Industry Training, Simulation, and Education Conference (I/ITSEC). Orlando, FL 2015.

[4] Murray K, Berking P, Haag J, Hruska N. Mobile Learning and ADL's Experience API. Connections: The Quarterly Journal. 2012 Dec 1;12(1): 45.

[5] Simpson E. Educational objectives in the psychomotor domain. Behavioral Objectives in Curriculum Development: Selected Readings and Bibliography. 1971; 60.

[6] Soller A. Supporting social interaction in an intelligent collaborative learning system. International Journal of Artificial Intelligence in Education (IJAIED). 2001; 12:40-62.

[7] Robert A. Sottilare, Keith W. Brawner, Benjamin S. Goldberg, Heather K. Holden. The generalized intelligent framework for tutoring (GIFT). Orlando, FL: US Army Research Laboratory–Human Research & Engineering Directorate (ARL-HRED). 2012 Jul 31.

[8] Will Thalheimer. Spacing Learning Events Over Time: What the Research Says. Retrieved December 29, 2016, from http://www.work-learning.com/catalog/. 2006 Feb.

[9] Art Werkenthin. 2016. Designing Your xAPI Data Strategy: xAPI-Statement Framework. Learning Solutions Magazine September 19, 2016. Retrieved January 10, 2017 from https://www.learningsolutionsmag.com/articles/2061/d esigning-your-xapi-data-strategy-xapi-statement-framework

[10] xAPI Vocabulary Working Group. 2015. Advanced Distributed Learning Vocabulary. Retrieved December 29, 2016 from http://xapi.vocab.pub/datasets/adl/#module

A Statistical Framework for Predictive Model Evaluation in MOOCs

Josh Gardner
School of Information, University of Michigan
Ann Arbor, MI 48109, USA
jpgard@umich.edu

Christopher Brooks
School of Information, University of Michigan
Ann Arbor, MI 48109, USA
brooksch@umich.edu

ABSTRACT

Feature extraction and model selection are two essential processes when building predictive models of student success. In this work we describe and demonstrate a statistical approach to both tasks, comparing five modeling techniques (a lasso penalized logistic regression model, naïve Bayes, random forest, SVM, and classification tree) across three sets of features (week-only, summed, and appended, from [7]). We conduct this comparison on a dataset compiled from 30 total offerings of five different MOOCs run on the Coursera platform. Through the use of the Friedman test with a corresponding post-hoc Nemenyi test, we present comparative performance results for several classifiers across the three different feature extraction methods, demonstrating a rigorous inferential process intended to guide future analyses of student success systems.

Author Keywords

Predictive modeling; machine learning; MOOC; evaluation

INTRODUCTION

Building predictive models of student success has emerged as a core task in the fields of learning analytics and educational data mining. As these fields continue to grow, and as offerings of Massive Open Online Courses (MOOCs) continue to expand, the need for building effective and reliable predictive models of student success grows too. Despite this, a literature survey[1] by the authors in these areas indicates that research on the creation of models of student success often neglects accepted statistical practices for model comparison. In particular, more than half of the predictive research surveyed did not utilize any statistical testing for the evaluation of model comparisons, despite performing these comparisons in situations where such testing is necessary (such as when model

[1]This survey reviewed the 2014-2016 years of the conference proceedings for the annual International Society for Educational Data Mining (EDM) and the International Learning Analytics and Knowledge (LAK) conferences.

L@S 2017, April 20 - 21, 2017, Cambridge, MA, USA

© 2017 Copyright held by the owner/author(s). Publication rights licensed to ACM.
ISBN 978-1-4503-4450-0/17/04... $15.00

DOI: http://dx.doi.org/10.1145/3051457.3054002

performance is estimated directly on the training set through 10-fold cross-validation). In many cases where significance testing was performed, details with respect to the precision or confidence of estimates were not reported. This leaves such research susceptible to potentially spurious results and low replicability due to concerns with multiple comparisons (comparing multiple algorithms often with multiple hyperparameter settings for each), uncorrected biased estimates caused by estimating model performance directly on training data, and the randomization inherent in sampling schemes such as cross-validation or repeated random subsampling that are used to obtain estimates of model performance.

The lack of adoption of statistical techniques for model evaluation in the field of learning analytics is not due to their nonexistence. Statistical testing of model significance is common in fields such as economics and public policy, where F-testing and ANOVA are frequently used to draw inferences about comparisons between regression models. The broader machine learning research community has produced several additional tools well-suited to evaluating more complex predictive models of student success. In particular, [1] catalogues several approaches for statistical inference about model comparison in various contexts, recommending a Friedman test paired with a post-hoc Nemenyi test for inference about comparisons between multiple models across multuple datasets. Also presented in [1] is an information-dense, interpretable visualization for displaying the results of this procedure, the Critical Difference (CD) diagram. This approach has been implemented in several comparative works, such as [5], but to our knowledge has not been applied to predictive models in learning analytics.

Thus this paper makes two contributions to the area of predictive modeling in education. First, we describe methodological deficiencies in the current practice and outline appropriate methods to mediate these issues, basing our discussion in the statistical machine learning literature. Second, we implement a procedure that addresses these issues through a comparison of five different machine learning algorithms applied to five diverse MOOCs. The results of this comparison demonstrate the value of this rigor-and the limits it enforces on overconfident interpretations of comparisons of multiple algorithms. We introduce this methodology here in context in order to better disseminate the approach and increase rigor and reproducibility in the field.

Course	# Offerings	# Students
Intro. to Thermodynamics	5	16,511
Instr. Meth. in Health Prof. Edu.	5	6,212
Fantasy and Science Fiction	8	26,580
Intro. to Finance	7	181,797
Inside the Internet	5	28,229

Table 1. Courses used to build feature sets. Data from all available runs of each course were combined into a single dataset to meet the independence assumptions described below.

Feature	Description
Forum Views	Count of pageviews of course forum pages.
Active Days	Count of days learner registered any activity in the course (maximum of 7).
Quiz Attempts	Count of attempted quiz questions.
Quiz Exams	Count of attempted exam questions.
Quiz Human Graded	Count of attempted human-graded quiz questions.
Forum Posts	Count of forum posts.
Direct Nodes	Count of distinct users a given user responded to on the forums (direct-reply).
Thread Nodes	Count of distinct uses a given user posted in the same forum with (thread-reply).

Table 2. Definitions of features used to build week-only, summed, and appended feature sets from raw clickstream logs.

DATASET

The dataset used in this analysis is extracted from the raw text clickstream files from 30 offerings of five unique courses at the University of Michigan between 2012 and 2016. A summary of this dataset is shown in Table 1.

We used three different feature engineering methods, described in [7], to derive weekly feature sets from the raw clickstream logs. These different feature approaches represent different methods for aggregating temporal data in predictive models of student success through replicable and platform-independent features. The three feature sets are built from the same basic set of feature definitions, shown in Table 2, using different methods of aggregation. The *week-only* feature sets contain only the values of each feature for the week at which the model is trained (and no data about any other week); *summed* feature sets contain the total values of each feature up to and including the training week; *appended* feature sets concatenate a new set of 8 columns for each week up to and including the training week (e.g. distinct columns for week 1 forum views, week 2 forum views, etc.). The training week in this experiment was the third week, with the goal of prediction being whether students would drop out in the following week of the course. These extraction methods each represent a different approach to capturing student behavior over time in the course, and we direct the interested reader to [7] for details.

After extracting features within each run of each course, data for all runs of each course were combined, because we assumed a high degree of dependence within courses, and therefore utilizing multiple runs of an identical course as "different" datasets would violate the assumptions of dataset independence underlying the comparison process outlined below. This yielded a total of 15 datasets (5 courses * 3 feature extraction methods).

METHODOLOGY

Our goal in this project was to demonstrate a statistical approach to the task of selecting the best of $k > 2$ models across $N > 1$ datasets. While a set of accepted statistical practices for comparing $k = 2$ models across a single dataset is also needed, the multiple-model-multiple-dataset case matches the practical situations learning analytics researchers face most often.[2] Using the feature sets applied above, we trained a set of five classifiers commonly used in predictive models of student success (a lasso penalized logistic regression model, naïve bayes, random forest, SVM, and classification tree) and evaluated their accuracy using 10-fold cross-validation across each of

the five datasets within each of the three feature extraction methods. No hyperparameter optimization was performed, and default or standard rule-of-thumb values were chosen for necessary hyperparameters to avoid conducting additional comparisons. The *performanceEstimation* package in R was used as the framework for model building and evaluation [6][3].

To draw inferences about the respective differences in model performance, we implemented a procedure from [1], applying it separately to each of the three feature sets. The procedure consists of two steps: first, a Friedman test (non-parametric equivalent of the repeated-measures ANOVA) is used to test the null hypothesis that all the algorithms are equivalent. The Friedman test compares the average rankings of the k algorithms across each of the N datasets, calculating a test statistic measuring the probability of the observed rankings under the null hypothesis of all algorithms having equivalent performance (and therefore equal expected average rankings). The observed value of the Friedman statistic

$$\chi_F^2 = \frac{12N}{k(k+1)} \left[\sum_j R_j^2 - \frac{k(k+1)^2}{4} \right] \qquad (1)$$

where R_i^j is the rank of the jth of k algorithms on N datasets and the statistic is distributed according to a chi-square distribution with $k - 1$ degrees of freedom, is compared to a critical value for the given values of N and k [3]. If the null hypothesis is rejected at the selected significance level ($\alpha = 0.05$ in this experiment), the post-hoc Nemenyi test is used to compare all classifiers to each other. The Nemenyi test is similar to the Tukey test for ANOVA, and uses a critical difference

$$CD = q_\alpha \sqrt{\frac{k(k+1)}{6N}} \qquad (2)$$

---

[2]See [4] for a discussion of the two-model, single-dataset case.

[3]The models utilized within this framework were from several different standard R packages; contact the authors of this paper for details of implementation and specific models used.

as a threshold to determine whether the performance between any two classifiers is significantly different, where the critical value q_α is based on the Studentized range statistic divided by $\sqrt{2}$.

One advantage of this method is that because the Friedman test uses only the *rankings* of the algorithms on each dataset, it does not require estimates of the variance of model performance. Instead, it only requires that the estimates of model performance and the measured rankings they produce are reliable and "...that enough experiments were done on each data set and, preferably, that all the algorithms were evaluated using the same random samples..." [1] and that the datasets, and therefore the rankings of the algorithms across each dataset, are independent. In contrast to many other statistical approaches to comparing model performance, such as ANOVA, the Friedman test makes no further assumptions about the sampling scheme (in contrast, discussion of the two-model-single-dataset case is almost entirely centered on methods for sampling schemes in an effort to estimate the variance of model performance and fit within the assumptions of the testing procedures used, for example, [2]).

RESULTS

The results of our comparisons are presented in the Critical Difference (CD) diagrams proposed in [1] in Figure 1, and in a more detailed tabular format displaying the performance and respective rankings of each algorithm in Table 3. The CD diagrams visualize the results of the post-hoc Nemenyi test in a compact, information-dense format. The colored line for each algorithm shows its average rank in comparison with the other algorithms across all five course datasets. The bold black line shows the critical difference for the comparison (based on the values of N, k, and α). Models separated by a distance of less than the CD are statistically indistinguishable–the data is not sufficient to conclude whether they have the same performance–and are connected by a black line segment. Models separated by a distance greater than the critical distance have a statistically significant difference in performance.

Our results demonstrate that, while there are several apparent differences in the model performance based on a cursory evaluation of the performance matrix in Table 3, the experimental data only allows us to conclude that a small number of these differences in performance are statistically significant, within any given feature set (*week-only*, *summed*, and *appended*). For week-only features (the top CD diagram in Figure 1), the only statistically significant difference in performance is between the naïve Bayes and rpart (classification tree) algorithms, with all others showing differences of average ranks less than or equal to the critical difference. For summed features (the middle CD diagram in Figure 1), we see a statistically significant difference between both the rpart and SVM algorithms and the naïve bayes, with no significant difference detected between the SVM and rpart algorithms. The appended feature set shows a more nuanced set of differences in performance, and detailed interpretation is left to the reader.

Several features of these comparisons are worth noting. First, the critical difference ($CD = 2.7$ in all three comparisons), calculated according to Equation 2, is already quite high. Adding

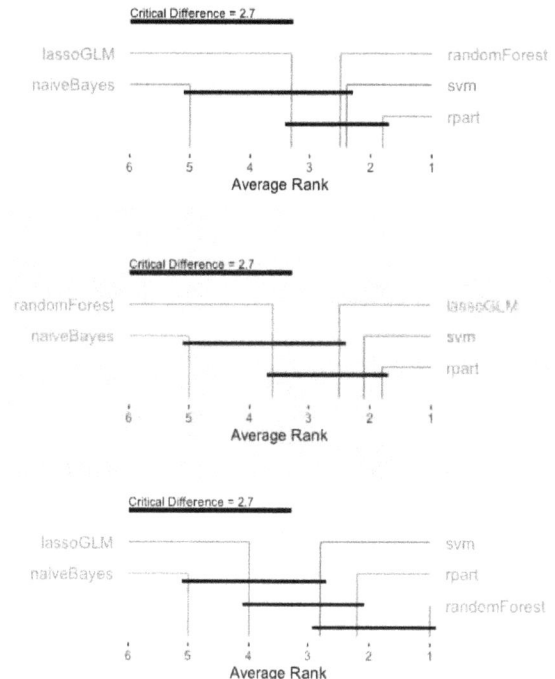

Figure 1. Critical Difference (CD) diagrams demonstrating the results of the Nemenyi post-hoc test for *week-only* features (top), *summed features* (middle), and *appended features* (bottom) with significance level $\alpha = 0.05$. Note that *rpart* refers to the classification tree algorithm. The performance of two classifiers is significantly different if the corresponding average ranks differ by at least the critical difference, calculated according to equation (2) above. Groups of classifiers that are not significantly different are connected by a black CD line. If an algorithm is within one CD of all other algorithms (such as naïve Bayes in the week-only diagram), the correct interpretation is that *the experimental data is not sufficient to reach any conclusion regarding this algorithm.*

additional comparisons between algorithms, and thus increasing k while holding N constant-as would be the case if multiple variants of each model with different hyperparameters were tested-would quickly inflate the value of CD due to an increased likelihood of spurious differences in performance. This calls into question the current practice of training many algorithms with a breadth of hyperparameter settings, which has become easy due to increased comprehensiveness of machine learning toolkits, and simply selecting the highest-performing. Second, this comparison (and the accompanying matrix of results shown in Table 3) demonstrates the effect of this procedure's analysis of algorithms' relative ranking, but not their absolute performance. While we can see that the lasso penalized logistic regression model (GLM) consistently achieved performance scores much higher than the naïve bayes (NB) across all datasets, the average rankings were still quite close-leading to statistically indistinguishable performance under this testing procedure. By contrast, the classification tree (rpart) algorithm, which only marginally outperformed the other algorithms (by an average of roughly 0.001), consistently achieved higher rankings, leading to statistically significant differences in its performance across many of the feature sets.

Feature	Model	IT	HPE	FSF	IF	ITI	Avg. Rank
Week-only	GLM	0.815 (4)	0.868 (4)	0.844 (4)	0.849 (2)	0.87 (2.5)	3.3
	SVM	0.818 (3)	0.871 (1.5)	0.847 (3)	0.849 (2)	0.87 (2.5)	2.4
	NB	0.264 (5)	0.285 (5)	0.32 (5)	0.249 (5)	0.226 (5)	5
	CART	0.835 (1)	0.871 (1.5)	0.861 (2)	0.849 (2)	0.87 (2.5)	1.8
	RF	0.835 (2)	0.871 (3)	0.861 (1)	0.848 (4)	0.87 (2.5)	2.5
Summed	GLM	0.818 (2)	0.871 (2)	0.847 (3)	0.849 (1.5)	0.87 (4)	2.5
	SVM	0.818 (2)	0.871 (2)	0.847 (1.5)	0.848 (3)	0.87 (2)	2.1
	NB	0.247 (5)	0.341 (5)	0.306 (5)	0.255 (5)	0.273 (5)	5
	CART	0.818 (2)	0.871 (2)	0.847 (1.5)	0.849 (1.5)	0.87 (2)	1.8
	RF	0.818 (4)	0.871 (4)	0.846 (4)	0.848 (4)	0.87 (2)	3.6
Appended	GLM	0.81 (4)	0.861 (4)	0.84 (4)	0.844 (4)	0.867 (4)	4
	SVM	0.849 (3)	0.893 (2)	0.881 (3)	0.874 (3)	0.891 (3)	2.8
	NB	0.252 (5)	0.334 (5)	0.301 (5)	0.256 (5)	0.256 (5)	5
	CART	0.855 (2)	0.892 (3)	0.885 (2)	0.874 (2)	0.892 (2)	2.2
	RF	0.857 (1)	0.895 (1)	0.886 (1)	0.878 (1)	0.894 (1)	1

Table 3. Detailed models results (accuracy; ranks shown in parentheses). Course codes: IT = Introduction to Thermodynamics; HPE = Instructional Methods in Health Practitioners Education; FSF = Fantasy and Science Fiction; IF = Introduction to Finance; ITI = Inside the Internet. Average ranks within a course/feature cell (a single column within a feature, e.g. 2.5 for the ITI course and *week-only* features) are the result of ties.

CONCLUSIONS AND FUTURE RESEARCH

In this work, we contribute to the growing field of predictive models in student success by (1) summarizing the state of the practice when it comes to comparing machine learned models and (2) demonstrating such comparisons using large scaled learning data from a diverse set of MOOCs.

While this project demonstrates a basic implementation of a statistical approach for evaluating predictive model performance in MOOCs, it also reveals the limits of contemporary approaches and the need for research in several directions. Further research is needed on methods for statistical comparison of different feature extraction approaches from raw datasets, a task that is beyond the scope of this study. Testing procedures and inferential methods used for model comparison do not appear to be appropriate for these cases, which violate the dataset independence assumption underlying the Friedman test and many other tools for statistical comparison. Evaluating feature extraction methods from raw data is a key task in

learning analytics and educational data mining, which often builds models on data derived from an unstructured source (such as clickstreams or other traces of learner activity), and such research is essential to valid, reproducible research on the application of such methods to MOOC datasets.

Additional research is also needed to extend this approach to the practical case of testing multiple hyperparameter settings of a given model. While we explicitly only used pre-selected hyperparameters for the models used in this analysis to avoid the confounding effects of additional comparisons, most statistical software packages optimize models by testing a grid of hyperparameter settings, which amounts to several additional layers of comparisons, substantially increasing the chance of observing spurious differences in model performance even when no true difference exists. Identifying approaches which can consider even large grids of hyperparameters to match the reality of current available toolkits will be an important next step for research in this area.

While machine learning algorithms are increasingly made available to researchers in open-source projects, tools for conducting statistical testing and evaluation of these models are far less common, and working within existing toolkits presented several challenges to the research team on this project. Future development efforts in this direction, such as providing built-in statistical testing of model comparison using the Friedman/Nemenyi procedure (and others) and visualization of the results in CD diagrams, would significantly advance researchers' ability to implement these practices in their work.

REFERENCES

1. Janez Demšar. 2006. Statistical Comparisons of Classifiers over Multiple Data Sets. *J. Mach. Learn. Res.* 7, Jan (2006), 1–30.

2. T G Dietterich. 1998. Approximate Statistical Tests for Comparing Supervised Classification Learning Algorithms. *Neural Comput.* 10, 7 (15 Sept. 1998), 1895–1923.

3. Milton Friedman. 1940. A comparison of alternative tests of significance for the problem of m rankings. *Ann. Math. Stat.* 11, 1 (1940), 86–92.

4. Josh Gardner and Christopher Brooks. Statistical Approaches to the Model Comparison Task. In *LAK 2017 Workshop on Methodology in Learning Analytics (MLA)* (in submission).

5. Gjorgji Madjarov, Dragi Kocev, Dejan Gjorgjevikj, and Sašo Džeroski. 2012. An extensive experimental comparison of methods for multi-label learning. *Pattern Recognit.* 45, 9 (2012), 3084–3104.

6. Luis Torgo. 2014. An Infra-Structure for Performance Estimation and Experimental Comparison of Predictive Models in R. (1 Dec. 2014).

7. Wanli Xing, Xin Chen, Jared Stein, and Michael Marcinkowski. 2016. Temporal predication of dropouts in MOOCs: Reaching the low hanging fruit through stacking generalization. *Comput. Human Behav.* 58 (2016), 119–129.

Suggesting a Log-Based Creativity Measurement for Online Programming Learning Environment

Lilach Gal
Tel Aviv University
Tel Aviv Israel
lilachgal90@gmail.com

Arnon Hershkovitz
Tel Aviv University
Tel Aviv Israel
arnonhe@tauex.tau.ac.il

Andoni Eguíluz Morán
University of Deusto
Bilbao, Spain
andoni.eguiluz@deusto.es

Mariluz Guenaga
University of Deusto
Bilbao, Spain
mlguenaga@deusto.es

Pablo Garaizar
University of Deusto
Bilbao, Spain
garaizar@deusto.es

ABSTRACT

Creativity has long been suggested as an important factor in learning. In this paper, we present a preliminary study of creativity in an online programming learning environment. We operationalize creativity using an existing scheme for scoring it, and then measure it automatically based on the system log files. We analyze the data in order to explore the associations between creativity and personal/contextual variables. Creativity is associated with contextual variables and is not associated with personal variables. Directions for continuing this research are discussed.

Author Keywords

Creativity; programming learning; log-based measurement; learning analytics.

ACM Classification Keywords

H.1.2. User/Machine Systems: Software psychology; K.3.2. Computer and Information Science Education: Computer science education.

INTRODUCTION

Creativity refers to the creation of something (a product, a solution, etc.) that has some value. The importance of creativity in learning and for learners has been suggested since the mid-20th century. Still, there is no single definition of this construct; actually, more than a hundred definitions of creativity have been suggested [14], a direct result of its multifaceted nature.

L@S 2017, April 20–21, 2017, Cambridge, MA, USA.
© 2017 ACM ISBN 978-1-4503-4450-0/17/04...$15.00.
DOI: http://dx.doi.org/10.1145/3051457.3054003

Overall, it is agreed that creativity has four dimensions: fluency, flexibility, originality (also referred to as novelty), and elaboration [13]. The latter is relevant to non-verbal settings, hence will be neglected here. To put it simply, these dimensions measure the number (fluency), nature (flexibility), and uniqueness (originality) of the learner's products. As was previously shown, creativity in computer science (CS) education might improve CS knowledge and skills [12], and teaching CS might improve learners' creativity at large [3,5,10,11].

Contrary to previous attempts to automatically measure creativity of computer programs [6,8], our operationalization is directly based on the common multi-dimensional definition of creativity and on analyzing the whole process of using a programming learning system.

RESEARCH GOAL

Our main goal in the current study is to explore characteristics of creativity among children (6-18y/o) in an online environment for computational thinking learning. The research questions are:

1. What are the associations between creativity and personal characteristics (gender, age, programming knowledge, tech affinity)?
2. What are the associations between creativity and task difficulty?
3. Is creativity a state or a trait?

METHODOLOGY

The Learning Environment: Kodetu

Kodetu is a Web app, built using Google's Blockly, for teaching basic programming skills. Each of Kodetu's 15 levels presents the user with a maze in which an astronaut should get to a marked destination; guiding the astronaut is done via a block-based code the user is editing. The game levels introduce simple forward/turn commands, loops and conditions. While using the app, the system logs any action taken by its users. An example is brought in Figure 1.

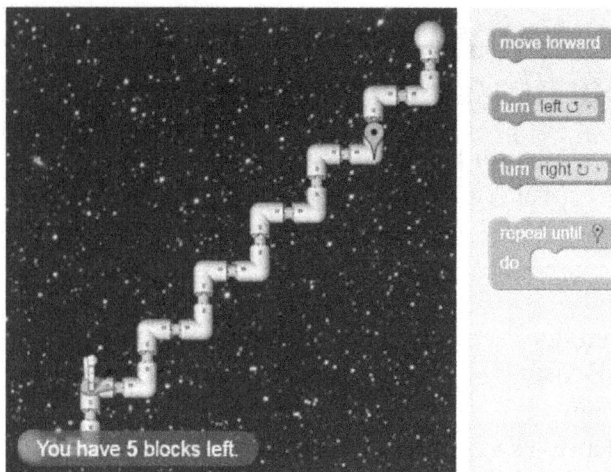

Figure 1. Level 9 of Kodetu. The user should edit a code, using the available blocks, to get the astronaut to the red mark (the coding-area is not shown here)

Population and Dataset

The dataset we analyzed is derived mostly from a set of technology workshops given to primary and secondary school students from the north-central part of Spain.

The original file included 307,608 rows, documenting 1,044 sessions taken between October 2014 and February 2015. The system logs the data anonymously, hence a session holds all the actions that occurred from start using the system until leaving it; therefore, a single user may be logged with multiple sessions. Logs document all users' suggested solutions and include timestamp, level [1-15], action result [Success, Failure, Timeout, Error, Unset], and the code. Triangulating with another file that held user's self-reported information, we also had for each session some personal characteristics of the user: age, gender, interface language [English, Spanish, Basque]; school-level [Primary School, Secondary School, High School, University, Professional Training, Not a Student]; programming background [Yes, No]; and technology affinity [1-10].

First, we removed rows that did not represent running a code (mainly, dragging a block to the editing windows – the resulting code was later documented when the user hit the "Run Program" button), as well as erroneously-logged rows. The final dataset includes 34,894 actions in 1,024 session. Overall, 45% of the sessions were reported to be taken by females and 55% by males, with an average reported age of 12.9 (SD=8.3), with about three-quarters of the sessions were taken by users at the ages 10-11y/o (756, 73.8%). About two-thirds (64.6%) of the sessions were taken by users who had no background in programming, and the average score for technology affinity was 8.7 (SD=1.6).

Operationalization of Creativity

We adapted Leikin's scoring scheme for creativity [7], developed in the context of multiple solution tasks in mathematics. As Kodetu lets the learners move to the next stage once a correct solution was given—just like many other CS learning environments, e.g., Code Monkey[1], Code.org, as well as other tutors in general, e.g., the mathematics tutor, ASSISTments[2]—we score for creativity in *solution attempts* rather than in *solutions*.

Scoring Fluency. Originally in [7], each student's solution got 1 point for each correct solution. We score with 1 point every solution attempt.

Scoring Flexibility. We establish groups of solutions based on the solution strategies. Our strategies are based on the use of control blocks (*While, If-Then, If-Then-Else*), presented from Level 7 and on. For levels 8-15, we defined 4 strategies:

- The solution attempt uses *While* and not using *If*;
- The solution attempt uses *If* and not using *While*;
- The solution attempt uses both *While* and *If*;
- The solution attempt uses neither *While* nor *If*.

Each solution attempt is scored with 10 points for a first time using a given strategy, and 0.1 points for any other solution attempt in a strategy previously used. (For levels 1-6, all solutions are referred to as belonging to a single strategy).

Scoring Originality

Instead of using a pre-defined rarity thresholds (15% and 40% in [7]), we decided to re-define these thresholds for each level separately, based on the distribution of unique solutions in it (by manually examining the solutions' distribution histogram and the knee of that curve).

Total Creativity Score for each Solution Attempt

Total creativity score for each solution was calculated by multiplying its flexibility and its originality scores.

Total Creativity Score for a Session

Total creativity score for a session is calculated as the average creativity score across all the solution attempts in it.

RESULTS

Taking the average of originality, flexibility, and creativity within each session (N=1,024), we get an average *Session Creativity* of 7.9 (SD=9.84), an average *Session Originality* of 9.8 (SD=13.5), and an average *Session Flexibility* of 12.8 (SD=4.2). Overall, the average of solutions attempts across all sessions was 3.9 (SD=3.4, skewness=4.7). All these variables are not normally distributed, hence we will use nonparametric statistical tests.

---

[1] http://playcodemonkey.com.

[2] https://www.assistments.org.

Next, we calculate averages of creativity, originality and flexibility for each level, across all sessions (see Table 1). Minimum and maximum values of originality in levels 8 and 13, respectively, reflect the number of unique solutions, which was minimal for level 8 and maximal for level 13.

Level	N	Mean Solution Attempts (SD)	Mean Originality (SD)	Mean Flexibility (SD)	Mean Creativity (SD)
1	857	1.4 (0.9)	1.1 (3.4)	10.0 (0.1)	5.9 (19.2)
2	833	2.7 (1.8)	6.5 (12.0)	10.2 (0.2)	9.0 (15.8)
3	787	2.5 (1.7)	2.8 (7.0)	10.1 (0.2)	4.7 (10.1)
4	756	2.8 (1.8)	3.8 (7.6)	10.2 (0.2)	7.2 (15.8)
5	721	2.3 (2.0)	3.8 (10.8)	10.1 (0.2)	4.6 (10.3)
6	704	3.5 (2.8)	8.9 (17.0)	10.3 (0.3)	10.9 (16.2)
7	665	4.1 (3.0)	9.6 (15.1)	10.3 (0.3)	10.3 (14.4)
8	639	2.1 (2.0)	0.8 (1.7)	12.3 (4.3)	1.6 (2.6)
9	638	3.9 (3.6)	9.6 (21.1)	12.5 (4.3)	5.4 (9.8)
10	619	3.4 (3.4)	10.1 (20.3)	12.3 (4.2)	8.2 (14.7)
11	589	6.5 (5.5)	22.0 (30.4)	22.8 (10.7)	10.8 (15.2)
12	530	5.0 (5.4)	17.1 (32.1)	16.5 (9.0)	9.9 (16.9)
13	456	8.3 (7.9)	48.1 (60.4)	18.9 (9.7)	14.8 (23.5)
14	344	6.1 (7.1)	5.1 (6.5)	17.2 (9.9)	3.9 (3.4)
15	283	8.0 (7.7)	6.9 (7.1)	16.2 (8.8)	3.0 (2.6)

Table 1. Descriptive statistics of creativity for each level

Creativity and User Characteristics

Two of the four user characteristics variables are binary: **gender**, and **background in programming**. We compare creativity between the two groups defined by each of these variables using Mann-Whitney U-test. No difference was found by **gender** in creativity, with Z=1.4 (p=0.17), respectively; same was found regarding fluency and flexibility. A marginally significant difference in creativity was found between those users with no **background in programming** and those with a programming background, with Z=1.89, at p=0.06, however with a negligible effect size[3] of r=0.06. Fluency and flexibility were shown with significantly different, again with very small effect sizes.

Technology affinity was found to be correlated with flexibility only, however with a low coefficient, ρ=0.1, at p<0.001; the other five comparisons of creativity dimensions and technology affinity/gender were not significant.

Creativity and Level

Correlating creativity measures with level, we get no significant results, with Spearman's ρ=-0.01, at p=0.96. It might be that Level 8, 14, and 15 are outliers in that context: Level 8 forces a two-block solution, which reduces significantly the possible solution space, hence affecting the *originality* score; Level 14 is rather an easy level; and Level 15 sets a very challenging task (solving a general maze),

which is difficult even for experienced programmers. Omitting these two levels, we get a marginally significant correlation of ρ=0.6, at p=0.055, that is, the more difficult the task is, the higher the creativity is.

In order to better understand if there are differences in creativity based among the game levels, we ran Kruskal-Wallis one-way analysis of variance, comparing between the 15 groups defined by the game levels. This was run on a dataset of all pairs of session-level, N=9,421. The result is statistically significant, with $\chi^2(14)$=882.6, at p<0.001. An eta-squared index (a measure of effect size for ANOVA) can be derived from this value[4], resulting in η^2=0.1, a medium effect size.

We ran a post-hoc test, comparing creativity values between each pair of levels (for users who played in both levels). As we run an overall of 105 tests, we correct for multiple comparisons using the post-hoc False Discovery Rate (FDR) method, which produces a q-value that can be interpreted the same way as a p-value. The results suggest that in most cases (80 of 105 pairs), creativity average was statistically significantly different between levels. Effect sizes[5] range from very small values (0.05) to medium values (0.5).

More on the State-or-Trait Question

For shedding more light on the state-or-trait question, that is, is creativity more associated with user characteristics (trait) or with contextual variables (state), we set up two linear regression models to predict creativity on the full dataset, which includes 9,421 user-level pairs.

The first model tries to predict creativity by level. It uses 15 variables that denote the game levels. We will refer to this model as the *State Model*. Similarly, we set up a *Trait Model* to predict creativity by user; this model uses 1024 variables that denote the users. This approach is similar to the one applied in [2].

The linear regression models were built with M5' feature selection[6] and their goodness of fit was measured using Pearson's correlation and Root Mean Squared Error (RMSE). To validate the generalizability of the models, we calculated their fitness using 2-fold cross-validation. The models were built using RapidMiner Studio Version 7.2.003.

---

[3] Computed as $r = \frac{z}{\sqrt{N}}$

[5] Here, $r = \frac{z}{\sqrt{2N}}$, as we run within-subject comparisons, hence number of observations is doubled.

[4] Computed as $\eta^2 = \frac{\chi^2}{N-1}$

[6] In each iteration, the attribute with the smallest standardized coefficient is removed and another regression is performed; if the result is improved (based on Akaike Information Criterion, AIC), this attribute is dropped. This process is repeated until no attributes can be removed.

The *State Model* resulted with a correlation of 0.21 and RMSE=14.4. The *Trait Model* resulted with a correlation of 0.06 and RMSE=16.1. Therefore, in accordance with the above results, state explanations are better predictors of user creativity than trait explanations.

DISCUSSION

Our operationalization of creativity as a multi-dimensional contsruct, based on an established scheme (though from a different domain [7]), is an important step forward to analyze creativity at scale, as it allows automatization of evaluating creativity measures. Such an automatization will benefit both CS students and instructors by enabling the development of creativity assessment mechanisms.

Originally considered as a fixed personality trait, it is now suggested that a few forces influence creativity, some of which are personality traits (e.g., openness to experience, or persistent work style), and some of which are contextual (e.g., intrinsic task motivation) [1]. In the context of CS, an analysis of creativity in programming resulted with different creativity scores for different teaching methods of the same teacher to the same class, which demonstrate the influence of state-related variables on creativity [6]. Our findings support the "contextual approach"; specifically, creativity was higher as level progressed. In Kodetu, it is not only difficulty that is getting higher as levels progress, but only constraints are being presented to users in terms of code-length. As previously shown, constraints might be a fertile ground to creativity [9].

Also note, in the context of personal-related variables, that age, gender, programming background and technology affinity – were all unrelated to creativity in our data. Previous studies were also not able to find direct associations between creativity and gender, age, or cognitive abilities. Future work will be dedicated to shed more light on the associations between personal characteristics and creativity.

One barrier that we will need to tackle with further research lies in the fact that our operationalization of creativity, which originates in *multiple solution* tasks (in mathematics [7]) is being used in *multiple solution-attempts* tasks, which is popular in many tutoring systems. Transforming the idea of multiple solutions to multiple solution-attempts might hinder the validity of the construct, although previous studies associated multiple attempts to give a correct solution to creativity [4]. In any case, the validity question is not as simple as it may look, as it is not clear which validation might be tested. This is an issue that we plan to seriously tackle in the near future.

REFERENCES

[1]   Amabile, T.M. & Pillemer, J. (2012). Perspectives on the social psychology of creativity. *Journal of Creative Behavior, 46*(1), 3-15.

[2]   Baker, R. (2007). Is gaming the system state-or-trait? Educational data mining through the multi-contextual application of a validated behavioral model. *Presented in the Workshop on Data Mining for User Modeling at the 11th International Conference on User Modeling (July 25-29, Corfu, Greece).*

[3]   Bustillo, J. & Garaizar, P. (2016). Using Scratch to foster creativity behind bars: Two positive experiences in jail. *Thinking Skills and Creativity, 19*, 60-72.

[4]   Karakok, G., Savic, M., Tang, G., & El Turkey, H. (2015). Mathematician's view on undersgraduate students' creativity. *Proceedings of the Ninth Congress of the European Society for Research in Mathematics Education (February 4-8, Prague, Czech Republic)*, 1003-1009.

[5]   Kobsiripat, W. (2015). Effects of the media to promote the scratch programming capabilities creativity of elementary school students. *Procedia – Social and Behavioral Sciences, 174*, 227-232.

[6]   Koh, K.H., Bennett, V., & Repenning, A. (2011). Computing indicators of creativity. *Presented at the ACM Creativity & Cognition Conference (November 3-6, Atlanta, GA).*

[7]   Leikin, R. (2009). Exploring mathematical creativity using multiple solution tasks. In R. Leikin, A. Berman, & B. Koichu (Eds.), *Creativity in Mathematics and the Education of Gifted Students (pp. 129–145)*. Rotterdam, the Netherlands: Sense Publisher.

[8]   Manske, S., & Hoppe, H.U. (2014). Automated indicators to assess the creativity of solutions to programming exercises. In *Proceedings of the 2014 IEEE 14th International Conference on Advanced Learning Technologies*, 497-501.

[9]   Moreau, C.P. & Dahl, D.W. (2005). Designing the solution: The impact of constraints on consumers' creativity. *Journal of Consumer Research, 32*(1), 13-22.

[10] Pardamean, B. (2014). Enhancement of creativity through Logo programming. *American Journal of Applied Science, 11*(4), 528-533.

[11] Scherer, R. (2016). Learning from the past – The need for empirical evidence on the transfer effects of computer programming skills. *Frontiers in Psychology,* doi: 10.3389/fpsyg.2016.01390.

[12] Shell, D. F., Hazley, M.P., Soh, L.K., Dee Miller, L., Chiriacescu, V., & Ingraham, E. (2015). Improving learning of computational thinking using computational creativity exercises in a college CS1 computer science course for engineers. *Presented at the 44th Annual Frontiers in Education (FIE) Conference (October 22-25, Madrid, Spain).*

[13] Torrance, E.P. (1974). Torrance tests of creative thinking. Bensenville, IL: Scholastic Testing Service.

[14] Treffinger, D.J., Renzulli, J.S., & Feldhusen, J.F. (1971). Problems in the assessment of creative thinking. *The Journal of Creative Thinking, 5*, 104-112.

Long-Term Peer Reviewing Effort is Anti-Reciprocal

Yasmine Kotturi[1], Andrew Du[2], Scott Klemmer[2], Chinmay Kulkarni[1]
[1]HCI Institute, Carnegie Mellon, [2]Design Lab, UC San Diego
{ykotturi, chinmayk}@cs.cmu.edu, {aadu, srk}@ucsd.edu

ABSTRACT

Many studies demonstrate that peer reviewing provides pedagogical benefits such as inspiration and developing expert vision, and changes classroom culture by encouraging reciprocity. However, much large-scale research in peer assessment has focused on MOOCs, where students have short tenures, and is unable to describe how reciprocity-oriented classroom cultures evolve over time. This short paper presents the first long-term analysis of peer reviewing with 304 students, conducted in three large physical classes in a year-long undergraduate series. Surprisingly, this analysis reveals that when students receive better reviews on their work, they write worse reviews in the future. This suggests that while students believe in the reciprocal nature of peer review, they act anti-reciprocally. Therefore, battling the emergent norm of anti-reciprocity is crucial both for system designers and practitioners who use peer assessment.

Author Keywords

peer assessment, peer review, reciprocity

INTRODUCTION

Peer assessment can be pedagogically powerful: it exposes students to ideas, supports reflection, enhances critical thinking, improves course performance, and decreases attrition [1, 4, 14, 16, 17]. Peer review at scale can also catalyze fast, formative feedback on in-progress open ended work at massive scale [12]. Such feedback and iteration are important for mastery learning [6].

However, why do students put in substantial effort in helping their peers, rather than the minimum effort required? Thus far, reciprocity, i.e. our desire to help those who help us [7], has been cited as a likely reason [2]. Does this desire diminish over time, or does seeing the others provide help build a stronger norm, strengthening reciprocity over the long-term? We believe the answer to this question is of fundamental importance to the long-term sustainability of peer review as an academic practice. Unfortunately, current large-scale research on peer review is unable to answer this fundamental question, because it has largely been conducted in large scale settings where students have short tenures (e.g. [8, 10, 11, 12, 13,

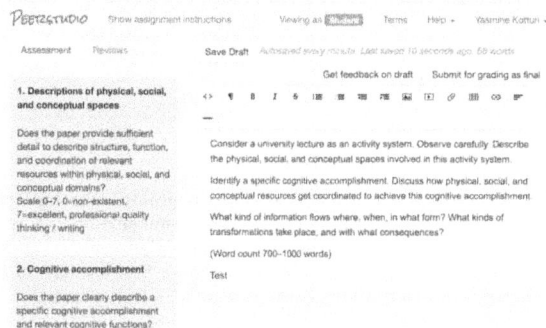

Figure 1. PeerStudio enables students to get fast peer feedback and iterate on their open-ended work.

18]). These short tenures are insufficient to study how peer assessment evolves over time.

We introduce the first long-term analysis, one academic year (2015-2016), of peer reviewing behavior in three large, physical classes. In total, we analyze data from 304 active students as they progress through all three classes which comprise an undergraduate year long series; each class used our peer review platform, PeerStudio (Figure 1) [12]. These analyses suggest an emergent norm of anti-reciprocity, where over time students perform reviews of declining quality.

Course and Assignment Format

We analyze data from 304 students who participated in a three-course series in UC San Diego's Cognitive Science undergraduate program, taught by the same instructor. Students learn about topics such as distributed cognition and cognitive ethnography. Students wrote essays (between 500-1000 words) for assignments, such as reviews of research articles. Rubrics evaluating these assignments comprised a number of Likert scales. Overall, our dataset comprises 10,845 reviews generated on 4,131 submissions.

Hypotheses

Our conversations with the course staff teaching this series revealed an increasing frustration with peer assessment over time. Often, course staff would ask for best practices to combat what they saw as an increasing lack of student interest over time. Based on these observations, we hypothesized that:

(H1) Review quality decreases over time.

Since peer reviewing is a reciprocal act, we believed that students' review quality (H1) was likely the result of visible norms: when students saw that poor reviewing went sans

L@S 2017, April 20-21, 2017, Cambridge, MA, USA

© 2017 ACM. ISBN 978-1-4503-4450-0/17/04. . . $15.00

DOI: http://dx.doi.org/10.1145/3051457.3054004

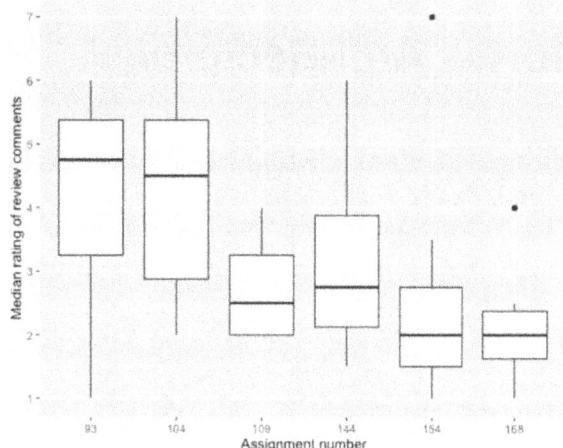

Figure 2. Review quality decreases as students progress through year long course series. Coders rated quality of 60 comments on 7-pt scale [3]. Assignments 93 and 104 are the first and last assignments in the first course, respectively. Assignments 109 and 144 are first and last in the second course, and so on. Assignments were about 6 weeks apart.

repercussion, they were less likely to put in effort themselves [9]. This leads to our second hypothesis:

(H2) Reviewers act on reciprocity: when students receive a good review, they are more likely to generate a good review on the next assignment.

Measures
We analyzed review comment length, quality of reviews, and their potential interaction. To analyze the quality of a review, we extracted a subset of 60 reviews: 10 reviews from the first and last assignments in each course. Four blinded-to-assignment coders–HCI graduate students–(1F/3M, ages 22-29), rated this subset of reviews on a continuous scale adapted from prior work [3]; from one to seven with the following coding schema: (1) Irrelevant or no discussion: review offers no actionable feedback (4) Merely stated edits: review suggests edits and changes, gives some justification or reasoning (7) Actionable and justified: Review articulates clear actionable edits with sound and succinct justification. Because our raters had fair agreement on this scale, we use the median rating as the aggregate.

RESULTS
We first analyzed review comment length from all 10,845 reviews and we saw that, generally, length decreased over time (Figure 3). We then examined the quality of reviews, as rated by the four coders. For the 60 rated reviews, we see that quality decreased over time (Figure 2). We therefore investigated the interaction between review length and quality.

Review quality increases with comment length
Across the 60 reviews that our coders rated, we found that the word length of the review was highly correlated with the median rating of quality (Spearman $\rho = 0.88$). Because the review length is much easier to compute, we use it as a proxy for comment quality for further large-scale analyses.

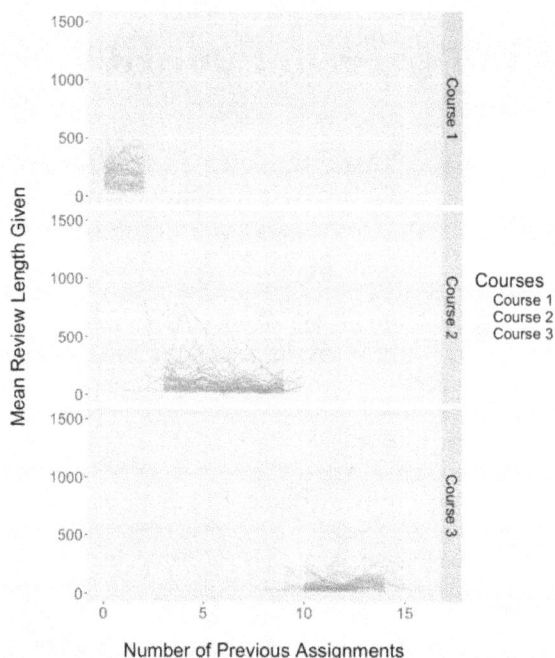

Figure 3. Data from 10,845 reviews: as number of assignments completed increases review length decreases.

Coefficients	β	F	p-value
Intercept	86.14165	17.74	<0.001
Previous Mean Review Length Given	0.61138	42.58	<0.001
Second Course	-54.91843	-12.08	<0.001
Third Course	-57.35288	-11.14	<0.001

Table 1. Students' previous reviewing quality significantly affects their current reviewing quality.

R1: Review quality decreases over time
To understand how review quality changes over time, we built a linear regression model that used the word length of a student's previous review to predict the length of their current review. The course name was included as a fixed effect covariate (since courses were chosen to be part of a series). This model has strong fit ($R^2 = 0.47$), and students' previous reviewing quality significantly affects their current reviewing quality ($F(1,2505) = 48.04, p < 0.001$) (See Table 1). On average, students write reviews that are only 66.9% as long as their reviews for the previous assignment. Adding the course as a covariate to the model significantly improves model fit ($R^2 = 0.51$), suggesting that review quality has significant variation within courses in the same series. On average, students write approximately 50 fewer words for each new course in the series. We then examined patterns of review behavior, based on the types of review students received. We see that within course variation in length of review is much lower than variation across courses (Figure 4).

R2: Changes in review quality are anti-reciprocal
To understand more specifically how the quality of reviews written by a student are influenced by the reviews they re-

Coefficients	β	F	p-value
Intercept	115.05531	18.88	<0.001
Previous mean review length given	0.63564	43.72	<0.001
Previous mean review length received	-0.16359	-7.70	<0.001
Second Course	-67.86219	-14.14	<0.001
Third Course	-74.16512	-13.39	<0.001

Table 2. When students see longer reviews on their previous work, they write shorter reviews

ceive, we added the average word length of reviews received on their previous submission as a covariate. Doing so slightly improves model fit ($R^2 = 0.52$), suggesting others reviewing significantly affects reviewing behavior. However, the direction of this influence is surprising. When students see longer reviews on their previous work, they write shorter reviews (See Table 2). On average, for every additional word in reviews students receive, they write 0.16 fewer words in their own reviewing: ($t(2502) = -7.70, p < 0.001$).

Adding an interaction variable (between previous comment length written, and previous comment length received) shows no significant interaction ($t(2501) = 0.12, p > 0.8$). This suggests that even the most motivated students (who initially write reviews of high quality) nonetheless write shorter (worse) reviews when they see longer (better) reviews on their own work.

Implications for Design

Our finding also has implication for the design of peer assessment systems: we suggest that relying exclusively on reciprocal social nature may be an insufficient design lever. Instead, other motivational methods, such as increasing social translucence [5], visible monitoring of students' progress, not only on assignments, but also on review quality, and more tightly integrating the platform with physical course activities [8]; for instance, highlighting positive review behavior by decomposing examples of good reviews during class meetings, or, if online, in class announcements.

DISCUSSION AND FUTURE WORK

Current peer review systems rely on student reciprocity. Our findings (admittedly based on one course-series at one university) offer preliminary evidence that peer review systems may lead to anti-reciprocal behavior in the long-term. While particular design features of the system may be responsible, we speculate our finding may represent more than a "bug" in the design of current peer assessment systems. Instead, we speculate three fundamental causal pathways, which future work could investigate. First, students who see well-formed reviews perhaps see the standard as unachievably high, and therefore do not put in further effort reviewing. We see similar results when students are shown extremely high-quality peer work as inspiration [15]. Second, seeing high quality reviews may encourage a diffusion of responsibility. In essence, once students see someone else is working hard on reviewing, they may believe they need to carry a smaller burden [19]. Third,

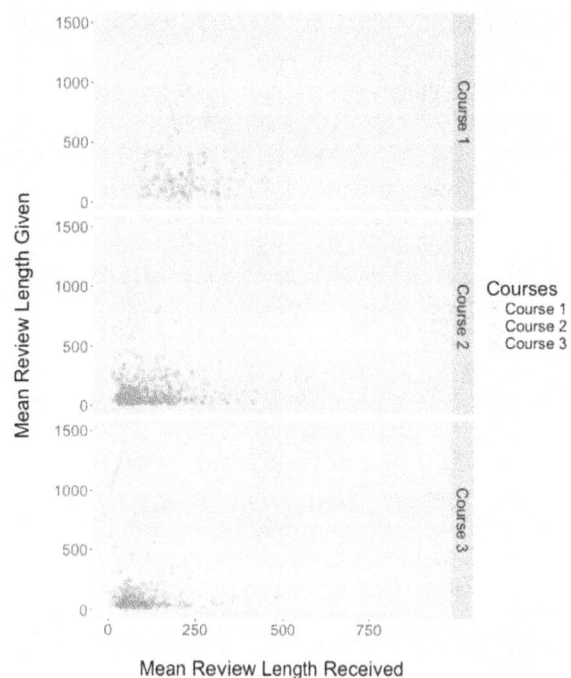

Figure 4. Students write shorter reviews when they see longer reviews on their own work

over time students who do not receive recognition for their high efforts may gradually become less driven to continue to generate high quality reviews. This work was conducted under IRB protocol #140267XX and was partially funded via NSF grant #IIS-0745320.

REFERENCES

1. David Boud, Ruth Cohen, and Jane Sampson. 2014. *Peer learning in higher education: Learning from and with each other*. Routledge.

2. Kwangsu Cho and Christian D Schunn. 2007. Scaffolded writing and rewriting in the discipline: A web-based reciprocal peer review system. *Computers & Education* 48, 3 (2007), 409–426.

3. Derrick Coetzee, Seongtaek Lim, Armando Fox, Bjorn Hartmann, and Marti A Hearst. 2015. Structuring interactions for large-scale synchronous peer learning. In *Proceedings of the 18th ACM Conference on Computer Supported Cooperative Work & Social Computing*. ACM, 1139–1152.

4. Catherine H Crouch and Eric Mazur. 2001. Peer instruction: Ten years of experience and results. *American journal of physics* 69, 9 (2001), 970–977.

5. Thomas Erickson and Wendy A Kellogg. 2000. Social translucence: an approach to designing systems that support social processes. *ACM transactions on computer-human interaction (TOCHI)* 7, 1 (2000), 59–83.

6. K Anders Ericsson and Paul Ward. 2007. Capturing the naturally occurring superior performance of experts in the laboratory toward a science of expert and exceptional

performance. *Current Directions in Psychological Science* 16, 6 (2007), 346–350.

7. Alvin W Gouldner. 1960. The norm of reciprocity: A preliminary statement. *American sociological review* (1960), 161–178.

8. Yasmine Kotturi, Chinmay E Kulkarni, Michael S Bernstein, and Scott Klemmer. 2015. Structure and messaging techniques for online peer learning systems that increase stickiness. In *Proceedings of the Second (2015) ACM Conference on Learning@ Scale*. ACM, 31–38.

9. Robert E Kraut, Paul Resnick, Sara Kiesler, Moira Burke, Yan Chen, Niki Kittur, Joseph Konstan, Yuqing Ren, and John Riedl. 2012. *Building successful online communities: Evidence-based social design.* Mit Press.

10. Chinmay Kulkarni, Julia Cambre, Yasmine Kotturi, Michael S Bernstein, and Scott R Klemmer. 2015b. Talkabout: Making distance matter with small groups in massive classes. In *Proceedings of the 18th ACM Conference on Computer Supported Cooperative Work & Social Computing*. ACM, 1116–1128.

11. Chinmay Kulkarni, Koh Pang Wei, Huy Le, Daniel Chia, Kathryn Papadopoulos, Justin Cheng, Daphne Koller, and Scott R Klemmer. 2015c. Peer and self assessment in massive online classes. In *Design thinking research*. Springer, 131–168.

12. Chinmay E Kulkarni, Michael S Bernstein, and Scott R Klemmer. 2015a. PeerStudio: rapid peer feedback emphasizes revision and improves performance. In *Proceedings of the Second (2015) ACM Conference on Learning@ Scale*. ACM, 75–84.

13. Tricia Ngoon, Alexander Gamero-Garrido, and Scott Klemmer. 2016. Supporting Peer Instruction with Evidence-Based Online Instructional Templates. In *Proceedings of the Third (2016) ACM Conference on Learning@ Scale*. ACM, 301–304.

14. Leo Porter, Cynthia Bailey Lee, and Beth Simon. 2013. Halving fail rates using peer instruction: a study of four computer science courses. In *Proceeding of the 44th ACM technical symposium on Computer science education*. ACM, 177–182.

15. Todd Rogers and Avi Feller. 2016. Discouraged by peer excellence: Exposure to exemplary peer performance causes quitting. *Psychological science* 27, 3 (2016), 365–374.

16. Donald Schön. 1987. Educating the reflective practitioner. (1987).

17. Michelle K Smith, William B Wood, Wendy K Adams, Carl Wieman, Jennifer K Knight, Nancy Guild, and Tin Tin Su. 2009. Why peer discussion improves student performance on in-class concept questions. *Science* 323, 5910 (2009), 122–124.

18. Thomas Staubitz, Dominic Petrick, Matthias Bauer, Jan Renz, and Christoph Meinel. 2016. Improving the Peer Assessment Experience on MOOC Platforms. In *Proceedings of the Third (2016) ACM Conference on Learning@ Scale*. ACM, 389–398.

19. Milena Tsvetkova and Michael W Macy. 2014. The social contagion of generosity. *PloS one* 9, 2 (2014), e87275.

The Changing Patterns of MOOC Discourse

Nia M. M. Dowell
Department of Psychology
Institute for Intelligent Systems
University of Memphis
Memphis, United States
ndowell@memphis.edu

Christopher Brooks
School of Information
University of Michigan
Ann Arbor, United States
brooksch@umich.edu

Vitomir Kovanović
School of Informatics
University of Edinburgh
Edinburgh, United Kingdom
v.kovanovic@ed.ac.uk

Srećko Joksimović
Moray House School of Education
University of Edinburgh
Edinburgh, United Kingdom
s.joksimovic@ed.ac.uk

Dragan Gašević
Schools of Education and Informatics
University of Edinburgh
Edinburgh, United Kingdom
dragan.gasevic@ed.ac.uk

ABSTRACT

There is an emerging trend in higher education for the adoption of massive open online courses (MOOCs). However, despite this interest in learning at scale, there has been limited work investigating how MOOC participants have changed over time. In this study, we explore the temporal changes in MOOC learners' language and discourse characteristics. In particular, we demonstrate that there is a clear trend within a course for language in discussion forums to be of both more on-topic and reflective of deep learning in subsequent offerings of a course. We measure this in two ways, and demonstrate this trend through several repeated analyses of different courses in different domains. While not all courses show an increase beyond statistical significance, the majority do, providing evidence that MOOC learner populations are changing as the educational phenomena matures.

Author Keywords

MOOCs; learning at scale; discussion forums; on-topic discussion; discourse complexity.

INTRODUCTION

Early research on the MOOC phenomena saw significant investment in understanding the makeup of the learner population, largely through demographic [1], performance, and activity-based measures [2]. With the phenomena now in its fifth year, we provide here a retrospective analysis of how learner engagement within MOOCs has changed based on the form of learner discussion. In particular, we demon-

strate here that discussions have (a) become more focused or on-topic over time, and (b) the linguistic features that characterize MOOC learners' discourse has become more complex over time.

This discovery has significant implications for instructional design and course iteration, as well as implications for future research in the area of learning at scale research. For instance, if students for future offerings of a course are a more selective population, and that this population tends towards more complex and on-topic discussions, course designers may focus future development efforts on expanding the disciplinary depth of assessments, or introducing additional depth-based learning activities (e.g. honor tracks in the Coursera platform). Researchers, meanwhile, need to be aware of not only the intra-course difference, especially when doing repeated trials and quasi-experimental designs, but also the inter-course difference when attempting to generalize findings. As we show, the population characteristics of a MOOC in its first offering are not the same as those of a population in the same course but in subsequent offerings, and direct comparisons (at least with respect to discourse) cannot be made.

METHODS

For this analysis, we chose five MOOCs on the Coursera platform which ran for several sessions (N= 59,017 participants). We worked with instructional designers to ensure that each of the courses chosen experienced minimal changes between course offerings, limited to corrections and minor additions of content. The instructors had consistent involvement in the course across subsequent offerings. Each course was different with respect to the first session start date, the length of the course, the instructor, learning objectives, participants, and domain being taught. The courses chosen had all been run between six and ten times ($\bar{x} = 8.2$ $\sigma = 2.05$), and the data from all offerings was included.

L@S 2017, April 20-21, 2017, Cambridge, MA, USA
©2017 ACM. ISBN978-1-4503-4450-0/17/04...$15.00
DOI: http://dx.doi.org/10.1145/3051457.3054005

A mixed-effects modeling approach was adopted for all analyses due to the structure of the data (e.g., courses over time) [7]. Mixed-effects models include a combination of fixed and random effects and can be used to assess the influence of the fixed effects (e.g. time) on dependent variables after accounting for any extraneous random effects (e.g. individual participant differences). The primary analyses focused on identifying the characteristics of MOOC participants discourse features over time. We were particularly interested in changes in discourse features related to message relevance (measured by the relevance of students' messages in the discussion with the course video transcripts)[1] and linguistic complexity (measured through Coh-Metrix's [4] Flesch-Kincaid reading level measure [3]). Therefore, we developed two mixed-effects models, with message relevance level and Flesch-Kincaid reading level as the dependent variables, and time and course as the independent variables.

In addition to constructing the models with the on-topic discussion and Flesch-Kincaid reading level as fixed effects, null models with the random effects (participant) but no fixed effects were also constructed. A comparison of the null random-effects-only model with the fixed-effect models allowed us to determine whether MOOC participants discourse has changed over time above and beyond the participant individual differences. Akaike Information Criterion (AIC), Log Likelihood (LL) and a likelihood ratio test were used to determine the best fitting and most parsimonious model. In addition, we also estimate effect sizes for each model, using a pseudo R^2 method, as suggested by Nakagawa and Schielzeth [5]. For mixed-effects models, R^2 can be characterized into two varieties: marginal R^2 and conditional R^2. Marginal R^2 (R^2_m) is associated with variance explained by fixed factors, and conditional R^2 (R^2_c) can be interpreted as the variance explained by the entire model, namely random and fixed factors. Both R^2_m and R^2_c convey relevant information regarding the model fit and variance explained, and so we report both here. The NLME package in R [6] was used to perform all the required computation.

RESULTS AND DISUCSSION

The likelihood ratio tests indicated that both the on-topic discussion and Flesch-Kincaid model yielded a significantly better fit than the null random effects only models with $\chi^2(9) = 9277.32$, $p = .001$, $R^2_m = .16$, $R^2_c = .38$ for the on-topic model, and $\chi^2(9) = 3024.47$, $p = .0001$, $R^2_m = .05$, $R^2_c = .37$, for the Flesch-Kincaid model. Several conclusions can be drawn from this initial model fit evaluation and in-

[1] Relevance was determined by building a custom LSA space using the instructor video transcripts for the course as source data. The amount of on-topicness of a students' post was then calculated by computing the semantic similarity between the LSA space and the students' post using LSA.

spection of R^2 variance. First, the model comparisons imply that temporality and course features were able to add a significant improvement in characterizing the trend of both MOOC participants' rate of on-topic posting and linguistic complexity, above and beyond individual participant differences. Second, for the on-topic model, time, course, and individual participant features explained about 38% of the predictable variance, with 16% of the variance being accounted for by the time and course features alone. However, for the Flesch Kincaid Model, time and course features were only able to explain a total of 5% of variance grade level. The observed difference in variance suggests temporal changes and the course are more accurate at characterizing changes in MOOC participants' on-topic discussion, than their linguistic complexity. Table 1 shows the coefficients for the main effects of each course and course by time interactions. To assess course-time interactions, a reference category was selected for the categorical predictor variable of course (i.e., Thermodynamics) for both models.

The main effect coefficients for each course in Table 1 represent the difference in the intercepts between a given course and the reference course, Thermodynamics, when the time variable is at its mean value. However, because we are more interested in the temporal changes in on-topic discussion and linguistic complexity, these main effects are of less relevance for the current research. The interaction coefficients for the on-topic model indicate that four of the five MOOC courses are increasing in linguistic complexity over time, as compared to the Thermodynamics reference course.

Variable	On-Topic Model		Flesch Kincaid Model	
	β	SE	β	SE
Main Effects				
Thermodynamics	**0.72***	0.007	**7.18***	0.11
Fantasy & Science Fiction	**0.07***	0.007	-0.12	0.11
Instructional Methods	**0.15***	0.010	**2.04***	0.16
Finance	**-0.13***	0.007	**-1.10***	0.11
Model thinking	**-0.07***	0.007	**-0.44***	0.11
Interactions				
Thermodynamics* Time	-0.005	0.006	0.01	0.09
Fantasy & Science Fiction* Time	**0.03***	0.006	0.11	0.10
Instructional Methods* Time	**0.02***	0.009	0.22	0.14
Finance * Time	**0.03***	0.006	**0.21****	0.09
Model thinking * Time	**0.02***	0.006	**0.37***	0.09

Table 1. All learner mixed-effects model coefficients for predicting changes in on-topic discussion with Flesh Kincaid over time. Note: * p < .09; **p < .05; *** p < .001. Fixed effect coefficient (β). Standard error (SE). N= 59,017.

For the Flesch-Kincaid model, we see two of the courses have increased in linguistic complexity, as compared to the Thermodynamics reference course. We further probed the Fantasy & Science Fiction and Instructional Methods courses to see if the temporal trend for linguistic complexity was significant when it is not being compared to the reference category. Specifically, we constructed additional models by regressing time on Flesch-Kincaid, for the Fantasy & Science Fiction and Instructional Methods courses separately. This analysis revealed that linguistic complexity was indeed increasing significantly for both the Fantasy & Science Fiction with $\chi^2(1) = 11.57$, $p < .001$, $\beta = .12$, $p < .001$, and the Instructional Methods course with $\chi^2(1) = 8.04$, $p < .01$, $\beta = .24$, $p < .01$.

These temporal changes in on-topic discussion and linguistic complexity are depicted in Figures 1 and 2, respectively. Note that the standardized time variable was used in the analysis, however this relationship is plotted across years in the below figures to visualize the relationship. Figure 1 illustrates the temporal trend of on-topic discussion, which appears to increase with subsequent offerings of a course, for all courses but thermodynamics. Figure 2 shows the temporal trend of grade reading level appears to increase with subsequent offerings of a course, for all courses but thermodynamics.

CONCLUSIONS

This paper shares some of our initial explorations of issues associated with discussion forums of course-based Massive Open Online Courses. In this work, we have demonstrated the increasing relevance and linguistic complexity of MOOC discussion fora over subsequent offerings. While not all courses have the same amplitude of increase, there is a general trend seen in all courses except for one, an introductory thermodynamics course. We have not addressed the question as to why discourse patterns are changing in MOOCs. It may be that the population for subsequent offerings is more niche, and new courses are generally taken by the broadest (in terms of interest) population. It could be an effect of habitual course takers: there are several anecdotes which we aim to explore more fully of learners taking courses repeated despite passing them, either to sign up as a formal mentor for the course, or to engage in continued on-topic learning with new cohorts. Or it could be an effect of the MOOC phenomena in general, with a steadily increasing user base and distribution of new courses. In our future work, we will also explore additional MOOC participant population characteristics, and incorporate the total number of posts per learner into the models.

Figure 1. Linear mixed-effect model fitted estimates for on-topic discussion over time for five MOOC courses.

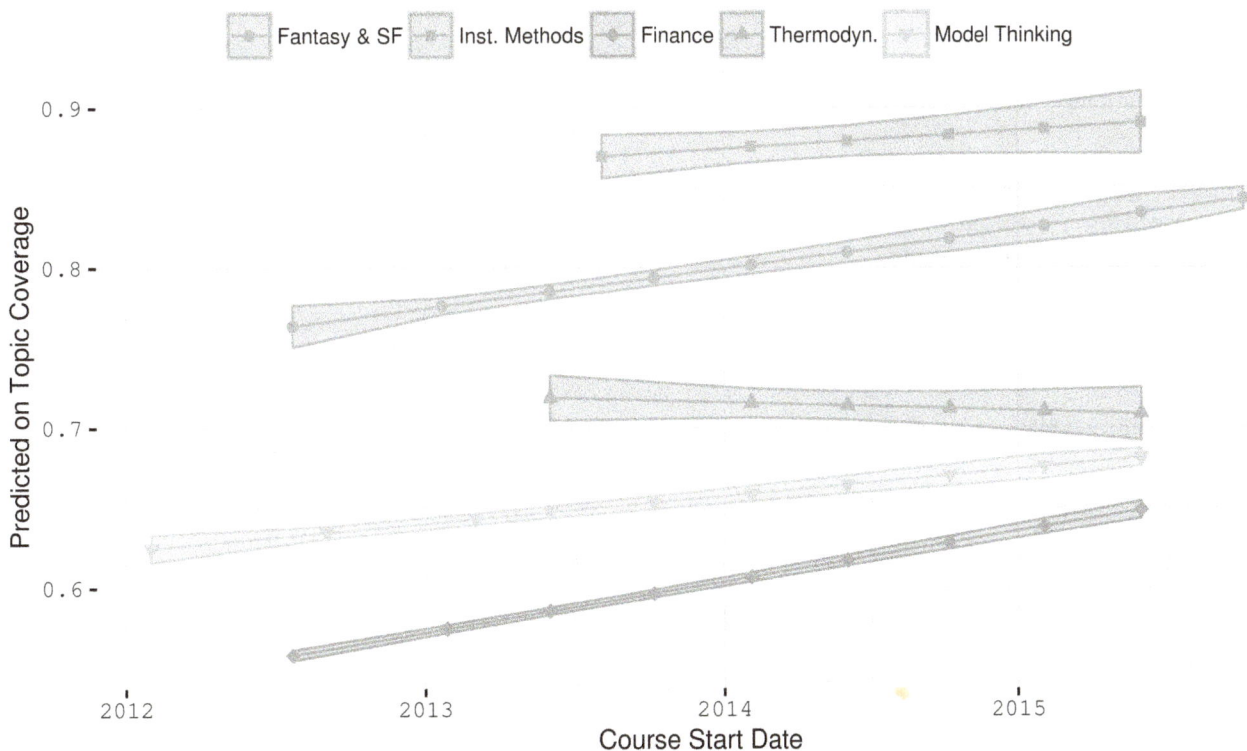

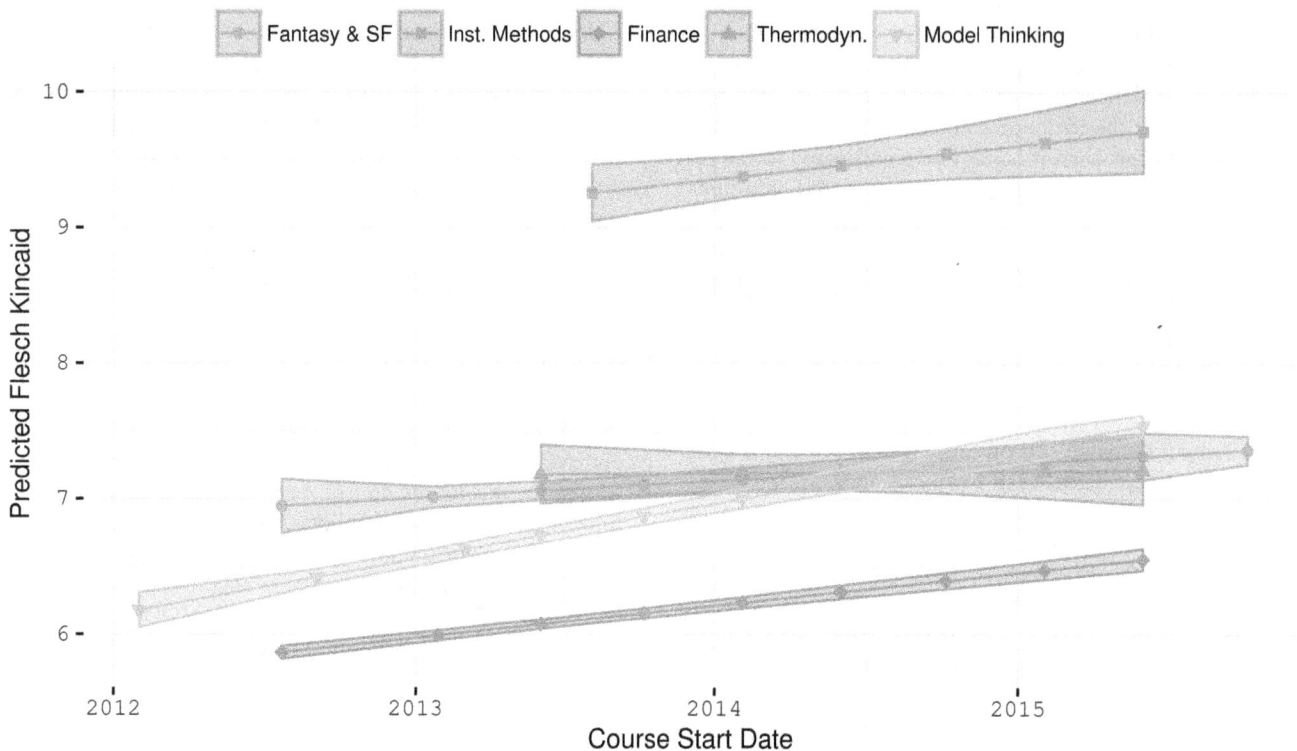

Figure 2. Linear mixed-effect model fitted estimates for Flesch-Kincaid Grade level over time for each of the five MOOC courses.

ACKNOWLEDGMENTS
This research was supported in part by the National Science Foundation under Grant No. BCC 14-517. Any opinions, findings, and conclusions or recommendations expressed in this material are those of the authors and do not necessarily reflect the views of these funding agencies.

REFERENCES
[1] Emanuel, E.J. 2013. Online education: MOOCs taken by educated few. *Nature*. 503, 7476 (2013), 342.

[2] Kizilcec, R.F. et al. 2013. Deconstructing Disengagement: Analyzing Learner Subpopulations in Massive Open Online Courses. *Proceedings of the Third International Conference on Learning Analytics and Knowledge* (New York, NY, USA, 2013), 170–179.

[3] Klare, G.R. 1974. Assessing readability. *Reading Research Quarterly*. 10 (1975 1974), 62–102.

[4] McNamara, D.S. et al. 2014. *Automated evaluation of text and discourse with Coh-Metrix*. Cambridge University Press.

[5] Nakagawa, S. and Schielzeth, H. 2013. A general and simple method for obtaining R2 from generalized linear mixed-effects models. *Methods in Ecology and Evolution*. 4, 2 (Feb. 2013), 133–142.

[6] Pinheiro, J. et al. 2016. *nlme: Linear and nonlinear mixed effects models*.

[7] Pinheiro, J.C. and Bates, D.M. 2000. *Mixed-effects models in S and S-Plus*. Springer.

MOOClets: A Framework for Dynamic Experimentation and Personalization

Joseph Jay Williams
Harvard University
Cambridge, MA, USA
joseph_jay_williams@harvard.edu

Anna N. Rafferty
Carleton College
Northfield, MN, USA
arafferty@carleton.edu

Samuel Maldonado
San Jose State University
San Jose, CA, USA
samuel.maldonado@sjsu.edu

Andrew Ang
Harvard University
Cambridge, MA, USA
andrew_ang@harvard.edu

Dustin Tingley
Harvard University
Cambridge, MA, USA
dtingley@gov.harvard.edu

Juho Kim
KAIST
Daejeon, South Korea
juhokim@cs.kaist.ac.kr

ABSTRACT

Randomized experiments in online educational environments are ubiquitous as a scientific method for investigating learning and motivation, but they rarely improve educational resources and produce practical benefits for learners. We suggest that tools for experimentally comparing resources are designed primarily through the lens of experiments as a scientific methodology, and therefore miss a tremendous opportunity for online experiments to serve as engines for dynamic improvement and personalization. We present the MOOClet requirements specification to guide the implementation of software tools for experiments to ensure that whenever alternative versions of a resource can be experimentally compared (by randomly assigning versions), the resource can also be dynamically improved (by changing which versions are presented), and personalized (by presenting different versions to different people). The MOOClet specification was used to implement DEXPER, a proof-of-concept web service backend that enables dynamic experimentation and personalization of resources embedded in frontend educational platforms. We describe three use cases of MOOClets for dynamic experimentation and personalization of motivational emails, explanations, and problems.

ACM Classification Keywords

H.5.m. Information Interfaces and Presentation (e.g. HCI): Miscellaneous; K.3.1. Computer Uses in Education

Author Keywords

A/B experiment; dynamic experimentation; MOOClet; personalization; multi-armed bandit; reinforcement learning; statistical machine learning; adaptive learning

INTRODUCTION

One of the promises of online education is to advance research on learning, and randomized experiments in online educational environments have yielded many insights into learning and motivation. However, it is important for academic research to yield not only generalizable principles, but result in enhancements to student learning. Unfortunately, there is a substantial delay and many obstacles between obtaining experimental results to making concrete changes to courses. Arguably, most published randomized experiments in online environments do not directly result in improvements to the context in which the study was conducted.

In contrast, when randomized experiments or "A/B tests" are used for product testing versions of websites and online advertisements, the software is designed so that versions that maximize user engagement or purchases are provided to subsequent users [3]. Instructors and students could benefit more directly from research studies if software for educational experiments was similarly designed to use data to dynamically transition from assigning versions of a lesson with equal probability to assigning effective versions more frequently for future students, rather than using data from an experiment in one course to impact design in a course occurring months later.

However, using data from randomized experiments to provide one version of a resource to everyone reflects a "one-size-fits-all" assumption, and could miss what are known as heterogeneous effects, where one version works well for one subgroup of learners, while another version works better for a different subgroup. Experiments could therefore lead to personalization, in the sense that different conditions are presented to learners with different characteristics. While personalization encompasses many different approaches, such as intelligent tutoring systems adapting how many activities are provided or customization of choices by individual learners (see [2] for a review), adaptive assignment to different versions of software suggests one way to bridge experiments with the large body of work on adaptive learning and personalization.

Despite the novel opportunities online environments provide for randomized experiments and their widespread use, relatively little work has examined how to design tools for instructors and researchers to conduct experiments. The major technical work on building tools for experiments has taken place in industry settings like website testing, where companies like Facebook and Microsoft invested resources to implement experiments and machine learning algorithms for product improvement, like creating programming languages for experiments [1]. This paper addresses the need for a more standardized way of conducting experiments in educational resources by proposing a software requirements specification that can be reused in different contexts and eases the burdens of customizing experiments through an API that facilitates experimentation, dynamic improvement, and personalization. We describe three case studies that used different implementations of this specification within learning resources.

DESIGNING SOFTWARE FOR EXPERIMENTATION, DYNAMIC IMPROVEMENT, AND PERSONALIZATION

We identify three major functions to support in the experimental specifications, which are closely related to each other: (1) Conducting an experiment on a resource, by assigning alternative versions of the resource with equal probability. (2) Dynamically improving a resource, by adding or removing which versions are presented over time, as new ideas arise or new data is collected. (3) Personalizing a resource, by presenting different versions to learners based on characteristics like prior knowledge or motivation.

Design Goals

Tools for conducting an online educational experiment can simultaneously enable dynamic improvement and personalization, if it is possible to:

- Add and remove versions at any point in time.

- Use multiple methods for deciding how versions are delivered to a particular learner, including but not limited to uniform randomization, weighted randomization, personalization based on a learner's characteristics.

- Change the method for assigning versions to learners, at any point in time, such as changing the weights/probabilities for assigning a version, changing the rules for assigning based on a learner's characteristics, or both.

- Collect and access data from past learners who received alternative versions, in deciding which versions are best and in dynamically improving a resource.

- Collect and use data about a specific learner, in deciding which version to assign to them for personalization.

MOOClet Specification for Software for Experimentation, Dynamic Improvement, and Personalization

To achieve the preceding design goals, we provide what is known as a *software requirements specification* for what components and functions should be satisfied by the software underlying an experiment on a digital educational resource. We name this the *MOOClet* requirements specification, and the

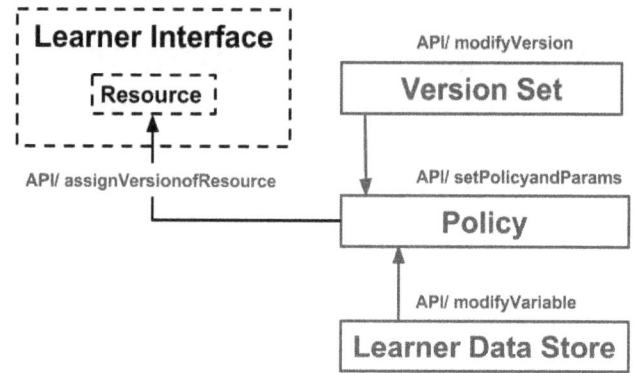

Figure 1. Components of the web service that enable an educational resource to function as a MOOClet. Before a learner interacts with the resource, the Learner Interface makes an API call to the web service, and the Policy associated with the MOOClet can use information from the Learner Data Store in selecting a version from the Version Set and serving it to the Learner Interface. API endpoints allow addition or modification of versions and variables, and changes to the current Policy.

API (Application Programming Interface) Specification		
Endpoint	Parameters	Function
assignVersionofResource	learner_id, mooclet_id	Assign version of resource using current policy
modifyVersion	version_id, mooclet_id, version_content	Add or modify a version for a MOOClet
modifyVariable	learner_id, mooclet_id, variable, value	Add or modify variable in Learner Data Store
setPolicyandParams	mooclet_id, policy, policy_parameters	Change policy and/or policy parameters

Figure 2. The key API endpoints for the DEXPER web service. DEXPER serves as the backend for MOOClets by providing versions to a frontend Learner Interface, and allowing modification at any point via API of Versions, Learner Variables, and a Policy or its parameters.

term *MOOClet*[1] is used to refer to any educational resource augmented to meet these requirements. Roughly, implementing a digital educational resource as a MOOClet associates the frontend software presenting the resource to learners with the backend software that maintains a set of versions, a store of learner data, and a suite of methods for assigning versions to learners (including rules for weighted randomization and personalization). A MOOClet must also provide functions that instructors or researchers can use at any time to modify the backend components, such as adding new versions or learner data, and changing the method for assigning versions to learners.

As depicted in Figure 1, an online educational resource implemented as a MOOClet – or more formally, using the software requirements specification for a MOOClet– has the following components:

- A *Learner Interface*, which displays the content a learner interacts with. The exact content the learner sees depends on which alternative condition or version of an educational resource they are assigned to. For example, one of two explanations for why the answer to a problem is correct. This is what would typically be called an educational resource,

---

[1] We introduce the novel term *MOOClet* because it is useful to have a label for educational resources that matches this precise specification, versus educational resources that only enable randomized experimentation, or only enable personalization. The approach applies to any digital educational resource, and to digital resources beyond education, from websites to emails to mobile apps. Another term we have used is *AdapComp*, short for Adaptive Component.

since there is usually just one version when no experiment is being conducted.

- A *Version Set*, which contains alternative versions of content that will be provided in the Learner Interface. For example, this structure could contain multiple different explanations a learner could be shown. Elements of the Version Set can be accessed, modified, and added at any point.

- A *Learner Data Store*, which contains a set of variables linked to each learner by their anonymous learner ID. This might include whether a learner had gotten a previous problem right, or their rating of an explanation. Variables can be added and modified at any point. All variables can be accessed and used by the *Policy* that determines which version is assigned to a particular learner.

- A *Policy*, which is a function for determining which version of a resource is presented to a particular learner, and can use any data in the *Learner Data Store*, about the current learner or the effects of versions on past learners. A MOOClet must always have access to the *Randomized Personalization* Policy Class, which enables uniform randomization, weighted randomization, and personalization using IF-THEN rules. Particular MOOClet implementations can optionally provide a range of other Policy Classes.

DEXPER Web Service: Enabling Resources to Function as MOOClets

We used the MOOClet specification to implement a proof-of-concept web service that enables cross-platform dynamic experimentation and personalization, which we call DEXPER. DEXPER can be used with text and HTML components of educational resources, which are ubiquitous across platforms and play an important role in learning, such as motivational messages, explanations, and problems or quizzes.

DEXPER is implemented using Django (a Python-based framework for web applications), with classes that allow the creation and modification of SQL database objects for text and HTML versions that are needed for a MOOClet's *Version Set*, variables and values that make up the *Learner Data Store*, and a range of Policy Classes. These components of the MOOClet can all be added or modified using a set of RESTful API calls, a specification of which are shown in Figure 2. We also use built-in Django capacity to provide a graphical user interface that allows manual editing of these data objects.

The DEXPER Policy Classes allow weighted random assignments (e.g., from [0.50, 0.50] to [0.20, 0.80] to [0.0, 1.0]). The weightings can be dependent on characteristics of the learner to combine experimentation and personalization (as shown in Figure 3). It also includes a policy for dynamic improvement using Thompson sampling, a multi-armed bandit algorithm from reinforcement learning [4]. In this policy, a target outcome variable from the Learner Data Store is identified, and the algorithm chooses condition assignments to maximize this value of this variable across learners. At any point an API call can be used to change the Policy being used for a specific MOOClet (or equivalently, to change the Policy's parameters). Figure 3 shows the use of specific Policies in the use cases discussed in the next section.

MOOClets provide an abstraction for reinforcement learning
More generally, the MOOClet specification serves as an abstraction for any reinforcement learning algorithm to provide the Policy for a MOOClet. To use the terminology of RL, Actions correspond to Versions, a State Space is implicitly defined by learner characteristics in the Learner Data Store, and Reward functions are based on data in the Learner Data Store about past learners' responses to versions. To provide extensibility so that any machine learning researcher or service can provide policies for a MOOClet/experiment, DEXPER provides a Policy that functions as a pass-through: it sends data from the Learner Data Store to another API or code base to obtain a recommendation, and then allows the external method to specify which version DEXPER selects and sends to the Learner Interface. This allows researchers to take advantage of existing implementations of algorithms without needing to design their own interface between the algorithm and the educational resource.

APPLICATIONS OF MOOCLETS

This section describes three educational resources that were implemented as MOOClets, which illustrate the use of the requirements specification and DEXPER.

Use Case 1: Personalizing Emails. Learners in a MOOC were sent emails that elicited feedback about why they were not continuing with a course [4]. Different introductory messages to the emails were written, with the goal of maximizing the number of people providing feedback. The *Version Set* consisted of three versions of email content (conditions in experiment) differed in the introductory line, labeled Survey, Acknowledgement, Brief. The survey/emailer software Qualtrics functioned as the Learner Interface, and was used to send emails and provide the survey to collect learners' feedback. The Number of Days Active for each learner was obtained from the MOOC provider and sent via API to the Learner Data Store, in which all learners were identified by an anonymous ID (that could be connected by us to their email address). The outcome variable, Provided Feedback, was whether a learner responded to an email within one week. The value of this variable was added to the Learner Data Store every time a participant finished a survey, via an API call from the survey software Qualtrics.

The first batch of 1883 learners were assigned to emails with equal probability, using the Policy Weighted Randomization with parameters [0.33, 0.33, 0.33*]. The second batch of 1882 learners were assigned to emails using two policies. The first policy was to "roll out the best version" by using `WeightedRandomization[0, 0, 1]` to assign only the version with the highest response rate from the first batch of learners, the Survey message. This produced a response rate of 10.4%. The second policy was to personalize to subgroups of learners, since analyzing data from the first batch revealed a "crossover" effect. Learners with high course activity were most likely to respond to the highest rate to the Acknowledgement message, but learners with lower course activity were most likely to respond to the Survey message. Using this *Personalization* Policy resulted in 11.2% of learners providing feedback. This increase of 0.8 in response rate corresponded to a 7.6% ad-

	Use Case 1	Use Case 2	Use Case 3
Learner Interface	Emailer Software (Qualtrics)	LTI Tool for quizzes, embedded in Canvas LMS	iframe in MOOC platform (edX)
MOOClet	Introductory Message to Email	Explanation	Problem
Version Set	HTML	Plain Text	URL
Policy	1. Weighted Randomization with different parameters [p1, p2, p3] resulted in: (a) Uniform choice of Versions 1, 2 or 3, [0.33*, 0.33*, 0.33*], (b) Drop V1, favor V3 over V2, [0, 0.49, 0.51], (c) Only V3, [0, 0, 1] 2. Personalization [Weighted]: IF Number of Days Active = 0 THEN Version 3 [0, 0, 1]; IF Number of Days Active = 1 THEN Version 3 [0, 0, 1]; IF Number of Days Active >= 2 THEN Version 2 [0, 1, 0].	Dynamic Randomization with target variable [Rating of Explanation Helpfulness]	External Policy: BKT - Bayesian Knowledge Tracing
Learner Data Store	Number of Days Active, Provided Feedback	Rating of Explanation Helpfulness	Accuracy on Previous Problems

Figure 3. Overview of three uses cases for a MOOClet, showing what played the role of Learner Interface, Version Set, Policy, and Learner Data Store.

vantage of personalization over choosing the apparently "best" condition.

Use Case 2: Dynamic Explanations. To provide learners with explanations of why the answer to a math problem is correct, the AXIS system [5] automatically enhances the explanations learners received by crowdsourcing them from learners, presenting them to future learners, and dynamically choosing the most highly rated. Anyone can create systems like this using DEXPER and MOOClets. We implemented the displayed explanation as the *Learner Interface* to a MOOClet. The *Version Set* contained different versions of explanations. The variables added to the *Learner Data Store* included: the version/explanation assigned to each learner, and each learner's rating of the explanation they received. The *Policy* was DEXPER's `DynamicRandomization`, with the variable to optimize being learners' rating of a version of an explanation.

Use Case 3: Problem Recommendation. We used DEXPER and MOOClets to provide individualized recommendations of problems for students in a MOOC, based on a student's performance on prior problems. The *Learner Interface* is provided by an LTI tool that allows the embedding of various problem "windows" inside an edX MOOC. The problems displayed in a window were native edX content, but the MOOClet allowed an external web service to decide which problem was displayed. This was enabled by the *Version Set* containing links to individual problems. Then, DEXPER allowed problem recommendation to be outsourced to an external web service. An organization provided an API to receive problem recommendations based on their implementation of Bayesian Knowledge Tracing, which obtained a user's variables from the *Learner Data Store*, such as performance on past problems and other course activities like video watching.

CONCLUSION

This paper presents the *MOOClet* requirements specification for designing software for experimentation, so that every randomized comparison of versions of a resource enables dynamic improvement and personalization of that resource. We

created a proof-of-concept web service, DEXPER, that provides the backend for a MOOClet: Version Set, Learner Data Store, and a suite of Policies. We described three applications of MOOClets and DEXPER: to experiment on and personalize emails to MOOC learners, automatically improve learners' satisfaction with explanations in math problems, and adaptively tailor problems in a MOOC based on learners' past performance. For future work, we plan to improve the specification and tools by working with more instructors and researchers and verifying improvements in their practice and course content. Furthermore, we will release our tools as open source.

REFERENCES

1. Eytan Bakshy, Dean Eckles, and Michael S Bernstein. 2014. Designing and deploying online field experiments. In *Proceedings of the 23rd International Conference on World Wide Web*. ACM, 283–292.

2. Peter Brusilovsky and Christoph Peylo. 2003. Adaptive and intelligent web-based educational systems. *International Journal of Artificial Intelligence in Education (IJAIED)* 13 (2003), 159–172.

3. Ron Kohavi, Roger Longbotham, Dan Sommerfield, and Randal M. Henne. 2009. Controlled experiments on the web: survey and practical guide. *Data Mining and Knowledge Discovery* 18, 1 (2009), 140–181.

4. Jacob Whitehill, Joseph Jay Williams, Glenn Lopez, Cody Austun Coleman, and Justin Reich. 2015. Beyond prediction: First steps toward automatic intervention in MOOC student stopout. *Available at SSRN 2611750* (2015).

5. Joseph Jay Williams, Juho Kim, Anna Rafferty, Samuel Maldonado, Krzysztof Z Gajos, Walter S Lasecki, and Neil Heffernan. 2016. AXIS: Generating Explanations at Scale with Learnersourcing and Machine Learning. In *Proceedings of the Third (2016) ACM Conference on Learning at Scale*. ACM, 379–388.

Criteria for Video Engagement in a Biology MOOC

Sera Thornton
MIT
Cambridge MA, USA
serat@mit.edu

Ceri Riley
MIT
Cambridge MA, USA
ceri.a.riley@gmail.com

Mary Ellen Wiltrout
MIT
Cambridge MA, USA
mew27@mit.edu

ABSTRACT

We have designed a Molecular Biology massive open online course (MOOC) for a global audience. Among the learning aids offered are two types of short video segments: lecture videos (delivered unscripted by a professor) and deep dives (fully scripted and animated). While the engaged learners overwhelmingly watched the lecture video segments through to completion, some watched only a portion of each deep dive. As the deep dives take pains to follow evidence-based best practices and are more labor-intensive to make, further study of this difference in viewer retention would inform future course development decisions. Notably, course organization, length of video, lack of on-screen narrator, and identity of narrator show no correlation with this trend. Interestingly, learners who complete lecture videos but not deep dives have slightly higher overall course grades on average. Thus, our model is that learners with a higher degree of knowledge about the subject matter may feel that they do not need to complete the deep dive videos, while they feel the lecture videos are valuable. Future research will test this model.

Author Keywords

biology; video engagement; online education; MOOC

INTRODUCTION

MITx 7.28.1x Molecular Biology: DNA Replication and Repair is a massive open online course (MOOC) that we designed in collaboration with MIT Department of Biology Professors Stephen Bell and Tania Baker, who have long taught the subject on campus. The MOOC offers several modes of learning, including two types of short videos: lecture videos (delivered unscripted by Professor Bell or Baker, overlaid with segments of animated graphics) and deep dives (fully animated and carefully scripted to address learning objectives, with an anonymous narrator).

Animated graphics are especially important in teaching biology because our field is so intrinsically visual. Biological descriptions – of the structure of DNA, for

example – are made more accessible, especially to the novice, by visual representations. In many biological processes, complex structures too small to be seen interact with each other in a highly concerted manner over time; moving graphics have thus been shown to improve student learning and retention of biology [7]. Research suggests that moving graphics, such as those used in both of our video types, are beneficial to learning when the visuals depict concepts central to the learning objective(s) [3]. Much work has been done on determining best practices for digital educational media to maximize the beneficial effect on the audience's learning. For example, Richard Mayer has developed a set of principles for multimedia learning that takes into account factors such as minimizing extraneous cognitive load to optimize the effectiveness of multimedia educational materials. Among Mayer's principles are that audio and visual should work seamlessly together, and that on-screen text should be minimal and in close proximity to the graphics [1]. We utilized Mayer's principles and other evidence-based practices in crafting our deep dives.

Despite everything we know about the design of and positive impact of educational multimedia, for a video to affect learning, the learner must be persuaded to actually watch it. Learners on the course discussion forum are vocally appreciative of our deep dives. We were thus surprised to notice that while engaged learners overwhelmingly watched the lecture video segments through to completion (93% +/- 3% of viewers watched to the end), many watched only a portion of each deep dive (only 65% +/- 5% of viewers watched to the end).

Our research questions are thus: What characteristics of lecture videos and deep dives might cause this difference in engagement? What characteristics of the learner might drive this difference in engagement? We explore position of the video within the course, length of video segment, presence of on-screen narrator, and identity of narrator, and show no correlation between any of these variables and viewer retention. We determined that only a quarter of the learners do not watch the deep dives through to completion, and that this group of learners has a slightly higher median grade than learners who do. Our working model is thus that learners who have a better grasp of the course materials may feel that the deep dives are not delivering enough new information, while the lecture videos are. To test this model, we will re-design an existing lecture video in the style of a deep dive, with the same information content, and perform A/B testing to determine whether the video style affects retention when information is held constant. The current and future results of this study will be invaluable in informing the design of educational video for MOOCs, both for our team and for the field as a whole.

RESULTS

After the first offering of *7.28.1x Molecular Biology* on the edX platform, we noticed a surprising trend. If a learner clicked play on a lecture video segment, they would watch that video to completion in 93% (+/-3%) of cases (Figure 1, top). However, if a learner clicked play on a deep dive, only 65% (+/-5%) of the time would they complete that video. This was surprising, as we had spent considerable time and effort to create the deep dives according to evidence-based best practices and deliver the material in a concise and logical manner. However, others have shown that tutorial videos can have higher dropout rates than lecture videos, indicating that this is not a pattern unique to our course [5]. Thus, we set about trying to determine what could be causing this decrease in viewer retention in the deep dives, so that we could improve engagement.

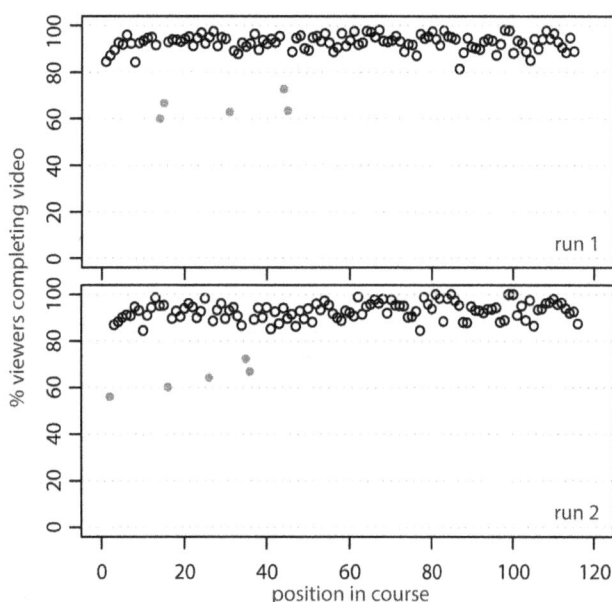

Figure 1. A smaller % of viewers watch each deep dive (blue circles) completely than do each lecture video segment (black rings), regardless of organization within the course. In the first run of the course (top), we positioned deep dives in a separate section from the lecture video, and viewer retention does not correlate with course position (R^2<0.03). In the second run of the course (bottom), we interspersed deep dives among the lecture video segments, as dictated by content, and viewer retention does not correlate with course position (R^2<0.1).

In the first run of the course, we had presented the deep dives in a separate section of the courseware from the lecture videos. We hypothesized that this organization sent the message to learners that the deep dives were less important than the lecture video. To test this hypothesis, in the second run of the course, we interspersed the deep dives

in amongst the lecture video segments, such that the subject matter covered in the successive videos had a logical flow. However, while the lecture videos maintained their high rate of completion, the deep dives also maintained their lower rate of completion, not supporting our hypothesis (Figure 1, bottom).

Video length is a characteristic of educational video that is much discussed in the context of engagement. As presented at Learning at Scale 2014, a study of four early edX MOOCs concluded that viewer engagement drops off after six minutes, and proposed a maximum video segment length of six minutes to maximize retention [2]. We thus next considered video length as a possible mediator of viewer retention. Using the aggregate data from course runs 1 and 2, we looked at completion rate as a function of video time (Figure 2A). We found no correlation between video segment length and completion rate in either run of the course. Moreover, in disagreement with the literature, we observe no drop off in learner engagement at 6 minutes of video length.

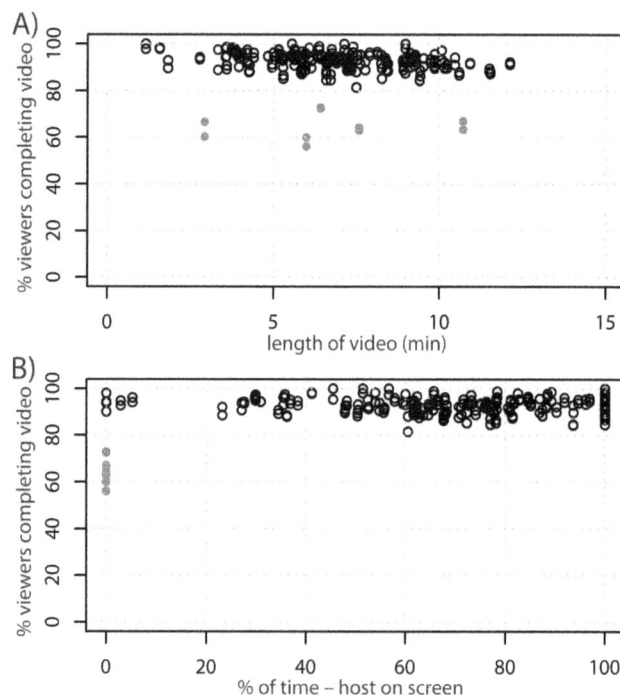

Figure 2. Viewer retention does not correlate with (A) length of video segment (average R^2=0.025) or (B) the percentage of the video that the professor is visible on screen. Neither characteristic separates the deep dives (blue circles) from the lecture video segments (black rings). Data from runs 1 & 2.

We next hypothesized that learners were not feeling an emotional or social connection to the instructor in the deep dives, since these videos are entirely animated and the narrator's face is not shown, while in most lecture videos, the professor's face is often seen. We thus plotted the completion rate as a function of the percentage of time the narrator's face is seen on screen (Figure 2B). We found no correlation between these variables, and moreover, the few lecture video segments that are entirely animated – due to the highly visual nature of the material discussed – still cluster with the rest of the lecture video segments with regards to completion rate, while the deep dives do not. These data thus do not support this hypothesis. This result agrees with studies showing higher cognitive load and lower perceived learning from video in which the instructor's face appears [4,6].

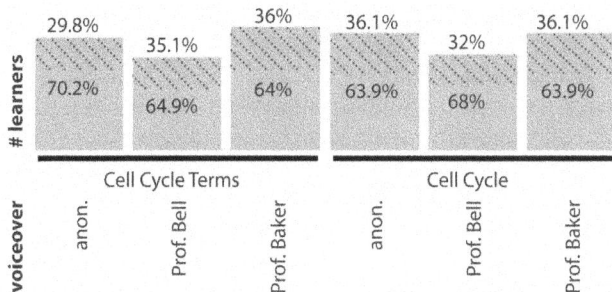

Figure 3. A/B testing shows no significant difference in percentage of viewers watching completely (green) or incompletely (gray with dots) between anonymous and professor voiceovers for two deep dives.

We next focused on an obvious difference between the two categories of videos: different hosts. Our hypothesis was that the learners were not completing the deep dives because a professor did not present the content. To test this hypothesis, we ran an A/B test during the third run of *7.28.1x Molecular Biology*. We edited two existing deep dives, "Cell Cycle" and "Cell Cycle Terms," to create three versions: one with the original anonymous voiceover, one with a voiceover by Professor Bell, and one with a voiceover by Professor Baker. We randomly assigned one host for these two video segments to each learner, and measured completion rates (Figure 3). We observed no significant difference in completion rate between the three different hosts. Moreover, the completion rate for these deep dives remained within the previously observed 60-80% range for deep dives, regardless of host. Our hypothesis is thus once again not supported by our findings.

At this point, we pivoted from characteristics of the videos to those of the learners. Are all learners behaving similarly, completing lecture video segments more than deep dives, or are different subgroups of learners exhibiting different viewing behaviors? For each learner who viewed any video in run 1 of *7.28.1x Molecular Biology*, we calculated the ratio of the mean fraction watched of deep dives to that of lecture videos. Around 1, this ratio means the learner watched approximately the same fraction of a video, whether a deep dive or a lecture video segment. A histogram shows that most learners are watching the deep dives and the lectures approximately equally, but that there are also categories of learners completing each of the video types more than the other (Figure 4A).

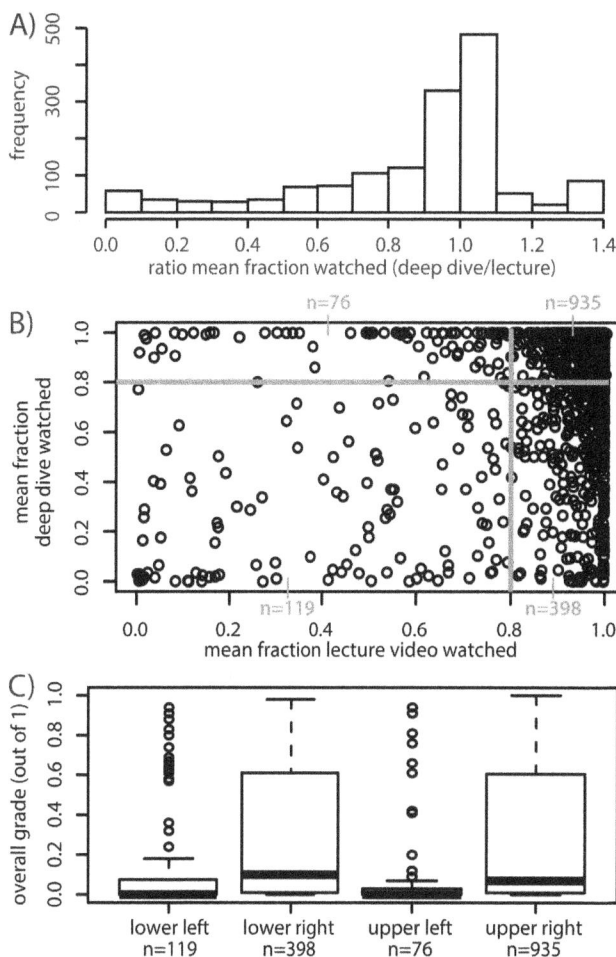

Figure 4. A) For each learner who viewed a video in run 1 of the course, we calculated the ratio of mean fraction of deep dive watched to mean fraction of lecture video watched. We capped this ratio at 1.4 to allow for inclusion of learners who watched nearly 0 lecture video. The distribution of these ratios is plotted here. B) Each learner's viewing pattern is plotted individually to visualize the distribution of behaviors in the course. C) The distribution of overall course grades differs between learner categories as defined in (B). The upper left and upper right quadrants are significantly different (p<3E-9).

To delve deeper into learners' viewing behaviors, we next plotted the average deep dive fraction watched against the average lecture video fraction watched, for each learner (Figure 4B). We found that the majority of learners (upper right quadrant) watched over 80% of any given video they viewed, regardless of category. There was a small number of learners (lower left quadrant) not watching any video to completion, and a small number of learners (upper left quadrant) watching deep dives to 80% completion or greater, but not lecture video segments. Additionally, approximately a quarter of learners (lower right quadrant) were watching over 80% of the average lecture video they viewed, but not deep dives.

Why is this last category of learners watching partial deep dives but entire lecture video segments? Elucidating this would be very useful in deciding whether this behavior is an issue we need to take steps to address, and how. When we looked at the distribution of overall course grades in the four categories of learners defined above, we found a step towards such an elucidation (Figure 4C). This category of learners has a slightly (though not significantly) higher median overall grade than those who complete both types of video. If this trend is meaningful, a model in which these learners have more background knowledge in the domain or are successfully searching out external resources, and thus may feel that the deep dives are not advanced enough to be worth their time, would be in agreement with these data.

CONCLUSIONS

As a course team still developing the third part of the Molecular Biology MOOC series to which *7.28.1x Molecular Biology* belongs, the findings described herein are already useful in informing how we create educational videos. Lack of evidence for subpar course organization, excess video length, lack of "facetime" with the host of deep dives, or a perception of inadequacy of a non-professor host allow us to not worry about changing those characteristics and instead focus our efforts where they are more likely to improve our learners' experience and learning. We believe other MOOC development teams will also benefit from our findings, as they can compare their learner data to our own and determine whether our conclusions should be extrapolated to their courses.

Based on our findings on video segment length, we would make more of an effort to stay under 10 minutes, as completion rate seems to drop 5-10% in videos longer than that, but the evidence does not support a 6-minute cutoff in our course. We would further advise developers of other MOOCs to take advantage of the huge amount of data they collect to evaluate the response of their specific population of learners to their particular video styles before potentially over-extrapolating the 2014 findings [2] and imposing a 6-minute cutoff on video segments in their MOOCs.

We are encouraged by the trends we find in the viewing patterns and overall grades of different categories of learners. First, the majority of our learners are completing >80% of the average video they view, be it a deep dive or a lecture video segment. Thus, the video learning resources we create *are* being utilized by our learners and *are* thus worth our effort and resources in making. Second, if the quarter of learners not finishing deep dives truly do not need them due to their knowledge background, this is not a problem in need of a remedy; rather, they are finding and utilizing the resources they need to accomplish their learning goals amongst the resources we provide. Third, the small population of low-performing learners who complete deep dives but not lecture videos is worth noting. If they are able to learn material due to the deep dives that would otherwise be out of reach, perhaps there is even more we could do to aid that population in their learning goals.

We plan to gather further evidence on this question by performing a new A/B test wherein we choose an existing lecture video segment to remake in deep dive style, adhering to the evidence-based best practices, but also maintaining the same information as in the original video. Whether learners' viewing patterns cluster this video with lecture video segments or with deep dives will illuminate the criteria they are using to inform their video engagement.

ACKNOWLEDGMENTS
MEW led the course team that developed 7.28.1x (ST and Nathaniel Schafheimer). CR created most deep dives and began research study. Thanks to Professors Bell and Baker for their role in this study and creating this course; to Swati Carr for her role in 7.28.1x run 3; and to Betsy Skrip for her deep dive work. ST thanks CMU LearnLab and Jon Daries of MIT Institutional Research for data mining help. 7.28.1x is funded by the MITx Grant Program, MIT Department of Biology, and MIT Office of Digital Learning.

REFERENCES
1. Ruth Colvin Clark and Richard E. Mayer. 2008. *e-Learning and the Science of Instruction: Proven Guidelines for Consumers and Designers of Multimedia Learning, Third Edition*. John Wiley & Sons, Inc.

2. Philip J. Guo, Juho Kim, Rob Rubin. 2014. How video production affects student engagement: an empirical study of MOOC videos. In *Proceedings of the first ACM conference on Learning @ scale conference*, 41-50. https://doi.org/10.1145/2556325.2566239

3. Tim N. Höffler and Detlev Leutner. 2007. Instructional animation versus static pictures: A meta-analysis. *Learning and Instruction* 17, 722–738.

4. Bruce D. Homer, Jan L. Plass, and Linda Blake. 2008. The effects of video on cognitive load and social presence in multimedia-learning. *Computers in Human Behavior* 24.3, 786-797.

5. Juho Kim, Philip J. Guo, Daniel T. Seaton, Piotr Mitros, Krzysztof Z. Gajos, Robert C. Miller. 2014. Understanding in-video dropouts and interaction peaks in online lecture videos. In *Proceedings of the first ACM conference on Learning @ scale conference*, 31-40. https://doi.org/10.1145/2556325.2566237

6. Alendra Lyons, Stephen Reysen, and Lindsey Pierce. 2012. Video lecture format, student technological efficacy, and social presence in online courses. *Computers in Human Behavior* 28.1, 181-186.

7. Phillip McClean, Christina Johnson, Roxanne Rogers, Lisa Daniels, John Reber, Brian M. Slator, Jeff Terpstra, and Alan White. 2004. Molecular and Cellular Biology Animations: Development and Impact on Student Learning. CBE Life Sci Educ. 4.2, 169-179.

Pass the Idea Please: The Relationship between Network Position, Direct Engagement, and Course Performance in MOOCs

Stacey L. Houston, II
Vanderbilt University
Department of Sociology
stacey.houston@vanderbilt.edu

Katherine Brady
Vanderbilt University
Department of Electrical
Engineering and Computer
Science
katherine.a.brady@vanderbilt.edu

Gayathri Narasimham
Vanderbilt University
Vanderbilt Institute for Digital
Learning
gayathri.narasimham@vanderbilt.edu

Douglas Fisher
Vanderbilt University
Department of Electrical
Engineering and Computer
Science
douglas.h.fisher@vanderbilt.edu

ABSTRACT

Extant research suggests that learner engagement in discussion forums is positively correlated with learner performance. In this paper we investigate which types of forum engagement are most strongly associated with final performance in MOOC courses. In particular, we compare the correlation between course final grade and two types of learner engagement: direct measures, which count the number of interactions, and indirect measures, which capture learners position in a social network. We found that direct measures have stronger correlations with final grade. However, in preliminary analyses, we also found that course instructors score higher than learners on some indirect measures. We discuss the implications of these findings and our plans for developing the work further in the future.

Author Keywords

MOOCs; Social Network Analysis; Course Performance

ACM Classification Keywords

K.3.1 Computer Uses in Education: Distance learning

INTRODUCTION

Models which treat the spread of information as a type of contagion have been verified by historical records [1, 7]. This, along with studies that have found word of mouth more effective than other forms of marketing [15, 11], provide strong evidence that interacting with classmates should increase learning in a course. In this paper we investigate whether learn-

ers benefit more from interacting directly with peers or positioning themselves to indirectly receive knowledge and ideas through the forum's social network.

We investigate whether learners' final grades are more closely correlated with direct or indirect connections to their peers. To capture these connections, we modeled learner interactions on course discussion forums for three massive open online courses (MOOCs) on the Coursera Platform as a social network. The **direct measures** were the number of threads on which a learner posted and the number of peers a learner interacted with on those threads. The **indirect measures** we explored were the frequency at which a learner serves as the link between peers (betweenness), a learner's connectedness to influential peers (Bonacich Power), and the number of peers through which a message from a learner would need to travel to reach all other learners (closeness).

Our findings indicate that direct measures of learner interactions are more consistently correlated with final grade than a learner's indirect interactions. However, we found some evidence that indirect metrics may be better suited for identifying the most influential members of a forum. Expanding on this evidence will be necessary for drawing any concrete conclusions.

BACKGROUND AND RELATED WORK

Researcher interest in the ways social networks affect learning has been around for some time. Martinez et al. established in 2003 that networks of social interactions in traditional classrooms are a good model of learner collaboration [10]. As online classrooms increasingly developed active forums which automatically record student interactions, methods were tailored for building social networks from forum data [9]. Research has demonstrated that, as in traditional classrooms, peer interactions in online discussion forums can foster learning [6]. Furthermore, more active networks pro-

L@S 2017, April 20–21, 2017, Cambridge, MA, USA
© 2017 ACM. ISBN 978-1-4503-4450-0/17/04...$15.00
DOI: http://dx.doi.org/10.1145/3051457.3054008

mote higher levels of cognitive engagement and critical thinking [14].

There has been some research into the type of interactions that best foster learning. A study that investigated networks of scientific publications suggests that networks with large diameters and many small tightly connected communities (like a company with many small departments) spread ideas best [4]. Studies which have looked at the benefits to individual learners have concluded, like us, that direct metrics like the number of posts a learner makes or the number of peers they interact with, are the most predictive of performance metrics such as dropping out or completing [16, 13]. These studies explored whether social statistics can predict learner outcomes. Our work differs from these studies in asking whether *some* statistics are better predictors than others.

Though our work suggests that indirect links are not as predictive of performance outcomes, research suggests closeness is correlated with having more influence within the network. Cho et al. found through surveys of an online master's program that learners who were close on the friendship network before the beginning of a course had a larger influence on how the social network developed during the course [2]. Dowell et al. found that learners in a MOOC who were close used longer, more narrative form language [3]. This findings suggests that measures of indirect interaction may have implications beyond course performance. The preliminary component of this study regarding course instructors intends to develop this line of thinking.

The present study contributes to the existing literature in three ways:

1. It utilizes data from three different courses to replicate findings from existing literature. In addition, we examined different time points in each course to determine the extent to which the timing of course interactions might influence, or moderate, the relationship between learner interactions and final course performance.

2. It compares the association between course performance and two specific types of learner interaction on online discussion forums: direct and indirect. Previous studies have tended to examine these types separately, neglecting to compare the usefulness of exploring one type of interaction over another.

3. It offers a preliminary look at instructor positioning in the social network. Given the implicit assumption that course instructors are most expert among the course participants, exploring the ways in their position differs from learners' is a fruitful avenue for continued research.

DATASET
The data used in this research came from three MOOC sessions. Two of these sessions were different offerings of Innovation, a course on entrepreneurship which heavily encouraged forum participation. The other session was Matlab, a course on programming. All three sessions had active instructor and teaching assistant involvement on the forums.

Course	Sign Ups	Assignment	Unique Posters
Innovation 1	47,000	7,200	6,100
Innovation 2	33,000	3,300	2,000
Matlab 1	63,000	7,700	1,500

Table 1: Number of learners in each course who signed up, did at least one assignment or posted on the forum.

Course	Sub-Forum	Posters	Threads
Innovation 1	Week 1	4329	532
Innovation 1	Week 4	1798	247
Innovation 1	Week 8	1236	112
Innovation 2	Week 1	1493	327
Innovation 2	Week 4	811	280
Innovation 2	Week 8	435	77
Matlab 1	Weeks 1-4	700	378
Matlab 1	Week 5	163	79
Matlab 1	Week 8	266	131

Table 2: This table shows the number of posters (including both learners and instructors) who participated in each sub-forum and the number of threads they generated in that sub-forum.

Course announcements were made on a separate announcements page, not the forums.

It is important to consider time in any analysis of the relationship between course interaction and grade. Learners who post in a discussion forum about the final project in a course are more likely to receive passing grades than students who post about the first lecture since some of the learners who watch the first lecture drop out before the final project [6]. The MOOC sessions under study here all had separate sub-forums for each week of the course. We take this into consideration in this study. Specifically, in each course, we modeled sub-forums from the beginning, middle and end as separate social networks rather than treating the whole forum as single social network. The number of participants in each session and sub-forum are shown in tables 1 and 2.

Method
In these MOOCs, after a learner made a post on a thread they were automatically added to a mailing list which would send out an email each time there was a subsequent new post on that thread. For this reason we modeled learners as being exposed to every post on threads to which they posted. To represent this as a social network, we modeled every learner as a node. Two nodes shared an edge if the corresponding learners had co-participated in at least one thread in a sub-forum. This method of modeling the forums has been corroborated by other researchers [8, 12, 6]. A popular alternative is to model the discussion forums as directed graphs [3, 9, 16] where edges point to the peer a learner is replying to. For the forums explored in this study there was no reliable means of recording if one post was in reply to another. Therefore, we used a model with undirected edges. To account for the difference in course commitment between learners who have

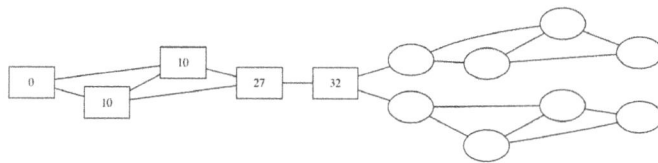

(a) The value inside each node shows the betweenness of that node.

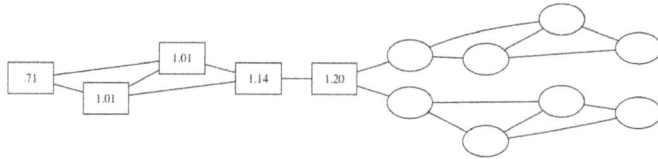

(b) The value inside each node shows the Bonacich Power of that node.

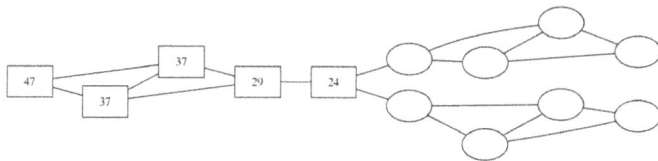

(c) The value inside each node shows the closeness value of that node. A node is considered "closer" if it has a lower value.

Figure 1: The above graph shows examples of the values for each indirect measure we looked at on a small example network.

just started the course and learners in the last week, we did not combine models across sub-forums.

The purpose of this study is to determine the relative correlation between grade and metrics of direct connections versus indirect metrics. We differentiate between direct learner connections and indirect learner connections based on the manner in which information is spread to learners. Direct metrics capture the extent to which one learner is exposed to the ideas or knowledge of another learner. Indirect metrics, on the other-hand, capture the extent to which a learner positions themselves to be exposed to a variety of other learners. Further, direct metrics are captured by counts of user activity, whereas indirect metrics must be calculated from social network models. The specific direct metrics we examined were the number of threads to which a learner posted and the number of peers with whom they shared at least one thread. We contrasted these with three indirect metrics of social network positioning: Betweenness, Bonacich Power and Closeness. Betweenness measures how often a learner lies on the shortest path between two peers. Bonacich Power is a reciprocal measure in which the connectedness of a learner's neighbors on the network determines their Bonacich Power. Closeness measures the sum of the shortest paths from a learner to each of their peers - thus, learners with lower closeness scores are more central. The values of all three of these metrics are shown in figure 1.

To provide examples of the indirect measures, a learner in a MOOC course with high betweenness is one who frequently engages with posts by peers from different groups, thereby hypothetically exposing themselves to a variety of diverse ideas. A learner with high Bonachich Power posts in threads

Course	Sub-Forum	Neigh	Thread
Innovation 1	Week 1	ns	0.08**
Innovation 1	Week 4	0.07**	0.05*
Innovation 1	Week 8	0.06*	ns
Innovation 2	Week 1	0.10**	0.16**
Innovation 2	Week 4	ns	0.08*
Innovation 2	Week 8	ns	ns
Matlab 1	Weeks 1-4	0.16**	0.15**
Matlab 1	Week 5	0.20*	0.15*
Matlab 1	Week 8	ns	ns

Table 3: The significant correlations with grade for direct interactions: number of neighboring peers (Neigh) and number of threads posted to (Thread). In this table ns = not significant, * = $p < .05$ and ** = $p < .01$

Course	Sub-Forum	Close	Bon	Bet
Innovation 1	Week 1	-0.05**	ns	0.05**
Innovation 1	Week 4	-0.09**	ns	ns
Innovation 1	Week 8	-0.09**	ns	ns
Innovation 2	Week 1	-0.12**	ns	0.09**
Innovation 2	Week 4	ns	ns	0.07*
Innovation 2	Week 8	ns	ns	ns
Matlab 1	Weeks 1-4	ns	ns	0.14**
Matlab 1	Week 5	ns	0.16*	ns
Matlab 1	Week 8	ns	ns	ns

Table 4: The significant correlations with grade for indirect interactions: Betweenness (Bet), Closeness (Close) and Bonacich Power (Bon). In this table ns = not significant, * = $p < .05$ and ** = $p < .01$

that are frequented by other highly engaged and active learners, thereby hypothetically exposing themselves to peers who have learned from others in the course. Lastly, a learner with a low closeness score interacts on threads in a manner that exposes them to ideas of many other learners in the course. The results of our analyses comparing these metrics are presented in the following section.

RESULTS

The number of threads a learner posted to was significantly correlated with grade more often than any of the other statistics (in 6 out of the 9 sub-forums). Furthermore, those six sub-forums are the ones from the beginning and middle of each course, suggesting that this statistic is most useful at earlier points in the course.

The next most promising statistic was the number of neighboring peers a learner has followed by betweenness and closeness. Bonacich Power was only significant in one sub-forum. These results suggest that direct measures of learner interactions are more consistently correlated with course performance than indirect measures. The significant correlations for each measure can be seen in tables 3 and 4.

In analyses not presented here, we estimated a few models which used linear combinations of indirect statistics to see if grade could be better predicted using multiple linear regression. None of these models explained more variation in learners final grade than number of threads. Thus, we concluded that combining the features does not add value if the outcome of interest is final course performance.

In addition to correlating each statistic with grades, we also explored the difference between the measurements for instructors and students. In the Matlab course, instructors were more engaged than the average learner, as measured by all the metrics we considered in this study. This was not true for the Innovation courses with the exception of closeness. In all sub-forums in which instructors participated, the instructor closeness scores were at least a standard deviation 'closer' than the mean closeness score. Dowel et al. found that forum participants who had high closeness scores tended to use more narrative language, much like instructors [3]. We hope to explore the implications of this in future work.

CONCLUSIONS AND FUTURE WORK
In this study we found that direct learner interactions on the forums are more often correlated with learners' final grades than indirect interactions. We hypothesize that this trend arises due to similar ideas being posted on multiple threads and plan to investigate the veracity of this hypothesis in future work. We also find that, in general, instructors are more indirectly connected than learners in the social networks.

In future work, we hope to further uncover ways in which the behaviors of learners are related to behaviors of instructors. Additionally we hope to do a qualitative assessment of the diversity of thread topics on each sub-forum. We would expect indirect measures to be more correlated with grade on sub-forums which rarely have the same ideas repeated on multiple threads and less correlated with grade on sub-forums where multiple threads contain similar ideas. Our current model treats all peers in the social network as more or less the same. However, research suggests that learners benefit more from interacting with peers with high GPAs [5]. We plan to look into whether interactions with instructors and teaching assistants lead to different benefits than peer interactions.

REFERENCES
1. Bettencourt, L. M., Cintrón-Arias, A., Kaiser, D. I., and Castillo-Chávez, C. The power of a good idea: Quantitative modeling of the spread of ideas from epidemiological models. *Physica A: Statistical Mechanics and its Applications 364* (2006), 513–536.

2. Cho, H., Gay, G., Davidson, B., and Ingraffea, A. Social networks, communication styles, and learning performance in a cscl community. *Computers & Education 49*, 2 (2007), 309–329.

3. Dowell, N. M., Skrypnyk, O., Joksimovic, S., Graesser, A. C., Dawson, S., Gašević, D., Hennis, T. A., de Vries, P., and Kovanovic, V. Modeling learners' social centrality and performance through language and discourse. *International Educational Data Mining Society* (2015).

4. Gasevic, D., Kovanovic, V., Joksimovic, S., and Siemens, G. Where is research on massive open online courses headed? a data analysis of the mooc research initiative. *The International Review of Research in Open and Distributed Learning 15*, 5 (2014).

5. Gašević, D., Zouaq, A., and Janzen, R. Choose your classmates, your gpa is at stake!: The association of cross-class social ties and academic performance. *American Behavioral Scientist* (2013), 0002764213479362.

6. Gillani, N., and Eynon, R. Communication patterns in massively open online courses. *The Internet and Higher Education 23* (2014), 18–26.

7. Gillani, N., Yasseri, T., Eynon, R., and Hjorth, I. Structural limitations of learning in a crowd: communication vulnerability and information diffusion in MOOCs. *Scientific reports 4* (2014), 6447.

8. Jiang, S., Fitzhugh, S. M., and Warschauer, M. Social positioning and performance in moocs. In *Workshop on Graph-Based Educational Data Mining* (2014), 14.

9. Laat, M., Lally, V., Lipponen, L., and Simons, R.-J. Investigating patterns of interaction in networked learning and computer-supported collaborative learning: A role for Social Network Analysis. *International Journal of Computer-Supported Collaborative Learning 2*, 1 (2007), 87–103.

10. Martınez, A., Dimitriadis, Y., Rubia, B., Gómez, E., and De La Fuente, P. Combining qualitative evaluation and social network analysis for the study of classroom social interactions. *Computers & Education 41*, 4 (2003), 353–368.

11. Nekovee, M., Moreno, Y., Bianconi, G., and Marsili, M. Theory of rumour spreading in complex social networks. *Physica A: Statistical Mechanics and its Applications 374*, 1 (2007), 457–470.

12. Poquet, O., and Dawson, S. Analysis of MOOC Forum Participation. In *Australasian Society for Computers in Learning and Tertiary Education* (2015), 224–234.

13. Romero, C., López, M.-I., Luna, J.-M., and Ventura, S. Predicting students' final performance from participation in on-line discussion forums. *Computers & Education 68* (2013), 458–472.

14. Thomas, M. J. Learning within incoherent structures: The space of online discussion forums. *Journal of Computer Assisted Learning 18*, 3 (2002), 351–366.

15. Trusov, M., Bucklin, R. E., and Pauwels, K. Effects of word-of-mouth versus traditional marketing: findings from an internet social networking site. *Journal of marketing 73*, 5 (2009), 90–102.

16. Yang, D., Sinha, T., Adamson, D., and Rosé, C. P. Turn on, tune in, drop out: Anticipating student dropouts in massive open online courses. In *Proceedings of the 2013 NIPS Data-driven education workshop*, vol. 11 (2013), 14.

Observing Personalizations in Learning: Identifying Heterogeneous Treatment Effects Using Causal Trees

Biao Yin
Worcester Polytechnic
Institute
Worcester, MA
byin@wpi.edu

Thanaporn Patikorn
Worcester Polytechnic
Institute
Worcester, MA
tpatikorn@wpi.edu

Anthony F. Botelho
Worcester Polytechnic
Institute
Worcester, MA
abotelho@wpi.edu

Neil T. Heffernan
Worcester Polytechnic
Institute
Worcester, MA
nth@wpi.edu

ABSTRACT

The incorporation of computer-based platforms in the classroom has introduced the ability to conduct numerous randomized control trials at scale with student-level randomization. Such systems are able to collect vast amounts of data on each student while completing work in the classroom and at home. It is often the case, however, that the effects of these trials are reported across all students, ignoring the potential for personalized learning. Personalized learning, or the observation of heterogeneous treatment effects, considers that the effects of a studied learning intervention may differ for individual students; while an intervention may work well for low-performing students, for example, it may have no effect for higher performing students. Personalized learning can lead to better instructional practices that maximizes the learning benefits for each individual student, and with the use of computer-based platforms, such individualized instruction is made feasible at large scales. In this work we use a causal decision tree to observe treatment effects in 9 experiments run in the ASSISTments online learning platform.

Author Keywords

Personalization; Heterogeneous Treatment Effects; Randomized Controlled Trials; Causal Tree

L@S 2017, April 20-21, 2017, Cambridge, MA, USA

© 2017 ACM. ISBN 978-1-4503-4450-0/17/04...$15.00

DOI: http://dx.doi.org/10.1145/3051457.3054009

INTRODUCTION

Many teachers employ computer-based learning platforms to assign content and track students' learning progress. While these systems provide many useful tools to teachers, their usage, or more specifically that of their students, provides the ideal setting to run randomized control trials aimed at identifying what interventions best help students learn. While the results of these trials, often described in terms of the effectiveness of treatment over a control condition, are useful to describe the effectiveness of interventions across all students, it is often the case that there is variance within each condition; the treatment may work very well for an identified subgroup of students and exhibit no effects on another subgroup. It is also possible that no significant effect of treatment is found in whole, but such an effect may exist specifically for a smaller subgroup. Identifying what works for whom is the goal of personalized learning, such that, knowing information about a student, one can apply the best instructional practices that maximize student learning.

This concept of personalization is often referred to in terms of heterogeneous treatment effects. Essentially this is the idea that treatment effects are not the same across all students, and can be more accurately measured by identifying the subgroups where the effect is present and testing for significance. This identification of subgroups could be formed in a variety of ways. While many clustering algorithms attempt to find groups of similar students, the method that has been applied to this problem in the past has instead utilized a form of decision tree, splitting students to maximize differences between the subgroups on some observed outcome metric. One such tree-based method, referred to as Causal Trees [1], has been introduced specifically to identify these heterogeneities, and employs a methodology to split students as well as measure differences in treatment effects.

While not fully explored in the field of education and learning analytics, the measurement of heterogeneous treatment effects has long existed in other fields. Commercial companies such as Microsoft [3][4], Ebay [2], and many others who often choose not to publish run large quantities of trials at scale on their respective websites and platforms. Often is the goal of these trials is to identify variations in design, layout, and incorporation of advertisement that optimizes an outcome metric of interest; more importantly, it is often the goal to identify who responds best to the tested variation in order to maximize indirectly, if not explicitly, revenue. Such companies understand that effects of treatment can exhibit, if perhaps rarely, significance in the presence of heterogeneous subgroups, so why has this not been widely implemented in the field of education?

The answer to this question in the past has been in regard to scalability. It is difficult in traditional classroom environments to implement individualized instruction practices. As the teacher usually addresses multiple students, using instructional practices that benefit the greatest number of students is more practical simply due to the infeasibility of one-to-one instruction. This changes, however, with the incorporation of computer-based instructional practices in the classroom and for homework. In this case, individualized aid can be given to students in addition to the in-class instruction. We expect that the combination of these two strategies will increase student learning by collecting and utilizing information about student performance.

Online learning platforms and intelligent tutoring systems already collect a breadth of student features as problems are attempted, and such information has been used in a range of predictive and performance measuring tasks. Similarly, such information can be used to better analyse the results of randomized control trials within these systems. Students who have experienced the experiment can be grouped based on features collected before condition assignment, after which treatment effects can be measured within each grouping. Identifying a significant effect within a subgroup can be then implemented for personalized instruction for future students. Future students beginning an assignment could be assessed using the same set of prior performance metrics to identify if one method of instruction is more beneficial than another, and then be given the better strategy.

The goal of this paper is to provide a preliminary analysis to demonstrate that heterogenous treatment effects exist in the field of learning. Beyond this, we show how a Causal Tree (CT) can be implemented to observe this effect.

METHODOLOGY

In order to explore the concept of heterogeneous treatment effects, we observe two approaches. The first explores the use of just one student feature to observe a qualitative interaction exemplifying this effect, while the second applies the more sophisticated method of Causal Trees [1]. This work utilizes a unique dataset consisting of student information from 22 randomized controlled trials run in the ASSISTments online learning platform.

Dataset

The ASSISTments online learning platform is a free web-based platform utilized by a large user-base of teachers and students. The system, based primarily in math content, allows

teachers to assign several types of assignments for classwork and homework, reporting on student performance and learning progress. Students are given immediate feedback on each problem, and are also presented with several forms of instructional aid including hints, that provide a useful message, and scaffolded questions that break the problem into smaller steps. The platform has been the subject of a recent study within the state of Maine [5], demonstrating significant learning gains for students using the platform.

The dataset used [7] in this work is unique in that it provides student information collected within the platform, comprising 22 randomized controlled experiments. These experiments were run in assignment types known as "skill builders" in which students are given problems until a threshold of understanding is reached; within ASSISTments, this threshold is traditionally 3 consecutive correct responses. Reaching this threshold denotes sufficient performance and completion of the assignment. In addition to this experimental data, information of the students prior to condition assignment is also provided in the form of problem-level log data providing a breadth of student information at fine levels of granularity.

Initial Approach

A preliminary analysis is performed to introduce a simple method of identifying heterogeneity within one of the experiments in our dataset. This selected experiment compared a treatment group that presented students with video-based hints to a control group that used text-based hints. The experiment was run within an assignment entitled the "Composition of Functions." This analysis observes differences in completion rates of the experimental assignment as an outcome measure.

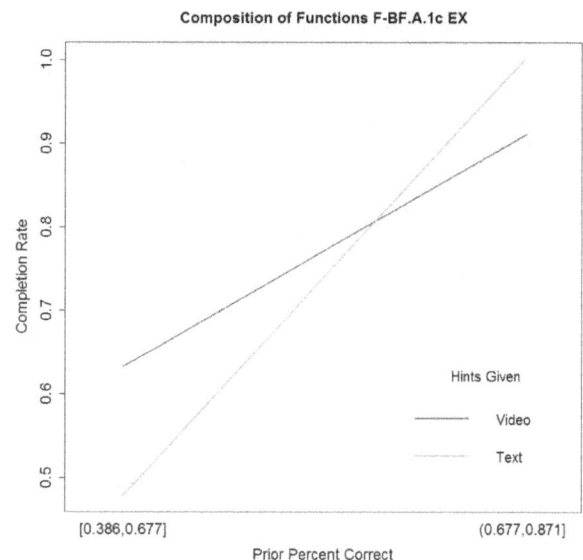

Figure 1. Qualitative interaction found using a median split of prior percent correctness.

After filtering observations in the dataset with missing values, two simple methods are applied to illustrate the heterogeneous effect. Each of these observes the student feature of prior percent correct, representing the average number of correct responses in all data prior to the experiment for each student. The data is filtered to remove missing values, leaving 110 observations. The first method, depicted in Figure 1 uses a median split of this metric to place students into one of two bins after which the completion rate is averaged within each bin. The second method, illustrated in Figure 2 uses a logistic regression including a term for condition, the prior percent correct covariate, and an interaction term of these two.

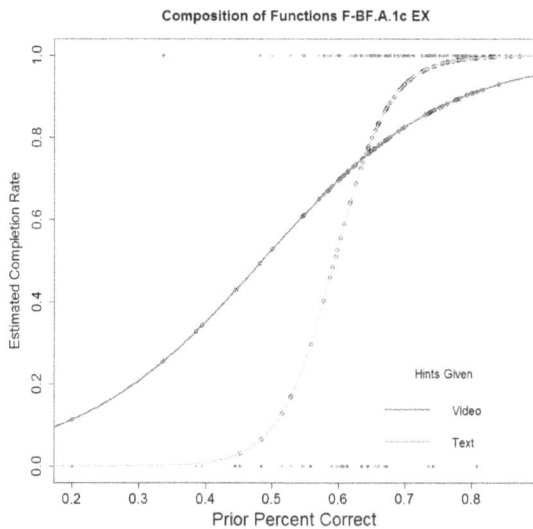

Figure 2. Qualitative interaction found using a logistic regression.

Each of these show an interaction indicative of heterogeneity. As is depicted in the second method, using the continuous representation of prior percent correct, the effect is not equally large for all types of students. This suggests that a more sophisticated method may be able to identify other effects using multiple features rather than just one to group students.

Causal Trees

Expanding upon the preliminary work depicted in the previous section, we also apply Causal Trees [1] to our dataset to identify and measure other such treatment effects. The technique is applied to 9 experiments of the existing 22 due to their similarity of intervention design. Each compares a variation of providing video versus text hints in different contexts. This subset is used for this comparison and as this is presented as a demonstration of the method's utility. Due to the small treatment effects found in the training data, it is expected that heterogeneity in these particular experiments within our dataset is rare.

First, we randomly split the data into two equal subsets; the first is to be used for model training, while the second will be used as a test set. Using the training data, we build a single causal tree across all experiments; as each experiment observes a similar intervention, the results will indicate more generalized effects of video- versus test-based hints. As input into the tree, we observe multiple covariates such as locality of the school, Guessed Gender (as data is anonymized, gender is inferred or left as unknown), Z-Scored Mastery Speed (a performance metric denoting the number of problems needed

to complete a skill builder), Prior Percent Completion (average number of completed assignments prior to the experiment), Prior Percent Correct, Prior Homework Percent Completion, Z-Scored HW Mastery Speed, and also the experiment identifier. Using the test set, students are grouped using into leafs using the constructed tree. Within each leaf, students are split by condition and compared to identify treatment effects.

RESULTS

Observing the analysis using the causal tree[1], the method of measuring differences between condition at each leaf can vary. In our analysis, we perform a Fisher test for odds ratios[6] with 95% confidence intervals. This odds ratio analysis provides a relative measure of effect of treatment as compared to the control condition. Again, completion of the experiment is our outcome metric of comparison. To interpret the ratio, a value less than 1 indicates higher effects in the experimental condition, while values greater than one indicate a higher effect in the control condition; values equal to one indicate that there is no effect. This analysis provides significance values and confidence intervals to evaluate the believability of the effect.

Breslow-Day X^2	22.71
p-value of Common Odds Ratio	0.01

Table 1. Breslow-Day test for heterogeneity between nodes in regard to odds ratio.

The causal tree odds ratio analysis is reported in Table 2. These results, generated from the test set applied to the constructed model from training, show two leafs with significant treatment effects. These leafs represent interactions of prior homework completion and prior percent correctness values of students as discovered by the tree. The number of students found to complete, as opposed to those who did not complete, the experimental assignment are also reported in Table 2.

The method is shown to identify heterogeneous effects, but one further step can be taken to ensure that the technique is splitting students such that there is heterogeneity between the leafs themselves. Using a Breslow-Day (B-D) test, we can validate that the causal tree is finding heterogeneous groups of students. The results of this test, reported in Table 1, indicate that there is significant heterogeneity between the leaf nodes.

DISCUSSION

The results of the causal tree analysis suggest that some heterogeneous effects do exist across all experiments. Based on this general analysis, however, it would appear that no qualitative interactions emerge from the results. It is found in the first two leafs that the text-hints condition is significantly better than the video-hint condition, while no other significant effects are found.

As this is merely an exemplary usage of such a model to identify areas for personalization, several limitations of our approach may be affecting our results. For example, a single

---

[1] The resulting tree can be viewed at http://tiny.cc/LaS_causal_tree

Leaf	Control N Complete	Control N Incomplete	Treatment N Complete	Treatment N Incomplete	Odds Ratio	Lower CI	Upper CI
1	33	18	23	3	2.45*	1.05	5.87
2	19	5	17	21	4.58*	1.30	19.06
3	54	4	65	1	2.07	0.56	9.54
4	51	17	48	8	0.50	0.17	1.37
5	42	15	39	5	0.36	0.09	1.18
6	100	8	78	10	1.60	0.54	4.90
7	28	6	32	7	1.02	0.26	4.15
8	24	1	17	3	4.11	0.30	231.08
9	34	18	33	13	0.75	0.29	1.91
10	25	8	28	11	1.22	0.12	4.12
11	35	27	48	27	0.73	0.35	1.54

Table 2. The number of students for each leaf in the causal tree and odds ratio analysis metrics. *Significance based on the confidence intervals.

tree is used to describe all 9 related experiments for sake of reducing the complexity of our presentation of the approach, but it may be more beneficial to train a separate tree on each experiment. Likewise, in place of using a single tree per experiment, it may also be beneficial to explore the usage of random causal forests [1] to explore a wider range of covariate combinations.

CONTRIBUTION

This paper stresses the need to apply focus toward improving personalizations in learning. As explored in both a simple analysis, and a more sophisticated approach using a causal tree, heterogeneous effects are observable in our dataset. This work is, to our knowledge, among the first to apply causal trees in an education context and thus acts as a pilot study to observe the efficacy of such an application.

In addition to the exploration of these effects, we introduce the application of a very simple statistical test to validate the splitting criterion of the causal tree. The B-D test validates that there is heterogeneity between leafs in terms of the effects of treatment as measured by the odds ratio.

In light of these findings, it becomes apparent that current instructional approaches could greatly benefit from the incorporation of such information. This is particularly the case in computer-based systems that often collect breadths of student information, the potential of which is perhaps not yet fully realized.

ACKNOWLEDGMENTS

We thank multiple current NSF grants (IIS-1636782, ACI-1440753, DRL-1252297, DRL-1109483, DRL-1316736, DGE-1535428 & DRL-1031398) , the US Dept. of Ed (IES R305A120125 & R305C100024 and GAANN), and the ONR.

REFERENCES

1. Susan Athey and Guido Imbens. 2015. Recursive partitioning for heterogeneous causal effects. *arXiv preprint arXiv:1504.01132* (2015).

2. Thomas Blake, Chris Nosko, and Steven Tadelis. 2015. Consumer Heterogeneity and Paid Search Effectiveness: A Large-Scale Field Experiment. *Econometrica* 83, 1 (2015), 155–174.

3. Alex Deng, Pengchuan Zhang, Shouyuan Chen, Dong Woo Kim, and Jiannan Lu. 2016. Concise Summarization of Heterogeneous Treatment Effect Using Total Variation Regularized Regression. *arXiv preprint arXiv:1610.03917* (2016).

4. Ron Kohavi, Alex Deng, Brian Frasca, Toby Walker, Ya Xu, and Nils Pohlmann. 2013. Online controlled experiments at large scale. In *Proceedings of the 19th ACM SIGKDD international conference on Knowledge discovery and data mining*. ACM, 1168–1176.

5. Jeremy Roschelle, Mingyu Feng, Robert F. Murphy, and Craig A. Mason. 2016. Online Mathematics Homework Increases Student Achievement. *AERA Open* 2, 4 (2016). DOI:http://dx.doi.org/10.1177/2332858416673968

6. Nova Scotia. 2010. Explaining odds ratios. *J Can Acad Child Adolesc Psychiatry* 19 (2010), 227.

7. Douglas Selent, Thanaporn Patikorn, and Neil Heffernan. 2016. ASSISTments Dataset from Multiple Randomized Controlled Experiments. In *Proceedings of the Third (2016) ACM Conference on Learning@ Scale*. ACM, 181–184.

A Probabilistic Approach for Discovering Difficult Course Topics Using Clickstream Data

Assma Boughoula
201 N Goodwin Ave
Urbana, IL 61801
boughou1@illinois.edu

Chase Geigle
201 N Goodwin Ave
Urbana, IL 61801
geigle1@illinois.edu

ChengXiang Zhai
201 N Goodwin Ave
Urbana, IL 61801
czhai@illinois.edu

ABSTRACT

One of the main factors affecting the success and effectiveness of Massive Open Online Courses is the ability of the instructor to acquire and incorporate student feedback in a timely manner, and preferably before assigning grades to student assessments. This research uses raw clickstream data from video watching sessions of the Coursera MOOC: "Text Retrieval and Search Engines"[1] to discover which topics are difficult for the students. We introduce a measure for topic difficulty based on these clickstream events, and rank the topics according to this measure. The validity of our ranking is evaluated by comparing it with the ranking of topics based on student votes and find that our method agrees with the ranking based on student votes with $> 63\%$ accuracy.

ACM Classification Keywords

K.3.1 Computer Uses in Education: Distance learning; K.3.2 Computer and Information Science Education: Self-assessment

Author Keywords

Topic difficulty; student feedback; probabilistic clustering

INTRODUCTION

Massive Open Online Courses are emerging as an increasingly important future direction for education around the world since they provide a globally accessible platform for courses where the learner can tailor their learning experience as needed. However, the learning environment in a MOOC is dramatically different than that of a traditional classroom where real-time, face-to-face interactions with individual students provides instructors with immediate and actionable feedback about the effectiveness of material presentation. Providing instructors of MOOCs this type of actionable feedback remains an important area of research, and it is necessary in order to allow instructors to improve the course in future offerings and/or react in real time as it is offered.

[1] https://www.coursera.org/learn/text-retrieval

L@S 2017, April 20 - 21, 2017, Cambridge, MA, USA

© 2017 Copyright held by the owner/author(s). Publication rights licensed to ACM. ISBN 978-1-4503-4450-0/17/04. . . $15.00

DOI: http://dx.doi.org/10.1145/3051457.3054010

In this paper, we outline a system to provide actionable feedback to MOOC instructors by ranking automatically discovered topics in a MOOC according to a proposed difficulty measure. These topics are learned by ingesting lecture material transcripts, and thus they provide insight into the difficulty of course material at multiple levels of granularity (at the level of an entire week, a single video, or a single section of a single video). Providing such interpretable feedback about which topics presented in course material might be proving difficult for students can inform instructors in many ways, such as: assigning grades (i.e. how to curve grades), allowing the identification of students needing additional support, or persuading the instructor to re-configure the course's syllabus layout and redo problematic course material.

METHOD

The first step in the implementation of our method[2] is to discover the list of topics that are taught in a MOOC and how they are covered in the lectures. We do this by applying topic modeling algorithms to a document corpus consisting of the transcripts of the video lectures of the MOOC.

The second step is ranking the discovered topics by "perceived difficulty," which is measured based on the level of video activity corresponding to each topic. We use raw clickstream data from video watching sessions to discover the most watched video segments, and from the subtitle text we deduce what topics those "hot" video segments correspond to. Our hypothesis is that the "hotter" a video segment is, the more difficult the topic covered by that segment is. This matches the intuition that if a student encounters a video segment confusing for them or dealing with a difficult topic, the student would most likely pause, rewind, or seek to replay this segment repeatedly. This in turn generates many entries in the clickstream log for that segment.

Finally, we use direct student feedback data in the form of text files submitted by students where they describe what the most difficult topics or concepts were for each lecture in order to evaluate the rankings. The topic that is mentioned most in this data is assumed to be the most difficult. We can then compute the average overlap of the two lists to empirically evaluate how effective our model is at identifying the most difficult topics covered in a MOOC.

[2] Implementation source code can be found at https://github.com/assmaboughoula/difficult_topics.git

Topic	Word Distribution
0	can + user + use + right + item + two + one + see + similar + system + look
1	user + document + go + can + re + just + look + will + like + filter
2	document + model + can + vector + word + queri + use + probabl + also + space + like + t + need
3	document + queri + can + user + use + model + word + relev + now + also
4	document + word + model + queri + function + rank + can + probabl + one + retriev
5	rate + user + gener + one + language + movi + object + actual + crawl + assum
6	can + document + one + see + use + right + now + page + will + relev
7	document + use + page + now + user + queri + word + search + also + web
8	model + can + use + word + queri + user + system + document + look + right
9	function + word + will + now + valu + can + count + reduc + key + probabl
10	can + search + use + system + data + also + engine + file + queri + text
11	can + function + will + valu + probabl + document + data + now + also + word
12	probabl + model + wor + can + comput + see + use + go + page + will
13	can + document + queri + use + user + data + search + relev + also + word
14	document + queri + term + can + one + relev + match + use + score + now
15	document + user + word + relev + differ + can + term + model + use + now
16	can + document + word + score + see + now + term + weight + use + vector

Table 1. Topic Word Distributions from PLSA for Text Clustering

Topic Discovery

The document corpus for this project is created using the transcript text of all video lectures in the MOOC "Text Retrieval and Search Engines" offered on Coursera. Although the lectures in this MOOC are reasonably short, they each still tend to contain multiple topics. Since our long-term goal for this work is to be able to provide actionable feedback for the instructors and point them to possibly problematic or confusing video segments and difficult topics, we thus want to partition each lecture into "topically coherent segments" where each segment should be short enough so that it covers only one main topic, but long enough so that no segment is purely background noise. After some experimentation, we discovered that a segment containing text from one minute of lecture results in a fairly good, coherent document generally covering one topic. This rule is not necessarily ideal for all MOOCs due to its dependence on the lecturer's style and rate of speech, but would be a reasonable starting point to explore this new problem; more sophisticated, lecturer-independent, segmentation methods such as the one in [2] can be applied in the future.

After performing this segmentation, we have a corpus D consisting of N text documents. We want to automatically discover the topics that are discussed across these N documents. A natural way to accomplish this is by applying a generative topic model such as PLSA [3], which models each document $d_i \in D$ as being generated from a K-component mixture model. To generate each word $d_{i,j}$ in a given document d_i, a "label" $z_{i,j}$ is sampled from the document-specific mixing distribution π_i. This label is then used to select one of the K components of the mixture model from which to generate the word $d_{i,j}$. Each of these components, θ_k, is a multinomial distribution over words. Thus, if we infer the parameters of a topic model like PLSA on a corpus D, we will obtain $\Theta = \{\theta_1^K\}$ which describe the latent topics discussed across the corpus (which are shared between all of the documents), and $\Pi = \{\pi_1^N\}$ which describe the coverage of each of the K topics in each document individually.

However, one problem with this approach for our scenario is that its generative process is too flexible—each word $d_{i,j}$ is allowed to be generated by *any* of the K topics. This is inconsistent with our deisre to have "topic coherent" documents that each cover precisely one topic. To remedy this issue, we instead use the Probabilistic Mixture Clustering Model[5] which is conceptually similar to PLSA, but instead requires that every word within a document d_i be generated from *the same* topic distribution. In other words, the "label" is sampled *once per document* instead of *once per word*. Thus in this model, the likelihood function will translate to

$$p(D \mid \Pi, \Theta) = \prod_{i=1}^{N} \sum_{k=1}^{K} p(z_i = k \mid \pi_i) p(d_i \mid \theta_k) \quad (1)$$

where

$$p(d_i \mid \theta_k) = \prod_{j=1}^{|d_i|} p(d_{i,j} \mid \theta_k). \quad (2)$$

The log-likelihood function is then

$$\log p(D \mid \Pi, \Theta) =$$

$$\sum_{i=1}^{N} \log \left(\sum_{k=1}^{K} p(z_i = k \mid \pi_i) \times \prod_{j=1}^{\|d_i\|} p(d_{i,j} \mid \theta_k) \right) \quad (3)$$

which is maximized via the use of the EM algorithm [1].

Table 1 displays the topic word distributions obtained when fitting this clustering model to our transcript dataset to discover topics. The table displays the 10 most probable words for each of the 17 discovered topics. We can judge the quality of the topic modeling since some topic word distributions in the tables have a clear title or topic name, for example: topic number 2 from the table can have the title "Vector Space Model," while topic number 12 may be "Probabilistic Modeling." Such phrase labels can be automatically generated to facilitate interpretation by the instructor (e.g., by using methods proposed in [5]).

Measure of Topic Difficulty

Given a corpus of D documents, a K-topic probabilistic clustering model produces a $D \times K$ "topic coverage" matrix π, where each entry $\pi_{i,k}$ indicates the probability that document i belongs to topic k. We can then combine this with the calculated activity level (or "heat") for all documents/video segments H to compute the perceived difficulty of a topic k. Specifically, we model the difficulty of a topic k with a binary random variable δ_k where 1 indicates a difficult topic and 0 indicates otherwise. The perceived difficulty of a topic is then the probability that δ_k takes value 1, which can be computed as the Euclidean norm of the fraction of video activity attributed to topic k:

$$p(\delta_k = 1 \mid k, H) \approx \frac{\sum_{i=1}^{N} H_i \times \pi_{i,k}}{\sqrt{\sum_{i=1}^{N} H_i^2} \times \sqrt{\sum_{i=1}^{N} \pi_{i,k}^2}} \quad (4)$$

The "Heatmap" matrix H is calculated by summing up all click events of types: "play," "pause," "rate change" (when the user changes the speed at which the video is played) and "seek" (when the user jumps to a specific location in the video) for each video segment and then normalizing by the number of students watching the video. Since the number of students fluctuates throughout the course and since the majority of students who register for the course drop-out after the first week of class, neglecting to normalize by the number of students will skew our ranking function in favor of topics covered in the first week of class. Table 2 displays the resulting rankings of the discovered topics.

EVALUATION

As an approximation of the ground truth of difficult topics in this MOOC, We use the submitted difficult topics by the students in a course offered at UIUC in Spring 2016 that used as its primary material this MOOC's lecture videos. For the duration of the course, the students were required to write a sentence that described the most difficult concept in each week's lectures. We aggregated all the student submissions of difficult concepts to obtain a long text document, from

Topic	P(Diff=1| Topic,H)
0	0.0595
1	0.0583
2	0.0576
3	0.0564
4	0.0506
12	0.0469
6	0.04669
16	0.04667
15	0.04664
11	0.0465
9	0.0463
13	0.0461
8	0.0458
14	0.0456
5	0.0453
10	0.0452
7	0.0437

Table 2. Difficulty Rankings from Video Activity

which we further compute a word distribution (a word profile of difficult topics, denoted by θ_Q) by normalizing the counts of all the words (a word in many student submissions would tend to have a higher probability, indicating that it is more likely part of a difficult concept). Given any set of topics $\{\theta_i\}$ discovered using our probabilistic clustering model, which are each themselves word distributions, we can compute the similarity between each topic word distribution θ_i and θ_Q; the similarity function we used is negative KL-divergence $D(\theta_Q \| \theta_i)$. Intuitively, the more similar a topic is to θ_Q, the more likely the topic is difficult. Thus the ranked list of these topics based on their similarity to θ_Q can be regarded as our "ideal" ranked list reflecting which topics are difficult (a highly ranked topic is more likely difficult).

To evaluate the effectiveness of the proposed measure of topic difficulty, we can then compare the ranking of the topics using our measure (shown in Table 2) with the ideal ranking generated using the submitted difficult concepts submitted by the students (shown in Table 3) by calculating the average size of intersections between sets of items in each list at each subsequent depth k in the lists. Let $T_H(k)$ be the set of top k topics in the ranking based on video activity, and let $T_{SV}(k)$ be the set of top k topics in the ranking based on student votes. If we have K total topics, then we calculate this similarity measure between the lists as

$$VID = \frac{\sum_{k=1}^{K} \frac{\{T_H(k)\} \cap \{T_{SV}(k)\}}{k}}{K}. \quad (5)$$

The maximum value for this similarity measure is 1 when the two ordered lists match perfectly. For the topic ranking we calculated using video activity as a difficulty measure, the above similarity measure is

$$VID = 0.636$$

We should take into account that the student voting data we used as the golden standard here should be taken with a grain of salt; students might not spend so much time thinking about

Topic	log P(Q| Topic,SV)
0	-61278
6	-81255
12	-87971
2	-90890
3	-106296
11	-123739
7	-126338
8	-126512
14	-160040
4	-162433
15	-168706
9	-177707
5	-188600
1	-201131
13	-223962
10	-237699
16	-242295

Table 3. Difficulty Rankings from Student Votes

what topics were difficult, for example they might merely put down whatever topic is freshest in their minds at the moment simply to complete the assignment that day. On the other hand, if students submit carefully thought-out votes, the voting data will give us a good subjective measure for difficulty from each student's perspective which can prove useful for future directions. Another possible standard for topic difficulty might be quiz grades. We will explore using quiz grades as an evaluation method in our future work.

CONCLUSION AND FUTURE WORK

In this work, we studied how to provide actionable feedback to instructors in MOOCs in the form of a topic ranking by difficulty. Our hypothesis is that topic difficulty is reflected by the activity level in lecture video segments that deal with the topic. We designed a measure of topic difficulty based on our hypothesis to automatically rank topics discovered using a probabilistic model. We leveraged the submitted difficult concepts by students as gold standard to evaluate the accuracy of the ranking produced using the proposed measure. The results are encouraging and support our hypothesis, suggesting the great potential for using the proposed method to develop a practically useful system to help instructors obtain useful real-time feedback about topic difficulty.

Our work is a preliminary step in studying the new problem of automated discovery of difficult topics from MOOC data, and can be further improved in multiple ways. First, the topic discovery can be further improved by using more intelligent topic segmentation algorithms and analyzing any additional content of course materials that might be available (e.g., syllabus, textbook). Second, while we have shown that video activity data provides useful signals about topic difficulty, we can potentially further improve the measure of topic difficulty by exploiting other data such as forum data, assignment data, quiz data. (However, we should note that using video activity data would generally allow us to detect difficult topics earlier than using other data, especially quiz data, which may sometimes be advantageous from application perspective.) Third,

we can explore the evolution of difficult topics in a MOOC series. Since We expect topics in a "specialization" course series to be closely related and dependent on one another, it would be interesting to see how difficult topics discovered in an earlier course can help us predict difficult topics in subsequent courses. One MOOC series we may look at is Coursera's Data Mining Specialization, the first course of which is Text Retrieval and Search Engines which we used for this project. Finally, another interesting future direction is to personalize our results and give tailored feedback to each student. Difficulty is a subjective concept; one student might find topic T to be very difficult while another student with a different background might find it easy. Personalized difficult topic discovery can be achieved by, e.g., ranking topics using only video activity and other data from one student.

ACKNOWLEDGMENTS

We thank Dr. Maryalice Wu for granting us access to the MOOC data. This material is based upon work supported by the NSF under Grant Number DGE-1144245 (GRFP) and Grant Number 1629161.

REFERENCES

1. A. P. Dempster, N. M. Laird, and D. B. Rudin. 1977. Maximum Likelihood from Incomplete Data via the EM Algorithm. *Journal of the Royal Statistical Society, Series B* 39, 1 (1977), 1–38.

2. J. Eisenstein and R. Brazilay. 2008. Bayesian Unsupervised Topic Segmentation. In *EMNLP SIGDAT*. 334–343.

3. T. Hoffman. 1999. Probabilistic Latent Semantic Indexing. In *SIGIR*. 50–57.

4. Shaohua Li, Tat-Seng Chua, Jun Zhu, and Chunyan Miao. 2016. Generative Topic Embedding: a Continuous Representation of Documents. In *Proceedings of the 54th Annual Meeting of the Association for Computational Linguistics*. 666–675.

5. Qiaozhu Mei, Xuehua Shen, and ChengXiang Zhai. 2007. Automatic Labeling of Multinomial Topic Models. In *Proceedings of the 13th ACM SIGKDD International Conference on Knowledge Discovery and Data Mining (KDD '07)*. ACM, New York, NY, USA, 490–499. DOI: http://dx.doi.org/10.1145/1281192.1281246

6. Hemant Misra, Fracnois Yvon, Joemon M. Jose, and Olivier Cappe. 2009. Text Segmentation via Topic Modeling: An Analytical Study. In *Proceedings of the 18th ACM conference on Information and knowledge management*. 1553–1556.

7. Kamal Nigam, Andrew K. McCallum, Sebastian Thrun, and Tom Mitchell. 2000. Text Classification from Labeled and Unlabeled Documents Using EM. *Machine Learning* 39 (2000), 103–134.

Congruency, Adaptivity, Modularity, and Personalization: Four Experiments in Teaching Introduction to Computing

David A. Joyner
Georgia Institute of Technology
Atlanta, Georgia, USA
david.joyner@gatech.edu

ABSTRACT

In January 2017, Georgia Tech launched a new online section of its CS1301: Introduction to Computing class. The course, offered both as a for-credit course to on-ground students and as an open MOOC, built on four unique design principles: congruency, adaptivity, modularity, and personalization. In this short paper, we describe the background of the course, the definitions of these design principles, and their application to the course design.

Author Keywords

Computing education, personalized learning, MOOCs.

ACM Classification Keywords

• Social and professional topics~CS1 • Applied computing~Computer-managed instruction

INTRODUCTION

The internet is replete with places to learn computer science and computer programming. There are dozens of open textbooks, MOOCs, YouTube tutorials, interactive development environments, and more. A few months ago, Georgia Tech set about creating its own online Introduction to Computing course, and one of our first questions was: what is going to make this course different? The last thing the world needs is *another* online computing course, but are there needs that are not fulfilled by the courses that are currently out there?

In researching how to address this, we uncovered several places where a new course could distinguish itself. Some of these are largely administrative: like many MOOCs, this new online course is custom-built to take advantage of the options presented by the internet, but yet we are experimenting with offering it to on-ground residential students. It will also ultimately be offered as a publicly-accessible MOOC with Georgia Tech credit attached: any "students who successfully demonstrate mastery will earn a

statement that may be recognized for credit if they later apply and are admitted to Georgia Tech" [2].

In addition to attaching credit to the course, however, we observed a number of experimental principles to leverage in the development of this course. Two of these, congruency and adaptivity, aim at creating a more complete pedagogical experience. These principles aim to inform a design for presenting content in multiple complementary mediums that adapt the learning experience to the student's current level of ability. The other two, modularity and personalization, inform a foundation for this course that preserves the potential to expand in new and innovative ways to encompass other programming languages and domains for application.

In this paper, we present the four principles that informed the design of this experimental Introduction to Computing course. It is important to emphasize that this course is very much a work in progress: it launched one week prior to this paper's submission deadline, and we are currently gathering enormous quantities of data to establish the usefulness and success of these principles and this course as a whole.

COURSE BACKGROUND

This Georgia Tech Introduction to Computing course is an online version of the school's foundational CS1301 course, which has no prerequisites for prior computing experience. Its designer and instructor (and this paper's author) is an award-winning instructor in Georgia Tech's online Master of Science in Computer Science (OMSCS) program, having taught and conducted research in it for two years [4]. The course features four primary technological components: the video course on edX, an adaptive textbook (authored by the instructor and built with McGraw-Hill Education), an automated evaluator for code (provided by Vocareum), and a digital proctoring service (Proctortrack, from Verificient).

The edX course is the central home of the course. The course is organized on the edX platform into nineteen chapters, each with an average of seven lessons. Each lesson is comprised of a handful of short videos (1 to 5 minutes), between which are interspersed interactive exercises (multiple choice and fill-in-the-blank). These exercises are graded for completion, and students have unlimited attempts to achieve the right answer; every wrong answer has dedicated feedback associated with it. Each chapter concludes with an additional page of suggested resources for further reading. The majority of chapters also

L@S 2017, April 20 - 21, 2017, Cambridge, MA, USA
Copyright is held by the owner/author(s). Publication rights licensed to ACM.
ACM 978-1-4503-4450-0/17/04...$15.00
DOI: http://dx.doi.org/10.1145/3051457.3054011

have an associated problem set, where students complete additional exercises but with a more limited number of chances per exercise (typically two). All of these are immediately and automatically evaluated.

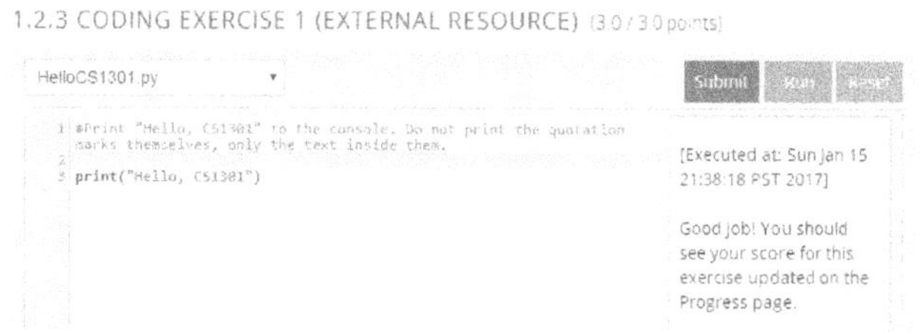

Figure 1: An example of a simple Vocareum coding widget. Here, the code window is on the left, and the window on the right shows the results of the student's submission. Students may also run the code on the left directly.

In addition to these multiple choice and fill-in-the-blank exercises, there are also programming exercises interspersed between the videos. These programming exercises all come with an embedded in-browser lightweight development environment, allowing students to write and run code directly in their browser. These exercises can be run against an instant auto-grader, which tests the code against a number of test cases and returns the result. These programming exercises are both interspersed in the chapters and included in the problem sets, with unlimited submissions in both locations. Additionally, each lesson concludes with a sandbox development environment featuring all the code shown in the lesson to allow students to easily jump in and experiment with the code featured in the videos. Exams are digitally proctored by Verificient's Proctortrack, but are comprised of the same kinds of exercises seen in the main course material, including multiple choice, fill-in-the-blank, and programming.

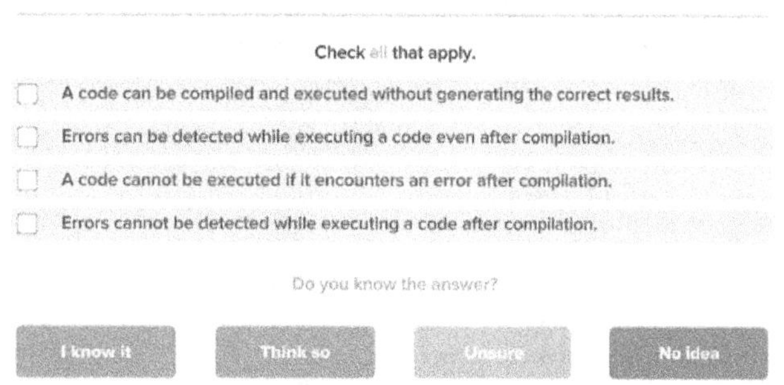

Figure 2: An example exercise from the adaptive textbook.

In parallel to this course is an adaptive textbook written by the course instructor and published on McGraw-Hill Education's SmartBook platform. As part of this SmartBook, McGraw-Hill Education has authored over a thousand exercises. Students complete these exercises as part of their completion of the edX course material. The next section contains significantly more information about the adaptive textbook, and an example exercise is shown in Figure 2.

Thus, a student's experience in the course is that each week, they complete one or two chapters and a problem set. In completing the chapters, they watch a series of short videos, most of which have exercises (multiple choice, fill-in-the-blank, or programming) interspersed at a rate of approximately an exercise per three minutes of video, and complete a series of exercises provided by the SmartBook. In completing the problem sets and exams, they complete similar sets of multiple choice, fill-in-the-blank, and programming exercises, with the added constraints of fewer attempts or digital proctoring.

CONGRUENCY

The first guiding principle behind the design of our Introduction to Computing course we dub "congruency". Congruency refers to a congruent structure between multiple presentations of the same course material. The principle of congruency comes from a lesson learned in Georgia Tech's OMSCS program. The program is built around several video-centric MOOCs, and students have repeatedly reported that while the production values and instruction in the videos are excellent, videos themselves are difficult to study. Searching, perusal, and rapid repetition are all unnatural interactions to have with a video compared to a textbook. To resolve this inadequacy, students have reflected on the value of transcripts, and a couple classes have gone so far as to share the course scripts or transcripts in a more textbook-like format that students can use to more easily seek the target material.

In many ways, this observation is consistent with a residential experience. Instructors assign class readings that overlap with lecture material because it allows the same material to be presented in two different ways. However, oftentimes mentally mapping the lecture material to the reading material requires expert-level knowledge in the first place.

This is where our principle of congruency comes in. As noted, the course is made of two primary sources of material: a video-based course on edX and an adaptive textbook on McGraw-Hill's SmartBook platform. These two sources of material, however, are congruent in their content, structure, and examples. They organize the content in the same way, use the same examples, and show the same visuals. Each chapter of the course contains a dedicated widget to launch the corresponding chapter of the SmartBook.

The goal is to facilitate easy alteration in the medium from which students choose to consume content. We hypothesize that students will generally choose to initially consume the material from the video-based course, but will use the textbook to recap the material later, take a deeper dive into some of the course material, and more slowly move through material they find confusing.

Complete data is recorded on students' interaction with both the video course and the adaptive textbook. This data will be used to create profiles of students' interaction patterns and connect those patterns with learning outcomes.

ADAPTIVITY

Adaptivity is not a particularly new idea in computer-assisted instruction; the general area of intelligent tutoring systems has built on computer-aided adaptivity for decades [e.g. 1, 6], and efforts are already under way to extend such features to online education [e.g. 3]. However, most similar efforts focus on adaptivity specifically within a practice environment with dedicated feedback. This experiment in teaching Introduction to Computing aims to instead integrate adaptivity into the instructional process.

This is achieved in two ways. First, as noted, the course and adaptive textbook are tightly integrated, and the adaptivity in the textbook comes from a collection of several dozen exercises for each chapter. These exercises are each tied to a learning objective present in the textbook, and as students complete these exercises, the platform constructs a model of students' mastery of those learning objectives. When students answer incorrectly to a particular exercise, they receive feedback from the textbook on the correct answer; however, they will then later be re-tested on the same learning objective using a different question to ensure they are developing their understanding of the material rather than simply recalling answers they have already seen.

Students' experiences within the textbook then change based on their current level of mastery of the objectives as communicated via the exercises. If a student continues to struggle with a certain learning objective's exercises, the textbook directs the student to the area of the book that covers that material. The congruency described previously also allows students to then jump to the identical corresponding area in the course videos, which are also launched from within the textbook. Additionally, whenever a student peruses the textbook, the adaptive platform applies a visualization on top of the text calling students' attention to the areas in which they have already demonstrated mastery in the exercises, as well as the areas in which they have struggled or not yet demonstrated mastery. In this way, the textbook experience adapts to students' current level of ability.

Similarly, the exercises integrated into the edX course facilitate some adaptivity as well. Each exercise is constructed with dedicated feedback on anticipated wrong answers. While this boils down to a straightforward mapping between answers and feedback in multiple-choice and fill-in-the-blank questions, the programming exercises allow additional adaptivity. Each programming exercise is itself evaluated by a Python script that can examine both the output of students' code and the code itself, allowing a complex tutoring system to be built that evaluates code style, efficiency, and function, along with providing dedicated feedback based on anticipated incorrect answers. In its initial incarnation, the feedback supplied by this system is largely implicit (such as providing students

desired output to compare to their code's actual output), but as a library of past student answers and mistakes accrues, detailed feedback will be developed based on the most common patterns of errors.

MODULARITY

The third guiding principle of the course's design is potentially controversial. Modularity in this context refers to a modularity between three general topic areas in computer science: foundational concepts, language fluency, and domain applications. Each video of the course falls into one of the three categories. Foundational lessons do not use any particular language's code; they focus on more abstract concepts. Language lessons then take those concepts and concretize them in code with actual syntax and execution. Domain lessons then take those principles (and sometimes that language) and apply them to a particular application domain, like computer graphics, data science, or robotics.

There have been unsuccessful efforts in the past that attempted to teach foundational concepts separate from instructing their application in a particular language. These have been unsuccessful due to the observation that understanding of core concepts is tightly tied initially to the syntax in which they are written; higher-level understanding comes with practice *with* that syntax, not from learning the concept prior to that syntax. We hypothesize, however, that our effort will be more successful because of a specific affordance of the online medium: whereas some efforts have split foundational concepts and language fluency into long, entirely different lectures, we instead rapidly switch between them. Five minutes of foundational material will be followed by five minutes of implementation of those concepts in a particular language before switching back to foundational concepts. We posit that this mirrors the way the subject matter is actually taught, and the online medium simply affords us the ability to concretely but rapidly switch back and forth between areas.

There are two goals of this modularity. First, it aims to equip students with an understanding of the fundamentals of computer science in addition to fluency with a particular programming language. Second, while we believe that this modularity will present a valuable way of learning computer science on its own, modularity is also a means to an end. Specifically, the plans for the course's personalization are derived from this modularity.

PERSONALIZATION

In its initial state, the course teaches Introduction to Computing in Python with computer graphics as its domain of application. However, the modular design of the course is with a strong eye toward individualization. Modularity in this sense is intended to allow for easy substitutions within the different areas of the course such that an experience may be constructed that is personalized to the learner's own interests.

In the near-term, the major application of this is expected to be in the domain material. The initial deployment of the course emphasizes computer graphics as its domain, but the advantage of the online environment is its potential to create an experience that allows students to choose their own learning path. Toward this end, additional domain modules are planned focusing on other topics, including robotics, data science, and artificial intelligence. Given that the class is often taken by students majoring in topics like engineering, science, business, and arts, additional modules are planned that focus on those topics. The hope is that while the course launches as an "Introduction to Computing", these domain options will allow for dynamically personalized courses like "Introduction to Computing for Accountants" and "Introduction to Computing for Musicians."

A second phase of personalization comes from the modularity of the language component. By separating out the foundational concepts from the language component of the course, the entire course could be redeployed in a different language by replacing only ~50% of the content rather than 100%, and much of that content demands only a syntax translation rather than a wholesale rewrite. Comparable Introduction to Computing classes are often taught in Java, Matlab, and C++, and ongoing trends suggest there may arise a demand for Introduction to Computing in Swift, Ruby, or JavaScript. Domain material could complement those as well, especially with popular JavaScript frameworks. Thus, with far less work than creating an all-new course, this Introduction to Computing could become "Introduction to Computing for Engineers in Matlab" or "Introduction to Computing for Graphic Designers in Swift."

Finally, an ideal third phase of personalization may come from the options to select instructors and spoken languages. To increase inclusivity, this drive for personalization may allow students to select an instructor based on the desired gender and race from which they would like to learn. This approach will allow us to showcase the diversity of individuals finding success in the computing field, thus letting students select an instructor who will most personally resonate with them [5]. Similarly, by translating the course into other languages, we hope to extend its availability to students around the world.

CONCLUSION: TO BE CONTINUED...
This Introduction to Computing course is an experiment in a number of different ways. First, the four principles outlined here that have guided the structure of the course are themselves experiments. We may discover that students do not leverage the congruency between presentation styles at all, or that the modularity confuses students more than it supports them.

The course represents an experiment in other ways as well. At the most general level, it is an experiment to see if an online course can succeed for a residential audience. It is similarly an experiment to see if the principles and expertise cultivated in a Master's program with at-a-distance students translate to an undergraduate program with residential students. Other experiments include whether or not access to a live development environment during test-taking enhances learning outcomes and whether or not an online course draws a different type of student compared to residential classes even from the same student body. Every element of this course is set up to learn, improve, and iterate through experiments like these.

ACKNOWLEDGMENTS
We are grateful to our partners in developing this course: Georgia Tech's College of Computing (especially but not limited to Zvi Galil, Charles Isbell, Melinda McDaniel, and Bill Leahy), Georgia Tech's Center for 21st Century Universities (especially but not limited to Pam Buffington, Jo Keith, Rob Kadel, Amanda Madden, and Rich DeMillo), Georgia Tech Professional Education (especially but not limited to Yakut Gazi, Shabana Figueroa, Brian Wilson, Stephen Murphy, Brian Armstrong, Aqueelah Sabir, and Nelson Baker), McGraw-Hill Education (especially but not limited to Tom Hinkley, Cal Alford, Jenny Bartell, Amber Cortez, Stephanie Wilson, and David Levin), edX, and Vocareum. We are also grateful to the teaching assistants authoring some content and helping run the first offering of the class: Marguerite Murrell, Joshua Diaddigo, and Jackie Elliott, Rachel Golding, and Christine Feng.

REFERENCES
1. Anderson, J. R., Boyle, C. F., & Reiser, B. J. (1985). Intelligent tutoring systems. *Science*, *228*(4698), 456-462.

2. Georgia Tech. (2016). Taking Undergraduate Computer Science Online. Retrieved from http://www.cc.gatech.edu/news/583367/taking-undergraduate-computer-science-online

3. Heffernan, N. T., & Heffernan, C. L. (2014). The ASSISTments ecosystem: building a platform that brings scientists and teachers together for minimally invasive research on human learning and teaching. *International Journal of Artificial Intelligence in Education*, *24*(4), 470-497.

4. Joyner, D. A., Goel, A. K., & Isbell, C. (2016, April). The Unexpected Pedagogical Benefits of Making Higher Education Accessible. In *Proceedings of the Third (2016) ACM Conference on Learning @ Scale* (pp. 117-120). ACM.

5. Kizilcec, R. F., Saltarelli, A. J., Reich, J., & Cohen, G. L. (2017). Closing global achievement gaps in MOOCs. *Science*, *355*(6322), 251-252.

6. VanLehn, K. (2011). The relative effectiveness of human tutoring, intelligent tutoring systems, and other tutoring systems. *Educational Psychologist*, *46*(4), 197-221.

Mobilizing the Crowd to Create
an Open Repository of Research Talks

Rajan Vaish
Stanford University
rvaish@cs.stanford.edu

Sharad Goel
Stanford University
scgoel@stanford.edu

Amin Saberi
Stanford University
saberi@stanford.edu

ABSTRACT

While most existing research knowledge is distributed in the form of papers, there has been a shift towards learning and consuming information through video. Limited time and resources, however, prevent individual researchers from making their work available in this format. Crowdsourcing this task is a promising alternative, but it requires solving complex coordination and collaborative video production problems. In this paper, we propose an end-to-end solution to crowdsource the creation of research videos. To assist coordination, we designed a structured workflow that enables efficient delegation of tasks, while also providing collaborative learning environment to the crowd for motivation. To facilitate video production, we developed an online system through which groups can make micro audio recordings that are automatically stitched together to create a complete talk. We tested this approach with a group of volunteers recruited from 24 countries through an open call. This distributed crowd produced five video talks based on the best paper winners and nominees from WWW 2016. Evaluations from the authors of the papers and outside reviewers rated the talks "very good" (giving a median score of 4 out of 5). We further applied this method to translate these talks and produce 11 additional videos in Spanish, Romanian, and Catalan. These results suggest that our crowdsourcing approach has the potential to significantly increase learning and the accessibility of the scientific knowledge.

Author Keywords

Crowdsourcing; online creative collaboration; peer video production; scientific knowledge/learning at scale.

INTRODUCTION

At present, most scholarly material is available only in the form of text, as books and papers. There is growing demand for learning and consuming scientific information through video [3], as evidenced by the popularity of efforts such as "Two Minute Papers" and "Papers We Love". Researchers and other individuals, however, typically lack the time and resources to create such content at scale, impeding the dissemination of academic knowledge.

L@S 2017, April 20-21, 2017, Cambridge, MA, USA

© 2017 ACM. ISBN 978-1-4503-4450-0/17/04. . . $15.00

DOI: http://dx.doi.org/10.1145/3051457.3054012

In this paper, we present an approach for creating an open repository of research talks that are developed collaboratively by volunteers around the world. The initial research videos are produced by distributed teams of individuals working in close collaboration; these videos can subsequently be edited and improved by any interested participant. With this effort, which we call the Stanford Scholar Initiative [1], we aim to make research more readily accessible and engaging, while also providing a collaborative learning environment to the participating contributors for motivation.

Crowdsourcing such an open-ended expert task poses two key challenges. First, we must facilitate extended and complex coordination between large groups of individuals of varying expertise. Second, we need to develop tools for groups to collaboratively produce editable videos. We address the first challenge by designing a scaffolding process to coordinate volunteers. Specifically, we divide the talk creation process into two phases: (1) converting a paper into a *slide deck* that includes both the talk slides and a slide-by-slide written transcript of the talk; and (2) transitioning the slide deck to a video talk. To address the second challenge, we created an online system, called "Audio Studio", where people can seamlessly create audio recordings for individual slides. These micro-contributions are then algorithmically stitched together to produce a complete video talk. This approach supports efficient editing, both during and after the initial video is created, requiring only audio segments to be recorded at a given time.

To test our process and the system, we issued an open call in the summer of 2016, attracting more than 200 people from 24 countries. This crowd of volunteers created 10-minute talks based on five papers that were winners or nominees for the best paper award at WWW 2016 [2]. These talks were entirely created by the crowd, from designing the structure to video production. To evaluate the talks, we solicited 97 responses from outside reviewers and 11 authors of the presented papers. The talks were typically rated "very good" and "very useful", receiving a median score of 4 out of 5 on both dimensions. To expand the reach of these talks, we applied our approach to translate them and created 11 additional videos in Spanish, Romanian and Catalan languages.

Our work points to the potential for scaleable creation and dissemination of video-based research content. Though still in its early stages, we hope that the Stanford Scholar Initiative will help bring academic knowledge to broader audiences and encourage aspiring researchers to pursue STEM education.

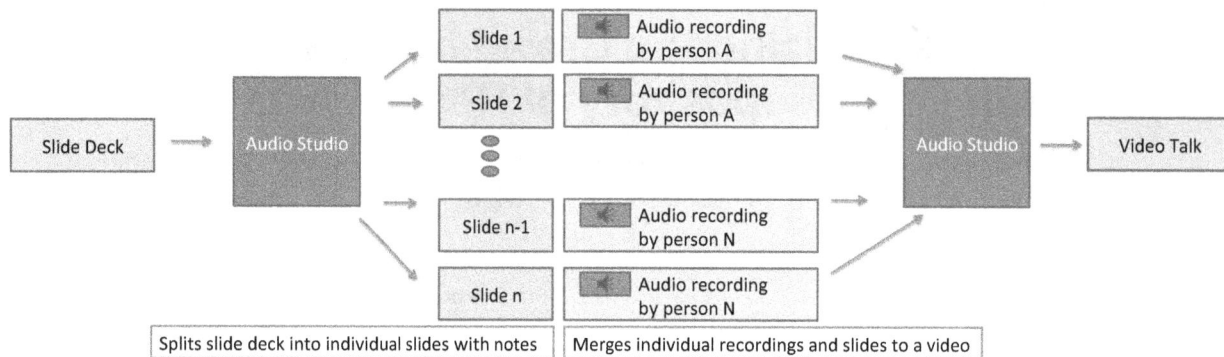

Figure 1. Workflow of the Audio Studio — a tool that lets anyone make micro contributions in the form of audio recording per slide, that are then stitched to create a complete video.

THE PROCESS AND THE SYSTEM

We propose a solution that divides the collaborative video production process into two phases: the 1st phase includes converting a paper to a slide deck, while the 2nd phase includes transitioning from a slide deck to a video talk.

Phase 1: Research Paper to Slide Deck — Coordination for Creating the Talk's Content

Step 1: Dynamic Team Creation and Onboarding
After an open call is made worldwide through different social media and online platforms, participants are onboarded on Slack to form teams on the basis of their interest in research topics and papers.

To facilitate onboarding and phased entry of new participants, we provide access to the "Getting Started" documentation, "Progress Log", and share instructions about the workflow, best practices, deadlines and ask to read and understand the paper. Overall, the team members play either of the two roles:

1. **DRIs (directly responsible individuals)**: Two or three topic experts from the crowd are chosen to make critical decisions, and to maintain the direction of the talk. They also verify the content, and help with logistical aspects, such as maintaining timeline and onboarding more members [4, 5].

2. **Crowd members**: Rest of the members.

Step 2: Learning and Designing the Talk Structure
Crowd members read and learn about the research topics from the paper, in a collaborative setup, and contribute towards the design of the talk structure. Through a series of divergence and convergence of ideas and transition proposals, the structure of the talk is evolved and synthesized by the DRIs.

Step 3: Creating Talk's Content in Slide Deck
After the structure is discussed and defined, crowd members and the DRIs self-organize and coordinate freely. To facilitate collaboration, we rely on Slack for communication and Google Drive/Slides for content creation. Though the crowd is free to collaborate in anyway they wish, their exploration and contribution follows the guidelines for *duration* (short 5-10 minute long talks), *target audience* (people who have minimal

familiarity for a given research topic), *collaboration* (anyone can edit/improve anyone's work), *script* (talk's narration to be used for audio recording), *timeline* (to maintain the momentum) and *credit distribution* (for positive reinforcement).

DRIs help facilitate the entire logistical effort during course content creation — logging contributions, updating progress and remaining time, and helping onboard new members that want to contribute.

Step 4: Iterative Peer-Review for Quality
Before a slide deck is converted into a video, each of them is reviewed by all the other active teams iteratively until every feedback has been addressed. As each talk was created by multiple crowd members of the team, their individual styles can bring inconsistency across the presentation. The review process helps with validating the quality, structure, and consistency of the talks. The iterative design allows the crowd to gather feedback in multiple rounds and improve accordingly.

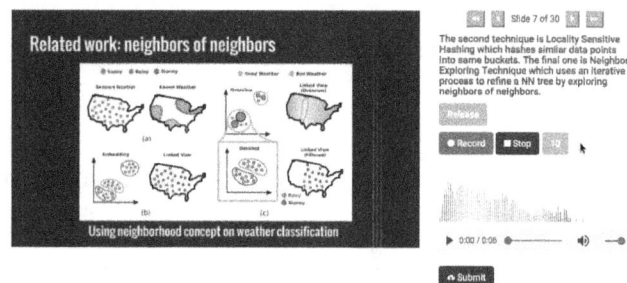

Figure 2. Audio Studio's audio recording interface, with slide and script next to each other. Narrator reads off from the script and can replay multiple times before submitting.

Phase 2: Slide Deck to Video — "Audio Studio" for Collaborative Audio Recording and Video Production

Once the slide deck for the talk is ready, we move to video production. Unlike collaboration on and editing text, editable video production is extremely challenging. Current state of the art text-to-speech systems (e.g. Google Deepmind's WaveNet) are not yet advanced to produce human-like natural audio.

Therefore, beyond creating the slide decks, crowd is also involved in this phase.

Traditionally, creating a video requires several retakes, until the complete recording is flawless. A recording mistake made around the end of the narration can cause one to re-record it. To overcome these limitations, we designed and developed "Audio Studio" — an online tool, where people can make micro contributions and seamlessly record audio per slide, that are then stitched to create a complete video. As shown in Figure 1, the workflow of the Audio Studio can be divided into three steps:

Step 1: Splitting the Slide Deck into Slides and Scripts
Audio Studio is designed to minimize per person contribution, minimize retake time, and to make re-recording and improving the video easier — by anyone, even if they were not involved in slide deck creation. This is possible when the entire slide deck is split into individual slides. Upon uploading a Google slide, Audio Studio, extracts and generates individual slides, along with their respective narrative script.

Step 2: Iterative Audio Recording as Microtasks
As shown in Figure 2, any person can self-assign a particular slide to themselves, and record the audio per slide by reading off the narrative script next to it. They can re-play recorded audio, iterate and re-record until satisfied, then submit. To maintain rich experience, we limit each talk's recording to a maximum of two people.

Step 3: Merges Recordings and Slides to a Complete Video
After the audio recording is received for all the slides in the slide deck, a complete video is generated, ready for download. Additionally, if the talk requires specific slide based improvement or editing, crowd members can re-record audio for a given slide, and a new video can be re-generated. Thereby, making video editing easier. Through our approach, content creation and video development are essentially separated, helping the crowd to focus on the content and creativity.

STANFORD SCHOLAR INITIATIVE
Stanford Scholar Initiative [1] is our early setup for an open repository of research video talks, aimed to address the recent shift in learning preferences for videos scalably and efficiently.

Real World Setup and Demographics
To put our process and system to test, we made an open call for volunteers, which resulted in 215 sign ups from 24 countries with the majority from United States and India. From these volunteers, 178 joined our Slack team for collaboration and 46 actively contributed to the development of the talks. Of the 46, 67.3% were undergraduate students, 13.2% were high school students and 19.5% were graduate students with a major in computer sciences and engineering. The average age of the participants was 21.8 years.

About 23.9% of the participants had never given a talk before, while 28.2% had given a non-research talk, and 36.9% had an experience of giving a research talk. Finally, the participants rated their own topical expertise. The mean was 3.15, on a Likert scale of 5, with 5 being an expert.

Outcome and Participation
Our field deployment lasted for three weeks, where 46 active people helped create five research talks based on the five papers nominated for the best paper and best student paper awards at WWW 2016 [2]. Together, these participants exchanged over 7,500 messages, made a total of about 6,000 edits and created five short videos with an average duration of 8.53 minutes. After the production of these talks, we facilitated an effort to "fork" existing assets of a slide deck, including individual slides and scripts to create the videos in other languages — producing additional 11 videos in Spanish, Romanian and Catalan. These videos were uploaded on YouTube [1] and have attracted over 700 views so far.

Collaboration Activity for Creating Talks
For collaboration and content creation, participants utilized Google Drive where they made a total of 889 edits while designing the talk structure, and 5,116 edits while working on the slide deck.

Communication Activity and Engagement
A campaign's success highly depends on the continued participation by its members in multiple capacities. On average, more than 300 messages were exchanged via Slack everyday. On any given day, an average of 24 people were communicating via Slack, while 49 people were reading or observing.

Audio Studio for Audio Recording
The process of audio recording started with an audio audition, where participants recorded a 30 second introduction of themselves. By a popular vote, nine of them were selected, who helped record audio for 110 individual slides, producing a total of 42.6 minutes of recording.

EVALUATION AND FINDINGS
We ran three studies to assess the effectiveness of our process and system to produce high quality talks. These studies were conducted via online surveys, and targeted the following:

- Authors of the Paper: We reached out to the authors of the papers based on which the five talks were created. Being subject matter experts and having given a talk earlier at WWW 2016, their feedback provided valuable insight and assessment of the quality of crowd-generated talks. Of the total 21 coauthors, 11 responded including the first authors of all the five papers.

- Outside Evaluator/Audience: The talks were created for anyone with an interest or familiarity in the topic of the paper can make use of it. We reached out to members of our Stanford Scholar community and outside, who were not involved in the talk creation. We got a total of 97 responses.

- Talk creators/Participants: Beyond assessing the quality of the talk, it was important for us to understand the effectiveness of the process, experience and the system we built for the volunteers. Therefore, we reached out to our crowd participants and collected 20 responses.

Quality, Usefulness and Learning
Here are our findings about the quality of the outcome — by the authors and the outside evaluators.

Authors find the talks to be high quality.
On the Likert scale of 1 to 5, with 5 being "excellent" and 1 being "poor" — 11 authors rated the overall quality of the talk as "very good" (average = 4.09, median = 4). Authors strongly appreciated the initiative and found the talks to be of high quality, as one of the quotes here demonstrate: *"The talk is extremely thorough despite its brevity. Its certainly better than the talk I gave at WWW."*

Authors find the talks to be very useful for someone interested in a quick overview of the paper.
Upon asking about the usefulness of the video, for someone trying to get a quick overview of their papers, authors rated the crowd generated talks to be "very useful" (average = 4.18, median = 4 — with 5 being "extremely useful", and 1 being "not useful"). On a higher level, authors' sentiments can be expressed through the following quote: *"You and your team have provided a great public service to science."*

Outside evaluators were able to learn and understand the paper's contribution and found the quality to be very good.
To understand how public will respond to these talks, we reached out to outside evaluators and collected 97 responses. Based on these responses, outside evaluators rated the overall quality of talks to be "very good" (average =3.6, median = 4 — where 1 is "poor" and 5 is "excellent"). For the same talks, they "very well" understood and learned the paper's contribution (average = 3.5, median = 4 — where 1 is "not at all" and 5 is "extremely well").

Experience of the Participants
Our process and approach was designed to attract and retain volunteers so they can collaborate, learn and create high-quality talks. Therefore, it is critical to understand their experience with the process and the system.

Audio Recording through Audio Studio
Audio Studio was our systems contribution to enable participants record audio with ease. The participants found it "absolutely simple" to use (average rating = 4.6, median = 5, with 5 being "absolutely simple").

Structure and the Process
To enable the crowd to create talks, we developed a unique structure and process, that begins from dynamic team creation to video production. Based on the survey response, participants expressed "great experience" (average rating = 4.4, median = 5, with 5 being "great").

Iterative Peer Review
Peer review was introduced to ensure high quality. It was iterative with and continuous until all the comments were addressed. Participants found this mandatory part of the process "extremely useful" (average rating = 4.6, median = 5, with 5 being "extremely useful").

Learning, Enjoyment and Experience
Stanford Scholar Initiative is a voluntary effort that requires substantial commitment from the participants. Therefore, it is extremely critical that the volunteers are motivated and learning, while enjoying the experience. Based on their responses,

participants seem to "extremely enjoy" their role and contributions (average rating = 4.5, median = 5 out 5, with 5 being "extremely enjoyable").

Overall, the participants were very motivated to contribute, as the effort provided them an opportunity to learn about research while they work. Their positive experience can be demonstrated by one of the quotes here: *"I had always wanted to read through research papers on hot topics of computer science. But I could never get started. This program not only inspires me to read through a paper but requires me to understand it enough, so as to create a talk on it. And learning is always fun when more people are learning with us."*

CONCLUSIONS AND FUTURE WORK
There is a growing shift in preferences for learning and consuming information by watching videos. At the same time, individual researchers fall short of resources to make such content. To address this gap, we developed and evaluated a two-phased crowdsourcing approach to creating research talks from papers. The first phase involves coordinating the crowd to convert a paper to a slide deck, and the second phase involves transitioning from the slide deck to a complete video using our Audio Studio platform. This process also provides a collaborative learning environment to the crowd that serves as their primary motivation. Ratings and comments from both the papers' authors and outside evaluators suggest the created videos were consistently high-quality.

Moving forward, we plan to focus our efforts on the following three fronts — applying the approach to other domains such as creating technical talks and courses, breadth of topics covered and languages supported, and quality. Through our open repository of research video talks, we hope to advance the dissemination of knowledge and provide an alternate way of learning and consuming novel scholarly contributions.

ACKNOWLEDGMENTS
We are grateful to Shirish Goyal, who helped us with the development of Audio Studio. We thank hundreds of crowd participants who collaboratively created the research talks.

REFERENCES
1. 2016. Stanford Scholar. (2016). http://scholar.stanford.edu/.

2. ACM. 2016. Nominees and winners for best paper and best student paper - WWW 2016. (2016). http://www2016.ca/program/bestpapercandidate.html.

3. Philip J. Guo, Juho Kim, and Rob Rubin. 2014. How Video Production Affects Student Engagement: An Empirical Study of MOOC Videos. In *Proceedings of the First ACM Conference on Learning @ Scale Conference (L@S '14)*. ACM, New York, NY, USA, 41–50.

4. Adam Lashinsky. 2012. *Inside Apple*. Hachette Book Group, New York.

5. Kurt Luther, Casey Fiesler, and Amy Bruckman. 2013. Redistributing leadership in online creative collaboration. In *Proceedings of the 2013 conference on Computer supported cooperative work*. ACM, 1007–1022.

Improving Assessment on MOOCs Through Peer Identification and Aligned Incentives

Dilrukshi Gamage
University of Moratuwa
Katubedda, Sri Lanka
dilrukshi.gamage@gmail.com

Mark E. Whiting
Carnegie Mellon University
Pittsburgh, Pennsylvania
mwhiting@andrew.cmu.edu

Thejan Rajapakshe
Rajarata University of Sri
Lanka
Anuradhapura, Sri Lanka
coder.clix@gmail.com

Haritha Thilakarathne
Rajarata University of Sri
Lanka
Anuradhapura, Sri Lanka
harithalht@gmail.com

Indika Perera
University of Moratuwa
Katubedda, Sri Lanka
indika@cse.mrt.ac.lk

Shantha Fernando
University of Moratuwa
Katubedda, Sri Lanka
shantha@cse.mrt.ac.lk

ABSTRACT

Massive Open Online Courses (MOOCs) use peer assessment to grade open ended questions at scale, allowing students to provide feedback. Relative to teacher based grading, peer assessment on MOOCs traditionally delivers lower quality feedback and fewer learner interactions. We present the *identified peer review* (IPR) framework, which provides non-blind peer assessment and incentives driving high quality feedback. We show that, compared to traditional peer assessment methods, IPR leads to significantly longer and more useful feedback as well as more discussion between peers.

ACM Classification Keywords

K.3.1. COMPUTERS AND EDUCATION: Computer Uses in Education

Author Keywords

Massive Open Online Course; Peer Review

INTRODUCTION

Peer assessment in Massive Open Online Courses (MOOCs) affords grading open ended assignments of many students, but this approach often can't provide the level of feedback that students need. Alternatives such as automated grading enable grading at scale, but require specialized assignment design to facilitate accurate algorithmic judgment, and can't deal well with open ended task designs, sacrificing student learning for ease of grading [13].

LAS'17, April 2017, Boston, MA, USA

© 2017 ACM. ISBN 978-1-4503-4450-0/17/04. . . $15.00

DOI: http://dx.doi.org/10.1145/3051457.3054013

Peer assessment on MOOCs often leads to inaccurate grades and low quality feedback [16], due to laziness, collusion, dishonesty, retaliation and a lack of time, experience or interest [13]. To counter this, humanizing feedback prompt phrasing [11] and offering bonus points to feedback deemed helpful by the receiver [19] have offered improved efficacy. In point systems, if a reviewer provided helpful feedback, the receivers will rate it, however without intrinsic motivation to provide a rating, this leads to single sides systems.

Additionally, MOOC peer reviews are carried out double blind where peers are not made aware of whom they are reviewing or who has reviewed them. This leads to a rising problem in MOOC assessment where due to increased anonymity, there is reduced accountability and eroded community affiliation [15]. Blind peer grading has been practiced in many face to face classroom environments and online learning environments to prevent grading bias and mitigate targeted criticism or bullying. A disadvantage of blind reviews arises in MOOCs when students provide lower quality and less insightful feedback because, being anonymous in review, they are not socially accountable.

Evaluating peers work is a great means of learning. In face to face classroom situations peer evaluation often leads to a conversation where both parties interact richly and gain important understandings about the work, through back and forth communication. MOOCs provide forums for communication and networking, however they are often flooded with community discussion, weeding out paired peer discussions because individual social connections are not readily made.

We introduce the *Identified Peer Review* (IPR) framework with reduced anonymity and matched incentives to counter these issues of current approaches and increase communication. We evaluated the design with an between subject field experiment. This paper presents preliminary results with a small number of participants (n=87), and describes a future implementation and further evaluation plans.

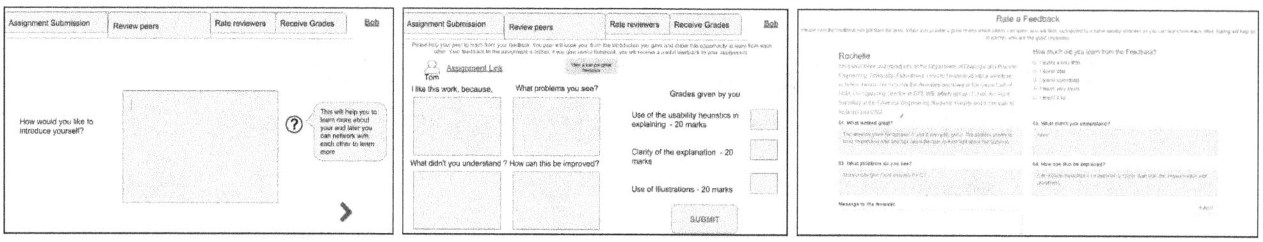

Figure 1. The interfaces of IPR: (1) the peer introduction form where reviewers provide a short introduction to be shared with those reading their reviews, (2) the review form where the four review prompts and grades are entered, (3) the feedback form displaying the feedback and prompting the receiver to rate its usefulness. Grades are not shown in this figure, but would appear after all feedback and ratings had been conducted.

RELATED WORK

Assessment is important to the pedagogy of MOOCs [3]. MOOCs utilize peer assessment to assess student's work in a scalable way, not dependent on a one to many teacher to student relationship, but, optimal methods of choosing graders and assignments to grade remains an open question [2]. The benefits of peer assessment include improvement of higher order thinking skills, consolidation of topical knowledge, and individualized feedback for each participant [6]. Giving and getting feedback has been identified as an effective way to learn in online [17] and in the classroom.

However, with the potential benefits, peer grading still faces challenges. Providing accurate grading where the performance of a novice is being judged by other novices is problematic. Students mistrust peer grades and anonymity lead students to be unscrupulous. Reviews are often short and not well considered, which is especially problematic when students work hard on an assignment and receive comments they can't learn from [20].

Our framework is design based on assessment interactions with visible incentivized peers. Anonymity is commonly practiced in online and in person class peer review systems. Due to the comfort of peers in providing critical feedback [4], the bigger problem in online reviewing is due to increased anonymity and reduced community affiliation [7, 15]. Visible identities lead to more constructive feedback than anonymous ones [22]. Thus through providing non blind review, our framework may encourage accountable reviewing.

Feedback improves performance by changing students' locus of attention, focusing them on productive aspects of their work [9, 13]. However, not all peers provide great feedback and some leave limited comments with no coherent message for improvement, or they are rogue reviews [16]. Rogue reviews are insufficient reviews caused by laziness, collusion, dishonesty, retaliation, competition, or malevolence [10]. To improve on this, PeerStudio [14] peer assessment system is designed to encourage more feedback comments by showing short tips for writing comments just below the comment box. For example, if a response has no constructive feedback, it may remind students with phrases like: "Quick check: Is your feedback actionable?" by triggering heuristics word count on feedback [14]. Students see such comments as more useful than rubrics in reviewing [11]. Similar techniques are used to improve the quality of product reviews online [8]. Our framework uses a simple interface design reflecting these lessons by integrating four pointed questions with separate response areas.

In MOOCs, social connections and networking are attractive features for improving learning and providing a platform for desperate learners to interact and learn together. Since MOOCs are often open to the public, the diverse nature of students can be an asset for improving learning performance, increasing innovations, creativity and critical thinking rather than negativity [1, 10]. The cMOOC [18] approach explains peers as a learning source and finds that the more connections achieved in network with diverse perspectives from participants leads to a richer learning environment. By providing feedback and interactions in viewing assignments, projects, and online discussions as opportunities for crowd-sourcing, this approach leads to superior results that otherwise cannot be achieved individually by students (or the instructor) [18]. However, the cMOOC approach requires significant integration and system familiarity, so it is not widespread. Peer assessment is a great way of learning from each others in the community, yet MOOC designs tend to be so complex that no student can simply choose a peer to align with for feedback. Our framework provides a connection and communication mechanism where peers can talk and learn directly. Such discussions and interactions with diverse groups increase the learning significantly [12]. In particular, an HCI course on Coursera encouraged students to post assignments to forums in getting feedback, leading to a conversation of feedback with identified peers and to more connectivity on fellow peers. In this HCI MOOC, more than 75% students were in favor of sharing their assignments on the public [13], where they assert that blind peer review only drives decreased social connection and availability of diverse perspectives.

IDENTIFIED PEER REVIEWING FRAMEWORK

The IPR framework is built upon 4 phases: submit assignments, review peers, rate feedback, receive grades (Figure 1). In the first phase, students submit their assignments. In the second phase, students are given a *peer introduction form* to provide a short public introduction to be displayed in reviews they conduct. Next students review peer's work with the *review form*, an interface with four targeted feedback fields and grade input field. Students then receive feedback on their own work from other peers in the *feedback form*, which initially shows only the feedback fields, a text input to converse with the reviewer, and a five point scale to rate the usefulness of the feedback. Once all rating is finished, students will receive the grades their reviewers assigned them.

Each student reviews three other students' work, and receives reviews from three students. Unlike most peer reviewing systems, IPR does not randomize peer review assignment, instead aligning incentives by matching a student with reviewers based on the usefulness of that student's previous feedback. Students are motivated to provide their peers with high quality feedback to get high quality peer feedback in return. The next round of review allocations are made when feedback has been rated. Only after a student has received and rated all their feedback are grades made visible, so good feedback ratings can't be bought with inflated grades.

EVALUATION AND RESULTS

We hypothesize that having identifiable peers and matched incentives will increase the feedback quality and lead to more communication than blind peer reviewing. To test this, we conducted a between subject experiment with 3 conditions.

1. **Control condition**: Blind peer review, randomized reviewers.

2. **IPR random condition**: Identified peer review, randomized reviewers.

3. **IPR incentive condition**: Identified peer review, incentivized reviewers.

87 participants collected from an online advertisement placed through authors social media channels and participants were randomly assigned one of three conditions. We created an assignment on the subject "Creativity and Innovation", requiring no previous lessons or special subject knowledge. We measured how students perform in each condition, and how useful the feedback was to them.

How does reviewer blindness influence feedback quality?

To test this, we ran an independent t-test using the control condition and the identified condition. Students in the control condition had an average feedback quality score of 1.21 out of 29 ($\sigma = .243$), and students in the identified condition had an average score of 2.43 out of 29 ($\sigma = 1.02$). An unpaired t-test confirmed that students in the identified condition is significant than other: $t(56) = 6.24$, $p = 0.000$, $\alpha = 0.05$. Which means identified peer reviewing had a large positive effect on the usefulness of feedback compared with double-blind peer-reviewing of assignments.

How does incentive alignment influence feedback quality?

To test this we ran another independent t-test using the identified condition and the aligned incentives condition. Students in the identified condition had an average feedback quality score of 2.43 out of 29 ($\sigma = 1.08$), and students in the aligned incentives condition had an average score of 2.12 out of 25 ($\sigma = 0.71$). The t-test confirmed that students in the identified peer grading condition is significant: $t(48) = 1.19$, $p = 0.009$, $\alpha = 0.05$.

A possible impact of the incentive alignment condition would be to make the gap between the best and worst students larger as the best students help each other, and the worst students are never given high quality feedback. In this initial study, we have not seen evidence of this effect, and hope to explore this in more detail in the future.

Students motivation to communicate

We analyzed the peer reviews done by all 3 conditions from the communicating message box shown in Figure 1. The control group blind peer reviews contained only 29 messages responding to the feedback they received while the identified condition contained 53 and the aligned incentives condition received 49. The control condition group messages did not contain meaningful communication while treatment groups both had students interested in further communicating together. For example control case messages were limited to one or two words such as "Thanks, OK" while the treatment groups had messages like "I like to network too, it is great to be connected to someone new, thanks for the advice - KIT." The message box also gave students means to ask and respond to questions about the assignment or feedback, for example, a student was able to inform their reviewer that a broken link to the assignment for review had been repaired.

DISCUSSION AND FUTURE WORK

We aimed to reintroduce identity in a humanize form where peers introduce themselves to each other. This shared identity showed value, driving conversation and improving feedback quality. Inspired by the design studio concept [21] and cMOOCs where learners make meaningful connections and learn by giving feedback, we designed the IPR framework and witness early results of students' response, compared to a control condition. At the same time adding incentive matching in which reviewers and those being reviewed both had the incentive to be honest in their responses. We believe these results introduce incentive compatible interaction design [5] to MOOCs and that this kind of design offers significant opportunities for ongoing improvement in this field.

This research will continue through testing the influence IPR has on larger cohorts' in a fully develop MOOC. For decades, online peer reviewing has been blind, we aimed to integrate identity in assessment on an MOOC, by carefully designing interactions leading students to discuss and have reason to improve their feedback quality. Initial experimentation showed minimal advantage using incentive alignment over randomized review assignment, but both test conditions performed significantly better in review usefulness and in starting conversations. We believe this is a consequence of the small sample size, so we will explore efficiency with a larger cohort where our ultimate goal is to provide effective feedback to students with meaningful connections, so they can benefit from the diverse crowd in a MOOC.

REFERENCES

1. Wilfried Admiraal, Bart Huisman, and Maarten Van de Ven. 2014. Self-and peer assessment in massive open online courses. *International Journal of Higher Education* 3, 3 (2014), p119.

2. Stephen P Balfour. 2013. Assessing writing in MOOCs: Automated essay scoring and calibrated peer review (tm). *Research & Practice in Assessment* 8 (2013).

3. Sian Bayne and Jen Ross. 2013. The Pedagogy of the Massive Open Online Course (MOOC): the UK View, the Higher Education Academy. (2013).

4. Stephen Bostock. 2000. Student peer assessment. *Learning Technology* (2000).

5. Snehalkumar Neil S Gaikwad, Durim Morina, Adam Ginzberg, Catherine Mullings, Shirish Goyal, Dilrukshi Gamage, Christopher Diemert, Mathias Burton, Sharon Zhou, Mark Whiting, and others. 2016. Boomerang: Rebounding the Consequences of Reputation Feedback on Crowdsourcing Platforms. In *Proceedings of the 29th Annual Symposium on User Interface Software and Technology*. ACM, 625–637.

6. Edward F Gehringer. 2000. Strategies and mechanisms for electronic peer review. In *Frontiers in Education Conference, 2000. FIE 2000. 30th Annual*, Vol. 1. IEEE, F1B–2.

7. John Hamer, Kenneth TK Ma, and Hugh HF Kwong. 2005. A method of automatic grade calibration in peer assessment. In *Proceedings of the 7th Australasian conference on Computing education-Volume 42*. Australian Computer Society, Inc., 67–72.

8. Soo-Min Kim, Patrick Pantel, Tim Chklovski, and Marco Pennacchiotti. 2006. Automatically assessing review helpfulness. In *Proceedings of the 2006 Conference on empirical methods in natural language processing*. Association for Computational Linguistics, 423–430.

9. Avraham N Kluger and Angelo DeNisi. 1996. The effects of feedback interventions on performance: a historical review, a meta-analysis, and a preliminary feedback intervention theory. *Psychological bulletin* 119, 2 (1996), 254.

10. Linda V Knight and Theresa A Steinbach. 2011. Adapting peer review to an online course: An exploratory case study. *Journal of Information Technology Education* 10 (2011), 81–100.

11. Yasmine Kotturi, Chinmay E Kulkarni, Michael S Bernstein, and Scott Klemmer. 2015. Structure and messaging techniques for online peer learning systems that increase stickiness. In *Proceedings of the Second (2015) ACM Conference on Learning@ Scale*. ACM, 31–38.

12. Chinmay Kulkarni, Julia Cambre, Yasmine Kotturi, Michael S Bernstein, and Scott R Klemmer. 2015b. Talkabout: Making distance matter with small groups in massive classes. In *Proceedings of the 18th ACM Conference on Computer Supported Cooperative Work & Social Computing*. ACM, 1116–1128.

13. Chinmay Kulkarni, Koh Pang Wei, Huy Le, Daniel Chia, Kathryn Papadopoulos, Justin Cheng, Daphne Koller, and Scott R Klemmer. 2015c. Peer and self assessment in massive online classes. In *Design thinking research*. Springer, 131–168.

14. Chinmay E Kulkarni, Michael S Bernstein, and Scott R Klemmer. 2015a. PeerStudio: rapid peer feedback emphasizes revision and improves performance. In *Proceedings of the Second (2015) ACM Conference on Learning@ Scale*. ACM, 75–84.

15. Ruiling Lu and Linda Bol. 2007. A comparison of anonymous versus identifiable e-peer review on college student writing performance and the extent of critical feedback. *Journal of Interactive Online Learning* 6, 2 (2007), 100–115.

16. Ken Reily, Pam Ludford Finnerty, and Loren Terveen. 2009. Two peers are better than one: aggregating peer reviews for computing assignments is surprisingly accurate. In *Proceedings of the ACM 2009 international conference on Supporting group work*. ACM, 115–124.

17. Roger C Schank, Tamara R Berman, and Kimberli A Macpherson. 1999. Learning by doing. *Instructional-design theories and models: A new paradigm of instructional theory* 2 (1999), 161–181.

18. George Siemens. 2005. Connectivism: Learning as network-creation. *ASTD Learning News* 10, 1 (2005).

19. Thomas Staubitz, Dominic Petrick, Matthias Bauer, Jan Renz, and Christoph Meinel. 2016. Improving the Peer Assessment Experience on MOOC Platforms. In *Proceedings of the Third (2016) ACM Conference on Learning@ Scale*. ACM, 389–398.

20. Hoi K Suen. 2014. Peer assessment for massive open online courses (MOOCs). *The International Review of Research in Open and Distributed Learning* 15, 3 (2014).

21. David Tinapple, Loren Olson, and John Sadauskas. 2013. CritViz: Web-based software supporting peer critique in large creative classrooms. *Bulletin of the IEEE Technical Committee on Learning Technology* 15, 1 (2013), 29.

22. Siri Vinther, O Haagen Nielsen, Jacob Rosenberg, Niels Keiding, and TV Shroeder. 2012. Same review quality in open versus blinded peer review in" Ugeskrift for Læger. *Dan Med J* 59, 8 (2012), A4479.

Using Student Annotated Hashtags and Emojis to Collect Nuanced Affective States

Amy X. Zhang
MIT CSAIL
Cambridge, MA, USA
axz@mit.edu

Michele Igo
University of California, Davis
Davis, CA, USA
mmigo@ucdavis.edu

Marc Facciotti
University of California, Davis
Davis, CA, USA
mtfacciotti@ucdavis.edu

David Karger
MIT CSAIL
Cambridge, MA, USA
karger@mit.edu

ABSTRACT

Determining affective states such as confusion from students' participation in online discussion forums can be useful for instructors of a large classroom. However, manual annotation of forum posts by instructors or paid crowd workers is both time-consuming and expensive. In this work, we harness affordances prevalent in social media to allow students to self-annotate their discussion posts with a set of hashtags and emojis, a process that is fast and cheap. For students, self-annotation with hashtags and emojis provides another channel for self-expression, as well as a way to signal to instructors and other students on the lookout for certain types of messages. This method also provides an easy way to acquire a labeled dataset of affective states, allowing us distinguish between more nuanced emotions such as confusion and curiosity. From a dataset of over 25,000 discussion posts from two courses containing self-annotated posts by students, we demonstrate how we can identify linguistic differences between posts expressing confusion versus curiosity, achieving 83% accuracy at distinguishing between the two affective states.

Author Keywords

Massive Open Online Courses (MOOCs); Forums; Emotion; Hashtags; Emojis; Confusion; Curiosity; Online Discussion.

ACM Classification Keywords

H.5.3. Group and Organization Interfaces: Asynchronous interaction; Web-based interaction

INTRODUCTION

Many large courses today use online discussion forums in order to allow educators and students to help one another understand the material. However, in a large course, it can be

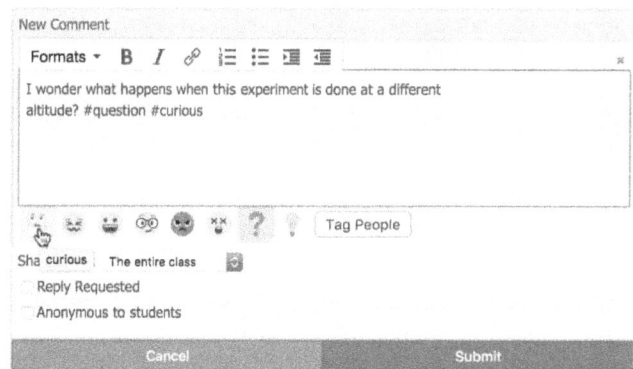

Figure 1. The comment box in Nota Bene that allows the author to add multiple hashtags, along with shortcut emoji buttons, to their post.

difficult for instructors to find the students and the comments that need the most assistance, especially if they do not have the capacity to read or respond to every comment. As a result, researchers have become interested in predicting the emotions that student convey in online discussion threads in order to provide further attention to particular students and threads. To do this, prior studies have developed labeled datasets through manually tagging students' posts with their affect using crowd workers hired from systems such as Mechanical Turk [1, 5]. Particular categories that have been annotated include confusion, sentiment, and urgency, among others. However, it is time-consuming and costly to have instructors or paid crowd workers annotate posts.

Additionally, annotations by paid crowd workers are made by people that are likely not acquainted with the course or the material in question. This may make it difficult to distinguish between more nuanced affective states, such as *confusion* and *curiosity*. In prior work predicting confusion, the appearance of a question mark was found to be the most important feature [5]. However, this does not adequately distinguish confusion from curiosity, as shown in the following examples that have been annotated by the author of the question:

- **Curious**: *I wonder why bacteria multiply so rapidly as opposed to other organisms? Could it be that they are mainly unicellular organisms?*

- **Confused**: *Why would ATP be higher in a cancer cell than in a white blood cell? I don't understand how this information helps us understand the cycle of ATP pools.*

This information, while perhaps difficult for paid annotators to infer, can be easily determined by the original poster, since they are intimately aware of their own feelings. We note that the *emotional* state of confusion, which is what we focus on, is different from a confused *understanding* of the material, which may be something best annotated by instructors. Given the nature of what we wish to collect, authors of the post may be a better source than crowd workers for gold data annotations.

To address these issues, we present a novel strategy of collecting annotations using student-provided hashtags and emojis. Self-annotated data from hashtags has been previously explored in the context of Twitter [2] and used towards capturing subtle variations in sentiment. We choose this method as student authors may be one of the best sources regarding their own affective state. Additionally, students may be eager to self-annotate their posts as another form of self-expression or if they know that instructors or other students are using the information to go through posts. Finally, given the prevalence of social media, they are likely comfortable with using hashtags or emojis in online conversation already.

We develop an interface supporting self-coding (shown in Figure 1), and from our deployment on a large discussion system, we collect a dataset of over 25,000 annotated posts. From this dataset, we show how we can develop models to distinguish between the affective states of confusion and curiosity at 83% accuracy. From this analysis, we are also able to learn indicative terms for each category. This suggests that there are indeed some lexical cues that can help convey curiosity versus confusion.

The contribution of our work is in presenting a practical strategy for collecting nuanced affective state in educational forums at scale. We additionally present a model to distinguish posts expressing confusion from posts expressing curiosity. Determining these nuanced affective states has ramifications for instructors aiming to provide interventions for their students, as an instructor would likely have different responses for a student expressing curiosity versus a student expressing confusion.

DATA COLLECTION
We now describe the interface for collecting annotations as well as the annotated dataset that was collected.

Discussion Interface
In the discussion system, buttons containing emojis appear below the comment textbox. As shown in Figure 1, clicking on an emoji adds a hashtag to the textbox. Students can write in their own hashtags but the emoji buttons provide a shortcut to a set of 8 default tags we chose with the help of instructors, as shown in Table 1. As can be seen, users can add as many hashtags as they like to their post. We deployed the buttons on

Hashtag	Count	Emoji	Hashtag	Count	Emoji
#interested	5550		#confused	2612	
#question	5493		#idea	2464	
#curious	5122		#help	840	
#useful	3311		#frustrated	172	

Table 1. Hashtags and associated emoji in the discussion interface.

Hashtags	Count	Hashtags	Count
#curious #question	697	#confused #help	321
#curious #interested	655	#help #question	307
#confused #question	601	#confused #curious	239
#interested #useful	540	#interested #question	221

Table 2. The top 8 pairs of hashtags that appear together in the same post.

Nota Bene (NB)[1] [6], a textbook annotation system that classrooms can use to have threaded discussions "in the margins", or anchored to a particular place on a page. With a single click, students can create a private or public post anywhere in the margins of the course material. While reading, students can see each others' public posts and respond to them, and instructors can respond to all posts in the course. The system has generated over a million posts and has been used in thousands of courses by over a hundred thousand students.

Data
The hashtag feature was rolled out to NB in the spring of 2016. While anyone using the system can make use of the buttons, we focus on the data provided by two courses using NB that explicitly encouraged students to use the hashtags. These included summer and fall quarter iterations of a course at University of California, Davis titled *Introductory Biology 2A*. Each iteration of the course enrolls over a thousand students. Reading assignments from textbooks were posted on NB, and course points were awarded for commenting in NB. The use of hashtags was not required for credit but was encouraged by the instructors as a means for communicating affect to others. From the two courses, 293,316 posts were made by 2,353 unique authors. 17.3% or 50,773 of these posts were replies to other posts. From the discussions, we extracted all the posts that contain a hashtag in the text of the post. From the two courses, we collected a total of 25,564 posts, 3,275 of which were replies, containing hashtags written by 1,356 unique authors. This constitutes 8.7% of all posts and 57.6% of all authors. In Table 1 and Table 2, we show counts for each of the hashtags as well as the most frequent pairs of hashtags that appear in the same post.

CLASSIFYING CONFUSION VERSUS CURIOSITY
While there are many use cases for our data, we now focus on the task of distinguishing confusion versus curiosity, an

---

[1]nb.mit.edu

Model	Accuracy	Precision	Recall	F1	AUC
Baseline	0.69	0.48	0.69	0.56	0.50
LR	**0.83**	**0.83**	**0.83**	**0.83**	**0.78**
SVM	0.81	0.81	0.81	0.81	**0.78**
ADT	0.77	0.77	0.77	0.76	0.71
RF	0.76	0.76	0.76	0.74	0.67

Table 3. Results for predicting confusion versus curiosity posts across the different models.

Feature Set	Accuracy	Precision	Recall	F1	AUC
All Features	0.83	0.83	0.83	0.83	0.78
Content	0.79	0.79	0.79	0.78	0.72
Author	0.71	0.70	0.72	0.69	0.61
Sentiment	0.68	0.64	0.68	0.58	0.52

Table 4. Results for predicting confusion versus curiosity posts using the LR model and using only one of the feature categories at a time.

Curiosity		Confusion	
Feature	Importance	Feature	Importance
wonder	3.055	confus	4.202
curious	2.728	understand	2.189
remind	2.143	write	1.913
scientist	2.080	strip	1.902
g2	2.023	wouldn	1.838
interest	1.950	sentenc	1.789
telophas	1.850	thought	1.729
similar	1.756	don	1.668
cool	1.692	explain	1.619
fascin	1.677	moment	1.603

Table 5. Important unigram word stem features for curiosity and confusion based on coefficients learned from a linear SVM.

issue of particular importance to instructors trying to target confused students or improve course materials. In the Introduction, we show an example of a post containing a #curious hashtag versus a post containing a #confused hashtag. As can be seen, both are posed as questions asking "why" a phenomenom occurs and might both be identified as "confused" by an outside annotator, though the author of the post labeled the first one as "curious".

As posts can have more than one hashtag, we gather all the posts that contain a #curious hashtag but no #confused hashtag and all posts that contain a #confused hashtag but no #curious hashtag. This led to 4,875 curious posts and 2,365 confused posts for a total of 7,240 posts, including replies. We also strip all hashtags from the posts.

Models

We experiment with four different classification algorithms and compare the performance. The algorithms we choose are Logistic Regression (LR), Support Vector Machines (SVM) with a linear kernel, Adaptive Boosted Decision Trees (ADT), and Random Forests (RF). We use 10-fold cross validation and average the results. We also have a baseline which is simply tagging all posts as curious.

Features

We make use of three feature categories.

Content: The first is unigrams from the text of the post. We use a word tokenizer that keeps punctuation as separate tokens. We also reduce words to their word stem using the Snowball stemmer. Finally, we use TF-IDF weighting, and set a minimum document frequency of 5 posts. Though we experimented with bigrams and trigrams, we found no improvements using these additional features.

Author: The second feature is the author of the post. This was chosen as some students may tend to post more curious or confused comments.

Sentiment: The sentiment of the post may be related to curiosity versus confusion as curiosity has positive connotations while confusion has negative connotations. We calculate the frequency of positive and negative terms used in the post using Linguistic Inquiry and Word Count (LIWC) dictionaries[2] [3].

We also experimented with other feature categories that have been used in the past towards predicting confusion [5] or engagement [4], such as certainty and tentativeness, use of negation or personal pronouns, and use of cognitive processes or insight words, all using dictionaries taken from LIWC. While several of these features had weak correlations with the two categories, they did not yield improvements in our best performing model so we omit them here.

Results

The LR model achieves the best accuracy score of 0.83 using all the features. However, as the dataset is unbalanced, area under the curve (AUC) may be more relevant, and here the LR and SVM models have the best score of 0.78. This constitutes a 28% absolute improvement in AUC over the baseline of 0.5.

Also, we note in Table 4 that the LR model with only unigram features has an AUC of 0.72, while the model with only author features achieves a 0.61 AUC. This demonstrates that the content features are the most important towards making the prediction. A model without author features is useful for cases when there is no prior information about the authors on which to train, for instance when needing to annotate posts from a new iteration of a course with new students.

In Table 5, we show the most important unigram features for confusion and curiosity using coefficients determined by a linear SVM model. For the curiosity class, important word stems include "wonder" and "interest". This echoes prior work showing terms signifying cognition or application can predict engagement [4], as curiosity is related to higher engagement. The terms "remind" and "similar" also suggest that the student is making comparisons to other topics. Finally, curiosity is positively correlated with positive emotion (Spearman's rank correlation, ρ=0.115, p<0.0001).

---

[2] https://liwc.wpengine.com

On the confusion side, terms such as "understand", "thought", and "explain" show a focus on comprehension. We also see the use of negation in word stems such as "wouldn" and "don", and we determine that confusion is positively correlated with negative emotion (Spearman's rank correlation, ρ=0.155, p<0.0001). As can be seen, features that signal whether a post contains a question, such as presence of a question mark, are not useful for distinguishing between confusion and curiosity.

DISCUSSION AND FUTURE WORK

Using a new method of collecting student-annotated hashtags, we build a dataset of 25,000 posts annotated with a variety of tags with little cost or effort on the part of instructors. With these annotations, we can build novel features within discussion systems, such as allowing educators and students to filter posts by certain hashtags or even augment the reading material with highlights based on emotions expressed. These additions to a discussion interface could further motivate students to voluntarily annotate their posts with affect. In the case of the two courses used in our data collection, the instructors encouraged the use of hashtags by mentioning it during lecture. In other iterations of the course where they did not explicitly discuss hashtags, we saw usage drop considerably. Thus more work is necessary to consider how instructors and system design can encourage annotation.

The creation of this dataset also allows us to differentiate between nuanced emotions such as confusion and curiosity at 83% accuracy and 78% AUC. Given that the most important feature category for our best model is unigrams, this demonstrates that there are indeed some lexical differences between the two categories of posts. This suggests that contrary to our assumptions, it may be possible for crowd workers to distinguish between the two to some degree, even though student self-annotations are still cheaper and faster. Future work will need to determine how well student and crowd annotations align. There may also be some interesting differences between student and instructor annotations. In the case of instructor annotations, the instructor may additionally be able to state whether the student has a confused *understanding* of the material, even if the student may not *feel* confused.

These results suggest future improvements in our model that can account for cases where the student feels confused but there are no clear lexical signifiers. In those cases, underlying knowledge of the course could be taken into account. For instance, to be able to separate confusion and curiosity, one might be guided by what the course has already covered as well as what topics are outside the scope of understanding the material and require inference. A question about a fundamental topic already covered would signify a misunderstanding of something important, or confusion, while a question musing about an unexplained connection would signify curiosity. This would be an interesting future line of work to explore, and our student-annotated dataset could be used for evaluation.

Finally, the ability to detect nuanced signals of affect is an improvement over models that ignore emotions such as curiosity when attempting to identify confusion, as this gives educators the ability to better tailor their actions in response. The differentiation between curiosity and confusion is particularly important as it suggests opposite actions though both types of posts may be asking questions. Students expressing curiosity might be directed to different resources or prompt different responses than students expressing confusion. Instructors may also wish to focus more attention towards helping confused students rather than curious students. Additionally, these different signals can help instructors with improving their course material. Course material that evokes curiosity should be promoted while material that evokes confusion should be targeted for improvement. Since we developed our tagging feature on a textbook annotation system where students can select arbitrary portions of the page on which to comment, we can determine down to the sentence or paragraph level which portions of the material evoke confusion or curiosity.

CONCLUSION

In this work, we develop a method for collecting annotations of nuanced affective states at scale by allowing students to self-annotate their forum posts with hashtags and emojis. For students, this is a new way to express themselves as well as a way to signal to their peers and instructors what kind of attention they want in response. After collecting over 25,000 annotated posts using this strategy from two courses, we demonstrate the usefulness of this data towards understanding nuanced emotions by developing models to distinguish posts expressing confusion from posts expressing curiosity. Our best model achieves an accuracy of 83%, and we also show the most important terms from the text of the post that signify confusion or curiosity.

ACKNOWLEDGEMENTS

We would like to thank Ya'akov Gal and Eran Yogev for useful discussions and Roy Fairstein for developing the hashtag feature.

REFERENCES

1. Akshay Agrawal, Jagadish Venkatraman, Shane Leonard, and Andreas Paepcke. 2015. YouEDU: addressing confusion in MOOC discussion forums by recommending instructional video clips. (2015).

2. Dmitry Davidov, Oren Tsur, and Ari Rappoport. 2010. Enhanced sentiment learning using twitter hashtags and smileys. In *COLING*. ACL, 241–249.

3. Yla R Tausczik and James W Pennebaker. 2010. The psychological meaning of words: LIWC and computerized text analysis methods. *Journal of language and social psychology* 29, 1 (2010), 24–54.

4. Miaomiao Wen, Diyi Yang, and Carolyn Penstein Rosé. 2014. Linguistic Reflections of Student Engagement in Massive Open Online Courses.. In *ICWSM*.

5. Diyi Yang, Miaomiao Wen, Iris Howley, Robert Kraut, and Carolyn Rose. 2015. Exploring the effect of confusion in discussion forums of massive open online courses. In *Learning@Scale*. ACM, 121–130.

6. Sacha Zyto, David Karger, Mark Ackerman, and Sanjoy Mahajan. 2012. Successful classroom deployment of a social document annotation system. In *CHI*. ACM, 1883–1892.

A Heuristic Method for Large-Scale Cognitive-Diagnostic Computerized Adaptive Testing

Jill-Jênn Vie
RIKEN Center for Advanced
Intelligence Project (AIP)
Tokyo, Japan
vie@jill-jenn.net

Fabrice Popineau
Laboratoire de recherche en
informatique (LRI)
Orsay, France
fabrice.popineau@lri.fr

Françoise Tort
ENS Paris-Saclay
Cachan, France
francoise.tort@stef.ens-
cachan.fr

Benjamin Marteau
French Ministry of Education
Paris, France
benjamin.marteau@education.gouv.fr

Nathalie Denos
Université Grenoble-Alpes
CNRS, LIG
Grenoble, France
nathalie.denos@univ-
grenoble-alpes.fr

ABSTRACT

In formative assessments, one wants to provide a useful feedback to the examinee at the end of the test. In order to reduce the number of questions asked in an assessment, adaptive testing models have been developed for cognitive diagnosis, such as the ones encountered in knowledge space theory. However, when the number of skills assessed is very huge, such methods cannot scale. In this paper, we present a new method to provide adaptive tests and useful feedback to the examinee, even with large databases of skills. It will be used in Pix, a platform for certification of digital competencies for every French citizen.

Author Keywords

adaptive testing; cognitive diagnosis; item response theory; knowledge space theory; q-matrices; knowledge components.

INTRODUCTION

In online assessments, it is crucial to uncover the latent knowledge of examinees efficiently, in order to tailor the learning experience to their needs. Therefore, the cost to be minimized is the number of questions asked during an assessment. In summative assessments such as the ones encountered in certifications (GMAT, GRE), several models have been proposed in order to reduce the number of questions asked, using item response theory [5]. In formative assessments though, one also wants to provide a useful feedback at the end of test. To address this outcome, several models based on cognitive-diagnostic computerized adaptive testing (CD-CAT) have been proposed [2]. However, most of them are not suitable for learning at scale, i.e., they cannot handle many knowledge components.

In this paper, we show how to provide a CD-CAT that can handle more knowledge components, that efficiently computes the next question to ask, and that provides useful feedback in few questions.

This paper is organized as follows. We first present the existing models for CD-CAT and their limitations. Then, we present the curriculum we want to assess, and our new heuristic method. Finally, we describe the context in which our method has been used: a certification of digital competencies for all French citizens. Our conclusions follow.

MODELS FOR COGNITIVE-DIAGNOSTIC COMPUTERIZED ADAPTIVE TESTING (CD-CAT)

In order to provide a feedback called cognitive diagnosis, most models rely on a *q-matrix* [6], i.e., a binary matrix that draws a link between questions and knowledge components (KCs) required to solve them. Formally, the (j,k) entry of the q-matrix q_{jk} is 1 if the KC k is involved in the resolution of the question j, 0 otherwise. Using this q-matrix, it is possible, based on the performance of a learner, to tell them their strong or weak points at the end of the test.

An adaptive test can be represented as a tree-shaped automaton called CAT tree, of which the states are the questions asked, and the edges are labeled with 0 or 1 according to a false or true answer from the learner. Thus, an execution of the adaptive test can be seen as a path in the automaton, according to the learner's performance.

We will now present two adaptive testing models based on a q-matrix: the DINA model and the attribute hierarchy model, also related to knowledge space theory.

L@S 2017, April 20 - 21, 2017, Cambridge, MA, USA

ACM ISBN 978-1-4503-4450-0/17/04. . . $15.00

DOI: http://dx.doi.org/10.1145/3051457.3054015

DINA model

In the DINA model (Deterministic Input, Noisy And), a learner should master every KC involved in the resolution of a certain question in order to solve it. This model is also robust to careless errors from the learners, using *slip* (s_j) and *guess* (g_j) parameters for every question j. The learner has a latent state $c \in \{0,1\}^K$ of which the k-th component c_k represents their mastery or non-mastery of the k-th KC. The probability that a certain learner answers the question j correctly is:

$$\begin{cases} 1 - s_j & \text{if the learner masters every KC involved in } j \\ g_j & \text{otherwise.} \end{cases}$$

Formally, a learner of latent state c masters every KC involved in j if for all KC k, $q_{jk} = 1$ implies $c_k = 1$.

Using this model, it is possible to infer the most probable latent state of the learner based on their answers, update the probability distribution of the 2^K possible latent states after each question in a Bayesian way. One can also compute which question is the most informative, i.e., reduces the uncertainty (entropy) over the latent state of the learner the most. For details on potential algorithms for next item selection using the DINA model, see [2].

When the number of KCs is high, say 30, the number of possible states is big (2^{30}), and so is the support of the probability distribution. Therefore, the next question to ask cannot be computed efficiently.

Attribute Hierarchy Model and Knowledge Space Theory

Prerequisite graphs have been suggested in order to reduce the complexity of CD-CAT: $G = (V, E)$ where the nodes V are the KCs and $(u, v) \in E$ whenever u should be mastered before v. Therefore, the possible latent states should verify $\forall (u, v) \in E, c_v = 1 \Rightarrow c_u = 1$. Thus the support of the probability distribution is reduced and the next question to ask can be computed efficiently. Such an approach has been referred to as the *attribute hierarchy model* [7].

Knowledge space theory follows the same principle, but the underlying models are not robust to careless errors [4]. They have been tested to provide an adaptive test at the beginning of a MOOC of mathematics [8]. See [12] for a review of models used for adaptive assessment.

If the prerequisite graph is large though, or composed of many connected components, the number of states is still intractable, therefore other approaches should be used.

OUR NEW HEURISTIC METHOD

We now present our method, based on a q-matrix together with a prerequisite graph. An extra requirement is that every KC should have an intrinsic value of difficulty level, which is a positive real number. Questions assess one main KC, and in what follows, we will call *difficulty* of question j the difficulty level of the main KC validated by j.

Curriculum Data

We had 48 knowledge components being assessed by 48 questions. Each question assesses the mastery of a single KC. Each

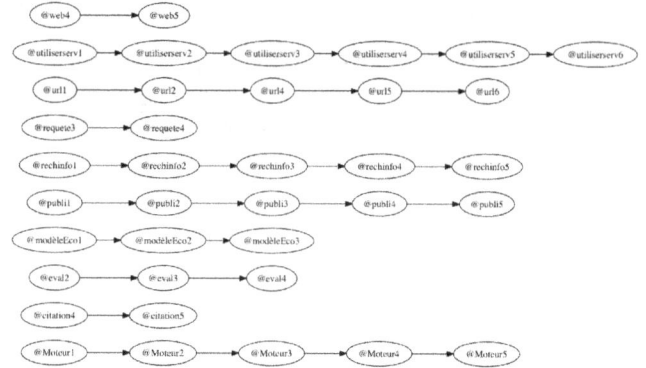

Figure 1. The prerequisite graph for our adaptive test in Pix.

of our KCs has a difficulty level comprised between 1 and 6 that will help choose the next question. The prerequisite graph is composed of 10 connected components that are simple paths, such as $web4 \rightarrow web5$ or $url1 \rightarrow url2 \rightarrow url4 \rightarrow url5 \rightarrow url6$, see Figure 1. Thus, validating a KC propagates the validation to its parents, while invalidating a KC propagates the non-validation to its children.

In our case, even with our prerequisite graph, the number of possible latent states is too big (15M), because the numerous connected components lead to a combinatorial explosion. Seemingly, edges are missing, but we did not want to force such extra connections before we could examine learner data. Based on this usage data, some extra prerequisites could be added, such as $url2 \rightarrow web4$, that could reduce the number of possible latent states.

Algorithm

Instead of maintaining a probability distribution over potentially millions of latent states, in order to build the CAT tree, we maintain two sets called `acquired` and `not_acquired` that collect the KCs seemingly mastered or non-mastered by a learner throughout the test. Those sets do not necessarily reflect the final diagnosis provided to the learner but will allow to choose efficiently the next question to ask. At the end of the test, one can compute a diagnosis of the learner based on the collected information, for example using the general diagnostic model [3], or models based on slip and guess parameters.

When a learner solves correctly a question that requires a certain KC, they also validate the parents of this KC in the prerequisite graph, all of them being added to the `acquired` set. When they provide an incorrect answer to a question validating a KC, they also invalidate the children of this KC in the graph, being added to the `not_acquired` set. For example, if the prerequisite graph contains the path $url1 \rightarrow url2 \rightarrow url4$, then solving correctly a question that requires $url2$ will add both $url1$ and $url2$ to the `acquired` set, while solving incorrectly such a question will add both $url2$ and $url4$ to the `not_acquired` set. It is thus possible to compute for each KC the number of KCs acquired N_{acquired} or not acquired $N_{\text{not\_acquired}}$, using a simple depth-first search. Those sets do not reflect the true knowledge of the learner, but allow choosing early questions of various difficulty levels.

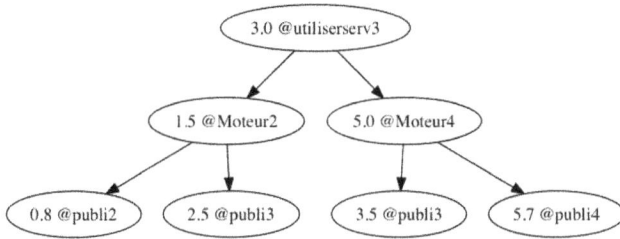

Figure 2. An example of CAT tree provided by our method.

The learner is modelled by a single parameter θ representing their proficiency. We denote R_j the outcome of the learner over the question j, either right (1) or wrong (0). This outcome verifies:

$$p_j(\theta) \triangleq \Pr(R_j = 1) = \Phi(\theta - d_j)$$

where d_j is the difficulty of question j and $\Phi : x \mapsto 1/(1+e^{-x})$ is the logistic function. This is the 1-parameter logistic model of item response theory.

At each step, we ask the question which achieves the highest expected number of KCs added either to the `acquired` set or the `not_acquired` set. This way, we can compute a value of the information collected at each question, based on the current estimated level of the learner:

$$score(j) = \Pr(R_j = 1) \cdot N_{\text{acquired}} + \Pr(R_j = 0) \cdot N_{\text{not\_acquired}}.$$

After some questions have been asked, parameter estimation of the learner's level θ is performed by maximizing the likelihood:

$$L(\theta) = \prod p_j(\theta)^{a_j}(1 - p_j(\theta))^{1-a_j}.$$

In other words, we just need to find the zeroes of:

$$\frac{\partial \log L}{\partial \theta} = \sum_{j=1}^{N} a_j(1 - p_j(\theta)) - (1 - a_j)p_j(\theta) \qquad (1)$$

which is usually performed using the Brent algorithm. When the samples are all-right or all-wrong, we add either a positive outcome for a question of difficulty 0 or a negative outcome for a question of maximal difficulty (in our case, 7), in order for the maximum-likelihood estimator to exist. Such an update of the parameter θ allows asking more difficult questions if the learner is performing well.

Computing the zeroes of Equation 1 is fast, therefore a 20-question-depth CAT tree (containing one million nodes) can be computed in 1 minute, using a Python implementation of our method. The CAT tree obtained this way is shown in Figure 2. An edge towards the right indicates a correct answer while an edge towards the left indicates a wrong answer. Within

each node are described the estimated level of the learner at this node, together with the main KC of the question that will be asked to them next. One can see on this figure that the questions are increasingly difficult whenever the learner performs well, and vice versa. Also, consecutive questions deal with different components of the graph, because it is more informative to test various subjects, according to the objective of maximizing the KCs added or removed at each step.

The test is available online at `http://pix.jiji.cat`.

CONTEXT: PIX, CERTIFICATION OF DIGITAL COMPETEN-CIES FOR FRENCH CITIZENS

Goal and curriculum

This method will be applied to Pix[1], an online platform for assessment and certification of digital skills for every French citizen. It is managed by the French Ministry of Education, in close relationship with public and private stakeholders. It aims at revealing and stimulating the training needs necessary to face the digital transformation of our societies, by measuring, promoting and developing digital competencies. It is built upon DigComp 2.0, the European Digital Competence Framework for Citizens [10] composed of five areas:

1. information and data literacy;
2. communication and collaboration;
3. digital content creation;
4. safety;
5. problem solving (in a digital environment).

The main goal of Pix is to provide a free assessment to any French citizen (scholar, student, professional, retired, etc.) that can assess their digital skills, and put a name on what they do not know (e.g., "most wiki-like websites have a publicly available history"). At the end of the test, they can receive a diagnosis, summarizing their strong and weak points, and possibly do the test again at will. Therefore, Pix provides a formative assessment, and people can learn more by sitting for the test again.

Pix allows citizens to monitor their progress using an account. After each test administration, they will be acknowledged with points on a 1024 pix scale, together with a competency profile. Progress will be encouraged with targeted recommendations of learning resources. Within a test, a level of proficiency between 1 and 8 is computed, together with the acquisition or non-acquisition of knowledge components called *acquix*, which are learning outcomes.

Impact

Within the next months, 4000 people will try the adaptive test. The next year, every student from grade 8 to 12 will try the platform: 3.5M students, potentially half of all French higher education students (1.25M), together with employment integration organizations. The source code of the platform is freely available on GitHub[2], under the license AGPLv3.

---

[1] `https://pix.beta.gouv.fr`
[2] `https://github.com/sgmap/pix`

Problem statements

Problem statements are built in a way similar to evidence-centered design [9], because in order to solve them, people have to bring to the system the proof that they managed to perform the requested task. For example, if the short-answer question is: "In the city Montrésor, what street leads to *Rue des Perrières*?" The answer is *Rue de la Couteauderie*, and the most straightforward way for anyone to find it — except if they unfortunately know Montrésor by heart — is to use a mapping service. No matter whether they used Google Maps or OpenStreetMap, if the answer is correct, the learner will prove they master the corresponding knowledge component *@utiliserserv3*, which means they can "find and use a service to get an answer, without a hint." The problems are thus challenge-based, and fun to solve. To date, there are 697 items in the database, designed by a team including teachers and researchers from French universities and educational institutions.

Research

Data collected by the platform will be sanitized (e.g., removing personal information in user input) and made publicly available for research purposes.

Problem statements will be continually improved according to usage data. For example, some of the questions expect a short answer, therefore new correct solutions may be added to the system, using approaches such as the Divide and Correct framework developed in [1].

CONCLUSION

In this work-in-progress paper, we showed how it was possible to provide a CD-CAT when the number of latent states is potentially very large, and few prerequisites over the KCs are known. Our method consists of a combination of the Rasch model from item response theory and existing techniques based on knowledge components. We applied this technique to Pix, the French platform of certification of digital skills.

After a first administration of this adaptive test to thousands of students, we will be able to calibrate other models that need existing data in order to be trained, such as adaptive testing models based on the general diagnostic model [11]. Such models could help suggest new links between KCs, or could express the fact that a single question could require two KC with different weights. We leave this for further work.

ACKNOWLEDGEMENTS

This project was funded by the French Ministry of Education. Pix has been designed since March 2016 and developed as a State Startup since June 2016 within the incubator of the SGMAP[3] (General Secretariat for the Modernization of Public Action), similar to task forces such as 18F[4] or the United States Digital Service[5].

---

[3] https://beta.gouv.fr
[4] https://18f.gsa.gov
[5] https://www.usds.gov

REFERENCES

1. Michael Brooks, Sumit Basu, Charles Jacobs, and Lucy Vanderwende. 2014. Divide and correct: using clusters to grade short answers at scale. In *Proceedings of the first ACM conference on Learning@ scale conference*. ACM, 89–98.

2. Ying Cheng. 2009. When cognitive diagnosis meets computerized adaptive testing: CD-CAT. *Psychometrika* 74, 4 (2009), 619–632.

3. Matthias Davier. 2005. A general diagnostic model applied to language testing data. *ETS Research Report Series* 2005, 2 (2005), i–35.

4. Jean-Claude Falmagne, Eric Cosyn, Jean-Paul Doignon, and Nicolas Thiéry. 2006. The assessment of knowledge, in theory and in practice. In *Formal concept analysis*. Springer, 61–79.

5. Ronald K. Hambleton, Hariharan Swaminathan, and H. Jane Rogers. 1991. *Fundamentals of item response theory*. Sage.

6. Alan Huebner. 2010. An Overview of Recent Developments in Cognitive Diagnostic Computer Adaptive Assessments. *Practical Assessment, Research & Evaluation* 15, 3 (2010), 7.

7. Jacqueline P. Leighton, Mark J. Gierl, and Stephen M. Hunka. 2004. The Attribute Hierarchy Method for Cognitive Assessment: A Variation on Tatsuoka's Rule-Space Approach. *Journal of Educational Measurement* 41, 3 (2004), 205–237.

8. Danny Lynch and Colm P. Howlin. 2014. Real world usage of an adaptive testing algorithm to uncover latent knowledge. (2014).

9. Robert J. Mislevy, John T. Behrens, Kristen E. Dicerbo, and Roy Levy. 2012. Design and discovery in educational assessment: Evidence-centered design, psychometrics, and educational data mining. *JEDM-Journal of Educational Data Mining* 4, 1 (2012), 11–48.

10. Vuorikari Riina, Yves Punie, Stephanie Carretero Gomez, and Godelieve Van Den Brande. 2016. *DigComp 2.0: The Digital Competence Framework for Citizens. Update Phase 1: the Conceptual Reference Model*. Technical Report. Institute for Prospective Technological Studies, Joint Research Centre.

11. Jill-Jênn Vie, Fabrice Popineau, Yolaine Bourda, and Éric Bruillard. 2016a. Adaptive Testing Using a General Diagnostic Model. In *European Conference on Technology Enhanced Learning*. Springer, 331–339.

12. Jill-Jênn Vie, Fabrice Popineau, Yolaine Bourda, and Éric Bruillard. 2016b. A review of recent advances in adaptive assessment. In *Learning analytics: Fundaments, applications, and trends: A view of the current state of the art*. Springer, in press.

Comment Ranking Diversification in Forum Discussions

Curtis G. Northcutt, Kimberly A. Leon, Naichun Chen
Massachusetts Institute of Technology
Cambridge, MA, USA
{cgn, kimleon, naichun}@mit.edu

ABSTRACT

Viewing consumption of discussion forums with hundreds or more comments depends on ranking because most users only view top-ranked comments. When comments are ranked by an ordered score (e.g. number of replies or up-votes) without adjusting for semantic similarity of near-ranked comments, top-ranked comments are more likely to emphasize the majority opinion and incur redundancy. In this paper, we propose a top K comment diversification re-ranking model using Maximal Marginal Relevance (MMR) and evaluate its impact in three categories: (1) semantic diversity, (2) inclusion of the semantics of lower-ranked comments, and (3) redundancy, within the context of a HarvardX course discussion forum. We conducted a double-blind, small-scale evaluation experiment requiring subjects to select between the top 5 comments of a diversified ranking and a baseline ranking ordered by score. For three subjects, across 100 trials, subjects selected the diversified (75% score, 25% diversification) ranking as significantly (1) more diverse, (2) more inclusive, and (3) less redundant. Within each category, inter-rater reliability showed moderate consistency, with typical Cohen-Kappa scores near 0.2. Our findings suggest that our model improves (1) diversification, (2) inclusion, and (3) redundancy, among top K ranked comments in discussion forums of online courses.

INTRODUCTION

Text ranking systems (e.g. Facebook post comments, Amazon product reviews, Reddit forums) are ubiquitous, yet many face a common problem. When posts (e.g. reviews or comments) are ranked primarily by text content and rating (e.g. like/unlike, ↑/↓, +/-, number of replies, etc.), similar posts tend to receive similar scores. Moreover, higher ranking posts tend to exclusively represent the majority opinion, since there are more users in the majority group to up-vote posts sharing their sentiment. For large forums with thousands of posts, viewers may only be exposed to the majority opinion when they only view top-ranked posts. If the ground truth semantics of each comment were known a priori, comment scores could be

normalized by the number of comments with similar semantics, avoiding this problem. Unfortuantely this is not the case. Instead, there are a multitude of techniques to approximate semantic similarity [12, 7, 13].

We consider the comment ranking diversity problem in the context of an online edX course, *Harvardx Christianity Through Its Scriptures*, where increased visibility of the diversity of comments across thousands of learners may aid in debunking misconceptions held by the majority of forum respondents. edX forums are organized hierarchically into topics > comments > replies (an example topic is depicted in Figure 1). Our focus is the ranking of comments and we use the number of replies as the score for each comment, although by default, edX comments are ranked chronologically.

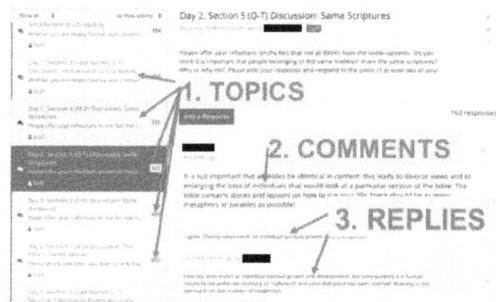

Figure 1. An example topic used to illustrate the organization of an edX discussion forum. edX forums are organized hierarchically into topics > comments > replies. Our focus is the ranking of comments.

In this paper, we develop an algorithm for forum comment ranking diversification using maximal marginal relevance (MMR) to linearly interpolate between the original ranking score (relevance) and the similarity of an item to higher-ranked items (diversity) estimated using PCA + TFIDF, and evaluate our model using a blind experiment requiring subjects to compare our diversified ranking to a baseline relevance ranking.

BACKGROUND AND RELATED WORK

The crux of diversification is a well-trained comment embedding model that accurately captures the semantic similarity between two documents. Text embedding is a well-studied problem at the word-level [12] and document-level [10]. In this section, we consider increasingly complex methods for comment similarity, followed by methods for ranking documents and how it relates to diversification.

One of the simplest document embedding representations is TFIDF [9] which uses a "bag of words" (nBOW) counts model, normalized by word count per document frequency. Although

TFIDF works well on some tasks [1], it ignores word ordering and suffers a performance loss for longer documents. TFIDF performs well when combined with matrix decomposition methods like PCA or LSA. More sophisticated approaches such as word2vec [12], LDA [2], and Gated CNN [11] offer classification accuracy improvements, but are task-specific. These models are compared in Table 1. A state-of-the-art (2016) LSTM similarity model uses a Siamese recurrent architecture to combine the word2vec embeddings of all words in a document, and trains using a Manhattan loss on the output of the two LSTMs [13]. Although this method would likely offer improvements, simpler models were sufficient for our task.

Model	Method	Scaling Sensitivity
TFIDF	F	False
PCA + TFIDF	M+S	True
LSA + TFIDF	M+S	True
NMF + TFIDF	M+S	True
LDA + TFIDF	T	False
Word2Vec + TFIDF	W+S	False
Word2Vec + nBOW	W+S	False
Gated CNN + TFIDF	W+S	False

Table 1. A comparison of the comment embedding models evaluated in this study. Method symbols are abbreviated as: T=Topic, M=Matrix Factorization, W=Local Window, F=Frequency, S=Semantic

The task of forum comment ranking can be thought of as a search task, where common methods like PageRank [14] and RankSVM [6]) are used to identify the most relevant document for a given query. In our case, relevance is determined a priori by comment score, and instead our focus is diversification of this ranking. Diversification has been successfully applied to the task of online shopping [4], with the task of reducing abandonment in shopping queries by providing a diversified selection of options. In this paper, we elect a more general approach, MMR [3], which we describe more in Section 3.2.

TECHNICAL APPROACH

Our methodology consists of four ordered components: (1) Automated generation of gold data, (2) Evaluation of comment embedding models, (3) Implementing diversification in comment rankings, and (4) Measuring efficacy of diversification. We describe these components in the following sections.

Dataset

edX forums are organized hierarchically by topic > comments > replies as shown in Figure 1. We consider diversification at the comments level (within a single topic). In the context of this study, we focus on the comment rankings for topics in the forum discussions of an edX course, *HarvardX: HDS3221.2x Christianity Through Its Scriptures*, obtained via web-scraping. Comment scores were set equal to the number of replies for each comment. Forum text was tokenized with stop-words removed and over 100,000 comments were analyzed.

Automated Gold Data Generation

We used a novel method to generate large gold datasets, without human labeling, by sampling comments across highly differing topics and generating a pairwise cosine similarity matrix for these comments. This matrix contains binary labels, a (1) if comments were taken from the same topic (Gold 1 pairs) or (0) if comments were taken from different topics

(Gold 0 pairs). For exclusive sets of topics, we generated both train and test gold datasets to evaluate our selection of different comment embedding models discussed in 4.1.

Maximal-Marginal Relevance (MMR)

MMR is an iterative algorithm, at each step selecting the comment which maximizes a modified score (Equation 1).

$$\hat{s} := \lambda \cdot s - (1 - \lambda) \cdot c \qquad (1)$$

A single parameter λ adjusts the trade-off between the original comment score, s, and its maximum cosine similarity among all comments that have already been added to the new ranking, c, to produce the updated score, s'. For example, $\lambda = 1$ ranks entirely by score and $\lambda = 0$ selects maximally diverse comments irrespective of score. In this study, we evaluate two settings of the parameter, $\lambda = 0.75$ and $\lambda = 0.25$ in comparison with a baseline where $\lambda = 1$.

Comment Embedding Model Selection

Diversification with MMR hinges on a comment embedding model that accurately captures the semantic similarity between two comments. Eight models were evaluated (Table 1).

Two evaluation metrics were used to compare these models. (1) The median quantile difference defined as the difference in average cosine similarity percentile rank (quantile) of Gold 1 pairs minus that of Gold 0 pairs. We recommend this metric as it is unbiased and captures relative ranking. (2) The accuracy of logistic regression using a given model's pairwise comment cosine similarity matrix as input and the gold binary labels as output. Our two metrics consistently ranked all models.

Using the best performing model for these two metrics, comment similarity was computed using cosine similarity [8]. In our case, the best model was PCA + TFIDF comment embeddings, as seen in Table 2 in the Results section.

MMR Evaluation Experiment

Since the comment order for the course we experimented on is chronological, we used ordering by score (number of replies, $\lambda = 1$) for our baseline ranking. We conducted a small-scale re-ranking evaluation experiment requiring subjects to choose among two unidentified ordered lists of comments: (1) the top 5 comments of our diversified ranking and (2) the top 5 comments of a baseline ranking ordered only by score, their true identities unknown. Three subjects evaluated 100 trials. The Cohen-Kappa score [5] was used to measure inter-rater reliability. For each trial, subjects were presented with three items (an example trial is shown in Figure 2):

1. The forum's topic question
2. Two lists, A and B. One of these lists is the top five comments ordered by score (baseline). The other is the top five diversified (re-ranked) comments
3. A random comment C from this forum not included in (2) where C's probability of being chosen was proportional to number of replies (higher rank = more likely to be chosen).

Both the order in which lists A and B were shown to subjects and trial order were randomized to ensure the true labels for

```
Trial 11

|------------|
| Question 0 |
|------------|
'Whether you are deeply familiar with Christianity or new to the tradition, please share 1-3 things...

|--------|
| List A |
|--------|

[1] 'Christianity was explained in just 4 minutes. Very good video.'

[2] "Interesting that so many listed as making up part of Christianity don't recognize each other as such!"

[3] "I appreciated the point about how Eastern Christianity emphasizes the Incarnation... "

[4] 'Christianity is based not on the writings of Jesus Christ, but the writings of others...'

[5] 'I have always found it interesting that Christianity has both condemned and enabled oppression. '

|--------|
| List B |
|--------|

[1] 'Christianity was explained in just 4 minutes. Very good video.'

[2] 'I found it interesting that some missions working in other cultures recognized the active presence of God...'

[3] "Interesting that so many listed as making up part of Christianity don't recognize each other as such!"

[4] 'Christianity is based not on the writings of Jesus Christ, but the writings of others...'

[5] 'Orthodox is newer to me.   I was raised in a Pentecostal church and converted... '

|-----------|
| Comment C |
|-----------|
'Two things that impressed me most in the text were:  the history and diversity of Christian movements..'
```

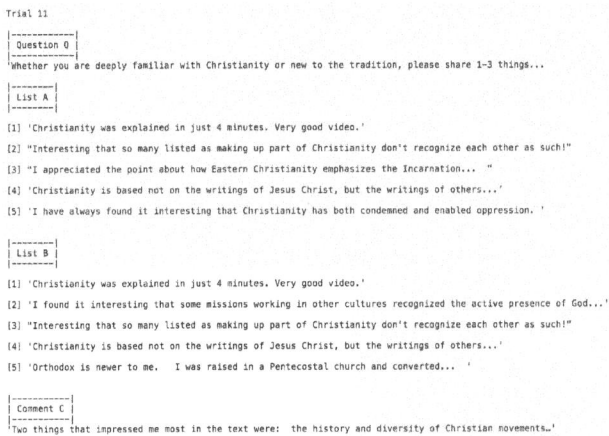

Figure 2. A trial in the MMR evaluation experiment.

list A and B were unrecoverable within and across subjects. For each double-blind trial, each subject answered 3 questions:

1. **Inclusion Experiment**: Which list, A or B, has a comment that resembles the semantics of comment C?

2. **Diversity Experiment**: Which list, A or B, best captures a diverse set of all potential answers to this question Q?

3. **Redundancy Experiment**: Which list, A or B, contains more redundant comments?

If our comment embedding model accurately captures pairwise semantic similarity, we would expect the diversified ranking to be chosen more often for "inclusion" and "diversity", and less often for "redundancy".

Among the 100 trials for each subject, 75 trials used $\lambda = 0.25$ (ranked more by diversity) and 25 trials used $\lambda = 0.75$ (ranked more by score). More trials were taken for $\lambda = 0.25$ to offset increased stochasticity when selecting low-scored (but diverse) comments. Neglecting comment score increases variation in ranking. Additional trials mitigated increased variance.

RESULTS AND DISCUSSION

This section is divided into two parts. Since diversification relies on accurate semantic similarity scores, in Section 4.1 we evaluate comment embedding models on our gold dataset. Then, in Section 4.2, we evaluate our model in a double-blind subject experiment comparing our diversified ranking against a baseline ranking ordered by score.

Model	Median Quantile Difference	Logistic Regression Accuracy
TFIDF	0.338009	0.841026
PCA + TFIDF	**0.433901**	**0.866738**
LSA + TFIDF	0.431401	0.867211
NMF + TFIDF	0.416625	0.860729
LDA + TFIDF	0.128716	0.815278
Word2Vec + TFIDF	0.204944	0.815278
Word2Vec + nBOW	0.166570	0.815278
Gated CNN + TFIDF	0.115584	0.786467

Table 2. Comparison of various comment embedding methods. Median quantile difference computes the difference in average cosine similarity rank (percentile) of Gold 1 pairs - Gold 0 pairs. Logistic regression predicts the accuracy of the gold labels trained using each model's pairwise cosine similarity matrix as input.

Comment Embedding Models

For our task, word-level comment embedding methods (word2vec, Gated CNN, LDA) performed worse than a simple TFIDF vector representation alone, with a classical application of dimensionality reduction using PCA achieving highest accuracy on our gold dataset. Table 2 captures the performance of different embedding models on our gold test set, for both median quantile difference and logistic regression accuracy. In the rest of this section, we discuss potential reasons for this.

Comparing the use of the TFIDF embedding to the use of PCA and LSA affirms that there is benefit to employing dense embeddings. More unexpectedly, word2vec and Gated CNN, when combined with TFIDF, did not perform as well as TFIDF. A likely suspect is that our word2vec model was trained on the Google News corpus, which is a semantically different and much broader corpus than learner comments in an online course. As a result, word embeddings related to the course content were compressed into a smaller space relative to the broader embeddings of the model.

Given that comments were on average 78 words in length, and "bag of words" ignores ordering and contextual information, it is less surprising that PCA and LSA outperformed nBOW and TFIDF models. As PCA offered a marginal performance improvement over LSA, PCA + TFIDF was chosen as our final comment embedding model.

MMR Evaluation

Table 3 lists the results of the blind evaluation experiment. The fraction of subject responses selecting the diversified (MMR) ranking is depicted in Figure 3. The MMR ranking with $\lambda = 0.75$ (ranked more by score) outperformed the baseline in every experiment (experiments are described in 3.3), while rankings with $\lambda = 0.25$ (ranked more by diversity) did not perform significantly better or worse than the baseline.

λ	Experiment	Trials	Baseline Trials	MMR Trials
0.25	inclusion	225	0.52	0.48
	diverse	225	0.46	0.54
	redundant	225	0.51	0.49
0.75	inclusion	75	0.32	0.68
	diverse	75	0.37	0.63
	redundant	75	0.61	0.39

Table 3. Depicts the aggregated subject counts of the blind evaluation experiment. For each (λ, experiment) group, the number of times either list was chosen is tallied. The two rightmost columns capture the normalized counts. The baseline ranking is generated with MMR and $\lambda = 1$ (ranked only by score).

For moderate diversification ($\lambda = 0.75$), the MMR ranking was chosen significantly more often than the baseline ranking for both diversity and inclusion experiments, and significantly less often than the baseline for the redundancy experiment, suggesting our model mitigates redundancy and majority biases in the top K comments. However, for extreme diversification ($\lambda = 0.25$) the fraction of responses choosing the MMR ranking was nearly 0.5 (completely random when compared with the baseline ranking) across all three experiment groups. The cause is likely two fold. Firstly, ranking correlates with relevance, therefore, replacing more high-ranking comments

Fraction of Responses Choosing
MMR Ranking (versus Baseline)

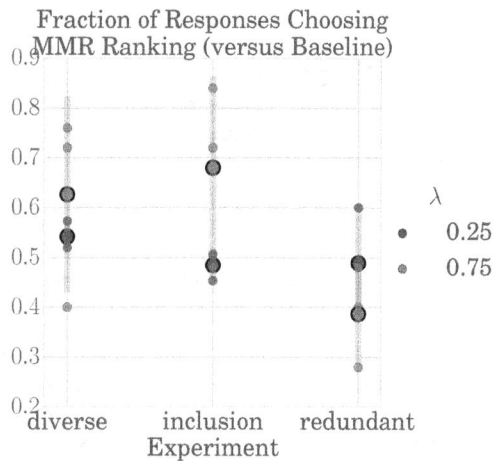

Figure 3. Depicts the fraction of trials choosing the diversified (MMR) ranking for each λ, experiment pair. Higher values for the "diverse" and "inclusion" experiments and lower values for the "redundant" experiment suggest MMR's efficacy, with $\lambda = 0.75$ outperforming $\lambda = 0.25$. The large, encircled points depict the means of each λ, experiment pair and the translucent bars depict the standard error of each mean. The smaller points depict individual rater scores.

with diverse, but lower-ranked (and less relevant) comments, may negatively impact all three experiments. Secondly, lower-ranked comments may be off-topic, lower quality, or harder to parse, leading to a simulated random choice.

Reliability and Agreement Among Test Subjects
Since only three subjects were included in our experiment, each evaluating 100 trials, we consider the inter-rater reliability among the three subjects to validate the consistency in our findings. Table 4 lists the Cohen's Kappa score for all pairs of subjects, for each experiment group. Although a small number of pairs were inconsistent, most showed moderate consistency.

		other1	other2
diversity	subject 1	-0.010918	0.273901
	subject 2	0.179319	0.273901
	subject 3	-0.010918	0.179319
inclusion	subject 1	0.033912	0.146825
	subject 2	0.185336	0.146825
	subject 3	0.033912	0.185336
redundancy	subject 1	-0.025851	0.135560
	subject 2	0.211045	0.135560
	subject 3	-0.025851	0.211045

Table 4. Cohen's Kappa pairwise inter-rater reliability scores.

CONCLUSION
Discussion forums play a vital role in online courses, yet due to the large scale of MOOCs, comment rankings often suffer from majority biases and redundancy. The primary contributions of this paper are (1) design and evaluation of a top K comment diversification re-ranking algorithm and (2) experimental evidence suggesting a significant increase in diversity and inclusion and decrease in redundancy when our algorithm is used to rank comments versus a baseline relevance ranking. We encourage MOOC and forum platforms to consider the importance of ranking diversification on learning and user experience, and hope our findings inspire future consideration.

ACKNOWLEDGEMENTS
We graciously thank Y-Lan Boureau (Facebook AI Research) for her mentorship and suggestion to use MMR and embeddings. We are also very grateful to Regina Barzilay (MIT) for her guidance in model selection and framework.

REFERENCES
1. Akiko Aizawa. 2003. An information-theoretic perspective of tf–idf measures. *Information Processing & Management* 39, 1 (2003), 45–65.

2. David M Blei, Andrew Y Ng, and Michael I Jordan. 2003. Latent dirichlet allocation. *Journal of Machine Learning Research* 3, Jan (2003), 993–1022.

3. Jaime Carbonell and Jade Goldstein. 1998. The use of MMR, diversity-based reranking for reordering documents and producing summaries. In *Proceedings of the 21st annual intl. ACM SIGIR conf. on Research and development in information retrieval*. ACM, 335–336.

4. Olivier Chapelle, Shihao Ji, Ciya Liao, Emre Velipasaoglu, Larry Lai, and Su-Lin Wu. 2011. Intent-based diversification of web search results: metrics and algorithms. *Info. retrieval* 14, 6 (2011), 572–592.

5. J. Cohen. 1960. A Coefficient of Agreement for Nominal Scales. *Educ. and Psych. Measurement* 20, 1 (1960), 37.

6. Yajuan Duan, Long Jiang, Tao Qin, Ming Zhou, and Heung-Yeung Shum. 2010. An empirical study on learning to rank of tweets. In *Proceedings of the 23rd International Conference on Computational Linguistics*. Association for Computational Linguistics, 295–303.

7. Susan T Dumais, George W Furnas, Thomas K Landauer, Scott Deerwester, and Richard Harshman. 1988. Using latent semantic analysis to improve access to textual information. In *Proceedings of the SIGCHI conference on Human factors in computing systems*. ACM, 281–285.

8. Anna Huang. 2008. Similarity measures for text document clustering. In *Proceedings of the sixth new zealand computer science research student conference (NZCSRSC2008), Christchurch, New Zealand*. 49–56.

9. Thorsten Joachims. 1996. *A Probabilistic Analysis of the Rocchio Algorithm with TFIDF for Text Categorization*. Technical Report. DTIC Document.

10. Quoc V Le and Tomas Mikolov. 2014. Distributed Representations of Sentences and Documents.. In *ICML*, Vol. 14. 1188–1196.

11. Tao Lei, Hrishikesh Joshi, Regina Barzilay, Tommi Jaakkola, Katerina Tymoshenko, Alessandro Moschitti, and Lluis Marquez. 2016. *Semi-supervised question retrieval with gated convolutions*. Association for Computational Linguistics (ACL), 1279–1289.

12. Tomas Mikolov, Ilya Sutskever, Kai Chen, Greg S Corrado, and Jeff Dean. 2013. Distributed representations of words and phrases and their compositionality. In *Adv. in neural information processing systems*. 3111–3119.

13. Jonas Mueller and Aditya Thyagarajan. 2016. Siamese Recurrent Architectures for Learning Sentence Similarity. In *Thirtieth AAAI Conference on Artificial Intelligence*.

14. Lawrence Page, Sergey Brin, Rajeev Motwani, and Terry Winograd. 1999. The PageRank citation ranking: bringing order to the web. (1999).

Access to Massive Open Online Labs through a MOOC

Wissam Halimi
EPFL
Lausanne, Switzerland
wissam.halimi@epfl.ch

Christophe Salzmann
EPFL
Lausanne, Switzerland
christophe.salzmann@epfl.ch

Denis Gillet
EPFL
Lausanne, Switzerland
denis.gillet@epfl.ch

ABSTRACT

Few MOOCs offer laboratory work as part of their educational material, yet it is known that hands-on sessions are important components of science and engineering education. Equally important is understanding how students are using labs as part of their learning activity without the constraints of space and time. In this work we present the initial results of the usage of a remote lab provided as part of a Control Systems MOOC.

ACM Classification Keywords

H.1.2 User/Machine Systems; K.3.1 Computers and Education: Computer Uses in Education

Author Keywords

MOOC; Massive Open Online Coourses; MOOL; Massive Open Online Labs; online education; e-learning; remote labs; experimentation; engineering education.

INTRODUCTION

Today MOOCs (Massive Open Online Courses) are a source of affordable and convenient knowledge. Most MOOCs offer knowledge evaluation tools such as quizzes or graded assignments, touching on the practice side of completing a course. But to the extent of our knowledge, very few of them offer laboratory work as part of the learning resources. The necessity of hands-on sessions as part of a complete science and engineering education is a given [2][4]. Some might argue that simulations can replace real hands-on experimentation, but research has shown that there are educational objectives which are only or better met when students deal with real physical laboratories [5]. Therefore, we identify the need to support lab work in MOOCs.

Nowadays there is a surge in remote labs use in blended and distance learning. The main motivations for developing and deploying remote labs are the unbounded accessibility by space and time, the sharing of resources among different institutions, and lowering costs of laboratory ownership, maintenance, and scalability as the number of students increases [1]. In this context, a remote lab is a real physical

L@S 2017, April 20 - 21, 2017, Cambridge, MA, USA

© 2017 Copyright held by the owner/author(s). Publication rights licensed to ACM.
ISBN 978-1-4503-4450-0/17/04. . . $15.00

DOI: http://dx.doi.org/10.1145/3051457.3054017

lab, which is accessible through the Internet at distance.

For more than ten years now, the Automatic Control Lab at EPFL (Ecole Polytechnique Fédérale de Lausanne) offers its students the ability to remotely connect to the lab of the Control Systems course. And recently, major efforts have been put into deploying the remote lab on a large scale, as part of its new MOOC: Control Systems [6][7].

In this work, we present the remote lab deployed as part of the educational resources of the mentioned MOOC. In order to extract interesting patterns in lab use, we gather activity tracks touching on different dimensions of students' interaction with the remote lab. This would give insight on how to enhance their learning experience and how to scale it for larger number of students thanks to learning analytics. Learning analytics is a major source of insight to infer learning patterns, identifying what makes a student successful, and often used for personalization and recommendation [3].

CONTROL SYSTEMS MOOC

Logistics

At EPFL, the Control Systems course taught at the undergraduate level, is delivered in an unconventional way: lectures are given in class, and hands-on sessions are available through the MOOC (flipped classroom). In the MOOC, students have lectures summaries, videos with instructions for experimentation to watch, quizzes to take, and remote access to the physical labs, interleaved in tabs. Each lesson or module can comprise one or several tabs with remote lab access. Typically, the student opens the MOOC and goes through a sequence of tabs (see Figure 1), each tab with relative material to study. The complete course is composed of 8 modules, the first of which is introductory.

There is an allocated and reserved time for students to use the MOOC at the premise, during which teaching assistants are present to answer any questions the students might have. Of course, the MOOC is continuously available 24/7 regardless of the pre-scheduled lab sessions.

Remote lab access

The remote lab is integrated in the MOOC in a separate tab than other kinds of learning material that might be grouped together. The user interface (UI) is shown in Figure 2. The UI allows the students to push parameters to the lab through the

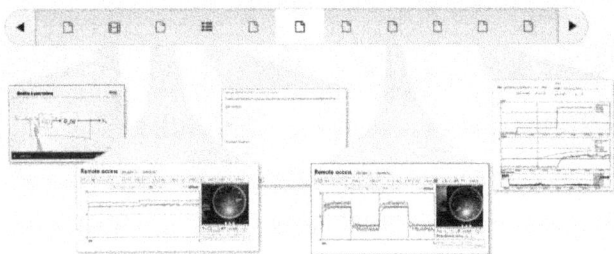

Figure 1. A typical lesson structure: consecutive tabs each comprising a different learning resource: videos, quizzes, remote lab...

control strip, they can see a graph of the collected measurements, and a live video of the status of the motor. The students can save their experimental results, and load them in another available tool for system modeling and interactive simulation, see [7].

THE LAB

The complete laboratory infrastructure services 25 installations of remotely accessible servo drives. At the time of writing, the MOOC is deployed on a local copy of edX hosted by EPFL, yet accessible to the world. The total number of students taking the course is around 250 for the current semester (and usually is in other semesters). The course ran from the 20th of September to the 23rd of December 2016. For the exception of some weeks, the students were required to go to the physical lab room twice a week.

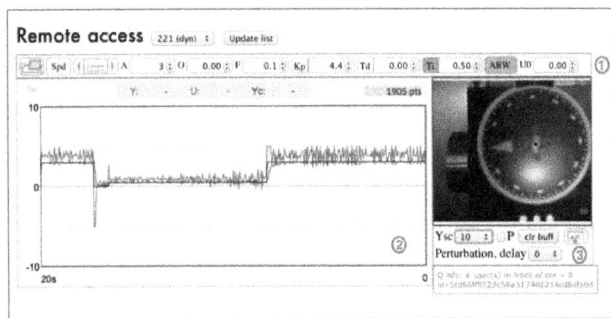

Figure 2. The user interface composed of a command strip ①, an oscilloscope screen ②, and a video feed as shown in the MOOC ③

DATA

For every connection, the lab saves activity tracks from the time of connection to disconnection. The tracks contain information regarding the time of connection, the role (*controller* who can act on the setup, or *observer* who can watch what the controller is doing and see the results), unique identifiers for location of connection and user, parameters pushed for experimentation, remaining time of experimentation, and other system specific logs for security and keeping the lab in a safe state. Over 500,000 activity tracks were gathered during the period of the course.

STATISTICS

Location of connection

We can see that 10.74% of the connections were made from the lab room (students can see the equipment). 8.54% came from the EPFL campus network, 61.16% from the either the EPFL Wi-Fi network or remote VPN access, and 19.56% from outside any EPFL provided connection. A considerable portion of the students is returning to the lab from outside the university, mostly between the hours 18:00 and 21:00 on the same day as the lab or the next.

Duration of experimentation

To handle queues, one strategy was to allocate to each experiment tab a fixed duration. If the allowed time expires and there are queuing users, the current user is pushed into the queue as an observer. If the allowed experimentation time expires but there are no waiting users, the current user can keep hold of control. We assume that students who didn't stay connected for more than 10 seconds, are not really using the lab. Depending on the experiments, the maximum allowed time ranged from 90 seconds to 2 minutes per session. Regardless of the fixed allocated time for experimentation and the expectation of the theoretical massive queuing (250 students for 25 setups with dynamical allocation), based on the data collected from all the lessons we found that the minimum connection time is 11 seconds, the maximum is 1 hour, the mean is 6 min and 22 seconds, with a standard deviation of 11 min and 29 seconds; hence the system is far from saturation.

Table 1 shows more granular statistics regarding the mean, standard deviation of experimentation time spent by the students in each module, in addition to the pre-allocated time to experiment, the number of connections to the lab setup, the number of experimentation tabs, and the allocated time per tab for each module . We notice that the mean and standard deviation of the experimentation time in all the course modules are close, regardless of the shortest allocated time (30 seconds) or the largest (4 minutes) per module, as well as of the number of connections and experimentation tabs per module.

To check whether students are returning to a Module after the time it was instructed, we inspect on which days students connected to the MOOC to access a specific module. The results for Module 4 are shown in Figure 3. We notice peaks at the beginning and around the twentieth of November. Then students are returning in smaller numbers. Other modules show similar measures, due to space constraints they are not included.

Queue Sizes

The maximum queue size encountered by students is 3 (0.1%). 2 users queued 2.89% of the time, and 97% of connections were for single users. Interestingly enough, when removing all students who spent less than 10 seconds connected, we don't observe any more queuing, i.e. no more observers and

Module	Mean	Std. Dev.	Allocated Exp. Duration	Num. of Connections	Num. Exp. Tabs	Allocated Duration per Tab
Intro	08:00	11:51	00:30	22	1	30
Module 1	09:50	13:09	01:00	57	2	30
Module 2	06:13	10:31	04:30	211	3	90
Module 3	06:15	11:43	08:00	228	4	120
Module 4	07:37	12:35	08:00	233	4	120
Module 5	06:52	11:25	04:00	211	2	120
Module 6	04:33	08:58	06:00	277	3	120
Module 7	06:27	11:04	04:00	76	2	120

Table 1. Mean, standard deviation, and allocated time in minutes:seconds format, number of connections, number of experimentation tabs, and allocated duration per experimentation tabs in seconds, for each module.

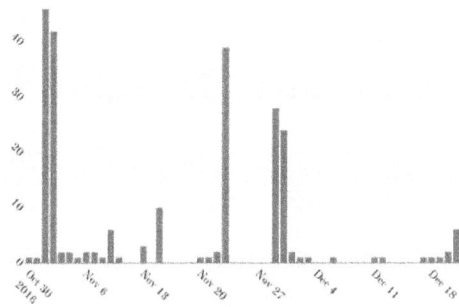

Figure 3. Number of connections for Module 4.

it seems that the 25 setups are successfully servicing the connected users. More specifically, no students waited more than a second in a queue. Queuing is only happening during the peak time for connections, which is during the pre-scheduled lab sessions, and it seems that students who are gaining control of the setup are leading the group work, and others are disconnecting or switching to other tasks.

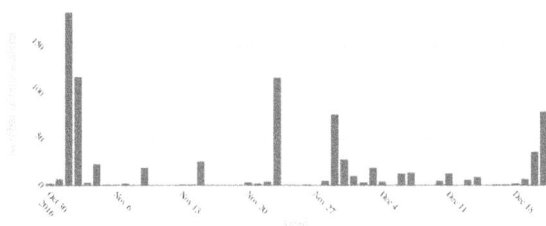

Figure 4. Number of connections throughout the whole period of the course.

CONCURRENT ACCESS

In Figure 4, we show all the days during which the students accessed the MOOC. Of the 49 days, on 37 days the lab was used. This shows that students are not only interested in the material offered by the course, but given the opportunity they will take it in order to experiment.

Knowing the dates of the lab sessions, we see that students mostly connected to the lab on those days. The maximum number of connections per day is 188, the minimum is 1, the mean is 17.75 and the standard deviation is 36.84. But more importantly, students were more enthusiastic about it during the beginning of the semester, mid-semester, and the end of it. Also, they seem to be more eager to use the lab around the time of the midterm: week of the 21st of November, and towards the end of the course.

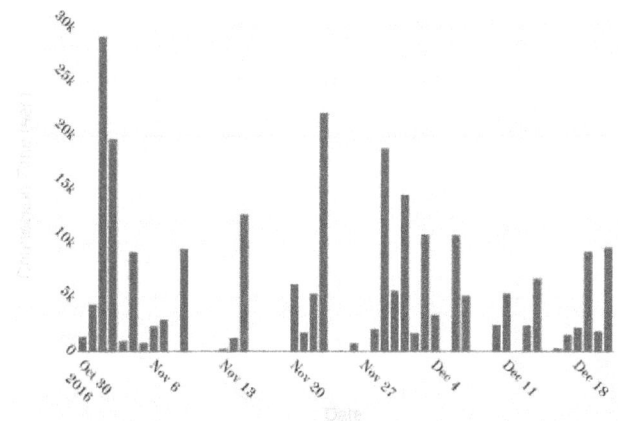

Figure 5. Time spent on experimentation through the whole period of the course

Figure 5 shows the time spent by students experimenting when they connect to the MOOC. In comparison with Figure 4, we see that the number of connections per day does not imply a longer usage time of the lab.

We isolate the connections made outside the lab session hours from the rest of the activity tracks, and observe the concurrent access behavior for one setup. In Figure 6 we can observe one of the busiest hours where 4 users tried to use the lab. There is no overlap between any of the users, yet the minimum elapsed time between 2 users is less than 30 seconds. This is mainly the result of having multiple setups servicing the requests: if one setup is busy the user is redirected to an available one, and there was never a time where users attempting to connect had to wait for access.

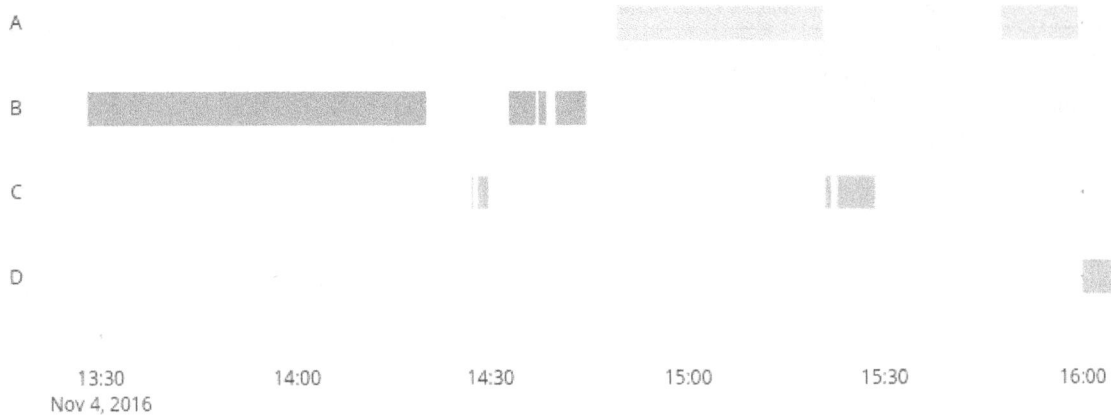

Figure 6. Occupation of one lab setup, outside lab hours, for one of the busiest hours

CONCLUSION AND FUTURE WORK

From the initial analysis of the data, we see that a 10:1 ratio is possible for servicing the students with the current configuration (25 setups-250 users with a round robin allocation scheme). While we cannot clearly differentiate between local Wi-Fi and VPN access, we notice that a large part of the MOOC accesses originates from outside the premise. The average experimentation time of 6 min is larger than the pre-allocated time, thus this duration could be dynamically set for each experiments. A similar result is obtained per module (Table 1) regardless of the varying allocated durations for experiments and the number of experiments per module. Additionally, we see that students are returning to a module after it is complete in class. Moreover, the collected data can be utilized to devise access management schemes to the lab given a larger number of users, especially through gamification. At the time of writing, the students had not yet taken the final exam, hence the correlation between grade and time spent on the MOOC is yet unknown.

REFERENCES

1. MJ. Callaghan, J. Harkin, TM. McGinnity, and LP. Maguire. 2004. Cost Effectiveness Issues in Remote Experimentation. *2004 IEEE International Conference on Systems, Man and Cybemetlcs* 5 (2004), 4700–4704. DOI: http://dx.doi.org/10.1109/ICSMC.2004.1401273

2. Balakrishnan Dasarathy, Kevin Sullivan, Douglas C. Schmidt, Douglas H. Fisher, and Adam Porter. 2014. The Past, Present, and Future of MOOCs and Their Relevance to Software Engineering. *FOSE 2014 Proceedings of the on Future of Software Engineering* (2014), 212–224. DOI: http://dx.doi.org/10.1145/2593882.2593897

3. Erik Duval. 2011. Attention please!: learning analytics for visualization and recommendation. In *Proceedings of the 1st International Conference on Learning Analytics and Knowledge.* ACM, 9–17.

4. David Lowe. 2014. MOOLs: Massive Open Online Laboratories: An Analysis of Scale and Feasibility. *2014 11th International Conference on Remote Engineering and Virtual Instrumentation (REV)* (2014), 1–6. DOI: http://dx.doi.org/10.1109/REV.2014.6784219

5. Jeffrey V. Nickersona, James E. Corterb, Sven K. Eschea, and Constantin Chassapisa. 2005. A model for evaluating the effectiveness of remote engineering laboratories and simulations in education. *Computers Education* 49 (2005), 708–725. DOI: http://dx.doi.org/10.1016/j.compedu.2005.11.019

6. Christophe Salzmann, Denis Gillet, and Yves Piguet. 2016. MOOLs for MOOCs: A first edX scalable implementation. In *Remote Engineering and Virtual Instrumentation (REV), 2016 13th International Conference on.* IEEE, 246–251.

7. Christophe Salzmann, Wissam Halimi, Denis Gillet, and Sten Govaerts. 2017. Deploying Large Scale Online Labs with Smart Devices. *Cyber-Physical Laboratories in Engineering and Science Education (In Press)* (2017).

Experimenting Choices of Video and Text Feedback in Authentic Foreign Language Assignments at Scale

Xiwen Lu
Brandeis University
Waltham, MA, USA
xiwenlu@brandeis.edu

Xiaolu Xiong
Worcester Polytechnic Institute
Worcester, MA, USA
xxiong@wpi.edu

Neil T. Heffernan
Worcester Polytechnic Institute
Worcester, MA, USA
nth@wpi.edu

ABSTRACT

With the development of "flipped classroom" concept and increasing usage of web-based learning platforms in foreign language teaching field, the effectiveness of online instant feedback come into researchers' focus, and whether or not teachers should provide choices of feedback medium also becomes an issue. The following study assesses the effects of feedback medium as well as the effectiveness of offering students feedback medium choices. This in-progress large-scale randomized controlled trial is conducted using ASSISTments, an adaptive online tutoring platform.

Author Keywords

E-learning, Flipped Classroom, Language Learning, Feedback, ASSISTments, Randomized Controlled Trial

INTRODUCTION

In the E-learning and adaptive tutoring field, many studies have done to compare video based learning and text based learning, mostly in the STEM education field. Kay and Edward [4] and Balslev et al. [1] compared VBL (Video-Based Learning) supported by a cognitive approach with text-based learning. The results showed statistically significant differences in improving learners' skills. Moreover, the authors reported that learners liked the followed cognitive approach in which knowledge was generated through step-by-step learning in video lectures. Ostrow and Heffernan [8] assessed the effects of feedback medium within a randomized controlled trial conducted using ASSISTments, and results suggest that video feedback enhances learning outcomes and is well perceived by student users. Most findings are focused on the STEM fields, and few randomized controlled trials are done in the field of second language education. Will the results also be proved in the field of second language education field?

Following the trend of "flipped classroom," more and more videos and web-based homework support systems have been adapted to foreign language teaching. Many empirical studies have been designed to determine the effect of video-based instruction on foreign language learning. Secules et al. [9] compared teacher-managed videotaped instructional materials featuring native speakers in everyday situations to more traditional pedagogical methods involving a variety of classroom exercises and drills, and found no significant difference between the two conditions in students' learning of grammatical structures. Herron et al. [2] conducted a longitudinal experiment to compare video based instruction and text supported instruction. Results showed a significant difference on the listening test, in listening comprehension between the experimental and control conditions at the conclusion of one year of French instruction, and no difference was found in grammar comprehension. Lin and Tseng [5] and Hsu et al. [3] conducted two studies to investigate the effect of different video-based learning designs to improve English language skills of K-12 students. The findings indicated that the groups which used VBL outperformed the other groups. However, very little research exists on the effectiveness of video feedback in the foreign language e-learning platform.

The survey results in Ostrow & Heffernan's study suggest that video feedback is well perceived by students, and 83% of students reported that they would at least somewhat prefer ASSISTments to use video more often. However this study didn't go deeper and investigate which kind of feedback students prefer during the homework, and how would their choice affect their learning results.

Thus, our research questions are:

- Are second language learning outcomes enhanced when scaffold feedback is delivered using video rather than text?

- Do students have preferences on choosing from video and text feedback?

- Will students with choices learn better than those who are not offered a choice?

METHODS

Participant

Participants are Chinese language learners in colleges and secondary schools in the U.S. We are expecting 600 students to enroll in this experiment.

Educational Content

Studies have shown that Mandarin is synchronically a typical VO (verb + object) language, in terms of text distribution of VO and OV orders (Sun & Givon, 1985[10]). Most Mandarin language learners also take Mandarin as a typical SVO language. However, there are several structures which do not follow SVO order. Language learners often make mistakes when dealing with a non-SVO structure, and for this reason, non-SVO structures are often key content in Chinese language classes. Normally word order is the same in Chinese for questions and statements. However, a question pronoun can appear in statements other than questions. When a question pronoun is used in a statement with 都(dou) appearing after it, it simply means "all" or "none" in the sense of being all-inclusive or all-exclusive [6]. Commonly used patterns of this structure are as follow:

a) 我什么中国菜都爱吃。
   Wo shenme Zhongguo cai dou ai chi.
   I love to eat all Chinese food.

b) 什么中国菜我都爱吃。
   Shenme Zhongguo cai wo dou ai chi.
   I love to eat all Chinese food.

c) 这些菜我哪个都不喜欢。
   Zhexie cai won age dou bu xihuan.
   I don't like any of these dishes.

d) 谁都喜欢这个颜色。
   Shei dou xihuan zhege yanse.
   Everyone likes this color.

e) 这个颜色谁都喜欢。
   Zhege yanse shei dou xihuan.
   Everyone likes this color.

The rules can be explained as 1) When Question word is used as a subject, the basic structure is QW + 都(dou) + V + Object; 2) When Question word is used as an object, the basic structure is Subject + QW + 都(dou) +V, and the subject and Question word can switch; 3) If you would like to mention that the statement you make is in a certain domain/range, the domain/range should be mentioned at the beginning of the sentence, no matter the question word is used as a subject or object. Structure: Range/domain + Subject + QW + 都(dou) + V; Range/domain + QW + 都(dou) + V.

While the structure "Question Word + 都(dou)" is the one that all students should have learned at the beginning level, the teachers we were working with identified it as a challenging structure for the students, and, in fact, many students were not sure how to correctly use this structure, even in advanced level. So in this study, we take this grammar structure as the target structure.

Design

The ASSISTments platform is used to compare the delivery methods of feedback messages.

Participants are asked to answer a set of 6 questions on ASSISTments which requires reordering given words to form a sentence to properly indicate the English meaning. Each three questions are in a section, and each question reflects one of the three rules. 6 questions are numbered as A1, B2, C3, D1, E2, F3.

All questions and feedback are available at [7]. We listed below one question as an example, which reflects rule 2 (When Question word is used as an object, the basic structure is Subject + QW+都(dou)+V, and the subject and Question word can switch):

English meaning: I like all colors.

Word bank: 什么(shenme)，颜色(yanse)，我(wo)，喜欢(xihuan)，都(dou)

Correct answer:

1) 我什么颜色都喜欢 。(Wo shenme yanse dou xihuan.)

2) 什么颜色我都喜欢。(shenme yanse wo dou xihuan.)

Students will receive feedback when given an incorrect response or if students request to see a hint. At the beginning of the assignment each student is randomly assigned to either the Choice or No Choice condition. Those assigned to No Choice conditions will receive either video feedback (Group 1) or text feedback (Group 2), and those assigned to Choice condition will be asked to choose the feedback medium from video and text (Group 3). See Table 1.

Video content as shown in Figure 1 was designed to mirror textual feedback (Figure 2) in an attempt to provide

Linear Order	1	2	3	4	5	6
Group 1	A1-VF	B2-VF	C3-VF	D1-VF	E2-VF	F3-VF
Group 2	A1-TF	B2-TF	C3-TF	D1-TF	E2-TF	F3-TF
Group 3	A1-VF/TF	B2-VF/TF	C3-VF/TF	D1-VF/TF	E2-VF/TF	F3-VF/TF

Table 1: Group design with question types and feedback types.

identical assistance through both mediums. Each video simply featured the lead researcher reading a feedback message while referring to the grammar structure on a screen.

Reorder given words to form a sentence to properly indicate the English meaning:
English meaning: I like all colors.
Words: 什么，颜色，我，喜欢，都

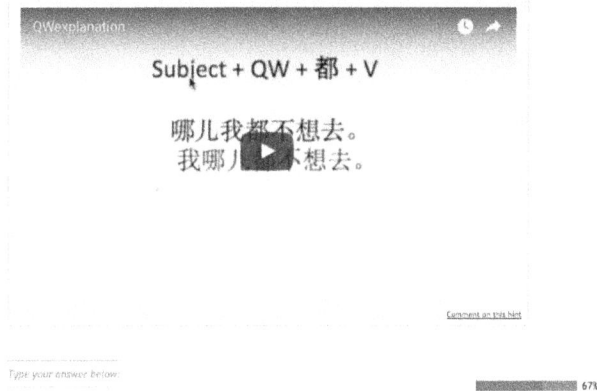

Figure 1: video feedback for question 1.

Reorder given words to form a sentence to properly indicate the English meaning:
English meaning: I like all colors.
Words: 什么，颜色，我，喜欢，都

When Question word is used as an object, the basic pattern is Subject + QW+都+V, and the subject and Question word can switch. For example, 哪儿我都不想去。or 我哪儿都不想去。

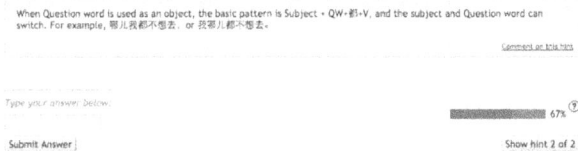

Figure 2. Text feedback for question 1

To make sure students are exposed to both types of feedback before asked to choose from them, an instruction is shown at the beginning of assignment. A video check is followed to remove students who cannot see video. Practices with text feedback is assigned to those who cannot see video.

A post-test is given to all participants' right after the assignment. Post-test contains three questions each reflecting one of the three rules, and it is also assigned to participants through ASSISTments.

Procedure
The problem sets are assigned to students as either classwork or homework. Students are free to work at their own pace. As shown in Fig. 3, when completing the introduction and video check, students are randomly assigned to one of the three groups. Data will be logged by ASSISTments automatically, which includes elements such as correctness, response time, attempts, hints requested, and more.

Hypotheses
Based on former research, our hypotheses are:

- Group 1 which receiving video feedback gets better grades comparing to group 2;

- Participants in group 3 prefer video feedback to text feedback;

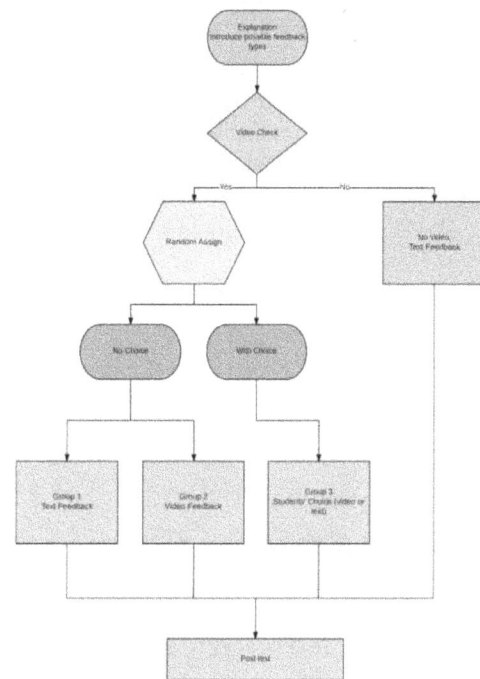

Figure 3. Procedure chart

- Students in Group 3 who are provided choices would excel No Choice groups.

REFERENCES

1. Thomas Balslev, Willem S. de Grave, Arno M. M. Muijtjens, and Albert J. J. A. Scherpbier. 2005. Comparison of a text and video case in a postgraduate problem-based learning format. Medical Education 39, 11: 1086-1092

2. Carol Herron, Matthew Morris, Teresa Secules and Lisa Curtis. 1995. A Comparison Study of the Effects of Video-Based versus Text-Based Instruction in the Foreign Language Classroom. The French Review 68, 5: 775-795

3. Ching-Kun Hsu, Gwo-Jen Hwang, Yu-Tzu Chang, and Chih-Kai Chang. 2013. Effects of Video Caption Modes on English Listening Comprehension and Vocabulary Acquisition Using Handheld Devices. Educational Technology & Society 16, 1: 403–414.

4. Robin Kay, Jaime Edward. 2012. Examining the Use of Worked Example Video Podcasts in Middle School Mathematics Classrooms: A Formative Analysis. Canadian Journal of Learning and Technology 38, 3.

5. Chih-cheng Lin, Yi-Fang Tseng. 2012. Videos and animations for vocabulary learning a study on difficult words. Turkish Online Journal of Educational Technology 11, 4: 346-355.

6. Yuehua Liu, et al. 2008. Integrated Chinese Level 1 Part 2, 3rd edition: 216-217. Cheng & Tsui publisher.

7. Xiwen Lu, 2016. Video and Text Feedback Study data. http://researches.chinesereadingmaterials.net/

8. Korrin S. Ostrow, Neil T. Heffernan. 2014. Testing the Multimedia Principle in the Real World: A Comparison of Video vs. Text Feedback in Authentic Middle School Math Assignments. In Proceedings of the 7th International Conference on Educational Data Mining.

9. Teresa Secules, Carol Herron, Michael Tomasello. 1992. The Effect of Video Context on Foreign Language Learning. The Modern Language Journal 76-4: 480-490.

10. Chao-Fen Sun and Talmy Givón. 1985. On the So-Called Sov Word Order in Mandarin Chinese: A Quantified Text Study and Its Implications. Language 61, 2: 329-35.

Author Index

www.ingramcontent.com/pod-product-compliance
Lightning Source LLC
Chambersburg PA
CBHW082106220326

41598CB00066BA/5517